Ethnicity, Social Mobility, and

This major comparative study of the social mobility of ethnic minorities in the USA and UK argues that social mobility must be understood as a complex and multidimensional phenomenon, incorporating the wealth and income of groups, but also their political power and social recognition. Written by leading sociologists, economists, political scientists, geographers, and philosophers in both countries, the volume addresses issues as diverse as education, work and employment, residential concentration, political mobilization, public policy, and social networks, while drawing larger lessons about the meaning of race and inequality in the two countries. While finding that there are important similarities in the experience of ethnic, and especially immigrant, groups in the two countries, the volume also concludes that the differences between the USA and UK, especially in the case of American blacks, are equally important.

GLENN C. LOURY is Professor of Economics and Director of the Institute on Race and Social Division at Boston University.

TARIQ MODOOD is Professor of Sociology, Politics, and Public Policy and founding Director of the Centre for the Study of Ethnicity and Citizenship, University of Bristol. He has published extensively and was awarded the MBE for services to social science and ethnic relations 2001.

STEVEN M. TELES is Assistant Professor of Politics at Brandeis University. He has published books and articles on a wide range of topics including welfare, affirmative action, devolution in the UK and EU.

Ethnicity, Social Mobility, and Public Policy

Comparing the USA and UK

Edited by

Glenn C. Loury, Tariq Modood,

and

Steven M. Teles

CAMBRIDGE
UNIVERSITY PRESS

CAMBRIDGE UNIVERSITY PRESS
Cambridge, New York, Melbourne, Madrid, Cape Town, Singapore, São Paulo

Cambridge University Press
The Edinburgh Building, Cambridge CB2 2RU, UK

Published in the United States of America by Cambridge University Press, New York

www.cambridge.org
Information on this title: www.cambridge.org/9780521823099

© Cambridge University Press 2005

First published 2005

Printed in the United Kingdom at the University Press, Cambridge

A catalogue record for this book is available from the British Library

Library of Congress Cataloguing in Publication data
Ethnicity, social mobility, and public policy: comparing the USA and UK / edited by
Glenn C. Loury, Tariq Modood, and Steven M. Teles.
    p.   cm.
Includes bibliographical references and index.
ISBN 0 521 82309 9 – ISBN 0 521 53001 6 (pb.)
1. Social mobility – United States.   2. Social mobility – Great Britain.
3. Minorities – United States.   4. Minorities – Great Britain.   5. Minorities –
Government policy – United States.   6. Minorities – Government policy – Great Britain.
I. Loury, Glenn C.   II. Modood Tariq.   III. Teles, Steven Michael.
HN90.S65E86   2004
305.5′13′0941 – dc22   2004051887

ISBN-13 978-0-52182309-8 hardback
ISBN-10 0-521-82309-9 hardback
ISBN-13 978-0-52153001-9 paperback
ISBN-10 0-521-53001-6 paperback

Contents

Figures

Tables

Contributors

FAWZIA S. AHMED, Analysis Group Inc., Boston, Massachusetts

RICHARD BERTHOUD, Institute for Social and Economic Research, University of Essex

DAVID M. CUTLER, Department of Economics, Harvard University

RONALD F. FERGUSON, Kennedy School of Government, Harvard University

EDWARD L. GLAESER, Department of Economics, Harvard University

NATHAN GLAZER, Professor Emeritus, School of Education, Harvard University

ANTHONY HEATH, Department of Sociology, Oxford University

MARY J. HICKMAN, Irish Studies Center, Metropolitan University London

MICHAEL HOUT, Department of Sociology, University of California at Berkeley

ROBERT LIEBERMAN, Department of Political Science, Columbia University

GLENN C. LOURY, Department of Economics, Boston University

LINDA DATCHER LOURY, Department of Economics, Tufts University

DORREN McMAHON, Institute for the Study of Social Change, University College Dublin

ROBERT MICKEY, Department of Political Science, University of Michigan

SUZANNE MODEL, Department of Sociology, University of Massachusetts, Amherst

TARIQ MODOOD, Department of Sociology, University of Bristol

BHIKHU PAREKH, Professor of Political Theory, University of Hull

ORLANDO PATTERSON, John Cowles Professor of Sociology, Harvard University

CERI PEACH, Social Geography and Environment, Oxford University

VAUGHAN ROBINSON, Department of Geography, University of Wales, Swansea

PETER SKERRY, Department of Political Science, Boston College

STEVEN M. TELES, Politics Department, Brandeis University

RINA VALENY, Context Research International, Harpenden, UK

JACOB L. VIGDOR, School of Public Policy and Department of Economics, Duke University

ROGER WALDINGER, Department of Sociology, UCLA

MIN ZHOU, Department of Sociology, UCLA

Acknowledgements

This book has taken much longer to materialize than we would have wished. We thank all the authors for their patience and willingness to go through multiple revisions in pursuit of an edited work that would genuinely operate as a coherent whole. The first drafts of chapters were presented at a workshop in Bath, England in 1999 and revised drafts were subject to further discussion at the follow-up workshop in Boston, USA in 2000. The two workshops were an expression of the partnership between scholars of two countries and involved many more experts than are authors to this volume. Each workshop included many discussants who made valuable contributions to the general comparative discussion as well as commenting on specific papers. The discussants are too numerous to be named individually but we thank them all.

We also appreciate the hard and patient work of the editors at Cambridge University Press, and in particular the painstaking copy-editing work of Jacque French, and Sarah Caro's continuing commitment to this project through a whole series of revised deadlines.

We are especially grateful to the W. K. Kellogg Foundation for underwriting this work through a very generous grant. This project began under the auspices of the Institute on Race and Social Division at Boston University, and we wish to thank IRSD Administrative Associate Bobbie Patrick for her tireless efforts which helped keep this project on track, as well as the support of Centre for the Study of Ethnicity and Citizenship at Bristol University.

It is an astonishing fact that, but for the current effort, no book exists today which systematically compares the social, economic, and political dimensions of "race" and ethnicity in America and Britain. So, we hope that the appearance of this volume will have been worth the wait.

GLENN LOURY
TARIQ MODOOD
STEVE TELES

Introduction

Glenn C. Loury, Tariq Modood, and Steven M. Teles

Edited volumes are, by their very nature, a compilation of the views of different minds. And yet, in most cases, those different minds are chosen for a purpose. In the case at hand that purpose can be intuited from the title of this volume: *Ethnicity, Social Mobility, and Public Policy: Comparing the USA and UK*. The assumptions underlying the editors' efforts in bringing these many scholars together are essentially twofold: that social mobility is a heterogeneous phenomenon – not functioning the same way in every society and for every social group; and, that the social markers of ethnicity and race matter in the study of social mobility. Ethnicity and race are causally related to social mobility for the obvious reason that actors in society at large distribute mobility – relevant goods with those markers in mind, but also because those markers represent real social formations in the context of which mobility-relevant goods are produced and nurtured. Our view is that, in discerning how these effects play themselves out, analytical leverage is gained by making reference to the broadest possible range of groups and social settings. This we attempt to do in this volume. This introductory essay will elaborate on and defend these assumptions, and then connect them to the structure and content of the book.

1   Social mobility – what is it?

The editors of this volume view social mobility not as a single, homogeneous phenomenon, but rather as a cluster of interdependent social processes. We saw no need to establish a single definition of social mobility but instead encouraged the authors to select a conception of mobility that seemed most appropriate for their area of study. It is convenient, if a bit oversimplifying, to delineate four different ways of thinking about social mobility that are used in this volume. First, and in the United States most common, mobility can be measured by income, in either absolute or relative terms. This approach tends to envision social classes defined basically in arbitrary terms (e.g., by income deciles), and to view the differences between individuals as incremental. Here the classes between which individuals are more or less mobile are creations of the researcher, but not "real" categories in the world. This approach is typified by Duncan (1984).

A second, and still partially an economistic approach to social mobility, looks to the labor market for the core of its analysis but conceives that market as strictly segmented into real professional classes: mobility is the shift from a lower-status profession to a higher one, and it is not so much the income derived from the profession as its power and prestige that matters. This is a more common approach in the Nuffield studies of, for example, Heath (Goldthorpe 1980, Erikson and Goldthorpe 1992).

A third approach shares an emphasis on power and prestige with the Nuffield school but does not insist on the centrality of the labor market. This approach sees social mobility in terms of "recognition" and social citizenship – that is, in the degree to which individuals are affirmed by others as being equal partners in the community. While the labor market is an important setting for processes of inclusion and exclusion, this third approach recognizes that there are many other important settings wherein distinctions of status and belonging are produced. Individuals make significant decisions about where to live, with whom to socialize, and with whom to engage in collective action. Whether a group is recognized as having "social citizenship" is partially independent of its position in the labor market. It is indeed possible for there to be large, and even permanent, lags between labor market position and social equality. Scholars in this tradition insist that social citizenship is as real as economic status and is perhaps even more foundational. For instance, while the Indian minority in Uganda were able to attain a high economic success in that country, their continuing outsider status in Ugandan society rendered their economic achievements ephemeral once challenged by state authorities. Students of social citizenship thus look for what is "beneath" labor markets and political institutions, and tend to think of social mobility less in terms of classes moving in a labor market hierarchy, and more in terms of racially and ethnically defined groups operating within a hierarchical system of social statuses.

A final approach to the subject looks at the capacity of groups to organize for collective action and to significantly influence the institutions that affect them. For lack of a better word we can call this the "political" school of mobility studies. This approach typically understands racial and ethnic minorities (particularly newcomers) to be outsiders to the major social institutions, and thus to be in an inferior bargaining position when critical social resources are being distributed. This outsider position creates strong incentives for group-based collective action, but these incentives may be undermined either by the structure of social and institutional rules, or by the cultural and economic attributes of the group itself. Mobility in this understanding is the process by which groups attain sufficient internal coherence to legitimately threaten existing social institutions with the loss of power, and thus to obtain a fair (or more than fair) slice of the collective pie. More sophisticated analyses in this vain look at the social "pie" not as fixed in content, but rather as sensitive to the needs of groups in power. Social mobility can thus be analyzed in terms of the ability of a group of people to shift the overall supply of social resources in a direction that matches their needs and tastes. A quintessentially political analysis of social mobility is Nathan Glazer and Daniel Patrick Moynihan's *Beyond the Melting Pot*, whose British equivalent is John Rex and Robert Moore's *Race, Community and Conflict* (Glazer and Moynihan 1963, Rex and Moore 1967).

It is unnecessary to decide which of these approaches is the "right" way of studying the subject. It is more fruitful to think of the income, professional class, and social citizenship schools as all having something true and significant to say about social stratification. Nor is it necessary to distinguish among these approaches as primary and secondary, or as sub-structural versus super-structural. It is a fundamental feature of modern societies that they exhibit what Daniel Bell called a "disjuncture of realms": social complexity produces multiple centers of power that themselves produce only loosely overlapping status hierarchies (Bell 1976). It is thus possible to obtain substantial and rising income in a field lacking social prestige or power, or, as we have noted, to obtain both rising incomes and power without those labor market outcomes producing substantial social acceptance of one's racial or ethnic group. Thus, consider the contrast between British Afro-Caribbeans and South Asians. While the former have achieved far inferior social mobility than have the latter in terms of the labor market, Afro-Caribbeans are widely accepted as being at the core of modern British identity, while suspicions of foreignness and a consequent cultural distance still bedevil those from the Indian subcontinent (Modood 1999).

2   What do race and ethnicity have to do with it?

Most accounts of social mobility study the matter from the perspective of an individual endowed with particular skills and capital, or by examining how individuals are able to transfer their status across the generations to others within their families or their racial or ethnic group. One way that race and ethnicity can come into the picture is that differential treatment in contractual relations (such as employment) of minority group members by others can impair the ability of these persons to translate their endowments into mobility outcomes (either within generations or between them). We can call this the *discrimination paradigm* in the study of social mobility.

The discrimination paradigm, while surely of some value in particular contexts and for certain groups, has probably become less important as an explanatory schema in both societies over the past quarter-century. But this does not mean that ethnicity or race have ceased to matter to the attainment and transfer of status across time – far from it. As noted briefly above, race and ethnicity matter in the production of social mobility in two ways: first, decisions which affect the life chances of persons belonging to a particular racial or ethnic group are sometimes made by non-group members on the basis of their perception of the group's habits, attitudes, and skills. Secondly, ethnicity and race may reflect real social formations – networks of mutual influence, like-mindedness, and reciprocal concern – that influence (either negatively or positively) the development of those habits, attitudes, and skills that, in turn, partially determine social mobility. These disparate channels of influence are worth describing in more detail.

Individuals often make choices on the basis of perceived group averages, choices that extend across a wide range of social contexts. These choices can range from the annoying but relatively trivial (store clerks distributing attention to customers based on their perception of customers' likelihood of making a high-priced purchase), to the significant but virtually undetectable (house-buyers estimating neighborhood "quality" on the basis of its ethnic and racial mix), to the significant and advantageous (high-tech employers preferring "Asians" because of their reputation for hard work and technological competence). What is significant is that, from the point of view of social mobility, outsiders' estimation of group averages and their imputation of those averages onto individuals may have very substantial consequences for the acquisition of job experience, education, and assets. If individuals use the racial and ethnic mix of a neighborhood as a proxy for "quality," it may serve to depress housing values in neighborhoods with the wrong mix, thereby affecting lenders' willingness to lend in such neighborhoods (thus keeping individuals out of the housing market altogether, and limiting their asset appreciation if they are able to get into the market). If employers evaluate Asian applicants on the basis of perceived group averages, applicants whose real qualities are well below the group average will obtain an unearned advantage in the labor market, the opportunity to build on the job skills and experience, and as a consequence may end up fulfilling the prediction implicit in the group stereotype (this example works in the opposite direction, of course, for groups with a perception of low quality) (Loury 2002: Chapter 2). In short, when mobility-relevant resources are controlled by individuals who make decisions on the basis of group averages, race and ethnicity can profoundly impact social mobility even in the absence of group-based animus.

But racial and ethnic groups are not just fictive categories that exist only in the minds of outsiders. They are also real social groupings, through which mobility-relevant skills, habits, and attitudes are produced. And, in some cases they harbor real institutions through which resources are hoarded and distributed. Decisions to invest in education, to defer consumption, to accept or resist superiors in the workforce, and to delay or accelerate childbearing come down, in part, to questions of what "people like me do." That is, they are affected by the meaning embedded in racial and ethnic identity, meanings that are produced by some combination of group insiders and outsiders. Groups that are constituted by a rich set of ethnically or racially specific institutions are likely to have more control of these processes of meaning production, while groups with weaker institutions are likely to find their identity produced at least as much by outsiders as by themselves (Loury 2002: Chapter 3).

Identity, however, is not the only mechanism through which race and ethnicity function as real social groupings that affect mobility. Institutions bounded by race and ethnicity also produce and distribute resources and discipline individuals to meet group norms. But it is with respect to this sense of "group-ness" that ethnic and racial groups vary most starkly. In short, not all racial and ethnic groups are constituted in the same way. The more an ethnic or racial group is constituted by well-functioning social institutions, the greater its ability to mobilize its members for ongoing collective action, to pool resources to guard against risk, to invest for long-term returns, and to discipline members into ongoing group identity by the (implicit or explicit) threat of the withdrawal of those opportunities. The weaker a group's institutions, conversely, the more identity will be enforced through symbolic means, and the less able the group is to coordinate its activities, and thereby to maximize group resources.

3   Comparative method and regime effects

While linking the study of race and ethnicity to that of social mobility makes sense, the reader might reasonably ask what the advantages are of doing so comparatively, and given a comparative method, why the choice of the United States and Great Britain? Our sense is that the deeper processes that structure social mobility, and the way that race and ethnicity interact with it, are brought to the surface by the method of comparison, and that the two countries have the right balance of similarities and differences to make comparison productive. To illuminate these points, the balance of this introduction will begin the comparison conducted by the authors in the rest of this book, looking particularly at the variation in political institutions in the two countries. We will also discuss how the analyses in this volume can help us better understand the intersection of "social capital" with race and ethnicity. The larger argument here is that a single-minded focus on the characteristics of ethnic and racial groups, or even on racism, will tend to obscure a central issue – how social and political institutions condition the effects of both group attributes and anti-group animus, in some cases magnifying and in others limiting them.

Institutions and policies vary across space and time. As similar as the two countries here under study may be, they are not the same. Britain fuses political power in a strong executive backed by disciplined political parties, has a strong and insulated civil service, and centralizes power in the national government, leaving localities to implement diktats from London. The United States de-concentrates power within a national government with relatively little party discipline, a weak civil service, and a decentralized federal system in which important decisions are made by states and localities. While the last twenty years have changed things somewhat, Britain has generally been characterized by a broader scope of state intervention in the economy and a more comprehensive welfare state, while the United States has had a stronger and more intrusive set of civil rights laws and protections.[1] These broad institutional and policy differences provide the context within which ethnic minorities make claims, are counted and labeled, seek allies, construct ideologies, organize and mobilize. They do not always influence those outcomes in the way one might first think. At least some of the authors of the chapters that follow arrive at counterintuitive conclusions about the influences of politics on group mobility.

An examination of political influences on group mobility must start with the obvious although often overlooked, fact that political institutions shaped the immigration policies that, in the first instance, caused ethnic and racial minority groups to enter Britain and the United States. In comparing the USA and Britain, the old saw is that the USA is a country of immigrants, while Britain is a country with immigrants. Cliché though it may be, this claim has a great deal to be said for it. While indigenous people are a tiny minority in the USA, whose massive population has been built up by the descendants of colonialists, refugees, forcibly transported slaves and migrant families over several centuries and from across the globe, large-scale, society-constituting inward population movements have a historical depth in the USA that dwarf the same in the UK. Britain has not been without a series of incomers that have changed its population mix and social structures, but (leaving aside the violent invasions of a thousand and more years ago) they have been on a smaller scale, more intermittent, and till recently, from fewer sources. The pre-1948 notable cases are the Huguenots (Protestant refugees from persecution from across the Channel), the Irish, as laborers in the late Victorian industrial expansion, and the Jews at various times and from different parts of Europe (the largest Jewish flow being those fleeing from Eastern Europe, especially Russia and Poland, in the late nineteenth and early twentieth centuries). Nineteen forty-eight, the year in which the steamship, *Windrush* brought some young West Indian male workers to Britain, witnessed the start of the large nonwhite, New Commonwealth migrations that are the source of social formations which, on its British side, form the subject of this book. The result, in racial terms, is that 8 percent of the UK today is not white according to census forms (ONS 2003), as compared to 75 percent in the USA (US Census Bureau 2000).

The form of the immigration to Britain has had significant impacts on the society. Most of the British immigration in the first decades of the post-1948 period came from colonies and recent ex-colonies of the empire and so the migrants, predominantly young men, had automatic citizenship status from the moment of arrival. In contrast, migrants to the USA were more likely to come as families and citizenship required periods of residency, could be withheld and, perhaps for these reasons, could be prized. A series of legislative and administrative changes, beginning in 1962 and culminating in the Nationality Act of 1981, restricted rights of entry and citizenship to new migrants in Britain. Family dependents were, however, allowed and thus congeries of temporary male workers steadily began to be transformed into ethnic minority families and settlements. Migration from new sources became very difficult, so reinforcing the presence of specific migrant communities, such as the Caribbeans and South Asians. This has to be qualified, however, by three important observations. First, in this same period Britain joined the European Union, which progressively integrated itself and created a common citizenship enabling the nationals of any one member state to work and live freely in another. Second, employees in multinational companies were becoming more mobile, and London, being a major financial, commercial, and communications hub, attracted many such workers; also, Britain was a major global player in higher education and many overseas students came to Britain and thereafter settled and worked in Britain at least for a period. Third, in the last decade the numbers of refugees and asylum-seekers (coming from, for example, Afghanistan, the Horn of Africa, and the former Yugoslavia and Soviet-bloc countries) has greatly increased and includes people who are really traditional economic migrants but if they declared themselves as such would be denied entry. Thus the last decade or so has seen a revival in inward flow which some commentators refer to as the "new migration." In the USA, by contrast, immigration (especially from outside Europe) opened up in 1965 (precisely the time it was closing up in the UK and later elsewhere in the EU) and has continued to grow with the economic boom years of the 1980s and 1990s.

Political institutions have played a central role in the US immigration story. Slavery, protected and regulated by the national government, is responsible for the presence in North America of the vast majority of black Americans. The desire to populate the continent in the early 1800s led successive American governments, both state and national, to actively encourage immigration through much of the nineteenth century. The incentives provided by closely competing political parties caused mass immigration to continue unabated well into the second decade of the twentieth century (when America abruptly stepped on the hose of further migration, largely in response to the shifting national background of immigrants combined with the increasing autonomy of the national state from political parties (Tichenor 2002). A similarly elite-driven process led to the removal of immigration restrictions in the 1960s, followed by a four-decade-long mass wave of migration that brought to American shores the groups most particularly under examination in this study. Despite rising opposition to further immigration among large parts of the American public, the peculiarities of American party competition and an increasingly insulated political system have kept the doors open to further migration, to the point where no national political candidate can now openly advocate immigration restriction.

The British story is quite different. Migration *within* the United Kingdom (primarily from Ireland) is an old story, and one critically connected to the tale of more recent years, as Mary Hickman observes in her contribution to this book. Such migration was not – could not be – formally restricted, and as a result substantial parts of England had a real, durably important experience of ethnic diversity. It was this same legal openness to immigration, combined with the tight postwar British labor market, that led to the sudden burst of Caribbean and Indian subcontinent immigration that began in the 1950s and carried on until the 1970s. Legally, all citizens of first the empire and then the Commonwealth had a right to move to Great Britain, and for a few decades large numbers availed themselves of this right, in part as a result of active government policies of encouragement. As in the United States (both in the early twentieth century and in more recent times), mass immigration led to popular support for restriction. Unlike in contemporary American experience, popular pressure for restriction in Great Britain led both Labour and Conservative governments to step hard on the hose of further migration. The result has been that the numbers of ethnic minorities in Britain are substantially below what would have resulted had immigration policy remained constant, as it has in the United States. It is difficult to speculate about the consequences of different immigration policies in Britain, but a more liberal policy would undoubtedly have led to ethnic minorities having a larger influence on national and local politics, and would thereby have made subsequent moves toward restriction that much more difficult.

To put it bluntly, immigration policies – influenced by the nature of the two political systems (whose study lies largely beyond the scope of this volume) – have guided the evolution of ethnic diversity in the two countries in ways that provide the largely silent background for many of the chapters in this book. Had these policies been different, the stories that the authors that follow tell would have been different as well.

In addition to critical differences in the origins and numbers of ethnic and racial minorities, our two cases diverge substantially in the political institutions and culture that groups have encountered, as well as the ways that ethnic and racial diversity have shaped those institutions (a point that Robert Lieberman emphasizes in his chapter). It would be difficult to tell the story of American political development without taking note of the ways that core state institutions have been constructed by, and in some cases against, racial and ethnic minorities. Thus, the persistent decentralization of American politics well into the twentieth century was supported largely by a Democratic Party coalition held together by a desire to protect the autonomy of ethnically and racially defined political projects. In the South, limiting the construction of an autonomous national state was necessary in order to protect first slavery and then segregation. This influenced both critical political rules (for instance, those supporting individualism in the Senate, such as the filibuster) and the contours of public policy (such as state control of the level and eligibility rules in welfare policy). On the other hand, ethnically defined Northern and Midwestern party machines, controlled primarily but not exclusively by the Irish persistently resisted state centralization and policymaking autonomy so as to maximize the patronage resources that fueled their typically urban organizations. Both of these groups supported the expansion of national government spending when it avoided touching their core prerogatives but fiercely opposed it when state expansion threatened to damage the maintenance of the ethnic and racial political status quo. So, American political institutions and the politics of race and ethnicity could be said to have evolved in tandem in the United States, to the point that efforts at policy change by racial and ethnic out-groups also required a substantial project of institutional reconfiguration.

Britain presents a sharp contrast to this story of political development. On the one hand, the sheer numbers of racial and ethnic minorities in Britain have always been so small as to make their influence on the country's institutional architecture relatively marginal. The greatest experience of dealing with diverse racial and ethnic groups occurred at the edges of British politics, in the empire and in the subordinate parts of the United Kingdom, specifically Ireland. As a general rule, Britain's polity is substantially more centralized than that of the United States, with a more autonomous bureaucracy and a substantial fusing of legislative and executive power. This basic institutional configuration predated the arrival of commonwealth immigration, and basic institutional reforms have occurred with little consideration of their impact on ethnic minorities, and without substantial input from them. As compared to the American experience (where there was a co-evolution of institutions and racial/ethnic politics), Britain's minorities have confronted a deeply institutionalized system that developed without them in mind.

This basic fact turns out to have substantial, and in some cases counterintuitive, effects on the groups of interest to this study. On the American side, dealing with racial inequality required a massive transformation of the fundamental structure of American politics. The civil rights movement of the 1950s and 1960s was forced to attack not just racial segregation, but American traditions of federalism and weak bureaucratic power. That is, policy change and institutional reform went hand in hand. Britain's ethnic minorities, by contrast, have exercised what influence they have through an essentially static set of institutions.

Political decentralization, which was a major obstacle to racial minorities in the USA in the 1950s and 1960s, has since served to magnify their influence in some ways and diminish it in others. The concentration of black Americans in central cities with still-substantial authority has given them access to real power in, among other places, Los Angeles, Atlanta, New York, Detroit, and Chicago (once they were able to use their voting franchise to help elect black mayors). At the same time, these mayors attained power just as the budgets of central cities were coming under stress, making it difficult for them to use their newfound influence to durably advance the fortunes of their groups (as immigrants were, arguably, able to do earlier in the century). Nevertheless, political decentralization combined with population concentration has given ethnic and racial minorities access to power as something more than a coalition partner in the national Democratic Party.

Compare this to the situation in Britain. Despite their relatively small numbers, Britain's ethnic minorities are highly concentrated in a few central cities. In a more decentralized system with powerful urban governments, at least the larger ethnic minorities would have serious incentives to mobilize their members to capture local government and use it to their advantage. But Britain's local government, never terribly strong, has grown progressively weaker in the period since commonwealth immigration hit its stride. Local governments are now, effectively, administrative instruments of central government. Having achieved substantially more power at the local level than they have managed in the House of Commons, Britain's ethnic minorities found they had access to few resources for their troubles. As a general rule, Britain's ethnic minorities are best represented where that representation is of least value – on the one hand, in local government, where the absence of real power has dampened competition from other groups, and in the House of Lords, where political parties can accommodate minorities without the fear that it will damage their electoral competitiveness. As a result, ethnic minorities in Britain therefore appear before government agencies not as bearers of electoral power, but as sources of advice to ministers and civil servants who find they have an interest in their condition.

In addition to this institutional effect of timing, there is another, less remarked-upon, effect – the way the sequencing of ethnic and racial groups into the polity affects their political mobilization and organization. Steven Erie has persuasively argued that because the Irish were the first major ethnic group to immigrate en masse to the United States after the creation of the Jacksonian party system, they were able to take control of urban political organizations and extract disproportionate resources from them. Later-arriving groups, such as Italians, Jews, and blacks, had to be processed through a system that the Irish had, more or less, designed for themselves, and which they controlled. The Irish, therefore, had substantial power to influence the terms of political incorporation that other groups received, especially where public jobs and contracts were concerned. This propelled other groups into mobility strategies that were less dependent upon the public sector but also had the paradoxical effect of, in Erie's terms, "proletarianizing" the Irish by keeping them in low-wage public jobs.

4   Social mobility and social capital

Comparative analysis is also useful in helping us to distinguish the effects of superficially similar but functionally different social phenomena. A good example of this is geographic concentration or, as it is sometimes called, "segregation." Comparative analysis – both across groups, and across nations – helps us see that concentration does not necessarily equal segregation, and that under certain cases geographic concentration may be highly functional where social mobility is concerned. One way to put the difference is to think in terms of the difference between "ghettos" and "enclaves." Both may exhibit a similar level of group concentration, but their functioning will be highly dependent upon the meanings, or social significations, that those inside and outside associate with the fact of concentration.

In brief, an ethnic enclave combines elements of closure and permeability. An enclave is enclosed in the sense that primarily a single ethnic or racial group populates it, and this demographic fact is maintained by a combination of individual preferences, economic and social incentives, and collective action. In the first instance, an enclave maintains itself by its reputation (both to those it attracts and those it repels) as open only to persons of a particular ethnic or racial identity. This reputational feature of enclaves is, at least in part, shared with ghettos. The second two features, incentives and collective action, are not similarly shared. An enclave maintains its ethnic identity in part by a continuous process of recruiting new entrants, who are attracted by the social interactions and resources that are exclusively available within its boundaries. It provides these resources and interactions in part because it is maintained by a continuous cycle of population, with individuals living in the enclave and engaging intensely in its activities, and then moving out of the enclave but returning for the resources and identity-maintenance that can be delivered only within its boundaries. This continuous attraction to those who have "graduated out" of living in the enclave provides an ethnic network that cuts, at least somewhat, across class lines. An enclave is, finally, policed through processes of collective action. Because enclaves are not just sites of identity but also of institution building, they have the resources necessary to defend themselves against outsiders whose presence would diminish the intense concentration necessary for an enclave to function. In brief, enclaves work by recruiting coethnics, retaining existing members through nonresidential ties, and defending themselves against those deemed outsiders. This is, broadly speaking, the process described by Min Zhou in her contribution to this volume.

Ghettos may seem very similar to enclaves, in that both are characterized by residential concentration of a single racial or ethnic group. The primary difference between the two phenomena is not the degree of concentration, but the mechanisms by which that concentration is maintained and the effects that concentration has. Ghettos are maintained partially by external constraints, such as discrimination in the housing market, but also by the limited opportunities for mobility present in the ghetto and the damaging form of social capital that ghettos cause or at least help to replicate over time. That is, while ghettos are created in the first instance by external action, they may not need substantial, on-going external pressure to maintain their racial or ethnic exclusivity and patterns of stunted social mobility.

Critical to the process of stunted social mobility in the ghetto is the stigma that becomes attached to a particular place and the persons within it. This stigma profoundly impacts social mobility in two ways – through the stereotyping of the individuals within the ghetto (thereby affecting outsiders' sight-unseen assumptions of residents' individual characteristics) but also through limiting the degree to which what individual mobility there is in the ghetto redounds to the benefit of other ghetto residents. Remember that in the case of an enclave, there are substantial incentives for those who have moved up economically (and residentially) to retain ties to the enclave, thus providing social ties for those at the bottom of the group hierarchy. But a place affected by stigma becomes somewhere to leave and never come back. Thus, for a ghettoized group, individual mobility may have few or no external impacts on group members, while in the case of an enclave, coethnics may derive substantial external benefits from the achievements of those no longer living there.

This abstract analysis should suggest that the critical thing to pay attention to in examining residential concentration is not the raw mathematical fact that racial and ethnic minorities are not distributed equally across space, but the social significations that come to be associated with that concentration, and the patterns of cross-class social interaction that accompany it. In examining concentration comparatively, as Ceri Peach does in this volume, one thing is immediately clear – the American pattern of black residential concentration is a radical comparative outlier. British Afro-Caribbeans are among the country's least residentially concentrated ethnic groups, despite their relatively low socioeconomic levels, while greater ethnic concentrations are, for the most part, found among South Asian groups that experience higher levels of mobility. In both countries, only native-born black Americans demonstrate a combination of residential concentration, low levels of intermarriage with the majority group, and persistently low social mobility.[2] Comparative analysis, therefore, provides strong evidence for what we might call, "African-American exceptionalism." The analyses in this volume supports the view that the African-American experience is sufficiently different from that of other minorities that, for both purposes of analysis and of

normative judgment, it may be best to avoid the immigration analogy when examining the problems of black Americans. Conversely, we
should avoid thinking about immigrants and their problems through an
African-American frame of reference – an argument taken up powerfully
in this volume by Peter Skerry.

The distinction between ghettos and enclaves suggests the need
for clarifying somewhat our understanding of the concept of social
capital. For our purposes, social capital may be understood as the internal institutions and patterns of social interaction within geographically
concentrated racial and ethnic groups that facilitate the attainment by
individuals in those groups of valued social outcomes. The analyses in
this volume suggest that social capital may not be best studied in terms
of "how much," but in terms of the match between group patterns and
structural factors. In some cases, a group's strong internal bonds may
retard the ability of individuals to move where economic opportunities
are, while in other cases those same bonds may be the foundation for
ample opportunities, if the group is situated in an economically vibrant
area. Some groups, like poorer African-Americans, may have very deeply
patterned social interactions and expectations of coethnic behavior, but
that form of social capital may cause low investment in human capital
and may encourage involvement in behavior that is a poor match for the
preferences of outside employers, teachers, judges, and other distributors
of mobility-relevant goods.

This suggests that we may want to think about social capital in three
ways, especially when our interest is the effect of social relations on subsequent social mobility. First, the bonds we talk about in terms of social
capital vary in the way that groups are constituted. Some groups are held
together primarily by social institutions like businesses, political organizations, and schools that can provide substantial material incentive for
group attachment, while other groups are held together by less formal
mechanisms, primarily through social processes that distribute honor and
identity. How the group is constituted will have substantial impacts on
whether it is capable of organizing individuals for collective action and
redistributing mobility-relevant goods within the group. Second, as suggested above, social capital is a function of regime – whether the way a
particular group is constituted enhances or detracts from social mobility
is highly dependent upon the match with larger political and economic
structures. Third, and finally, social capital may be helpful at one stage of
group social mobility, but those same habits and institutions may become
deleterious at later stages.

5   The plan of the book

This volume is divided into five sections: (1) historical overviews; (2) informal social networks; (3) formal structures; (4) political institutions and processes; and (5) normative analysis. Section (1) consists of a pair of essays that provide a broad, historical overview of the demographics of racial and ethnic diversity in the two countries. In sections (2), (3), and (4) we present essays prepared for this volume by the sociologists, economists, and political scientists whom we recruited from either side of the Atlantic. These three sections form the core of this book. Each is introduced by a brief editors' commentary that surveys the key issues at stake, provides some historical or theoretical background while making clear the contribution of the individual chapters to the larger plan of the book. The essays in these middle three sections are descriptive and empirical. In section (5) we offer some explicitly prescriptive reflections on the ethical concerns raised by racial and ethnic inequalities in the two countries.

Here is a brief preview of what the reader can expect to find in sections (2), (3), and (4). Informal networks, which substantially determine what economists might call the "pre-market" experience of individuals, are essential to understanding differential group patterns of social mobility. These networks, such as the family, neighborhood, and ethno-racial group, interact in the production of social and human capital, and ultimately group development. These papers do not, however, investigate informal networks in a vacuum, instead examining their roots in specific historical processes (such as slavery and migration) and ongoing social policies and patterns (such as neighborhood racial composition). The identities of groups, their cultural meanings and the processes of group formation are matters not just of interest to cultural studies. As these chapters make clear, these processes through which groups come to be constituted have very clear effects on social and economic outcomes.

These outcomes start to become clear in the second section, on the formal structures of the labor market and education. By necessity and design, this section and the one preceding overlap substantially. The reason for this is simple: family, neighborhood, and ethnic group all deeply interpenetrate formal institutions. Schooling is strongly influenced by the cultural habits, group identities, and racial perceptions of the students and teachers who come in the door. Individuals do not enter the labor market as racially neutral clusters of skills, but as racially and ethnically identified and connected persons networked into labor markets where those identifications and networks matter. The formal, in sum, is incomprehensible in the absence of an understanding of the informal.

The third section examines how political institutions and processes interact with forces examined earlier to help produce social mobility outcomes. But these chapters also move away from the more economic definition of outcomes of the previous chapters. Mobility has dimensions that cannot be measured in dollars or pounds, encompassing also the recognition of group members as equal citizens, political power, health and safety. In some cases these other dimensions of social mobility act as critical leverage for economic mobility, but in other cases they are understood as ends desirable in and of themselves. A final section steps back even further, considering the normative consequences of the empirical analyses found in the rest of the book, and pointing the reader to how these should alter our thinking on fundamental questions of political and social theory.

NOTES

1. To some degree this reflects the tendency of the American state to intervene in society through regulatory and legal instruments, rather than direct government spending – a tendency that is less prevalent, but growing, in Great Britain.
2. It may be that Bangladeshis fit this pattern somewhat, but it is simply too early in this group's history in Britain to say with any confidence.

REFERENCES

Bell, D., 1976, *The Cultural Contradictions of Capitalism*, New York: Basic Books.

Duncan, G., 1984, *Years of Poverty, Years of Plenty: The Changing Economic Fortunes of American Workers and Families*, Ann Arbor, MI: Institute for Social Research.

Erikson, R. and J. Goldthorpe, 1992, *The Constant Flux: A Study of Social Mobility in Industrial Societies*, Oxford: Clarendon Press.

Glazer, N. and D. P. Moynihan, 1963, *Beyond the Melting Pot*, Cambridge, MA: MIT Press.

Goldthorpe, J., 1980, *Social Mobility and Class Structure in Modern Britain*, Oxford: Clarendon Press.

Loury, G., 2002, *The Anatomy of Racial Inequality*, Cambridge, MA: Harvard University Press.

Modood T., 1999, "New Forms of Britishness: Post-Immigration Ethnicity and Hybridity in Britain," in R. Lentin (ed.), *The Expanding Nation: Towards A Multi-Ethnic Ireland*, Dublin: Trinity College, pp. 34–40.

Office for National Statistics (ONS), 2003, *Census, April 2001*, Office for National Statistics.

Rex J. and R. Moore, 1967, *Race, Community and Conflict*, New York: Oxford
   University Press for the Institute of Race Relations.
Tichenor, D., 2002, *Dividing Lines: The Politics of Immigration Control in the United
   States*, Princeton University Press.
US Census Bureau, 2000, *Decennial Census*, Summary Files 1 and 3.

Part I

Historical overviews

1   Ruling an empire, governing a multinational state: the impact of Britain's historical legacy on the contemporary ethno-racial regime

Mary J. Hickman

1   Introduction

The ethno-racial regime in Britain is discussed usually in terms of the impact of the end of empire and the post-1945 immigration of people, mostly in possession of British citizenship, from the New Commonwealth and Pakistan. This chapter extends the discussion to bring into simultaneous consideration the formation of the multinational state and the light this can shed on the management of national/ethnic relations within the domestic sphere. It is the articulation of these two realms, those of empire and that of the multinational state, which will be explored to reveal the extent to which common practices inform both, and the specificity of each which explains the particularities of the British case.

Much of the literature about the post-1945 immigrants and their British-born children argues that as populations they are distinguished by their experiences of colonialism and subsequent related experiences after migration to the imperial centre. It is assumed, quite correctly, that this history of colonial relations has been important in developing British attitudes to ethno-racial differentiation. I am not challenging these fundamental points but I am arguing against any reduction of this history to a matter of white/black relations. A major reason for arguing against this is that in Ireland empire and multinational state formation intermeshed and produced a history which both explains the centre and the periphery and had an impact on the developing ethno-racial regime.

These opening remarks have referred to Britain rather than the United Kingdom. In the nineteenth century, after the last Act of Union in 1801 between Great Britain and Ireland, the United Kingdom comprised England, Wales, Scotland, and Ireland. The partition of Ireland in 1920 altered the boundaries of the United Kingdom so that it was made up of England, Wales, Scotland, and Northern Ireland. Britain or Great Britain refers only to England, Wales, and Scotland and, therefore, Britain and the United Kingdom are not synonymous. England which is only one part of either is often used to refer to all parts of the union and its people. The frequent terminological conflation of the terms England, Britain, and the United Kingdom is directly linked to and reflects the unequal relations between parts of the union. This historical account will focus on Britain (meaning England, Wales, and Scotland) because I am differentiating Northern Ireland from the rest of the United Kingdom because the relationship of Ireland to Britain has been qualitatively different from that of Scotland and Wales. This difference, as I intend to show, is informative about the relationship between ethnicity and public policy.

In contemporary Britain ethnicity is most frequently cited within public discourses in relation to "ethnic minorities." Any reference to ethnic minorities is assumed to be to people who are black or Asian and who by definition must be migrants or descendants of migrants, because ethnic minorities is the term used for groups formerly represented as "immigrants" and prior to that as "colored," and therefore people whose origins are represented as "external" to the United Kingdom (Lewis 2000). By definition ethnic minorities are British subjects but their classification as members of minorities securely locates them in a subordinate position in the hierarchy of "Britishness."

On various assessments of social mobility the Irish in Britain are located in an intermediate position, doing less well than Indians and Chinese, better than Black Caribbeans (although Irish women and Black Caribbean women are very similar in socioeconomic profile) and Pakistanis in Britain (see Heath and McMahon 1997, Hickman and Walter 1997, Scully 1997, and Model 1999 on the blocked mobility of the Irish). In the mid-1990s the Commission for Racial Equality recommended the inclusion of the Irish in ethnic monitoring and followed up by publishing a report on discrimination and the Irish (Hickman and Walter 1997). The 2001 census included "Irish" as a category in the ethnic origin question for the first time in England, Wales, and Scotland. The experiences of the Irish in Britain are useful to consider when examining the historical contextualization of ethnicity, social mobility, and public policy for the following reasons. First, the longevity of their experiences of racialization and differentiation challenges assimilationist arguments. Second, the different relationship of Ireland compared with England, Wales, and Scotland to the United Kingdom warrants an understanding of variegated ways in which ethno-racial differences have been incorporated into practices of governance in Britain/the United Kingdom. Third, as a long-term source of labor and in particular for the argument here, unskilled manual labor, the Irish can help explicate the relationship between ethnicity and class in Britain. Fourth, bringing the Irish into a broader historical examination of ethnicity and public policy will provide a fuller account of the relationship than those provided on the basis of a narrow definition of ethnicity (that is, color). Fifth, focusing on the Irish, in addition to the Asian, African, and Caribbean populations in Britain, will facilitate an articulation of two histories: that of empire and of the multinational state.

Below I commence with a brief account of the British Empire, beginning in the sixteenth century which saw significant developments that foreshadowed key directions of English/British global expansion, the reconquest of Ireland, the slave trade, and the establishment of the East India Company. The next section provides a summary of the origins and formation of the multinational United Kingdom, including an analysis of English hegemony within the UK. The following section examines social hierarchies and racialization processes in the nineteenth century and details the institutional strategy developed in response to the Irish immigration at that time and its legacy. The final section deals with immigration controls and the consolidation of public policies towards those positioned as "external" to the nation despite holding British citizenship and the contradictions inherent in these policies regarding Irish nationals.

2   Empire

The relationship of England, and later of the unitary formation, Britain, to the various parts of the empire was differentiated but involved a common thread of racializing "native" and slave populations. Although the specificity of the characterization of various populations underwent changes, the notion of hierarchy and the tendency to racialized representations has persisted down to the twenty-first century. There is only space here to indicate briefly how English, later British, colonial endeavors were manifested in a variety of arenas. The aim is twofold. First, to demonstrate the extent to which Ireland was part of the colonial sphere as well as part of nation-state formation in the domestic context; second, to illustrate some aspects of the history of contact between England/Britain and colonial territories/subjects. These histories framed not only developments in the colonies, but the impact of empire on the British "domestic" sphere and the influence across/between colonies.

2.1   Ireland

For four centuries after the initial Anglo-Norman invasion of Ireland in 1169 there were various attempts to gain effective control of Ireland, which met with only temporary success. In the sixteenth century, under

Elizabeth I, a sustained re-conquest was made to control and exploit Ireland on a permanent and persistent basis. Ireland was subject to this re-colonization project as part of a wider process of English expansion in the sixteenth century. By the end of the sixteenth century: "Ireland came to be treated differently from England, it in turn provided a model for the management of those transoceanic territories that were soon to come under the control of the English government" (Canny 1988: 29). The ambivalence of Ireland's positioning in this period was rooted in Ireland being juridically a kingdom though treated practically by the English as if it were a colony. Ireland was therefore linked both to Britain's overseas empire and to the processes of state-building that characterized the early modern European composite monarchies (Armitage 2000).

After the joining of the Scottish and English crowns under James VI/I, a policy of subduing Ireland by plantation was promoted as a specifically British enterprise involving both lowland Scots and English settlers. Plantation aimed at the imposition of cultural, religious, and legal uniformity, although the eradication of cultural diversity at this point went in tandem with toleration of constitutional diversity. The plan failed for a variety of reasons and the native Irish rose up to slaughter the colonists in 1642. The consequence was the Cromwellian invasion which dispossessed the native Catholic population and redistributed the land to new, non-Irish colonists, and sent thousands of indentured Irish people to the West Indies. These policies aimed at both cultural and constitutional uniformity, although this was never fully achieved. The Cromwellian campaign was of such "rigour and cruelty" and resulted in such a ruthless land settlement that it left a mark, a cultural memory, that succeeding centuries have not been able to wipe out (Beckett 1979: 75). The majority of landlords of large estates from this period onwards were divided from their tenants by religion and language and regarded themselves as English or Anglo-Irish and as part of the Protestant Ascendancy. By the middle of the eighteenth century Catholics, who made up 80 percent of the population, owned 5 percent of the land (Beckett 1979).

Through the periods of conquest, rebellions, and re-conquest in Ireland "evidence" for the necessity of these campaigns was generated. The Anglo-Norman invasion of Ireland in the twelfth century was accompanied by "justifications" which relied upon conceptions of the Irish as inferior and alien. The evidence for dominating Ireland has involved lengthy discursions on the Irish national character, directly linked to notions about the Celts as a "race" or the Irish as a nation (Lebow 1973: 6; Hechter 1975). This is an example of the racialization of the *interior* of Europe (Miles 1993: 88). The civilization project so integral to later European colonial empires began within Europe. Ireland's location in

Europe and its Christianity was divided by imputing that its Christian practices were more nominal than real and suffused with superstition. This defined the Irish as an aberration compared with the rest of the continent. A key text was Edmund Spenser's *A View of the Present State of Ireland* published in 1596 (see Spencer 1970). It devoted considerable attention to the barbaric condition of the Gaelic Irish and identified a series of stages of social development, situating the Irish, with their supposed progenitors the Scythians, at the least developed stage (Canny and Pagden 1987).

Spenser argued that the Irish must be compelled to be free by a sustained policy of war followed by good government. This meant the Irish had to become English. These themes were explored by David Hume. Writing in the eighteenth century, he argued that from the beginning of time the Irish had been buried in the most profound barbarism and ignorance; primarily because, having never been conquered by the Romans, they had never acquired civilization, and thus were not tamed by education, or restrained by laws (Hume 1778, Vol. I: 424). Hume asserted that the British/English have benefited from the inter-breeding of different peoples and cultures, and that the Irish are "beyond the Pale" because of their isolated inbreeding/incest (see also Kohn 1940). Implicit in this view is that the Irish are not only alien but inferior and should be compelled to conform to the laws of civilized man. Subsequently, religious antipathy had inflamed this fundamental cleavage between the English and the Irish (Hume 1778, Vol. V: 397–8). It is the backwardness (still mired in superstition and not engaged in critical re-evaluation) and barbarity (wildness of manners) of Irish culture which clearly differentiates the Irish from the rest of Europe. English assumptions were of an undeniable relationship between civilization, the common law and Protestantism (Deane 1983).

2.2   West Indies

British islands in the West Indies were intended as settler colonies. However, because of the crop economies that developed the importing of African slaves increased. England's interests in the slave trade accelerated with the expansion of plantation crops in North America and the West Indies during the sixteenth and seventeenth centuries, including Oliver Cromwell seizing Jamaica from Spain in 1655. Finally in the Treaty of Utrecht in 1713, Britain acquired from France the contract to supply African slaves to the Spanish colonies from its Caribbean territories. Within fifty years Britain became the leading slave-trading nation in the world, the foremost slave carrier for other European nations, and the

centre of the Triangular Trade (Hiro 1992). The slave trade was trans-
forming the basis of these colonies as well as the European powers themselves. These were therefore settler societies in which the native people
had been exterminated and another subordinate population was now in
place as a labor force.

Slave-merchants' and sugar planters' financial needs meant that in
Bristol and Liverpool, as in London, very close connections were established between the slave trade and the banks. In this way and in the
barrage of commission agents, absentee proprietors and political agents
of the West Indian colonies, who made up the West Indian lobby, the
slave trade and the colonization of the Caribbean became interwoven into
British institutions, commercial activities, and political priorities (Fryer
1984: 46). As British involvement in and profits from slavery and the
slave trade increased, the concept of the African slave as a commod-
ity or, at best, a workhorse began to emerge. On plantations, African
slaves were catalogued along with livestock and treated as work-animals,
"to be worked to the maximum at the minimum cost of maintenance"
(Hiro 1992: 2). By the end of the long seventeenth century Africans
became thoroughly racialized as negroes and this was linked to slavery (see
Vaughan 1989 for a fuller discussion). Religious and cultural justifications
were often advanced to establish the inherent inferiority of negroes as a
race.

David Hume wrote about the inferiority of blacks compared with whites
in the following terms:

I am apt to suspect the Negroes . . . to be naturally inferior to the Whites. There
scarcely ever was a civilized nation of that complexion, nor ever any individuals,
eminent either in action or speculation. No ingenious manufacturers among
them, no arts, no sciences. On the other hand, the most rude and barbarous
of the Whites such as the Germans, the present Tartars, still have something eminent about them in their valour, form of government or some particular. (Hume
1997: 33)

Possession of or lack of civilization is a key attribute which is associated
with "race" and is thought by Hume to clinch the argument for superiority or inferiority. The Germans despite being "barbarous" and therefore
lower in the European hierarchy than the English, have been able to benefit to some degree from Western civilization (a point he was unprepared
to concede in relation to Ireland).

In many of the West Indian colonies forms of (limited) representative government were established. For example, Jamaica from the 1860s
had a Governor, Council, and Assembly. One significant difference
compared with Ireland was that the people being governed were an

imported population rather than natives. When emancipation for slaves was achieved in 1837, as in most other Caribbean societies this did not entail rights of political representation being conferred on the former slaves in the British Caribbean. Their rights were restricted by the property requirements that effectively disenfranchised all but a few of the black and colored population.

2.3   India

The East India Company was launched in England in 1599. Elizabeth I granted the company a charter which gave it a monopoly of trade with India and the East and in 1612 the Mughal Emperor granted the Company the vital "firman" (mandate), allowing it the privilege of Indian trade. Operating from its headquarters in London, the Company's main interest was trade and profit, and familiar British institutions like law courts, churches, theatres were transplanted to India with a growing army of professionals and other employees, all slotted into the Company's strictly defined hierarchy (Visram 1986).

By the middle of the eighteenth century the vast Mughal Empire was fast disintegrating and the East India Company, utilizing its own regiments, emerged as an influential political and military power in South India. The East India Company now had unbridled power over large areas in which they possessed trade monopolies, were exempt from taxes, and determined what was produced and the wages to be paid. The result was gross abuse of their authority as members of the Company sought to enrich themselves. In 1773 parliament intervened and a Governor General was appointed to the Company's Indian possessions with instructions to halt the corruption. From this time therefore the government was directly overseeing the affairs of the Company in India and after the loss of the American colonies in 1783 the centre of the empire effectively shifted to India.

Many administrators and soldiers were required to protect the growing empire in what was a captive market and a vast reservoir of resources for Britain. England and Scotland obtained most of their raw materials from India at very cheap prices and sold most of their manufactures at arbitrary prices back to India. Gradually Indian ways and customs, which in the eighteenth century had been encouraged, began to disappear from the British community. In the nineteenth century interventionist policies were embarked upon with often very disruptive effects: social and religious practices viewed as "barbaric" were abolished (and evangelical Christian missionaries encouraged), Indian classical education was reformed, that is, Europeanized, and Indian laws, customs, and practices were all remodeled on the English pattern. In the grip of bequeathing "civilization" to India, the Indian National Rising of 1857 came as a considerable shock to the British. They responded with terrible reprisals, although it still took eighteen months to quell the rebellion. However, the uprising represented a watershed in British rule. The East India Company was wound up, direct rule from Westminster was instigated, and Queen Victoria became Empress of India. With the reassertion of control the British Raj was established, paid for by Indian taxes, and British supremacy became synonymous with arrogance, a hardening of racial attitudes and "the white man's burden" (Judd 1996).

In the aftermath of imposing direct rule the viceroys sent to India recognized that in order to oversee such a vast territory it was necessary to reinforce the support of an already courted Hindu elite. Indian social institutions were left alone, thereby securing a degree of acquiescence to British rule from the upper classes, and this enabled the colonizers to exploit class, ethnic, and regional differences (Visram 1986). A prototype of dual mandate was implemented by which the British sought to operate through the existing structures and to use them as points of mediation and effective control in an elaborate system of domination (Goulbourne 1998). As in the West Indian colonies the mass of people were not politically enfranchised.

In India, the awe with which the British had initially greeted contact with the riches of Indian civilization had been in retreat by the second half of the eighteenth century. It was during this period that the British ceased to be obsequious traders in India and became rulers and with this went a growing sense of superiority and authority. The vast plundering of this period was accompanied by increasingly contemptuous views. Charles Grant, a British historian, in 1792 described the Indian people as "a race of men lamentably degenerate and base, retaining but a feeble sense of moral obligation . . . governed by a malevolent and licentious passion." Soon descriptions of Indians echoed with phrases familiar from their application to African slaves. For example, another historian Herbert Edwardes referred when discussing Indians to "wild barbarians, indifferent to human life . . . yet free, simple as children, brave, faithful to their masters" (cited in Hiro 1992: 6).

English, later British, colonization of these three areas proceeded in different ways but there were also important similarities and important points of contact. Both in the early period of colonization and later in the nineteenth century, common personnel and policies developed in one area were applied with or without modification and with varying degrees of success in other areas (see Canny and Pagden 1987, Cook 1993). In each domain processes of racialization and inferiorization developed – immediately in Ireland, as a result of local labor policies in the West Indies, and in India as exploitation became more vigorous and widespread. In all arenas the "native" or slave populations were deemed not to be civilized and the theme of colonization was rectifying this situation.

3   The multinational state: origins and formation

It required an enormous effort to "naturalise the link between physical and political geography" in the British Isles and central to this process was the fictive narrative of the island race who had not been invaded since 1066 (Cohen 1999). The English constructed themselves as the backbone of a more inclusive sense of British nationhood which subsumed all differences within an overriding principle of identity. Part of the myth of England, for which the establishment of the multinational state has been central, is the notion that at the heart of English success has been the ability of English identity and institutions to evolve by peaceful commingling and the absorption of various groups and influences, and this underpinned its claim of superiority.

Modern state formation in England commenced during the Tudor period in the sixteenth century. The Reformation in England was a political and legal revolution as well as a religious one and took place for both external and internal reasons. The subjection of the Catholic Church formed the most striking, but not the sole, manifestation of a general policy designed to create the unitary realm of England under the legislative sovereignty of the King in Parliament (Elton 1955). Steps towards forming a multinational state soon followed. The 1536 Act of Union legislated for the unification of Wales with England. This imposed English land law, English courts and judges, the Anglican Church, and a requirement to speak English for public office in Wales. Since the sixteenth century, therefore, the two countries have been treated as one administrative unit.

The union of Scotland with England and Wales, as will be seen, represented a more equal combination, and distinct legislation has always been passed for Scotland. In the case of Ireland union followed a violent rebellion. What emerged from the Civil War in the seventeenth century was a constitution and national identity which were based on the strengthened sovereignty of Parliament and Protestantism. The Act of Union in 1707 reinforced the role of religion in the nation state. It linked Scotland to England and Wales in one united kingdom of Great Britain, with one Protestant ruler, one legislature, and one system of trade. Scotland retained a distinctive religious organization (the Kirk) and also separate legal and education systems. Nairn (1981) writes that the 1707 Act represented a patrician bargain between two ruling classes in which Scotland relinquished its statehood (its parliament) but preserved a set of institutions normally associated with independence.

Ireland was granted a legislature of some autonomy in 1782. This reform did not satisfy everyone, and the Society of United Irishmen demanded radical reforms including universal suffrage for Catholics as well as Protestants. A nationalist uprising in 1798, led by Theobold Wolfe Tone and supported by French troops, was the most violent in Ireland's history, with a death toll of almost 30,000. Many potential supporters of the rebellion amongst the Anglo-Irish ascendancy, however, had come to recognize that, regardless of their resentment of Britain, they could never aspire to complete separation from the "mother country" as it would result in their being eventually engulfed by the native population. Instead of a bid for independence they settled for union with Britain to assure a continuation of their privileged position in Ireland (Canny 1987: 211). After the rebellion had been crushed, Ireland was united with Britain through the Act of Union and brought under the direct sovereignty of the Westminster parliament.

A quasi-colonial relationship persisted in the nineteenth century despite incorporation into the domestic state. Although Ireland enjoyed parliamentary representation at Westminster (which was of critical significance during the struggle for Home Rule) and was frequently subject to the same legislation as the rest of the United Kingdom its political integration was imperfect at best; Ireland was subject to a vast body of legislation that was not applied anywhere else in the British Isles (this was true of Scotland, though to a lesser extent and for different reasons). Ireland retained (unlike Scotland and Wales) a civil service and policy administration that was wholly separate from that of England's and far more centralized. Like India, the British administration in Ireland was headed by a viceroy (Cook 1993: 18–19).

Old English Tories were ruthless in maintaining English political dominance. They came to tolerate national cultural identities (although more so in Wales and Scotland than in Ireland) as long as state power was not challenged (Crick 1991). They shared the spoils of empire while confident that advantages of numbers, wealth, and territory would ensure English dominance within the United Kingdom and the colonies. Sharing the spoils of empire was crucial with respect to Scotland. Scotland was allowed full trading access to England's colonies as a consequence of the 1707 Act of Union, and the wealth brought back to Scotland during the eighteenth and nineteenth centuries transformed its economy (Maan

1992). The case of Ireland was rather different. There was little transition to large-scale industrial production so Irish industries could not compete on a world market. The main exception was the eastern part of the province of Ulster where industrial progress was made during the nineteenth century. A native Catholic population was concentrated in the lowest-paid occupations and the worst housing, while workers who were descendants of a settler, Protestant population dominated the more skilled occupations. This was, therefore, the only region which was integrated into the wider UK industrial economy and hence the empire. This is one of the reasons why Home Rule was regarded as undesirable by the majority of Protestants.

Protestant Ireland was therefore far more enthusiastic in pursuit of imperial projects than Catholic Ireland (Kennedy 1996). The chief ways in which any member of the Irish Catholic peasantry participated in the empire was by emigration to one of the settler dominions, by joining the Catholic Church, or by joining the British army or navy (the officer-class was mainly Anglo-Irish). The archetypal Irishman in India during British rule was neither a missionary nor a merchant, neither doctor nor administrator, but a soldier. Hence the oft-cited characterization of the contribution of the peoples who made up the United Kingdom to the British empire: "The Irish fought for it, the Scottish and Welsh ran it, but the English kept the profits" (Kapur 1997: 6). By the time of the rebellion in 1857 Irish soldiers constituted over 40 percent (some 16,000 men) of the combined regular army and the East India Company's regiments in India (Bartlett 1997).

An overarching identity developed as the British came to define themselves as a single people not because of political or cultural consensus at home but rather in reaction to war with Catholic France in the eighteenth century (Colley 1992). Catholic Ireland was also a significant other of emerging Britishness. By the nineteenth century the heart of the Catholic question was the peculiar relationship between Britain and Ireland, one in which Irish Catholics were simultaneously inside and outside the national polity even after the 1801 Act of Union and the 1829 Catholic Emancipation Act (Hall 2000). Closely intertwined with Catholicism in the popular imagination, it was the Irish issue which raised fundamental issues of English national identity. The Church of England and the Tory party mobilized to defend the institutions of an ethno-cultural constitution against the encroachments of popery (Best 1958, Hickman 1995). On many occasions a cross-class, cross-Protestantism alliance was possible on the basis of antipathy to Catholicism, whose corrupting and contaminating influence was perceived as manifest in every city in the form of Irish immigrants. They were perceived as threatening the union of Church and State, which was the embodiment of "the English people" (Robbins 1982: 469), because of their allegiance to a foreign authority and resistance to English rule.

By the nineteenth century a modern state had been formed which was in the process of constructing its own ancestry and inventing its own traditions in which ethnic and national identifications were marginalized or carefully controlled from London (Morgan 1985–6). The whole process of centralization in the British state, the fact that the English parliament, between 1540 and 1801, had become the British parliament, the idea of the sovereignty of that parliament and the lack of any distinct Celtic representative in the Cabinet, all reinforced the idea that the United Kingdom was "a coat that fitted snugly and firmly over all the peoples who dwelt in the British Isles" (Boyce 1986: 231). Britishness has been an incorporating identity. The existence of other ethno-national identities (for example Welsh, Scottish) is recognized, but these are positioned as sub-national identities. They are not hyphenated with Britishness because the latter overarches them, the symbol of this hierarchical system being the supremacy of the Westminster parliament. The legitimacy of this distinction, and the material resources it has delivered, is in part what has sustained the Union. Because of the history of British-Irish relations this was not to be a satisfactory basis for incorporating Irish national identifications. The constitutional and land struggles in Ireland challenged the notion of the "snug fit" of the cloak of the United Kingdom.

4   Social hierarchies and institutional arrangements in the nineteenth century

The transformation of Britain into the first industrial capitalist nation carried with it the erosion of old divisions and forms of belonging, and new ways of imagining the nation became imperative. What can be traced in the nineteenth century is the construction of a code of breeding which enabled the alliance of the new hybrid elite (aristocracy and industrial capital on the one hand, and different national elites, English, Welsh, Scots, and the Anglo-Irish Protestant Ascendancy, on the other hand) to be cemented. Positioned as members of a superior island race this code enabled the English/British to classify and hierarchize all human beings (see Cohen 1988, Dodd 1986).

At different times in the nineteenth century, therefore, the English working class was designated by the ruling class as "a different breed" or an uncivilized "race," but in other circumstances, as a constituent part of the English (British) "race." As Miles comments:

The result was a racialized nationalism or a nationalist racism, a mercurial ideological bloc that was manipulated by the ruling class (or rather by different fractions of it) to legitimate the exploitation of inferior "races" in the colonies, to explain economic and political struggles with other European nation states, and to signify (for example) Irish and Jewish migrants as an undesirable "racial" presence within Britain. (Miles 1993: 96)

Immigrants with political demands came to be identified with an invasive and highly contagious virus, which must be isolated if the body politic is to survive. It is important to note that this distinction between immigrants and the indigenous population powerfully combined elements of class and racial signification in an ideology that was the basis of a nation-state underpinned by both class and ethnic/national differentiations. The two arenas of differentiation intermesh: calls to the national interest mask class relations; and debates about the primacy of socioeconomic divisions mask important ethno-racial hierarchies.

Ideas of race and hierarchy were a constant feature of much of the public discourse in the domestic arena as well as in various parts of the empire (Hall 2000). Empire is in the centre of the work of many of the literary and scientific establishment. In the formation of notions of hierarchy in Britain in the nineteenth century, the domestic realm of the multinational state and the realm of empire were often linked and were as significant as conceptions of class relations for the construction of social and political hierarchies. My theme is making connections because many histories are written as if they are distinct and separate realms. Ireland consistently belies this. Even the argument that each part of the empire was ruled very differently has to be qualified when we remember the extent to which rule in Ireland was used as an exemplar in India and how India functioned as an intermediary between parts of Africa and Southeast Asia as supplier of troops, labor, policy precedents and forms of indirect rule (Cook 1993). There was a complex interaction between forms of governance and the management of ethno-national relations which had a direct significance for developments in the metropolitan center as the impact of the Indian National Uprising (1857), the Morant Bay rebellion (1865), and the Fenian rebellion (1867) demonstrate. These events led to constitutional and institutional responses as well as intertwining social subordination, cultural alienness, and political threat in the framing of black Caribbeans, Indians, and Irish Catholics. I now turn to examine one institutional response to Irish Catholic immigrants in nineteenth-century Britain which demonstrates the dual constitution as internal and external that characterized Irish positionings in the nation.

The "social" is a distinct domain and can be seen to emerge within a specific conjuncture in relation to various attempts to resolve the "social question," that is, the problematic question of population management and political order which the nineteenth century defined in "social" terms (Squires 1990). This can be illustrated with reference to the institutional response to Irish immigration. In the nineteenth century approximately 1 million Irish people migrated to Britain (Ó Gráda 1975) both before and after the Great Famine and augmented substantial settlements already established in London, Liverpool, Manchester, and Glasgow. The discourses generated about the Irish at both national and local levels in the 1830s and 1840s differentiated them as immigrants from the rest of the working class. The Irish in Britain were constituted as both a social and a political threat and the three most important aspects of these discourses were: the fear that the Irish would socially contaminate the indigenous working class, the fear of their role in producing public disorder, and the fear of the possibility they would combine with the indigenous working class in political revolt (Hickman 1995). It was specifically the Irish Catholic working class who were problematized in this way; they failed tests of acceptability and were deemed to be "unEnglish."

Both the types of jobs the Irish did and the conditions in which they were compelled to live were transmuted into corroborative evidence of their degenerative nature. They were also deemed a threat to public order because of perceived Irish habits of ingrained drunkenness and "faction fighting." Examining the relationship between the agencies of "law and order" and Irish immigrants casts a different light. The Irish bore the brunt of the early police drive to assert their authority in urban Britain (Swift 1985). The categories of crime statistics in which the Irish were concentrated reflected both their vulnerability to certain types of prosecutions because of their popularized image and decisions by police forces to implement legislation (for example, the Beer Act 1848, the Lodging House Act 1851) aimed at the working class in general, specifically in Irish areas (see Cockcroft 1974, Philips 1974, Swift 1985).

This example of how the Irish were a specific target of policing practices indicates one of the ways in which anti-Irish prejudice was an influence on policy formation and implementation at a local level. Finnegan in a study of the Irish in York states that:

there was a marked degree of anti-Irish prejudice in the city, stemming mainly from the middle classes and apparent in the attitudes and utterances of the Poor Law Guardians, Sanitary Inspectors and magistrates, and particularly evident in newspaper editorials and the coverage of local news. . . . Those in authority, English, middle-class respectable Protestants, were prejudiced against the immigrants, and the prejudice led them to make stereotypes, misleading judgements about the Irish . . . (Finnegan 1985: 77)

The deduction is often made that because there was an absence of specific legislation to deal with the "Irish menace" they were, despite being noticeable in nineteenth-century cities, fundamentally not treated differently from the rest of the working class. In Britain it was repeatedly in the differential implementation of legislation of general applicability that the problem of the "Irish immigrant" was dealt with (see Williams 1996 on the operation of the 1834 Poor Law in this respect).

Examining state education policy in the nineteenth century reveals another institutional response to Irish Catholic immigrants and shows how ethnic diversity and the construction of social problems was a feature of policymaking (Hickman 1995). Liberal accounts of the development of the state assume that state grants were extended to Catholic schools as a corollary of the emancipation of Catholics in 1828. A separate Catholic elementary school system *did not* develop for this reason or because of the demands of the Catholic Church in Britain. Government policy in the 1830s–1840s (Whig/Peelite administrations) was to encourage inter-denominational schooling, funded in part by government grants, for reasons of national cohesion and economy. However, strong objections to this policy centered on a fear of contamination. Specifically that the children of Irish Catholic working-class migrants would be a contaminant influence if schooled with other working-class children. These objections came from other denominations, especially the Church of England, and from certain political forces, in particular the Conservative Party. Their efforts to differentiate and segregate the children of the Irish working class were forcibly expressed at local level through the Protestant Association and by the local and national press through discourses of anti-Catholicism and anti-Irishness (see Murphy 1959, Hickman 1995).

Despite the wish of central government to develop a national system of education opposition to interdenominational education became acute whenever the suggestion was made of including Irish Catholics in any state-funded arrangements. Eventually the state successfully introduced grant aid for Catholic schools in 1847, against still significant opposition, by stressing the dire educational need, and the consequences if neglected, of the poorest and most alien section of the population being outside the national framework (for greater detail see Hickman 1995). Central government was concerned with re-constructing the Irish in Britain as political subjects (Curtis 1983) and the Catholic Church was to be the chief agency in a process of incorporating and denationalizing the Irish working class; this was similar to the strategy pursued in Ireland after 1796 of funding the Catholic Church as a means of co-opting it as an institution and diffusing political rebellion. Within the Enlightenment, education was the means by which 'man' was perfectible and

thus schooling was to confer access to civilization. Education was, therefore, central to the construction of modernity. However, the racialized
discourse which ensured that Irish Catholic children were not educated
with other working-class children established an ethnically segregated,
religiously distinctive, state-education system with far-reaching consequences for both the Irish Catholic children educated within Catholic
schools and those educated in the rest of the sector (Hickman 1995).
Modern subjects were being created and in particular the political subjects of the nation.

Catholic schools became the institutional means of containing Irish
children and became the symbol of differentiation of Irish Catholics from
the indigenous working class, all of whom, whatever their other differences, shared Protestantism and British national identity. The Catholic
Church and Catholic school were local symbols of an "enemy within"
and were frequently attacked (Hickman 1995). Most important from the
perspective of the government of the day was that on both ethno-national
grounds and class criteria the Catholic Church could be trusted with
the task of incorporating and denationalizing the Irish. This was because
English and Scottish Catholics were anxious in the post-Emancipation
context to demonstrate their loyalty to the state, and as members of the
gentry/aristocracy they shared a similar ideological outlook with the newly
established elite. The church hierarchy often expressed the view that its
interests were coterminous with those of central government. There was
no takeover of the Catholic hierarchy in Britain by the Irish as there was
in the United States of America and Australia.

Issues about the integration and segregation of an ethnic minority were,
therefore, of crucial significance in shaping the development of the British
education system in the nineteenth century. The processes which ensured
that Irish Catholic children were not educated with other working-class
children established an ethnically segregated education system. One consequence was the masking of Irishness within official discourses. Simultaneously, Catholic schools, which adopted a curriculum approved by
government inspectors and specifically devoid of general references to Ireland, held up a mirror to their pupils in which was reflected their Catholic-
ity rather than their Irishness. The important point here is that state
funding of denominational schools is not necessarily a sign of cultural
belonging. Thus we see that at the same time that Irish Catholics were
being excluded from the "nation" as an "imagined community" they were
simultaneously included within the welfare relations which were developed around state-financed schooling, but in a subordinated, marginalized position (Hickman 1995). These differences remained as crucial
markers in the twentieth century prior to renewed large-scale immigration from Ireland in the 1950s. Irish Catholics (that is the descendants

of the nineteenth-century migrants) continued to be distinguished "as a race apart" in local communities in the 1930s and 1940s (see Priestley 1934, Archer 1986, Hoggart 1988, Fielding 1993, Lennon, McAdam, and O'Brien 1988). They were segregated within a marginalized, poorer-funded, institutional framework run by the Catholic Church. These institutional arrangements, established in the nineteenth century, became a crucial framework for the settlement of Catholics from the Republic of Ireland in the renewed heavy immigration of the 1940s–1960s.

There were some similarities in the changes of discourse about New Commonwealth migrants and their children in the 1980s, with those described above about the Irish. In the 1980s a change of discourse from "immigrant" to "ethnic minority" took place which signified that migrants from the New Commonwealth and their children and grand-children were no longer being discursively addressed as foreign. An ethnic minority is quite another "subject" compared with an "immigrant." She or he is defined as "inside" the political and geographical borders of the nation-state and usually has full citizenship. However, an ethnic minority is *in* the nation but not necessarily *of* the nation in the way this is understood as an "imagined community" (Lewis 1998). An effect of the 1988 Education Reform Act was in part to shift power away from the Local Education Authorities and towards parents who through "opt out" and local management of schools could reinforce tendencies towards "racial" and/or ethnic segregation in schools. It is worth noting that it had been parents backed by the Tory establishment that won out in Liverpool in 1841 ensuring that segregated education was the result.

This section has shown that the correlations made between the Irish Catholic working class and disease, poverty, crime, and political rebellion ensured that they were the object of government attention. Irish immigrants were citizens of the state as well as subjects of the monarch, but they were consistently treated in discriminatory ways. This reflected the religio-ethnic cleavage in the nation which shifted to the center after the 1801 union and heavy migration from Ireland in mid-century. The differential treatment of the Irish orchestrated differences and antagonisms amongst the working class. These differences occurred along lines which reinforced a hierarchy of skills with that of respectability and cross-cut this class stratification with ethno-national, ethno-racial, and religious differences.

6 Immigration controls, public policies and the racialization of the nation

At various times in British history the boundaries of the nation and of the imagined national community have been reconstructed. In the twentieth century the boundaries of the nation were reinscribed in 1905, the 1920s, and in the 1950s after, respectively, the passage of the first immigration controls of the century, the granting of Irish independence, and in the wake of considerable inward migration from the Caribbean, the Indian subcontinent, and Ireland.

The 1830s–1840s had seen various social policy developments in a context of discourses about Irish contamination and disruption of order resulting in a subordinated inclusion of Irish immigrants. The period 1905 to 1918 marked another crucial phase of social policy developments when a range of welfare benefits and services were enacted including old age pensions and national insurance. At the same time, in 1905, the Aliens Act imposed immigration controls amid an anti-Semitic response, expressed especially by the Labour movement, to Jewish refugees from Eastern Europe and Russia. The Jewish population in England, which was about 60,000 in 1880, had increased to a quarter of a million by 1914 as a result of the arrival of people fleeing Tsarist pogroms in Russia (Krausz 1973: 132). The Aliens Act required that any person who could not support herself or himself or who might need welfare provision should not be allowed to enter the country, and that anyone who within twelve months of entry was homeless, living in crowded conditions, or living off poor relief should be deported. The Act did not specifically identify Jews as "aliens" but sought to exclude those deemed "undesirable immigrants," those without the means of supporting themselves, or likely to become a charge on the rates or become a "detriment to the public."

In turn, therefore, "nationality" became a qualifying condition for the Liberal Welfare Reforms (see Squires 1990, Williams 1996). The 1908 Pensions Act denied a pension to anyone who had not been both a resident and a British subject for twenty years; and the 1911 National Insurance Act provided that non-British residents who had not been resident for five years received lower rates of benefits even though they paid full contributions. Williams (1996) comments that it is interesting that in 1920, when the Aliens Order tightened up immigration further, the Special Irish Branch was given the task of enforcement (the SIB, the forerunner of the Special Branch, was established in the wake of Fenian activities in Britain in the 1860s). During this period, immigration controls became synonymous with protecting welfare provisions and the labor market for the white British male working class. This legitimated a strategy of deportations and repatriation as a solution to the perceived problem of "scroungers."

In 1922 the Irish Free State was established after a bitter war of independence. It was to be a dominion within the British Commonwealth.

This represented the first, and so far only, contraction of the borders of the United Kingdom. Irish citizens, like all residents of the Commonwealth, were still recognized as British subjects. By a series of actions in the next three decades the Irish government asserted its separate nationhood both by challenging its membership of the Commonwealth and by rejecting the status of British subject for its citizens (Paul 1997). In the 1940s Irish neutrality during World War II was a logical step in a context where relations with Britain were an overdetermined factor in policy-making in Ireland. Despite this thousands of Irish citizens were recruited into the army and for work in munitions factories. Similarly regiments formed in India and the West Indies were relied on in Britain's efforts in two world wars. Indeed recruitment of soldiers in the British Caribbean during World War I represented the first utilization of the area for more than provision of foodstuffs and raw materials.

In Britain between 1922 and the 1940s there were regular calls for controls on immigration from the Irish Free State. In the 1920s and 1930s the issue was persistently raised in parliament and was the subject of a number of Cabinet discussions (Glynn 1981). Investigations into Irish immigration were reported to Cabinet which eventually concluded that there was no significant increase in Irish migration but there was a real problem with the Irish already in Britain due to their high degree of concentration and rate of natural increase. The only solution it was agreed was wholescale repatriation but this appeared out of the question without the cooperation of the Irish Free State government. Instead the Home Secretary recommended that a state-sponsored policy of pauperization be employed to reduce the number of "Southern Irishmen" in Britain. It was thought if employers could be persuaded through informal approaches by the Government to dismiss their Irish-born workers then the Irish elements in employment would eventually be forced on to poor relief and might become eligible for repatriation (Douglas 2002). This plan was proceeded with but had mixed results. In the 1930s the issue was again discussed a number of times in Cabinet and was accompanied by a constant focus by some MPs and other interested parties such as the Church of England on the subject of Irish immigration and the resulting drain on the benefit system. The Bishop of Birmingham in 1929 argued that Britain should close her doors to immigrants from "Southern Ireland" so that she might "try to breed, not more citizens, but better citizens" (*Birth Control News* 1930, No. 8: 9).

These discussions about the problems of Irish immigrants took place against a backdrop of renewed racialized discourses about the Irish in the aftermath of the granting of independence to Ireland. The "shock" of Ireland's secession from the United Kingdom underpinned part of the racialization of the Irish in the interwar years. It amounted to a redrawing of the boundaries of the national community and included miscegenationist fears about mingling and breeding with the "Mediterranean Irish." The incompatibility of the two peoples served to provide an explanation for Britain's failure to assimilate the Irish to Anglo-Saxon norms. The Anglo-Irish Treaty was a demonstration of the failure after seven centuries of the civilization mission in Ireland and could be explained only by representations of the Irish as an atavistic human strain that intense struggle elsewhere in Europe had rendered extinct. These views of the Irish were propagated by members of Britain's academic, political, ecclesiastical, and journalistic elite, those whose chagrin at perceived postwar decline in Britain ran deepest (for a full discussion see Douglas 2002).

The post-1945 period which saw the end of empire, was a period of national reconstruction, and extensive immigration forced Britain to redefine its notions of citizenship and belonging. Britain's unwritten constitution and English common law traditions meant that rights flowed from "being a subject," whereas being a citizen conferred right of entry but little else. Over the next twenty-five years a strategy of strong, racialized immigration controls developed, which effectively altered the concept of a British citizen, alongside a dual policy of social problematization and assimilation of immigrants "already here."

Immediately after the war the government turned to various European sources for labor for the rebuilding program, European Volunteer Workers, mostly drawn from Poland and other Europeans "displaced" by the war. While ruling out a concerted plan to bring West Indian workers to Britain, the Europeans were welcome if of "good stock" and the idea was that they would intermarry and become completely absorbed into the population. In this case aliens were being preferred to subjects of the Crown (Miles 1993, Paul 1997).

However, as it turned out the three prime sources of labor for Britain's reconstruction program were people from the Caribbean, the Indian subcontinent, and Ireland. Irish citizens were consistently the largest group to enter postwar Britain, between 50,000 and 60,000 entered every year throughout the 1950s. For example, in 1959 there were 64,494 "new" Irish workers, compared with 30,842 from the colonies, 35,198 from the Commonwealth, and 46,965 from the rest of the world (Paul 1997: 93). The first migrants of this period from Jamaica landed in 1948 and migration from the island increased dramatically between 1952 and 1956 after the USA restricted immigration from Jamaica. Although the African-Caribbean population in Britain has its origins in a wide range of countries from Anguilla to Trinidad and Tobago, in the 1991 census those of Jamaican background made up over 50 percent of people of Caribbean heritage in Britain. In the long run, though, Asians from the Indian subcontinent (predominantly Sikhs and Gujarati Hindus from India, migrants from the Mipur in Pakistan, and from the districts of Sylhet and Chittagong in Bangladesh) and Africa became the main source of post-1945 Commonwealth migration to Britain (Goulbourne 1998).

When, on arrival in Britain in the 1950s and 1960s, members of these three groups looked for housing they met with notices which said "No Irish, no Blacks, no Dogs." In some areas "No Irish" signs were the more numerous (Holmes 1988). Despite this similarity of experiences, as the "problems" of immigration began to be addressed the Irish were excluded from the official discourses of the public debate on race relations. This was in part due to a carefully orchestrated government strategy of the day. As early as 1950 a secret Cabinet working party had been set up to consider how black workers might be prevented from coming to the UK, while maintaining the notion of free entry and preserving the unity of the Commonwealth. The working party's conclusion was that the numbers were too small to warrant legislative action (Carter, Green, and Halpern 1996). However, the issue of immigration continued to be addressed in Cabinet throughout the 1950s and in these debates the Irish figured as a problem on a number of counts.

The 1948 Nationality Act had reconfirmed British citizenship as an inclusive category. With substantial immigration from the New Commonwealth in the 1950s what was sought was a form of citizenship which would enable the restriction of immigration from these countries while enabling British settlers and their descendants throughout the Commonwealth to retain the right of return. This was sought initially due to fears expressed within the political elite about the possible "disruption" that could be caused by the immigration of people of a different "race" and culture. The 1958 Notting Hill Riots and later the Conservative win on a "race" ticket at the Smethwick by-election in 1964 reinforced these concerns with those of the potential threats to public order. The "problem," endlessly discussed in Cabinet, was that the vast majority of potential immigrants were British citizens and as such had right of entry to live and work.

The specific problem that immigration from the Irish Republic presented (there was relatively little migration from Northern Ireland at this point) was that it involved the entry of people who were foreign nationals. In 1949, after the declaration of an Irish Republic, the Ireland Act had confirmed that an Irish citizen on entering Britain was to be treated "as if he were a British subject" (Attlee speaking in the second reading of the Ireland Bill, Hansard 1949, Vol. 464, Col. 1859). The motives of the Labour government in maintaining the position whereby the citizens of two foreign countries would not be aliens to each other were varied. It was a position they came to reluctantly. It was viewed as impossible to treat Ireland as a foreign state because of the possible protest within the Commonwealth, just as it was impracticable to establish immigration control along the Northern Ireland border under peacetime conditions, or to distinguish Irish citizens from British citizens on the electoral role throughout the United Kingdom. In addition, the importance of Ireland for security issues in the postwar world was a constraining factor as also was the Irish vote, which was made clear by Herbert Morrison (Hansard 1948–9, Vol. 464, Cols. 1854–5). Thus it was more in Britain's interests (as it was in the Irish government's, which was concerned to maintain an outlet for a "surplus" population although not at the cost of retaining Commonwealth membership), not to treat the Irish as aliens (for a fuller discussion see Hickman 1998; for a different emphasis see Paul 1997).

After this apparent settling of the relationship between the Republic of Ireland and the United Kingdom the ambiguity with which relations remained shot through was revealed in discussions about immigration during the next decade. Cabinet papers of the 1950s reveal that the Irish continued to be seen as different from the English/British but that for reasons of expediency were included in the same "race." The decision was taken in Cabinet to assert that the "British Isles" was one unit not only geographically but historically (that is, culturally). The Irish were declared the "same" as the inhabitants of Great Britain (England, Wales, and Scotland) whether the Irish "liked it or not" (CAB 129/77; CP [55] 102; for further discussion of this extraordinary phrase, see Hickman 1998). These declarations of "propinquity" ignored the hostility and discrimination that many Irish people experienced at the time and became an important part of the genesis in the 1950s and 1960s of the myth of the cultural homogeneity of Britain in parallel with the arrival of immigrants from the New Commonwealth.

The Commonwealth Immigration Act in 1962 like all subsequent legislation hinged on notions of who belonged to the United Kingdom. In 1962 it was defined as birth in the United Kingdom and the holding of a passport issued by the UK government. The legislation that followed in 1968 and 1971 was much more clear-cut in its discriminatory ability to allow entry to those people who were viewed as "kith and kin." The 1968 Commonwealth Immigrants Act created a distinction between people who had exactly the same citizenship. It was aimed at excluding East African Asians who held UK-issued passports and was accomplished by stating that not only was a UK passport required but also "substantial connection" with the UK: this could be birth or alternatively a parental or grandparental connection. The 1971 Immigration Act created a number of categories of British citizens but the critical distinction was between "patrials" and "non-patrials," "the patrial and non-patrial principles of the legislation sanctioned the distinction Enoch Powell had made from 1968 between people who belonged to Britain and those who did not" (Goulbourne 1998: 53).

In its original form the 1962 Commonwealth Immigration Bill made the Irish subject to immigration control, but by the second reading the government had dropped this provision. In the debate on the Bill it was broadly accepted that it would be impossible to enforce immigration controls between Britain and Ireland because of the border with Northern Ireland and the political unacceptability of introducing identity controls in Northern Ireland. It was also broadly accepted that Irish labor was needed, especially for the unskilled labor slot. This did not prevent many MPs expressing their views that the "Southern Irish" were a social liability, a source of contamination and a drain on the public purse. Significantly, no arguments were advanced that the Irish represented "kith and kin" or that as formerly one of the "home nations," there would be some objection to placing immigration controls on them. The one aspect of the 1962 Act in which the Irish were included was that which gave power to the Home Secretary to deport immigrants from the Commonwealth who offended against British laws. By May 1965, 716 immigrants had been deported using these powers, 452 of them were Irish. The rate of Irish deportations ran at more than twice the rate for the next highest group, West Indians, 193 of whom were deported in the same period (Foot 1965).

The 1962 Act was a defining moment in the state's strategy of re-racializing the boundaries of the nation. This was the "moment of differentiation" and it has been reinforced by many means since. However, in order to achieve this the state had to address the issue of Irish immigration and this led to a strategy of "forced inclusion" of the Irish within the parameters of the nation. What is more it represented a complete volte-face from the official discourses problematizing Irish immigration that had marked the nineteenth and first half of the twentieth centuries. A disjunction existed between the ongoing reformulation of official discourse about Irish immigration and the continued racialized representations of Irish immigrants as socially undesirable in popular discourses, for example, in anti-Irish jokes, in adverts, and in MPs' testimonies.

This official myth of homogeneity assumed that all people who were white smoothly assimilated into the "British way of life" and that "the problems" all resided with those who migrated and possessed a different skin color. Different skin color was taken to represent different culture.

The same skin color was taken to mean the same culture. The myth of homogeneity therefore had to entail the denial of differences amongst the white population. The "whiteness" of the Irish therefore facilitated continued access to their labor power for British employers and served to render them invisible within a reformulated British claim about the cultural homogeneity of the "British Isles." My interpretation of this period of re-racializing the boundaries of the nation is, therefore, different from many other accounts which unproblematically assume that the whiteness of the Irish had always ensured that they "passed an unwritten test of potential Britishness measured according to a racialized conception of the world's population" (see Paul 1997: 90, who chronicles the discrimination and prejudice experienced by the Irish, but posits that they were thought of as first cousins although she provides no evidence to substantiate this). The point is that whiteness was a factor in the re-positioning of the Irish but the assumption that a "simple" color divide fully explains the reconfiguring of the nation in this period masks the subtleties of the processes of (re)racialization which were invoked. In the black–white dichotomy which was installed, whiteness masked suppressed ethnicities, hidden racializations, and pre-existing hierarchies.

Famously British immigration controls were accompanied by the mantra that the more effective they were the more they would contribute to improving community relations. The Labour government of 1964–70 was critical for the explicit formulation and extension of both policies. In two periods of government the Labour party introduced Race Relations Acts which were not subsequently removed by Conservative administrations, just as Labour implemented immigration controls and the 1981 Nationality Act introduced by the Conservatives when in office. Interestingly, only one other area of government policy in the same period, also one which involved managing ethno-national relations, has been the subject of such sustained bipartisanship: Northern Ireland.

Lewis (2000: 36–7) makes the case that the immigration legislation, by progressively redrawing the lines of demarcation between ex-colonial subjects who could or could not make a claim for full citizenship/subjecthood, established the juridical framework within which a move from "immigrant" to "ethnic minority" could be accomplished. In this way black and Asian people became encompassed within the field of governmentality. For groups whose difference was demarcated around notions of essential cultural "otherness," the time would come when representatives of these populations would be required to ensure the delivery of "ethnically sensitive" welfare services. These representatives, that is a range of welfare professionals, had to be brought into being as part of the racially governed populations, through the provision of specifically targeted schemes and professional training courses. As should be clear from the historical account above, a significant difference in the nineteenth century, a period when religio-ethnic definitions of a racialized group dominated determinations of cultural "otherness," was that the state could utilize the services of an already existing institution, the Catholic Church, whose political and cultural characteristics were "reliable" compared with those of the "problematic minority population."

7   Conclusion

The significance of the Irish as a group lies in their contradictory positioning as both inside and outside the nation, as both a "home nation" and a colony. In the nineteenth and the first half of the twentieth century, the conviction that the Irish constituted a separate race was regularly aired, a presupposition which was only challenged in official discourses in the 1940s/50s. Ireland was a colonial project in the domestic realm and one element of the multinational state albeit treated differently from the other parts. In the shape of Irish immigrants in nineteenth-century Britain, Ireland/"the Irish" represented a disturbing phenomenon in the heart of the state/nation 100 years ahead of the New Commonwealth migration of the mid-twentieth century.

The differentiated implementation of general legislation which is a hallmark of the British ethno-racial regime (thus preserving a façade compatible with liberalism) means that those designated in subordinated, minority positions have to wage a constant struggle to assert and claim their rights. Many of these struggles have had to take to the streets as the political processes often accommodate them with difficulty (this is as true in England as it is in Northern Ireland). The Irish in the 1990s had to claim "ethnic minority" status in order to gain recognition of ongoing but hidden disadvantages and discrimination, masked by a myth of white homogeneity.

Although it is wise to guard against making assumptions about the permanence or stability of categories across time and space (Brah 1992), my aim has been to attempt what I consider a historical perspective within the social sciences which should have as one of its aims: the explication of structures, processes, and categories which are currently "taken for granted." In other contexts writers discuss the impact of cultural or collective memory (see Gilroy 1993, Loury in this volume). Just as there are specific cultural memories of different groups, as this chapter has sought to demonstrate, so there are also proactive processes of "forgetting." Much of what I have written about in this chapter concerning Ireland/Britain and about the Irish in Britain is either "forgotten" or presumed secure in the repository of history. But qualitative research reveals that many of the contemporary experiences that black, Asian, and Irish people report are threaded with the vestiges of complex colonial/domestic encounters of the past and the present, as are their interpretations. In Britain this has not produced an underclass correlated with ethnicity/"race" as is argued either directly or indirectly has occurred in the USA but it has produced a hierarchical society which is underpinned by disparities of social class, cross-cut by ethno-racial cleavages in which religion continues to play a significant part.

REFERENCES

Archer, Anthony, 1986, *The Two Catholic Churches: A Study in Oppression*, London: SCM Press.

Bartlett, Thomas, 1997, "The Irish Soldier in India, 1750–1947," in M. Holmes and D. Holmes (eds.), *Ireland and India. Connections, Comparisons, Contrasts*, Dublin: Folens.

Beckett, James C., 1979, *A Short History of Ireland*, Hutchinson: London.

Best, Geoffrey F. A., 1958, "The Protestant Constitution and its Supporters 1800–1829," *Transactions of the Royal Historical Society* 13: 105–27.

Boyce, George, 1986, "The 'Marginal Britons': The Irish," in Robert Colls and Philip Dodd (eds.), *Englishness, Politics and Culture 1880–1920*, Beckenham, Kent: Croom Helm, pp. 230–53.

Brah, Avtar, 1992, "Difference, Diversity and Differentiation," in James Donald and Ali Rattansi (eds.), *"Race," Culture and Difference*, London: Sage, pp. 126–45.

Canny, Nicholas and Anthony Pagden (eds.), 1987, *Colonial Identity in the Atlantic World, 1500–1800*, Princeton: Princeton University Press.

Canny, Nicholas, 1988, *Kingdom and Colony: Ireland in the Atlantic World*, 1560–1800, Baltimore and London: Johns Hopkins University Press.

Carter, Bob, Marci Green, and Rick Halpern, 1996, "Immigration Policy and the Racialization of Migrant Labour: The Construction of National Identities in the USA and Britain," *Ethnic and Racial Studies* 19, 1: 135–57.

Cockcroft, W. R., 1974, "The Liverpool Police Force, 1836–1902," in S. P. Bell (ed.), *Victorian Lancashire*, Newton Abbot: David and Charles, pp. 150–68.

Cohen, Phil, 1988, "The Perversions of Inheritance: Studies in the Making of Multi-racist Britain," in P. Cohen and H. S. Bains (eds.), *Multi-racist Britain*, London: Macmillan, pp. 9–118.

1999, *The Last Island*, London: Centre for New Ethnicities Research, University of East London.

Colley, Linda, 1992, *Britons. Forging the Nation*, New Haven: Yale University Press.

Cook, Scott B., 1993, *Imperial Affinities. Nineteenth Century Analogies and Exchanges between India and Ireland*, London: Sage.

Crick, Bernard (ed.), 1991, *National Identities: The Constitution of the United Kingdom*, Oxford: Blackwells.

Curtis, Bruce, 1983, "Preconditions of the Canadian State: Educational Reform and the Construction of a Public in Upper Canada 1837–1846," *Studies in Political Economy* 10: 99–121.

Deane, Seamus, 1983, *Civilians and Barbarians*, Derry: A Field Day Pamphlet.

Dodd, Philip, 1986, "Englishness and the National Culture," in R. Colls and P. Dodd (eds.), *Englishness, Politics and Culture 1880–1920*, Beckenham, Kent: Croom Helm, pp. 1–28.

Douglas, Raymond M., 2002, Anglo-Saxons and Attacott: The Racialization of Irishness in Britain between the World Wars, *Ethnic and Racial Studies* 25, 1: 40–63.

Elton, Geoffrey Rudolph, 1955, *England under the Tudors*, Methuen History of England Vol. 4, London: Methuen.

Fielding, Steven, 1993, *Class and Ethnicity. Irish Catholics in England, 1880–1939*, Buckingham: Open University Press.

Finnegan, Frances, 1985, "The Irish in York," in R. Swift and S. Gilley (eds.), *The Irish in the Victorian City*, Beckenham, Kent: Croom Helm, pp. 59–84.

Foot, Paul, 1965, *Immigration and Race in British Politics*, London: Penguin.

Fryer, Peter, 1984, *Staying Power: The History of Black People in Britain*, London: Pluto.

Gilroy, Paul, 1993, *The Black Atlantic: Modernity and Double Consciousness*, London: Verso.

Glynn, Sean, 1981, "Irish Immigration to Britain 1911–1951: Patterns and Policy," *Irish Economic and Social History* 8: 50–69.

Goulbourne, Harry, 1998, *Race Relations in Britain since 1945*, Basingstoke: Macmillan.

Hall, Catherine, 2000, "The Rule of Difference: Gender, Class and Empire in the Making of the 1832 Reform Act," in J. Blom, K. Hagerman and C. Hall (eds.), *Gendered Nation. Nationalism and Gender in the long Nineteenth century*, London: Berg, pp. 107–35.

Heath, Anthony and Dorren McMahon, 1997, "Education and Occupational Attainments: The Impact of Ethnic Origins," in V. Karn (ed.), Ethnicity in the 1991 census, Vol. IV: *Education, Employment and Housing among Ethnic Minorities in Britain*, London: HMSO.

Hechter, Michael, 1975, *Internal Colonialism. The Celtic Fringe in British National Development 1536–1966*, London: Routledge and Kegan Paul.

Hickman, Mary. J., 1995, *Religion, Class and Identity*, Aldershot: Avebury.
    1998, "Reconstructing Deconstructing 'Race:' British Political Discourses about the Irish in Britain," *Ethnic and Racial Studies* 21, 2 (March): 288–307.

Hickman, Mary. J. and B. Walter, 1997, *Discrimination and the Irish Community in Britain*, London: Commission for Racial Equality.

Hiro, Dilip, 1992, *Black British, White British: History of Race Relations in Britain* (expanded and updated edition), London: Paladin.

Hoggart, Richard, 1988, *Life and Times, Vol. I: A Local Habitation*, London: Chatto & Windus.

Holmes, Colin, 1988, *John Bull's Island, Immigration and British Society*, 1871–1971, London: Macmillan.

Hume, David, 1778, *A History of England*, Vol. I, London: Cadet.

Hume, David, 1997, "Negroes . . . Naturally Inferior to the Whites," In Emmanual C. Eze (ed.), *Race and the Enlightenment*, Oxford: Blackwell, pp. 29–37.

Judd, Denis, 1996, *Empire: The British Imperial Experience from 1765 to the Present*, London: Harper Collins.

Kapur, Narinder, 1997, *The Irish Raj*, Antrim: Greystone.

Krausz, Ernest, 1973, "The Jews in Britain: The Sociography of an Old Minority Group," *New Community* 11, 2, Spring.

Kohn, Hans, 1940, "The Genesis and Character of English Nationalism," *Journal of the History of Ideas* 1: 69–94.

Lebow, Ned, 1973, "British Historians and Irish History," *Eire-Ireland* 8: 3–38.

Lennon, Mary, Marie, McAdam, and Joanne O'Brien, 1988, *Across the Water. Irish Women's Lives in Britain*, London: Virago.

Lewis, Gail (ed.), 1998, *Forming Nation, Forming Welfare*, London: Routledge with the Open University Press.

  2000, *"Race," Gender, Social Welfare. Encounters in a Postcolonial Society*, Cambridge: Polity.

Maan, Bashir, 1992, *The New Scots: The Story of Asians in Scotland*, Edinburgh: Donald.

Miles, Robert, 1993, *Racism after "Race Relations,"* London: Routledge.

Model, Suzanne, 1999, "Ethnic Inequality in England: An Analysis Based on the 1991 Census," *Racial and Ethnic Studies* 22, 6: 966–90.

Morgan, Glenn, 1985–6, "The Analysis of Ethnicity: Conceptual Problems and Policy Implications," *New Community* 12, 3 (Winter): 515–22.

Murphy, James, 1959, *The Religious Problem in English Education. The Crucial Experiment*, Liverpool: Liverpool University Press.

Nairn, Tom, 1981, *The Break-Up of Britain*, London: Verso.

Ó Gráda, Cormac, 1975, "A Note on Nineteenth Century Irish Emigration Statistics," *Population Studies* 29: 143–9.

Paul, Kathleen, 1997, *Whitewashing Britain. Race and Citizenship in the Postwar Era*, Ithaca: Cornell University Press.

Philips, David, 1974, "Riots and Public Order in the Black Country 1835–1860," in R. Quinault and J. Stevenson (eds.), *Popular Protest and Public Order: Six Studies in British History, 1790–1920*, London: George Allen and Unwin.

Priestley, John Boynton, 1934, *English Journey: Being a Rambling but Truthful Account of What One Man Saw and Heard and Felt and Thought during a Journey through England in the Autumn of 1933*, London: William Heinemann; Victor Gollancz.

Robbins, Kenneth, 1982, "Religion and Identity in Modern British History," in S. Mews (ed.), *Religion and National Identity* (Studies in Church History, Vol. 18), Oxford: Basil Blackwell.

Scully, Judy, 1997, "A 'Stage Irish Identity' – an example of 'symbolic power,'" *New Community* 23, 3: 385–98.

Spenser, Edmund, 1970, *A View of the Present State of Ireland* (ed. W. L. Renwick), Oxford: Clarendon Press.

Squires, Peter, 1990, *Anti-Social Policy. Welfare, Ideology and the Disciplinary State*, London: Harvester Wheatsheaf.

Swift, Roger, 1985, "Another Stafford Street Row: Law and Order and the Irish Presence in Mid-Victorian Wolverhampton," in R. Swift and S. Gilley (eds.), *The Irish in the Victorian City*, Beckenham, Kent: Croom Helm, pp. 179–206.

Vaughan, Alden T., 1989, "The Origins Debate: Slavery and Racism in Seventeenth-Century Virginia," *Virginia Magazine of History and Biography* 97: 311–54.

Visram, Rozina, 1986, *Ayahs, Lascars and Princes: Indians in Britain, 1700–1947*, London: Pluto.

Williams, Fiona, 1996, "'Race,' Welfare and Community Care: A Historical Perspective," in W. Ahmad and K. Atkin (eds.), *"Race" and Community Care*, Buckingham: Open University Press, pp. 15–28.

2 American diversity and the 2000 census

Nathan Glazer

The census is not the only way to enter into the problems of American diversity, and may not be the best way, but it clearly provides the most authoritative information on the enormous range of races and peoples and ethnicities that make up the American people. It tells us a great deal about their economic situation, their educational progress, the way they are distributed spatially, the degree of their segregation or separation from others, who they marry, and how they conceive their race and ancestry. It is not information that is unaffected by political considerations. The census is directed by an official appointed by the President of the United States – a political appointee – but generally one with some competence in the issues that the census deals with, and his staff is a professionally qualified one. Congress will also get into the act of directing the census. And shaped as it is by politics, the census will also in return shape how Americans see and interpret their diversity. But most important, the census tells us how Americans conceptualize their diversity, and how their views of this diversity and its significance change over time.

The first reports of the census of the year 2000, on which the Census Bureau started issuing information as early as March and April of 2001, reflected the two central enduring themes of American racial and ethnic diversity, present since the origins of American society in the English colonies of the Atlantic coast: first, the continued presence of what appears to be an almost permanent lower caste composed of the black race in the United States; and second, the ongoing process of immigration of races and peoples from all quarters of the globe, who seem to within a few generations – with some variation, and aside from the marked special case of African-Americans – merge into a common American people.

To make two such large generalizations is admittedly a somewhat over-bold move. Undoubtedly, as further data from the census are released, we will have evidence of the continuing progress of American blacks, in education, in occupational diversity, in income. We will have grounds for arguing that the effects of integration into a common people can be seen, at long last, among American blacks. And when it comes to the new waves of immigration of the past few decades, we will have further evidence on the large question of whether the process of assimilation and incorporation, which has swallowed up so many groups and races and religions into a common American people, is continuing to work its effects in similar ways on the new groups now gathered together under the terms "Hispanic" and "Asian."

Yet I believe that this large distinction in the processes of assimilation and integration that have persisted during the three- or four-century history of American diversity, the distinction between blacks and others, still shows itself, and still poses some of the most difficult questions for American society.

The distinction makes itself evident in the very history and structure of the census, and in the character of the data that it first presents to the public today. In the first census of 1790, required for purposes of apportionment by the United States Constitution adopted in 1787, the separation between blacks and whites was already made. Indeed that separation was itself foreshadowed by the Constitution, which, in a famous compromise, decreed that "Representatives . . . shall be apportioned among the several states . . . according to their respective numbers, which shall be determined by adding to the whole number of free persons . . . three-fifths of all other persons." Those "other persons" were slaves. The "three-fifths" was a compromise between excluding all slaves for purposes of apportionment (which would have reduced the weight of the Southern slave states in the union) or counting them simply as persons (which would have given the slave states too great weight).

The census could have fulfilled the requirements of the Constitution by counting only slaves. But what was to be done with free blacks? There were, even then, free blacks, but their civil status was sharply below that of whites. It was apparently decided that they could not be simply numbered among the "free persons" referred to in the Constitution but had to be clearly distinguished from whites. The first census went beyond the Constitution: it counted "free white males and females" as one category, "other persons" as another, but then added a category of "all other free persons." The count of "other persons" – slaves – and "all other free persons" – free blacks – gave us the total number of blacks. White could thus be differentiated from black from the beginning. That has remained the most enduring distinction in the United States census.

In that first census, following the apportionment provision of the Constitution, "Indians not taxed" were also excluded. "The apportionment rule incorporated into the census and the political fabric of the new nation a tradition of 'differentiating these three great elements

of the population' – the free, the slave, and the Indian populations"
(Rodriguez 2000: 67; for the passage within quotes, Anderson 2000:
12).

Over time, this simple scheme has been extended to cover other races
and ethnic groups as they entered the new nation through immigration,
to a degree which is possibly unique among national censuses, and which
we will explore below. But the census begins crucially with the distinction
between white and black. As Rodriguez writes:

> Between the drafting of the Constitution of 1787 and the taking of the first census
> in 1790, the term white became an explicit part of [the free population] . . .
> Theoretically, those in political charge could have chosen another definition for
> the [free population] . . . They could have chosen 'free English-speaking males
> over sixteen' or 'free males of Christian descent' or 'of European descent.' But
> they chose color. Having named the central category 'white' gave a centrality
> and power to color that has continued throughout the history of the census.
> (Rodriguez 2000: 69)

But of course this reflected the centrality of the black-white distinction in
American society and the American mind. Rodriguez goes on to note that
on occasion in the censuses preceding the Civil War "aliens and foreigners
not naturalized," separately numbered, are combined in one table with
native whites and citizens in a table of "total white." "In the 1850 census,
the category 'free whites' is changed to simply 'whites', which suggests
by this time it was evident that all the people in this category were free"
(Rodriguez 2000: 71).

Color – race – has since been elaborated to a remarkable degree in
the United States census. The most striking aspect of the American census of 2000 – as of the few before – is that the short form, which goes
to all American households, consists mostly of questions on race and
"Hispanicity." Two large questions ask for the respondent's race, and
whether the respondent is of "Spanish/Hispanic" origin, and both go into
considerable detail in trying to determine just what race, and just what
kind of "Hispanic," the respondent is. The race question lists many possibilities to choose from, including, to begin with, "white" and "black,"
and going on to "Indian (Amer.)," with an additional request to list the
name of the tribe, "Eskimo," "Aleut," and then under the general heading "Asian or Pacific Islander (API)," it lists as separate choices Chinese,
Filipino, Hawaiian, Korean, Vietnamese, Japanese, Asian Indian,
Samoan, Guamanian, "Other API", and finally "Other race (print
name)." The respondent is informed – in the 2000 census, the first time
this has been possible – that he or she can also check more than one race.
This was the decision made after an extended discussion in the 1990s

as to how to account for the children of parents of different race, who wanted to check off both, or perhaps more than two.

The question on whether one is Spanish/Hispanic also goes on to list a range of possibilities: "Mexican, Mexican-Am. [for "American"], or Chicano" (to account for the fact that Mexican Americans choose different terms to describe themselves), "Puerto Rican," "Cuban," and "other Spanish/Hispanic," with again the request to print one group, and a host of examples – "Argentinean, Colombian, Dominican, Nicaraguan, Salvadoran, Spaniard," and so on.

The observant and conscientious citizen may note that many other matters of interest to the census and the polity – whether one is of foreign birth or not, a citizen or not, one's education, one's occupation, one's income, one's housing status, etc. – are all relegated to the long form, which goes to a large sample of citizens, and may ask why the census pays such great and meticulous attention to race and ethnicity (or rather one kind of ethnicity, that of Spanish-Hispanic background).

Many answers, going back to the first census of 1790, and before that, to the Constitution that prescribed a regular decennial census, and before that, to the first arrival of black slaves in the English colonies in the early seventeenth century, are available to explain why the first statistics the census makes available today, along with the raw number of the population in each state and locality, is the breakdown by race and ethnicity. But there is also an immediate and proximate answer of much more recent currency: Congress requires that ethnic and racial statistics be available within a year of the census for the purpose of redrawing the boundaries of Congressional districts, and the other electoral districts for state legislative assemblies, and where relevant for city and county elected officials.

Ethnic and racial statistics have become so significant for redistricting because of the Civil Rights Act of 1964 and the Voting Rights Acts of 1965, and its amendments of 1970, 1975, and 1982. Admittedly these acts, which simply proscribe discrimination on the basis of race and national background, did not necessarily require such detailed minority statistics to check on the presence of discrimination in various spheres of life and in particular in the free exercise and effect of the vote, but the course of the law has been to use statistical tests to determine whether there is such discrimination. The right given directly in the Voting Rights statute, to the free exercise of the vote, has been extended through litigation and administrative and judicial rule-making to cover rights to the drawing of Congressional and other district boundaries in such a way as to protect or enhance the ability of minority groups, blacks in particular, but others too, to elect representatives of their own group. If blacks are to be protected from discrimination, interpreted as the creation of voting

districts that enhance the power of blacks to choose a black representative, if they are so inclined, the statistics of how a race is distributed in
the finest detail is necessary (Thernstrom 1987, Canon 1999).

That is why the first statistics that come out of the census are those
that make it possible to immediately go about the business of redrawing
district lines on the basis of the new census, and for various groups to
challenge the new district lines if they are aggrieved. "Growing minority
groups will likely face lawsuits over redistricting," reads one news headline, with the subtitle, "One California assemblyman says his caucus 'will
sue' regardless of the rationale for redrawing districts." The story tells
us: "Here in Orange County [California], . . . a dozen Latino officials
last week huddled in a spartan conference room over a map of Southern
California as Art Montez, felt-tipped marker in hand, lopped the city of
Westminster off the state's 68th Assembly District. Westminster's large
population of conservative whites makes it 'impossible for a minority
candidate to win there,' Mr. Montez, a political activist and school board
member, explained to the group" (Porter 2001).

But this is only the beginning of a struggle that will move through the
state legislature and almost inevitably to the Department of Justice and
the Federal courts, where the racial and ethnic statistics and the role they
have played in drawing up new districts will be carefully examined and disputed. For those with the responsibility of drawing up the new districts –
the state legislatures primarily (Fund 2001) – the central concern is generally the maximization of the number of representatives of the party in
power in the lower house of Congress and in the state legislature. A second concern is to maintain for the incumbents of the favored party district
boundaries that secure their return. But overlaying these historic political reasons for drawing district lines, which courts accept as in measure
legitimate, is a new imperative, the protection of minority groups.

The official minorities

"Portrait of a Nation" is the title of a major story on the first results of the
census in the *New York Times*, and it is accompanied by elaborate colored
maps. The colors provide information on the distribution of the minority population – blacks, Hispanics, Asians, American Indians (Schmitt
2001d).

To explain how these have become the American minorities – to the
exclusion of many other possible minorities – and why information on
the numbers in these groups is in every newspaper report considered the
most important information to look for in the census would require a
précis of American history and the choices that have been made in it.

It is hardly necessary to explain why blacks are the first of the minority groups. They have been a significant presence in the United States and its predecessor colonies from the beginning. Our greatest national trauma – the Civil War – was directly occasioned by the problem of black slavery, and the most significant amendments to the Constitution became part of that quasi-sacred document in order to overcome the consequences of black slavery.

American Indians were there even before the beginning but were considered outside the society and polity unless they individually entered into non-Indian American society, as many have, through intermarriage and assimilation. Their status has changed over time, from outside the polity as semi-sovereign foreign nations, or savages to be exterminated, to subjects almost without rights, to a population confined on reservations, to one now that increasingly becomes part of the society, in which American Indian heritage somewhere in one's past may be a plus for one's social status. This is too complex a history to be reviewed here. There is good reason to maintain a separate count of Indians, though there are great complexities in doing so: relatively few Indians today, as numbered in the census, are of unmixed Indian ancestry.

"Hispanics," too, were there from before the beginning, if we take into account the Spaniards and Creoles moving up from Mexico who had already established colonial settlements in northern Mexico, what is now the southwest of the United States, before the first English colonists had established permanent settlements on the Atlantic coast. Of course they were not "Hispanics" then. Two hundred and fifty years later, this mixed population became part of the United States as a result of the annexation of the northern part of Mexico after the Mexican American war. But it contained then a small population, of Mexicans and Indians, and interestingly enough, despite the sense of racial difference and superiority felt by the Anglo-Americans, and despite the prejudice against Mexicans, they were not differentiated in the census as a separate group until 1930. Until then, one presumes, they were "white." In that year, a census publication, responding to the increase in immigration from Mexico as a result of the revolutionary wars and troubles of the 1920s, reported that "persons of Mexican birth or parentage who were not definitely reported as white or Indian were designated Mexican" and included in "other races." In 1940, this policy was changed, and Mexicans became white again (Rodriguez 2000: 82–3). By 1950, added to the growing number of Mexicans in the southwest as a result of immigration in the previous decades, was a large number of Puerto Ricans in New York City, migrants from the island of Puerto Rico which had been annexed after the Spanish American war of 1898. In that census year, the two were combined in the census – along with smaller numbers of other groups – into a "Spanish-surnamed" group.

In the wake of Castro's victory in Cuba, a third large group of Latin Americans emigrated to the United States. Whether or not one could make a single meaningful category out of Mexicans, Puerto Ricans, and Cubans, separated as they are by culture, by history, to some extent by racial characteristics, they were so combined, with a host of other Spanish-speaking groups, into a "Hispanic" category in the census of 1970. The creation of the category was owing to political pressure from Mexican Americans (Rodriguez 2000: 102–3). It is surprising that Mexican Americans, then relatively few, could exert such influence: but perhaps the Nixon administration saw some political advantage in responding to it. "Hispanics" now include large numbers of Nicaraguans, Guatemalans, Salvadorans, Dominicans, Colombians, Ecuadorans, and others fleeing the political and economic troubles of their homelands.

Racial and ethnic groups are conventionally described today as "constructed," but it is worth noting that this "construction" is not simply the result of white determinations – it is also the result of group insistence, at least to some degree. According to Peter Skerry:

> The finalized questionnaires for the 1970 census were already at the printers when a Mexican American member of the US. Interagency Committee on Mexican American affairs demanded that a specific Hispanic-origin question be included. . . . Over the opposition of Census Bureau officials, who argued against inclusion of an untested question so late in the process, [President] Nixon ordered the secretary of commerce and the census director to add the question. As former bureau official Conrad Taeuber recalls, "The order came down that we were to ask a direct question, have the people identify themselves as Hispanic." (Skerry 2000: 37–8)

And so Hispanics were born. The pressure to maintain the category, with all its subdistinctions, persists. A distinguished demographer has written about a well-intentioned intervention at a conference preparatory to the 1990 census:

> I naively suggested that there was no reason to have an Hispanic question separate from the ethnic ancestry question [an ancestry question has been part of the long form since 1980] since the former . . . could be classified as a subpart of the latter. Several participants from prominent Hispanic organizations were furious at such a proposal. They were furious, by the way, not at me (just a naive academic), rather it was in the form of a warning to census personnel of the consequences that would follow were this proposal to be taken seriously. (Lieberson 1993: 30)

The last of the four minorities distinguished in the census is the "Asian," a creation – or construction – which has as complex a history as that of the Hispanic. Chinese and Japanese individuals were undoubtedly present in the United States before they were first listed as "races" in 1870 – by then there was a substantial population of Chinese in California, and they were already the subject of racist legislation. In 1930, "Filipino," "Hindu" [sic], and "Korean" were added as separate races, and it became the pattern to add a new "race" for each Asian immigrant group as it became numerous. Eventually, we have the complex category of "Asian and Pacific islander" (API), with all its listed subgroups, that we have described above.

As in the case of the Mexicans, the initial discrimination that made each of these a separate group was undoubtedly racist and reflected a sense of white superiority. The Asian groups were all subjected to discriminatory legislation. One could be naturalized as a citizen only if one were "white" (or, after the Civil War, black). All sorts of restrictions, from land ownership to the pursuit of certain professions or occupations, were imposed by various states on noncitizens, or persons of a group that was denied because of race the right of becoming citizens, particularly in the west. These groups were indeed nonwhite, but their separate classification was more than a matter of keeping neat statistics. An identity was being selected for a group considered inferior. This identity may well have been the one the members of the group would have chosen, had they had the power to do so, but it was not they who decided they should be numbered aside from the dominant whites.

In more recent decades, the power to name and describe has shifted: the groups themselves, or those who speak for them, now shape in large measure how they are to be described, named, differentiated, counted. And the political and administrative process bends to their desires. Why do we distinguish so many subgroups among the "Asian and Pacific Islanders"? There is a separate story for each category. But note one account from the political history of the census: the Census Bureau tried to simplify and shorten the Asian and Pacific Islander question for the 1990 census. Congressman Robert Matsui introduced legislation "in which the formatting of the API race question was spelled out, even to the point of stipulating that 'Taiwanese' be one of the subgroups. . . . It was only President Reagan's pocket veto that blocked this extraordinary degree of Congressional involvement in what is ordinarily considered the technical side of questionnaire design" (Skerry 2000: p. 41).

How "ethnics" become "whites"

These then are the four "official" minorities, though it should be clear no law names these and only these as minorities. But what has happened then to all those others once considered "minorities," the ethnic groups that were in the first quarter of the century in the eye of public attention because of the recency of their immigration, because of their lower social and economic status, because of concern as to whether they would or could be assimilated as Americans? Immigration was largely cut off by law in the 1920s because of these concerns. The United States has been a country of immigration since its origins, and by some measures the immigration of the first two decades of the twentieth century was much greater than the immigration of the last three decades which has swelled the numbers of the new minorities (Ueda 1994: 10–11). Had one picked up a textbook on American minorities and race relations in the 1950s, Jews might have been presented as the typical minority. Much of the social theory and social psychology on minority status was formulated with the position of Jews in mind. Jews were a major element in the mass immigration that preceded the present one, from the 1880s to the 1920s. Other major components of this immigration were Italians, Poles, Hungarians, Czechs, Slovaks, Slovenes, Croats, Serbs, Greeks, Armenians, Lebanese, Syrians, and there were many other peoples of Eastern and Southern Europe and the Near East. Are they no longer included in the story of American minorities?

One can go further back and ask, what has happened to the Irish, the Germans, the Swedes and Norwegians and Danes and the host of immigrants who came earlier, and were also once sharply distinguished as separate groups, different from the founding group, the English? Does not the story of American diversity include all these too? How has the palette become restricted to the four minorities which play so large a role in the current census?

The simple answer is that integration and assimilation – a move into higher-paying occupations, more education, more intermarriage – reduce over time the differences that distinguish one group from another, or from the original settler group, what Tocqueville called the "Anglo-Americans." We have no good term for this group. WASP ("white Anglo-Saxon Protestant") has been used in recent decades, ironically or derisively, for the founding element and their descendants, but the fact is that aside from the necessity to distinguish such a group historically, no term is currently really necessary: immigrants merge in two or three generations into a common American people, and ethnic distinctions become less and less meaningful. Ethnicity becomes symbolic, a matter of choice, to be noted on occasion on the basis of name or some other signifier, of little matter for most of one's life (Waters 1990).

At one time the census distinguished the foreign-born by place of birth, and the foreign-born parents of the native-born, by place of birth, permitting us to track ethnic groups over two or three generations, but somewhat uncertainly, owing to the lack of fit between ethnicity and national boundaries, and the radical change of national boundaries in Europe after World War I. The rest of the population was classed as "natives of native parentage," not further distinguishable, at least in the census, on the basis of their ethnicity. In 1980, the question on birthplace of parents was dropped, to the distress of sociologists and students of ethnicity. A new question on "ancestry" was added. That in theory would permit us to connect people to ethnic group in the third generation and beyond. But the amount of mixture among groups, through marriage, is today such that the answers to the ancestry question, if one is not an immigrant or the child of an immigrant with a clear sense of ancestry, are not very helpful in distinguishing an ethnic group much beyond the second generation. The answers then become so variable, so dependent on cues from the census itself – such as the examples the census form gives to the respondent as to what is intended by the term "ancestry," which is by no means clear to many people – as to be hardly meaningful. It is a question that permits some 40 million Americans, seven times the population of Ireland, to declare that they are of "Irish" ancestry (see Lieberson and Waters 1988).

There are indeed differences of some significance based on ethnicity among the native white population, and sometimes these become evident – when home countries are involved in conflict, for example – or even paramount. This is particularly evident for Jews, who are doubly marked not only as a religion (but the census rigorously refrains from asking or accepting any question on religion) but also by ethnicity (but to the census Jews are not an ethnic group, but a religion). The exceptional history which has resulted in the killing of most of the Jews of Europe, and the creation of a regularly imperilled State of Israel, ties Jews to their past and to their coreligionists abroad much more than other ethnic groups. They are excluded from any census count – they are not a "race" and not even, for the census, an "ancestry," even though that answer would make the most sense for most Jews. The Jewish community, in the absence of census statistics. makes do with compiling its own from sample surveys.

Sociologists and political scientists can plumb for differences among the native white population, and they are not insignificant in income, occupation, in political orientation, and so on. So Jews, for example, are exceptional among "whites" for regular overwhelming support for Democrats. Indeed, the differences among native whites ethnically distinguished, as in the case of political orientation, may be as great or greater than those that distinguish minority groups from the native white population. Yet for the most part the ethnic groups of the great immigrations of the nineteenth and early twentieth centuries have sunk below the horizon of official attention. They have merged into the "white" population, become integrated and assimilated, and emerge as a special interest only on occasion, stimulated by a conflict or crisis involving the home country.

Recently this somewhat benign view of American history, one in which immigrant groups steadily assimilate to and become part of the common American people, has been challenged by a group of historians who argue that this was a strictly limited process, available only to whites, and, further, that many of those who were eventually included as full Americans had to overcome a presumption that they were not "really" white. Race in other words is crucial, both at its beginning, and by implication throughout American history, for full inclusion. To take one powerful and clear statement of this position:

> The saga of European immigration has long been held up as proof of the openness of American society, the benign and absorptive powers of American capitalism, and the robust health of American democracy. "Ethnic inclusion," "ethnic mobility," and "ethnic assimilation," on the European model set the standard upon which "America," as an ideal, is presumed to work; they provide the normative experience against which others are measured. But this pretty story suddenly fades once one recognizes how crucial Europeans' racial status as "free white persons" was to their gaining entrance in the first place; how profoundly dependent their racial inclusion was upon the racial exclusion of others; how racially accented the native resistance was even to their inclusion for something over half a century. (Jacobson 1998: 12)

The implication of this point of view is that the present minorities as commonly understood exist not only because of recency of immigration, which characterizes some of them, but primarily because of color: they are not white. Their ability to become full and equal participants in American society is thereby limited because of its racist character.

I believe the whiteness theorists are wrong. The racist character of the past is clear, and a degree of racism in the present is also evident, despite radical changes in public opinion and major changes in law and legal enforcement. But there has been a striking and irreversible change between the 1920s, when immigration from Eastern and Southern Europe was sharply reduced, and immigration from Asia was banned entirely, and the postwar decades and in particular the period since the 1960s. Public institutions and significant private institutions today may take account of race only for the purpose of benefiting minorities. Race, or ethnicity considered akin to race, is not the barrier to full inclusion it was half a century ago.

The whiteness theorists have a story to tell about the past, but it is one that has limited bearing on the present. The new immigrant groups are for the most part distinguished by race or quasi-racial characteristics from the population of European white origin, yet it seems likely they progress pretty much at the same rate, affected by the same factors – their education and skills, their occupations, the areas of the country in which they settle, and the like – as the European immigrants of the past.

They merge into the common population at the same rate too. We know that the number and percentage of such intermarriages between persons from the minorities and from the majority has grown greatly in recent decades. One analysis of the previous census reports that "for married people between the ages of twenty-five and thirty-four, 70 percent of Asian women and 39 percent of Hispanic women have white [sic] husbands." The same account asserts, however, that only 2 percent of black women in the same age group were married to white men (Canon 1999: 32). The theme of black difference on the one hand, intermixture and merger for other groups on the other, is clearly sounded in these and other statistics.

The black difference

The first analyses conducted by independent analysts of the census statistics brought up sharply the degree to which blacks are still distinguished from other minorities or subgroups in the United States by residential segregation. "Analyis of Census Finds Segregation Along With Diversity," reads one headline. "Segregation" in this analysis is measured by the diversity of census tracts, as experienced by the "average" person of a given group or race. So, the average white person lives in a tract that is 80 percent white, down from 85 percent in 1990; the average black person lives in a tract that is 51 percent black, down from 56 percent in 1990; the average Hispanic is less "segregated" by this measure – his tract is 45 percent Hispanic, and increased from 43 percent in 1990. But one may explain this degree of "segregation" and its rise since 1990 by the huge increase, based on immigration, much of it illegal, of the Hispanic population. The average Asian lives in a tract that is not particularly Asian – 18 percent, as against 15 percent in 1990 (Schmitt 2001e). This rise reflects to some degree the 50 percent increase in the Asian population, mostly through immigration, in the decade.

Local reporting focused on the relative proportions of the minority groups in each community, and also on the degree of segregation. Integration proceeds, but for blacks slowly. There are black census tracts in Boston with almost no whites, white tracts with almost no blacks (Cindy

Rodriguez 2001b, Schmitt 2001c). We calculate these figures every census, as if watching a fever report. The overall picture is that the segregation of blacks is great, the segregation of Hispanic groups, despite the recency of their immigration and their foreign tongue, is rather less, and little segregation is noted among Asians.

The big news of the census was that "Hispanics" had for the first time surpassed blacks in number, but that was only the case if one excluded from the black population those individuals who had chosen the race "black" along with another race. The number of Hispanics rose to 35.3 million, a 61 percent increase in ten years, the number of blacks rose at a much lower rate to 34.7 million, 36.4 million if one added those who chose more than one race. Blacks account for 12.3 percent of the population, about the same percentage they have maintained for the past century. The increase in Hispanics was much greater than expected: it was generally agreed that one reason for this increase was a larger number of illegal immigrants than had been previously calculated, 9 million according to one demographer instead of 7, perhaps as much as 11 million according to another demographer (Cindy Rodriguez 2001a).

Making the comparison between the two largest minorities was complicated by the fact that respondents could choose more than one race for the first time, and 7 million did so. Analysis of these mixed-race choices, even reporting on them, is not easy. A reporter writes: "Five percent of blacks, 6 percent of Hispanics, 14 percent of Asians and 2.5 percent of whites identified themselves as multiracial" (Schmidt 2001b). But why are these multi-race choosers labeled "black" or "Asian"? Is the one-drop rule once used by southern states operating here? If someone chooses "American Indian" and another race, do we include that person in the count of American Indians? If we do, that would increase the number of American Indians more than 50 percent. The Office of Management and Budget overseas the race and ethnic statistics compiled by federal agencies and it has determined that for their purposes (affirmative action monitoring and the like) all multi-race choosers who chose white and a minority race are to be counted as being part of the minority, a decision that has pleased minority advocates (Etzioni 2001). But does it reflect how these individuals see themselves?

The mixed-race choices complicate the issue of choosing a base on which to measure the progress of, or possible discrimination against, minorities, an important step in programs of affirmative action. That is one reason some minority leaders opposed allowing this option. But the more important one is that any measure that reduces the number of the groups is felt to be a diminution of their political weight.

Now that the option exists, it is clear many are eager to choose two or even more races. Even among blacks, where there may be less willingness to choose two races than among Asians and American Indians – because it may be seen as something like race betrayal (Schmitt 2001c) – it is noteworthy that younger persons are much more willing to choose two races than older ones. Or perhaps simply more of the younger groups is indeed the offspring of parents of different race. If one creates a combined black group by putting together blacks with those who choose black as one of the races they tick off, 2.3 percent of this combined group who are fifty years of age or older are multi-race choosers, but 8.1 percent of those seventeen and younger choose more than one race (Schmitt 2001c). But those who choose the options of black–white are still few – fewer in percentage terms than those who choose white-other ("other" in the racial category generally means Hispanic) or white-Asian or white-American Indian.

When the statistics of intermarriage are analyzed, one can be sure there will be a considerable rise in white–black marriages over 1990, even if the percentage of such intermarriages is considerably less than white–Asian or Hispanic–non-Hispanic marriages. Blacks are still more segregated, more separated, in residence, than other minority groups. They are more sharply defined in their consciousness and majority consciousness as separate: history has made them so. But one sees the processes of assimilation and integration working among blacks, as measured by intermarriage, by presence in high-status occupations, and to a more modest degree by residential integration. By the census of 2010, or 2020, these processes will be further advanced.

Choosing a future

What is the upshot of this story of counting and differentiating, by race and ethnicity? One can take a neutral position, insisting that it merely records what exists, but we are today far from that innocence. What exists, in terms of race and ethnicity and group differentiation, is a product of choices, of dominant groups primarily, but by those who are dominated too. They are "constructed," and whatever their significance in reality, for us they don't exist apart from what we make of them. We have in this account noted a number of times the political factors that have created the current scheme of racial and ethnic accounting, a scheme now deeply implanted in the American mind. Leaders of groups have helped create the scheme, as in the case of the Hispanics. The scheme once created helps also to create a group. Hispanics for certain purposes become a reality, even though they did not exist before a name was coined and a category created. This does not mean they cannot come into conflict – where they come together in number, they become aware of their differences and there may be conflict (Feuer 2003). Today, Mexicans and Puerto Ricans may create their own groups on campus – there is hardly much cultural connection between them – but for other purposes, such as calling for a Hispanic studies center, they will unite and present themselves as one.

There are significant and important differences among Hispanics, among Asians, among whites, and among blacks too. Conflicts divide minority from minority, as in California, where blacks and Hispanics compete over jobs and political appointments and representation, a competition that seems fated to be resolved in favor of Hispanics owing to their growing huge demographic advantage. There is generally some political advantage for leaders to aggregate groups, to take advantage of the large category the authorities have created, like "Hispanics," and so to claim they speak for more people than they actually do represent.

I would not exaggerate the role of bureaucratic and administrative measures in creating or maintaining groups: there are realities that make groups, commonness of culture, experience, history, misfortune. But that reality changes over time. Groups change their culture, forget their history, overcome misfortune, and that is the most common experience of groups in the United States. It is not the universal experience: for some, and for some leaders in particular, the effort may be to focus on and exaggerate misfortune, and keep a history of oppression alive. But whatever the fashionability of a multicultural maintenance of difference, or the advantages that an emphasis on past discrimination may give, assimilation persists, and changes every group. The great divide between blacks and others is still marked – but it is less than it was, and who can doubt it will be less in the future?

Perhaps the most important current role of the system of naming and differentiating and counting is to measure the degree to which groups change and assimilate. From that point of view, the proposal being presently debated in California – to delete all reference to race and ethnicity in state statistics and administration – is premature. The groups exist, the reality of difference persists, and it will not fall below the horizon of public attention if the statistics that describe them become less available. But the boundaries between groups do soften, the distinctions decline, and the degree to which this has been happening is indicated by the necessity to accommodate multiple race choices in the 2000 census, and in the complexities, ever greater each year, in accounting for race and ethnicity, for sorting the population into meaningful groups.

For one of the large groups, African–Americans, these processes of assimilation and integration operate on a much-reduced schedule. Counted from the beginning, it is essential if we are to have a sense of progress or lack of progress, to continue counting. It would be no great loss if the scheme of counting by race and ethnicity were abandoned for all the other groups. Statistics of place of birth and parents' place of birth would give us all we need to know, or can really know with any great degree of accuracy (Glazer 2002). Indeed, one may perhaps look forward to a time when our complex system of racial and ethnic counting is made so confusing by the number of possible choices, singular and multiple, that the whole scheme is abandoned. Many Americans hope so.

REFERENCES

Anderson, M., 2000, *The American Census*, New Haven: Yale University Press.

Canon, D. T., 1999, *Race, Redistricting, and Representation*, University of Chicago Press.

Etzioni, A., 2001, "To Diversity and Beyond: The New Census Manufactures Minorities," *Weekly Standard*:19.

Feuer, A., 2003, "Ethnic Chasm in El Barrio," *New York Times* (September 6).

Fund, J. H., 2001, "The Ghost of Elbridge Gerry," *Wall Street Journal* (April 23): A22.

Glazer, N., 2002, "Do We Need the Census Race Question?" *The Public Interest*, 149.

Jacobson, M. F., 1998, *Whiteness of a Different Color*, Cambridge, MA: Harvard University Press.

Lieberson, S., 1993, "The Enumeration of Ethnic and Racial Groups in the Census: Some Devilish Principles," in *Challenges of Measuring an Ethnic World*, Proceedings of the Joint Canada–United States Conference on Measurement of Ethnicity, Washington, DC: Bureau of the Census, US Department of Commerce.

Lieberson, S. and M. Waters, 1988, *From Many Strands*, New York: Russell Sage Foundation.

Porter, E., 2001, "Growing Minority Groups Will Likely Face Lawsuits Over Redistricting," *Wall Street Journal* (March 14): B1.

Rodriguez, Clara, 2000, *Changing Race: Latinos, the Census, and the History of Ethnicity in the United States*, New York University Press.

Rodriguez, Cindy, 2001a, "Census Bolsters Theory Illegal Immigrants Undercounted," *Boston Globe* (March 20): A4.

2001b, "Census shows a Boston still divided," *Boston Globe* (April 20): A1, 18.

Schmitt, E., 2001a, "New Census Shows Hispanics Are Even With Blacks in US," *New York Times* (March 8): A1, A15.

2001b, "For 7 Million People in Census, One Race Category Isn't Enough," *New York Times* (March 13): A1, 14.

2001c, "Blacks Split on Disclosing Multiracial Roots," *New York Times* (March 31): A1, 15.

2001d, "Portrait of a Nation: US Now More Diverse, Ethnically and Racially," *New York Times* (April 1): 20.

2001e, "Analysis of Census Finds Segregation Along With Diversity," *New York Times* (April 4): A15.

Skerry, P., 2000, *Counting on the Census: Race, Group Identity, and the Evasion of Politics*, Washington, DC: Brookings Institution.

Thernstrom, A., 1987, *Whose Votes Count?* Cambridge, MA: Harvard University Press.

Ueda, R., 1994, *Postwar Immigrant America: A Social History*, Boston and New York: Bedford Books of St. Martin's Press.

Waters, M. C., 1990, *Ethnic Options: Choosing Identities in America*, Berkeley, CA: University of Califronia Press.

Waters, M. C., 2000, *Black Identities: West Indian immigrants and American Realities*, Cambridge, MA: Harvard University Press; New York: Russell Sage Foundation.

3   Four modes of ethno-somatic stratification: The experience of Blacks in Europe and the Americas

Orlando Patterson

Introduction

In this chapter I argue that there are four modes of ethno-somatic stratification in Europe and the Americas: the North American mode of binary mobilization, the Afro-Caribbean mode of pluralistic underdevelopment, the North European mode of proletarian incorporation, and the Latin mode of hegemonic *blanqueamiento* or whitening.[1] Each mode refers to a unique configuration of ethno-racial ideology, ethno-demographic mix, ethno-class stratification, and level of societal racialization. Each is the product of distinctive socio-historical trajectories, as well as modern economic, political, and migratory processes. All four modes will be briefly outlined, but because of space constraints and the special interests of this volume, the paper will concentrate on the first three modes mentioned above.

The paper begins with a demographic portrait of the black diaspora populations circa 2000. We then move to an analysis of the broad patterns of adjustment by the post-diasporic populations of African-ancestry people in the Americas. Part three discusses the origins and formation of the three modes of the Americas. The fourth, and major, part of the chapter discusses the North European ethno-somatic mode then focuses on the nature and interactions between the three modes of special interest: the North Caribbean, Afro-American, and the British version of the North Atlantic. We end with some concluding observations.

1   A demographic overview

Somewhere around 2000–3 some 164,208,800 persons of whole or part-African ancestry lived in Europe and the Americas.[2] In comparative global terms, the African-ancestry diaspora population is not especially large. There are three countries, having no persons of African ancestry, with larger populations: China, India, and Indonesia. As migratory

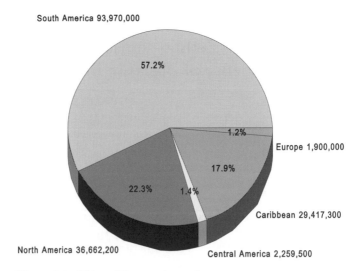

South America 93,970,000

57.2%

1.2%

Europe 1,900,000

17.9%

22.3%   1.4%

Caribbean 29,417,300

North America 36,662,200

Central America 2,259,500

Figure 3.1 African Diaspora by region

populations go, however, it ranks second only to the Neo-European in size. In spite of the far greater number of Chinese and Indians, the African diaspora is substantially larger than those of these two peoples and it dwarfs those of the Jewish, Armenian, Kurdish, and other diaspora peoples. The African diaspora population is almost completely confined to the Atlantic lands, with the notable exception of the Pacific Afro-Colombian and Afro-Peruvian communities and, of course, Afro-Americans in the US Pacific coastal areas. Circa 2003 the diaspora populations were distributed as follows: 36,662,200 live in North America, of whom 36 million reside in the United States and 662,000 in Canada. There were 2,259,500 living in Mexico and Central America (not including Belize), the largest concentrations being in Mexico (approx. 1 million), Nicaragua (461,500), and Panama (414,500). Outside of Africa, South America is the continent with the largest number of persons of African ancestry (not counting Surinam, French Guiana, and Guyana). A total of 93,979,000 live on that continent, of whom 85 percent are to be found in Brazil. With 80,094,300 persons of self-identified African ancestry, Brazil is by far the country with the largest number of such persons outside of Africa. Indeed a little over one in two of all persons in the African diaspora live in Brazil and more persons of African ancestry live there than any other country except Nigeria. It should be noted also that this is a moderate estimate of the Afro-Brazilian population, restricted to persons who identify themselves as being of African ancestry in the most recent (2000) census.[3] By all accounts, a far greater proportion of Brazilians are actually of some African ancestry, something to which I return below. Colombia and Venezuela, with 8.7 million and 2.5 million persons conservatively estimated of African ancestry are, respectively, the second and third largest groups in South America.

At least 29,417,300 persons of identified African ancestry live in the Caribbean, of whom15,042,700 live in the Latin islands of Cuba, Puerto Rico, and the Dominican Republic, while 14,374,600 live in the non-Hispanic Caribbean region which includes, culturally, Guyana, French Guyana, Suriname, and Belize.

Finally, there is Western Europe where, by 2002 there were at least 1,900,000 persons of African ancestry from Africa and the Caribbean: 1,148,700 live in Britain, at least 200,000 in the Netherlands; at least 500,000 in France, and about 50,000 in Portugal. Britain has by far the best data: 565,870 blacks are of Caribbean ancestry, making up 1 percent of the total British population and 12.2 percent of its total minority population. There are 485,270 people from Africa and another 97,585 designated "other blacks" by the UK census.

Migration history

Diasporas are the products of forced or voluntary migrations, and we turn now to a consideration of the population movements that resulted in the present distribution of African-ancestry peoples. In any such consideration, we have to distinguish between primary, secondary, and even tertiary migration eras. The primary phase was the product of the Atlantic slave trade between the middle of the fifteenth century and the 1870s. Between the start of the seventeenth century and the ending of slavery in the 1880s some 9.9 million Africans were transported as slaves to the Americas nearly all coming from the West Coast of Africa, an area extending from Senegal to Angola (Curtin 1969, Lovejoy 1982). It has been estimated by Patrick Manning that the delivery of some 9 million slaves to the New World between 1700 and 1850 entailed the capture of 21 million Africans, suggesting a devastating demographic impact on this part of the continent. In addition, the trade almost certainly had many negative social and political consequences for the region.[4]

The second migration era began in the late eighteenth century. There was a not insubstantial movement of US slaves to Canada and the Caribbean during and after the American Revolution, followed in the nineteenth century by the movement of runaway slaves via the *Underground Railroad* to that country. From the first half of the nineteenth century Afro-Caribbean peoples began to move to the United States and

Table 3.1 *Legal immigration from the Caribbean 1950–2002 and totals for 1820–2002*

	1951–60	1961–70	1971–80	1981–90	1991–2000	2001–2	1951–2	1820–2002
Caribbean	123,091	470,213	741,126	872,051	978,787	347,369	3,532,636	3,873,162
Cuba	79,984	208,536	264,863	144,578	169,322	86,204	953,487	971,625
Dom. Rep	9,897	93,292	148,135	252,035	335,251	78,916	917,526	889,117
Haiti	4,442	34,499	56,335	138,379	179,644	80,179	493,478	456,125
Jamaica	8,869	74,906	137,577	208,148	169,227	59,769	658,496	628.383
Other Carib	20,935	58,980	134,216	128,911	125,343	42,383	510,768	927,902

Source: Bureau of Citizenship and Immigration Services, 2003, *2002 Yearbook of Immigration Statistics*, Washington, DC.

Central America. By the end of the century over 100,000 West Indians had moved to the United States and well over 50,000 had moved to Central America. West Indians were the core of the labor force that dug the Panama Canal. Later they spread out across Central America where they worked as laborers and clerks on the large banana plantations. Today, most English-speaking pockets of peoples in Central America are from the Caribbean.

The movement of Caribbean peoples to the United States was halted by the explicitly racist immigration act of 1923, at which time over 150,000 had migrated there. The movement of peoples from the islands was reduced to a trickle between 1924 and 1965. However, with the change in US immigration laws in 1965 there was a sudden huge movement of peoples from the islands to the USA (see Table 3.1). Of all legal immigrants entering the USA from the Caribbean between 1820 and 2002 – a total of 3,873,162 persons – 91.2 percent came after 1960. Of the 2,012,410 coming from the non-Hispanic Caribbean, 82.6 percent came between 1960 and 2002.[5] A third of all Jamaicans (more properly, Jamaican-identified persons), and nearly a half of the population of some of the smaller islands now live in America, especially the North East. The fact is little known, but one in three of all persons of African ancestry in New York state are of Caribbean ancestry.

Immediately preceding the renewal of the secondary diaspora to the US was the secondary diaspora of West Indians to Europe between the early fifties of the last century and 1962. The present African-ancestry populations of Western Europe are largely the product of this secondary Caribbean migration. Between 1948 and 1973, when it largely ended, over 300,000 West Indians had migrated to Britain. There were only 17,218 West Indian immigrants living in Britain in 1951. By 1961, the year before the British immigration act that ended unrestricted entry to Britain, the West Indian born population had soared to 173,659. And by

1971, near the end of this migratory wave, the figure stood at 304,070. Along with 244,000 children born in Britain to these migrants, the population of West Indians had soared from an estimated total of 18,000 in 1951 to 548,000 in 1971 (Peach 1991).

West Indians from the French West Indies in France and Dutch-speaking Caribbean in Holland constitute the other half of Caribbean peoples living in Europe. Net migration from the French Caribbean to France surged only in the early 1970s, resulting in an increase in the Caribbean-born population of France from 61,160 in 1968 to 180,448 in 1982 and a total (including children born in France) of 265,988 that year (Peach 1991: p. 3, Table 2a). The flow from the Dutch Caribbean to the Netherlands began slowly during the 1960s and took off only in the mid-1970s. As late as 1970 there were only 28,985 immigrants from the region in the Netherlands; by 1975 this had climbed to 104,154 and to 247,000 in 1988. Along with second-generation persons the total Caribbean-origin population in the Netherlands in 1988 was 308,000.

In the late eighteenth and first half of the nineteenth centuries there was a secondary migration of freed slaves from the Americas to Sierra Leone and Liberia. We know little about the numbers that went to Sierra Leone, but it could not have been more than a few thousands. Between 6,000 and 11,000 African-Americans went to Liberia, mainly with the assistance of the Colonization Society from 1820 to 1865. They were joined there by a few hundred West Indians. There has also been a demographically insignificant but culturally meaningful secondary migration of West Indians to Africa, mainly Jamaican Rastafarians who moved to Ethiopia during the second half of the twentieth century.

Both in North America and Western Europe, West Indian migrants and their descendants are increasingly being joined by a new primary diaspora from Africa. Between 1960 and 1989 there was a net emigration of 138,719 Africans to different regions of the world. Of this total 71,193 went to North America, mainly the United States; 48,146 went to Western Europe; and the remainder, 19,380, went to various parts of Oceania. As we saw earlier, 24 percent of the African-ancestry population of Britain come directly from Africa.

Afro-Caribbean peoples are, in both absolute and relative terms, the most mobile of the peoples of African ancestry and account for well over 90 percent of the secondary diaspora movements across the Atlantic. They are also the only people of African ancestry who have engaged in tertiary diaspora movements. The most important of these have been the movement of people of color from central America to the United States which has been gaining momentum in recent years, and the small, still demographically insignificant, re-migration of Caribbean people from Britain to Canada and the US.

Other New World people have also engaged in secondary diaspora movements although nothing approaching the scale of West Indians in international movements. There was a movement of Afro-Brazilians between Brazil and Africa during the late nineteenth and first half of the present century. However, it is doubtful whether there was a net migration back to Africa of any significance.

So far I have considered only international migrations across the Atlantic. However, no discussion of movements of people of color would be complete without mention of the large-scale movement of Afro-Americans from the rural South of the USA to the urban north. In scale, range, and sociological consequences this was one of the great movements of peoples in modern times. However, it was internal and some may question whether it constituted a secondary diaspora movement. At the very least, it may be contested, a diaspora should involve a change of states. Others may dispute this. At any rate, no one doubts the social, economic, and political significance of this secondary, if internal, movement of African-ancestry people.

One major consequence of this movement, the urbanization of the Afro-American population, brings me to my final demographic observation. It is the fact that while homeland Africans are still predominantly rural, the great majority of diaspora peoples of color in the Atlantic region are predominantly urban. Afro-Americans are now among the most urbanized of Americans. Most Afro-Caribbean peoples in the Caribbean live in urban areas, although many in miserable squatter settlements and other slums. Afro-Caribbean peoples in North America and Europe tend to have far higher rates of urbanization than average; indeed, they are almost 100 percent urban (I exclude the annual movement of contract farm workers). And in most areas of Latin America people of African ancestry tend to be more urban than average although living under less than adequate conditions.

2   Patterns of adjustment in the New World

At least five major factors influenced the adjustment of Africans to the New World: the kind of slave system; geography; the African cultural background; the ethnic demography of the society; and the nature of the European culture of the contact group. These factors together account for the important variations found among peoples of African ancestry in the Americas today, and we will have occasion to return to them.

However, at this point I wish to emphasize the sociocultural commonalities of the New World black experience, for it is these that justify any talk of a black Atlantic. The most important common experience of all diaspora peoples was the generative, historical trauma of slavery which left in its wake certain critical uniformities that are still important.

Like slaves everywhere, the ancestors of all New World blacks were natally alienated from the communities into which they were forcibly inserted. By that I mean, not that the slave did not have a social life of his or her own, but that he or she had no legitimate place in the political, legal, and civic life of his or her society (Patterson 1982: Introduction). The centuries of enslavement suffered by the Afro-Atlantic peoples led to an ingrained view of them, by the dominant and all other nonblack groups (including the descendants of European immigrants who were to arrive centuries after the ancestors of blacks), as people who did not belong to the society at large, only to individuals and private estates. That view was to persist, with devastating consequences, long after the formal abolition of slavery. And it still plagues the experience of African-descended peoples in many parts of Latin America, including Brazil where they are, by most estimates, the majority.

Whether slavery resulted from, or was the cause of the racism experienced by blacks everywhere is a socio-historical issue we cannot debate here. What is certain is that it fully institutionalized the racist view of blacks as an inferior group. The actual cultural expression of these views varied, resulting in the different ideologies of racism to be discussed below.

Unlike many pre-modern slave systems, the primary motive for enslavement in the Atlantic Basin was the labor exploitation of blacks. In the dominant plantation systems this meant incorporation into a harshly regulated, gang-structured regime requiring little skill for the vast majority. There was, to be sure, a minority who were trained in semi-skilled and occasionally even skilled work. But for most blacks, slavery meant centuries of illiteracy and commodified labor. Slavery also denied blacks the right to hold and accumulate property. Hence blacks emerged from centuries of incorporation in the emerging capitalist systems of the Americas with little skill, near complete illiteracy, and no property. What's more, every effort was made to keep these disadvantages in place for another century or so after emancipation. Indeed, in some places like the US South, the proportion of blacks with skills that could facilitate mobility in the broader economy actually fell from their already low levels following emancipation.

Bereft of skill, literacy, and wealth, black people throughout the Americas entered the emerging capitalist orders after slavery with crippling disadvantages compared with all white native or immigrant workers. Even without the added scourge of racism, it would have taken decades to catch up with descendants of non-slaves in the acquisition of social, cultural, and material capital.

There was, however, another equally devastating de-skilling of the black populations of the Americas which rarely gets mentioned, partly because discussing it is historiographically out of favor. Slavery denied blacks not only the security of dual parenting, but of effective parenting itself. On all plantation systems women had to labor at the same level as men. Indeed, in most Caribbean and many US and Brazilian plantations, women made up a higher proportion of the laborers in the fields than men. Not only were they given little time off during their pregnancy but were ordered back to the fields within weeks, sometimes days, of giving birth. Child-rearing, if one may call it that, was left in the hands of old and often incapacitated and certainly very tired slave women who were simply overwhelmed by the inhuman burden placed upon them during their final months of living. This was true even of the USA, in spite of the greater tendency to encourage slaves to reproduce there (Steckel 1986). The tragic result was not simply the fact that slave children were hardly socialized or trained – their childhood "stolen" as one scholar recently described it (King 1995) – but that the all-important social skill of effective child-rearing was severely attenuated.

Slavery also had certain harmful internal social consequences. The most important of these was the way it violated and distorted familial and gender relations.[6] Throughout the Americas the female-headed family is the norm among African-ancestry peoples. Further, this household type emerges, not from the dissolution of marriages (as is true of most cases among nonblacks), but from nonmarital childbearing and paternal abandonment. While all Afro-Atlantic peoples continued to value kinship, the erosion of West African household patterns was replaced by ad hoc, slaveholder-conditioned household arrangements that could not provide structures for secure marital relations or stable child-rearing. The view that slavery largely accounts for present household and parenting patterns among New World African-ancestry peoples has been strongly contested in recent decades although the scholarly tide has once again shifted back to the slave-genesis position (Patterson 1998). Poverty cannot explain existing household and gender relations (most peoples of the world are poor but do not find themselves with populations in which 60 percent of children have been abandoned by their fathers or in which the typical household type is headed by a lone parent).

Closely related to this, indeed originating in it, is another modern Atlantic social commonality: the distinctive role of women. Slavery forced women to be independent. As noted earlier, they were equally exploited as manual laborers in the fields, and in many cases even more so than men. The frequent absence of a male partner (including cases of stable unions in which the male partner lived on another estate, so called "away marriages" in America) and the sole responsibility for parenting after slavery, led to higher labor force participation rates than those for other women. In recent decades, with increased educational opportunities, black women throughout the Atlantic diaspora have been closing the income gap not only with black men, but with white women. They also far surpass black men in the educational systems of all these societies, and in America they are now far ahead in professional training (Patterson 1998). Exactly the same holds for the Caribbean and most Latin American societies as well as Europe.

Finally, the African-descended peoples of the Americas emerged from the experience of slavery with creolized cultural constructions that, in spite of considerable variations, had certain underlying themes and deep structures that partly reflects their common West African cultural ancestry, and the adaptation of these transmitted traditions to the slave and post-emancipation environments. These commonalities are found mainly in the expressive-symbolic areas of their cultures, especially music, folklore, language, and other communicative patterns, and, of course, religion. I noted above that slavery was especially destructive of West African social organization. However, there were two areas of West African social life that survived the crossing and devastation of slavery. One of these was the strong emphasis on kinship and the tendency to use the idiom of kinship to express all close relations. My fieldwork in the Caribbean, as does the work of many others, certainly confirms this. However, it is easy to misunderstand what this means and revisionist historians have all but confounded the issue. Thus Herbert Gutman assumed that the evidence he found for strong emphasis on kinship relations was further proof of the existence of strong families. It was nothing of the sort. Indeed, the strong emphasis on kinship at best compensates for, at worst works against, stable conjugal or other cohabitational relations and broader affinal ties. This explains a paradox of New World black life that has long bothered anthropologists: that in spite of the fact that they so greatly value kinship, the network ties of black people, while dense, tend to be unusually narrow.

3   The consolidation of ethno-somatic modes

It is in the post-emancipation era that major differences were to emerge in the socioeconomic condition and cultural experiences of the peoples of the Afro-Atlantic. Slavery ended in very different ways throughout the New World with important differences in socioeconomic consequences for the ex-slaves. In the Caribbean the slave owners were paid off and many left, offering opportunities for the construction of a semi-independent peasantry that most ex-slaves in the larger colonies took advantage of. This, however, was the exceptional outcome in comparative terms, as Engerman has emphasized, and even here conditions began to deteriorate for the newly established peasantry by the last third of the nineteenth century (Engerman 1966). In the USA slavery ended only after a savage civil war engendering deep bitterness in the Caucasian population that displaced the ex-slaves. Indeed, what emerged in the USA was a neo-slavery system in which the personal ownership of the master was ended but the culture of slavery persisted. This was the worst possible situation for the ex-slave population which was later abandoned by its northern liberators. The result was a vicious system of terrorization which culminated in the lynching era that lasted from the 1880s to about 1950, during which some 5,000 Afro-Americans were slaughtered, many of them burnt alive. I have recently argued that a significant minority of these lynchings were classic instances of human sacrifice engaging entire communities and often officiated by an ordained clergyman (Patterson 1998).

What emerged from the conjunction of inherited peculiarities of the slave past, the new forms of labor exploitation, the political and social constraints placed on the ex-slave population and their descendants, the demographic mix and migratory policies of the neo-doulotic systems in which blacks found themselves, and the cultural, especially the religious and intellectual preoccupations of the dominant white groups, were the different modes of ethno-somatic stratification. As indicated earlier, there were four such modes which will now be briefly adumbrated.

The North American binary mode

The pattern of racism and "racial" domination that consolidated in America during this period constituted one of the four main forms of ethno-somatic ("racial") stratification that emerged in the Americas (see Figure 3.2). North Americans developed what may be called a *binary* conception of race, more commonly known as the one-drop rule: the classification of all persons either as "white" or "black," including in the latter category all persons with any known African ancestry, however somatically light-skinned they may be. Contrary to what is commonly believed, this system, though long in the making, was consolidated nationally only during the late nineteenth century. Important parts of the South, such as the Carolinas, more closely resembled the Latin mode discussed below. And, of course, Louisiana's mode was very Latin until the late

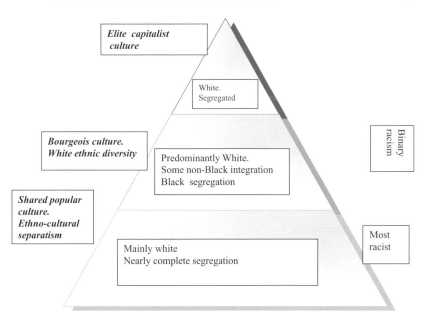

Figure 3.2 The North American binary mode

nineteenth century. Nonetheless, by the late nineteenth century the entire United States had converged into what is being called the North American binary mode.[7] Its demographic base is a majority white population with deep internal class cleavages, and the fact that for most of American history, blacks were the major distinctive people of color. Native Americans had been largely exterminated and those that survived had been banished to reservations and were largely out of sight and out of mind. The binary system was developed in the South as a means of dividing the dominated groups and, at the same time, a way of establishing a hegemonic bond of solidarity between white elite and the mass of poor whites. Racial solidarity, notions of racial purity and avoidance, became a powerful means of diverting poor whites from the inequities of the system and their own exploitation (Morgan 1975). It is possible that this system was reinforced by the fundamentalist religion of the South, with its belief in a moral and social universe polarized between good and evil, God and Satan, elect and damned, sinners and saved, black and white.

In the North an equally powerful version of the binary system developed as a means of unifying the many disparate immigrant groups from Europe. Whiteness was reconstructed during the nineteenth century as a precious positional good – unknown in the European homeland where, because everyone was white, whiteness had no meaning or social reality – which the immigrants eagerly grasped and consumed (Roediger 1991). It instantly gave them a sense of oneness with the dominant group, and a quick means of identity with the emerging mass democratic demos of Jacksonian America. Ironically, antislavery agitation was as much motivated by anti-black racism as it was by the noble struggle of principled, pro-black abolitionists (Davis 1984). The white working class and its leadership despised blacks as much as they despised slavery, seeing both as a threat to their dream of yeomanric independence on the frontier (Foner 1995). The high mortality rate of the Civil War reinforced this racist trend. When the capitalist classes later in the century began to use black labor as a way of breaking strikes, the die of northern binary racism was cast.

It is important to note, further, that northern whites used the binary conception of whiteness even more effectively than their Southern elite counterpart. In the South, whiteness was easily acquired: if a person had no black ancestry (true of all European immigrants) and looked vaguely white, he or she was included. In time, even the Chinese of Mississippi found that they could negotiate their way across the the boundaries of whiteness by placing enough distance between themselves and their former black neighbors (Loewn 1988). Not being black was the iron test. In the north it was more difficult. Being born in Europe was not enough, especially during the nativist era of hostility to immigrants. Many immigrant groups had to struggle for "racial" acceptance and inclusion into the fold of whiteness. These included the Jews (who only finally acquired full, pure white status after World War II), the Irish (for all their freckles, pale skin, and light hair), Italians and other Southern Europeans. Indeed, as is well known, the restrictive immigration act of 1923 was passed primarily to keep out the inferior European races who were not really "pure" white (Ignatiev 1995; Brodkin 1999).

Eventually northern and southern variants merged into the brutal anti-black binary system that persisted up to the end of the sixties, becoming the sociocultural foundation of a fully racially structured and stratified society. Other groups entering this system such as pre-1965 Hispanics, anxiously played by the binary ethno-somatic rules, sometimes agitating to get the census to define them as Caucasian, as Mexican-Americans successfully did during the thirties.

A final, very important, point to note about the binary system is that it was highly gendered. White women became the living symbol of white purity and Negrophobia focused obsessively on sexual relations between white women and black men. The great dread of the binary system was race dilution through miscegenation and preventing this was a major political and cultural preoccupation. Very often anti-black hostility was rationalized as the protection of the white woman's honor, whatever may have been the original cause of the conflict. Many lynchings, I have argued, were elaborate rituals of human sacrifice meant not only to terrorize blacks, but to give communal expression to the sacredness of white women and, by extension, the inviolability of Jim Crow laws and the system of white supremacy. Of course, laws against intermarriage were universal in the South and were finally declared unconstitutional only in 1966, when sixteen states still had them.

The gendered element of binary racism, it should be emphasized, rested on a paternalistic view of women. Anti-miscegenation laws clearly assumed that women could not be trusted to keep the racial faith. Women were weak, precious extensions of male honor who were to be protected at all costs. As many feminist writers have pointed out, the conception of women and women's status implicit in the binary view of race was that of a group that was almost as dependent and inherently inferior as blacks. Where the dependency of the latter entailed their exlusion and degradation, the dependency of the former was expressed in their elevation on a pedestal. Both, however, were "owned" by white men – as despised laborers and cherished icon – and both were equally excluded from the public household (Wyatt-Brown 1982, Genovese 1988, Cash 1991).

The Afro-Caribbean mode

In South America and the Caribbean two different ethno-somatic systems emerged. They have in common the fact that they are non-binary. "Race" in all these societies is conceived of in denotative terms, ranging on a continuum from white, through various mixed shades (each with a given name) to black. Only people who are somatically black are so designated. An elaborate phenotypic terminology exists, especially in Spanish and Portuguese, to describe the different shades and types of somatic mixtures. A study by the Brazilian Institute of Geography and Statistics in 1976 found 134 self-designated terms for various shades of color in Brazil (Instituto Brasileiro de Geografia e Estatistico 1976).

However, there are extremely important differences between the Latin and Non-Latin societies, based on differences in the relative demographic mix of the various color types and on the composition and racial ideology and behavior of the elite groups.[8] In the Afro-Caribbean system – the second major ethno-somatic type – people of visibly African ancestry constitute the majority of the population. The lower and working classes in these societies are also visibly and (with the exception of Trinidad and Tobago and Guyana where East Indians

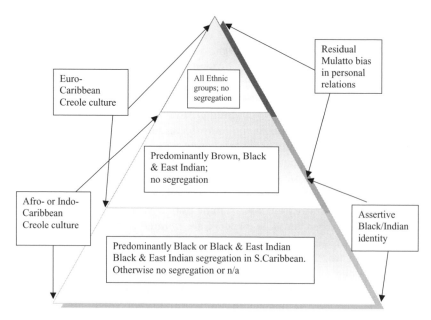

Figure 3.3 The Caribbean plural mode

make up approximately a half of the populations and a good part of the lower classes) almost exclusively of African ancestry. The unusual light-complexioned or European ancestry person of lower-class status is invariably classified as "red" (in Barbados, "Redlegs"). Until the 1950s, there was a close correlation between color and class and rampant color prejudice between shades, especially in personal relations and an elaborate trade-off between income and shade emerged in the marriage market.[9] At the same time, there has never really been any legal segregation in the islands and intermarriage was not uncommon.

Since the early sixties – with political independence, modernization programs, and the growth of the middle class – an important change took place marking off this system from both the American and Latin modes. Significant upward mobility of black and brown people into the upper classes has resulted in elites that are now predominantly nonwhite and increasingly made up of persons of visibly black ancestry. Black and brown people dominate the political system, the professions, and play significant and increasing roles in business. This is found in no other part of the Americas or, indeed, anywhere else except Africa.

Non-Hispanic Caribbean societies are culturally pluralistic. Most are at least bicultural. There is an Afro-Caribbean Creole culture that emerged from the syncretism of African and European cultural patterns and survival and adaptation to the exigencies of slavery, plantation life, and peasant communities. This was the culture of the black masses which, until the middle of the last century, was largely denigrated by all upwardly mobile West Indians, including those who were black. The other culture was the creolized version of European colonial cultures – French, English, and Dutch – of the ruling classes and middle-class groups. A very important and distinctive feature of all Afro-Caribbean societies is that this creolized elite culture was, for the late nineteenth century, largely mastered and transmitted by brown and black people in the region. The white plantocratic and commercial elites in most of them were both too small and too busy making money to attempt any direct hegemonic control of the system. Instead, it was left to the brown and upwardly mobile blacks to take over the professions and the teaching of the elite culture. Unlike America and the Latin regions, then, there is no identification of the culture of the elite, or things culturally European, with whites.

It should be noted, further, that West Indians, including those from the black poor, either are or aspire to be bicultural. Upwardly mobile blacks and browns learn the Afro-Caribbean base culture in the course of growing up. Mobility requires learning the Euro-Creole culture of the elites. People experience little problem in this, or in shifting between one culture and another in their daily interactions. Lower-class West Indians also move freely between the public areas of the Creole high culture and their own, most noticeably in their joint commitment to European Anglicanism or Catholicism (as in Jamacia and Haiti) on the one hand, and to the Cumina or Voudon Afro-Caribbean religion, on the other.

Nonetheless, there was until the last third of the last century a general slighting of things black and Afro-Caribbean in the traditional system and a major change in the evolution of the present Afro-Caribbean mode was the successful struggle for ethno-somatic respect and a change in the reputation of the Afro-Caribbean Creole. Under pressure from successful darker bourgeois persons, as well as assertive proletarian, black-pride movements such as the Rastafarians, and partly also under the influence of the African-American civil rights and black-identity movements, traditional phenotypical distinctions have faded, though by no means disappeared. They still operate in personal relations and, to a declining degree, in mate selection among middle- and upper-class browns and blacks. The enormous international success of the cultural creations of the Afro-Caribbean working classes – especially Reggae, Rastafarianism, and Calypso – and the rise of black political leadership before and after independence reinforced this trend, in the end creating a virtual social revolution in the role and reputation of Afro-Caribbean Creole.

The Caribbean mode is even more complex in its Southern Caribbean variant, especially Trinidad, Guyana, and Surinam.[10] The main difference is the greater multiculturalism of these societies with their large demographic mix of East Indians and, in Surinam, people from Java as well. We find here the same set of contested color–class relations as well as two stratified Creole cultures. East Indians, who came as indentured servants during the nineteenth century, constitute nearly a half of the populations of Trinidad and Guyana. Furthermore, they too developed a flourishing Creole alongside that of the blacks. Indians, of course, brought over their own color values with them, which dovetailed only too well with the pre-existing Afro-European pattern. Although they came from the lowest castes in the poorest part of India and were generally very dark – often much darker than most Afro-Caribbeans – they looked more European and had straight hair. It was not long before they had plunged into all the nasty little nuances of the trade-off between features, hair type, color, status, and class that characterized colonial Trinidad and the Guyanas.

The Latin American mode: hegemonic blanqueamiento

As mentioned earlier, I will have less to say about this mode due to the focus of our volume. For context, comparison, and completeness, however, some account must be taken of it. The Latin mode, found in Spanish America and Brazil, blends important features of the binary and Afro-Caribbean modes although, let me hasten to add, it has several quite unique features of its own.[11] Between the lower and middle classes these societies behave much like the Afro-Caribbean with two important differences. Demographically, people of European (Hispanic) ancestry and very light-skinned persons are more prevalent and can be found among the lower classes, which is rare in the non-Hispanic. What is more, people of all colors mix freely among the lower classes. Here these systems differ sharply from the USA, where most Euro-Americans emphasize racial differences and segregation, especially the poorer groups. In Latin-America poverty integrates; in North America it segregates; and in the Afro-Caribbean it is demographically irrelevant to ethno-somatic issues since the poor are entirely nonwhite (with a few exceptions here and there).

The second, decisive, difference from the Afro-Caribbean system, however, is the fact that above the middle classes there is a sharply demarcated ceiling in the operation of the denotative pattern of race and interracial interaction. The elites in these systems are almost entirely white or white identified. They differ from the North American Caucasian elites in their

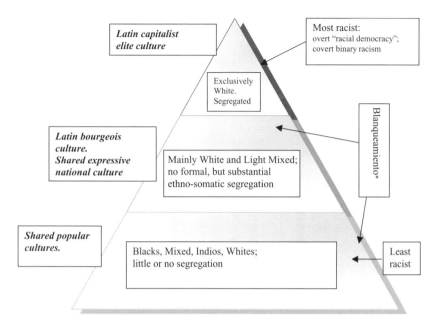

Latin capitalist
elite culture

Most racist:
overt "racial democracy";
covert binary racism

Exclusively
White.
Segregated

Latin bourgeois
culture.
Shared expressive
national culture

Blanqueamiento*

Mainly White and Light Mixed;
no formal, but substantial
ethno-somatic segregation

Shared popular
cultures.

Blacks, Mixed, Indios, Whites;
little or no segregation

Least
racist

* Spanish: Literally = "whitening." Brazilian Portuguese cognate: *esbranquecimento*

Figure 3.4 The Latin mode: hegemonic *blanqueamiento*

public acceptance of the denotative system below the elite levels, in the fact that they did not find it necessary to use binary racial solidarity as a means of hegemonic division and control (perhaps because of their use of direct, authoritarian means), in the absence of anxiety over interracial marriages at the middle and lower levels of the society, and in their celebration of hybridity and the myth of racial democracy. But they have very similar practices and private attitudes in their racist exclusion of all persons of color from elite positions, whether in government, the economy, the army, or in their own intimate relations. Though never formally legislated, elite occupations, neighborhoods, and intimate relations were, and still are, as segregated as anywhere in the deep South at the height of the Jim Crow era.

It has long been claimed that upwardly mobile lower-class people of color tend to marry up somatically – a process called blanqueiamento (*embranqecimento* in Brazil) or "whitening" – with the hope that their progeny will thereby climb the color-class ladder intergenerationally. While the whitening process certainly seems to operate in male mate selection (obviously this does not apply to women, since for every male

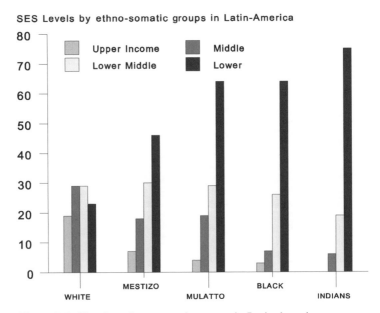

Figure 3.5 Class by ethno-somatic groups in Latin America

who marries lighter, there must be a female who marries darker), it seems to make little difference in terms of economic mobility, or in generating any close correlation between income and shade, as is commonly believed. This was the rather surprising recent finding of Edward Telles who discovered that blacks and browns in Brazil have very similar family income profiles, and are equally distinct from whites: the income of browns being 44.7 percent of whites, that of blacks 40.2 percent (Telles 1999: 86, Table 1). More recent work by Roland Soong confirms this (see Figure 3.5) as well as showing the high level of impoverishment among both.

The Latin mode of ethno-somatic stratification consolidated nation-wide during the decades after emancipation in much the same way that the binary system did in the USA.

As Katia M. de Queriós Mattoso noted, in the post-emancipation era whiteness became even more important for those who could claim it:

The old families, bankrupt or not, prided themselves on their supposed all-white ancestry, despite all the evidence to the contrary. Everywhere there was racism, and everywhere it was denied. "Purification became a necessary prerequisite for upward mobility. In relations between individuals, the imperatives of humility, obedience, and fidelity were even stronger than they had been during the time of slavery." (1996: 211–12)

A similar consolidation took place in the Latin Caribbean during the late nineteenth century and intensified after emancipation. Governments pursued immigration policies that encouraged Europeans to immigrate to Cuba with the explicit aim of whitening the population, resulting in a significant demographic shift from a predominantly mixed and black, to a predominantly mixed and white one.

In many ways Brazil was, and remains, the worst possible system of racial stratification for people in the African diaspora. Their poverty levels approach 50 percent. They experience chronic unemployment. Nearly 40 percent of them are illiterate compared with a 25 percent rate among Caucasians. Most live in abysmal slums or *favelas*. They have extremely high rates of criminal victimization. Delinquency is a major issue and begins from early childhood. There are some 7 million abandoned children on the streets of Brazil, nearly all of whom are of African ancestry, who have no hope of sanctuary from the state and are regarded as human vermin by the light-skin and Caucasian elites. Periodically, Caucasian death squads, often hired by merchants, hunt them down and slaughter them like wild beasts. And their incarceration rates are horrendous: over 80 percent of imprisoned Brazilians are of marked African ancestry. This is what Brazilians used to call, with Orwellian bombast, "racial democracy." It has been more recently called, with some truth, a system of "de facto" and "unwritten apartheid." Although there are no segregation or apartheid laws, extreme Negrophobia remains rampant at all levels of the society (Vieira 1995; U.N. Foundation 2003). Nonwhite Brazilians are systematically excluded from all major positions in their society as well as all minor ones having to do with the public, including the job of office-boy. It is claimed that the public would not put up with a nonwhite person in any such position, in spite of the fact that the majority of the population is of African ancestry. Recent research suggests that the color bar works as viciously against mulattos as against dark-skinned educated persons, contrary to what was commonly believed. It has also been shown that in recent decades the Caucasian group has, if anything, become more exclusive and discriminatory (Telles 1999: 82–97). Telles' observation that "black–white relations in Brazil are less separate but more unequal" (ibid.: 91) holds true for the mass of lower-class Brazilians, is less true of middle- and upper-middle-class communities, and is simply not true of the elite (Reichmann 1999).

At the same time, it has been difficult for Afro-Brazilians to mobilize against this system of racism and racial discrimination because they have so thoroughly bought into the *embranqecimento* ideology. Only in recent years has there been significant activism by educated Afro-Brazilians against this system. Their efforts have had some modest effects. It is now generally agreed that the myth of "racial democracy" is well and truly dead. And in 1994 Fernando Henrique Cardoso, the president and a former sociologist of race and class, publicly acknowledged the reality of racism, racial inequality, and the need for state action. More recently the Brazilian government has introduced an affirmative action program for its higher educational system.

4   Continuity and change in contemporary Europe and the Americas

Beyond the different systems of ethno-somatic stratification, the most important external developments after slavery were the different patterns of economic development. The USA was to emerge as the major industrial power of the world in the century after slavery; while Brazil was to become the typical semi-peripheral Latin American economy and the Caribbean classic underdeveloped, plantation- and peasant-based systems. The socioeconomic and political conditions of the ex-slave populations varied with regard to their involvement in these economic systems. In America, Afro-Americans became trapped in the share-cropping system and were systematically excluded from the mainstream industrial economy in the North and the urban South. In the Caribbean all workers were caught in a moribund economic system, whether they were peasants attempting to eke out a living on farms that were nonviably small and getting smaller, or plantation workers being paid reservation wages. In Latin America rampant economic discrimination confined most persons of African ancestry to the plantations or domestic service.

This pattern of post-emancipation entrapment was broken by three developments in the second half of the twentieth century. One was the achievement of independence and subsequent attempts at economic development in the Caribbean; the other was the historically parallel civil rights movement of blacks in the USA. However, for the mass of non-US blacks in the Americas, including the Caribbean, the secondary migrations mentioned earlier were the major means of escape from permanent poverty. Caribbean blacks have made far greater use of migration as an escape mechanism than their Latin counterpart. This has resulted in both higher levels of income as well as greater exposure to the culture, ethno-somatic consciousness, and strategies of political mobilization of US blacks.

African-Americans

In a recent review of the Afro-American condition over the past forty years I concluded that considerable progress has been made – in the growth of the Afro-American middle class (now 35 percent), in educational gains, in declining poverty rates (now 24 percent), in declining joblessness, in the integration of the armed forces and subsequent rise to high office in them by African-Americans, especially the Army where over ten of the officer corps is black, in the enormous influence of Afro-Americans on the nation's popular and elite cultures, and in the political clout of the group (Patterson 1997).

Overall, racism has declined substantially in the United States over the past thirty-five years. Only one in five Euro-Americans are now hardened racists. While this still means that for every two Afro-Americans there are three Euro-American racists, it is still a far cry from mid-century when over three-quarters of Euro-Americans were racists.[12]

For several reasons, America's traditional binary conception of race is currently undergoing considerable change. An important factor in the view of many scholars is the large inflow of people from Latin America and the Caribbean since 1965.[13] The 2000 US census found that people of Latin ancestry are now the largest minority group in the nation, although the exact significance of this demographic change is not entirely clear.[14] However, slightly over a half of them refused to designate themselves as either white or black in their census returns. Such a large "third" group undermines one of the basic assumptions of the binary racial model – that matters of "race" concern only blacks and whites. The binary construct is being further challenged by the growth of a still small but vocal mixed population. Some have suggested a long-term Latinization of America's racial attitudes, which would be different, though not necessarily a gain for the nation. A multicultural strategy is favored by many in the academic community but appears to have only modest support outside of Academe and is intellectually contested on many fundamental issues.[15]

At the same time, it is ironical that it is Afro-American leadership that is now most committed to the binary conception of race and the preservation of the "one-drop" rule of descent. A major reason is the fear of losing or diluting its political base as a result of any changing of ethno-somatic identities. The experience of Brazil clearly suggests certain political advantages in the binary conception of race for political mobilization and elite penetration by successful members of the black minority. But there are clear risks in clinging too ardently to this strategy since it reinforces the self-segregation of Afro-Americans from the rest of the society as well as its mainstream norms and networks, major factors explaining persisting failures not only among residents of the isolated inner-city ghettos, but middle-class students who perform below what their more privileged background would predict.

Serious problems remain with the bottom quarter of the population which is marginalized from the mainstream economy. While their rate of poverty may now be near the historic low of 22.7 percent reached in 2001, the current rate of 24 percent still places the group as the poorest in the nation.[16] African-Americans also continue to experience unemployment rates that stubbornly remain twice the national average. The main factors behind these rates are the skill-gap between the group and Euro-Americans,[17] the historically high and still-growing proportion of female-headed families, and the paternal abandonment of children. Some 60 percent of African-American children are now being brought up in single-parent (overwhelmingly female) households, the majority of them in poverty. Significantly, African-American households headed by married couples have substantially closed the household income gap with their Euro-American counterpart.

While the proportion of the poor who live in segregated and highly concentrated areas of poverty has declined somewhat in the past few years (Jargowsky 2003), Afro-Americans as a group are still the most segregated population in the country (Massey and Denton 1993).[18] As is well known, this segregation originated in legal restrictions and economic discrimination in the past. Today, however, it is not clear to what degree segregation results from persisting discrimination, inertia, or ethnic preference by blacks. Whatever the reasons, we share the view of Douglass Massey and others that the resulting cultural and economic isolation are major causes of black poverty and inequality. More recently, public-health officials have added yet another deleterious consequence of living in segregated ghettos: alarmingly high rates of stress and hypertension.

An important problem among African-Americans is the fraught nature of their gender relations and the growing gender gap in educational performance.[19] Survey data suggest that these tensions exist in all types of unions. They are reflected in the low marriage rate of the group, their high rates of marital and cohabitational disruption, their low rates of re-marriage, and in extremely high rates of intimate, inter-gender violence.[20]

A related problem is the growing gender gap in educational attainment among African-Americans especially at higher educational levels. Black women are now almost twice as likely to attain a bachelors degree than black men and are 20 percent more likely to achieve a first professional degree. In striking contrast with other ethno-somatic groups, this holds for all disciplines, including business, law, and medicine (Patterson 1998: Chapter 1).

The issue of gender deserves special attention because it is one of the major continuities across the Atlantic diaspora as we will see when we come to discuss the present Caribbean.[21] Three major additional features of the group should be noted, especially in light of similar rates elsewhere in the black Atlantic. These are, the high rate of criminal victimization, nearly all at the hands of fellow blacks, astonishingly high incarceration rates, and extremely high rates of HIV infection.

In 2002, according to the US Bureau of Justice, 32 of every 1,000 African-Americans suffered some violent crime, compared with 24.5 of whites. The lifetime odds of a black male being murdered in 1997 has been estimated at 1 in 35, an improvement on earlier years. Even so, it was still five times greater than the odds of a white man being murdered (Akiyama and Noonan 2000). The incarceration rate of African-Americans, especially men, has drawn considerable attention because it may well be the highest in the world. A staggering 10 percent of black men between the ages of 25 and 29 are in jail or prison, and black men, a mere 12 percent of all males, make up 45 percent of America's inmate population. The main causes of this rate, as is well known, is the high involvement of blacks with illicit drug use and sale as well as the nation's draconian, and largely ineffective, drug laws.

The AIDS epidemic has recently emerged as one of the most serious problems confronting African-Americans and if present trends persist it will soon overshadow all other problems. Although only 12 percent of the US population, the CDC reports that in 2001 African-Americans accounted for half of all new HIV infections in the country: African-American men accounted for 43 percent of new cases among males, and African-American women made up 64 percent of all new cases among women. AIDS is now the leading cause of death among African-American women between 25 and 34, and among men aged 35 to 44. Since the beginning of the epidemic, 168,000 African-Americans have died of the disease (CDC 2003). It is important to note that poverty is not a risk factor for AIDS. The distinctive sexual practices of African-Americans, substance abuse, higher STD rates, higher turnover of partners, and reluctance to use condoms by men are major factors explaining the greater incidence of the diseases. African-American women suffer high rates of infection largely through heterosexual contact, often with partners who either refuse to acknowledge their infection or are unaware of it. Indeed, denial is a major cause of the rapid spread of the disease among African-American men. Not only do heterosexual men deny having the disease, but gay men often deny their homosexuality – the practice of living "down low" – and thus avoid prevention measures and messages directed at gay men (CDC 2003). In fact, a half of all AIDS cases among black men results from sex with other men.

Table 3.2 *Some basic socioeconomic indicators for selected Afro-Caribbean countries*

	GDP per cap PPP US$ (2001)	GNI per capita US$ (2002)	HDI Index 2001	Life expectancy at birth	Adult literacy rate % 15+ years
Antigua	10,170	9390	.798	73.9	86.6
Barbados	15,560	9750	.888	76.9	99.7
Haiti	1,860	480	.467	49.1	50.9
Jamaica	3,720	2800	.757	75.5	87.3
Surinam	4,599	1810	.762	70.8	94.0
Trinidad and Tobago	9,100	5,960	.802	71.5	98.4
USA	34,320	30,941	.937	76.9	100

Source: United Nations, 1993; World Bank, 1992.

The Afro-Caribbean

Most of the Afro-Caribbean economies are currently experiencing difficult times. Barbados, the Bahamas, Trinidad and Tobago, and Antigua are ranked among the better-off countries by the World Bank, measured in terms of their rates of growth, per capita income, and human development index. However, with the exception of Barbados, the economies of these better-off countries are all precariously dependent on only one or two industries – mainly tourism or some extractive industry such as oil. Furthermore, they still share many of the social problems found among African-Americans, such as high crime rates, drug dependency, fragile female-headed families, and high rates of HIV incarceration.

Haiti stands at the other extreme. It has the largest black population in the Caribbean; indeed, with 7 million persons of identified black ancestry (not counting the color-conscious 300,000 who explicitly reject a black identification), its population is larger than all the other black populations of the region put together. Haiti, sadly, has only its revolutionary anti-slave past to be proud of. With a GNI per capita of $440, over half its population over fifteen years of age illiterate, a life expectancy at birth of only fifty-two years, and its economy currently shrinking, Haiti ranks as the poorest country in the hemisphere, and one of the poorest in the world.

Jamaica is typical of Afro-Caribbean societies and we will briefly focus on it. The first decade of development after independence in 1962 appeared impressive on the surface. However its 4.5 percent average growth rate during this period was based on a flawed import-substitution model of growth, royalties from the highly capital-intensive bauxite industry, investment in tourist infrastructure, and a large inflow of foreign loans (Girvan 1971, Jefferson 1972). Improvement in educational and job opportunities led to a significant growth in the local managerial and middle classes. But accompanying this were the neglect of agriculture and a massive internal migration to the urban areas resulting in vast shanty-town settlements. Job growth never kept up with employment losses and chronic underemployment in agriculture, the result being the rapid rise of unemployment with so-called economic growth (a pattern found all over the Caribbean, including Puerto Rico with its once vaunted Operation Bootstrap model of growth).

Jamaica changed course in the seventies with the election of the People's National Party to power and its shift toward a democratic social-ist strategy. However this incited the wrath of the United States and alien-ated the managerial classes who fled with their capital. Compounding this were sharp internal ideological differences within the ruling party. The result was economic chaos. The economy shrank during the last half of the seventies and came close to bankruptcy (Stephens and Stephens 1986). During the eighties, with the return to office of the conservative Jamaica Labor Party, Jamaica returned to the straight capitalist, open-market path and has remained steadfastly on it in spite of changes of government. While these structural adjustment policies have satisfied the IMF and other foreign lenders, on almost every social and economic indicator Jamaica has either stagnated or fallen behind over the past two decades. As the most recent United Nations Development report makes clear, after forty years of economic planning and change, Jamaicans are on average poorer now than they were on the eve of independence. The nation has one of the highest debt ratios in the world, a trap from which it is now impossible to extricate itself. The society is substantially more unequal. Social services and subsidies for the poor declined markedly dur-ing the eighties in the effort to meet IMF conditionalities (Looney 1987).

The abysmal and ever-worsening condition of the urban masses, com-bined with a traditional soft-drug (ganja) culture which has metastasized into hard drug use and absorption into the international trade in illicit drugs, and murderous political rivalries, has led to one of the highest crime rates in the world. The homicide rate of the island rose from 7 per 100,000 in the 1960s to 23 in the 1980s, to over 36 in the 1990s (Moser and Holland 1997).

One of the most serious problems currently threatening the black Caribbean is the AIDS pandemic, although it is still not given the priority it deserves by the region's leaders. The most recent UN reports indicate that outside of Africa the Caribbean region has the world's worst infection rates (UNAIDS 2002). Over 6 percent of all adults in Haiti are infected with HIV and in some poor areas over 13 percent of pregnant women were tested HIV-positive. Although the Bahamas, as indicated earlier, is among the higher income states of the region, it ranks next to Haiti with an adult infection rate of over 3.5 percent. And Trinidad, another one of the better-off states, has adult infection rates over 1 percent. This is consistent with the finding, reported earlier, that low income is not an important risk factor for HIV infection. As in Africa and the USA, the high infection rates in the Caribbean are rooted in the region's traditional sexual and familial patterns: early entry into sexual relations, frequent turnover of partners, low rates of marital stability, and a strong reluctance on the part of men to use condoms. As in Africa, the sexual exploitation of young girls by older men results in much higher rates of infection among girls between 15 and 19: they are twice as likely to be infected than boys of the same age group in Jamaica, and five times more likely in Trinidad.

I have argued elsewhere that the future of the Caribbean lies in what I have called the emerging West Atlantic system (Patterson 1987). More recently, a growing number of scholars have interpreted this as part of a trend toward transnational communities. Unfortunately, this scholarship suffers, substantively, from a too great preoccupation with American ethnic and identity issues and, methodologically, from a rather too narrow ethnographic focus and a reluctance to place these transnational movements within the broader framework of Caribbean underdevelopment.[22]

Caribbean societies have gone farther in this process than those in any other part of the world. Indeed, their migratory histories, forced and voluntary, seriously call into question the qualitative newness of transnationalism as a social process. The "social remittances" which Peggy Levitt recently found among the returned migrants and villagers she studied in the Dominican Republic would be familiar to anyone with the slightest acquaintance with Barbadian or Jamaican cultural history from the late nineteenth century (Levitt, P. 2001). For example, the Panama Canal was dug by vast numbers of Jamaican and other West Indian workers at the end of the nineteenth century, most of whom returned home with Latin economic and "social remittances" that greatly influenced the popular cultures and gender attitudes of the then British islands. West Indian contract farm workers in America have been bringing back such cultural remittances to the islands for decades, one major outcome of which being the international music we now know as reggae. And to get a bit personal, my own very Latin, and most un-British first name –

Orlando – was derived from Jamaican transnational cane cutters who brought the name back with them after cutting cane in Cuba during the "dance of the million" years of the twenties sugar boom in Cuba.

In quantitative terms, however, there is no gainsaying the growth of the transnational process. Caribbean economies are not just dependent – as they have been since the late fifteenth century – but increasingly enveloped by the United States, and their populations increasingly live in both the USA and the islands in so-called transnational communities. Over a third of all Jamaicans, and more than a half of many of the smaller island states of the Lesser Antilles, live in communities that are, in effect, colonies of settlement in America. The typical Afro-Caribbean migrant no longer considers himself as being abroad when he is located in the stateside part of his society, whether in Brooklyn, Miami, or Toronto. This process is likely to accelerate in coming years as the island economies become less and less viable.

We should be careful, though, in our predictions about this transnational process. The big question here is the extent to which second and later generations of West Indians in North America will identify with their ancestral Caribbean societies. It may be that transnationalism is a single-generation phenomenon, largely restricted to the generation that migrated. Oddly, in spite of the large number of studies of second-generation migrants from the region, there has been no rigorous attempt to assess the extent to which the transnational process is multi-generational. My own anecdotal experience talking to scores of second-generation students and other persons over the past thirty years suggests that while many of them use their Caribbean background in negotiating distinct ethno-somatic identities in America, as many studies have emphasized,[23] very few of the second generation return home or have any plans of doing so, and a surprisingly large number have rarely even visited the region as tourists.

The migration and settlement of Caribbean people in the USA has raised the question of their relative performance in this society when compared with black Americans and with West Indian migrants in Britain. Afro-Caribbean peoples in the United States are reputed to be moderately successful and are indeed even cited as classic upwardly mobile migrants (Sowell 1981). In contrast, West Indians in the UK are said to exhibit the usual set of problems associated with the Afro-American poor: low educational performance; little success in the occupational ladder; high unemployment; high crime rates and problems with the police.[24]

Why the difference, scholars have come to ask? It is doubtful how useful this comparison is. Some scholars have recently argued that the popular view of West Indian success in the USA is itself largely a myth, and can be explained away once we control for labor force participation (Model 1995). Others, along with Model, have also argued that income differences, insofar as they exist, pertain mainly to English-speaking Caribbean immigrants, but that being black remains the decisive factor in the occupational and income achievement of all Afro-Caribbean people in the USA.[25] One may reasonably conclude that earlier waves of West Indian migrants were successful, especially when the formidable hurdles of racism in the earlier half of the twentieth century are taken into account (Kasinitz 1993) and that Anglophone West Indians do indeed earn more and are better placed occupationally than their Afro-American counterparts (Kalmijn 1996).

The contrast with West Indian migrants to Britain is easily explained by the different migratory flows and by the selection process accompanying the movements to Britain and America. West Indians who migrated to the United States went in two major waves, as we noted earlier. The wave that ended in 1923–4 was a highly selected one. Many were among the most educated persons of color in the islands from which they came. It is remarkable, for example, that the mother of US Secretary of State Colin Powell – possibly the most famous and successful West Indian American of this earlier wave – was a high school graduate in the 1920s. This would have placed her in the top 2 percent of educated persons of color in Jamaica. In addition, the America that these early West Indian migrants entered offered considerable opportunities to act as brokers between the still politically unorganized Afro-Americans and the Euro-American power elite (Kasinitz 1993). One is hardly surprised at the success of this wave. Indeed, there is evidence of a persisting difference in the residence pattern and success rates of Jamaicans whose ancestors came in the earlier wave and those who came later. A study commissioned by the *New York Times* found that residents of the Williamsbridge-Wakefield area of the Bronx where Colin Powell grew up are the most prosperous of all Jamaican communities in New York (Nossiter 1995).

By contrast, the migrants who went to England between 1955 and 1962 came predominantly from the peasant and proletarian classes of the West Indies and, with the exception of Barbadians – many of whom have actually done moderately well in the UK – were not anywhere as educated as the earlier wave of migrants who went to America. They were also incorporated at the bottom of the manual labor hierarchy to do jobs that English workers did not want. Nor was there a politically undeveloped native Afro-British group offering the prospect of middlemen roles as was true of West Indians in New York in the earlier decades of the century.

In comparing the earlier wave of West Indian migrants with those of the post-fifties migrants to Britain we are really comparing apples and pineapples. A better comparison would be with the working- and lower-class migrants who moved to America in the post-1965 wave that is still in full swing. When we observe the economic performance of these less-educated migrants we find really little difference between them and their British counterparts, or for that matter between them and their lower-class Afro-American counterparts. They are failing at the same rates in schools and have income levels that, on a per hour basis, is lower than that of poor Afro-Americans. A recent study by Mary Waters (1999) suggests that West Indian migrants of the recent wave differ from earlier waves also in the tendency of a significant proportion of them to assimilate into Afro-American lower-class urban society. She argues, along with others such as Alejandro Portes (1993), that there is now a "segmentary assimilation" pattern among immigrants from the Caribbean and other areas of the Americas. Unlike earlier West Indians and European migrants, assimilation into American society means incorporation into Afro-American life, attitudes and problems, the argument goes. Hence, in sharp contrast with the past, it is precisely those second-generation West Indians who remain unassimilated and maintain close ties to parents and home who are likely to be more successful. While this argument may be true of New York and a few other northeastern cities, it hardly holds for all or even most West Indians in America today. Selective migratory factors, as Model, Sullivan, and others have noted, both before *and after* migrating to the USA sufficiently explain differences in outcomes. Many successful West Indians in New York, for example, re-migrate to Florida, which makes it problematic to generalize about the experience of the group from studies of New York.

Actually, this latest wave of West Indian migrants to the United States is highly bimodal. Migrants are coming more and more not from only the lower end of these societies but also increasingly from the top end. Intellectuals, professionals, and others who traditionally would have migrated to Europe now move to the USA. Hence the seeming paradox that although West Indians are disproportionately among the trouble-makers and deviants of America (the drug posses of the eighties having been a major problem) the islands have handed the USA two nobel laureates, a disproportionate number of its nurses, and an unusually large number of its academics of color. Milton Vickerman is correct in describing the West Indian situation in the USA as "multifaceted," one in which they share many of the burdens of racism along with Afro-Americans and have developed a strong sense of ethno-somatic consciousness as a

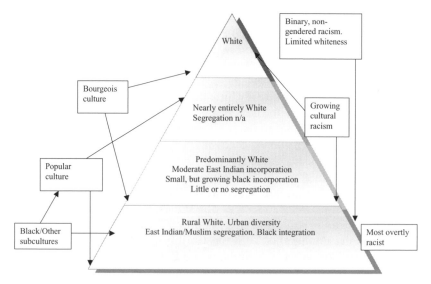

Figure 3.6 North Atlantic mode: proleterian incorporation

result, but have maintained distinctive commitments to achievement and mobility. "Indeed," he observes further, "their presence tends to show that opportunities for upward mobility blacks exist, but these commingle with, rather than displace, racism. Thus, West Indians help to illustrate the complexity, especially for blacks, of race in present day America" (Vickerman 1999: 126–7).

The North Atlantic mode: proletarian incorporation

Earlier we discussed three of the four modes of ethno-somatic stratification. In turning to Europe we come to the fourth mode, which will be discussed through the case of Britain where a half of all people of African ancestry on the continent live. As indicated earlier, there are 1,148,700 black identified persons in Britain, making up 2 percent of the total British population and 24.8 percent of the minority population. In addition, there is a mixed, black–white group of 225,705, constituting another 10 percent of minority Britons.

The first thing to note about the North Atlantic mode (see Figure 3.6) is that these are not racially constituted societies.[26] By this I mean that, unlike the USA and Latin American societies with large black populations, "race" never became a fundamental principle of social organization and social identity. Let me emphasize at once that this is not to say that racism was and is not important here. From as early as Elizabethan times we find evidence (including the utterances of the Virgin Queen herself) of rampant racist attitudes in Britain. Britain, however, never made "race" a principle of social organization, for the simple reason that the black – and nonwhite – population there was, until the short wave of commonwealth migration between the late forties and early sixties, demographically insignificant. Whiteness becomes a salient basis of identity only where there is a continuous demographic, sociocultural, and psychological presence of blacks or other nonwhite groups and a history of *domestic* enslavement of this other group. To be sure, the English person who met a black person (in the colonies, on the docks, wherever) was often likely to interact with racist assumptions, but such meetings were rare for the mass of British people. And it is still the case that the typical British person who lives outside of the large metropolitan areas rarely encounters people of color.

Unlike the sharp, binary conception of race that was so constitutive of US identity, Britishness, as Robin Cohen observed in his very supple analysis, is a rather fuzzy and malleable identity: "Multiple axes of identification have meant that Irish, Scots, Welsh and English people, those from the white, black, brown Commonwealth, Americans, English-speakers, Europeans and even 'aliens' have had their lives intersect one with another in overlapping and complex circles of identity construction and rejection" (1994: 35). What is of even greater significance is Cohen's argument that the more exclusive identity of Englishness carries "connotations of class, linguistic and cultural superiority" from which some whites are excluded. Being white may be assumed in this identity, but it carries little or no definitional weight and is in no way constitutive. In other words, in striking contrast with the answer one would most certainly receive from a white person from the US South – the classic region of binary racial identification – if one were to ask the typical English person to state what most defines his identity, it is very unlikely that being white would ever be mentioned. To be sure, the fact that being white is taken for granted has significance for those who are not white, but there is an important asymmetry here which cannot be neglected: the fact that nonwhiteness is important for nonwhites, in no way implies that whiteness is in any way meaningful for whites. And this is itself very important, both in distinguishing the British ethno-somatic mode from the others, and in the kind of interactions it makes possible in Britain.

To take one major implication of this asymmetry, miscegenation does not have anything like the same emotional, sociological, and political potency that it had, and in many areas, still does in the USA and Latin America. The binary system, as we have pointed out, is obsessed with notions of racial purity and traditionally considered black–white unions the greatest social evil with laws forbidding intermarriage in America as late as 1967. It still remains true that mixed couples, while no longer lynched or stoned in America, still find themselves stared at even in the most cosmopolitan metropolitan areas of the country, by whites *and* by blacks. And in Latin America the Negrophobia of the racist elite means that not only are white–black marriages rare, but in the highly unusual case where it happens the white person is immediately ostracized from elite circles.

There is simply no parallel to this anywhere in Britain or Northern Europe generally. Mixed couples draw virtually no notice in the metropolitan areas where they tend to reside. I know this to be true not only from my own experience living for many years in different parts of Britain, but from the experience of every one of the numerous mixed British couples I have known. These anecdotal experiences are supported by almost every national survey that has probed British attitudes on mixed unions. As we will document later, 91 percent of British whites said that they would not oppose the marriage of their child to a black person. What is remarkable about this poll is the fact that more than half these whites claim that Britain is racist and a third admitted that they themselves have behaved in racist ways. What this means is that in Britain, unlike the multiethnic societies of the Americas, being racist is not necessarily correlated with being racially purist or positively valuing whiteness.

This brings me to the second important difference between British racism, and white–nonwhite relations generally, and those of the USA. It is the fact that British ethno-somatic relations are largely non-gendered. There is nothing there remotely comparable to the obsessive symbolic use of women as embodiments of the honor and purity of "the race." This is partly due to the absence of a domestic history of slavery, and of a tradition of obsessive preoccupation with the fearsome, uncontrollable sexuality of males of a natally alienated, "inferior," and wretchedly oppressed group. It may also be due to the greater secularism of North Europeans and, consequently, the non-moralizing of sex and women's status. Whatever the reason, as we will see, the ungendered nature of British racism has meant that unusual levels of intermarriage and interethnic cohabitation are possible without this becoming a basis of interethnic conflict.

The mass migration of Caribbean and Asian peoples to Britain after the late forties marked a new era in British (as well as Dutch and French) societies, converting them to multicultural and multiethnic systems in their metropolitan areas. Even so, they still make up only 7.9 percent of the total. In addition, they are concentrated in the large metropolitan areas of the country, as Ceri Peach has pointed out.[27] What this means is that for the mass of British people ethnic minorities are not part of daily social interactions. They are, however, now very much a part of the national and political landscape and a very real sociological presence in the most vital part of the country.

Multiethnic Britain has gone through three critical periods.[28] The first period of entry and settlement lasted for about three decades, between the late forties and 1980. It was characterized by periodic expressions of cultural shock and growing resentment on the part of the native population and, on the immigrants' part, adjustment to the lower ranks of the laboring classes, as well as political passivity. Increasing waves of racist attacks by natives as well as harassment by the police culminated in the anti-police riots of the early eighties.[29] This marked the second era of adjustment characterized, on the one hand, by growing political awareness and antiracist activism by the minority populations and, on the other hand, the reluctant acceptance of the fact that Britain had become a multiethnic society by the natives. Immigrant political activism went through a period of defensive coalition by the different ethnic groups facilitated by a shared construction of political "blackness" vis-à-vis the white majority. This construction, however, was wholly expedient and was bound to be temporary. It was undermined by the cultural diversity of the immigrant groups, by their homeland hostility to each other (especially tensions between Indians and Pakistanis), by their own ethno-somatic values, including South Asian distaste for dark-complexioned people, by their very different pre-migratory experiences with, and attitudes toward the English, and by marked differences in economic performance and incorporation. This resulted in very different modes of adjustment to British society by the various ethnic groups, as we will see shortly.

The native British leadership during this second era was dominated by the Conservative Party under Thatcher and by a shift in attitude toward the immigrant population. The Conservative reaction moved in two apparently opposing directions. One was the rise of what Barker has called "the new racism" (1981). Old-fashioned biological racism – the view that nonwhites were genetically inferior – was replaced by the ideology of primordial cultural differences: the view that people had a natural preference for their own traditional ways of life and that these differences were so great and immutable that integration was unrealistic and may even be undesirable. A benign version of this view informed the activism of some of the new antiracist activists. In this view, people were culturally different but such differences were desirable. Here was the genesis of the new ideology of multicultural diversity, aided by intellectual imports from the United States which had moved in this direction in its post-civil-rights period.

However, as the realization sunk in that the immigrants were in Britain to stay, especially with the growth of the second generation of black British, a more ancient British attitude toward immigrants reappeared. In a nutshell, this view amounted to a close-the-door-and-absorb-the-aliens policy. In less homely terms: end immigration and integrate. I say it is an ancient British view because this is exactly how Britain had solved its immigrant "problem" over the centuries of its post-Anglo-Saxon history at all levels of its society: consider the Normans and the Danes; consider the history of its own royal families.[30] As we will see, whether consciously pursued or not, this approach has worked with precisely the group of immigrants we are most concerned with.

The third era of British ethnic adjustment began somewhere during the late eighties and early nineties. This era has been marked not only by intensifying activism, but a growing involvement in municipal politics – begun from the mid-seventies – and the emergence of minority participation in national politics, a "major breakthrough" coming with the election of four black Members of Parliament in 1987 (Fitzgerald 1990). By the nineties however, the ethnic coalition of the earlier era had fallen apart due to the underlying differences mentioned earlier. Ethnic Indian and other South Asian groups rejected the overarching identity of political "blackness" and began to assert their own separate identities. This was partly in response to the intensifying black identity movement among Afro-Caribbean and African British leadership, itself in part an adoption of black American identity politics, in part a homegrown Afro-Caribbean movement rooted in the popular music and culture of the Caribbean. As in America, the ideology of diversity has been adopted as the overarching rationale for activism in this new era.

Britain, however, is not America. The underlying differences in the total size and demographic mix of its ethnic populations, along with the different sets of ethno-somatic attitudes on the part of the British and the ethnic groups themselves, and the very different experiences of the ethnic groups in the British labor market and economic system generally, have resulted in a peculiar dissonance between the imported ideology of diversity and the realities of ethnic incorporation. As Figure 3.7 indicates, there are striking ethnic and gender differences in unemployment rates. Bangladeshi, Pakistani, and African men and women are not faring well in the labor market. Nor are Caribbean men. Indian men and women are participating at much higher rates, as are Caribbean women, whose participation and unemployment rates are nearly equal to that of white British women.

Much the same pattern holds for the proportion of the different groups in low income households, as Figure 3.8 shows, except that Caribbean

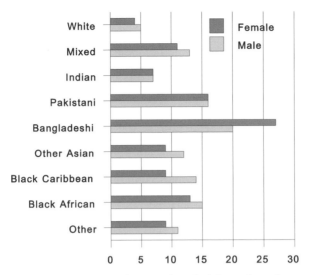

Figure 3.7 UK unemployment by ethnicity and gender
Source: UK Census, National Statistics On-line, posted 10/2/2003

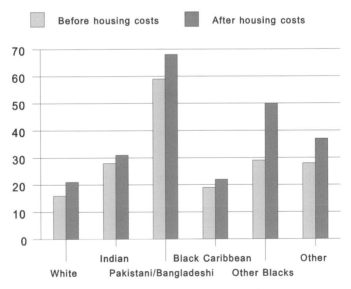

Figure 3.8 Households on low income by ethnicity
Source: UK Census, National Statistics On-line, posted 10/2/2003

Table 3.3 *Percentage of students aged 16 who achieved 5 or more GCSEs, 1999*

England and Wales	Percentages
Indian girls	66
White girls	55
Indian boys	54
Black girls	46
White boys	45
Other group girls	44
Other group boys	40
Pakistani/Bangladeshi girls	37
Black boys	31
Pakistani/Bangladeshi boys	22

Source: UK Census, National Statistics On-line, posted 10/2/2003.

blacks and Indians are about on par in this regard. Indeed, if income before housing costs is considered, a smaller proportion of black Caribbean households than Indian households are in the low-income category. At the same time, this table does not register the fact that Indians are doing much better at the higher income levels and occupational structure than Caribbean blacks. One of the main reasons for this is the much better educational attainment of Indian men compared with Caribbean men and other men from South Asia.

Table 3.3 is interesting for two reasons. It partly explains the very different income and occupational outcomes of the different groups. However, it also shows that one of the striking continuities in the black Atlantic persists here: the gender gap between black men and women. In their GCSE results – the closest parallel to America's SAT tests – black boys perform next to last of all the ethnic-gender groups, above only the Pakistani and Bangladeshi boys. The disciplinary and educational problems of black students has been a major issue in the British educational system.[31] At the same time, it is remarkable that black girls are performing near the top end of the ethnic-gender groups. Indeed, they outperform white British boys in these exams.

Closely related to this is another sociocultural continuity with other black groups across the Atlantic: the high proportion of lone-parent families and low rates of marriage.[32] A recent study summarizes the black Caribbean situation in Britain in terms that could apply equally to blacks in the United States, Latin America, or the Caribbean: "The key feature of family life in the (British) Caribbean community is the low rate of marriage. Caribbeans are less likely to live with a partner than white people; those who have a partner are less likely to have married them;

those who have married one are likely to separate or divorce" (Berthoud 2000). As is true also of the Americas, single female parenting is on the increase, the combined impact of traditional values and greater female independence. Thus 24 percent of immigrant Caribbean mothers were single compared with 48 percent of mothers born in Britain or brought up there (ibid.: 8–9).

Another continuity with the rest of the black Atlantic is the high rates of crime and incarceration of young Caribbean men. This is a highly contested issue in Britain. Young Caribbean men were, and to a lesser extent still are, profiled and harassed by the British police, the indiscriminate and clearly racist use of the notorious SUS laws of the past being the main reason for riots in numerous towns and cities all over Britain in 1981 (Colman and Gorman 1982: 1–4). It has been suggested that the high rate of crime among young Caribbean men is partly the result of the greater tendency of the police to search and arrest them, exacerbated by biased crime reporting that emphasizes precisely those crimes most likely to be committed by young black men.[33] While there is certainly some truth to this, there is no denying the fact that young Caribbean men commit a disproportionate number of serious crimes and experience relatively high rates of incarceration. Seven percent of arrests in 1997 and 1998 were of black people and 11 percent of all who were stopped and searched (UK Home Office 1998: 19–26). Much of this criminal activity is related to drug use and trading, as is the case in the United States and the Caribbean.

There is one set of statistics that is largely free of police reporting bias: namely, homicide. Though only 2 percent of its population, in cases where both victims and offenders have been identified, blacks in Britain were 6.3 percent of its murder victims between 1977 and 1999 and were the principal suspects in 7.8 percent of its homicides (UK Home Office 1999: 17, Tables 4.2–4.3). Regarding incarceration, the figures in absolute terms seem better than those for black Americans, but this is largely a reflection of the much smaller rate of imprisonment in Britain. Black Caribbean men make up 7.4 percent of the total prison population and the total black percentage was 11.8; and black Caribbean women were 9.5 percent while the total black female incarcerated population stood at 17.9 percent (UK Home Office 1999: 42–43, Tables 7.1–7.4). Hence their overrepresentation rate in Britain's prisons (slightly over eight times what their proportion of the population would predict for Caribbean men, and 9.5 times for Caribbean women) is actually twice the overrepresentation rate of black Americans.

With such data, it is easy to exaggerate the negative aspects of the condition of blacks in Britain, a tendency that both British antiracist activists and those conservatives convinced that there is no hope for blacks in Britain, find hard to resist. In fact, the overall trends in the condition of blacks in Britain are generally positive, and in one respect quite extraordinary. The first generation who migrated from conditions of economic hopelessness in the Caribbean all improved their situation, even if it meant employment at the bottom rung of the British labor market. More importantly, the second generation of Caribbean blacks have significantly improved their standing in the British occupational structure. Whereas the first generation of immigrants were nearly all unskilled or semiskilled manual laborers, by 1990 31 percent of black Caribbean people in the labor force – primarily the second generation of British-born blacks – were in professional or other non-manual occupations (Jones 1996: 99–100). Susan Model concluded from her analysis of the 1991 census data that, "Native-born Indians and Black Caribbeans attain significantly higher class positions than their foreign-born counterparts" (1999: 969–90). Indeed, by the end of the century Black Caribbean women had not only caught up with white British women in the attainment of higher education qualifications but had slightly surpassed them. A downside of this, however, is the fact that black men and women do not get the same returns to educational achievement as whites do, suggesting the persistence of a significant level of employment discrimination.

There are two respects in which the experience of blacks in Britain differ markedly from those in the Americas, and it is these which largely justify our claim that this is a distinct mode of ethno-somatic stratification. These are their much lower rates of segregation and their unusually high rates of inter-marriage with native white British persons. The segregation patterns of blacks and South Asians in Britain are the very opposite of what pertains in the United States. Overall, Britain remains a remarkably unsegregated society. Ceri Peach has neatly summarized the different patterns of socioeconomic and residential adjustment (1998). There is what he calls an Indian profile which is white-collar, suburban, and owner-occupying; a Pakistani profile that is blue-collar, inner-city and owner-occupying; a Bangladeshi profile that is blue-collar and council-housed in the inner city; and a Caribbean pattern that is blue-collar, council housed "but far less segregated than the Bangladeshis and with a pronounced tendency to decentralisation." Indeed, it turns out that although Caribbean blacks are more blue-collar and inner-city than Indians, and are on the lower rungs of the occupational structure, they are far less segregated than any of the groups from Asia.

Even more remarkable are the rates of interethnic unions (both cohabitational and marital) between Caribbean and native white British persons. These are easily the highest rates of interethnic unions of any two groups in Britain and they far surpass any such rate in the Americas, including Brazil.[34] The 1991 census indicates that 40 percent of all British-Caribbean men and 20 percent of women between the ages of 16 and 34 are living with a Euro-British partner (See Table 3.4). Even more telling, however, is the marital behavior of the second generation, those who identify themselves as "Black Other." Over a half of all men *and women* who are partnered are living with or married to a Caucasian-British person (Barrington 1996: 199). This clearly implies an exponential growth of the mixed population. What is equally significant is that this mixed group largely identifies itself as simply British. Thus there is both a physical and an identity-stimulated leakage from the Afro-British population. The data bear this out. The Caribbean British population reached a peak of 590,000 in 1976 and began to decline thereafter. Thus there was a 3 percent decline between 1976 and 1981, followed by a 14 percent decline between 1981 and 1991. Since there has been no decline in the birth rate of Caribbean-British people and only negligible out-migration (which may have been compensated for with inflows, resulting in negligible net migratory flows), the only explanation for this dramatic decline is passage into the Euro-British population through miscegenation.

The high intermarriage rate of Caribbean blacks cuts across economic groups and is clearly a survival of Caribbean homeland ethno-somatic and culture-class attitudes. Although West Indian, especially Jamaican, popular singers endlessly celebrate black pride, and the Rastafarian religion has made a virtual cult of it, West Indians still have a strong preference for British people. There is some reason to believe that the attraction is not simply physical but cultural and the best evidence of this is their intermarital behavior when they migrate to another majority white society, the United States. Suzanne Model and Gene Fisher have found that while US-born Caribbean black men intermarry with white US women at three times the rate of African-American men, the rate itself is still quite modest (11.9 percent of partnered men are married to whites compared with 3.87 percent of African-American men). What's more, immigrant black Caribbean men actually marry white US women at an even lower rate than African-American men. An even smaller proportion of immigrant and US-born Caribbean women marry white US men (Model and Fisher 2002). The contrast with the intermarriage rate of both immigrant and native-born black Caribbeans in Britain is remarkable: almost 18 percent of partnered immigrant and 40 percent of partnered British-born Caribbean men in their sample are married to white women, and a quarter of all partnered British-born Caribbean women are married to white Britons compared with only 8 percent of their US-born Caribbean counterpart.

Table 3.4 *Interethnic unions of all married and cohabiting UK residents, 1991*

Ethnic group of male partner	Ethnic group of female partner									
	White	Black Caribbean	Black African	Black Other	Indian	Pakistani	Bangladeshi	Chinese	Other	Total
White	*126,150*	102	41	63	71	10	0	79	287	126,803
Black Carib	225	*559*	8	10	4	2	0	2	15	865
Black Afric.	48	16	*208*	4	2	1	0	0	2	281
Black-Other	76	3	2	*62*	1	0	0	0	3	147
Indian	134	2	4	1	*1,762*	18	0	5	9	1,935
Pakistani	42	0	0	1	6	*775*	0	0	7	831
Bangladeshi	7	0	2	0	4	1	*217*	0	2	233
Chinese	34	0	0	0	2	0	0	*234*	0	270
Other	273	6	2	3	11	8	1	4	*498*	806
Total	126,989	728	267	144	1,863	815	218	324	823	132,171

Source: Berrington 1996: 199, Table 7.9.

Obviously, the different attitudes of white British and white American men and women toward interracial partnering partly explains this. But it does not explain as much as one might think. Although a majority of white Americans say they would not intermarry with a black person, a substantial minority are quite willing to do so, perhaps as much as one in five from surveys and other indicators. When we take account of the demographic fact that West Indians are a tiny fraction of the US population, this means that for every one of them desiring to marry a white person there would be several hundred potential takers on the marriage or partner market. The fact that Caribbeans in America are heavily concentrated in the large metropolitan areas also means that they are in the most liberal centers of America where most whites willing to marry blacks are likely to be found. Hence other factors are needed for a sufficient explanation of the low intermarriage rate in the USA, when compared with Britain. Since British whites and US whites are physically similar (well, sort of) the explanation must be a cultural bias in favor of British mates by West Indians.

This bias was, and remains, part and parcel of the Afro-Caribbean mode of ethno-somatic stratification. These societies are all culturally stratified with elites adhering to a creolized version of European cultures. It remains true even of Haiti, over two centuries after its successful revolt from France. Unlike African-Americans, what upwardly mobile Caribbean people most desire is not the rejection but the assimilation of this thinly islandized shoot of European culture, an assimilation that is vital for class mobility but no longer carries the burden of white ethno-somatic identification since the elites who practice and transmit it are now almost all black or brown. Among the masses, who rarely make it into this elite, there are still ways of appropriating the desired culture, the most powerful instance of which being the almost obsessive assimilation of the quintessentially British game of cricket. Nor should it be forgotten that British imperial propaganda was no idle hegemonic snare. The generation of West Indians who migrated to Britain on the eve of empire did sincerely believe that they were going to the mother country,[35] unlike those who went to America right after. It is easy to say now that they were soon to be disabused of such false consciousness, but the truth, as always, was far more complex than that. Contrary to the vexatious and proudful talk of racial spokesmen, the typical immigrant of the first generation was, on the whole, largely grateful for the opportunity to work a regular job and earn a living wage – a simple dignity which the society he had left behind had never allowed him to enjoy. For the first time in his life he could live in a real house rather than a corrugated, wattle and daub coop, with the privacy of his own and his woman's room, could enjoy the domestic miracle of indoor plumbing, the unfamiliar regularity of three round meals a day and dress each morning as if it was Sunday. Even more, he could quietly marvel at the fact that his children would all attend high school – an elite assumption back home – and could even dream of them moving beyond his unskilled condition. These were pleasing things that made his passage worthwhile and largely compensated for the anxieties of displacement and the intermittent shock of racist abuse.

There was satisfaction, too (no doubt a trifle ironic), of laboring side by side with working men looking exactly like the people who, back home, naturally assumed the air of rulers. What's more, the typical British worker with whom he worked was not the compulsive racist bigot of antiracist abstractions. Whatever their misgivings about the immigration policies of their government and their bosses, most had the simple decency to live and let live and, in time, even befriend. It is this that explains the repeated finding of surveys, compulsively explained away by social analysts, that the typical black and white worker made friends at work. It also explains, along with the ethno-somatic values brought over by the immigrant, the tendency to intermarry with the natives.

With all this in mind, then, let us look more closely at a recent poll conducted in 2002 by the BBC, what is perhaps the most thorough and professionally executed survey of "racial" attitudes and experiences in modern Britain (BBC, 2002). The range of answers suggest that black and Asian as well as white British people have a realistic, but not pessimistic, view of the present and future of ethno-somatic relations in Britain. A slight majority of whites did not believe that immigrants integrated and made a positive contribution to Britain, a view not shared by minority respondents. At the same time, an identical majority (51–52 percent) across all groups that immigrant communities could do more to integrate. Over 70 percent of blacks and Asians thought that the police were doing a poor job, a view equally shared by whites, and 55 percent of blacks thought they discriminated on grounds of race. Most, however, thought they would get a fair trial in the courts. Speaking of their experiences in the labor market, some 40 percent of blacks claimed to have experienced personally, or witnessed, racism in employment, compared with 22 percent of whites and 34 percent of Asians; and approximately a third of blacks and 29 percent of Asians claimed to have actually suffered racial or religious discrimination at work. Finally, on the negative side, both whites (52 percent) and blacks (53 percent) were in near agreement that Britain is still racist: six in ten blacks and Asians claimed to have experienced some verbal or racial abuse, and about one in five physical racial abuse, and over a third of whites actually admitted that they had said or done something that others could consider racist. These answers are consistent with expert accounts and observations of ethno-somatic relations in Britain in recent years which, in conjunction with their remarkable candor, increases our confidence in them and makes their other more positive responses all the more persuasive.

Apart from their candor, many of the above answers could easily have come from a sample of African-Americans speaking about their own country. It is when we turn to personal relationships and opinions about where Britain is headed in its ethnic relations that fundamental differences between the two societies emerge. There was striking agreement among a majority (54 percent whites, 57 percent blacks and 52 percent Asians) that Britain is a more tolerant place today than it was ten years ago.

One remarkable feature of British ethnic attitudes which marks it sharply off from the Americas, especially the United States, is the finding, confirmed by another recent poll, that white Britons express *more* liberal attitudes in those areas where there are higher proportions of immigrants and black British (*Economist* 2003). As *The Economist* observes, "assimilation has done a lot to dissolve prejudice." This is in stark contrast with the United States where a large number of polls and academic studies have confirmed what is now a virtual sociological truism: that the greater the proportion of blacks in a metropolitan area or state, the greater tends to be the level of prejudice and segregation.[36]

Returning to the BBC poll, we come upon another distinctive feature of British ethno-somatic attitudes and relations. When asked if their circle of friends included people from different ethnic backgrounds, a half of all whites, 82 percent of Asians and 87 percent of blacks said yes. Attitudes towards intermarriage seem consistent with the observed behavior of the different ethnic groups. Only 46 percent of both whites and Asians said they would marry or have a relationship with someone "from a different race" whereas 71 percent of blacks said that they would. However, very few whites (9 percent) said they would oppose the marriage of a child to someone of another ethno-somatic group (an inconceivable response anywhere in the Americas) and there was overwhelming agreement that there was either some or a lot of tolerance for mixed marriages in Britain.

If this trend, in conjunction with the high rates of intermarriage between blacks and white British, continues the Afro-British population of Caribbean ancestry, for all its cultural verve and assertions of black consciousness, will be absorbed into the mainstream British population over the course of the next three or so generations. Ironically, the very cultural vitality that now informs its identity, will contribute to its integration, since it is precisely what appeals most to the dominant popular culture which rapidly adopts it.[37] Britain will have solved this part of its "racial problem" by one of its most ancient methods: through physical absorption and cultural appropriation. Before that day arrives, however, the Afro-Caribbean population will find itself in the paradoxical situation of experiencing serious problems of unemployment, poverty, crime, and racism, even as it fades into the lower-and lower middle reaches of the British populace.

It is worth noting that an almost identical pattern of high intermarriage and high levels of assimilation among the second generation are found among black immigrants in the Netherlands from the Dutch Caribbean, especially Suriname (Mollenkopf 2002).[38]

Conclusion

We have argued that there are four major contexts in which blacks in Europe and the Americas live. Nonetheless, striking continuities are still to be found among them. Variations in their present condition result from the interplay of these different contexts and underlying uniformities.

Let us first briefly summarize the uniformities. We may roughly distinguish between uniformities that are primarily external in origin (i.e., externally imposed or resulting mainly from their disadvantaged socioeconomic condition) and those that emerge mainly from internal patterns of behavior and attitudes, although it should be clear that the two are closely related, both historically and contemporaneously.[39] Throughout the Atlantic Basin, being black is still socially significant, and racism remains a major problem, although the consequence of this for their life chances vary from Latin America, at one extreme in which it is usually economically catastrophic, to the West Indies, where its impact is now largely confined to intimate relations. Throughout the Atlantic communities, also, blacks and African-ancestry people are disproportionately among the poorest groups and have the least opportunities for advancement. Everywhere they are disproportionately among the least educated, the worst housed, the least healthy and have the lowest life expectancies at birth. Throughout the Atlantic Basin blacks are incarcerated at rates that are usually more than twice that of other groups. This is in part due to the fact that they commit a greater proportion of crimes, but of equal importance is the fact that behaviors they are more likely to engage in tend to be criminalized to a far greater degree by the dominant white classes, the most egregious instance of which being the radically different sentences meted out to crack as opposed to powdered cocaine users in America. And apart from the non-Hispanic Caribbean, blacks throughout the Atlantic tend to be racially profiled and harassed by police forces whose members tend to exhibit greater levels of racism and Negrophobia than their populations at large.

The internal uniformities are equally striking. Throughout the Atlantic blacks experience significantly higher rates of criminal victimization, usually at the hands of fellow blacks. As noted above, they also commit a disproportionately higher number of crimes, even after taking account of the greater tendency to criminalize their antisocial behaviors. Poverty and racial discrimination cannot explain much of this. Its origin is, rather, another major internal uniformity among all black communities of the Atlantic Basin: the fragility of their families and deep tensions in their gender relations. Throughout, we find far lower rates of marriage or stable cohabitational unions, far higher rates of union disruption where these do occur, far lower rates of re-marriage, far higher rates of single status among adults over thirty, extremely high rates of lone-parent, female-headed households, high rates of paternal abandonment, and resulting child-rearing arrangements in which over 60 percent of children are being brought up without the emotional or material security of their fathers.

However, the internal cultural adaptation of blacks to their Atlantic environments have resulted in a uniform pattern of disproportionate contributions to their respective national cultures. Much of what is distinctive culturally in the Latin societies where they reside are the outcome of syncretic constructions in which the African element is usually prominent. This is certainly true of the music, religion, dance, and literature of Afro-Latin societies. The case of the United States is unusual, but of great importance. Blacks, though a mere 13 percent of the population, have a powerful, sometimes predominant influence on the nation's popular culture – its sports, dance, popular music, fashion, literature, theatre, TV, and film – and were the primary creators of the nation's pre-eminent contribution to the world's heritage of advanced civilized practice, namely jazz. The fact that America is now not only the world's only superpower, but the major source of the emerging global popular culture has meant that the disproportionate black influence at its source is now rapidly being diffused as a primary global cultural agent.

Let us, finally, turn to a summary of the ways in which the black experience differs in the four socioeconomic and political environments we have distinguished. Each has its own distinctive configuration of constraints and opportunities, depending on the class and color of blacks we are considering. For those born in the elite and upper-middle classes, as well as the most talented of the upwardly mobile, the non-Hispanic Caribbean apart from Haiti offers the best prospects for African-ancestry people. Only here do blacks dominate the elites and control the economic and political course of the nations in which they live. But as we have seen, these are all precarious economic systems, increasingly dependent on the American giant hovering over them. The mass of black people in most of these societies are impoverished and, other than an insecure life in their large informal and underground economic sectors, external migration is often their only hope. In seizing this opportunity, whether legally or illegally, they have created transnational systems which, contrary to current sociological views, have long been in the making. While these systems undoubtedly benefit those who participate in them, it is still not clear what their consequences are for those in the region who are not directly participating in them.

North America, especially the United States, undoubtedly offers the best prospects for the greatest number of blacks. Located in the wealthiest and most powerful country in the world, with an articulate and politically skilled leadership, with a vibrant and sophisticated culture that is, as we just noted, the foundation of the entire nation's popular culture, the majority of black Americans enjoy a level of income, and have opportunities, that are almost unimaginable anywhere in Latin America and in most regions of the black Caribbean. In recent years, too, black Americans have begun to penetrate the upper ruling and entrepreneurial elites of the country in numbers and proportions that now go well beyond mere tokenism. At the same time, the bottom quarter of the black population seems trapped in concentrated urban and rural ghettoes of poverty and despair. Identity politics and ethno-racial mobilization, which has served the group well in its successful struggle for inclusion over the past four decades, may well now be on the verge of becoming a liability. A too racialized interpretation of their problems obscures the recognition of profound internal issues that thwart the acquisition of educational skills by youth of the lower classes that are essential for survival in a post-industrial society. Recent research suggests that even middle-class black Americans, especially young men, now risk being ensnared by these self-destructive processes.

Without doubt, Latin America is presently the very worst environment for black people of the Atlantic. They are at the bottom of land-starved rural wastelands and desolate urban barrios. They are denied all entry to the leadership of their societies in a systematic pattern of total racist exclusion that is reminiscent of South Africa's former apartheid regime. Trapped in the self-denigrating psycho-phenotypic miasma of *blanqueamiento*; obscured and diverted by mass pageantry, carnivals, saints and spirits, and the Orwellian double-speak of "racial democracy"; blacks in Latin America – for all but the lightest *triguenos*, *mulatinha*-, and *acastanhada*-colored – are truely the wretched of the earth.[40]

For the working classes and poor, Europe is without doubt the best environment for black people. While disproportionately placed at or near the bottom of the class system, blacks in these welfare states are at least ensured minimum standards of living and are spared the indignity of homelessness and the class- as well as racial contempt for the "losers" at the bottom found elsewhere in the Atlantic Basin. At the same time, as we have argued, it seems unlikely that there is a long-term future for blacks, especially black Caribbean people, at least in Britain. For some, this may be all for the good: racial tensions will have abated, and the melanin-impoverished British gene pool could use the infusion. For others, especially those engaged in the promotion and celebration of black identity, this may seem like a "racial" nightmare.

NOTES

1. This classification builds on earlier comparative work, most of which will be cited below. For now I wish to acknowledge the classic earlier individual and collected studies which shaped my thinking on the subject: Frazier 1957, Wagley 1957, Harris 1964, Smith 1965, Hoetink 1967, Franklin 1968, Morner 1970, Lowenthal 1972.

2. This portrait is based on annual reports of the UN Population Division, 1999; various national censuses; and annual reports of the US Department of State, 1999.

3. The 1980 Brazilian census counted 53.3 million of the nation's 119 million people as persons of African ancestry. However, it is generally acknowledged that these official reports grossly underestimate the true count because of Brazilians' tendency to overemphasize their "whiteness." Estimates by Afro-Brazilian scholars place the proportion as high as 75 percent, or more than 100 million persons. See Andrews (1991: 2).

4. Manning 1982, 1989. But see Eltis 1991, who suggests that the economic impact was minor.

5. See Bureau of Citizenship and Immigration Services 2002.

6. For a detailed discussion on the USA, see Patterson 1998: Chapter 1; on Jamaica, see Patterson 1967 and Dorsey 1995.

7. For a still valuable discussion of the late emergence of this mode and the complex reasons for it, see Williamson 1980, see also Davis 1993, Dominguez 1986.

8. See Hoetink 1967, for a discussion of variations between the Latin and Non-Latin Caribbean, as well as variations within the Latin system.

9. For classic accounts on Jamaica, see Henriques 1950, Smith 1965, Stone 1973; on the black Caribbean generally, see Lowenthal 1992.

10. On Trinidad, see Yelvington 1993, Ryan 1972; and on Guyana, Premdas 1996.

11. For what is still one of the best accounts, see Hoetink 1967. Of more recent studies, see Carrion 1997; and Oostindie 1996.

12. While there is little disagreement that racist attitudes have declined in the USA there is still a considerable debate about the extent of this decline and the new forms that racism has taken over recent decades. My own interpretation of the abundant data tend to be more optimistic than others. See Lawrence Bobo 2001.

13. See, for example, Rodriguez 1992, Omi and Winant 1996, Vickerman 1999.

14. For one thing, it lumps all persons of Hispanic ancestry into a single category, which many consider sociologically questionable. The category "Hispanic" like "Asian" is largely the construction of the American Census Bureau, one that has been eagerly embraced by Latino and Asian political leaders anxious to play the politics of numbers.

15. See Schuck 2003.

16. All figures are from the US Census Bureau (2002). For a brief profile, see McKinnon 2003.

17. See Patterson (1967); Jencks (1998).

18. See, however, Jargowsky (1998), who emphasizes the critical additional role of economic segregation as opposed to purely racial factors.

19. I have examined these issues at great length in a recent study. See Patterson 1998: 3–167.

20. Overall, black women are 67 percent more likely to report incidents of intimate violence. In the mid-seventies black men killed their girl-friends at 6.5 times the rate of nonblacks and their wives at 7.5 times the white rate. More remarkable, however, was the fact that black women were driven to kill their lovers and their husbands at a greater rate than girlfriends and husbands were being killed by black men. The rate at which irate black women were killing both lovers and husbands was 18 times greater than that of their white sisters. Since then, mercifully, the rates have declined dramatically by over 75 percent for both genders, as have the black–white differences, although they remain substantial. US Department of Justice, Bureau of Justice Statistics (2002).

21. There is a mushrooming, and very contentious, literature from scholars in the region. See Miller 1991, Momammed and Perkins 1998.

22. See Foner (2001), Cordero-Guzman, Smith, and Grosfoguel (2001).

23. See, for example, Waters 1994; see also Mary Waters and Peggy Levitt (2001).

24. See, for example, Foner (2001).

25. See Sullivan and Gilbertson 1990, Model 1991.

26. Here I am in complete disagreement with Ira Katsnelson who argues that both Britain and America are racially stratified societies (Katsnelson 1973: 199).

27. See Peach (this volume).

28. I have drawn on the on-line publications of the British Office of National Statistics for 2001 and more recent data as well as the two valuable collections of papers based on the 1991 census: Coleman and Salt 1996; Peach 1996. In addition to works cited separately, I have also found the following useful: Anwar and Roach (1998), Luthra 1981, Husband 1987, Skellington 1992, Goulbourne 1998, Goulbourne 1990.

29. Racial harassment by the police, while it has abated somewhat after a series of high-profile scandals, remains a serious problem in British interethnic relations. See Clancy 2001; for one of the most detailed, locality-based studies of the problem see Hess et al. 1992.

30. See Cohen 1994: Chapter 1. The Irish may seem to be an exception here. See the chapter on the group in this volume. However, it is hard to say just how much assimilation of the Irish has taken place, since earlier generations may have become wholly absorbed but were quickly replaced by new immigrants, given the open borders between England and Ireland.

31. For an analysis critical of the British school system, see Troyna 1988. For a different approach see Heath and McMahon 1996 and the paper by the same authors in this volume.

32. See Berrington 1996, Murphy 1996.

33. For the earlier period of police lawlessness and irresponsible racialization of minor offences, see Hall et al. (1978); on the 1980s see Carr-Hill and Drew (1988). For the standard social science account of more recent developments, see FitzGerald and Hale (1996).

34. For a somewhat understated comparison, see Model and Fisher (2002).

35. See James and Harris (1993).

36. Indeed, American sociologists have restated this observation as a sociological law in a well-known theory of ethnic relations. See, for example, Blalock (1970).

37. The process of cultural infusion began within a few years of the arrival of the first postwar wave of migrants, a process I observed and discussed in an early paper (see, Patterson 1966). On more recent developments, see Paul Gilroy's fascinating discussion of the rise and decline of Jamaican Rastafarianism in the UK and the influence of Black British youth on British punk (Gilroy 1987: Chapter 4).

38. John Mollenkopf, 2002.

39. For a more detailed discussion of this distinction and the ways they interact, see Patterson (2000).

40. *triguenos*, Spanish: literally "wheat-hued"; *mulatinha*, Brazilian Portuguese: literally a lighter-hued white negro; *acastanhada*, Brazilian Portuguese: literally cashew-colored; *alva*, Brazilian Portuguese, "pure white"; *bem-branca*, Brazilian Portuguese, "very white." As noted earlier, The Brazilian Institute of Geography and Statistics found 134 racial terms for describing different color and physical combinations on the path to whiteness in Brazil. This was not a joke, but the results of a serious, well-designed study by one of the nation's most reputable research institutes.

REFERENCES

Akiyama, Y. and J. Noonan, 2000, "Lifetime Chance for Murder Victimization," paper presented at the American Society of Criminology Conference, 2000, California State University, Los Angeles.

Andrews, G., 1991, *Blacks and Whites in Sao Paulo Brazil, 1888–1988*, Madison, University of Wisconsin Press.

Anwar, M. and P. Roach (eds.), 2000, *From Legislation to Integration*, London: Macmillan Press.

Barker, M., 1981, *The New Racism*, London: Junction Books.

Berrington, A., 1996, "Marriage Patterns and Inter-ethnic Unions," in D. Coleman and J. Salt (eds.), *Ethnicity in the 1991 Census*, Vol. I: *Demographic Characteristics of the Ethnic Minority Populations*, London: HMSO, pp. 178–212.

BBC, The, 2002, 'BBC Race Survey' (May 7–11). Internet release.

Berthoud, R., 2000, "Family Formation in Multi-Cultural Britain: Three Patterns of Diversity," Working Paper 2000-34, Institute for Social and Economic Research, University of Essex.

Blalock, H., 1970, *Toward a Theory of Minority Group Relations*, New York: Capricorn.

Bobo, L., 2001, "Racial Attitudes and Relations at the Close of the Twentieth Century," in N. Smelser, W. J. Wilson, F. Mitchell (eds.), *America Becoming: Racial Trends and their Consequences*, Washington DC: National Academy Press.

Brodkin, K., 1999, *How Jews Became White Folks and What That Says About Race in America*, New Brunswick, NJ: Rutgers University Press.

Bureau of Citizenship and Immigration Services, 2003, *2002, Yearbook of Immigration Statistics*, Washington, DC.

Carr-Hill, R. and D. Drew, 1988, "Blacks, Police and Crime," in A. Bhat, R. Carr-Hill, and S. Ohri (eds.), *Britain's Black Population*, London: Gower.

Carrion, J. (ed.), 1997, *Ethnicity, Race and Nationality in the Caribbean*, San Juan, PR: Institute of Caribbean Studies.

Cash, W. J., 1991, *The Mind of the South*, New York: Vintage.

CDC, 2003, "HIV/AIDS Among African Americans," Division of HIV/AIDS Prevention.

Clancy, A., 2001, *Crime, Policing and Justice: The Experience of Ethnic Minorities*, London: Home Office Research Directorate.

Cohen, R., 1994, *Frontiers of Identity: The British and the Others*, Harlow, Essex: Longman.

Coleman, D. and J. Salt (eds.), 1996, *Ethnicity in the 1991 Census*, Vol. I: *Demographic Characteristics of the Ethnic Minority Populations*, London: HMSO.

Colman, A. M. and C. P. Gorman, 1982, "Conservatism, Dogmatism and Authoritarianism in British Police Officers," *Sociology* 16: 1–4.

Cordero-Guzman, Hector, Robert C. Smith, and Ramón Grosfoguel (eds.), 2001, *Migration, Transnationalization, and Race in a Changing New York*, Philadelphia: Temple University Press.

Curtin, P., 1969, *The Atlantic Slave Trade: A Census*, Madison: University of Wisconsin Press.

Davis, D. B., 1984, *Slavery and Human Progress*, New York: Oxford University Press.

Davis, F. J., 1993, *Who is Black: One Nation's Definition*, University Park, PA: Pennsylvania State University Press.

Dominguez, V., 1986, *White by Definition: Social Classification in Creole Louisiana*, New Brunswick: Rutgers University Press.

Dorsey, J., 1995, "Women Without History," *Journal of Caribbean History*, 28: 165–208.

Economist, The, 2003, "You-Gov and MORI polls" (Oct. 11–17): 58–9.

Eltis, D. and D. Richardson, 1997, "West Africa and the Transatlantic Slave Trade: New Evidence of Long-Run Trends," in D. Eltis and D. Richardson (eds.), *Routes to Slavery: Direction, Mortality and Ethnicity in the Transatlantic Slave Trade, 1595–1867*, London: Frank Cass.

Engerman, S., 1966, "Emancipation in Comparative Perspective: A Long and Wide View," in G. Oostindie (ed.), *Fifty Years Later: Antislavery, Capitalism and Modernity in the Dutch Orbit*, University of Pittsburgh Press, pp. 223–41.

Fitzgerald, M., 1990, "The Emergence of Black Councillors and MPs in Britain," in H. Goulbourne (ed.), *Black Politics in Britain*, Aldershot: Avebury, pp. 17–32.

FitzGerald, M. and C. Hale, 1996, *Ethnic Minorities: Victimisation and Racial Harassment: Findings from the 1988 and 1992 Crime Surveys*, London: Home Office Research Study 154.

Foner, D., 1995, *Free Soil, Free Labor, Free Men*, New York: Oxford University Press.

Foner, N., 2001, "West Indians in New York City and London: A Comparative Analysis," *International Migration Review* 13: 284–97.

Foner, N. (ed.), 2001, *Islands In the City: West Indian Migration to New York*. Berkeley: University of California Press.

Franklin, J. H. (ed.), 1968, *Color and Race*, Boston: Beacon Press.

Frazier, E. F., 1957, *Race and Culture Contacts in the Modern World*, Boston: Beacon.

Genovese, E. F., 1988, *Within the Plantation Household*, Chapel Hill: University of North Carolina Press.

Gilroy P., 1987, *There Ain't No Black in the Union Jack: The Cultural Politics of Race and Nation*, University of Chicago Press.

Girvan, N., 1971, *Foreign Capital and Economic Underdevelopment in Jamaica*, Mona, Jamaica: Institute of Social and Economic Research.

Goulbourne, H. (ed.), 1990, *Black Politics in Britain*, Aldershot: USA.

1998, *Race Relations in Britain Since 1945*, London: Macmillan.

Hall, S. et al. 1978, *Policing the Crisis: Mugging, the State and Law and Order*, London: Macmillan.

Harris, M., 1964, *Patterns of Race in the Americas*, New York: Walker.

Heath, A. and D. McMahon, 1996, "Education and Occupational Attainment: The Impact of Ethnic Origins," in V. Karn (ed.), *Ethnicity in the 1991 Census*, Vol. IV: *Education, Employment and Housing*, London: HMSO.

Henriques, F., 1953, *Family and Color in Jamaica*, London: Eyre and Spottiswoode.

Hess, B. et al. 1992, *Beneath the Surface*, Aldershot: Avebury.

Hoetink, H., 1967, *The Two Variants of Caribbean Race Relations*, London: Oxford University Press.

Husband C. (ed.), 1987, *Race In Britain: Continuity and Change*, London: Hutchinson.

Ignatiev, N., 1995, *How the Irish Became White*, New York, NY: Routledge.

Instituto Brasileiro de Geografia e Estatistico, 1976, *Servico Nacional de Recenseamento*, Rio de Janeiro: O Servico.

James, W. and C. Harris (eds.), 1993, *Inside Babylon: The West Indian Diaspora in Britain*, London: Verso.

Jargowsky, P. A., 1998, *Poverty and Place: Ghettos, Barrios, and the American City*, New York: Russell Sage Foundation.

Jargowsky, P. A., 2003, "Stunning Progress, Hidden Problems: The Dramatic Decline of Concentrated Poverty in the 1990s," Living Cities Census Series, Center on Urban and Metropolitan Studies. Washington, DC: Brookings Institution.

Jefferson, O., 1972, *The Post-War Economic Development of Jamaica*, Mona, Jamaica: Institute of Social and Economic Research.

Jones, T., 1996, *Britain's Ethnic Minorities: An Analysis of the Labor Force Survey*, London: Policy Studies Institute.

Kalmijn, M., 1996, "The Socioeconomic Assimilation of Caribbean American Blacks," *Social Forces*, Vol. 74.

Kasinitz, P., 1993, *Caribbean New York: Black Immigrants and the Politics of Race*, Ithaca: Cornell University Press.

Katsnelson, I., 1973, *Black Men, White Cities: Race, Politics and Migration in the US, 1900–1930, and Britain 1948–1968*, London: Oxford University Press.

Kershen, A. (ed.), 1998, *A Question of Identity*, Aldershot: Ashgate.

King, W., 1995, *Stolen Childhood: Slave Youth in Nineteenth Century America*, Wilmington: University of Indiana Press.

Lev, P., G. Fouron, and N. Schiller, 2001, "The Generation of Identity: Redefining the Second Generation Within a Transnational Social Field," in H. Cordero-Guzman, Robert C. Smith, and Ramón Grosfoguel (eds.), *Migration, Transnationalization and Race in a Changing New York*, Philadelphia: Temple University Press, pp. 58–86.

Levitt, P., 2001, *The Transnational Villagers*, Berkeley: University of California Press.

Loewn, J., 1988, *The Mississippi Chinese*, Prospect Heights, IL: Waveland.

Looney, R. E., 1987, *The Jamaican Economy in the 1980s: Economic Decline and Structural Adjustment*, Boulder, CO: Westview Press.

Lovejoy, P., 2000, *Transformations in Slavery: A History of Slavery in Africa*, Cambridge University Press.

Lowenthal, D., 1972, *West Indian Societies*, New York: Oxford University Press.

Luthra, M., 1997, *Britain's Black Population*, London: Arena.

Maingot, A. P., 1992, "Race, Color and Class in the Caribbean," in A. Stepan (ed.), *The Americas*, New York: Oxford University Press.

Manning, P., 1990, *Slavery and African Life: Occidental, Oriental and African Slave Trades*, Cambridge University Press.

Massey M. and M. Denton, 1993, *American Apartheid*, Cambridge, MA: Harvard University Press.

Mattoso, Katia M. de Queirós, 1996, *To Be A Slave in Brazil 1550–1888*, New Brunswick, NJ: Rutgers University Press.

McKinnon, J., 2003, *The Black Population of the United States, March 2002*, US Census Bureau, Current Population Reports, Series P20–S41, Washington, DC.

Miller, E., 1991, *Men at Risk*, Kingston: Jamaica Publishing.

Minority Rights Group (eds.), 1996, *No Longer Invisible: Afro-Latin Americans Today*, London: Minority Rights Publications.

Model S., 1991, "Caribbean Immigrants: A Black Success Story?" *International Migration Review* 25 (Summer): 248–76.

1995, "West Indian Prosperity; Fact or Fiction," *Social Problems* 42: 535–53.

1999, "Ethnic Inequality in England: An Analysis Based on the 1991 census," *Ethnic and Racial Studies* 22: 969–90.

Model, S. and G. Fisher, 2002, "Unions Between Blacks and Whites: England and the US compared," *Ethnic and Racial Studies* 25: 728–54.

Mohammed P. and A. Perkins (1998), *Caribbean Women at the Crossroads: The Dilemma of Decision-making Among Women of Barbados, St. Lucia and Dominica*, New York: UWI Press and IPPF.

Mollenkopf, J., 2002, "Assimilating Immigrants in Amsterdam: A Perspective from New York," Amsterdam: Amsterdam Study Center for the Metropolitan Environment: Internet Release (9/17/2002).

Morgan, E., 1975, *American Slavery, American Freedom*, New York: Norton.

Morner, M. (ed.), 1970, *Race and Class in Latin America*, New York: Columbia University Press.

Moser, C. and J. Holland, 1997, *Urban Poverty and Violence in Jamaica*, Washington, DC: The World Bank.

Murphy, M., 1996, "Household and Family Structure among Ethnic Minority Groups," in Coleman and Salt (eds.), pp. 213–42.

Nossiter, A. 1995, "A Jamaican Way Station in the Bronx," *New York Times* (Oct. 25).

Omi M. and H. Winant, 1996, "Contesting the Meaning of Race in the Post Civil Rights Movement Era," in S. Pedraza, and R. Rumbaut (eds.), *Origins and Destinies: Immigration, Race and Ethnicity in America*, Belmont, CA: Wadsworth, pp. 470–78.

Oostindie, G. (ed.), 1996, *Ethnicity in the Caribbean*, London: Macmillan.

Parry O., 2000, *Male Underachievement in High School Education in Jamaica, Barbados, and St Vincent and the Grenadines*, Kingston, Jamaica: Canoe Press.

Patterson, O., 1966, "The Dance Invasion of Britain," *New Society*, 207.

1967, *The Sociology of Slavery: Jamaica, 1838*, London: McGibbon & Kee; Associated University Press, 1969.

1968, "West Indian Migrants Returning Home," *Race* 4(1): 69–77.

1982, *Slavery and Social Death*, Cambridge, MA: Harvard University Press.

1987, "The Emerging West Atlantic System: Migration, Culture and Underdevelopment in the U.S. and Caribbean," in William Alonso (ed.), *Population in an Interacting World*, Cambridge, MA: Harvard University Press, pp. 227–60.

1997, *The Ordeal of Integration: Progress and Resentment in America's "Racial" Crisis*, Washington, DC: Civitas.

1998, *Rituals of Blood: Consequences of Slavery in Two American Centuries*, New York: Basic Books.

2000, "Taking Culture Seriously: A Framework and an Afro-American Illustration," in L. Harrison and S. Huntington (eds.), *Culture Matters*, New York: Basic Books, pp. 202–18.

Peach, C., 1991, "The Caribbean in Europe: Contrasting Patterns of Migration and Settlement in Britain, France and the Netherlands," Research Paper in Ethnic Relations, No. 15, Center for Research in Ethnic Relations, University of Warwick.

(ed.), 1996, *Ethnicity in the 1991 Census*, Vol. II: *The Ethnic Minority Populations of Great Britain*, London: HMSO.

1998, "South Asian and Caribbean Ethnic Minority Housing Choice in Britain," *Urban Studies* 35: 1657–80.

Portes, A. and Zhou, M., 1993, "The New Second Generation: Segmented Assimilation and its Variants," in *The Annals of the American Academy of Political and Social Science* 530: 74–97.

Premdas, R., 1996, "Race and Ethnic Relations in Burnhamite Guyana," in D. Dabydeen, and B. Samaroo (eds.), *Across the Dark Waters: Ethnicity and Indian Identity in the Caribbean*, London: Macmillan–Warwick University Caribbean Studies, pp. 39–65.

Reichmann, R. (ed.), 1999, *Race in Contemporary Brazil: From Indifference to Inequality*, University Park, PA: Penn State University Press.

Rodriguez, C., 1992, "Race, Culture and Latina 'Otherness' in the 1980 Census," *Social Science Quarterly* 73: 931–37.

Roediger, D., 1991, *The Wages of Whiteness: Race and the Making of the American Working Class*, New York: Verso.

Ryan, S., 1972, *Race and Nationalism in Trinidad and Tobago*, Toronto: University of Toronto Press.

Schuck, P., 2003, *Diversity in America: Keeping Government at a Safe Distance* Cambridge, MA: Harvard University Press.

Skellington, R. 1992, *Race In Britain Today*, London: Sage and Open University.

Smith M. G. 1973, *The Plural Society in the British West Indies; Carl Stone, Class, Race and Political Behavior in Jamaica*, Mona, Jamaica: Institute of Social and Economic Research.

Smith, M. G., 1965, *The Plural Society in the British West Indies*, Berkeley: University of California Press.

Sowell, T., 1981, *Ethnic America*, New York: Basic Books.

Steckel, R. H., 1986, "A Dreadful Childhood: The Excess Mortality of American Slaves," *Social Science History* 10: 427–65.

Stephens, E. H. and J. D. Stephens, 1986, *Democratic Socialism in Jamaica*, Princeton University Press.

Sullivan, T. and G. Gilbertson 1990, "Caribbean Immigrants in the US: The Effects of Race and Language on Earnings," Austin, TX: Population Research Center, University of Texas, pp. 911–30.

Telles, E. E., 1999, "Ethnic Boundaries and Political Mobilization Among African Brazilians," in M. Hanchard (ed.), *Racial Politics in Contemporary Brazil*, Durham: Duke University Press.

Troyna, B., 1988, "British Schooling and the Reproduction of Racial Inequality," in M. Cross and H. Entzinger (eds.), *Lost Illusions: Caribbean Minorities in Britain and the Netherlands*, London: Routledge, pp. 166–84.

UK Home Office 1998, and 1999, *Statistics on Race and the Criminal Justice System, 1998*, London UK: Home Office Publications.

US Census Bureau, 2002, *Annual Demographic Supplement to the March 2002, Current Population Survey.*

US Department of Justice, Bureau of Justice Statistics 2002, "Homicide Trends in the US: Intimate Homicides," Internet Release (November).

UNAIDS, 2002, Report on the Global HIV/AIDS Epidemic (July).

U.N. Dept. of Economic and Social Affairs, 1993, *Report on the World Social Situation 1993*, New York: U.N. Publications.

United Nations Foundation, "Brazil's Police Death Squads Accused of Terror Campaign," U.N. Wire, Oct. 27, 2003.

Vickerman, M., 1999, *Crosscurrents: West Indian Immigrants and Race*, New York: Oxford University Press.

Vieira, R. M., "Brazil" in P. Perez-Sarduy and J. Stubbs (eds.), *No Longer Invisible: Afro-Latin Americans Today*, New York: Paul & Co., 1995.

Wagley, C., 1957, "Plantation America: a Culture Sphere," in Rubin, V. (ed.), *Caribbean Studies: A Symposium*, Mona, Jamaica: Institute of Social and Economic Research.

Waters, M., 1994, "Ethnic and Racial Identities of Second-Generation Immigrants in New York City," *International Migration Review* 28: 795–820.

1999, *Black Identities: West Indian Immigrant Dreams and American Realities*, Cambridge, MA: Harvard University Press.

Waters, M. and P. Levitt, 2001, "The Changing Face of Home: The Transnational Lives of the Second Generation," in H. Cordero-Guzman et al. (eds.), *Migration, Transnationalization and Race in a Changing New York*, Philadelphia: Temple University Press.

Williamson, J., 1980, *New People: Miscegenation and Mulattoes in the United States* New York: Free Press.

World Bank, 1992, *World Development Report, 1993*, Oxford University Press.

Wyatt-Brown, B., 1982, *Southern Honor: Ethics and Behavior in the Old South*, New York: Oxford University Press.

Yelvington, K. (ed.), 1993, *Trinidad Ethnicity*, London: Macmillan Press.

Part II

Informal social networks

Towards a synthetic introduction re households, families, and neighborhoods

The social mobility that we track in formal institutions of politics, the workplace, and education is powerfully influenced by the less formal social structures of the family, neighborhood, and ethnic group. It is in these less formal structures that the tastes, habits, disciplines, and capacities of individuals are formed. What is more, these informal structures penetrate into formal institutions, providing leverage for some and disadvantages for others. It is impossible to explore the relationships between race, ethnicity, and social mobility without examining the sites in which the capacities that allow individuals to move up are produced, or are hindered. The chapters in this section explore the way that social mobility and ethno-racial stratification are produced by the interaction of these formal and informal structures.

The process of social mobility for ethnic and racial minorities is almost without exception a geographic process. Ethnicity and race feed into the process by which individuals sort themselves (and others sort them) out in space. On the one hand, most ethnic and racial groups have strong reasons to prefer geographic clustering, since such a pattern puts them in easy association with those who speak the same language, profess the same religion, and who can provide networks into the labor market, while also providing a degree of concentration necessary for the provision of group-specific services. On the other hand, clustering is often driven not so much by the preferences of groups as by the limited space the larger society is willing to make for them. Where groups get sorted in space is thus frequently a matter of political and even violent contestation, as the indigenous population and new groups fight over turf. The desire to cluster therefore explains why we are likely to see some degree of ethnic and racial concentration but doesn't explain how much or where that concentration will occur. To explain that, forces outside the group must be examined.

In this volume, the papers by Cutler, Glaeser, and Vigdor (CGV), Peach, and to some degree Zhou examine this process of clustering and concentration. They all suggest that geographic concentration is driven by very deep forces within the migration process and within the political economy of racial and ethnic geography. But, as suggested in the introduction to this book, racial and ethnic geography can be sorted into two quite distinct groups. There is, first, an immigrant pattern, in which high (but rarely exclusive) levels of concentration in the early generations give way to a more dispersed pattern in later generations, often accompanied by the maintenance of a few clusters in which new immigrants settle and substantial group services are delivered. While there are variations in these patterns (for instance, a greater propensity to maintain enclaves over time among the Chinese in the USA, and greater concentration despite substantial social mobility among Indians in Britain), the general outlines seem fairly strong across both the US and British cases.

On the other hand, there is a pattern which seems to hold only for American blacks, of what Douglas Massey has called "hypersegregation," where a single group is not just a majority or significant plurality of a neighborhood (as in the immigrant pattern), but where they are close to the *only* residents. In this section, Ceri Peach persuasively argues that no ghettoes on the American pattern exist in Britain, while CGV provide additional evidence not only that such a pattern holds for the United States, but that it is highly durable intergenerationally and largely exceptional in its durability across groups in American history. What is more, the high degree of isolation of American blacks extends also to intermarriage, in sharp contrast to the situation of British Caribbeans, who are the British ethnic group most likely to be intimately assimilated. So while the papers in this book suggest that there are great commonalities in the immigrant experience, they also place, once again, in sharp relief the distinctive, perhaps exceptional, status of American blacks.

Peach finds that neither the ghetto nor the enclave pattern fully fits the British case. Instead, the dualistic model that he sees as fitting Britain is the contrast between the Irish and the Jews. The "Irish" model stands for full sociocultural integration, though with a working-class bias; while the Jews represent middle-class economic integration and the maintainance of some sociocultural distinctiveness. Using this pairing, and using quantitative data in relation to occupational levels and (inter)marriage, he suggests that the Caribbeans are on an Irish path and the South Asians are on a Jewish path. This is an insightful approach and has the virtue of understanding today's nonwhites in terms of a previous migration of whites, but one could perhaps refine it further. Expanding Peach's categories somewhat, we might describe the main minority groups as follows:

i) Caribbeans: broadly integrated with a working-class bias and some extremes: elite contributors to sport and popular culture at one end and ghetto-type outcasts at the other.

ii) African Asians and Indians: upwardly mobile, partly through self-employment, but some cultural distinctness and endogamy, especially amongst the working class, but loosening with social mobility.

iii) Pakistanis and Bangladeshis: high levels of disadvantage, high levels of segregation/exclusion, cultural distinctness and political conflict.

iv) Chinese: some residential segregation though the mini-Chinatowns are primarily business "theme-parks" but both the cultural and economic distinctness are being eroded by high levels of educational-economic mobility.

The ghetto/enclave distinction, however, does not apply to just the depth and durability of geographic concentration, but also the social meaning and functioning of these forms of ethno-racial clustering. Where social meaning is concerned, ghettos carry the taint of stigma both to outsiders and, to some degree, to group members as well. The intense concentration of disadvantage in ghettos both helps to reproduce that disadvantage, while also helping to create a social stereotype of ghetto residents as pathological and untrustworthy. That is, ghettos effect both the reality and the social image of social dysfunction – and the two will tend to reinforce one another. Once such a pattern has become locked in, ghettos become places simply to escape from, leading the most successful former ghetto-residents to place as much social distance (to avoid the "taint" of the ghetto as well as the very real dangers present) as possible from those still there. The absence of any meaningful presence of successful members of the group means that those most likely to build institutions, provide networking and police norms are absent, and social interactions become anarchic, and thus are set by the strongest and most fearsome (Anderson, 1990). This pattern means that, in ghettos, the social mobility of any individual resident or family has little or no external impacts on continuing residents, and the absence of those individuals from social life only exacerbates the ghetto's limited structure of opportunity.

The absence of stigma, hyper-concentration, and disorganization in enclaves causes them to function quite differently. Enclaves become centers for ethnically oriented business and a service-center for ethnic identifiers who reside both within the enclave and outside it. Because they tend to attract for residence those lower on the economic scale and more recent in migration, while pulling in the wealthier and better assimilated for services and business, enclaves tend to encourage networking across class lines within ethnic and racial groups. In contrast to ghettos, the constant cycle of successful coethnics back into the enclave provides a durable source of leadership for institutions, economic networking and opportunity, and a respected source of norm-enforcement. But neighborhoods are not the only – perhaps not even the most – important informal institution affecting social mobility. The family is of at least equal importance, but it is critical to view the family as embedded in larger ethnic and racial groups. Both the chapters by Berthoud and Patterson make the point that the structure of families varies enormously across ethnic and racial groups, and the chapters by Linda Loury and Ron Ferguson (and to some degree those of Hout, Heath, and Modood in the following section) suggest that the family is a critical factor in educational outcomes, that essential building block of social mobility. Patterson, no doubt controversially, argues that the family structures of the descendants of slaves – African-Americans and British Afro-Caribbeans – carry with them the legacy of that searing experience. For these individuals in both countries, Patterson argues the nuclear family has always been a fragile thing, and its fragility has only increased over time.

It is this change over time that Berthoud emphasizes, suggesting that, at least for British Afro-Caribbeans, the family has increasingly taken on what he calls a "modern" configuration, one more individualized and less rigidly institutionalized than for other groups – a pattern with obvious parallels in the American experience. But even here there are important differences. While the fragility of the black family in America has operated within an intimate environment still remarkably segregated from that of the white population, in Britain that increasingly individualized pattern has gone hand in hand with a remarkable level of intimate assimilation. Levels of British Afro-Caribbean intimate assimilation rival the levels seen by Mexican- and Asian-Americans and are substantially in excess of groups who trace their heritage to the subcontinent. While the deprivation that seems to accompany the "modern individualized" family that Berthoud describes appears to affect the descendants of slaves in both countries, in Britain it is accompanied by a rather rapid melting into the indigenous population. This is yet further evidence that the scale of the stigma and isolation that marks American blacks is not matched in the case of Afro-Caribbeans.

Berthoud finds that, for the descendants of the Indian subcontinent, on the other hand, a very different family form reveals itself, which he calls, with some justification, "old fashioned" or "traditional." While certain aspects of that traditional pattern seem to moderate over time (such as women's low labor force participation rate and arranged marriage), other parts seem quite durable, especially high rates of marriage and at least some level of multi-generational family ties. It may be that this family pattern is reinforced by the stronger institutional ties within the ethnic group, everything from religion to neighborhood concentration to ethnic businesses and social organizations – all of which provide a high level of social control by the elder over the younger generations, a pattern which Zhou observes in the United States as well.

How, if at all, do these family patterns matter? This is, to say the least, a more contentious issue. Both Linda Loury and Ferguson find that family background factors explain a great deal of the difference in educational outcomes between blacks and whites in America, and we can speculate that there is probably some similar connection in Britain as well. Both find that these factors are evident very early, even before children have entered schooling. But family background is far from an iron cage, as more conservative commentators suggest. On the one hand, variations in school quality and content seem to lead to quite different outcomes, even for similarly situated individuals – policy matters, regardless of family (dis)organization. What is more, ethnically and racially encoded cultural norms, which Ferguson suggests are quite powerful in explaining success in school, are highly volatile. The "culture" which influences school performance may not be as deep as some observers suggest. If it was, how can we explain the rapid improvements in black American test scores through the 1970s, followed by the disturbing decline thereafter? Apparently, the "meanings" that individuals associate with ethnic and racial group attachment seem to have altered in this period – and while those meanings could shift in a direction that led to lower school performance, they could also shift back.

In the end, both neighborhood, group, and family factors, as powerful as they are, must be seen within the context of public policy. To pay attention to such factors is not to ignore the fact that differences in educational performance – and ultimately the social mobility that this volume is concerned with – are sensitive both to the generic policy environment but also to the meaning that policymakers attribute to the inequalities that result from them. Do those inequalities call out for public action, both to change the resources available to ethnic and racial minorities, and also, perhaps, to help shift the cultural norms that seem to influence educational performance? Do policymakers have an obligation to help rectify these inequalities, understood in specifically racial and ethnic terms? This is an issue that will be taken on directly by both Glenn Loury and Bhikhu Parekh in the final section of this volume.

REFERENCE

Anderson, E., 1999, *Code of the Street*, New York: Norton.

4   Ethnicity as social capital: community-based institutions and embedded networks of social relations

Min Zhou

Past and recent studies have consistently found that ethnicity significantly affects varied outcomes of social mobility among different immigrant groups and that such divergent outcomes in turn lead to further changes in the character and salience of ethnicity. Much of the intellectual debate on ethnic differences is between the cultural perspective – emphasizing the role of internal agency and the extent to which ethnic cultures fit the requirements of the mainstream society – and the structural perspective – emphasizing the role of social structure and the extent to which ethnic groups are constrained by the broader stratification system and networks of social relations within that system.

Social scientists from both perspectives have attempted to develop statistical models to measure quantitatively the effects of "culture" and "structure" for the upward social mobility of immigrant groups. Under ideal circumstances, these models would include indicators illuminating pre-migration situations. But because of data limitations, many social scientists typically attempt to control for "structure" by documenting specific contexts of exit, identifying aspects of post-migration social structures, and operationalizing those components for which they have data. This is not only a conventional practice but also a reasonable approach, since many post-migration social structural differences (in the socio-economic status of persons who came to the United States as adults) are likely to either reflect, or be carryovers from, pre-migration differences. However, even the most sophisticated statistical model accounts for only a proportion of the variance, leaving a large residual unexplained. More intractable are questions of how to conceptualize the ethnic effect and how to measure it. Given the constraints of the data, many social scientists have tried valiantly to make progress on this front and have come up with measures that are ingenious, though not fully convincing. In the end, many have had to place much weight on the effect of the ethnic dummy, the exact meaning or contents of which remains a black box. I argue that ethnicity cannot be simply viewed as either a structural or a cultural measure, rather it encompasses values and behavioral patterns that are constantly interacting with both internal and external structural exigencies.

The purpose of this chapter is to examine the organizational structure of one immigrant community to illustrate where culture and social structure intersect and what it is that causes ethnicity to yield positive outcomes for some groups and negative outcomes for others. In doing so, I begin with a brief review of empirical findings and theoretical explanations of ethnic differences. I then delve into the social structures of New York City's Chinatown – an ethnic enclave as opposed to an urban ghetto – to explore ways of unpacking ethnicity, delineating conditions under which an ethnic enclave affects the social mobility of its members.[1]

Social mobility of racial/ethnic minority groups

Interethnic differences in social mobility

The sociological literature empirically measures individual or group progress by the extent to which racial/ethnic minority groups achieve parity with society's dominant group in education, occupation, income, and political power, which, in Gordon's term, constitutes "structural assimilation" (1964). On the social mobility of immigrants, the body of writing identified as "classical assimilation theories" stresses the effect of length of stay in the host society since immigration. Time, or generational status, denotes the processes of learning the English language, acquiring labor market skills, establishing contact with other social groups, especially the dominant group in society, adopting American ways, and ultimately becoming American. In sum, time moves groups ahead, while also producing intergroup convergence.

The mobility trajectories for the children and grandchildren of earlier European immigrants appear to confirm the linear model of structural assimilation. Between the 1920s and the 1950s, the United States indeed absorbed the great waves of immigrants and melted the racialized European ethnic groups – the Irish, Italians, and Jews – into an indistinguishable white (Wytrwal 1961, Sandberg 1974, Greeley 1976, Chiswick 1977 and Alba 1985). Recent studies have also shown trends of upward movement from the first generation to the next among new immigrants in terms of educational and occupational attainment (Hirschman and Wong 1984, Chavez 1989, Cheng and Yang 1996).

But time does not appear to work equally for all, neither does it matter much for upwardly mobile immigrants and their children. As Steven Thernstrom showed more than twenty-five years ago, the Irish,

Italians, and Jews moved ahead at very different rates, and in very different ways (Thernstrom 1973). Joel Perlmann's more sophisticated analysis of the Irish, Italians, Jews, African Americans, and Yankees of Providence, Rhode Island, underscored wide differences in both educational and occupational attainment among the second generation, which persisted after controlling for an extensive array of background variables (Perlmann 1988). Recently, the burgeoning literature on the children of contemporary immigrants, who are mostly of Asian or Latin origin, also points to diverse adaptational outcomes, with Asian origin groups approaching parity with, or even surpassing, the socioeconomic status of average Americans, and Latin-origin groups lagging significantly behind and, for some, trailing native-born minorities (Gans 1992, Portes and Zhou 1993, Landale and Oropesa 1995, Steinberg 1996, Vernez and Abrahamse 1996, Zhou 2001).

Significant ethnic differences in mobility rates and outcomes persist even after controlling for social class status of the individual or the group. Empirical research points to two major conclusions about the effect of ethnicity. First, ethnicity exercises its own effect, regardless of time or social class factors that might otherwise distinguish, or lump together, diverse ethnic groups (Rumbaut 1995, Steinberg 1996). The significance of the ethnic effect indicates that different ethnic groups not only face varied structural conditions but also develop varied strategies of coping that directly influence mobility outcomes. Second, the ethnic effect is distinctively linked to particular ethnic groups – positive for some and negative for others – which suggests that ethnicity interacts with broader structural factors in such a way as to reinforce the advantages or disadvantages associated with racial/ethnic group membership (Portes and MacLeod 1996, Hao and Bonstead-Bruns 1998). Thus, ethnicity can work to accelerate the upward progress of some groups, while keeping others from advancing, or possibly even pushing them further down toward the bottom.

Accounting for interethnic differences: the cultural explanation   Why is the effect of ethnicity diminishing for some groups in succeeding generations but persistent for others even after long periods of US residency? Why is it that ethnicity exerts opposite effects on the same outcome measures for different groups? Specifically, why is it that being Asian or Chinese gives immigrant children a significant advantage for educational achievement, but being black or Mexican distinctly disadvantages immigrant children, holding constant other key socioeconomic and contextual factors? The cultural interpretation of the ethnic effect emphasizes an ethnic group's traits, qualities, characteristics, or behavioral patterns with which the group is either inherently endowed or which it develops in the process of adaptation. Based on the primordial view, different ethnic groups possess identifiable characteristics, encompassing cultural values, practices, and social networks that were formed in the homeland and transplanted with minor modifications by immigrants in the new land and there transmitted and perpetuated from generation to generation. The cultural inventory that facilitates success includes high achievement motivation, industriousness, perseverance, future orientation, and ability to postpone immediate gratification for later rewards. Thomas Sowell calls this "whole constellation of values, attitudes, skills and contacts" human capital and believes that group differences in IQ tests and scholastic achievement represent real differences in cultural assets with which a group is endowed (1981). Francis Fukuyama takes a step further to argue that, just as some aspects of immigrant cultural patterns may continue in a state of uneasy coexistence with the requirements of the host country, other aspects of immigrant cultural patterns may "fit" the requirements of life there (1993).

The emergent view, in contrast, posits that cultural traits and related behavioral patterns are not necessarily intrinsic to a group but can exert an independent effect on social mobility once transmitted from the previous generation and reconstructed through interaction with the structural conditions of the host society. Oscar Lewis maintained that urban ghettos gave rise to a particular way of living constrained by poverty, which in turn generated particular value systems that encouraged fatalism, a lack of spiritual concerns and aspirations, and a present orientation fostering the desire for instant gratification, authoritarianism within the family, and male superiority. While poor families relied on these values and behaviors as a means of coping with poverty, they absorbed these values and behaviors. As a result, the urban poor established a stable and persistent way of life and passed it on from generation to generation (Lewis 1966). Following similar reasoning, the contemporary public debate on the urban underclass also stresses the devastating effect of a deficient culture. From this view, an underclass culture, arisen from economic marginalization and extreme conditions of ghetto living, nurtures values that are at odds with those of mainstream society in regard to work, money, education, home, and family life. It gives rise to a set of self-defeating behavioral problems, such as labor force nonparticipation, out-of-wedlock birth, welfare dependency, school failure, drug addiction, and chronic lawlessness (Wilson 1996).

Accounting for interethnic differences: the structural explanation
Like the cultural perspective, the structural perspective takes ethnicity as a key determinant for social mobility but assigns different meanings

to it. From the structural perspective, broader social structural factors, interacting with ethnic social structures, define the meaning of success, prescribe strategies for status attainment, and ultimately determine a group's chance of success. Three such structural factors – a group's socioeconomic standing in the host society, economic restructuring, and residential segregation – are of paramount importance. William Wilson argued that past racism essentially delayed the entry of racial minority members into full participation in the American economy until the old blue-collar opportunities largely disappeared, leaving behind non-white minority groups in economically deprived neighborhoods (Wilson 1978). However, he also saw the declining significance of race in determining contemporary racial inequality (Wilson 1987). Douglass Massey and Nancy Denton disagreed, providing compelling evidence to suggest that the physical and social isolation of many black Americans were produced not simply by racism in past historical periods that put blacks down, but by ongoing conscious, discriminatory actions and policies despite significant socioeconomic achievements (Massey and Denton 1987). Joleen Kirschenman and Kathryn Neckerman found that employers often emphasized the color of a person's skin when it came to describing workers' work ethics, attitudes toward work, and causes for tensions in the workplace, and that these employers tended to associate one's racial minority membership with low productivity, poor work ethics, and interracial tensions. They concluded that racial discrimination exacerbates the negative impact of economic restructuring (Kirschenman and Neckerman 1991). Roger Waldinger found from his study of ethnic succession in New York City's labor market that blacks were pushed out of the labor force not due to a lack of jobs but due to a lack of access to informal employment networks which were organized around ethnicity (1996).

The disappearance of industrial jobs in urban areas where racial minorities concentrate has detached the middle class from the working poor, leading to the formation of contemporary urban ghettos that are plagued by severe living conditions, high rates of unemployment, out-of-wedlock births, single parenthood, drug abuse and crime, and other social problems (Anderson 1990). Consequently, ghettoization traps the poor in extreme social isolation in the most impoverished stratum of society. Living in urban ghettos bears important implications for intergenerational mobility. Ghetto residents, predominantly racial/ethnic minorities, suffer from an unequal distribution of economic and educational resources and face multiple adverse conditions – poverty, unemployment, single parenthood, poor schools, violence and drugs – and a generally disruptive social environment, which greatly circumvents their chances for success.

Moreover, children living in the inner city are vulnerable to the negative influence of an "adversarial subculture" that entails the willful refusal of mainstream norms and values about mobility (Anderson 1990, Portes and Zhou 1993, Kohl 1994, Fordham 1996, Wilson 1996). This adversarial subculture can exercise a powerful negative influence on newcomers and their children in inner cities (Portes and Zhou 1993).

According to the structural argument, cultural values are conducive to upward social mobility only when they interact with a wider set of structural factors, including a relatively advantageous class status with which a particular group arrived and a favorable structure of opportunity that the group encounters. For example, the children of Jewish immigrants fared better academically than their Italian counterparts who arrived in the United States at the same time. Their educational attainment was not simply accounted for by the value Jews place on education but was attributed to their more advantageous class background – higher literacy, better industrial skills, and greater familiarity with urban living – and to the fact that they typically immigrated as families with the intention to settle, not to sojourn. Also, because of middleman minority status in the homeland, Jews had already developed a complex array of ethnic institutions and organizations which allowed them to maintain extensive Jewish networks and synagogue ties to cope with adversity and settlement problems (Goldscheider and Zuckerman 1984). Thus, the value Jews traditionally place on education is activated, redefined, and given new direction only when education carries with it compelling social and economic rewards (Steinberg 1981). Pre-migration and current socioeconomic status also account for second-generation mobility outcomes. Georges Vernez and Allen Abrahamse demonstrated that the lower educational attainment of Hispanic students, relative to Asians, blacks, and white students, was largely explained by their generally lower scores on all key socioeconomic characteristics, such as family income and parental education (Vernez and Abrahamse 1996). The fact that immigrant groups come from diverse socioeconomic backgrounds washes away the effect of time, with class status accelerating structural assimilation for higher-status groups while stifling the progress of lower-status groups.

In explaining Asian-American educational achievement, Stanley Sue and Sumie Okazaki advanced the notion of relative functionalism, which hypothesized that the greater the entry barriers into noneducational areas, the more salient education becomes a means for mobility. They argued that Asian Americans were constrained by the structure of opportunity for upward mobility in areas such as politics, sports, and entertainment, to which education is not the only ticket for admission. The experience and perception of blocked mobility in those noneducational areas thus allowed Asian Americans to devote more energy to education and disproportionately succeed in it (Stanley and Okazaki 1990).

Variations in context: enclaves vs ghettos

The structural perspective has considerable plausibility in that it takes into account the varied effects of structural constraints on ethnic groups. But this perspective is constructed at the "grand" level to predict macroprocesses and general patterns of social mobility. It thus lacks explanatory power on how to deal with the varied and disparate outcomes of a given process or a given pattern for diverse ethnic groups and the members of these groups who themselves display diverse socioeconomic characteristics. Overemphasis on ethnic cultures and ethnic characteristics can also create problems in the use of the cultural perspective as an explanatory tool. In reality, the enduring influence of ethnicity reflects the structural impact of the broader ethnic stratification system. Some portion of the ethnic disparities that existing research has detected is related to class differentials (e.g., pre-migration and/or parental socioeconomic characteristics and family wealth), different histories of societal subjugation, varied levels of residential segregation among different groups. Thus, specific cultural values and behavioral patterns of a particular group are not innate or static but arise from structural exigencies of societal as well as ethnic systems.

Different ethnic groups develop different cultural models and strategies, based on historical and current experiences, for responding to differential societal treatments and coping with survival and mobility. Some groups may respond to structural disadvantages in an active and empowering way to reject the dominant group's standards. Others may rely on the ethnic community or ethnic networks of social relations to overcome structural disadvantages and achieve structural parity with the dominant group.

However, culture interacts with structure not only at the macro-societal level, but also at the level of an ethnic community where a group establishes itself within a particular context of societal reception. Different ethnic groups vary in the availability of and access to tangible and intangible resources, and the ability to mobilize these resources at the neighborhood level. The contrast between an ethnic enclave and an underclass ghetto is a case in point. High levels of segregation by race/ethnicity and class characterize both urban forms. Enclave and ghetto residents both are unlikely to have white or middle-class coethnic neighbors, tend to be low-skilled, and work in dead-end jobs if employed. Their neighborhoods are beset by poverty and various problems, such as demeaning standards of living, run-down housing, street gangs, and crime. And their children are likely to attend public schools where fellow students are predominantly racial/ethnic minorities and from underprivileged socioeconomic backgrounds.

However, significant differences exist between the two. The first difference lies in the make-up of residents. Generally speaking, residents in an ethnic enclave are mostly first-generation immigrants with a strong sense of common ancestry, history, and culture, despite diasporic migration experiences. Enclave residents are poor but not socioeconomically downtrodden: some are of middle-class status prior to migration and maintain a middle-class outlook while experiencing downward mobility because of language and cultural barriers; most are employed, often by their coethnics within the enclave; and most live in two-parent households. Many enclave residents regard their current disadvantaged status as temporary and adopt an optimistic attitude and orientation toward upward "making it" in mainstream society. Some of those who have succeeded would aspire to return to the enclave to pursue entrepreneurial opportunities or perform community services, while others would return to patronize various ethnic businesses, social services, and cultural activities. Residents in a typical underclass ghetto, in contrast, are predominantly native-born minorities; many are unemployed; those who are employed tend to work for non-coethnics; and many live in single-parent households. Many ghetto residents are demoralized by societal stigmatization and structural barriers that segregate them from their more successful coethnics and mainstream society, and they adopt a fatalist attitude and respond to their disadvantaged status with defiance and withdrawal (Wilson 1996). Those who have "made it" would never return or look back, leaving the ghetto severely isolated without "tangible role models or instructive agents of social control" (Anderson 1990).

Another marked difference lies in social organization. The enclave is characteristic of high density and multiple levels of coethnic economic and social institutions. Ethnic businesses are diversified ranging from labor-intensive work and low-cost and basic services to knowledge-intensive work and professional services. The enclave economy provides entrepreneurial opportunities for the ambitious and employment opportunities for both the skilled and the unskilled and serves various needs of local residents, suburban middle-class coethnics, and tourists. Civic and voluntary organizations provide tangible supports as well as social control at the local level. The multiple levels of community-based business establishments and organizations consolidate the enclave social structure and functions as a strong stabilizing force for that structure. The underclass ghetto, in contrast, experiences a rapid depletion of coethnic-owned businesses and neighborhood-based civic organizations as the more successful members leave the ghetto. Suburban middle-class coethnics do not aspire to entrepreneurship nor to services in the ghetto (Anderson 1990). Most local businesses are non-coethnic owned, frequently harboring misunderstanding, distrust, and interethnic tension between owners and clients or workers; and they do not tend to have close ties to other neighborhood-based social structures. Of the neighborhood-based organizations, such as churches and social services, that survive, many suffer from work overload and lack funding and personnel.

A third difference lies in the patterns of social relations and networking. In the ethnic enclave, social relations and networking are extensive, transcending class and geographic boundaries. Since the enclave social and economic activities are diverse and coethnics who are involved in the enclave as entrepreneurs, workers, or customers are socioeconomically diverse, social relations and network ties that emerge from enclave participation tend to extend beyond geographic and class boundaries. Even though many ethnic ties may be weak, they function as bridge ties that cut across class, occupation, and generation (Granovetter 1973, Johnston 2000). So enclave residents benefit from these bridge ties that provide access to more advantageous resources facilitating mobility. In the underclass ghetto, social relations are truncated and network closure is constrained by class and race. Because of extreme social isolation and a lack of the types of economic and social organizations that attract coethnics from diverse backgrounds, social ties generated from the ghetto are unlikely to be bridge ties, and the cultural and social capital resources that exist in the ghetto are often barely enough to serve survival needs, much less mobility goals (Fernandez-Kelly 1995).

These neighborhood-level variations can provide clues to what allows a socioeconomically disadvantaged ethnic group to arise from poverty in one generation and how neighborhood-level factors operate to facilitate mobility. When an individual from a poor family is oriented toward upward mobility, the odds are beyond his/her control because his or her family lacks resources to provide support and the neighborhood social environment is not conducive to customary means of social mobility. Also, when poor families are socially isolated from established institutions of the mainstream society, it is extremely difficult for parents to enforce cultural values, work habits, and goal orientations necessary for their children's socioeconomic advancement. In inner-city neighborhoods, many immigrant parents speak little or no English and have little contact with the larger society. They also face the situation where their children have to translate for them and take on parental roles. This role reversal can severely undermine parental authority while also enabling children to mature early (Valenzuela 1999). Thus, the ability of poor families to socialize children in the right direction – i.e., integrating into mainstream middle-class America – is extremely limited.

Thus, what enables immigrant and minority children to withstand the leveling pressures from poor inner-city neighborhoods depends, to a large extent, on how parents can muster resources outside the family. Here, the concept of social capital is most relevant. Glenn Loury has argued that social connections associated with varied class status and human capital give rise to differential access to opportunities (1977). James Coleman has suggested that social capital, defined as closed systems of social networks in a community, would allow parents to "establish norms and reinforce each other's sanctioning of the children" (1988, 1990). Alejandro Portes and J. Sensenbrenner have defined social capital as "expectations for action within a collectivity that affect the economic goals and goal-seeking behavior of its members, even if these expectations are not oriented toward the economic sphere" (1993).

Poor neighborhoods are not poor in social capital in the form of social ties or relations. However, the value of social capital emerging from local social ties, which can facilitate access to resources conducive to mobility, varies from enclaves to ghettos. In neighborhoods with strong social organization, as in the case of ethnic enclaves, residents can benefit from multiple social ties that cut across class to help alleviate the negative effects of social isolation. In contrast, in neighborhoods with weak social organization, as in the case of underclass ghettos, residents may draw on social ties to help with their daily survival, but these local ties tend to be truncated by social isolation and are unlikely to provide resources beyond survival needs.

Thus, in accounting for intergroup differences in mobility outcomes, it is necessary to consider whether a particular ethnicity should be seen as a source of social capital (or as a disadvantage). One way to unpack ethnicity is to examine the density, diversity, and multiplexity of community-based institutions and embedded networks of social relations arising from these local social structures. Next, I zoom in on an ethnic enclave – New York's Chinatown – to illustrate how ethnicity functions to affect mobility outcomes of immigrant offspring. Although my analysis focuses on the case of one Chinatown, I believe that the substantive issues are well beyond the boundaries of a single urban enclave. By focusing on one enclave, however, I hope to develop a conceptual framework for studying inner-city neighborhoods across race/ethnicity.

Understanding ethnicity in an institutional context: the case of Chinatown

Ethnicity emerges from a paradoxical process. On the one hand, it develops in the context of frequent association and interaction with others of common origin and cultural heritage in a community setting. On the other hand, it depends on the interaction of the group with structural conditions that characterize the group's position in American society. This dynamic process leads to common experiences and interests, thereby setting the potential for collective mobilization around shared goals (Zhou and Gatewood 2000). Ultimately, ethnicity is "a manifestation of the way populations are organized in terms of interaction patterns, institutions, personal values, attitudes, lifestyle, and presumed consciousness of kind" – the result of a process that continues to unfold (Yancey, Juliani, and Erikson 1976).

Pre-existing ethnic communities represent the most immediate context for immigrant reception and ethnic identification (Portes and Rumbaut 1990). If ethnic communities are interpreted in terms of social capital, it becomes possible to suggest a mechanism by which the adherence to ethnic systems of support and control can provide an adaptive advantage for coethnic members and their offspring to achieve upward social mobility in American society (Zhou and Bankston 1998). However, this mechanism is never stagnant; it constantly accommodates changes in the larger society, in ethnic organizational structure, and in a group's struggle for survival or the social mobility process of immigration. New York's Chinatown offers an exemplary case for understanding the internal dynamics of an ethnic enclave, in contrast to an urban ghetto. I focus on three specific aspects of the ethnic enclave: group orientation, social organization, and multiplicity of ethnic involvement.

Group orientation: from sojourning to settlement   Individual goals and society treatment affect an ethnic group's orientation toward mainstream society. Earlier Chinese immigrants came to the United States in the hope of making a fortune and returning home with "gold." Many left their families behind in China and were drawn to this community by extensive kinship networks. During the time when legal and institutional exclusion set barriers and American society made available few life options, immigrant Chinese had to isolate themselves socially in Chinatown and to work in odd jobs that few Americans wanted. Since they had no families with them and had no intention of staying a long time, they built Chinatown initially as a place of refuge that resembled home. In old Chinatown, immigrant workers could speak their own language, eat their own food, play their own games, exchange news from home, and share common experiences with fellow countrymen day in and day out.

New York City's Chinatown started as a bachelor society in the late nineteenth century and remained so until the 1940s. During the exclusion era, ethnic institutions arose to meet the sojourning needs of immigrants. The level of coethnic interaction was high, almost entirely through various family, clan or kinship associations, hometown (district or regional) associations, and tongs (merchants' associations) (Kuo 1977, Wong 1979). When Chinese immigrants were oriented to the eventual return to their homeland, ethnic social organizations and patterns of social relationships in Chinatown supported that orientation, and broader structural forces such as legal exclusion also reinforced it.

After World War II, however, the bachelor's society began to dissolve when Chinese women were allowed into the United States to join their husbands and families. The repeal of the Chinese Exclusion Act and the passage of the War Brides Act facilitated the migration of Chinese women. However, it was not until after the enactment of the Immigration Act of 1965 (also referred to as the Hart–Celler Act) that Chinatown itself changed fundamentally. Between 1960 and 1998, the size of the ethnic Chinese population in New York City increased multiple times, from 33,000 to over half a million. Most of the post-1965 Chinese immigrants are family-sponsored immigrants: 75 percent were admitted as immediate family members, and the rest as employer-sponsored immigrants or other types. As immigrant women and children arrive to join their families or immigrate with families, the old Chinatown has undergone a dramatic transformation. Socially, the ethnic enclave has been transformed from a bachelor society to a full-fledged family community. As of 1990, about 80 percent of the Chinese in New York City live in married-couple households and few live in male-headed households. Economically, an enclave economy has been expanded and diversified with the influx of foreign capital, family savings, and human capital. Physically, Chinatown has expanded in all directions beyond its traditional ten-block boundaries, taking over decaying neighborhoods in surrounding areas and giving rise to "satellite" Chinatowns in Queens and Brooklyn (Zhou 1992).

Most significantly, Chinatown has reoriented itself toward integration, aspiring to "make it" in America. Although the majority of Chinatown residents are poor and recent immigrants, many conform to this community orientation, as in the words of a garment worker, "we want to buy a home and move out, and we want our children to get a job in those office buildings down the street [Wall Street]." Chinese immigrants also hold a strong sense of optimism that they can eventually make it through

hard work and perseverance. There is a general consensus on the means
of achieving integration, that is, through the educational achievement
of the second generation. In Chinatown, most immigrant parents firmly
believe that education is the only way out of Chinatown, and the fact that
hard work and education pay off further reinforce this belief. With the
socially mobile coethnics serving as role models, the achievement goal
has credibility and is accepted by the second generation, thus leading to
behavior that supports that goal.

*Social organization: density and diversity of community-based
institutions*   When the ethnic group is oriented toward mainstream society but is constrained by broader structural disadvantages, effective community organizing can mobilize ethnic resources to counter the negative
effects of adversarial conditions. The strength of social organization
can be measured by density and diversity of community-based institutions and establishments. In Chinatown, various densely situated ethnic
economic, civic, and religious organizations create an extensive ethnic
system of support and control for the achievement orientation. Such
a diverse organizational structure produces tangible resources in the
form of employment and self-employment opportunities and family-
oriented and children-oriented services. It also provides a physical site
for coethnics from diverse socioeconomic backgrounds to reconnect to
one another in multiple ways and form social networks that, in turn,
produce both tangible and intangible benefits.

The ethnic organizational structure can be measured by density
and diversity of institutions and establishments within a geographically
bounded area. Prior to World War II, Chinatown was a socially isolated
enclave and a self-governing and self-sustaining community. Residents
sojourning in Chinatown were supported and controlled by their family,
clan, or district associations. They depended heavily on an ethnic economy that was highly concentrated in restaurant and laundry businesses
along with small businesses catering to the basic needs of coethnics. By
the 1970s, the laundry business had shrunk substantially and the garment industry took over as one of Chinatown's backbone industries.
The restaurant business, another backbone industry in Chinatown, has
continued to grow and prosper. In addition, various other businesses
have also experienced tremendous growth, ranging from grocery stores,
import/export companies, barber shops, and beauty salons to such professional services as banks, law firms, financial, insurance, and real estate
agencies, and doctors' and herbalists' clinics. As a striking contrast to
Chinatown's self-sustaining economy in the old days, the economic development today has become highly diversified (Zhou 1992).

While low-wage employment, unskilled labor, sidewalk peddling, and crowding or slum living still characterize the community, upscale redevelopment, in the areas of professional services, highly skilled employment, knowledge-intensive investment, financial and real estate development, transnational businesses, and modern tourism, has become a new defining feature of Chinatown. Although ethnic businesses within the enclave may be short-lived and may last only one generation, they nonetheless form a unique opportunity structure to enable disadvantaged coethnics to gain a foothold in society. Moreover, ethnic businesses allow coethnics to interact with one another and rebuild social ties that were disrupted through the process of migration. Most importantly, an enclave with thriving ethnic businesses can attract suburban middle-class coethnics to return for business or leisure, thus reducing social isolation.

In the past three decades Chinatown has also witnessed a rapid growth of civic and religious institutions. In old Chinatown, family or clan associations and merchants' associations (tongs) used to be the major community-based organizations. The ethnic community was self-governed by the Chinese Consolidated Benevolent Association (CCBA), an apex group representing some sixty different family and district associations, guilds, tongs, the Chamber of Commerce, and the Nationalist Party (Kuo 1977, Sung 1987). These organizations functioned primarily to meet the basic needs of sojourners, such as helping them obtain employment and offering different levels of social support, and organizing economic activities. Powerful tongs controlled most of the economic resources in the community, and some formed underground societies to profit from such illicit activities as partitioning territories, extortion for business protection, gambling, prostitution, and drugs (Dillon 1962, Kuo 1977, Sung 1987). The key function of most traditional organizations was to shield Chinatown from outsiders and preserve the status quo within the community (Kuo 1977).

The drastic demographic change in the nature of Chinese immigration has created pressing demands for services associated with resettlement and adjustment problems that have overwhelmed the existing traditional organizations in Chinatown. To accommodate these changes, traditional organizations have been pressured to redefine their roles as the community's orientation is shifting from sojourning to settlement and assimilation. For example, to appeal to the settlement needs of new immigrants and their families, the CCBA has established a Chinese language school, an adult English evening school, and a career training center, and has instituted a variety of social service programs, including employment referral and job training services. The CCBA-operated New York Chinese School is perhaps the largest children- and youth-oriented organization in

Chinatown. The school annually (not including summers) enrolls about 4,000 Chinese children, from preschool to twelfth grade, in their 137 Chinese language classes and over ten specialty classes (e.g., band, choir, piano, cello, violin, T'ai chi, ikebana, dancing, and Chinese painting). The Chinese language classes run from 3:00 to 6:30 pm daily after regular school hours. Students usually spend one hour on regular school homework and two hours on Chinese language or other selected specialties. The school also has English classes for immigrant youths and adult immigrant workers (Zhou 1997).

Various new service organizations, both nonprofit and for-profit, have also been established in Chinatown. A glance at one Chinese business directory, for example, reveals over 100 voluntary associations, 61 community service organizations, 41 community-based employment agencies, 16 day-care centers, 27 career training schools, 28 Chinese and English language schools, and 9 dance and music schools in New York City in the early 1990s.[2] Most of these organizations are located in Old Chinatown; some are located in new satellite Chinatowns elsewhere in New York City. The Chinese-American Planning Council (CAPC, formerly the Chinatown Planning Council), established in the late 1960s in Chinatown, is one of the most important community-based organizations. Rivaling the CCBA, the CAPC represents an integration agenda. Led by educated second- or 1.5-generation Chinese Americans who are devoted to the community, the CAPC challenges the traditional patriarchal structure and conservative stance of the CCBA through grass-roots class mobilization and the support of federal and local governments and private foundations. The CAPC offers a broader array of services to families and children than the CCBA (though the CCBA Chinese school has a much larger enrollment than the CAPC's). Its aim is to provide "access to services, skills and resources toward the goal of economic self sufficiency and integration into the American mainstream."[3] During the 1970s, the CAPC initiated a number of youth-targeted programs, such as drug prevention, outreach, and recreational programs to help immigrant children and at-risk youths adapt to their new environment. These children- or youth-targeted programs not only offered counseling and opportunities for young people to voice their concerns and problems, but also provided recreational activities, such as renting places where they could read, party, and play pool or video games and furnishing free field trips, shows, and museum visits (Kuo 1977). Most of these programs have continued, expanded, and diversified in the 1990s.

Many smaller civic and voluntary ethnic organizations have also been established to address the concerns and demands of new immigrants and their children. The Chinatown History Museum, now the Museum of

Chinese in the Americas, was established in 1980 primarily as a history project for reclaiming, preserving, and sharing Chinese American history and culture with a broad audience. The member-supported museum offers historical walking tours, lectures, readings, symposia, workshops, and family events year round, not only to Chinese Americans but also to the general public. The museum also provides school programs for grades 1 to 12, guided and self-guided visits for college-level students, and a variety of videotapes, slide presentations, and exhibits.

Ethnic religious institutions have continued to play an important role in helping immigrants adjust to life in the United States. Although Chinese immigrants are mostly nonreligious, many initially affiliate with religious institutions for practical support and later are converted through intense participation. In the larger Chinese community in New York City, the number of churches and temples has doubled since 1965 including over eighty Christian churches and eighteen Buddhist and Taoist temples; about three-quarters are located in Manhattan's Chinatown. While Buddhist and Taoist temples tend to attract adults, including some college students and the elderly, Christian churches generally have well-established after-school youth programs, in addition to their regular Sunday Bible classes.

Civic and religious organizations are particularly beneficial to immigrant families and their children. Interviews with community leaders, organizers, and activists indicate that the functions of new community organizations specific to the younger generation are manifold. Instrumentally, community-based organizations provide a safe, healthy, and stimulating environment where youngsters, especially those whose parents are at work, can go after school. For example, Chinese schools and various after-school programs not only ensure that time is spent on homework or on other constructive activities, but also help to keep children off the streets and to reduce the anxieties and worries of working parents. More importantly, these organizations provide some space where children can express and share their feelings. A Chinese school teacher said, "It is very important to allow youths to express themselves in their own terms without parental pressures. Chinese parents usually have very high expectations of their children. When children find it difficult to meet these expectations and do not have an outlet for their frustration and anxiety, they tend to become alienated and lost on the streets."

Community-based civic and religious organizations also serve as a bridge between a closed immigrant community and mainstream society. Immigrant children and youths growing up in Chinatown are relatively isolated. Their parents, usually too busy working to put food on the table, tend to expect their children to do well in school and to have successful careers in the future but are unable to give specific directions to their children's educational and career plans, leaving a gap between high expectations and realistically feasible means of meeting these expectations. Community-based civic organizations fill this gap to help young people to become more aware of their choices and potentials and to help them find realistic means of moving up socioeconomically into mainstream society instead of being stuck in Chinatown. After-school programs, tutor services, and test preparation programs are readily available in the enclave, making school after school possible and an accepted norm. An educator said, "when you think of how much time these Chinese kids put in their studies after regular school, you won't be surprised why they succeed at such a high rate."

Culturally, community-based organizations function as ethnic centers, where Chinese traditional values and a sense of ethnic identity are nurtured. Students participating in after-school programs, especially the US-born and reared, often speak English to one another in their Chinese classes, and they actually learn a limited number of Chinese words each day. However, they are exposed to something which is quite different from what they learn in school and are able to relate to Chinese "stuff" without being teased about it. They also listen to stories and sing songs in Chinese, which reveal different aspects of Chinese history and culture, and learn classical Chinese poems and Confucian sayings about family values, behavioral and moral guidelines, and the importance of schooling. A Chinese school principal made it clear that "these kids are here because their parents sent them. They are usually not very motivated in learning Chinese per se, and we do not push them too hard. Language teaching is only part of our mission. An essential part of our mission is to enlighten these kids about their own cultural heritage, so that they show respect for their parents and feel proud of being Chinese." Like ethnic businesses, civic organizations also attract suburban middle-class Chinese immigrants to return to the enclave regularly, even though some may do so less frequently than others. The day-to-day interaction between members of the middle class and those of the working class occurs in various community-based businesses and organizations.

The growth and diversification of the ethnic economy and community-based ethnic institutions furnishes a protective social environment and a cultural core, effectively preventing the ethnic enclave from the ghettoization that has affected many inner-city neighborhoods. Even though the suburbanization of the affluent is an ongoing process and residents left behind are disproportionately poor, Chinatown gives reasons for the affluent coethnics to come back on a regular basis – to do business, to shop, to entertain, and to attend religious or cultural activities, and to send their children to learn an ancestral language and culture. It also provides a wide range of entrepreneurial and employment opportunities as well as culturally specific goods and services for both enclave residents and suburban coethnics (Zhou 1992). However, there are social costs attached to the benefits offered by the current organizational structure. The ethnic community reinforces the traditional patriarchy and privileges the elite, while exacerbating intraethnic conflicts and working-class disadvantages (Kwong 1997, Lin 1998). It also requires obligations that may constrain individual drive at certain points of the mobility path.

Multiplicity of ethnic involvement   Given its extensive social structures and the wide variety of economic, social, and cultural activities, ethnic involvement in the enclave is likely to be multiple and intertwining. For example, an enclave resident may be simultaneously a worker in an ethnic business, a patron of an ethnic shop, a member of a family association or a temple/church or a civil organization, to which his/her employer, co-workers, friends, or neighbors belong. The interacting individuals are likely to be heterogeneous in socioeconomic status and the social ties that are reestablished are likely to be coethnic but cut across class lines. These patterns of ethnic interaction function to reinforce common values and norms, strengthen common bonds, and create new mechanisms for sanctioning nonconformity while also facilitating the flow of information about mobility opportunities and strategies between middle-class coethnics and working-class residents.[4]

The experience of immigrant women in Chinatown's garment industry is illustrative of the ways in which multiple involvements in the ethnic community provide intangible resources that channel socioeconomically disadvantaged coethnic members out of the poverty trap. Chinatown's garment industry is dominated by immigrant women. Most of these women have little English and few job skills, are married with small children, and come from low-income families. Juggling paid work and household responsibilities defines their life which seems quite isolated. However, many find working in Chinatown a better option despite low wages, because the enclave enables them to fulfill their multiple roles more effectively as wage earners, wives, and mothers. In Chinatown, jobs are easier to find, working hours are more flexible, employers are more tolerant of the presence of children, and private child-care within close walking distance from work is more accessible and affordable. Convenient grocery shopping and the availability of various takeout foods also make dinner preparation easier. More importantly, women are able to socialize at work with other coethnic women, who come from similar cultural backgrounds, experiencing similar hardships, sharing similar goals and concerns about the family, child-rearing, and mobility. By the sewing machine, immigrant women can spread gossips, complain about insensitive husbands, disobedient children, and nagging relatives back in the homeland, share coping strategies, brag about children's or family's achievements, and comfort each other over problems.

So working in the garment industry gives immigrant women an indispensable source of income. Interaction with co-workers at work becomes an important source of emotional support and psychological comfort as well as a source of pressure to conform. But these women are not as isolated as one would expect since they are involved in other activities in the community at the same time. They would shop, send their children to after-school programs or Chinese language schools, visit a church or temple, attend social events of families and friends (e.g., birthday dinners, weddings, funerals), and participate in activities in various community-based organizations. They are also able to develop a more personable relationship with their coethnic employers than they would with non-coethnic employers. Moreover, they are able to read newspapers, listen to the radio, and watch TV programs, all in Chinese (Zhou and Cai 2002). This multiple involvement gives them the opportunity to extend their social network beyond their working-class status. Through these various contacts and exposure, the garment workers become better informed about what is going on around them and others. For instance, many mothers who work by sewing machines all day long not only know about the names of the best public high schools but also some of the students who attend these schools and their parents. They usually do not have co-workers or neighbors who are middle-class professionals, but they often meet these middle-class coethnics at church or temple or in Chinese schools on a regular basis and establish weak ties to be called upon when in need. Thus, intense involvement in the ethnic community – at work and in different community-based institutions – reduces isolation and reinforces community-prescribed goals of integration.

Social networks, embedded in the enclave, function to reinforce common norms and standards and exercise control over those who are connected to it. A tofu and noodle factory worker in Chinatown, who used to be a college professor before immigration, talked about this network sanctioning effect, "In the beginning, I felt very, very bad to work in this factory, it hurt my ego. But I didn't really have a choice for not working. Here people don't seem to care about what you were before because everybody is on the same starting point here whether you were a peasant or an intellectual. But they will certainly point their fingers at you if you are not working because you think you are worth more." A restaurant worker explained this community pressure from a different approach:

America is a free society, and nobody forces you to do anything. But when the guy arriving here at the same time as you and working side by side with you quits to open up his own business, or buys a house somewhere else, that makes you feel several inches shorter. When people around you mention this guy's success, you fear that they are talking about you, like a loser.

Parents who are tied to the network also feel the pressure of pushing their children to succeed. Immigrant mothers, most of whom work long hours in garment shops or other ethnic businesses in Chinatown, are very aware which public high school is the best in the city. Each year many Chinese elementary school graduates are getting into prestigious magnet public high schools, such as Hunter College High School, Stuyvesant High School, and the Bronx High School of Science. This information is circulated among mothers working in the same factory, or through parents who send their children to the same after-school programs. So going to Hunter, or Stuyvesant High, or Bronx High becomes a standard, and the mother would go home and tell her children to prepare for that school. "My mother used to scold me and called me a dummy because I couldn't get into Hunter. She didn't have a clue how hard it was to get in these elite schools," said a college freshman who grew up in Chinatown. A community organizer explained,

the pressure comes from the mothers and from those whom their mothers work with. When a mother hears that other mothers are sending their sons or daughters to the Hunter College High School, or to the Stuyvesant High School, or to the Bronx High School of Science, she would naturally think, "Why shouldn't my son [daughter] go to that school?" It's the peer pressure of the parents.

Children who are tied to ethnic networks endure the pressure for achieving most directly. Most children in Chinatown live in two-parent, nuclear families, and some in families with grandparents or other relatives. They are taught to conform to Confucian values of the family, education, hard work, discipline, and face-saving, which have been transplanted with minimum modifications and have become the normative behavioral standard in Chinese-American families. They are expected to attain the highest level of achievement possible, and they know that their parents rely on them to move the family up to middle-class status. Deviation from these values, standards, and expectations is considered shameful or "losing face" and thus sanctioned by the family.

It is not easy, however, for immigrant families to enforce these values and behavioral standards and guarantee that familial expectations are met because of vulnerabilities and the intense bicultural conflicts facing these families. In Chinatown, immigrant families are extremely vulnerable to problems associated with low social class status. Most parents work in restaurants, garment factories, and other low-wage, low-skilled jobs.

Two-thirds of the garment workers and over half of restaurant workers do not have any education beyond elementary school and speak very little English. Out of economic necessity in most immigrant Chinese families both parents work. Working parents, particularly those at low-wage jobs, tend to work long hours each day, six or seven days a week, and sometimes on different shifts. Although parents are very concerned about their children's schooling and well-being, they have very little time, very little energy, and very little human capital to be directly involved, to help their children with their homework, much less to talk with them or play with them. Moreover, most of the parents have to depend upon their children to translate, review household bills, manage all communication with the English-speaking world, and even read report cards sent from school. Such role reversal can undermine parental authority. Chinatown's immigrant families, especially those with pre-teen and adolescent children, are also vulnerable to the problem of street gangs. In Chinatown, gangs were formed for the same reasons as other gangs in Little Italy, Little Saigon, Mexican American *barrios*, or South Central Los Angeles (Kuo 1977, Sung 1987, Vigil 1990, Vigil and Yun 1990). Gang recruits are typically those immigrant youth who have severe adjustment problems, such as poor English language proficiency, difficulties relating to schoolwork, and a lack of a sense of belonging at home.

Children, especially pre-teen and adolescent new arrivals, also encounter a lot of adjustment problems in school. Because of linguistic and cultural difficulties, many newly arrived children are unable to express themselves and are thus misunderstood by teachers and fellow students; they are frequently teased, mocked, or harassed by other students because of their different looks, accent, and dress; and they are reluctant to bring these problems up at the dinner table for fear that their parents will get upset or blame them. When their problems are not addressed, children become discouraged; and discouragement is sometimes followed by a loss of interest, plunging grades, eventually dropping out of school and joining gangs. These problems are summed up in a community organizer's remark:

It is sometimes easier to be a gangster. These kids were generally considered "losers" by their teachers, parents, and peers in school. In school or at home, they feel uncomfortable, isolated, and rejected, which fosters a sense of hopelessness and powerlessness and a yearning for recognition. In the streets, they feel free from all the normative pressures. It is out there that they feel free to be themselves and to do things wherever and whenever they want, giving them a sort of identity and a sense of power.

Parents and children also face intense bicultural conflicts, which emerge from culturally distinct ways of raising children. First, immigrant Chinese parents tend to believe that discipline and hard work, rather than natural ability or innate intelligence, are the keys to educational success. They tend to think (and also tend to make their children believe) that their children can all get As in their tests in school if they just work hard and practice self-discipline. Second, immigrant Chinese parents tend to de-emphasize the American values of individualism and personal freedom and are expected to bring up their children in ways that honor the family. Since children's success in school is very much tied to face-saving for the family, parents consistently remind their children that achievement is a duty and an obligation to the family rather than to an individual goal and that if they fail, they will bring shame to the family. Third, immigrant Chinese parents tend to emphasize submission to authority – the parent is the authority in the home, as is the teacher in the school, and seldom treat their children as equals and friends. Fourth, immigrant Chinese parents also rely on the value of thrift as an important means of achieving future goals. Parents often bluntly reject material possessions and conspicuous consumption on the part of children and perceive spending money on name brand clothes, luxurious accessories, and fashionable hairstyles as a sign of corruption, which they often term as becoming "too American" (code word "bad"). However, these parents seldom hesitate spending on whatever they consider good for their children, such as books and computer software, after-school programs, Chinese lessons, private tutors, private lessons on the violin or the piano, and other educational-oriented activities. They do not just do it in the best interest of their children but are also driven by the mentality of "turning sons into dragons" (and daughters into phoenixes).

Family vulnerabilities and intense bicultural conflicts, coupled with American popular culture that glorifies self-indulgence and youth rebellion, severely circumvent the role of the family in socializing children in the expected direction. Immigrant families living in isolation may find it hard to instill proper values and expectations in children. However, when the ethnic community in which families are embedded also insists on consistent values, standards, and expectations and is organized in such a way that it offers support and control, these families are in a better position to guide their children.

In Chinatown, families and children are tied to one another through community-based institutions. While adults are involved in the community in many respects besides work, children are also involved quite extensively besides school, most commonly being in various after-school programs, family gatherings, and holiday celebrations in the ethnic enclave where they meet other coethnic adults and children. For example, to obey and to respect elders are some of the core cultural precepts in Chinese families. Relatives or adult family friends often greet children with, "Have you been obeying your parents?" or "Have you been good?" If a youngster shows disobedient and disrespectful conduct, he/she is considered without *gui-ju* or *jia-jiao* and *li-mao* (discipline or family principles and manners), and his/her parents may be blamed for bad parenting. So in the ethnic enclave where behavioral standards are enforced through everyday interaction, children tend to conform either willingly or as a way to avoid public disapproval and embarrassment.

Similarly, the pressure for academic achievement comes not only from within the family but also from the ethnic community. Again, in everyday conversation with children in the homes, streets, and restaurants in Chinatown, adults would frequently greet children in Chinese with, "How was school?" "Did you behave in school today?" "Did you do your homework?" "Have you got your grades yet? Are they any good?" or "An A-minus? How come you didn't get an A-plus?" Children are expected to give positive answers to these simple everyday adult-to-child greetings. Also, young people who receive good grades and awards in school, win academic competitions, and gain admissions to ivy league colleges are honored in Chinese language newspapers and TV programs and civic organizations. Owing to high levels of participation and interaction in the ethnic enclave, Chinatown's children generally develop a heightened sense of "Chineseness" and act upon this identity based on community approved values, standards, and expectations. Even though many children would much rather shed this Chineseness, they have fewer options to do so than their more fortunate peers who live in middle-class suburbs, because they are surrounded by so many "watchful" eyes and by a social environment where consistent signals are sent through not just parents, but also relatives, neighbors, business owners, and community organizers.

However, the ethnic effect is by no means uniform. Tremendous pressures for achieving both on parents and on children can lead to even more intense intergenerational conflict, rebellious behavior, withdrawal from school, and alienation from the networks that are supposed to help. Alienated children fall easy prey to street gangs. Even those children who do well in school and hope to make their parents happy and proud are at risk of being rebellious. A high school student said, "But that [doing well to make parents happy] never happens. My mother is never satisfied no matter what you do and how well you do it." This remark echoes a frustration felt by many other Chinatown youths who voiced how much they wish not to be compared with other children and how much they wish to rebel. Ironically, pressures and conflicts in a well-integrated ethnic community can serve to fulfill familial and community expectations.

Children are motivated to learn and do well in school because they believe that education is their only way to get out of their parents' status and out of their parents' control. This motivation, while arising from parental pressure and being reinforced through their participation in the ethnic community, often leads to desirable outcomes. A community youth program organizer summed up in these words:

Well, tremendous pressures create problems for sure. However, you've got to realize that we are not living in an ideal environment. Without these pressures, you would probably see as much adolescent rebellion in the family, but a much *larger* [emphasis in tone] proportions of kids failing. Our goal is to get these kids out into college, and for that, we have been very successful.

However, the utility of this form of ethnic social support and control mechanism can be effective only to a certain point. Once it gets beyond that point, this mechanism can become a pulling-back force. For example, the community and the family pressurize children to graduate from high school and go on to college and succeed in doing so. But beyond high school, the social capital available in the community is not sufficient to help children choose academic and career paths that are right for them. When applying for college, many Chinatown children are forced to choose the ones close to home. At college, they tend to concentrate in science and engineering because their families want them to do so and their friends are doing so. When graduating from college, they often lack the type of networks that facilitate their job placement and occupational mobility.

Conclusion

I have presented the case of New York's Chinatown to illustrate how cultural and structural factors interact to affect mobility. Even though Chinatown is beset by many structural disadvantages associated with poverty which are compounded by low-wage work and intense bicultural conflicts, Chinatown's families are experiencing upward social mobility within a generation. Many immigrants are able to attain homeownership and move out of Chinatown. Their children are generally adapting well and are indeed doing much better academically, in terms of GPAs (Grade Point Averages), high school graduation, and college attendance, than their American counterparts attending the same schools, and they are expected to enter mainstream labor markets rather than return to the enclave upon completion of their college education. What accounts for this success? How it is possible that immigrants and their children withstand the adversarial conditions of the inner city? How do families ensure that their children live up to their expectations?

   In the Chinese immigrant enclave, setting the goal of eventual integration into mainstream American society is only the first step and realizing this goal requires tremendous community support particularly among those who lack human capital and economic resources. Since the 1970s, Chinatown has transformed itself to meet the settlement needs of new immigrants, establishing various economic, civic, and religious organizations to provide jobs, job referral services, career training, language learning facilities, child-care, after-school programs, family counseling, and various youth-oriented crisis-prevention and rehabilitation programs. Involvement in these various ethnic institutions binds families and individuals to an interlocking network of ethnic relations. These ties have directly or indirectly broadened the base of ethnic interaction and thus increased the degree of ethnic cohesion, which in turn sustains a sense of identity, community, and ethnic solidarity. Because many parents and children are involved, in one way or another, in these intense networks in the ethnic enclave, it becomes possible for the community to reinforce norms and to promote a high level of communication among group members and a high level of consistency among standards. In this sense, the community, as an important source of social capital, not only makes resources available to parents and children, but serves to direct children's behavior. The density and diversity of Chinatown's economic, social, and cultural institutions provide tangible resources that help disadvantaged Chinese immigrants and their families cope with settlement hardships, poverty, and inner-city social problems, while fostering a sense of origin, orientation, purpose, and identity. Equally important, involvement in the ethnic enclave helps immigrants rebuild social ties that may be defined as weak ties but nonetheless serve as bridge ties to counter the negative impacts of social isolation and ghettoization. While this type of social capital helps immigrant families and their children to overcome intense adjustment difficulties and unfavorable conditions, such as linguistic and social isolation, bicultural conflicts, poverty, gang subculture, and close proximity to other underprivileged minority neighborhoods, its value is tied to an ethnic context. Once moving beyond Chinatown, this form of social capital can lose its utility. Among those who are successfully integrated into the mainstream society, the ethnic ties may become more symbolic than instrumental. Nonetheless, the fact that these upwardly mobile coethnics continue to return to Chinatown indicates that ethnic ties embedded in Chinatown cut across class and geographic boundaries. Thus, social capital should be treated as "a process," rather than as a concrete object, facilitating access to benefits and resources that best suit the goals of specific immigrant groups (Loury 1977, Fernandez-Kelly 1995).

Chinatown may be a unique case. It nonetheless provides evidence in support of an institutional approach to ethnicity that takes into account both structural and cultural factors in explaining intergroup differences in mobility outcomes. Although the Chinatown case is undoubtedly limited in its generalizability, it is beginning to suggest that cultural patterns – community orientation, ethnic organizational structure, and multiplicity of ethnic involvement – are not intrinsic to a particular group. Rather these patterns arise from a group's adaptation to society, which is largely determined by immigrant history, class backgrounds of immigrants, and societal reception. Since these cultural patterns not only interact with the various levels of social structures within the ethnic community but also in larger society, further study is necessary to delve in greater detail into how the broader ethnic stratification system affects social capital formation.

NOTES

The author thanks Gerald Jaynes, Nazli Kibria, Roger Waldinger, and the editors for their helpful comments.
1. The case study of Chinatown presented in this chapter draws primarily on findings from Zhou (1997). I conducted this study in selected homes, streets, community-based organizations, ethnic businesses, and garment factories in Chinatown during the months of September and October in 1994. Chinese and English were used in face-to-face or telephone interviews. I also made numerous field observations with the help of a group of high school students in Chinatown. All quotes are anonymous.
2. Chinatown Today Publishing 1993. Note: The actual number of community organizations in Chinatown was approximately twice as many as this list because many were not listed in this particular directory.
3. Chinese-American Planning Council (CAPC), 1993.
4. The development of the enclave economy is of course full of cut-throat competition and intense internal conflicts, making the sanctioning of nonconformity one of the key functions of ethnic economic institutions. Whether this function is effective or not, however, is the topic of another paper.

REFERENCES

Alba, R. D., 1985, *Italian Americans: Into the Twilight of Ethnicity*, Englewood Cliffs, NJ: Prentice-Hall.
Anderson, E., 1990, *Streetwise: Race, Class, and Change in an Urban Community*, University of Chicago Press.
Chavez, L., 1989, "Tequila Sunrise: The Slow but Steady Progress of Hispanic Immigrants," *Policy Review* 1989: 64–7.
Chinatown Today Publishing, 1993, *Chinese-American Life Guide*, Hong Kong: Chinatown Today Publishing.

Cheng, L. and P. Q. Yang, 1996, "Asians: The 'Model Minority' Deconstructed,"
    in R. Waldinger, and M. Bozorgmehr (eds.), *Ethnic Los Angeles*, New York:
    Russell Sage Foundation, pp. 305–44.
Chinese-American Planning Council (CPC), 1993, *Chinese-American Planning
    Council: Program List*, New York: CPC.
Chiswick, B. R., 1977, "Sons of Immigrants: Are They at an Earnings
    Disadvantage?" *American Economic Review* 67: 376–80.
Coleman, J. S., 1988, "Social Capital in the Creation of Human Capital," *Amer-
    ican Journal of Sociology* 94: 95–120.
Coleman, J. S., 1990, *Foundations of Social Theory*, Cambridge, MA: Belknap
    Press.
Dillon, R. H., 1962, *The Hatchetmen: Tong Wars in San Francisco*, New York:
    Coward McCann.
Fernandez-Kelly, M. P., 1995, "Social and Cultural Capital in the Urban Ghetto:
    Implications for the Economic Sociology and Immigration," in A. Portes
    (ed.), *The Economic Sociology of Immigration: Essays on Networks, Ethnicity,
    and Entrepreneurship*, New York: Russell Sage Foundation, pp. 213–47.
Fordham, S., 1996, *Blacked Out*, University of Chicago Press.
Fukuyama, F., 1993, "Immigrants and Family Values," *Commentary*: 26–32.
Gans, H. J., 1992, "Second Generation Decline: Scenarios for the Economic
    and Ethnic Futures of Post-1965 American Immigrants," *Ethnic and Racial
    Studies* 15: 173–92.
Goldscheider, C. and A. S. Zuckerman, 1984, *The Transformation of the Jews*,
    University of Chicago Press.
Gordon, M., 1964, *Assimilation in American Life: The Role of Race, Religion, and
    National Origins*, New York: Oxford University Press.
Granovetter, M., 1973, "The Strength of Weak Ties," *American Journal of Soci-
    ology* 78: 1360–80.
Greeley, A. M., 1976, "The Ethnic Miracle," *The Public Interest* 45: 20–36.
Hao, L. and M. Bonstead-Bruns, 1998, "Parent-Child Differences in Educational
    Expectations and the Academic Achievement of Immigrant and Native Stu-
    dents," *Sociology of Education* 71: 175–98.
Hirschman, C. and M. G. Wong, 1984, "Socioeconomic Gains of Asian Ameri-
    cans, Blacks, and Hispanics: 1960–1976," *American Journal of Sociology* 90:
    584–607.
Johnston, M. F., 2000, "Bridge Ties: Weak Ties as a Proxy and Gender as a
    Confounder," unpublished manuscript, Department of Sociology, UCLA.
Kirschenman, J. and K. M. Neckerman, 1991, " 'We'd love to hire them,
    but. . . .': the meaning of race for employers," in C. Jencks and P. E.
    Peterson (eds.), *The Urban Underclass*, Washington, DC: Brookings Insti-
    tution, pp. 203–43.
Kohl, H., 1994, *"I Won't Learn from You" and Other Thoughts on Creative Malad-
    justment*, New York: New Press.
Kuo, Chia-Ling, 1977, *Social and Political Change in New York's Chinatown: The
    Role of Voluntary Associations*, New York: Praeger.
Kwong P., 1997, *Forbidden Workers: Illegal Chinese Immigrants and American Labor*,
    New York: New Press.

Landale, N. S. and R. S. Oropesa, 1995, "Immigrant Children and the Children of Immigrants: Inter- and Intra-Group Differences in the United States," Research Paper #95-02, Population Research Group, Michigan State University.

Lewis, O., 1966, "The Culture of Poverty," *Scientific America*: 19–25.

Lin, J., 1998, *Reconstructing Chinatown: Ethnic Enclave, Global Change*, Minneapolis: University of Minnesota Press.

Loury, Glenn, 1977, "A Dynamic Theory of Racial Income Differences," in P. A. Wallace and A. Le Mund (eds.), *Women, Minorities, and Employment Discrimination*, Lexington, MA: Lexington Books.

Massey, D. S. and N. A. Denton, 1987, "Trends in Residential Segregation of Black, Hispanics, and Asians: 1970–1980," *American Sociological Review* 52: 802–25.

Perlmann, J., 1988, *Ethnic Differences: Schooling and Social Structure among the Irish, Jews, and Blacks in an American City, 1988–1935*, New York: Cambridge University Press.

Portes, A. and R. G. Rumbaut, 1990, *Immigrant America*, Berkeley, CA: University of California Press.

Portes, A. and D. MacLeod, 1996, "The Educational Progress of Children of Immigrants: The Roles of Class, Ethnicity, and School Context," *Sociology of Education* 69: 255–75.

Portes, A. and J. Sensenbrenner, 1993, "Embeddedness and Immigration: Notes on the Social Determinants of Economic Action," *American Journal of Sociology* 98: 1320–50.

Portes, A. and M. Zhou, 1993, "The New Second Generation: Segmented Assimilation and Its Variants among Post-1965 Immigrant Youth," *Annals of the American Academy of Political and Social Science* 530: 74–98.

Rumbaut, R. G., 1995, "The New Californians: Comparative Research Findings on the Educational Progress of Immigrant Children," in R. G. Rumbaut and W. A. Cornelius (eds.), *California's Immigrant Children: Theory, Research, and Implications for Educational Policy*, La Jolla, CA: Center for US-Mexican Studies, University of California, San Diego, pp. 17–69.

Sandberg N. C., 1974, *Ethnic Identity and Assimilation: The Polish-American Community*, New York: Praeger.

Sewell, T., 1981, *Ethnic America: A History*, New York: Basic Books.

Stanley, S. and S. Okazaki, 1990, "Asian-American Educational Achievement: A Phenomenon in Search of an Explanation," *American Psychologist* 45: 913–20.

Steinberg, L., 1996, *Beyond the Classroom: Why School Reform Has Failed and What Parents Need to Do*, New York: Simon and Schuster.

Steinberg, S., 1981, *The Ethnic Myth: Race, Ethnicity, and Class in America*, Boston: Beacon Press.

Sung, B. L., 1987, *The Adjustment Experience of Chinese Immigrant Children in New York City*, New York: Center for Migration Studies.

Thernstrom, S., 1973, *The Other Bostonians*, Cambridge, MA: Harvard University Press.

Valenzuela, A., 1999, "Gender Roles and Settlement Activities among Children and Their Immigrant Families," *American Behavioral Scientists* 42: 720–42.

Vernez, G. and A. Abrahamse, 1996, "How Immigrants Fare in US Education," RAND: Institute for Education and Training, Center for Research on Immigrant Policy.

Vigil, J. D., 1990, "Gangs, Social Control, and Ethnicity: Ways to Redirect," in S. B. Heath, and M. W. McLaughlin (eds.), *Identity and Inner-City Youth: Beyond Ethnicity and Gender*, New York: Teachers College Press, pp. 94–119.

Vigil, J. D. and S. Yun, 1990, "Vietnamese Youth Gangs in Southern California," in R. Huff (ed.), *Gangs in America: Diffusion, Diversity, and Public Policy*, Thousand Oaks, CA: Sage, pp. 146–62.

Waldinger, R. 1996, *Still the Promised City? African-Americans and New Immigrants in Postindustrial New York*, Cambridge, MA: Harvard University Press.

Wilson W. J., 1978, *The Declining Significance of Race: Blacks and Changing American Institutions*, University of Chicago Press.

1987, *The Truly Disadvantaged: The Inner City, the Underclass, and Public Policy*, University of Chicago Press.

1996, *When Work Disappears: The World of the New Urban Poor*, New York: Vintage Books.

Wong, B. P., 1979, *A Chinese American Community: Ethnicity and Survival Strategies*, Singapore: Chopmen Enterprise.

Wytrwal, J. A., 1961, *America's Polish Heritage: A Social History of Poles in America*, Detroit: Endurance Press.

Yancey, W., Juliani, R., and E. Erikson, 1976, "Emergent Ethnicity: A Review and Reformulation," *American Sociological Review* 41: 391–403.

Zhou, M., 1992, *Chinatown: The Socioeconomic Potential of an Urban Enclave*, Philadelphia: Temple University Press.

1997, "Social Capital in Chinatown: The Role of Community-based Organizations and Families in the Adaptation of the Younger Generation," in L. Weis and M. S. Seller (eds.), *Beyond Black and White: New Voices, New Faces in the United States Schools*, Albany, NY: State University of New York Press, pp. 181–206.

Zhou, M., 2001, "Second-Generation Prospects: Progress, Decline, Stagnation?" in R. Waldinger (ed.), *Strangers at the Gate: New Immigrant in Urban America*, Berkeley, CA: University of California Press, pp. 272–307.

Zhou, M. and C. L. Bankston, 1998, *Growing Up American: How Vietnamese Children Adapt to Life in the United States*, New York: Russell Sage Foundation.

Zhou, M. and J. V. Gatewood, 2000, "Introduction: Revisiting Contemporary Asian America," in M. Zhou and J. V. Gatewood (eds.), *Contemporary Asian America: A Multidisciplinary Reader*, New York: New York University Press, pp. 1–46.

Zhou, M. and G. Cai, 2002, "The Chinese Language Media in the United States: Immigration and Assimilation in American Life," *Qualitative Sociology* 25, 3: 419–40.

5 Intergenerational mobility and racial inequality in education and earnings

Linda Datcher Loury

1 Introduction

Most analyses of group differences in earnings examine a cross-section of the population in a given year or compare across two or more different years. A full understanding of the relative standing of racial or other groups requires, however, an analysis of the size and determinants of intergenerational mobility. If an individual's position in the distribution of earnings is determined largely by that of his parents, then the ability of disadvantaged groups to alter their economic status over time will be hampered. In addition, uncovering the causes of intergenerational mobility is necessary to determine to what extent the distribution of society's resources is fair and to find out which policies are most likely to change the circumstances of those at the bottom. In order to address these issues, this paper first discusses the overall level of intergenerational mobility in years of schooling and income. It then outlines factors that either magnify or reduce the effects for African-Americans and ethnic groups in the United States.

The theoretical economics literature examining the effects of family of origin on children's outcomes states that children's earnings and income depend on investment in human capital (as measured, for example, by years of schooling). The amount of that investment depends, in part, on children's endowed capacities and, in part, on parents' earnings and the quantity and quality of other nonpecuniary resources. Literature in sociology and psychology specifies in more detail the exact nature of these nonpecuniary resources. A variety of different models are offered. Three of the most common categories include (1) socialization models that focus on the importance of adults and peers in determining behavioral norms and aspirations, (2) family stress models which emphasize the role of negative events (such as divorce), and (3) developmental models that examine the timing of events in the individual's life and the context in which the events occur.

In addition to the hypothesized effects of the family of origin, Jencks and Mayer (1990) list possible ways to account for observed effects of neighborhoods on children's outcomes. These include (1) conformity models that center on the importance of peers, (2) collective socialization models which emphasize the roles of neighborhood adults outside the family, (3) institutional models which focus on schools, the police force, and other neighborhood institutions, (4) relative deprivation models which posit that disadvantaged individuals will do less well in affluent neighborhoods because of poorer relative performance, and (5) competition models where affluent neighbors more effectively compete for scarce resources than their disadvantaged counterparts.

Subject to the qualifications mentioned below, the main findings of this paper are as follows:

1) Overall, background characteristics explain at least 50 percent of the inequality in years of schooling for men and 40 percent for women. Family background factors account for most of this variation. Less than 10 of the 50 percent total for men results from differences in neighborhoods of origin.

2) Overall, background characteristics explain about 40 percent of inequality in earnings for men and about 30 percent for women. Sixteen of the 40 percent of inequality in earnings for men resulting from background is due to family income. Variation in the neighborhood of origin accounts for much less of this variation than in the case of schooling. The sources of the neighborhood effects differ across studies. In addition, some evidence suggests the neighborhood effects result from the degree of urbanicity rather than differences across neighborhoods in a given location.

3) Family income influences children's income more than it does children's schooling. A 10 percent increase in family income would increase years of schooling by no more than one percent. The same change would raise children's incomes by about 4 percent.

4) Parents' education is more highly correlated with children's education than it is with children's income. Father's schooling generally had no effect on children's income independent of family income. The results for mother's schooling were more mixed. Even in cases where the effect was positive, it was often limited to daughters. In contrast, each additional year of schooling for at least one parent (studies varied on whether it was the father or the mother) raised both sons' and daughters' years of education by 0.2 years. The remaining parent contributed an effect about 1/2 to 2/3 as large.

5) Beside parents' schooling and father's income, number of siblings and family structure are the two most widely analyzed family

background characteristics. While these had no effect on children's income, each additional sibling reduced children's schooling by as much as one year less of mother's or father's schooling. Furthermore, living in single-parent and stepfamilies was correlated with lower children's schooling across almost all studies. The effects appear to be larger for sons than for daughters.

6) While other family background characteristics have no effect on children's earnings, a wide variety of parental attitudes and behavior alter children's schooling outcomes. These include parental practices (as measured by education aspirations, mothers and fathers monitoring school work, and general supervision), the time mothers spend with children, and educational resources as measured by whether there is a specific place to study in the home, whether there are reference books, a daily newspaper, or a dictionary/encyclopedia in the home.

7) Background effects for African-Americans differ from whites in a variety of ways. The effects on father's education on children's schooling are smaller for African-Americans than for whites even after controlling for number of years in a single-parent household. In contrast, family income effects on children's earnings are larger. Community background effects may be larger for African-Americans than for whites because of negative effects of residential segregation and concentration in urban areas with extreme poverty.

8) There are large differences in education and earnings by ethnicity that, in part, reflect differences in family background characteristics. The size of family background effects varies by ethnic group.

9) Initially it appears that there are effects of ethnicity independent of family background. However, most of these differences actually result from variations in the characteristics of the neighborhoods in which children grow up. Ethnic effects persist only in the case of those who grow up in ethnically segregated communities.

10) All correlations between background and children's outcomes should be viewed with caution. A variety of problems, among which are simultaneity, omitted variables, selection bias, and measurement error, may generate over- and underestimates of the true causal relationships.

2   Overall effects of measured background characteristics

A.   *Children's years of schooling*

The literature examining the effects of parents' education shows that each additional year of parents' schooling adds between 0.1 and 0.2 years to both son's and daughter's schooling. Mother's schooling generally has a larger effect for daughters than for sons (Behrman and Taubman 1985, 1986, and Teachman 1987). In some cases, the effects of mother's schooling are higher than father's schooling for both sons and daughters (Hill and Duncan 1987, Datcher-Loury 1988, Krein and Beller 1988 and Kuo and Hauser 1995). Looking in more detail, parents' education both reduces high-schooling dropout rates (Brooks-Gunn et al. 1993 and Kane 1994) and increases post-secondary schooling (Kane 1994 and Behrman, Rosenzweig, and Taubman 1994).

Economic resources available to offspring as measured by family income (Haveman and Wolfe 1994) or parents' occupation (Kalmijn 1994) also significantly raise children's years of schooling. According to Hill and Duncan (1987), a 10 percent increase in family income raises children's educational attainment by about 1 percent. Brooks-Gunn et al. (1993) found that a one-standard deviation change in family income would reduce the likelihood of dropping out of high school by 7.5 percentage points.

Economic resources actually available to offspring depend on competing demands for parents' resources. Each additional sibling reduces years of schooling by roughly the same amount as each additional year of father's or mother's schooling. (See, for example, Behrman and Taubman 1986, Datcher Loury 1988, Haveman and Wolfe 1994, Kuo and Hauser 1995). Siblings that are closer to the individual in age have a more detrimental effect on educational performance than siblings who are farther away (Powell and Steelman 1990).

There are a variety of family characteristics other than parents' education that are correlated with children's outcomes. These include family structure, parental activities, and home resources. McLanahan and Sandefur (1994) estimated that, controlling for other family background characteristics, the difference in college enrollments rates was as high as 12 percentage points between those from single-parent or parent/step-parent families compared to those from intact families. The difference in high-school graduation rates was as much as 16 percentage points (see also Sandefur, McLanahan, and Wojtkiewicz 1992). The effects of single-parent households on schooling are higher if more total years or if more preschool years are spent with a single parent (Krein and Beller 1988, Haveman and Wolfe 1994, Wojtkiewicz 1993).

Astone and McLanahan (1991) showed that single-parent and step-parent families engaged in fewer positive parental educational practices (as measured by education aspirations for children, mothers and fathers monitoring school work, and general supervision) and that these practices had large and significant effects on dropping out of high school. The estimated effects largely occurred because parental practices alter the child's educational aspirations, grades, school attendance, and attitudes toward school.

Teachman (1987) and Krein and Beller (1988) found that educational resources as measured by whether there is a specific place to study in the home, whether there are reference books, a daily newspaper, or a dictionary/encyclopedia in the home had a large and significant effect on daughters but not sons. Ribar (1993) also reported that the presence of reading material in the home is correlated with lower dropout rates for teenage girls. According to Datcher-Loury (1988), children's years of schooling increased with the amount of time that educated mothers (those with at least a high-school diploma) spent with the children. In addition, she showed that sons and daughters of parents who expect their children to attend college average at least 0.2 more years than others (see also Sandefur, McLanahan, and Wojtkiewicz 1992). The effects of mothers' employment on high-school graduation, college attendance, and college graduation are mixed (Haveman, Wolfe, and Spalding 1991, Kalmijn 1994, Haveman and Wolfe 1994). Overall, the measured family background characteristics account for about 20 to 30 percent of the total variation in years of schooling (Behrman and Taubman 1986, Datcher Loury 1988, Kuo and Hauser 1995).

Compared to family background studies, there are fewer analyses of the effects of the neighborhood of origin on children's schooling. Brooks-Gunn et al. (1993) reported that, of the large number of neighborhood variables examined, only the fraction of female-headed families with children, the fraction of families in the neighborhood with incomes greater than $30,000 and whether less than 5 percent of workers were in the managerial or professional categories had the expected large and significant effects. For example, a one-standard deviation increase in the fraction of affluent families would reduce dropout rates by almost 5 percentage points. This is equivalent to a one-standard deviation change in mother's schooling. Crane obtained similar results for professional and managerial workers. Datcher (1982) and Corcoran et al. (1987) found that average neighborhood income (measured at the 5-digit zipcode level) and living in neighborhoods with more whites substantially raised years of schooling. According to Haveman and Wolfe (1994), individuals living in neighborhoods with a large percentage of youths who are high-school dropouts were less likely to complete high school. Similar results were reported by Case and Katz (1991).

These types of findings may explain the outcome of the Gautreax program. The Gautreaux program (Rosenbaum 1991) is an experiment with random assignment of families to different suburban and urban neighborhoods in and around Chicago. Those who moved to the city dropped out of high school much more often than those in the suburbs and they were less likely to attend college. A more recent random assignment program, the Moving to Opportunity Demonstration, reported related positive outcomes for children (Katz, Kling, and Liebman 2001).

B.   *Children's earnings and income*

Literature on the effects of specific family background variables on earnings and income largely focuses on estimates of the effects of parents' income on children's earnings. The most reliable estimates suggest that a 10 percent increase in parents' income would raise son's annual earnings by around 4 percent (Corcoran et al. 1992, Solon 1992, Zimmerman 1992). Analyzing men's wages and occupational status instead of annual earnings generates similar results (Zimmerman 1992). Note, however, that the sources of parental income matter since, for example, welfare receipt is correlated with lower children's earnings (Corcoran et al. 1992).

There are many fewer estimates of the effects of long-run parents' income for daughters. Lower labor force participation rates for women make women's earnings a less reliable measure of socioeconomic status than men's earnings. The existing estimates are roughly equal to those of men (Hill and Duncan 1987 and Altonji and Dunn 1991).

According to Corcoran et al. (1992), the estimated effects of various measures of family income do not change when son's educational attainment is added to the analysis. This suggests that these measures of family background do not operate primarily through son's years of education. Eide and Showalter (1999) obtained similar results. Adding son's years of schooling to the analysis of son's earnings reduces the effects of father's earnings only by about 25 percent. The largest drops are for sons with higher incomes.

Looking at the effects of parents' schooling on son's earnings, Corcoran et al. (1992) report that neither father's nor mother's education have any significant effects on son's income after controlling for family income characteristics (see also Kiker and Condon 1981 and Datcher 1982). Other researchers report that same finding for father's schooling. However, the results for mother's schooling are more mixed. Behrman and Taubman (1986) and Hill and Duncan (1987) found, even though father's education did not raise earnings for sons or daughters, mother's education had a significant effect for daughters but not for sons. Each additional year of mother's education raised daughter's income by about 3.5 percent.

Various family composition indicators had little effect on earnings. Behrman and Taubman (1986) and Hill and Duncan (1987) reported that number of siblings had no significant effect for either gender. Li and Wojtkiewicz (1993) and Lang and Zagorsky (2001) showed that growing up in a single-parent or stepfamily did not affect income holding education constant. Corcoran and Adams (1997) found that whether children lived in a female-headed household, percent of years in female-headed household, and percent of years where the family head was disabled generally had no or small effects on children's income.

Looking at the literature estimating neighborhood background effects on occupation and earnings, Jencks and Brown (1975) show that, while attending schools with higher average socioeconomic status increased subsequent occupational status, the size of the estimated effects were small for both men and women. Datcher (1982) found that, holding constant only other background variables, the racial composition of the neighborhood had large and significant effects on earnings for both white and African-American men. However, this effect fell to insignificance for African-Americans once controls for years of schooling were added to the analysis. This suggests that the initial estimated effects of neighborhoods on earnings may have largely occurred through changes in human capital. Similarly, Corcoran et al. (1992) found that a variety of community background variables (i.e., log median income and the male unemployment rate, and percentage of female-headed families with children) had no large or significant effect on son's economic outcomes as measured by annual labor earnings, annual hours of work, hourly wage rate, or annual family income.

C.   Evaluation of studies of measured background characteristics

While this work examining particular characteristics provides insight into the effects of intergenerational mobility, the findings are difficult to interpret because of a variety of problems (Manski 1993, Moffitt 1998, and Duncan and Raudenbush 1999). The simultaneity problem means that not only do family and community background affect children's outcomes, but children also shape family and community characteristics. Higher parents' educational expectations may raise children's education performance. On the other hand, higher children's early educational performance may raise parents' expectations. Similarly, choices of sons and daughters may be affected by the behavior of peers just as behavior of peers may be changed by behavior of sons and daughters.

The omitted variables problem occurs if observed characteristics included in the analysis capture the effects of unobservables. Suppose estimates show that higher parents' education increases children's income. The effects of higher parents' education on childrens' outcome may result from differences in child-rearing practices of more educated parents or it may reflect higher permanent family income. Clearly, policy implications to be drawn from the finding differ depending on which interpretation is correct. Similarly, correlation between community affluence and higher children's earnings may result from community income itself or from better schools in the community which is itself correlated with community income.

The selection problem often arises in the case of neighborhood background effects. Many important family characteristics that alter outcomes may be unobservable and may be correlated with parents' residential choices. Thus, any observed neighborhood effect could, in fact, result from differences in family characteristics. The selection problem can also occur in other contexts. Any estimated effects of high-achieving peers may not result from the causal effects of peers. Instead those who choose high-achieving peers may not be a random sample of the population but instead themselves be high-achievers along some unobserved dimension.

The last two problems lead to underestimates of neighborhood effects. First, neighborhood may affect family characteristics. For example, high unemployment rates or community receipt of welfare income may reduce parents' earned income. If community background effects are measured holding family characteristics, the analysis will understate the role of the neighborhood of origin. Second, the effects of neighborhood characteristics may be limited to specific neighborhood contexts. Most likely examples include segregated or especially low-income communities. In this case, overall measures of neighborhood effects would obscure important influences for particular population segments.

Work confirming the importance of some of these problems includes, for example, Evans, Oates, and Schwab (1992), Plotnick and Hoffman (1999), Lang and Zagorsky (2001). Evans, Oates, and Schwab (1992) analyzed the effects of peers on dropout rates. Their results indicated that large and significant initial effects of peers, as measured by the percentage of students in the individual's school who were classified as economically disadvantaged, disappeared when peer effects were treated as endogenous. Similarly, Plotnick and Hoffman (1999) focused on the effects of a variety of neighborhood characteristics including the proportion of families receiving public assistance, the proportion of families with low income, the proportion of families with high income, and the proportion of families that were headed by a single female in the individual's census tract. They showed that, while cross section estimates of these neighborhood effects on post-secondary schooling and income were large and significant, fixed effects estimates were insignificant. These fixed effects estimates were made by comparing sisters who lived in different neighborhoods with different characteristics.

Not all work controlling for selection and other problems concludes that there are no neighborhood effects. Aaronson's studies (1997, 1998) are based on comparing outcomes for siblings who have grown up in different neighborhoods in order to lessen omitted family variables problems. His results show that a 10 percent increase in the neighborhood dropout rate reduces the likelihood of graduating from high school by about 2 percent and a 10 percent increase in the neighborhood poverty rate reduces it by 7 percent. Holding a wide variety of family background characteristics constant, Ginther, Haveman, and Wolfe (2000) reported that the prevalence of neighborhood high-school dropouts and white persons continued to have significant effects on high-school graduation and years of completed schooling.

Similarly, not all work controlling for selection and other problems eliminates the effects of particular family characteristics. Using both parametric latent-variable models and nonparametric models, Manski et al. (1992) find that children from intact families are more likely to graduate from high schooling than those who are not. Painter and Levine (2000) find that larger high-school dropout rates for those with divorced parents does not result from pre-existing characteristics of the individuals or their families.

3   Sibling and neighborhood correlations in earnings and education

More recently, work aimed at estimating the overall effect of background has relied on correlations in earnings and education outcomes between siblings. This work assumes that, if background is important, siblings should have similar outcomes since they share the same background. Sibling correlations capture both observed and unobserved family effects and neighborhood effects as well as the correlation between family and neighborhood characteristics.

Note, however, that sibling correlations of schooling or income may understate background effects. They may be based on poor measures of permanent income either because analysts use single-year instead of multi-year earnings or because analysts calculate correlations when siblings are relatively young. Similar problems occur if school quality is not measured. Sibling correlations may also understate the effects of background because family or community characteristics differ between siblings. For example, birth-order effects may alter children's outcomes, siblings may spend different proportions of their youth growing up in different neighborhoods, children may try to differentiate themselves from brothers and sisters, parents may attempt to compensate for or highlight children's abilities and weaknesses, and as parents age, they may change their child-rearing practices.

A.   Years of schooling

Correlations in brothers' years of schooling have generally been estimated to be between roughly 0.5 to 0.65 (Griliches 1979, Bound, Griliches, and Hall 1986, Hauser and Sewell 1986, Solon, Page, and Duncan 2000, Hauser and Featherman 1976). The higher figures come from correcting for errors in measuring years of schooling. According to Bound, Griliches, and Hall (1986), the correlation between sisters and the correlation between brothers and sisters are only slightly smaller (both 0.44) than the correlation between brothers (0.47). The fraction of the variation in years of schooling due to measured and unmeasured family characteristics has remained relatively constant over time (Kuo and Hauser 1995).

One technique for determining the effects of neighborhood of origin on educational attainment is to estimate correlations across individuals from the same communities. The correlations between neighborhood children are due to (1) living in the same neighborhood, (2) similarities between families of neighborhood children, and (3) similar families choosing similar neighborhoods. Only the first is wholly the effect of neighborhood characteristics. The second is due to family effects, and the third is a combination of family and neighborhood characteristics. This implies that correlations between neighboring children are an upper-bound of neighborhood background effects.

According to Solon, Page, and Duncan (1999), neighborhood correlations in education attainment equal roughly 0.1 and are, therefore, about one-fifth of the sibling correlation of 0.5 and account for only 10 percent of the overall variation in years of schooling. This means that, if neighborhood backgrounds were equal, more than 90 percent of the inequality in years of schooling would remain.

B.   Earnings and income

Early estimates of the sibling earnings correlations were, in some cases, relatively small (0.112 for brothers in Bound, Griliches, and Hall 1986) due partly to poor measures of permanent income. Brother correlations using multiyear earnings are roughly 0.3–0.4 (Altonji 1988, Altonji and Dunn 1991, Solon et al. 1991). This implies that 40 percent of the inequality in permanent annual earnings results from variation in family and community origin. About 16 percent out of the 40 percent correlation between brothers' income is due to parents' income. Correlation between identical twins is somewhat higher at 0.56–0.64 (Ashenfelter and Krueger 1994 and Ashenfelter and Rouse 1997). The smaller body of work on sister correlations reports figures between 0.3 and 0.45 for annual earnings (Solon et al. 1991, Bound, Griliches, and Hall 1986, Altonji and Dunn 1991).

According to Page and Solon (1999a and 1999b), the estimated neighborhood correlation for men's earnings at 0.16 and for women's earnings at 0.12 are similar to neighborhood correlations for schooling. More than half of the neighbor covariance in earnings results from the size of the community of origin. This suggests that the particular neighborhood matters less than whether one grows up in a city or small town.

4   Racial and ethnic differences in background effects

The findings above indicate that a wide variety of background characteristics alter children's outcomes. These findings imply that racial and ethnic differences in outcomes occur in part because of different levels of background characteristics. In addition, non-linearities in background effects would result in different outcomes since African-Americans and Hispanics are more concentrated at lower levels of background characteristics where the effects on children's education and incomes are often larger. Finally, racial and ethnic differences would occur if African-Americans, Hispanics, and other ethnic groups with the same background characteristics as whites do not achieve the same outcomes.

A.   Racial differences in background effects on schooling

Less favorable family background characteristics have historically accounted for a substantial fraction of the gap in schooling between African-Americans and whites (Hauser and Featherman 1976). Eliminating all background differences would be likely to wipe out all schooling differences since current studies find that African-Americans achieved about one-half more years of schooling than whites holding background constant (see Hill and Duncan 1987, and Haveman and Wolfe 1994).

While background effects are important for both blacks and whites, the process by which background alters outcomes varies by race. For example, Kuo and Hauser (1995) report that the proportion of the variation of years of schooling due to measured and unmeasured family characteristics is slightly higher for African-American men at about 58 percent than for white men at about 50 percent. While a higher fraction of variation due to unmeasured family characteristics is the main cause, the impact of a given set of family background factors also differs by race. According to Kane's analysis of college enrollment (1994), the effects of father's schooling are generally higher than mother's education as reported above. The opposite is true for African-Americans. Consequently, the effects of mother's schooling are actually higher for African-Americans than for whites, while the effects of father's schooling are lower. Racial differences are much smaller in the case of high school graduation. According to Krein and Beller (1988), father's years of schooling raised white sons' and daughters' education by about 0.15 years but had no effect for either African-American men or women. This result holds even after controlling for the number of years in a single-parent family.

African-American family income effects may differ from whites because a larger portion comes from mother's earnings and government transfers. Neither of these have as much beneficial effect as father's earnings (Hill and Duncan 1987, Li and Wojtkiewicz 1992). There also is evidence of racial differences in the effects of neighborhood of origin on schooling. While affluent neighbors reduce the likelihood of dropping out for whites, they have little effect on African-Americans (Brooks Gunn et al. 1993).

B.   Racial differences in background effects on income

Some researchers have found that there are racial differences in the effects of family characteristics on children's income. While mother's years of schooling had no effect on African-American sons, it consistently raised family incomes of white sons, African-American daughters and white daughters according to Corcoran and Adams (1997).

Looking at parents' income Corcoran and Adams (1997) found that an increase had a much larger effect on incomes of African-American compared to white children. This is true for both sons and daughters. These effects, however, appear to occur mainly because the effects of family income are larger for those at the bottom of the education or income distribution. When Corcoran and Adams estimated separate parental income effects for different levels of parents' income, the race differences became smaller for women and disappeared completely for men. Furthermore, according to Eide and Showalter (1999), the effect of father's earnings on son's earnings declines from 0.77 for the 0.05 quantile to 0.19 for the 0.95 quantile of son's earnings. This implies that father's earnings are not as important for accounting for son's earnings at the top of the earnings distribution as at the bottom. Peters' (1992) findings are consistent with this result. She shows that the effects of parents' income are significantly lower for sons whose fathers attended college.

Not all of the difference in income mobility by race results from class differences. According to Rodgers (1995), 8.8 percent of whites growing up in poor families could expect to be poor themselves compared to 3 percent of the non-poor. The numbers for African-Americans are 31.6 and 14 percent respectively. This suggests that there is both less upward mobility for African-American poor and more downward mobility among the African-American non-poor.

There may be racial differences in the effects of neighborhood characteristics due to nonlinearities. Massey, Gross, and Eggers (1991) found that increases in residential segregation and group poverty substantially raise the likelihood that the individual will live in a neighborhood with a high poverty rate. Furthermore, they show living in a neighborhood with a poverty rate of 30 percent or more reduced the probability of working for both men aged 16–19 and aged 20–35. Thus, high level of residential segregation for African-Americans combined with high poverty rates would generate lower employment probabilities even in the absence of racial differences in the effects of concentrated poverty.

The effects of neighborhood segregation may also be particularly troublesome for African-Americans. O'Regan and Quigley (1996) found that exposure to whites (as measured by the probability that a randomly picked resident of his census tract is white) significantly increases employment probabilities for out-of-school African-American youth. Similar results are found for exposure to poverty. Cutler and Glaeser (1997) found that a one standard deviation increase in segregation would reduce earnings of African-Americans aged 25 to 30 years by 7 percent. The earnings effects appear to be largest for less-educated African-Americans or African-Americans from less-educated families. Furthermore, the effects do not diminish when instrumental variables are used to correct for endogeneity or when family background measures are included in the analysis. In contrast, Cutler and Glaeser found that segregation may have a small, positive effect on earnings of whites.

C.   Ethnic differences in background effects

Borjas (1992) comprehensively explores the relationship between ethnicity and intergenerational mobility. Looking at two nationally representative datasets, he finds large differentials in education, occupational prestige, and wages across ethnic groups in the USA. Some ethnic groups (e.g., those with ancestors from China, Denmark, Japan, Russia, Scotland, and Switzerland) currently average over fourteen years of schooling, while others (e.g., those with ancestors from Mexico and Puerto Rico) average roughly twelve or fewer years. Similarly, actual wage differences and those implied by occupational prestige scores are as large as 25 percent across groups.

A large part of the differential in sons' outcomes can be attributed to the correlation in socioeconomic status between sons and fathers described earlier. In addition, Borjas (1992) shows that mean schooling of the father's generation is correlated with son's education and that mean occupational prestige score for the father's generation is correlated with the son's occupational score. In a later paper Borjas (1995) argues that about half of the correlation between son's education and earnings and the average of his father's generation results from a small number of neighborhood characteristics. These include the percentage of the neighborhood's population with at least a high-school diploma, the percentage with a college diploma, the labor force participation rates of men and women, the percentage of workers in professional occupations, the percentage of families below the poverty line, and the percentage of families with high incomes. Thus, it appears that, on average, much of the ethnic correlation between generations is simply neighborhood effects rather than ethnicity per se. More complete controls for neighborhood effects reduce the ethnic-capital effect on son's education to zero. The only case where ethnicity has an independent effect is on son's education for those who lived in ethnically segregated neighborhoods.

While Borjas (1992) shows the average effect of ethnicity across generations, other studies focus more specifically on particular ethnic groups. For example, Rong and Grant (1992) find that years of schooling increase dramatically between Asian immigrants and the second generation. Further gains between subsequent generations are smaller. Schooling differentials between Hispanic immigrant and child-of-immigrant generations are even larger than those for Asians. In addition, gains continue to be made by later generations. The same immigrant and child-of-immigrant pattern holds for non-Hispanic whites but the differences between immigrants and the second generation are smaller.

5   Summary

The reviewed literature indicates that family background effects have a large and robust influence on the education and adult economic status of children. In addition, neighborhood effects appear to be important especially in the case of racially or ethnically segregated communities. These results taken together imply that a complete understanding of inequality across groups cannot rely solely on examining individual characteristics of current populations. Instead historical circumstances exert an independent influence over outcomes. Understanding the implications of these effects requires additional research work. The exact mechanisms by which background affects outcomes are not well-understood.

REFERENCES

Aaronson, D., 1997, "Sibling Effects of Neighborhood Effects." in J. Brooks-Gunn, G. Duncan, and J. L. Aber (eds.), *Neighborhood Poverty: Policy Implications of Studying Neighborhoods*, Vol. II, New York: Russell Sage Foundation.

    1998, "Using Sibling Data to Estimate the Impact of Neighborhoods on Children's Educational Outcomes," *The Journal of Human Resources* 33: 915–46.

Altonji, J., 1988, "The Effects of Family Background and School Characteristics on Education and Labor Market Outcomes," unpublished manuscript.

Altonji, J. and T. Dunn, 1991, "Relationships among Family Incomes and Labor Market Outcomes of Relatives," *Research in Labor Economics* 12: 269–309.

Ashenfelter, O. and A. Krueger, 1994, "Estimates of the Economic Returns to Schooling from a New Sample of Twins," *American Economic Review* 84: 1157–73.

Ashenfelter, O. and C. Rouse, 1998, "Income, Schooling and Ability: Evidence from a New Sample of Identical Twins," *Quarterly Journal of Economics* 113: 253–84.

Astone, N. M. and S. McLanahan, 1991, "Family Structure, Parental Practices, and High School Completion," *American Sociological Review* 56: 309–20.

Behrman, J., R. Pollack, and P. Taubman, 1982, "Parental Preferences and Provision for Progeny," *Journal of Political Economy* 90: 52–73.

Behrman, J., M. Rosenzweig, and P. Taubman, 1994, "A Sequential Model of Educational Investment: How Family Background Affects High School Achievement, College Enrollments, and Choice of College Quality," Working Paper, Department of Economics, Williams College, Williamstown, MA.

Behrman, J. and P. Taubman, 1985, "Intergenerational Earnings Mobility in the United States: Some Estimates and a Test of Becker's Intergenerational Model," *Review of Economics and Statistics* 67: 144–50.

    1986, "Birth Order, Schooling, and Earnings," *Journal of Labor Economics*: S121–45.

Borjas, G., 1992, "Ethnic Capital and Intergenerational Mobility," *Quarterly Journal of Economics* 107: 123–50.

    1995, "Ethnicity, Neighborhoods, and Human-Capital Externalities," *American Economic Review* 85: 365–90.

Bound, J., Z. Griliches and B. Hall, 1986, "Wages, Schooling, and IQ of Brothers and Sisters: Do the Family Factors Differ?" *International Economic Review* 27: 77–105.

Brooks-Gunn, J., G. Duncan, P. Klebanov, and N. Sealand, 1993, "Do Neighborhoods Influence Child and Adolescent Development?" *American Journal of Sociology* 99: 353–95.

Case, A. and L. Katz, 1991, "The Company You Keep: The Effects of Family and Neighborhood on Disadvantaged Youth," National Bureau of Economic Research Working Paper No. 3705.

Corcoran, M. and T. Adams, 1997, "Race, Sex, and the Intergenerational Transmission of Poverty," in G. Duncan, and J. Brooks Gunn (eds.), *Consequences of Growing up Poor*, New York: Russell Sage Foundation.

Corcoran, M., R. Gordon, D. Laren, and G. Solon, 1987, "Intergenerational Transmission of Income. Education and Earnings," Unpublished Working Paper.

1992, "The Association between Men's Economic Status and Their Family and Community Origins," *The Journal of Human Resources* 27: 575–601.

Crane, J., 1991, "The Epidemic Theory of Ghettos and Neighborhood Effects on Dropping Out and Teen Childbearing," *American Journal of Sociology* 96: 1226–59.

Cutler, D. and E. Glaeser, 1997, "Are Ghettos Good or Bad?" *Journal of Political Economy* 107: 455–506.

Datcher, L., 1982, "Effects of Community and Family Background on Achievement," *Review of Economics and Statistics* 64: 32–41.

Datcher Loury, L., 1988, "Effects of Mother's Home Time on Children's Schooling," *Review of Economics and Statistics* 70: 367–73.

Duncan, G. and S. Raudenbush, 1999, "Neighborhoods and Adolescent Development: How Can We Determine the Links," unpublished paper.

Eide, E. and M. Showalter, 1999, "Factors Affecting the Transmission of Earnings Across Generations: A Quantile Regression Approach," *Journal of Human Resources* 34: 253–67.

Evans, W., Oates W., and R. Schwab, 1992, "Measuring Peer Group Effects: A Study of Teenage Behavior," *Journal of Political Economy* 100: 966–91.

Ginther, D., R. Haveman, and B. Woolfe, 2000, "Neighborhood Attributes as Determinants of Children's Outcomes," *Journal of Human Resources* 35: 603–42.

Griliches, Zuin, 1979, "Sibling Models and Data in Economics Beginnings of a Survey," *Journal of Political Economy* 87(Part 2): 537–64.

Hauser, Robert and David Featherman, 1976, "Equality of Schooling: Trends and Prospects," *Sociology of Education* 49: 99–120.

Haveman, R. and B. Wolfe, 1994, *Succeeding Generations*, New York: Russell Sage Foundation.

1995, "The Determinants of Children's Attainments: A Review of Methods and Findings," *Journal of Economic Literature* 30: 1829–78.

Haveman, R., B. Wolfe and J. Spaulding, 1991, "Childhood Events and Circumstances Influencing High School Completion," *Demography* 28: 133–57.

Hill, M. and G. Duncan, 1987, "Parental Family Income and the Socioeconomic Attainment of Children," *Social Science Research* 16: 39–73.

Hauser, P. and W. Sewell, 1986, "Family Effects in Simple Models of Education, Occupational Status, and Earnings: Findings from the Wisconsin and Kalamazoo Studies," *Journal of Labor Economics* 4: S83–115.

Jencks, C. and M. Brown, 1975, "The Effects on High Schools on Their Students," *Harvard Educational Review* 45: 273–324.

Jencks, C. and S. Mayer, 1990, "The Social Consequences of Growing Up in a Poor Neighborhood," in L. E. Lynn, and M. McGeary (eds.), *Inner-City Poverty in the United States*, Washington, DC: National Academy Press.

Kalmijn, M. 1994, "Mother's Occupational Status and Children's Schooling," *American Sociological Review* 59: 257–75.

Kane, T., 1994, "College Entry by Blacks since 1970: The Role of College Costs, Family Background, and the Returns to Education," *Journal of Political Economy* 102: 767–911.

Katz, L., J. Kling, and J. Liebman, 2001, "Moving To Opportunity in Boston: Early Results of a Randomized Mobility Experiment," *Quarterly Journal of Economics* 2001 (May): 607–54.

Kiker, B. F. and C. Condon, 1981, "The Influence of Socioeconomic Background on the Earnings of Young Men," *Journal of Human Resources* 16: 94–105.

Krein, S. and A. Beller, 1988, "Educational Attainment of Children From Single-Parent Families: Differences by Exposure, Gender, and Race," *Demography* 25: 221–34.

Kuo, H. D. and R. Hauser, 1995, "Trends in Family Effects on the Education of African-American and White Brothers," *Sociology of Education* 68: 136–60.

Lang, K. and J. Zagorsky, 2001, "Does Growing Up With A Parent Absent Really Hurt?" *Journal of Human Resources* 36, 2: 535–73.

Li, J. H. and R. Wojtkiewicz, 1992, "A New Look at the Effects of Family Structure on Status Attainment," *Social Science Quarterly* 73: 581–95.

McLanahan, S. and G. Sandefur, 1994, *Growing Up with a Single Parent*, Cambridge, MA: Harvard University Press.

Manski, C., 1993, "Identification of Endogenous Social Effects: The Reflection Problem," *Review of Economic Studies* 60: 531–42.

Manski, C., G. Sandefor, S. Mclanahan, and D. Powers, 1992, "Alternative Estimates of the Effects of Family Structure During Adolescence on High School Groduation," *Journal of the American Statistical Association* 87: 25–37.

Massey, D., A. Gross, and M. Eggers, 1991, "Segregation, the Concentration of Poverty, and the Life Chances of Individuals," *Social Science Research* 20: 397–420.

Moffitt, R., 1998, "Policy Interventions, Low-Level Equilibria, and Social Interventions," Johns Hopkins University Working Paper.

Page, M. and G. Solon, 1999a, "Correlations between Brothers and Neighboring Boys in Their Adult Earnings: The Importance of Being Urban," University of Michigan Working Paper.

    1999b, "Correlations between Sisters and Neighboring Girls in Their Subsequent Income as Adults," University of Michigan Working Paper.

Painter, G. and D. Levine, 2000, "Family Structure and Youth Outcomes," *Journal of Human Resources* 35: 524–49.

Peters, H. E., 1992, "Patterns of Intergenerational Mobility in Income and Earnings," *Review of Economics and Statistics* 74: 456–66.

Plotnick, R. and S. Hoffman, 1999, "The Effect of Neighborhood Characteristics on Young Adult Outcomes: Alternative Estimates," *Social Science Quarterly* 80: 1–18.

Powell, B. and L. C. Steelman, 1990, "Beyond Sibship Size: Sibling Density, Sex Composition, and Educational Outcomes," *Social Forces* 69: 181–206.

Ribar, D., 1993, "A Multinomial Logit Analysis of Teenage Fertility and High School Completion," *Economics of Education Review* 12: 153–64.

Rodgers, J., 1995, "An Empirical Study of Intergenerational Transmission of Poverty in the United States," *Social Science Quarterly* 76: 178–94.

Rong, X. L. and L. Grant, 1992, "Ethnicity, Generation, and School Attainment of Asians, Hispanics, and non-Hispanic Whites," *Sociological Quarterly* 33: 625–36.

Rosenbaum, James E., 1991, "Black Pioneers: Do Their Moves to the Suburbs Increase Economic Opportunity for Mothers and Children?" *Housing Policy Debate* 2, 4: 1179–214.

Sandefur, G., S. McLanahan, and R. Wojtkiewicz, 1992, "The Effects of Parental Marital Status during Adolescence on High School Graduation," *Social Forces* 71: 103–21.

Solon, G., 1992, "Intergenerational Income Mobility in the United States," *American Economic Review* 82: 393–408.

Solon, G., M. Corcoran, R. Gordon, and D. Laren, 1991, "A Longitudinal Analysis of Sibling Correlations in Economic Status," *Journal of Human Resources* 26: 509–34.

Solon, G., M. Page, and G. Duncan, 1999, "Correlations Between Neighboring Children in Their Subsequent Educational Attainment," Working paper, Ann Arbor: University of Michigan.

2000, "Correlations Between Neighboring Children in Their Subsequent Educational Attainment," *Review of Economics and Statistics* 82: 383–92.

Teachman, J., 1987, "Family Background, Educational Resources, and Educational Attainment," *American Sociological Review* 52: 548–57.

Wojtkiewicz, R., 1993, "Simplicity and Complexity in the Effects of Parental Structure on High School Graduation," *Demography* 30: 701–17.

Zimmerman, D., 1992, "Regression Toward Mediocrity in Economic Stature," *American Economic Review* 82: 409–29.

6 Social integration and social mobility: spatial segregation and intermarriage of the Caribbean population in Britain

Ceri Peach

Introduction

This chapter deals with the social, economic, and spatial mobility of the Caribbean and other ethnic populations in Britain between 1948 and 2000. It draws comparisons, on the one hand, with the Indian, Pakistani, and Bangladeshi populations and other recent ethnic minorities in Britain, and on the other hand, with the African-American population in the United States. The Caribbean population is taken as the best available comparator for the African-American population in the UK/US analysis. The thrust of the chapter is that the British Caribbean male population is economically disadvantaged but socially integrated, while the Caribbean female population has a bimodal distribution, being both socially and economically more marginalized than Caribbean males in its lower levels but economically more advantaged in its upper levels.

One of the illuminating, if tendentious, generalizations about ethnic minorities in Britain has been to divide them into the Jewish and the Irish models of settlement. In broad terms, the Irish model is seen as having been more blue-collar, manual-labour dominated, council-house-tenured, and inner-city located, while the Jewish model is seen as white-collar, self-employed, owner-occupied and suburban. The Irish model (*pace* Mary Hickman, this volume) is similar to and convergent with the population as a whole. The Jewish model has been seen as pluralistic, maintaining its cultural distinctiveness despite economic integration. As with most broad generalizations, there are many exceptions, but it nevertheless is an instructive framework.

Broadly speaking then, the Caribbean population seems to be following the trajectory established by the Irish before them of convergence with the population as a whole. On the other hand, the Indian population seems to have progressed some way already along the Jewish trajectory of white-collar, self-employed, suburbanized and owner-occupier

178

route. The Pakistanis and Bangladeshis are rather more ambiguously following this latter route. Despite a fair degree of self-employment and a high degree of owner occupation in the case of the Pakistanis, they are economically more marginal than the Indians. However, all three South Asian groups have maintained a high degree of social exclusiveness as far as marriage patterns are concerned. Thus, while the Caribbean population is economically disadvantaged but increasingly socially assimilated, the Indian population is generally economically advantaged but has retained its social distinctiveness. The Pakistanis and Bangladeshis are economically challenged, but socially encapsulated (Ballard 1996, Eade, Vamplew, and Peach 1996).

The British discourse, from the beginning of the 1950s through to the 1980s, was one of *racial* discrimination (Rex and Moore 1967, Smith 1976, Brown 1984). However, in the 1990s and the 2000s, although racist discrimination persists, the racial category has been unpacked and the discourse has become more nuanced and focused on *ethnic* differentiation in which sociolinguistics and ethno-religious groupings, gender differences, and generational differences play a significant part (Modood et al. 1997). The discourse has moved from color to culture, from immigration to minorities, from minorities to gender and religion.

There are two main sources to track the changing trajectories of minority ethnic populations over time. The most heavily used is the decennial census which gives a snapshot every ten years from which change to individuals is inferred. Less used, but in some ways more revealing, is the Longitudinal Study (LS). The LS tracks the same individuals from census to census so that mobility can be tracked for an identical population, rather than for one with an identical nomenclature but a changing composition. In addition, there have been four surveys of British race relations by the Policy Studies Institute and its predecessors (PEP 1966, Smith 1974, Brown 1984, Modood et al. 1997).

The main conclusions to be drawn from the 1961, 1971, 1981, and 1991 cross-sectional census snapshots of the population is social and spatial progress for the Caribbeans, but continuing economic disadvantage. This is despite a history interspersed with violence and harassment (Scarman 1981, Peach 1986, Keith 1993). The Indian population shows economic upward mobility but little social assimilation, while the Pakistani and Bangladeshi populations as a whole show both social closure and economic marginality. The Chinese population shows both social and economic integration (Peach 1996a). Paradoxically, while the decennial censuses show the continuing disadvantaged state of the Caribbean population, the LS shows upward mobility.

British–American contrasts

In terms of comparison with the USA, the Caribbean population in Britain is sharply contrasted. It is not ghettoised (Philpott 1978, Peach 1996c) and it is socially integrated to a much greater extent than African-Americans in terms of intermarriage and cohabitation. However, it does not have the ability to reach the top of the hierarchies that seem open to African-Americans. There is not yet a British Colin Powell. British South Asian minorities, on the other hand, have been notably successful in industry, business, politics, medicine, and academia. Although the broad lines of comparison are clear, the amount of detailed census information is much smaller than for the USA.

The 1991 Census was the first in Britain to pose an ethnic question. In effect it was a racialized question posing as an ethnic question since it addressed only non-European groups. It showed a minority ethnic population of 3 millions out of a total British population of 55 millions. This is a much smaller percentage of the population than is the case in the USA. Britain is a country with minorities, the USA is a country of minorities.

Although there have long been non-European minority people in Britain and exaggerated attempts to invent for Britain a colorful ethnic past (Hickman, this volume), these populations consisted largely of individual men. British experience of large-scale non-European minority family groups dates back only fifty or so years to 1948 and the arrival of the first migrant ship, the *Empire Windrush*, from the Caribbean. The American experience is centuries old. The size of the British and American total populations and the proportions formed by minorities is also very different. The British total population is about one-fifth of the size of the US population. In the USA, the minority populations amount to about 25 percent of the total compared to 5.5 percent for Britain. The composition of the minority populations is also very different. The British minority ethnic populations are largely South Asian and Afro-Caribbean or of African origin. In the USA, the minority populations are largely African-American and Latino, but there is an important Asian component. Britain has nothing comparable to the American Latino population (Table 6.1).

The African-American population of the USA is about 12 percent of the total, while the Black Caribbean, Black Other, and Black African populations combined make up 2 percent of the British total. However, although the British minority percentage is small, it is also the product of a very short period of time. Black and Asian people numbered about 80,000 in 1951 (Peach 1996a). The current figure of 3 million is the product of the last fifty years of the twentieth century. The composition of

Table 6.1 *Comparison of the 1990 race population of the USA with the British 1991 ethnic composition*

	US number	US percent	GB number	GB percent
Total population	**248,709,873**	**100.0**	**54,888,844**	**100.0**
White	199,827,064	80.3	51,873,794	94.5
Black	29,930,524	12.0	890,727	1.6
American Indian	2,015,143	0.8		
Asian	6,876,394	2.8	1,834,117	3.3
Other	9,710,156	3.9	290,206	0.5
Hispanic (any race)	21,900,089	8.8		

Source: US Census 1990, OPCS, 1993.

the US Asian population is very different from that in Britain. In Britain, "Asian" is generally used as a shorthand term for the 1.5 million Indians, Pakistanis, and Bangladeshis. This is nearly double the number of such people in the USA (787,000 in the 1990 Census). On the other hand, the US Chinese population in 1990 of 1.6 million was ten times that of the British Chinese population in 1991 (157,000). The 1.4 million Filipinos in the USA have only a tiny counterpart of some 20,000 in Britain. The British have no equivalent to the Hispanic population.

The 1991 Census showed that the "Black Caribbean" ethnic population (the census term) numbered some 500,000, or just under 1 percent of the British population. The numbers had grown rapidly from about 15,000 in 1951 to reach a peak of about 550,000 in 1971, since when they had shown a light decrease to their present level (Peach 1991). This slight decrease masked a fairly significant return (and some re-migration to the USA and Canada) of perhaps 60,000 Caribbean-born persons. It also hides the substantial increase in the number of British-born Caribbeans (Peach 1991, 1996b) who now account for over half of the Caribbean population in Britain.

The Caribbean primary immigration started in 1948 and was completed by 1974, when the oil shock following the Yom Kippur War produced a massive economic recession in Britain. Caribbean immigration over this period showed a remarkable correlation with indicators of the British economy, directly with unfilled vacancies and inversely with unemployment (Peach 1991). Indian and Pakistani immigration peaked about eight years later than the Caribbean flow and the Bangladeshi migration peaked ten years later than the Indian and Pakistani peak. Indian and Pakistani immigration showed a similar, but less sensitive, adjustment to the British economic cycle (Robinson 1986: 27–31) while the Bangladeshi immigration was counter-cyclical (Peach 1990).

Table 6.2 *Relative concentration of ethnic groups in large metropolitan areas of Great Britain, 1991*

	Total	White	Black Caribbean	Black African	Black Other	Indian	Pakistani	Bangladeshi	Chinese
Great Britain	54,888,844	51,873,794	499,964	212,362	178,401	840,255	476,555	162,835	156,938
Greater London	6,679,699	5,333,580	290,968	163,635	80,613	347,091	87,816	85,738	56,579
West Midlands Metropolitan County	2,551,671	2,178,149	72,183	4,116	15,716	141,359	88,268	18,074	6,107
Greater Manchester Metropolitan County	2,499,441	2,351,239	17,095	5,240	9,202	29,741	49,370	11,445	8,323
West Yorkshire Metropolitan County	2,013,693	1,849,562	14,795	2,554	6,552	34,837	80,540	5,978	3,852
Percentage ethnic group in named areas	25.04	22.58	79.01	82.66	62.83	65.82	64.21	74.45	47.70

Source: OPCS, 1993, Table 6.

The Caribbean migrants, and later the Indians and Pakistanis, were essentially a replacement population. This was true of both their occupational and their geographic position. The native British were moving up occupationally and out of the major conurbations. Occupationally, the immigrants filled jobs in the service and manufacturing sectors which were low paid, had antisocial hours, and which had difficulty in attracting white workers. Large employers were British Rail, London Transport, and the National Health Service for the Caribbean population and Midland foundries and Northern textile mills for the South Asians.

Geographically, the minority ethnic populations were concentrated in a small number of large urban areas. These cities had already begun to lose population before the arrival of the immigrants. Immigrants thus filled a vacuum; they did not create a space. Demographic decrease in the large British conurbations was not white flight; it was not precipitated by immigration (Peach 1968, 1999). By 1991, nearly 80 percent of the Caribbean population was living in Greater London, Greater Birmingham (West Midland Metropolitan County), Greater Manchester, and the Bradford–Leeds conurbation (West Yorkshire Metropolitan County), compared with only 25 percent of the population as a whole (Table 6.2). Three-quarters of the Bangladeshi population was found in these same places, two-thirds of the Indians and Pakistanis, and nearly half the Chinese.

The 1991 Census gave mixed messages about the social and economic position of the different groups. If we interpret employment in the service sector (I, II, and III Non-manual) as desirable and manual employment as undesirable, the Indians and the Chinese were doing well; and the Caribbean, Pakistani, and Bangladeshi populations badly (see Figures 6.1 and 6.2). The census showed a predominantly blue-collar socio-economic distribution for Caribbean, Pakistani, and Bangladeshi men but a predominantly white-collar distribution for the Indians and Chinese (Figure 6.1). The census showed high rates of unemployment for Caribbean, Pakistani, and Bangladeshi men: 19, 21, and 22 percent respectively, compared with 7.7, 7.5, and 10.5 percent respectively for white, Chinese and Indian men aged 16+ (OPCS 1993, Table 10). Both Caribbean men and Caribbean women have the lowest percentages of any group in Professional class I.

Only about a third of the Caribbean men are in white-collar occupations compared with nearly half of the total male workforce (Figure 6.1) and two-thirds of the Caribbean women (Figure 6.2). On the other hand, if the ambiguous census-termed Black Other population is considered as substantially representing second-generation Caribbeans in Britain (Ballard and Kalra 1994, Owen 1996), then its male population shows

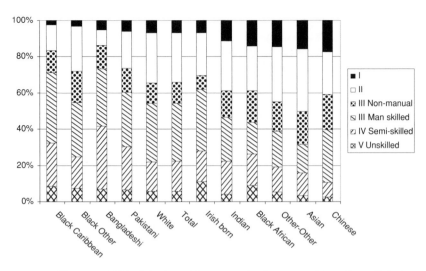

Figure 6.1 Ethnicity by socioeconomic class, men 16+, Great Britain, 1991

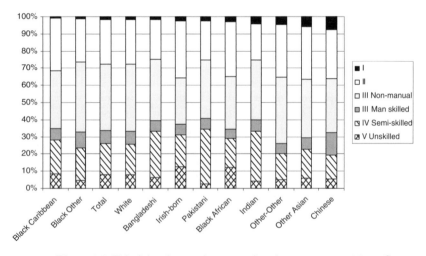

Figure 6.2 Ethnicity by socioeconomic class, women 16+, Great Britain, 1991

a significant advance in terms of white-collar employment (nearly half), compared to the Black Caribbean male population proper (Figure 6.1).

Caribbean women show a similar position to men in having the lowest percentage in the Professional class, but they show much less difference from women as a whole than do men to the overall male population.

Furthermore, about 65 percent of Caribbean women were in white-collar occupations (higher than for Indian, Pakistani, or Bangladeshi women) and their socioeconomic profile does not look dissimilar from that of white women or Irish-born women (the best-available comparator white immigrant group). Caribbean women had, at 67 percent, one of the highest participation rates in the formal labor force. On the other hand, their unemployment rate, 13.5 percent, was twice as high as that for white women, 6.3 percent (Peach 1996b: 34). However, in evaluating the female employment picture, it is important to recognize the very low rate of economic activity of Pakistani and Bangladeshi women.

Family structure

Although household size is similar to that of the white population, the Caribbean population shows significant differences in family structure. In particular, the Caribbean pattern of lone-parent families (and allied to this, single-parent, female-headed households with dependent children) is three times more common (28 percent) than in the white population (9 percent) or in the South Asian groups (whose percentages are similar to whites). Figure 6.3 illustrates these contrasts. Extended family households are significant for the Indians, Pakistanis, and Bangladeshis but not for the other groups.

Ethnically mixed households

The British Census contains a Sample of Anonymised Records (SARs) similar to the Public-Use Microdata Samples (PUMS) US Bureau of the Census. These allow us to examine the ethnic composition of households. Of the households in which either the head or partner gave their ethnic group as Black Caribbean, 37.2 percent were headed by a female with no male present, 18.1 percent were headed by a male with no female present. In 26.8 percent of cases, both the head and partner were Black Caribbean; in 10.1 percent of cases there was a Black Caribbean male with a white female partner while the obverse case obtained only half as frequently (4.8 percent of cases). There were very few cases of other ethnicities being partners in Black Caribbean households, although, given the relative sizes of the different ethnic populations, this is to be expected. One of the consequences of mixed partnership is children of mixed heritage. More than a third of the children in "Caribbean" households in the fourth PSI survey who lived with both parents, had one white and one black parent (Modood et al. 1997: 15). A complex process of ethnogenesis is taking place, which it is difficult to disentangle from census

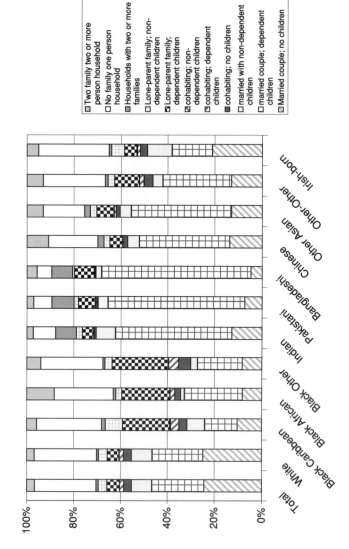

Figure 6.3 Family type by ethnicity, Great Britain, 1991

data. Black Caribbeans who wrote in their identity on the census form as "Black British" were assigned to the Black Other category. Thirteen percent of the Black Caribbeans in the fourth PSI survey characterized themselves as Black British whereas only 1 percent counted themselves as "Black Other" (Modood et al. 1997: 15).

Evidence of mobility: housing and suburbanization

Although the socioeconomic position of the Caribbean population seems disadvantaged compared to the total population, there is, nevertheless, evidence of significant upward mobility in the areas of housing tenure and suburbanization. In 1961, at the beginning of the immigration movement, West Indians were excluded from the social housing sector of council housing (Peach and Shah 1980) and were dependent upon private rentals. At that time, council housing accounted for about a quarter of the British housing stock, so that discriminatory exclusion of a working-class population from the main sector of working-class housing was a major constraint on dispersal. Essentially the Caribbean population was an exploited class at the mercy of racist private landlords (Glass and Westergaard 1965, see also Rex and Moore 1967). Some were forced into home buying (Byron 1994: 140). In 1961, in the conurbations which accounted for the large majority of Caribbean immigrants, private rentals provided 69 percent of the tenures and council housing only 2 percent (Peach and Byron 1993). Owner occupation accounted for 27 percent of Caribbean tenures (Figure 6.4).

By the 1970s, a breakthrough had taken place and the percentage living in council housing rose dramatically from 2 percent in 1961 and 7 percent in 1966 to 21 percent in 1971. By the 1981 Census, 45 percent of Caribbean-born headed households in England and Wales lived in social housing and an almost equal percentage lived in the owner-occupied sector. (For comparison, 42 percent of all tenures in the conurbations were owner-occupied and 24 percent were in local authority property.) By 1991 the position had changed significantly again, with a further rise in Caribbean owner occupation, and although social housing seemed to remain the same this seems to have been due to new households being created, while many previous social tenants became owner-occupiers (Figure 6.4).

It is important to indicate for an American readership that council housing in Britain is very different from Project housing in the USA. Council housing spans the whole range from suburban semi-detached (duplex) housing to high-rise inner-city flats (apartments) accommodation. Although "sink estates" exist and Caribbean households were

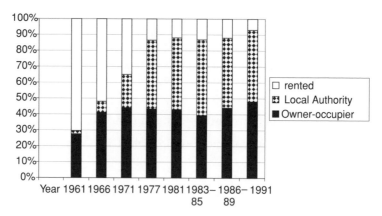

Figure 6.4 Changes in Caribbean housing tenure 1961–1991

disproportionately concentrated into the least desirable high-rise property, council housing in Britain did not bear the same stigmatized reputation as American inner-city Projects.

Longitudinal Survey data

The British Census contains a Longitudinal Survey (LS) which is more
important in demonstrating social mobility of the Black Caribbean population than the snapshot pictures obtainable from the decennial censuses. Since 1971, the census has identified a sample of individuals who
have been traced from census to census. The LS data show an even
more startling change for Caribbean tenures, with the Caribbean owner
occupation increasing from 47 percent in 1981 to 63 percent in 1991
(Table 6.3). Local Authority and housing association tenures decreased
from 49 percent to 33 percent. Moreover, the change was directly
attributable to households changing from social housing to owner occupation. Over 40 percent of those who were in social housing in 1981
changed to owner occupation in 1991. These figures support the field
survey work of Peach and Byron (1993) who found that 27 percent of
their 1992 London and Birmingham sample of Caribbean council-house
tenants had bought their homes since the Thatcher government had introduced the Right to Buy legislation in 1980 (Peach and Byron 1994).

African-American and British Caribbean contrasts in segregation

The most dramatic contrast between the situation of the Caribbean population in Britain and the African-American population lies in the degree

Table 6.3 *Tenure mobility 1981–1991 for the Black Caribbean population in Great Britain*

	Owner occupiers	LA housing assoc rent	Rent with job	Private rental	1981 Total	
Owner-occupiers	1245	153	11	25	1434	Frequency
	40.8	5.0	0.4	0.8	47.0	percent
	86.8	10.7	0.8	1.7		Row %
	64.6	15.0	33.3	34.7		Col. %
LA housing assoc rent	629	822	18	37	1506	
	20.6	26.9	0.6	1.2	49.3	
	41.8	54.6	1.2	2.5		
	36.6	80.7	54.6	51.4		
Rent with job	12	8	2	0	22	
	0.4	0.3	0.1	0.0	0.7	
	54.6	36.4	9.1	0.0		
	0.6	0.8	6.1	0.0		
Private rental	42	36	2	10	90	
	1.4	1.2	0.1	0.3	3.0	
	46.7	40.0	2.2	11.1		
	2.2	3.5	6.1	13.9		
1991 Total	1928	1019	33	72	3052	
	63.2	33.4	1.1	2.4	100.0	

Source: Special tabulations by the Longitudinal Survey Unit from 1991 Census
LA = Local Authority.
Note: To read this table, first compare the values in the right-hand (1981) column with the corresponding figure in the bottom (1991) row. For example, Caribbean owner-occupiers formed 47 percent of Caribbean tenures in 1981 but 63.2 percent in 1991. Those macro changes can be decomposed into their micro components of the 47 percent owner-occupiers in 1981, 5 percent had moved to LA housing by 1991 (read across the row). However, this loss was more than compensated by the fact that 20.6 percent of the 49.3 who were in LA housing in 1981 had moved into owner occupation.

of residential segregation. Massey and Denton (1993) have memorably represented the African-American population as hypersegregated. By this they mean that African-Americans score very high values on five different measures of geographical separation. However, levels of Caribbean segregation in British cities are just over half the level of African-American segregation. Segregation, in this instance, is measured by the Index of Dissimilarity (ID) (Duncan and Duncan 1955). ID measures the percentage of a given population that would have to move tract or district to replicate the distribution of the whole population or the population group with which it is being compared. Underlying the use of this index

Table 6.4 *Indices of Dissimilarity for 17 cities containing 1,000 or more Black Caribbeans, 1991, ward level*

City	White/Caribbean ID	ID	IS	Caribbean N
Leeds	69	66	66	5,102
Kirklees	64	62	62	4,452
Bristol	59	56	57	5,949
Manchester	56	49	51	10,390
Birmingham	54	40	42	42,341
Liverpool	54	52	52	1,479
London	49	43	45	289,712
Sheffield	49	47	48	4,994
Bradford	47	39	40	3,323
Oldham	44	38	39	1,042
Sandwell	43	36	37	7,837
Leicester	38	29	30	4,070
Wolverhampton	35	29	30	9,974
Oxford	33	32	32	1,732
Coventry	28	24	24	3,275
Slough	26	19	20	2,714
Luton	24	17	18	6,243
Average ID Unweighted	45	40	41	
Total				404,629

Source: based on Peach 1996c: Table XI.

is the hypothesis that the greater the likeness of groups (i.e., the lower the index), the lower the degree of social distance between them (Peach 1975). Table 6.4 shows that the average unweighted Index of Dissimilarity (ID) for the Caribbean population at ward level in 1991 for the seventeen cities containing 1,000 or more Caribbeans was 40. The average Caribbean/White ward level ID was 45. At enumeration district (ED) level, broadly comparable to US blocks, values are about ten percent higher. In London, for example, Caribbean/White ID at ED level is 54 compared with 49 at ward level (Peach 1996c: Table V). For Birmingham, the comparable figures are 58 versus 54. In the USA, on the other hand, Massey and Denton (1993: 222) show that the average level of black–white segregation in northern metropolitan areas in 1990 was 77.8 (compared with 84.5 in 1970 and 80.1 in 1980). Only Boston (68.2) and San Francisco-Oakland (66.8) had indices below 70. The average for southern cities was about 10 points lower. The overall unweighted average for the thirty metropolitan areas with the largest black populations in 1990 was 73.3 (Table 6.5). In Britain, on the other hand, the average ID

Table 6.5 *Trends in black-white segregation in thirty metropolitan areas with the largest black populations, 1970–1990*

	1970	1980	1990
Northern Areas			
Boston	81.2	77.6	68.2
Buffalo	87	79.4	81.8
Chicago	91.9	87.8	85.8
Cincinnati	76.8	72.3	75.8
Cleveland	90.8	87.5	85.1
Columbus	81.8	71.4	67.3
Detroit	88.4	86.7	87.6
Gary-Hammond-E Chicago	91.4	90.6	89.9
Indianopolis	81.7	76.2	74.3
Kansas City	87.4	78.9	72.6
Los Angeles-Long Beach	91	81.1	73.1
Milwaukee	90.5	83.9	82.8
New York	81	82	82.2
Newark	81.4	81.6	82.5
Philadelphia	79.5	78.8	77.2
Pittsburgh	75	72.7	71
St. Louis	84.7	81.3	77
San Francisco-Oakland	80.1	71.7	66.8
Average Northern	84.5	80.1	77.8
Southern Areas			
Atlanta	82.1	78.5	67.8
Baltimore	81.9	74.7	71.4
Birmingham	37.8	40.8	71.7
Dallas-Ft. Worth	86.9	77.1	63.1
Greensboro-Winston Salem	65.4	56	60.9
Houston	78.1	69.5	66.8
Memphis	75.9	71.6	69.3
Miami	85.1	77.8	71.8
New Orleans	73.1	68.3	68.8
Norfolk-Virginia Beach	75.7	63.1	50.3
Tampa-St. Petersburg	79.9	72.6	69.7
Washington DC	81.1	70.1	66.1
Average Southern	75.3	68.3	66.5
Overall Average	**80.8**	**75.4**	**73.3**

Source: Massey and Denton 1993 222, Table 8.1.

Table 6.6 *Comparison of Caribbean-born IDs in Greater London 1961–1991*

Year	Borough level ID	Ward level ID	Enumeration district ID	Source
1961	Not available	56	Not available	Lee (1973)
1971	38	49	65	Woods (1976)
1981	37	46	53	1981 census
1991	34	41	50	1991 census

Source: Peach 1996c.

for the Caribbean–White comparisons for the seventeen cities in which there were 1,000 or more Caribbeans in 1991 was 45 and there were only two cities, Leeds (69) and Kirklees (64), where the index was higher than 60 (Peach 1996c) (Table 6.4).

However, while US levels of black/white segregation are high and have remained so over a long period of time (Denton 1994), Caribbean levels are much lower and decreasing. Successive measures of Caribbean spatial patterns in London, which accounts for about 60 percent of the Caribbean population of Great Britain, indicates a progressive decrease in spatial segregation (Table 6.6). Cartographically, the evidence is similar. The Caribbean population appears to be moving from Inner London outwards to the suburbs (Figure 6.5). The Longitudinal Survey is again helpful in ascertaining the nature of this inner-city decrease. The LS data confirm the outward movement of the Caribbean-born from Inner London to Outer London during the period 1981 to 1991. The percentage of the London Caribbean-born living in Inner London decreased from 61 percent to 55 percent. Over 13 percent of the Inner London Caribbean population moved to Outer London and only 1 percent moved in the opposite direction (Table 6.7).

To read the mobility tables, see the explanation at the foot of Table 6.3.

Nevertheless, the general perception was of little socioeconomic change for the Caribbean ethnic population. However, the LS tracks the same individuals from census to census (while at the same time refreshing the LS sample with new entries). This allows us to measure whether mobility is taking place. The answer is remarkably positive. Although the cross-sectional picture of socioeconomic groups shows the Caribbean population in a lowly position (Figures 6.1 and 6.2) the LS data show significant improvement between 1981 and 1991. Table 6.8 shows the socioeconomic mobility of the ethnic population aged 27+ living in Inner London in 1991 as compared with their 1981 class. (The 27+ age is taken

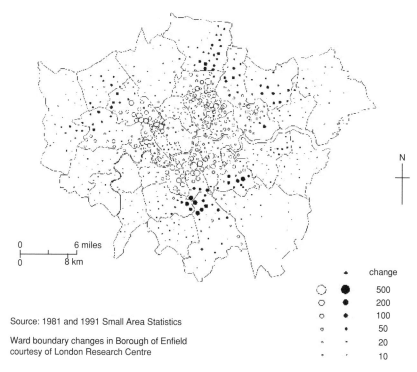

0 _____ 6 miles
0 _____ 8 km

Source: 1981 and 1991 Small Area Statistics

Ward boundary changes in Borough of Enfield
courtesy of London Research Centre

		change
○	●	500
○	●	200
○	●	100
○	·	50
●	·	20
●	·	10

Figure 6.5 1981–1991 change in Caribbean-born distribution in London

in order to capture those who would have been 16+ in 1981.) The total numbers are small (503), so genders have been amalgamated. Table 6.8 shows that there has been upward mobility. While 13.5 percent were in classes I (Professional) and II (Managerial) in 1981, this had increased to 20.7 percent by 1991. Class III Non-manual (Clerical, etc.) had increased from 14 to 15 percent over the same period. To read the mobility tables, see the explanation at the foot of Table 6.3 above.

Segregation and intermarriage

One of the main ways in which the British and American situation differ is in respect of the degree of ethnic intermarriage and cohabitation. Tables 6.9 and 6.10 present data for couples in Britain in 1991, by ethnicity. These data are drawn from the Sample of Anonymised Records (SARs). Table 6.9 presents the figures as percentages of males by ethnicity of partner. Table 6.10 presents the data as percentages for females, by ethnicity of partner. Table 6.9 shows that 27 percent of married or cohabiting

Table 6.7 *Caribbean-born geographic mobility 1981–1991*

LS data	Caribbean-born ethnic mobility 1981–91			1981 Total		Frequency percent Row %
	Inner London	Outer London	Elsewhere			
Inner London	605	96	26	727	**34.64**	Col. %
	28.82	4.57	1.24			
	83.22	13.2	3.58			
	93.8	18.22	2.8			
Outer London	24	419	24	467	**22.25**	
	1.14	19.96	1.14			
	5.14	89.72	5.14			
	3.72	79.51	2.59			
Elsewhere	16	12	877	905	**43.12**	
	0.76	0.57	41.78			
	1.77	1.33	96.91			
	2.48	2.28	94.61			
Total	645	527	927	2099	**100.0**	
1991	**30.73**	**25.11**	**44.16**	**100.0**		

Inner London decreased from 727 in 1981 to 645 in 1991.
83.2% of those in Inner London in 1991 had been there in 1981 and 13.2% had moved from Inner to Outer London and 3.6% elsewhere.
89.7% of those in Outer London in 1991 were there in 1981. 3.7% moved to Inner London and 2.6% elsewhere.
Source: Longitudinal Survey, special tabulations.

Caribbean men had a white partner. Over half of the Black Other men had white partners. The percentage for Caribbean men with white partners is almost double the rate for Caribbean women (15 percent; see Table 6.10). However, Black Other women have almost as high a rate of white partners (44 percent) as Black Other men. Interestingly, Chinese women have twice as high a proportion of white partners as Chinese men (24 percent versus 13 percent). The South Asian groups all have high endogamous rates (over 90 percent) although slightly lower for men than for women. The culture of arranged marriage is still very powerful for these groups (Ballard 1990). Other-Asian women also show a high rate of out-marriage or cohabitation (32 percent). There are also significantly high levels of marriage and cohabitation for both African men and women with white partners (17 and 15 percent respectively).

Taken overall, these figures show a remarkable degree of intermarriage and cohabitation for black groups, particularly in a white society that regularly castigates itself for racism. Attention is drawn to the Caribbean

Table 6.8 *1981–1991 occupational change for Caribbeans in Inner London*

		I Professional and managerial	II Non-manual	III Skilled manual	IV and V Part or unskilled	Insufficient description	Total 1981
I Professional and managerial							
	Frequency	53	5	1	5	4	68
	Percent	10.5	1.0	0.2	1.0	0.8	**13.5**
	Row %	77.9	7.4	1.5	7.4	5.9	
	Col. %	51.0	6.5	1.0	2.6	14.8	
II Non-manual							
		17	46	5	3	0	71
		3.4	9.2	1.0	0.6	0.0	**14.1**
		23.9	64.8	7.0	4.2	0.0	
		16.4	59.7	4.8	1.6	0.0	
III Skilled manual							
		7	2	71	29	12	121
		1.4	0.4	14.1	5.8	2.4	**24.1**
		5.8	1.7	58.7	24.0	9.9	
		6.7	2.6	67.6	15.3	44.4	
IV and V Part or unskilled							
		8	10	17	121	10	166
		1.6	2.0	3.4	24.1	2.0	**33.0**
		4.8	6.0	10.2	72.9	6.0	
		7.7	13.0	16.2	63.7	37.0	
Insufficient description							
		19	14	11	32	1	77
		3.8	2.8	2.2	6.4	0.2	**15.3**
		24.7	18.2	14.3	41.6	1.3	
		18.3	18.2	10.5	16.8	3.7	
Total 1991		104	77	105	190	27	503
		20.7	**15.3**	**20.9**	**37.8**	**5.4**	**100.0**

Source: Special tabulations from the Longitudinal Survey.

population whose patterns contrast with those of African-Americans, but even more notable is the position of the Black Other population. This census category is somewhat difficult to unpack (Ballard and Kalra 1994, Owen 1996), but a significant part of the group seem to be the offspring of black/white unions. The fact that the partners of this group are almost equally divided between Black Other and white partners seems to indicate high permeability of the race line and evidence against what has been termed in the USA or Caribbean the "one-drop rule" (Patterson, this volume), that is to say offspring of black/white unions are regarded as black.

Table 6.9 Interethnic unions. All married and cohabiting men and women. Resident population, Great Britain, 1991 (Unions expressed as percentage of male's ethnic group)

| | Ethnic group of female partner | | | | | | | | | | | |
	White	Black Carib	Black African	Black Other	Indian	Pakistani	Bangladeshi	Chinese	Other-Asian	Other-Other	Total	Total
Ethnic group of male partner												
White	**99.49**	0.08	0.03	0.05	0.06	0.01	0.00	0.06	0.12	0.11	100	126803
Black Carib	27.27	**67.76**	0.97	1.21	0.48	0.24	0.00	0.24	0.36	1.45	100	825
Black African	17.08	5.69	**74.02**	1.42	0.71	0.36	0.00	0.00	0.00	0.71	100	281
Black Other	51.70	2.04	1.36	**42.18**	0.68	0.00	0.00	0.00	1.36	0.68	100	147
Indian	6.93	0.10	0.21	0.05	**91.06**	0.93	0.00	0.26	0.21	0.26	100	1935
Pakistani	5.05	0.00	0.00	0.12	0.72	**93.26**	0.00	0.00	0.48	0.36	100	831
Bangladeshi	3.00	0.00	0.86	0.00	1.72	0.43	**93.13**	0.00	0.00	0.86	100	233
Chinese	12.59	0.00	0.00	0.00	0.74	0.00	0.00	**86.67**	0.00	0.00	100	270
Other-Asian	14.71	1.07	0.27	0.27	1.07	1.07	0.27	0.53	**79.14**	1.60	100	374
Other-Other	50.46	0.46	0.23	0.46	1.62	0.93	0.00	0.46	1.16	**44.21**	100	432
												132131

Source: Based on data from Berrington in Coleman and Salt 1996: 199, Table 7.9.

Table 6.10 *Interethnic unions. All married and cohabiting men and women. Resident population, Great Britain, 1991, (Unions expressed as percentage of female's ethnic group)*

					Ethnic group of female partner						
	White	Black Carib	Black African	Black Other	Indian	Pakistani	Bangladeshi	Chinese	Other-Asian	Other-Other	Total
Ethnic group of male partner											
White	99.34	14.83	15.36	43.75	3.81	1.23	0.00	24.38	32.03	38.50	126803
Black Carib	0.18	81.25	3.00	6.94	0.21	0.25	0.00	0.62	0.65	3.32	825
Black African	0.04	2.33	77.90	2.78	0.11	0.12	0.00	0.00	0.00	0.55	281
Black Other	0.06	0.44	0.75	43.06	0.05	0.00	0.00	0.00	0.43	0.28	147
Indian	0.10	0.29	1.50	0.69	94.58	2.21	0.00	1.54	0.87	1.39	1935
Pakistani	0.03	0.00	0.00	0.69	0.32	95.09	0.00	0.00	0.87	0.83	831
Bangladeshi	0.01	0.00	0.75	0.00	0.21	0.12	99.54	0.00	0.00	0.55	233
Chinese	0.03	0.00	0.00	0.00	0.11	0.00	0.00	72.22	0.00	0.00	270
Other-Asian	0.04	0.58	0.37	0.69	0.21	0.49	0.46	0.62	64.07	1.66	374
Other-Other	0.17	0.29	0.37	1.39	0.38	0.49	0.00	0.62	1.08	52.91	432
Total	100	100	100	100	100	100	100	100	100	100	132131
Total	126989	688	267	144	1863	815	218	324	462	361	132131

Source: Based on data from Berrington in Coleman and Salt 1996: Table 7.9.

One of the driving forces behind the interest in residential segregation is its impact on social interaction between groups and in particular, its impact on intermarriage. The greater the degree of residential segregation between groups, the lower the degree of social interaction. The lower the degree of social interaction, the lower the degree of intermarriage. The higher the degree of segregation, the higher the degree of inmarriage. Low levels of segregation correlate with high degrees of intermarriage (Duncan and Lieberson 1959, Peach 1980).

However, the relationship between residential segregation and social interaction, while necessary, is not sufficient. In Britain, one can divide ethnic groups into the patriarchal and the individualistic. In the patriarchal, concepts of control, family honor, and status dominate. Children's marriage partners (cohabitation does not exist as a choice) are determined by parental decision and marriages are not simply the union of couples, but the alliances of families (Ballard 1990).

South Asian households in Britain fall into this patriarchal category. Marriage patterns are strongly endogamous. Indeed, arranged marriages are prevalent and among the Pakistanis, cousin marriages predominate (Ballard 1990). Under such circumstances, ethnic residential patterns have little effect on social interaction (Clarke 1971). Endogamous relationships would dominate even were residences to be ethnically intermixed.

Where individual choices rule, however, cohabitation and marriage choices will tend to reflect the ethnic residential mix. Beshers (1962) has argued that where patriarchal rule can no longer be exercised, residential choice assumes a greater importance. Parental choice gives way to spatial inertia in guiding the choice of potential spouses. Where parents can no longer choose, they let neighborhood geography do the persuasion.

Thus, Indians in Britain, with levels of residential segregation not very different from those of the Caribbean population, have very much more endogamous marriage patterns. Indeed, while the segregation levels of Indians, Pakistanis and Bangladeshis are very different, their marriage patterns are notably similar (see Tables 6.9 and 6.10).

Having noted that residential intermixture is a necessary condition for social interaction, we return to the stark contrast between the hyper-segregation of African-Americans and the comparatively moderate levels for the Caribbean population in Britain (Tables 6.4 and 6.5). We note also that racial intermarriage in the USA is minuscule in relation to British figures. Regrettably the US and British figures are not directly comparable because the US figures deal only with marriage while the British figures include both marriage and cohabitation. However, the marriage data for the USA in 1993 are given in Table 6.11. It can be seen

Table 6.11 *United States race and origin of spouses,*
1993

	N	Percent	
Married couples total ('000s)	54,199	100	
Race			
Same race couples	51,437	94.9	
White/white	47,782	88.2	
Black/black	3,655	6.7	
Interracial couples	1,195	2.2	
Total Interracial couples	1,195	100	
Of which			
Black/white	242	20.25	of which
Black husband / white wife	182		15.23
White husband / black wife	60		5.02
White/other race	920	76.99	
Black/other race	33	2.76	

Source: Statistical Abstract of the United States 1993.

that while there were 3,655 black/black marriages there were only 242 black/white unions.

Conclusion

The position of ethnic minority populations in Britain has become more differentiated since the 1950s, with markedly different trajectories. The Caribbean population shows a mixed position. Economically, it occupies the lower end of the class structure, with males disproportionately concentrated in manual occupations. Caribbean women have a much more white-collar profile but are still underrepresented in the Professional class. The LS data, however, show significant upward mobility for the Caribbean population as a whole.

Socially, the Caribbean population shows a significant gender divide. There is a very high proportion of single-parent, female-headed families with dependent children. Thus although Caribbean women have a higher economic profile than Caribbean men, there is considerable economic disadvantage that flows from female family circumstances. For Caribbean men, although their socioeconomic position is generally disadvantaged, there is a high degree of social integration into white society witnessed by the high degree of intermarriage and cohabitation. For the Caribbean population as a whole, the moderate and decreasing levels of residential segregation, the signs of suburbanization, and the increase in the degree of owner occupation indicate some promise. While the picture is mixed, the Caribbean trajectory seems to be towards convergence with the majority white society of Britain.

The Black Other population, which in some ways seems to represent both the second-generation Caribbean population in Britain and the children of intermarriage, suggests a different and more positive outcome for British interethnic relations than that suggested by Patterson's "one-drop" rule (Patterson, this volume). The socioeconomic class position of the Black Other men shows a higher white-collar proportion than that of the Black Caribbean male population (Figure 6.1). This suggests an upward mobility for Caribbean men which is supported by the LS data (Table 6.8). The intermarriage and cohabitation data for both Black Other men and women show them selecting Black Other and white partners in almost equal proportions (Tables 6.9 and 6.10). This suggests that the patterns of high intermarriage and cohabitation seen for the Black Caribbean population are found in an even more marked way for the younger generation.

Broadly speaking then, the Caribbean population seems to be following the trajectory established by the Irish before them of convergence with the population as a whole. On the other hand, the Indian population seems to have progressed some way already along the Jewish trajectory of economic success with social encapsulation (white-collar, self-employed, suburbanized and owner-occupier but with significant degrees of in-marriage). The Pakistanis and Bangladeshis are rather more ambiguously following this latter route. Despite a fair degree of self-employment and a high degree of owner occupation in the case of the Pakistanis, they are economically more marginal than the Indians. However, all three South Asian groups have maintained a high degree of social exclusiveness as far as marriage patterns are concerned. Thus, while the Caribbean population is economically disadvantaged but increasingly socially assimilated, the Indian population is generally economically advantaged but has retained its social distinctiveness.

The main conclusion from this survey, however, is the marked difference between the position of the Black Caribbean population in Britain compared with the African-American population of the USA. The USA seems to offer greater opportunities for the black elite to rise than does the British situation. The African-American population is larger in absolute numbers and in percentage terms than the Caribbean population in Britain, or even the combined minority ethnic population. As a result, the black and other minority American population has a political power not possessed by the British minority ethnic populations. This power has been wielded to gain jobs for black and minority Americans in a huge range of public and private sector occupations from which the black British population is notably absent. On the other hand, Black Caribbeans have established themselves more solidly in the housing market than African-Americans. Even more impressively, Black Caribbeans are not ghettoized. In Britain in 1990, there were no wards in which the black population, however assessed, amounted to 100 percent of the population. Taking all ethnic minorities together, the highest percentage that they formed of a single ward was 90 in Northcote, Ealing (Peach 1996c). The highest percentage that the Caribbean ethnic population formed of a ward was 30.1 percent in Roundwood in Brent. The highest percentage that Indians formed was 67.2 in Northcote, Ealing. For Pakistanis, the figure was 52.8 percent in University ward in Bradford and for Bangladeshis it was 60.7 percent in Spitalfields, Tower Hamlets. Not only was there no ward in which these groups amounted to all of the population, but there were very few in which they accounted for even a majority of the population.

By contrast, if we take the black population of the United States, there are extensive blocks and tracts where they form 100 percent of the population. In Chicago PMSA in 1990, for example, 8.4 percent of the black population lived in tracts which were 100 percent black. Over two thirds of the black population of Chicago lived in areas which were 90 percent or more black and 82 percent lived in areas that were over 50 percent black. Reflect that if we aggregate all of the ethnic minority population of London, as defined by the 1991 Census, it would amount to 20 percent of the total population, yet there were hardly any wards in which such an aggregated population constituted a majority of the population. In London in 1991, 2.6 percent of the Caribbean population was living in enumeration districts (equivalent to US blocks) where they formed 30 percent or more of the population. Caribbean segregation levels are moderate and decreasing. Social intermixture is significant and rising.

NOTE

Work on this research was assisted by funding from ESRC Grant R 45126463797. Grateful acknowledgement is made to the Cathie Marsh Micro Census Unit, University of Manchester, for access to the Samples of Anonymised records from the 1991 census. Grateful acknowledgement is made to the Longitudinal Study, University of London, for production of tables from the LS.

REFERENCES

Ballard, R., 1990, "Migration and Kinship: the Differential Effect of Marriage Rules on the Processes of Punjabi Migration to Britain," in C. Clarke, C. Peach and S. Vertovec (eds.), *South Asians Overseas: Migration and Ethnicity*, Cambridge University Press, pp. 219–49.

Ballard, R., 1996, "The Pakistanis: Stability and Introspection," in C. Peach (ed.), *The Ethnic Minority Populations of Britain*, London: HMSO, 121–49.

Ballard, R. and V. S. Kalra, 1994, *The Ethnic Dimension of the 1991 Census. A Preliminary Report*, Census Microdata Unit, University of Manchester.

Berrington, A., 1996, "Marriage Patterns and Inter-ethnic Unions," in D. Coleman and J. Salt (eds.), *Ethnicity in the 1991 Census*, Vol. I: *Demographic Characteristics of the Ethnic Minority Populations*, London: OPCS, HMSO, pp. 178–212.

Beshers, J. M., 1962, *Urban Social Structure*, New York: Free Press.

Brown, C., 1984, *Black and White Britain: The Third PSI Survey*, London: Gower.

Byron, M., 1994, *Post-War Caribbean Migration to Britain: The Unfinished Cycle*, Aldershot: Avebury.

Clarke, C. G., 1971, "Residential Segregation and Intermarriage in San Fernando, Trinidad," *Geographical Review* 61: 198–218.

Denton, N. A., 1994, "Are African-Americans Still Hypersegregated?" in R. D. Bullard, J. E. Grigsby, and C. Lee (eds.), *Residential Apartheid: The American Legacy*, Los Angeles: Center for Afro-American Studies, UCLA, pp. 49–81.

Duncan, O. D. and B. Duncan, 1955, "A Methodological Analysis of Segregation Indexes," *American Sociological Review* 20: 210–17.

Duncan, O. D. and S. Lieberson, 1959, "Ethnic Segregation and Assimilation," *American Journal of Sociology* 64: 364–74.

Eade, J., T. Vamplew, and C. Peach, 1996, "Bangladeshis: The Encapsulated Community," in C. Peach (ed.), *The Ethnic Minority Populations of Britain*, London: HMSO, pp. 150–60.

Glass, R. and J. Westergaard, 1965, *London's Housing Needs: Statement of Evidence to the Committee on Housing in Greater London*, London: Centre for Urban Studies (Report No. 5).

Keith, M., 1993, "From Punishment to Discipline? Racism, Racialisation and the Policing of Social Control," in M. Cross, and M. Keith (eds.), *Racism, the City and the State*, London: Routledge, pp. 193–209.

Lee, T. R., 1973, *Race and Residence: The Concentration and Dispersal of Immigrants in London*, Oxford: Clarendon Press.

Lieberson, S., 1963, *Ethnic Patterns in American Cities*, New York: Free Press of Glencoe.

Massey, D. S. and N. A. Denton, 1993, *American Apartheid*, Cambridge, MA: Harvard University Press.

Modood, T., R. Berthand, J. Lakey, J. Nazroo, P. Smith, S. Virdee, and S. Beishon, 1997, *Ethnic Minorities in Britain: Diversity and Disadvantage*, London: Policy Studies Institute.

Owen, D., 1996, "Black-Other," in C. Peach (ed.), *The Ethnic Minority Populations of Britain*, London: HMSO, pp. 66–94.

OPCS (Office of Population Censuses and Surveys), 1993, *1991 Census of Great Britain, Ethnic Groups and Country of Birth Great Britain*, Vol. II, London: HMSO.

Peach, C. 1968, *West Indian Migration to Britain*, London: Oxford University Press.

1975, *Urban Social Segregation*, London: Longman.

1980, "Which Triple Melting Pot?" *Ethnic and Racial Studies* 3, 1: 1–16.

1986, "A Geographical Perspective on the 1981 Urban Riots in England," *Ethnic and Racial Studies* 9, 3: 386–94.

1990, "Estimating the Growth of the Bangladeshi Population of Great Britain," *New Community* 16: 481–91.

1991, *The Caribbean in Europe: Contrasting Patterns of Migration and Settlement in Britain, France and the Netherlands*, Research Paper in Ethnic Relations 15, Centre for Research in Ethnic Relations University of Warwick.

1996a, "Introduction," in C. Peach (ed.), *The Ethnic Minority Populations of Britain*, London: HMSO, pp. 1–24.

1996b, "Black-Caribbeans: Class, Gender and Geography," in C. Peach (ed.), *The Ethnic Minority Populations of Britain*, London: HMSO, pp. 25–43.

1996c, "Does Britain have Ghettos?" *Transactions of the Institute of British Geographers* 22: 216–35.

1997, "Postwar Migration to Europe: Reflux, Influx, Refuge," *Social Science Quarterly* 78, 2, 269–83.

1999, "London and New York: Contrasts in British and American Models of Segregation," *International Journal of Population Geography* 5: 319–51.

Peach C. and S. Shah, 1980, "The Contribution of Council House Allocation to West Indian Desegregation in London, 1961–1971," *Urban Studies* 17: 331–41.

Peach, C. and M. Byron 1993, "Caribbean Tenants in Council Housing: 'Race', Class and Gender," New Community 19: 407–23.

1994, "Council House Sales, Residualisation and Afro Caribbean Tenants," *Journal of Social Policy* 23: 363–83.

PEP, 1966 but undated, *A P.E.P. Report on Racial Discrimination*, London: Political and Economic Planning.

Philpott, T. L., 1978, *The Slum and the Ghetto*, New York: Oxford University Press.

Rex, J. and R. Moore, 1967, *Race, Community and Conflict: A Study of Sparkbrook*, London: Oxford University Press.

Robinson, V., 1986, *Settlers, Transients and Refugees*, Oxford: Clarendon Press.

Scarman, X., 1981, *The Brixton Disorders 10–12 April, 1981*, Report of an enquiry by the Rt. Hon. The Lord Scarman, OBE, Cmnd. 8427, London: HMSO (The Scarman Report).

Smith, D. J., 1976, *The Facts of Racial Disadvantage: A National Survey*, London: Political and Economic Planning.

Woods, R. I., 1976, "Aspects of the Scale Problems in the Calculation of Segregation Indicos," *Tijdschift voor Economische en Sociale Geografie* 67, 3: 169–74.

7   Ghettos and the transmission of ethnic capital

David M. Cutler, Edward L. Glaeser, and Jacob L. Vigdor

1   Introduction

African-Americans have experienced high levels of residential segregation from the racial majority for at least a century (Massey and Denton
1993, Cutler, Glaeser, and Vigdor 1999). Over the same time period,
black socioeconomic outcomes have persistently lagged behind those of
the majority, even as other initially disadvantaged ethnic and racial groups
have experienced convergence (see Figures 7.1 and 7.2). Social scientists
have developed and tested two causal explanations linking the former
trend with the latter. First, the spatial mismatch hypothesis, proposed
by John Kain in 1968, posits that residential segregation introduces a
physical separation between blacks and centers of employment, which
in turn adversely affects black outcomes. Empirical tests of this hypothesis (see Kain 1992, Ihlandfeldt and Sjoquist 1998 for recent reviews)
have provided varying degrees of support for the hypothesis. Second,
recent literature emphasizing the importance of neighborhood effects,
peer groups, and social interactions proposes that segregation negatively
affects blacks by separating them from positive role models, high-quality
local public goods, or other important inputs into the human capital production function (Wilson 1987, Case and Katz 1993, Cutler and Glaeser
1997).[1]

A natural question to ask upon examining this previous research is
whether residential segregation per se has negative effects on socioeconomic outcomes, or whether the relationship between segregation and
outcomes depends on specific factors, such as the proximity of ghettos
to employment centers or the collective human capital of the segregated
group.[2] Are inhabitants of an isolated ethnic enclave consistently harmed
by their isolation, even in cases where they can productively trade with one
another and count many positive role models among their group? This
chapter investigates the relationship between segregation, characteristics
of the segregated group, and subsequent outcomes for group members,

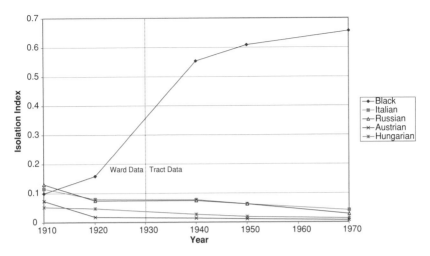

Figure 7.1 Isolation of blacks and new immigrant groups

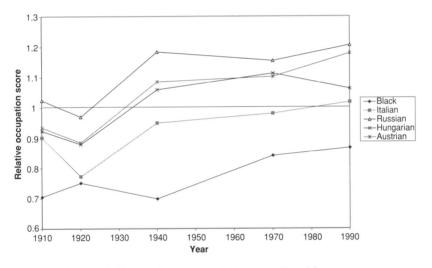

Figure 7.2 Occupation scores relative to native whites

expanding on the groundwork laid by Borjas' (1995) investigation of ethnicity, neighborhoods, and human capital.

The focus of this study, and to some degree its motivation, is the experience of blacks and white immigrant groups in the early part of the twentieth century.[3] In this chapter we introduce ethnic group segregation measures derived from census data beginning in 1910. These indices measure the degree to which foreign-born individuals are isolated within enclaves composed of persons of their nationality. In 1910, as Figure 7.1 illustrates, some white ethnic groups – Russians and Italians – were actually more segregated, on average, than blacks in cities across the United States. Similar to blacks, these immigrant groups had socioeconomic outcomes that lagged behind those of native whites. This can be seen in Figure 7.2, which plots an occupation-based measure of income over time for each group.

Since 1910, blacks and these immigrant groups have traveled widely divergent paths. Immigrant segregation essentially dissipated within one generation, while immigrant outcomes rapidly converged to native white levels. Black segregation, by contrast, skyrocketed between 1910 and 1970, and black outcomes continue to lag behind those of native whites. There are some obvious hypotheses to explain this striking divergence. Race was undoubtedly a significant barrier to assimilation. Continued migration of blacks from rural to urban settings weighed down average group characteristics well after the flow of immigrants from Europe had stopped.

At first glance, it might appear that elevated initial segregation levels could not have played a strong role in subsequent black outcome disparities – after all, many other groups with similarly high segregation in 1910 converged rapidly to native white means. If the effects of segregation differ systematically across ethnic groups, however, the potential for a causal relationship persists. This potential relationship motivates an interesting hypothetical question. How much of the black trend in outcomes since 1910 can be explained by their persistently high residential segregation? Had blacks experienced residential integration as immigrants did, what would their socioeconomic relationship to native whites look like today?

The central hypothesis we test, that the effects of segregation depend on the characteristics of the segregated, has an alternative, equivalent interpretation. We hypothesize that the rate of intergenerational *ethnic capital* transmission increases as ethnic group members experience greater exposure to one another within neighborhoods. Ethnic capital can be thought of as the set of individual attributes, cultural norms, and group-specific institutions that contribute to an ethnic group's economic productivity.[4] The transmission of ethnic capital across generations might occur for several reasons – the inheritance or emulation of parent-generation characteristics, internalization of norms and values, or cross-generational partnership in networks or institutions (Borjas 1992; see also Zhou, this volume). Each of these avenues of transmission might theoretically depend on the degree of within-group exposure at the neighborhood level.

The transmission of ethnic capital between generations should generate a correlation in socioeconomic outcomes between generations, even after controlling for correlations between individual parents and their children. Thus, to evaluate our hypothesis empirically, we test to see whether average ethnic group outcomes are more highly correlated across generations in segregated environments. To accomplish this, we match racial and ethnic segregation indices to individual socioeconomic characteristics reported in the census Integrated Public Use Microdata Samples (IPUMS).[5]

The results, based on cross-sectional samples of the urban population in 1910 and 1940, reveal some striking patterns. We find consistent evidence that the effect of segregation on subsequent outcomes for white ethnic groups depends on the ethnic capital of the group in question. This pattern does not, however, extrapolate to blacks, whose ethnic capital values in 1910 were substantially below those of any white ethnic group. Thus, we find evidence to suggest that segregation affects the transmission of ethnic capital between generations, at least for some ethnic groups. Since blacks do not fit into this pattern, however, we cannot say that low initial human capital coupled with high initial segregation contributed to consistently low black outcomes, at least in the early part of the twentieth century.

2   Data and methods

Our measures of ethnic segregation utilize data from the decennial censuses beginning in 1910. In that year, the Census Bureau began reporting the distribution of foreign-born persons by country of birth at the ward level for cities with at least 50,000 inhabitants.[6] Similar reports are available from the 1920 Census. There are no ward-level country of birth reports for any cities after 1920. In 1940 and 1950, country of birth is reported at the census tract level for a relatively small sample of cities.[7] This series is replaced by reports of "country of origin" for persons of foreign stock – foreign-born individuals (first-generation immigrants) and their native-born children (second-generation immigrants) – in 1960. Finally, the 1970 Census reports the census tract-level distribution of country of origin for both first- and second-generation immigrants separately.[8]

Segregation can be measured along many dimensions (Massey and Denton 1988). In this paper, we will be focusing on ethnic and racial *isolation*. To understand the definition of isolation, first consider a relatively simple measure, which we'll call the *exposure index*:

$$\text{Exposure index} \equiv E = \sum_{i=1}^{N} \frac{group_i}{group_{total}} \times \frac{group_i}{persons_i}, \tag{1}$$

where i indexes one of N neighborhoods (wards or tracts) in a city, $group_i$ indicates the number of racial or ethnic group members present in neighborhood i, $persons_i$ the total population of i, and $group_{total}$ the total number of group members across all neighborhoods in the city. The exposure index simply measures the ethnic group's share of population in the average group member's neighborhood.

The exposure index will always increase when group members form a larger share of the overall population. The isolation index attempts to purge this source of variation by subtracting off the overall citywide ethnic group share of population. Thus, when a group is evenly distributed across neighborhoods, the isolation index will always equal zero. To give the index a maximum of one, we divide by the theoretical maximum value. The end result is the following formula:

$$\text{Isolation index} = \frac{E - \left(\frac{group_{total}}{persons_{total}}\right)}{\min\left(\frac{group_{total}}{persons_i}, 1\right) - \left(\frac{group_{total}}{persons_{total}}\right)}, \tag{2}$$

where $persons_i$ represents the total population of the ward or tract with minimum population.[9] The isolation index thus measures the degree to which a group's exposure exceeds the level that would result from an even distribution of members across wards or tracts.

To determine how segregation levels in a city relate to individual outcomes, we will match our segregation data to the Integrated Public Use Microdata Samples (IPUMS), which provide detailed demographic and economic information for a 1 percent sample of the US population in each census year.

3   Modeling segregation, ethnicity, and outcomes

Previous research has sought to illuminate the relationship between ethnic group characteristics and individual outcomes (Borjas 1992) and between neighborhood characteristics and individual outcomes (Case and Katz 1993, Cutler and Glaeser 1997; see Ellen and Turner 1997 for a recent review). Borjas (1995) unites the two strands of literature, finding

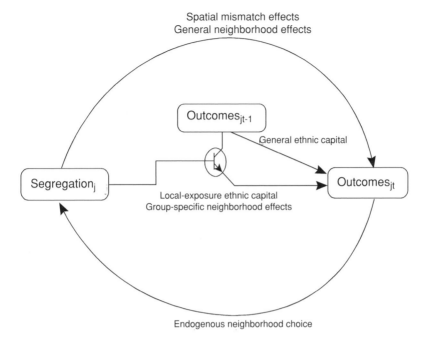

Figure 7.3 Causality in the relationship between segregation and outcomes (j = group; t = generation)

evidence to support the hypothesis that the intergenerational correlation of economic outcomes is strongest in neighborhoods where groups are highly concentrated.

The potential avenues of causality between segregation, ethnic group outcomes in the parent generation, and group outcomes in the child generation are diagramed in Figure 7.3. Potential causal relationships of one factor on another are indicated by arrows linking cause to effect. Underlying most of these arrows is the supposition that an individual's human capital is determined in part through their interactions with others. Both an individual's long-range goals, such as career paths, and short-term decisions, such as whether to commit a crime, are presumably influenced by interpersonal contact, as well as shared values, networks, institutions, and role models. Interpersonal contact occurs most frequently between physically proximate individuals. Potential role models are quite plausibly drawn from the ranks of an individual's neighbors and fellow ethnic group members. Each of the potential avenues of causality depicted in Figure 7.3 merits discussion here.

Segregation might have an impact on outcomes completely independent of the characteristics of the segregated group. The effects posited by the spatial mismatch hypothesis, for example, have little to do with the inherent characteristics of ghetto residents. According to the spatial mismatch argument, any group housed at great distance from employment centers will have difficulties in the labor market. Even if ghettos are not located far from employment centers, segregation might predict worse (or better) outcomes to the extent that regular interaction with a diverse group of people enhances (or detracts from) human capital accumulation. Aside from effects on human capital accumulation, segregation may positively impact groups by yielding opportunities for within-group trade. In Figure 7.3, these potential general effects of ghettoization are referred to as "general neighborhood effects."

As segregation may have independent effects on outcomes, ethnic groups might display correlations in outcomes across generations regardless of their degree of neighborhood concentration. One reason for this link is the well-documented correlation between parent and child outcomes (Becker and Tomes 1986, Solon 1992). Above and beyond this within-family correlation, the transmission of ethnic capital simply might not operate through frequent interaction with members of one's own group. A child's interaction with his or her own parents, or with a small number of individuals of the same ethnicity, might be sufficient to impart the shared norms or characteristics that create intergenerational outcome correlations. We refer to ethnic capital that can be transmitted without extensive within-group contact as "general ethnic capital."

While both segregation and parent-generation characteristics might have independent effects on child-generation outcomes, it is quite reasonable to suspect that the two purported causes are linked with one another. From one perspective, it is reasonable to expect that the influence of ethnic group characteristics (from the parent generation) on individual (child-generation) outcomes depends on the individual's degree of exposure to other group members. From another perspective, it is equally reasonable to expect the effects of high ethnic exposure to depend on the average characteristics of the ethnic group in question. Growing up in a poverty-stricken ethnic enclave should have different effects from growing up in a community of highly educated, skilled immigrants.

Since this interacted effect of ethnic capital and segregation has two equivalent interpretations, it is described with two names in Figure 7.3. The interacted effect represents the component of ethnic capital transmission between generations that depends on the degree of ethnic exposure. Equivalently, this effect can be described as the effect of segregation on outcomes that depends on the characteristics of the segregated group.

It is important to note that some components of ethnic capital might work to reduce, rather than increase, the intergenerational correlation of economic outcomes. Some ethnic groups, for example, might gravitate towards low-paying occupations in the first generation but create social institutions and norms that encourage higher achievement in the second generation. From this perspective, the effect of ethnic isolation on outcomes might vary across ethnic groups, but in a way not directly related to the socioeconomic outcomes of the parent generation. Embedded in our hypothesis, then, is the supposition that transmittable ethnic capital is, at least in the aggregate, positively correlated with measurable outcomes in the parent generation.[10]

There is one remaining, and potentially troubling, arrow in the diagram. There may be a reverse-causal relationship between outcomes and segregation levels. More broadly, there may be some factor omitted from this diagram that directly affects both outcomes and segregation, creating a correlation between the two when (potentially) no causal relationship exists. Any study of the relationship between segregation and outcomes is hampered by the fact that researchers, under most circumstances, cannot randomly assign treatment subjects to neighborhoods with varying characteristics.[11]

Our strategy for circumventing this potential endogeneity problem relies on the cross-generational nature of the study.[12] In our empirical analysis, we will examine the impact of segregation, as measured in the *parent* generation, on outcomes in the *child* generation. Since we consider an individual's outcomes to be a function of various factors influencing that person's development, it is quite natural to use past rather than present values of variables such as segregation in our empirical work. Use of this strategy clearly limits our ability to measure spatial mismatch effects and other hypothesized links between current segregation and current outcomes. Since our primary purpose here is to quantify the role of segregation in ethnic capital transmission, and not to identify all the effects of segregation on outcomes, we are comfortable with this limitation.

If causality runs only from outcomes to segregation, we might still observe a spurious relationship with this strategy if the outcomes that determine segregation levels, or omitted factors that determine both outcomes and segregation levels, are correlated across generations. Any such problematic relationship will be greatly reduced, if not eliminated, by controlling for outcomes in the preceding generation. We discuss this strategy in greater detail in the following section.

We focus on one outcome in particular: educational attainment, as reported for the "child" generation of blacks and second-generation

Table 7.1 *Ethnic capital measures*

Group	Mean standardized occupation score, 1910
Native whites	0.168
Blacks	−0.715
Canadians	0.077
English	0.123
Scottish	0.170
Irish	0.002
Greek	−0.386
Italian	−0.326
Austrian	−0.248
German	0.042
Hungarian	−0.336
Romanian	0.189
Russian	−0.015

Note: Occupation scores are standardized to mean zero and standard deviation one.

immigrants in the 1940 IPUMS.[13] Having defined our segregation measures in Section 2 above, we'll devote some attention here to our measure of ethnic capital, as well as the other control variables that appear in our regression models.

To measure ethnic capital of the "parent" generation, we will use one of the few socioeconomic indicators available from the 1910 Census, the occupation score. This measure, available for all census years in the IPUMS dataset, maps individuals' occupations into standardized 1950 classifications, and then into average annual earnings for individuals working in those occupations in 1950. Persons working in more remunerative occupations, then, are assigned higher occupation score values. We transform individual occupation scores to have mean zero and standard deviation one, then find the average value for all ethnic group members in the 1910 IPUMS sample.[14] Table 7.1 presents the ethnic capital measures for the set of ethnic groups included in our analysis.[15] Several immigrant groups, as well as native whites, have mean occupation scores above the national average. Most of the "new" immigrant groups, though, lag behind native whites, as documented in Figure 7.2 above. Blacks display the lowest ethnic capital score, by a fairly wide margin.

In addition to ethnic capital and segregation measures, our regressions include a number of control variables to separate out various factors that influence individual outcomes. Some of these factors, such as gender and age, are individual-specific.

As we alluded to in our discussion of the possible endogeneity of segregation levels above, selective migration might lead to systematic differences between children of a particular ethnic group who grew up in a segregated environment and children of the same ethnic group who grew up in an integrated environment. That is to say, parents choosing to reside in a ghetto might differ in important respects from parents who choose not to. To mitigate the potential selection bias associated with these parental differences, we include a set of control variables measuring characteristics of members of an individual's ethnic group who lived in the same city in 1910. These characteristics include the average standardized occupation score of employed males, literacy rates, the fraction of English-speakers, the average number of years since arrival in the USA for first-generation immigrants, and the proportion of married males with spouses belonging to a different ethnic group.[16] This set of parent-generation characteristics is clearly not exhaustive, but we feel it provides a reasonable check against the potential omitted variable bias associated with selective migration.

To ensure that our estimates of the effects of segregation for different groups do not simply reflect the impact of residing in different cities, we include city fixed effects in our regression models. This restricts our analysis to comparisons of ethnic groups within cities – we will determine whether ethnic groups that are more segregated than others in their city have different outcomes than less segregated groups in the same city.

The sample in each regression consists of individuals between 19 and 48 years old in 1940 who were born in their state of residence. The age restriction ensures that no individuals used to calculate parent-generation statistics in 1910 are included in our child-generation sample. The birthplace restriction limits the sample to include only those individuals most likely to have actually grown up in their 1940 city of residence.[17] For these individuals, the characteristics of the city as of 1910 are sure to be more relevant than to others who migrated later in life. The regressions include both second-generation immigrants and native whites; most parent-generation statistics, except for the occupation-score based measures, are set to zero for natives.

4   Results

Table 7.2 presents the results of probit regressions investigating the determinants of individual educational attainment in 1940. The dependent variable takes on a value of one for individuals who graduated from high school, and zero for all others. The first column presents coefficients from

Table 7.2 *Ethnic capital, segregation, and educational attainment, 1940*

Independent variable	Dependent variable: High school graduate indicator			
Group isolation index (1910)	3.435** (0.392)	4.074** (1.706)	3.227* (1.674)	4.169** (1.709)
Ethnic capital (1910)	−0.815 (1.185)	−1.699 (1.263)	−0.426 (1.115)	−1.729 (1.246)
Ethnic capital (1910)* Isolation index	32.17** (11.32)	20.98** (5.526)	5.829* (2.988)	20.40** (5.384)
Black group indicator	–	–	−1.268** (0.473)	−2.128** (0.570)
Black* isolation index (1910)	–	–	–	11.47** (3.019)
Individual characteristic controls	Yes	Yes	Yes	Yes
City fixed effects	Yes	Yes	Yes	Yes
Ethnic group-city level characteristics (1910)	No	Yes	Yes	Yes
Pseudo-R^2	0.070	0.074	0.076	0.076
N	23,397	23,397	25,265	25,265

Note: Entries in the table are coefficients from maximum likelihood probit estimation. Standard errors, corrected for grouped observations, in parentheses. Ethnic capital is measured by the standardized group mean occupation score in 1910. Observations are weighted by square root of sample size used to calculate mean group occupation score in city (1910). Sample consists of all individuals age 19–48. Individual characteristic controls include categorical age dummies and sex. Ethnic group/city-level characteristics include intermarriage rate, literacy rate, English-speaking rate, average standardized occupation score, and average years since immigration for first-generation immigrants. Native whites, included in all regressions, have the following variables set to zero: isolation index (1910), English-speaking rate (1910), literacy rate (1910), intermarriage rate (1910), and average years since immigration (1910). The regression contains a dummy variable to identify native whites.
** denotes a coefficient significant at the 5 percent level, * the 10 percent level.

a regression model including controls for age and gender, as well as city fixed effects, but omitting city/ethnic group specific parent-generation characteristics. The sample includes second-generation immigrants and native whites, but omits blacks. The first three rows of the table report the coefficients on the isolation index, ethnic capital measure, and interaction of isolation with ethnic capital, respectively. The pattern of results is consistent with the model of ghettos as conduits for ethnic capital transmission described above. For a group with an ethnic capital measure equal to zero, higher degrees of segregation in 1910 actually predict higher high school graduation rates in 1940. For groups with average standardized occupation scores of −0.1, however, the positive effect of segregation disappears. As ethnic capital descends below this level, the effect of segregation becomes more negative.

These results also indicate that residentially integrated groups display little, if any, intergenerational correlation in outcomes. As the degree of isolation increases, however, the correlation between generations becomes more clearly positive. According to these results, exposure to members of one's ethnic group at the neighborhood level plays a strong role in the transmission of ethnic capital.

As discussed above, there is some reason to be concerned that these results reflect selective migration – that outcomes for some groups were worse in segregated cities because individuals more disposed to poor outcomes settled there in the first place.[18] Adding controls for the parent-generation characteristics of ethnic groups by city, as in the second column of Table 7.2, we see evidence that selective migration might indeed explain some part of our results. The ethnic capital-isolation interaction coefficient retains statistical significance in this model, but the estimated magnitude falls by roughly one-third. The point estimates now suggest that segregation has negative effects for those groups with ethnic capital values below −0.2. As in the first regression, the rate of ethnic capital transmission appears to be essentially zero in cities where groups are fully integrated into the population.

Neither of the first two regression specifications in Table 7.2 incorporate data on blacks. Since blacks have a mean standardized occupation score substantially below that of any immigrant group in 1910, and the results presented to this point suggest that the effects of segregation on outcomes are more negative for groups with this characteristic, one might predict that the correlation between segregation and outcomes in the black population would be strongly negative. In fact, this is not the case. The third regression reported in Table 7.2 introduces blacks to the sample, adding an indicator variable to the specification to mark the added black observations. Expansion of the sample results in a substantial 75 percent reduction in the ethnic capital-isolation interaction coefficient – suggesting that the relationship between segregation, ethnic capital, and outcomes noted in the immigrant population does not extrapolate well to the black population. The coefficient on the black indicator variable is statistically significant and negative, suggesting that black high-school graduation rates were lower than one would predict on the basis of other observable characteristics.

The table's final regression verifies this impression, adding a new interaction effect that allows the effect of segregation on outcomes to stray from the model generated with immigrant group data. The interaction of the black indicator variable with the isolation index measures the extent of black deviation from the immigrant-based model. As we would expect, the first three coefficients reported are essentially the same as their counterparts in the table's second regression. For immigrants, the effect of segregation on outcomes is negative for groups with ethnic capital measures below -0.2.

For blacks, we calculate the effect of segregation by summing the main isolation effect, the black-isolation interaction term, and the ethnic capital interaction effect multiplied by -0.7 (the black ethnic capital value). Putting these terms together yields 1.4, a value statistically indistinguishable from zero. In 1940, black high-school graduation rates, although universally lower than one would otherwise predict, were essentially independent of blacks' relative segregation in the preceding generation.[19]

The results presented here tell a somewhat complicated story. First, there is evidence to suggest that the effects of immigrant segregation depend on the characteristics of the segregated group. Ethnic isolation tends to perpetuate differences between ethnic groups – leading to better outcomes for relatively advantaged groups, and worse outcomes for disadvantaged groups. The relationship does not extrapolate to the black population. Parent-generation segregation levels carried few implications for urban blacks in 1940.

5   Discussion and conclusions

At one time, blacks and white immigrant groups experienced roughly equivalent rates of segregation in American cities. Simultaneously, both black and immigrant economic outcomes lagged behind those of native whites. Since that time, most of the white ethnic groups have witnessed near complete integration and a gradual convergence in outcomes. African-Americans, by contrast, saw an escalation of segregation to unprecedented levels and continue to face a gap in outcomes.

These observations provoked a hypothesis, that perhaps the post-1910 divergence between black and immigrant segregation levels and outcomes can be explained by differential effects of segregation that depend on the initial characteristics of the segregated group. Our empirical investigation found evidence to support this hypothesis, but only in the sample of white ethnic groups. Among immigrant groups, residence in a segregated city predicts poor outcomes only for groups with low initial levels of ethnic capital, as measured by mean standardized occupation scores. As this measure of average group skills increases, the negative relationship evaporates. Extrapolating this result from the immigrant sample to the black population, one would expect higher segregation levels to predict significantly worse outcomes. As our results show, this is in fact not the case. Elevated 1910 segregation levels predict neither higher nor lower black outcomes in 1940.

How might we explain this intriguing discrepancy? While a full explanation is beyond the scope of this chapter, several facts and arguments made in existing literature suggest that our findings are really not all that surprising.

The social forces underlying black and European immigrant segregation were not entirely the same. In the early twentieth century, black segregation was enforced by a number of official and quasi-official barriers. While some white immigrant groups faced similar barriers, it is difficult to argue that external restrictions on their residential choices were more severe than those facing blacks. Segregation in 1910 was more a matter of individual choice for immigrants than blacks.

The benefits of exiting a ghetto were most likely limited for blacks, especially Southern blacks, by the extent of legal segregation outside the residential sphere. Whereas an immigrant family living in a ghetto in 1910 might wish to move in order to place their children in higher-quality public schools, a black family in the South faced no such incentive.

The option to exit the ghetto was probably most valuable to upwardly mobile members of an ethnic group – individuals who experienced success in economic and social assimilation. White immigrants were able to exercise this option to a greater extent than their black counterparts. The relatively high degree of class integration within black ghettos in the early decades of the twentieth century has been extensively documented (Wilson 1987). Quite possibly, black ghettos distinguished themselves from enclaves of similarly disadvantaged ethnic groups because of their greater degree of class integration. This distinction would not be captured by the measure of ethnic capital that we use in this chapter. Class integration within a ghetto permits the development of neighborhood culture, social networks and institutions that would factor into a more comprehensive measure of ethnic capital.

Our results here conflict with earlier research documenting a negative relationship between segregation and socioeconomic outcomes in the black population in 1990 (Cutler and Glaeser 1997). Recent research has confirmed, however, that this relationship was not in evidence in earlier census years (Collins and Margo 2000, Vigdor 2002a). The changing significance of segregation for black outcomes mirrors a change in the socioeconomic composition of black ghettos (Wilson 1987). As economic advancement, Federal laws against housing discrimination, and changing white attitudes have enabled some black families to exit the ghetto, the selected group left behind has suffered a loss of ethnic capital. While it is interesting to note that the pre-1940 black experience does not fit neatly into the immigrant-based model in the results we present here, it is perhaps more interesting to note that recent black experiences do appear to resonate with the immigrant model.

This chapter ends with an answer posed to its initial question – how much of the black trend in outcomes since 1910 can be explained by their persistently high residential segregation. The answer, at least covering the period between 1910 and 1940, is very little, if any. With this answer comes a new question – why were the implications of segregation so different for low ethnic-capital immigrant groups and blacks? As we begin a new century, with even newer "new" immigrant groups striving to assimilate in many developed nations, the answer to this question is of great importance.

NOTES

George Galster, Robert Margo, and seminar participants at the NBER Summer Institute and the Boston University Institute on Race and Social Division provided helpful comments on earlier versions of this research. Joe Geraci and Susan Dunn provided outstanding research assistance. We thank Kerwin Charles and the editors for invaluable comments, and the National Science Foundation for research support. Remaining errors are the authors' responsibility.

1. Our conceptualization of human capital follows from the traditional labor economics literature (Becker 1964) and can be thought of as the stock of knowledge, skills, and abilities that determine an individual's productivity.
2. In this chapter, we use the term "ghetto" to refer to any ethnically concentrated neighborhood. A ghetto, by our construction, need not be socioeconomically disadvantaged.
3. Lieberson (1963) and Taeuber and Taeuber (1964) compare the segregation patterns of blacks and immigrant groups over a similar time period. Lieberson, in his analysis of ten northern cities, observes the same patterns evidenced in our Figure 7.1. Taeuber and Taeuber, who focus on ethnic and racial groups in Chicago, note patterns similar to our Figures 7.1 and 7.2.
4. For sake of brevity, the term "ethnic group" will be used in this paper to refer to groups identified by either ethnicity or race.
5. The IPUMS represents a 1 percent sample of the US population in each census year. Individual observations are not linked across years.
6. Wards are political divisions of cities that vary substantially in size and shape. For this reason, there are some difficulties associated with comparing segregation levels across cities (see Cutler, Glaeser, and Vigdor 1999 for a discussion). Since we are able to construct segregation measures for multiple groups per city, in our empirical work we will employ city fixed effects in order to focus on the within-city variation in segregation levels.
7. Census tracts are geographically contiguous areas, delimited by major streets, railways, or other natural features, each containing approximately 4,000

residents. Tracts are in many ways more useful approximations of neighborhoods than are wards, since they are defined in a way that makes them comparable across cities and over time.

8. In 1970, we use metropolitan statistical area (MSA) level data rather than city level. Previous analysis (reported in Cutler, Glaeser, and Vigdor 1999) shows that there is a strong degree of correlation between city- and MSA-based segregation indices. When using the term "city" for the years 1970 and later, we are referring to MSAs.

9. See Cutler, Glaeser, and Vigdor 1999 for additional discussion and analysis of the isolation index.

10. The failure of this supposition to hold might explain some of the results we describe in section 4 below.

11. The recent Moving To Opportunity (MTO) programs undertaken in several American cities provide an exception to this. Several researchers have used MTO programs, which randomly assign central city households to neighborhoods with varying characteristics, to make inferences about the effects of neighborhoods (Katz, Kling, and Liebman 2001; Ladd and Ludwig 2003).

12. Galster (1987) identifies this simultaneous equation problem and uses an instrumental variable strategy to surmount it.

13. We obtained qualitatively similar results using the logarithm of earned income as an outcome measure.

14. The averages are calculated using only males who reported being in the labor force in 1910.

15. Many individuals classified as Russian, German, or Austrian in the 1910 IPUMS data would be categorized as Poles in later census years. The ethnic capital measures for these groups, in particular the German and Russian values, are effectively measured with error. Thus, we would expect a lower correlation between ethnic capital, as we measure it, and subsequent outcomes for these ethnic groups. As both the German and Russian estimates are relatively close to zero, we do not expect this measurement issue to have much impact on our results. First- and second-generation Polish immigrants, and members of other immigrant groups for which we have no segregation data in 1910, are deleted from the 1940 sample used in our empirical work.

16. These city/ethnic group characteristics are based on 1910 IPUMS data, a 1 percent sample of the entire population. Consequently, these measures will be subject to sampling error. Since sample sizes vary by ethnic group and city, this introduces heteroskedasticity problems. We combat these problems by estimating weighted regressions. Weights are equal to the square root of the sample size used to calculate the mean standardized occupation score.

17. This is an especially important restriction for our analysis of outcomes in the black population, since a considerable amount of black migration from rural areas to cities took place between 1910 and 1940. Even with this restriction, it is possible that we may include some individuals who grew up outside their 1940 city of residence. For example, we include blacks born in rural Georgia who had moved to Atlanta by 1940. We expect this "contamination" of our sample to reduce our estimates of intergenerational outcome correlation, especially within the black population.

18. Bear in mind that for the results in the first column of Table 7.1 to reflect selection bias, it must be true that both (1) unobservably *worse-off* members of low ethnic capital groups disproportionately choose to reside in ghettos, and (2) unobservably *better-off* members of high ethnic capital groups disproportionately choose to reside in ghettos. If worse-off members of all groups choose to reside in ghettos, we would predict the overall (non-interacted) effect of isolation to be negative, but it is not clear that we would make any prediction regarding the interaction term.

19. This finding corroborates some existing research. Both Vigdor (2002a) and Collins and Margo (2000) report that the negative correlation between black segregation and black outcomes, documented in 1990 by Cutler and Glaeser (1997), is not present in earlier data. This correlation may reflect selective migration: more educated blacks migrated disproportionately to highly segregated cities before 1940 (Vigdor 2002b).

REFERENCES

Becker, G. S., 1964, *Human Capital; A Theoretical and Empirical Analysis, with Special Reference to Education*, New York: National Bureau of Economic Research.

Borjas, G. J., 1992, "Ethnic Capital and Intergenerational Mobility," *Quarterly Journal of Economics* 107: 123–50.

1995, "Ethnicity, Neighborhoods, and Human Capital Externalities," *American Economic Review* 85: 365–90.

Case, A. and L. Katz, 1991, "The Company You Keep: The Effect of Family and Neighborhood on Disadvantaged Youth," NBER Working Paper #3705.

Collins, W. and R. A. Margo, 2000, "Residential Segregation and Socioeconomic Outcomes: When Did Ghettos Go Bad?" *Economics Letters* 69, 2: 239–43.

Cutler, D. M. and E. L. Glaeser, 1997, "Are Ghettos Good or Bad?" *Quarterly Journal of Economics* 112: 827–72.

Cutler, D., E. Glaeser, and J. Vigdor, 1999, "The Rise and Decline of the American Ghetto," *Journal of Political Economy* 107: 455–506.

Ellen, I. G. and M. A. Turner, 1997, "Does Neighborhood Matter? Assessing Recent Evidence," *Housing Policy Debate* 8: 833–86.

Galster, G. C., 1987, "Residential Segregation and Interracial Economic Disparities: A Simultaneous-Equations Approach," *Journal of Urban Economics* 21: 22–44.

Ihlandfeldt, K. R. and D. L. Sjoquist, 1998, "The Spatial Mismatch Hypothesis: A Review of Recent Studies and Their Implications for Welfare Reform," *Housing Policy Debate* 9: 849–92.

Kain, J. F., 1968, "Housing Segregation, Negro Employment, and Metropolitan Decentralization," *Quarterly Journal of Economics* 82: 175–97.

1992, "The Spatial Mismatch Hypothesis: Three Decades Later," *Housing Policy Debate* 3: 371–460.

Katz, L. F., J. R. Kling, and J. B. Liebman, 2001, "Moving to Opportunity in Boston: Early Impacts of a Randomized Mobility Program," *Quarterly Journal of Economics* 116: 607–54.

Ladd, H. F. and J. Ludwig, 2003, "The Effects of MTO on Educational Opportunities in Baltimore: Early Evidence," in J. Goering and J. Feins, eds., *Choosing a Better Life*, Washington, DC: Urban Institute Press.

Lieberson, S., 1963, *Ethnic Patterns in American Cities*, New York: Free Press of Glencoe.

Margo, R. A., 1990, *Race and Schooling in the South, 1880–1950: An Economic History*, University of Chicago Press.

Massey, D. and N. Denton, 1988, "The Dimensions of Residential Segregation," *Social Forces* 67: 281–315.

  1993, *American Apartheid: Segregation and the Making of the Underclass*, Cambridge, MA: Harvard University Press.

Taeuber, K. E. and A. F. Taeuber, 1964, "The Negro as an Immigrant Group: Recent Trends in Racial and Ethnic Segregation in Chicago," *American Journal of Sociology* 69: 374–382.

Vigdor, J. L., 2002a, "Locations, Outcomes and Selective Migration," *Review of Economics and Statistics* 84: 751–5.

  2002b, "The Pursuit of Opportunity: Explaining Selective Black Migration," *Journal of Urban Economics* 51: 391–417.

Wilson, W. J., 1987, *The Truly Disadvantaged*, University of Chicago Press.

8 Family formation in multicultural Britain: diversity and change

Richard Berthoud

Interpreting diversity

The living arrangements of Britain's ethnic minorities have been of interest to researchers ever since the first wave of West Indians arrived in the 1950s. Early consideration was primarily focused on the direct effects of a recent migration. In some migrant groups, for example, there was an initial preponderance of unattached men. In some areas, restricted access to accommodation led many recent arrivals to crowd together in the same house or flat, and so create large "households." But these characteristics were temporary and in a sense artificial consequences of the movement of populations, and have not been considered as primary issues in more recent analyses.

All four of the national surveys of ethnic minorities conducted by the Policy Studies Institute at about ten-year intervals have collected data about family and household structures, and each of the reports has presented summaries of the evidence (Daniel 1968, Smith 1977, Brown 1994, Modood et al. 1997). There has been extensive analysis by demographers of other large-scale sources, especially the 1991 Census (e.g., Coleman and Salt 1996) and the Labour Force Survey (e.g., Berrington 1994). It seems fair to say, though, that most of this work has been demographic and descriptive, rather than sociological or evaluative. The national surveys provided analyses of household structure in the form of background pictures of the population under study, before the authors moved on to the "real issues" of employment, housing, race relations, and so on. Variations in household structure have been used as part of the narrative of housing issues such as levels of overcrowding, or as explanatory variables in the analysis of employment or income. But few quantitative studies have attempted to explain (as opposed to describe) the variations in family structure between ethnic groups; the outcomes have been presented as "given." Still less have family formation and/or dissolution been discussed in a way which helps us to understand the social and economic processes at work in a multicultural society. Nor have the implications of particular patterns of living been much discussed in terms of their potential consequences for the people concerned.

This paper is mainly based on analyses of family formation derived from the Fourth National Survey of Ethnic Minorities and the Labour Force Survey, most of which have already been published. A note at the end of the paper briefly describes five papers from which the empirical findings are drawn. To avoid repetitive bibliographical citation of the same papers, the references are given in the text as EMiB (Ethnic Minorities in Britain), YCM (Young Caribbean Men and the Labour Market), IEM (The Incomes of Ethnic Minorities), EMCG (Ethnic minority children and their grandparents) and TB (Teenage births to ethnic minority women).

The paper will be useful as a summary of some of the key findings for readers who are new to them. But the facts have been organized here in such a way as to highlight some of the issues surrounding family formation which ought, perhaps, to be the subject of more debate within and around minority communities. The presentation is not, itself, evaluative (at least, I hope, not in a tendentious way). But it focuses on some of the key questions. Why do some ethnic groups adopt particular family structures? What influences will affect stability or change in these patterns? What are the implications for the sense of identity of the minorities themselves? Do people's decisions about partnering and parenting affect their or their children's chances in other spheres of life such as education or employment? I do not claim to answer many of these questions; but I think they should be asked.

It is appropriate to frame those questions within a broader discussion of normative social values in a multicultural society. One extreme position is to argue that the behavior of migrant groups should be judged exclusively by the standards of the host society. That tends to lead to a pathological interpretation of minority family patterns as deviant, rather then merely diverse. The other extreme position is to argue that minorities' behavior should be judged exclusively according to the conventions of their own societies, in their countries of origin. That overlooks the essential fact that the minorities' current social structures are no longer in their countries of origin but are located in multicultural Britain. Some of these issues are well discussed by Song and Edwards (1996) and in the concluding chapter of Beishon, Modood, and Virdee (1998).

It is not the aim of this paper to judge anyone, by any set of standards. It is to raise some questions about what is happening within and across community boundaries, in a Britain where young people of black and Asian origin share classes and lectures with white boys and girls who are also beginning to think about their approach to "the family"; and where white social norms are changing too.

The first thing to say about ethnic minorities is that they are a plural, not a collective. All nonwhite minorities may face a common experience of racism and harassment; but in most other spheres, it is the diversity between minority groups that is their most striking characteristic. In the crucial linked fields of education, employment, and income, for example, Indians and Chinese are, if anything, slightly better off than the white population, while Caribbeans, Bangladeshis, and Pakistanis are to various degrees worse off than average. Nowhere is this diversity more apparent than in family structures.

The family is the subject of intense moral and political debate on both sides of the Atlantic. Given the trends over time identified in the next section, it is fair to say that Caribbean family patterns are more "modern" than those of whites, while South Asians adopt more "old-fashioned" practices. I have been criticized for using these value-laden words. It is true that they carry values – but the interpretation of the time dimension depends on the point of view of the individual. "Conservatives" regret a moral decline from traditional to untested family patterns. "Progressives" welcome the replacement of archaic ("Victorian") social conventions with more liberal relationships. So, while readers will identify moral issues at every stage of the analysis, they should recognize that their interpretation may depend as much on their own set of values, as on that of the writer.

Comparisons over time and place

A key point is that diversity of family patterns is not a feature specifically of ethnic minorities. It is worth diverting from the focus on minority groups, for a page or two, to consider parallel changes affecting wider communities in Britain, Europe, and the USA.

There has been a huge change in routes to family formation within Britain over the past generation. Young people nowadays face a set of choices which itself can be interpreted as a form of diversity. And there are wide differences between the conventional patterns accepted in neighboring countries within Europe. These diversities – over time, between countries and among minorities – all help to show that there is no absolute ideal of family structure which needs to be defended against all rivals. The family is an organism whose successful evolution may be promoted by the introduction of diverse strains.

A generation or two ago, there was a standard trajectory of family formation in Britain whereby young people completed their education,

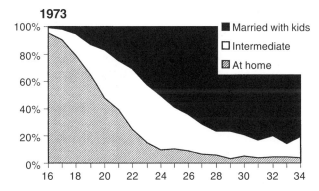

Source: General Household Survey. "Intermediate" includes living alone
or with friends, lone parent, cohabiting (with or without children)
and married with no children.

Figure 8.1 Family positions of British women age 16 to 34 in 1973

got married, and had children – and stayed that way until their own
children left home. This was never an obligatory or universal path, but
it was recognizably the standard thing to do. Figure 8.1 shows young
women's family positions at each year of age in 1973. Almost all were
single and living with their parents at the age of sixteen. The great majority
were married, and had children, by the time they were thirty-five. In
those days, the route from family of origin to family of procreation was
rather short. Very few women in their twenties were in an intermediate
position, no longer with their parents, not (yet) with their husband and
children.

Only a generation later, by 2000, the pattern had changed dramatically
(Figure 8.2). Young women were staying at home just as long. They were
reaching the stage of "married with children" much later (if at all). A
whole range of alternative or intermediate situations was now available –
single but living away from their parents; one-parent families; cohabiting;
or married but without children. A single statistic sums up this change: in
1973, more than two-thirds (69 percent) of women in their late twenties
were (legally) married and had children. By 2000, the proportion had
fallen to less than a quarter (24 percent).

Indeed, the label "intermediate" for those who lived neither with their
parents, nor with their husband and children, is no longer appropriate.
An increasing proportion of women will remain in one of the alternative

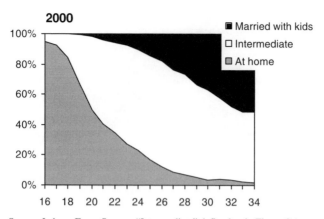

Source: Labour Force Survey. "Intermediate" defined as in Figure 8.1.

Figure 8.2 Family positions of British women age 16 to 34 in 2000

positions without ever moving to the destination that would once have been their primary expectation.

This increasing diversity of family form for British men and women in their twenties and thirties suggests a much wider range of options than was available and socially acceptable in the past. For many, it will have offered a greater degree of flexibility and perhaps choice, though not everyone would necessarily have chosen the positions they found themselves in. It has also led to a substantial degree of economic polarization, as the gap has widened between DINKYs (double income, no kids yet) at one extreme and non-working lone parents at the other.

There is diversity, too, between countries in Europe (Figure 8.3). Nearly half of women in their late twenties continue to live with their parents in Italy and Spain; hardly any do so in Denmark and the Netherlands. Among those who have left home, the great majority are married and with children in countries such as Greece, but "intermediate" family forms predominate in Denmark and the Netherlands. A clear regional pattern has been identified (Iacovou 2002). "Southern and/or Catholic" countries – Italy, Spain, Greece, Portugal, and Ireland – have "traditional" patterns whereby young men and women live with their parents until they get married; and they have children soon after that. In "northern/Protestant" countries – Denmark, the Netherlands, Finland, the UK, Germany, Belgium, France, and Austria – few people live with their parents, and many adopt intermediate living arrangements before (or perhaps instead of) getting married and starting a family.

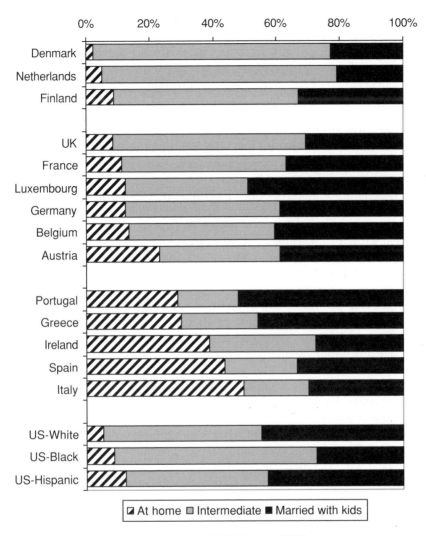

Source: European Community Household Panel 1994, Iacovou (2002)

Figure 8.3 Family positions of women aged 25 to 29: European Union and USA

Figure 8.3 also compares family formation patterns in the United States with those in Western Europe. Few American women are still single and living with their parents in their late twenties. A high proportion of white and Hispanic American women are "married with kids"; a higher proportion than is observed in most European countries. Black American women, on the other hand, are highly likely to have adopted one of the "intermediate" family forms.

In fact (not shown directly in the chart) African-Americans show very low rates of marriage, and high rates of lone parenthood (Iacovou 2002) – a subject of fierce controversy between "pro-family" and "black-feminist" commentators in the United States (Patterson 1998). The next section of this paper will show that Caribbean women in Britain are similar to African-American women in these two respects, and this immediately raises the possibility that the two black communities are following similar trajectories. There are clearly some major points in common; but there are also some important differences.

- Most families of Caribbean origin migrated to Britain in the 1950s and 1960s. The families of most Afro-Americans have remained in the USA for many generations – longer, in fact, than the families of most white Americans. (Though there was, of course, a substantial migration from southern to northern states *within* the USA in the first half of the twentieth century.)
- A high proportion of black Americans, especially those with poor economic prospects, live in areas where most of the other residents are also black. British people of Caribbean origin are not nearly so concentrated into "ghetto" districts (Peach 1996) and are likely to have much more regular personal contact with white and other ethnic communities.
- Mixed partnerships are much less common in the USA than they are in Britain. In America, it is possible to assume that unmarried men and women would have chosen someone from the same ethnic group if they had decided to marry. That assumption is not nearly so credible in Britain.

These considerations mean that it is not possible simply to treat African-Americans and British Caribbeans as essentially the same community on either side of the Atlantic.

The comparisons over time and between countries offered in this section set the diversity between British ethnic groups in context. Family patterns are not fixed in time or across space. Every generation in every society has its own ideas about what young people ought to do, and wags its beard if individuals deviate too far from that expectation. The fact that norms vary does not, though, mean that they are irrelevant. They are changeable – perhaps more restrictive in some societies, more liberal in others. They are changing now in Britain. They are changing, and will no doubt change again, within the minority communities. We need to understand the directions and the implications of these changes, rather than idealize current patterns (on the one hand), or bemoan them (on the other).

Caribbean families in Britain: "modern individualism?"

The key feature of family life in the Caribbean community[1] is the very low rate of marriage. This is true across all age groups, but can be seen most clearly by focusing on the late twenties (Table 8.1). Two-thirds of white men and women in that age group have lived with a partner; little more than one-third of Caribbeans have done so. Among those with a partner, three-quarters of whites, but only half of Caribbeans, are in a formal marriage. Among those who have married, the proportion who have separated or divorced is twice as high for Caribbeans as it is for whites (across all age-groups under sixty).

As a result of these three factors – low partnership rates, low marriage rates, and high separation rates – only 39 percent of Caribbean adults under the age of sixty are in a formal marriage, compared with 60 percent of white adults under sixty. Actually, most Caribbeans in the older half of that age range are married, or at least have been; it is among younger people that marriage rates are so low. That is partly an ageing effect (young people will eventually get married) but also partly a cohort effect (today's young people are less likely to marry than their predecessors were).

Of course most of those who migrated to this country as adults are married to (or live with) a man or woman of their own ethnic group. But among British-born Caribbeans, half of men with a partner live with a white woman; a third of women with a partner live with a white man (YCM, Table 22).

These mixed partnerships are much more common than is found, for example, among African-Americans, and they have attracted some interest. Whereas worry about "miscegenation" has always been a central

Table 8.1 *Marital status: Caribbeans compared with whites*

	Percentages	
	Caribbean	White
Ever had a partner (age 25–9)	38	68
Is (or was) married to their partner (age 25–9)	51	73
Separated or divorced from their spouse (16–59)	18	9

Source: Fourth National Survey of Ethnic Minorities (EMiB Tables 2.5, 2.7, and 2.9).

issue for white racists, many liberal commentators see cross-cultural relationships as a welcome sign of increasing mutual acceptance between the white and the black communities. Mixed marriages are widely accepted among Caribbeans – more than among whites, and much more than among Asians (EMiB Table 9.18 and 9.20). For some black people, though, there remains a suspicion that marrying into a white family is disloyal to one's ethnicity of origin, an opportunist move into white society (Modood, Beishon, and Virdee 1994, Beishon, Modood, and Virdee 1998). Insofar as objective measures can contribute to such issues, the indications are that the high rate of mixed marriage among Caribbean men is not associated with their social standing, in either direction: mixed relationships are about equally common among those with high and low levels of education, and among those with good and bad employment experiences (YCM, Table 22 and p. 51).

From the point of view of our immediate interest in family formation, though, the number of mixed partnerships among Caribbeans, combined with the low rate of partnership and marriage in the first place, means that *very* few Caribbean men and women are married *to each other*. This has obvious implications, which will be discussed later, for the future structure of the Caribbean community. But another point of interpretation is that this helps to emphasize the relative unimportance of marriage to the Caribbean self-image (in contrast, as we will see, to the South Asian self-image). It is not in marriage, but in other activities, that one asserts membership of the Caribbean community.

Because such a small proportion of Caribbean men and women are living with each other in nuclear families, more detailed analysis of family structures has to start with women. Most surveys do not ask respondents to record all the children of which they are the father or mother, but only the children living with them at the time. It will be seen that a large proportion of Caribbean children do not live with their father. All we can do is describe the families of the women and make inferences from that about the probable position of the men.

One-third of Caribbean women in their early twenties have children; about half of those in their late twenties; three-quarters of those in their early thirties (YCM Table 13). These figures suggest that Caribbean women are slightly earlier into the child-rearing phase than white women, but the two ethnic groups are broadly similar in their fertility rates.

Again, it is on the question of partnership that the two groups diverge most widely. One in ten white women with children (and under the age of thirty-five) are single (never-married) mothers (YCM, Table 13). No less than half of Caribbean mothers are single parents on this definition.[2]

Table 8.2 *Estimated proportion of mothers who remained single, by age and date, holding other characteristics constant*

	Logistic regression estimates, expressed as cell percentages	
	Caribbean	White
Age of mother at birth of first child		
20	66	11
25	48	7
30	31	5
Age of oldest child		
0	53	9
5	48	7
10	42	6
15	37	4
Date of mother's 20th birthday		
1975	27	1
1980	37	3
1985	48	7
1990	59	15

Source: Labour Force Survey (YCM, Tables 14 and 23).
The shaded band indicates some characteristics of the standard case against which variations are tested: the woman was born or schooled in Britain; she has O levels, GCSE, or equivalent qualifications (i.e. basic secondary qualifications obtained usually at age 16); she reached the age of twenty in 1985; she was aged twenty-five at the birth of the first child; that child is now five.

The patterns of single parenthood within each ethnic group are not easy to analyze, because all of the potential influences are inter-related. A multivariate logistic regression equation has been used to estimate the probability of a mother remaining single, depending on the age at which she first had children, the age of her oldest child, the year she passed her twentieth birthday, whether she was a migrant or a non-migrant, and what her educational qualifications were. The analysis can be used to show what happens if each of these characteristics is varied one at a time, holding the other four constant (Table 8.2). For both whites and Caribbeans, women who had been young when their first child was born were much more likely to be single mothers at the time of their interview – in both groups, mothers who had started a family at twenty were about twice as likely to be in that state as those who had waited another ten years. But Caribbean women retained six times as high a risk as white women, whatever their age at first birth.

The age of the oldest child can be seen as the number of years since the woman became a mother. Both groups of women were less likely to be single, the longer the period of their motherhood. This can be interpreted in terms of about half of white single mothers, and about one-third of Caribbean mothers, marrying (or forming a live-in partnership) later.[3] That is, single motherhood is not necessarily a temporary stage prior to marriage; many Caribbean women have children single and stay single.

The estimates in the first two panels of the table are all based on a notional cohort of women whose twentieth birthday occurred in 1985. It is well known that there has been a substantial increase in the number of single parents over the years (Haskey 1998), and we would expect such a change in social expectations to be reflected in a cohort effect. The third panel confirms this: women who reached the potential childbearing phase of their lives in the most recent period were much more likely to be a single parent than their predecessors. In absolute terms this trend seemed strongest for the Caribbean women: the increase from 27 percent to 59 percent over fifteen years represents one-third of all Caribbean women with children. But in relative terms, the increase was even stronger for whites: the number of white single mothers multiplied more than ten-fold over fifteen years.[4]

Much has been written about single mothers of Caribbean origin (Dench 1996, Song and Edwards 1996). The practice of living independently of the children's father can be traced to West Indian social and economic traditions – themselves, perhaps, a hangover from the days of slavery when husbands and wives might be sold to separate plantations. What is striking about these findings, though, is that behaviour said to be derived from Caribbean cultural values is becoming more, not less, common over the years in Britain. The same conclusion is supported by another result from the logistic regression equation: after controlling for the age and cohort effects shown in Table 8.2, the proportion of Caribbean mothers who were single was 48 percent among those who had been born in Britain or had arrived as children; it fell to only 24 percent among women who had come to Britain at the age of sixteen or later. Thus it is the second generation which has adopted the "West Indian" tradition, rather than the migrants themselves.

Research among white women has tended to show that those with lower levels of educational qualifications tend to have children younger than their better-educated counterparts, and that women who have children at an early age are often single mothers (Rowlingson and McKay 1998). So Table 8.3 distinguishes the two components of single motherhood – whether women had children, and whether those with children were single. Less than a third of women with degrees had children (at the "standard" age of thirty); four-fifths of women with no qualifications

Table 8.3 *Estimated proportion of mothers who remained single,*
by qualifications, holding other characteristics constant

	Logistic regression estimates, expressed as cell percentages				
	Degree or equivalent	A level or equivalent	O level or equivalent	Lower quals	None
Caribbean					
% Women who had children	29	57	72	78	79
% Mothers who were single	37	47	48	54	59
% Women who were single mothers	11	27	34	42	46
White					
% Women who had children	30	57	69	78	83
% Mothers who were single	5	5	7	10	15
% Women who were single mothers	2	3	5	8	12

Source: Labour Force Survey (YCM, Table 15).

were mothers. The strong and consistent effect of qualifications on the proportion of women who had children was almost identical for both whites and Caribbeans. In both groups there was a parallel tendency for less-qualified women with children to have remained single. The relative effect was stronger among white women (a ratio of 3 to 1 between unqualified women and graduates); but education was still an important source of variation in the much higher rate of single parenthood among Caribbeans. Putting the two sets of findings together, the analysis suggests that nearly half of all unqualified (thirty-year-old) Caribbean women were single mothers, compared with just 2 percent of white women with degrees.

What does the high rate of single parenthood among Caribbean women imply for the family positions of Caribbean men? The frequency of mixed partnerships means that we cannot automatically assume that the non-resident fathers of Caribbean single mothers are necessarily of Caribbean origin too. Nevertheless, the fact that a very large proportion of young Caribbean women with relatively low educational qualifications are single parents suggests that young Caribbean men with relatively low qualifications are unlikely to be living in the standard partner-plus-children family relationship. Qualitative evidence has suggested that some Caribbean couples have retained the "visiting partner" relationships that are common in the West Indies (Beishon, Modood, and Virdee 1998), and that this often involves the man in financial and other paternal responsibilities. Quantitative evidence, though, suggests these "active" nonresident

Table 8.4 *Frequency of contact between nonresident fathers and their children (as reported by lone mothers)*

	White mothers	Black mothers
Formerly married or cohabiting		
Father sees child(ren) once a week or more	38	25
Less often	30	34
Never, or father's whereabouts unknown	32	41
Mother has never cohabited		
Father sees child(ren) once a week or more	19	8
Less often	17	23
Never, or father's whereabouts unknown	64	69

Source: Families and Children Survey, 1999, new analysis.

fathers are very uncommon. Only 8 percent of black single mothers taking part in the Families and Children Survey reported that their children's father saw them at least once a week (Table 8.4). Two-thirds said that he never saw them, or that she did not know where he was. On this evidence, black single mothers really do raise their children on their own.

Nearly two-thirds (63 percent) of young adult Caribbean men (aged 22 to 35) are "unattached" – that is, they have neither a live-in partner nor live-in children. The equivalent figure for white men is less than half (47 percent). As before, it is difficult to sort out the influences of a range of potentially overlapping influences on men's family status, and a logistic regression equation has been used to measure the effect of each, independently of all the others.[5] The first panel of Table 8.5 shows the expected tendency for the proportion remaining unattached to fall as young men grew older, and illustrates the clear divergence between white men and Caribbean men by age.

The comparison between the cohorts of young men who entered adulthood at various periods over the past two decades is more important. For both white and Caribbean men, the proportion estimated to remain unattached at the age of thirty doubled in fifteen years. There appears to have been what amounts to a transformation in young men's family relationships. Most young men in the 1975 cohort lived with a partner and/or children by the age of thirty. By the 1990 cohort, most white and black young men remained single. Caribbeans were running ahead of whites throughout the period, but the trend was equally strong for both groups.

Among Caribbeans, men who had been born in Britain (or migrated as children) were more likely to remain unattached (60 percent) than those who had arrived age sixteen or more (43 percent).

Table 8.5 *Estimated proportion of men who remained unattached, by age and cohort, holding other characteristics constant*

	Logistic regression estimates, expressed as cell percentages	
	Caribbean	White
Age		
20	88	81
25	77	65
30	60	45
Date of 20th birthday		
1975	37	27
1980	48	35
1985	60	45
1990	70	55

Source: Labour Force Survey (YCM, Tables 18 and 24).

The high proportion of young black men who remain unattached may be related to their poor employment prospects. This hypothesis, which has been very influential in the United States (Wilson 1987), suggests that black women are reluctant to marry (or live with) a man whose chances of getting or keeping a good job make him an unreliable source of income for themselves and their children. Better to remain single (and claim social assistance if necessary). Young men's family position has therefore been analyzed by some of the factors which might make a difference to their employability. Comparison across educational qualifications is complicated by the fact that better qualified people tend to form partnerships later in their twenties, simply because they spend longer in the education system. So Table 8.6 shows how long it took men to get married or cohabit, in terms of the duration of the period since they completed their studies. For both white men and Caribbean men, those with lower than average levels of qualification took longer than others to form partnerships. The relationship was strongest for Caribbeans – in the extreme, a Caribbean man with no qualifications would expect to live without a partner for twenty years after leaving school.

Caribbean men living in regions with high levels of unemployment also have lower than average partnering rates (LFS, new analysis). The relationship is much weaker for white men. This provides further evidence of a link between Caribbean men's job prospects and their marriage prospects.

Table 8.6 *Estimated number of years following education before half of men had a partner, by educational qualifications*

| | Logistic regression estimates | |
	Caribbean	White
Degree	12.8	8.2
A level	15.0	9.8
O level	16.4	11.2
Other	16.5	10.7
None	20.2	12.0

Source: Labour Force Survey (new analysis).

Table 8.7 *Composition of families with children, where at least one parent was Caribbean*

| | Global percentages | | |
	Caribbean father	White father	Father not present
Caribbean mother	24	10	48
White mother	15		
Mother not present	3		

Note: Stepfathers and stepmothers are included as though they were natural fathers and mothers. A small number of mixed Caribbean-African couples have been included as both Caribbean.
Source: Labour Force Survey, 1992–95, new analysis.

The two most striking aspects of Caribbean family formation are the large number of men and women who live without a partner; and the high proportion of those, with a partner, whose partner is white. Both findings are summarized in Table 8.7, for families with children. Only a quarter of "Caribbean" children live with two black parents.

Most commentators seem to welcome the increase in the number of mixed relationships, as an indicator of reducing cultural, social, and economic barriers between ethnic groups. Perhaps it is a sign of declining racism within the white community. The fact that some black people are anxious about the trend nevertheless needs to be recognized. There is little evidence that men and women in mixed marriages are any better off or worse off than those who have chosen partners within their own ethnic group. There are nevertheless some consequences of mixed relationships which need to be taken into account in the analysis of multicultural Britain.

The first, and obvious one, is that a significant proportion of the children of Caribbeans will be of mixed origin. The sample of babies born in 2000 selected for the Millennium Cohort Survey is the only source which records the ethnic group of both fathers and mothers, including those of children born to single mothers. Of the 625 babies with any black parentage:[6]

> 53 percent had two black parents;
> 4 percent had one black parent and one of mixed origin;
> 29 percent had one black and one white parent
> 14 percent had one parent of mixed origin, and one white.

So mixed parentage means an increase in the number of members of the next generation who are in some way Caribbean, and a reduction in the number who are unambiguously Caribbean.

None of the quantitative surveys available in the past provided accurate information about people of mixed origin, though the 2001 Census offers a much more effective classification. In the meantime, it is rather assumed that people of mixed origin perceive themselves, and are perceived by others, to be black. It seems likely that they have a more complex identity than that, reluctant to throw over one half of their heritage. This is a major issue for further research.

From the point of view of Caribbeans as a community, though, the trend may lead either to the decline, or the increasing isolation, of blackness as an independent identity. Whereas early commentators were eager for minorities to be assimilated into the majority culture, the essence of multiculturalism is that Britain should learn to value the diversity of communities making their various contributions to national life. In that context, a long-term reduction in the number of people firmly rooted in the Caribbean tradition might be seen to impoverish us all.

The other main feature of Caribbean family formation is the number of single mothers, on the one hand, and of unattached men, on the other. It was emphasized at the beginning of this paper that the proportion of young people in "intermediate" family forms is much higher in "northern/Protestant" European countries than in "southern/Catholic" ones, and has risen rapidly in Britain over the last quarter of a century. Caribbeans could therefore be considered to be very "northern/Protestant"; or very modern. In this light, they are ahead of the trend (while South Asians are behind the trend). But the scarcity of co-resident partnerships during the child-rearing years is so far ahead of the national trend as to represent a real difference of social convention, rather than the kind of variation between groups which might be expected in any society. While the different convention is often explained in terms of the matriarchal family structures common in the West Indies, it is important to take account of the fact that Caribbeans are not converging on the European norm – the evidence clearly points to an increase in the number of unpartnered parents from generation to generation and from year to year.

Qualitative evidence suggests that Caribbeans' own views of these trends may be ambivalent. My former colleagues Beishon, Modood, and Virdee (1998) found three potentially conflicting points of view.[7]

- "Some Caribbeans . . . emphasised an individualism – the importance of individual choice, the value of commitments generated by the quality of relationships rather than custom, duty or marriage certificate, and independence . . . Marriage has come to be regarded as just a lifestyle option, which one may or may not wish to choose, depending on individual circumstances." Thus there is a theoretical and principled preference for the less committing family forms that can be labeled *modern individualism*.

- On the other hand, Caribbeans said that "their own communities were more family-orientated than the white British, and instilled more discipline and respect for age than their white contemporaries. Indeed, there was unity among the minorities in their criticism of what they perceived as a lack of commitment to parenting amongst whites, and they talked of white children as not having respect for their elders, and as being out of control." This apparently older-fashioned view is not necessarily inconsistent with a preference for lone-parenthood, since it might be argued that a mother (and a grandmother[8]) could exert a firmer discipline on children than a mother and father together. "Fathers were in practice dispensable; there was no particular role or responsibility that fathers performed which could not be performed in their absence by mothers."

- Nevertheless "it was noticeable that the ideal of marriage and joint parenting between resident fathers and mothers still exerted a considerable appeal among the Caribbeans . . . For the majority . . . marriage is an ideal which unfortunately only some achieve – mainly because, in the view of women, men lack commitment." On this latter view, single motherhood may be accepted by Caribbean women, but it is the men who should bear the responsibility for their position.

There is a large literature on the question of whether children brought up by one parent experience worse outcomes than those with two (Kiernan, Land, and Lewis 1998). Having only one resident parent may be a disadvantage, but the primary mechanism may be the poverty experienced by most such families, rather than the lack of a father as

Table 8.8 *Proportion of families with children who depend on Income Support*

	Cell percentages		
	Couples with children	One-parent families	All families with children
Whites	9	63	22
Caribbeans	13	53	36

Source: Family Resources Survey 1994/5 and 1995/6, new analysis.

such. Whatever the overall conclusion, little of the research can be applied directly to Caribbean families, where single parenthood is now a conventional rather than a deviant family form.

There is little doubt, though, about the financial position of Caribbean one-parent families. It is often remarked that Caribbean lone parents are more likely to support themselves through work than their white equivalents. The Fourth National Survey reported that only 27 percent of white lone parents living in an independent household had any employment; the figure for Caribbeans was 42 percent (EMiB, p. 152). The Family Resources Survey, analyzing lone parents regardless of their household position, recorded 37 percent of white lone parents and 43 percent of Caribbean lone parents to have any earnings (IEM, p. 11). Caribbeans may be ahead of whites on this measure, but still, more than half of Caribbean lone parents have no job. There is no evidence to suggest that many of them receive the substantial and regular maintenance payments which would be needed to float them and their children above the poverty line. As Table 8.8 shows, the majority of one-parent families – whether white or Caribbean – have to claim Income Support.[9] It is difficult to avoid the conclusion that it is the number of lone parents in the Caribbean community, rather than high levels of unemployment, which confines more than a third of all families with children to the safety net. This may be regarded as unfair on the social security system (which was never designed to shoulder the primary long-term responsibility for large numbers of families). And it is unfair on the mothers and children, who are obliged to accept the poverty and the sense of dependence with which Income Support is inevitably associated.

This analysis may conjure up a picture of prosperous Caribbean men selfishly keeping their earnings to themselves. It is true that an exceptionally high proportion of young men of Caribbean origin are unattached. On the other hand, the analysis in Table 8.6 suggested that many of these bachelors have limited educational qualifications and poor prospects in the labor market. Moreover, marital status itself has an independent effect on men's employment rates: for both whites and Caribbeans, a young man living on his own is about twice as likely to be unemployed as a young man who lives with a partner, holding other characteristics constant (YCM, p. 50). So the low rate of partnership in the Caribbean community may create poverty among men as well as among women and children.

South Asian families in Britain: "old-fashioned family values?"

All four of the South Asian groups[10] identified in the Fourth National Survey have features of family life which are similar to each other, different from whites and even more different from Caribbeans. Depending on the measure used, there are some variations between the four South Asian groups, with Bangladeshis and Pakistanis showing the most characteristic Asian pattern while Indians, and especially African Asians, sometimes appearing closer to the white position.

In contrast to Caribbeans, the key feature of family life in South Asian communities is the very high rate of marriage. Around three-quarters of Pakistanis and Bangladeshi women are in partnerships by the age of twenty-five, compared with about two-thirds of Indian women and just over half of African-Asian and white women (Table 8.9). South Asian men tend to be rather older than their wives, so the differences between ethnic groups would be smaller if the analysis focused on men. But the important point is that virtually all South Asians with a partner are in a formal marriage. And the proportion who have separated or divorced is less than half that recorded among whites.

Table 8.9 *Marital status: South Asians compared with whites*

	Percentages				
	Bangladeshi	Pakistani	Indian	African-Asian	White
Ever had a partner (women aged 25 born in Britain)	71	78	67	52	55
Is (or was) married to their partner (25–9)	------------- 97 -------------				73
Separated or divorced from their spouse (16–59)	------------- 4 -------------				9

Source: Fourth National Survey (EMiB, Tables 2.7, 2.8, and 2.9). The first line is based on a logistic regression equation controlling for age, sex, and place of birth.

Table 8.10 *South Asians' parents' decision about the choice of marriage partner, by age at which child came to Britain*

	Cell percentages				
	Men	Women	Hindu	Sikh	Muslim
Born in Britain or arrived up to age 10	30	26	9	34	40
Arrived age 11 to 24	43	62	30	60	69
Arrived age 25 or more	56	80	59	78	73

Source: Fourth National Survey (new analysis). The table shows the sum of "my parents made the decision" and "I had a say, but it was my parents' decision."

So for South Asians, the key questions are not whether they are married but how they married and who they chose. It is well known that young men and women in India, Pakistan, and Bangladesh commonly have their marriage partners chosen for them by their parents or other family elders, and that this practice continues, at least in part, among the communities that have migrated to Britain. Qualitative research (Stopes-Roe and Cochrane 1990, Anwar 1994) suggests that the attitudes of young South Asians on "arranged" marriages have been moving away from those of their parents, though this seemed to be much less true among Muslims than among Sikhs and Hindus. It is not necessarily a clean split between those who think it "my" decision and those who think it "their" decision, since an amicable negotiation might take account of both points of view. The FNS showed that the majority of South Asians who came to Britain at the age of twenty-five or more (most of whom are assumed to have been married before they came), reported that their parents had decided on their partner (Table 8.10). This was especially true among women; it was more true among Muslims and Sikhs than among Hindus.[11] For South Asians who were born here or arrived as young children (who must have married some years after they arrived) less than half of Muslims and Sikhs, and only a very small proportion of Hindus, felt that their partner had been chosen by the family, rather than by themselves. Interestingly, there was no apparent difference between men and women in the second generation.

Opinion questions in the Fourth National Survey suggested that South Asians were a good deal less likely to accept mixed marriages than Caribbeans were – indeed, less likely than white people. Well over half of Indians, Pakistanis, and Bangladeshis felt that most members of their group would mind if a close relative were to marry a white person. It was

Table 8.11 *Two indicators of gender roles within South Asian marriages*

	Row percentages	
	Proportion of women whose activity is looking after the house and family	Husband has the final say in financial decisions
Bangladeshi	81	39
Pakistani	70	
Indian	36	28
African-Asian	26	
White	27	20

Source: Fourth National Survey (EMiB Tables 4.1 and 5.20). The first column is based on women aged 16–59 not in full-time education. The second column is based on all couples.

not uncommon for respondents to claim that they themselves would not mind (even though most members of their group would). Both of the primary sources show that mixed marriages are much less common among South Asians than among Caribbeans. About one in five British-born men of Indian or African-Asian origin have a white wife; the equivalent figure for women is about one in ten. Very few Bangladeshis and Pakistanis have entered mixed relationships. It stands to reason that in communities where arranged marriages are common, mixed marriages are rare; in fact new analysis of the FNS shows that very few Indian Muslims or Sikhs had a white partner – most of the mixed marriages involved Hindus or the small number of Indian Christians.

Asians may also be "old-fashioned" in the nature of the relationships adopted between men and women within marriage. As Table 8.11 shows, Indian women are rather more likely to be a full-time homemaker than white women; but a clear majority of Bangladeshi and Pakistani women report their primary activity to be looking after the house and family. These are the sort of proportions that would have been observed among white women in the 1950s and 1960s. The fact (see below) that Bangladeshi and Pakistani women have significantly more children than members of other groups provides a partial explanation for their low rates of economic activity, but differences remain after taking family structure into account (EMiB, p. 87).

There are some signs, though, that the situation may be changing. Muslim women may be allowed to take professional-level jobs, even though they are still discouraged from accepting low-prestige occupations. Bangladeshi and Pakistani girls are holding their own in the British education system (YCM, Table 5). The Labour Force Survey shows that qualifications can make a big difference. Among married Bangladeshi and Pakistani women born or brought up in Britain:

- of those with no qualifications, 74 percent are full-time homemakers
- of those with qualifications up to GCSE level, 52 percent
- of those with qualifications above GCSE level, 22 percent.[12]

The strong implication of these findings is that more Muslim women will find their way into the labor market as more of them obtain educational qualifications.

Beishon, Modood, and Virdee (1998) report that South Asian men retain family authority over their wives, even in households where the wife has a job. Very few data are available with which to measure variation between communities in the quality of relationships within families. A question in the FNS asked whether it would be the husband or the wife who had the final say in big financial decisions (Table 8.11). Few families in any ethnic group said that the wife was the prime decision-maker – the issue was whether it was husbands on their own or couples as a partnership who decided these things. Indian and African-Asian couples were rather more patriarchal, on this measure, than white couples. Bangladeshis and Pakistanis were substantially more likely to assign responsibility to the husband, though even in these Muslim communities, power-sharing was the most commonly reported arrangement. More worrying, perhaps, for Bangladeshi and Pakistani men's sense of authority, their wives were much less likely to attribute power to them, than they were to claim it (EMiB, p. 179).

Three-quarters (76 percent) of white women have had children by the time they are in their early thirties (YCM, Table 13). The figures are rather higher for Indian women (83 percent) and very high indeed for Bangladeshi and Pakistani women (92 percent). In fact Indian women's fertility is very similar to white women's, right across the relevant age-ranges (Figure 8.4). The birth rate is substantially higher in the Pakistani community, and higher again among Bangladeshis, whose fertility is about double that of white and Indian women's at all stages. A striking point is the number of births to Bangladeshi teenagers – but, unlike white teenage mothers, the Bangladeshi women are already married (TB). Another striking point is the size of Bangladeshi and Pakistani families. Large families were a significant area of British social policy interest until the 1970s (Land 1969) but are so rare now that they have virtually disappeared from the research agenda. They are not rare in Asian communities though: more than half of Bangladeshi and Pakistani women in their late thirties have four or more children (EMiB, p. 41).

Table 8.12 *Average number of children
among Bangladeshi and Pakistani women, by
age of woman and date of her 20th birthday*

	Date of 20th birthday		
Age of woman	1980–4	1985–9	1990–4
20 to 24		1.3	0.5
25 to 29	2.0	1.8	1.5
30 to 34	3.1	2.0	

Source: Labour Force Survey (new analysis).

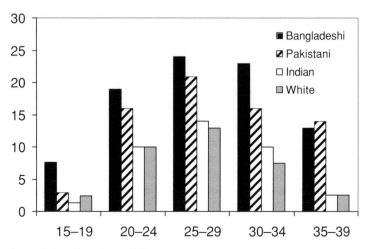

Source: Labour Force Survey (TB)

Figure 8.4 Women's fertility rates by age group

There are some signs, though, that these very high levels of fertility have also been reducing over recent decades. For example the annual rate of teenage motherhood among Bangladeshi women is estimated to have fallen from 61 per thousand in the mid-1980s to 38 per thousand in the mid-1990s (TB). Table 8.12 compares successive cohorts of women age for age and suggests a decline in family sizes. Thus there are some indications of convergence on white fertility rates.

Another well-known feature of Asian family life is the number of three-generation households, where couples continue to live with their parents after they have started a family of their own. Detailed analysis both confirms and contradicts this stereotype (EMCG). Take Indian families as an example, and focus on the paternal grandmother. (She is the most likely candidate to live with the family, because young Asian families live more often with the young man's than the young woman's family; and because she is likely to outlive her husband, the paternal grandfather.)[13]

- 70 percent of Indian paternal grandmothers are still alive.
- 51 percent of the surviving paternal grandmothers live in Britain.
- 67 percent of British-resident Indian elders live with one of their adult children. This is a very high proportion, compared with only 15 percent of white elders.
- 36 percent of Indian families, whose paternal grandmother lives in Britain, include her in their household. This is not much more than half of the number of elders living with their children, presumably because some grandparents were living with other children, the siblings of the family under consideration. This 36 percent is also a very high figure: only 1 percent of white families live with their paternal grandmother.
- So, because a large number of grandmothers are dead, or in India, or living with another sibling, the proportion of all Indian families who live with their paternal grandmother is only 13 percent.[14]

The outcome is that Indian families have a very strong tendency to live with the father's parents if those parents are available. But in most cases they are not available, so it is quite wrong to imply that most families have paternal grandparents living with them.

These figures all refer to Indian families. The four South Asian groups are compared with each other, and with white families, in Figure 8.5. It is immediately clear that most white grandmothers are alive, living in Britain, but not living with their children. Among South Asians:

- A large proportion of Bangladeshi grandmothers have died. This is probably not caused so much by high mortality in Bangladesh as by the fact that Bangladeshi men do not have children till relatively late in life. Their mothers are/were relatively old.
- Many Pakistani grandparents are alive, but still in Pakistan. On the other hand, most African Asian grandparents are in Britain; probably because the whole family came to Britain together from Kenya or Uganda.
- The four Asian groups have similarly high rates of co-residence among those where a grandmother is available in this country.
- But because many grandparents are dead, or living abroad, the over-all proportion of children living with their paternal grandmother is reduced, to 17 percent for African Asians, 13 percent for Indians, 9 percent for Pakistanis, and only 4 percent for Bangladeshis.

It is difficult to predict which way these figures will move over time. It is possible that a preference for three-generation families may reduce

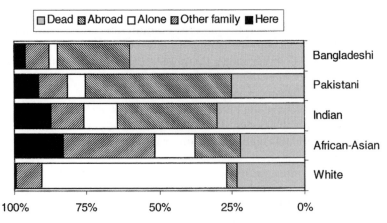

Figure 8.5 Where are paternal grandmothers?

over the years, as Asian family patterns are increasingly influenced by white norms. On the other hand, the supply of grandparents available in Britain is bound to rise, as the current generation of children start to have families of their own. It is therefore possible that the number of families living with grandparents will hold up or even increase.

To sum up, all four of the South Asian communities in Britain have some elements in common, that are distinct from the current white position. The key characteristic is the continued importance of marriage. All four groups provide evidence of distinctive South Asian forms, such as arranged marriages, a reluctance to marry out, and a preference for living with paternal grandparents. In some respects, Bangladeshis and Pakistanis are distinctive again, especially in the proportion of women spending their whole time looking after the house and family, and in the number of children they have.

The Asian patterns can clearly be labeled "old-fashioned" in the sense that many of their characteristics now could have been observed among white families in the past. They are "old-fashioned," too, in the sense that loyalty to their own communities' histories and traditions is one of the driving forces behind the preservation of these cultural patterns.

"Old-fashioned" can be a value-laden term, but it is one of those adjectives which could be complimentary or critical, depending on the context. It could mean "traditional" – tried and trusted; or it could mean "archaic" – out-of-date and inappropriate. Many of the old-fashioned characteristics of Asian family life are likely to resonate with a substantial body of white opinion, which favors a commitment to marriage and tight-knit families in preference to the current trends towards

Table 8.13 *South Asian household incomes*

	Percentages		
	Bangladeshi/ Pakistani	Indian	White
Proportion of non-pensioner, non-lone-parent households containing no worker	42	28	17
Poverty rate among:			
Working households	50	15	9
Non-working, non-pensioner households	72	54	43

Source: first line – Fourth National Survey (EMiB, Table 5.1); second and third lines – Family Resources Survey (IEM Table 2.3). Pensioners and lone parents are excluded as indicated, as there are very few of either group among South Asians. Poverty is defined conventionally as an income, adjusted for family size, below 50 percent of the national average.

open relationships and loose loyalties. Other features of Asian family life, though, have now been rejected decisively within white families: these include arranged marriages, husbands' authority over wives, women's obligation to keep house, and large numbers of children. These are the areas where future generations of British-educated Asians (perhaps especially the girls) are most likely to question traditional patterns and face conflict with their parents.

It is also appropriate to consider the possible effect of family patterns on economic prosperity. Table 8.13 makes use of data and concepts established by the Department of Work and Pensions for the measurement of poverty in Britain (DSS 2001). As one might expect, households where no-one has a job are much more likely to be poor than those with some earnings, and the distribution of poverty between ethnic groups is partly a simple function of the distribution of employment.

Although a number of data sources indicate that Indians have high rates of employment, and occupations and earnings which are on a par with those of white people, household-based measures tend to show that more Indian than white households have no earner; and that both working and non-working households have higher poverty rates than their white equivalents. It is not quite clear why these things are so, but the variations between whites and Indians are not large, and there is no particular reason to attribute them to the family patterns which are the subject of this paper.

In the Bangladeshi and Pakistani communities, though, the proportion of households containing no worker (and therefore living on social security) is far higher than in the other two groups shown in the table. Again, this is more likely to be a function of problems in the labor market, rather than any specific aspect of family structures. Non-working Bangladeshi and Pakistani households have very high poverty rates – higher even than non-working whites or Indians. But it is when we turn to working households that family factors may have an important part to play. Astonishingly, as many as half of Bangladeshi and Pakistanis *working* households are below the poverty line. Their earnings simply do not stretch far enough – in spite of in-work social security benefits which account for a fifth of their income (IEM, p. 15). This is partly due to low pay. But it is also, undoubtedly, due to the large number of children in each family, and to the fact that so few wives and mothers have jobs of their own.

Diversity and change

So, just as "modern individualism" contributes substantially to family poverty among Caribbeans, "old-fashioned values" play a similar role among Bangladeshis and Pakistanis.

Perhaps there is no contradiction in this. It can be argued that the disadvantage, the high rates of poverty, are a consequence of each minority group's difference from the standard white pattern, rather than from their position on a single scale running from old-fashioned values at one end to modern individualism at the other. It was no special disadvantage to have one earner and many children when most white families were like that. It will not be a special disadvantage to be a single parent when most white families are like that. It is just that the minority patterns do not fit the current standard mould.

On the other hand, it might be argued that a standard mould no longer exists. An interpretation of the changing patterns of family formation among white people in northern Europe, summarized at the beginning of this paper, is that increased diversity within that ethnic group provides such a wide range of choices that there is no longer a "recognized thing to do."

The single scale running from "old-fashioned values" to "modern individualism" may nevertheless be more helpful as a base for interpreting ethnic variations. Of course there are all sorts of detailed differences which do not quite fit the model. Nevertheless, it is fair to say that:
• White people in Britain, and elsewhere in northern/Protestant Europe, have substantially widened the range of family options available, especially to young people in a transitional stage between living with their parents and living with their own husbands/wives and children. This can

be seen as a significant shift along the continuum from old-fashioned values to modern individualism.

- Indians and African-Asians are further back along the old-fashioned values end of the continuum: there is a strong emphasis on the traditional marriage; the continued interest in such practices as arranged marriages helps to emphasize the primacy of family over personal preferences. On the other hand, Indians and African-Asians are indistinguishable from white families on some measures, and these groups are probably converging rapidly on the majority position – away from old-fashioned values, if not positively towards modern individualism.

- Bangladeshis and Pakistanis adopt the practices most consistent with the old-fashioned values model. This is especially visible in the proportion of women remaining outside the labor market, and the size of their families. This paper has found signs that these groups, too, are moving away from their exceptional position, though it is clear that such movement involves the reform of marriage rather than its rejection. The very strong emphasis on a particular set of family standards in Islamic teachings may mean that the pace of change will be slower among Muslims than among Sikh and Hindus. (The parallel may be between Catholic and Protestant churches in Europe.)

- If the white direction of change lies from old-fashioned values towards modern individualism, and South Asians are behind the trend, Caribbeans are well out in front. The Caribbean family, in the traditional and formal sense of a Caribbean man married to a Caribbean woman, may be dying out. Like all the other groups, they are moving away from old-fashioned values towards modern individualism. The relative acceptability of nonmarital and nonresidential partnerships may be traced to West Indian cultural traditions. But whereas the South Asians' movement along that scale can be described as a convergence on the patterns common in the society they have recently joined, Caribbeans are moving away from, not towards, the standard white family structure (though that is moving rapidly too).

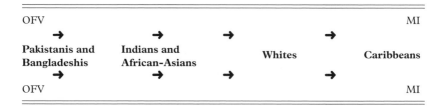

So the ethnic groups compared in this paper have one thing in common – they are all moving in the same direction. Of course, the fact that all groups are moving in approximately the same direction does not mean that there is anything inevitable about the trend – that it will affect all groups equally, or that it will carry on forever. More systematic research on the nature and direction of change is a key priority.

The current family structures of Bangladeshis and Pakistanis, on the one hand, and Caribbeans, on the other, could hardly be more different from each other. This provides plenty of scope for moralizing, from a white perspective, about the subordination of women to men and family (in one case) and irresponsible parenting (in the other). These issues are better sorted out within the relevant communities, rather than on the basis of a single (white-dominated) set of values. Nevertheless, both of the exceptional groups face the possibility of internal conflict, between fathers and daughters, between husbands and wives, or between lovers, if within-group norms remain or become too widely differentiated from those in Britain as a whole. Moreover, as the analysis in this paper has shown, the family structures at both ends of the OFV–MI continuum are associated with poverty.

Note on sources

This paper draws mainly on two large-scale surveys.

The **Fourth National Survey of Ethnic Minorities** was carried out by the Policy Studies Institute and Social and Community Planning Research in 1993/4. A nationally representative sample of 5,196 Caribbean, South Asian, and Chinese adults were interviewed, using matched interviewers and (where necessary) translated questionnaires, and 2,867 whites were also interviewed. A technical report is available from the National Centre for Social Research (Smith and Prior 1997). The principal report on the survey, *Ethnic Minorities in Britain* (EMiB, Modood et al. 1997), included a chapter on family structures; attitudes to marriage were also covered in the chapter on culture and identity. A subsequent reanalysis of the FNS, *Ethnic Minority Children and their Grandparents* (EMCG, Berthoud 2000b) has provided data about three-generation families.

The **Labour Force Survey** is commissioned annually by the Department for Education and Employment. All the adults are interviewed in about 50,000 households each year. The data analysed here are based on combining the eleven years from 1985 to 1995 to build up large samples of ethnic minorities. Between 1992 and 1995, when the LFS adopted a rolling quarterly design, the data were taken from the spring quarters, and omit respondents who had contributed the previous spring. Much of the material here has been taken from the chapter on family patterns in *Young*

Caribbean Men and the Labor Market (YCM, Berthoud 1999, summarized in Berthoud 2000a). Another analysis of the same data has provided evidence about fertility rates – see *Teenage Births to Ethnic Minority Women* (TB, Berthoud 2001).

The **Family Resources Survey** (combining 1994/5 and 1995/6), an annual sample of 25,000 households, has been analyzed to provide data on incomes – see *The Incomes of Ethnic Minorities* (IEM, Berthoud 1998a). Figure 8.1 is based on direct analysis of the **General Household Survey** of 1973. Figure 8.3 is based on the **European Community Household Panel**, and the **Panel Survey of Income Dynamics**, and is derived from Iacovou (2002).

NOTES

This paper was written as part of the ESRC-funded program of the Research Center on Micro-Social Change at the Institute for Social and Economic Research, University of Essex. Thanks to Nick Buck and Elena Bardasi for providing data, and to John Haskey, Tariq Modood, and Karen Rowlingson for extended and valuable comments on a draft.

1. The "Caribbean" group analyzed here includes LFS categories "black Caribbean" and "black other" on the grounds that most of the latter are the British-born children of people of Caribbean origin (Berthoud 1998b). Some data about African families are available from the LFS (YCM) but are not discussed here.

2. Throughout this paper, the term "single" mother always refers to a woman who is currently living with no partner, and who has never been married. Separated, widowed, or divorced mothers are covered by the term "lone parent" but are not included under "single parent" – note that this differs from American usage. Those currently cohabiting do not count as single (though they may never have been married). Those who cohabited in the past (perhaps with their child's father) and who never married are still counted as single – most data sources do not identify them separately. Former cohabitations are an increasing group within the single-mother category among white women (Ermisch 1997) but probably still represent a minority in the Caribbean community.

3. If 9 percent of white mothers were observed to be single when their child was born, and 4 percent when the child was fifteen, then 5 percent, about half of the original 9, must have married in the mean time.

4. The ratio in Table 8.2 appears to be fifteenfold, but is very sensitive to rounding. Tenfold is a better summary.

5. The table shows the estimated probability of remaining single for a "standard" member of each ethnic group: a man aged thirty, whose twentieth birthday fell in 1985, who was born in Britain (or migrated before the age of sixteen), and who had O levels or equivalent qualifications.

6. Millennium Cohort Survey preliminary data, new analysis.

7. All the quotations in this paragraph are taken from Beishon et al. 1998, pp. 77–8.

8. The Fourth National Survey suggests that a fifth of Caribbean single mothers live with their own mother and/or father; compared with one tenth of white single mothers (EMCG). Among families where grandparents were not living in the same household, Caribbean and white children both had similarly high levels of contact with their grandparents.

9. Non-British readers should note that Income Support is the means-tested benefit available to non-working individuals and families whose other sources of income are insufficient for their minimum needs. In the context of one-parent families, the direct American equivalent is TANF; but Income Support is also available to a wide range of other client groups, including pensioners, and does not always carry the strong moral stigma associated with "welfare" in America.

10. The Labour Force Survey, like the census, identifies Indians, Bangladeshis, and Pakistanis. The Fourth National Survey (FNS) introduced a fourth category, African-Asians, defined as people of South Asian origin whose family had lived in Africa before migrating to Britain. The majority of these were of Indian pre-origin, so the LFS's "Indian" category is roughly equivalent to the FNS's combination of Indians and African Asians. The main source reports (EMiB and YCM) provide some information about Chinese families, but they are not referred to here.

11. Note that the quantitative evidence and the qualitative research quoted earlier in the paragraph agree that Muslims are more and Hindus less traditional on this issue. But the quantitative figures place Sikh on the more traditional side, where the qualitative approach placed them on the less traditional side.

12. Labour Force Survey, new analysis.

13. Adults in the FNS were asked about the location of their own parents; the answers are interpreted as describing the grandparents of the respondent's children.

14. $70\% \times 51\% \times 36\% = 13\%$.

REFERENCES

Anwar, M., 1994, *Young Muslims in Britain: Attitudes, Educational Needs and Policy Implications*, Leicester: The Islamic Foundation.

Beishon, S., T. Modood, and S. Virdee, 1998, *Ethnic Minority Families*, London: Policy Studies Institute.

Berrington, A., 1994, "Marriage and Family Formation Among the White and Ethnic Minority Populations in Britain," *Ethnic and Racial Studies* 17, 13: 517–47.

Berthoud, R., 1998a, *The Incomes of Ethnic Minorities*, Institute for Social and Economic Research, Report 98–1, Colchester: University of Essex.

1998b, "Defining Ethnic Groups: Origin or Identity?," *Patterns of Prejudice*, 32, 2: 56–63.

1999, *Young Caribbean Men and the Labour Market: A Comparison with Other Ethnic Groups*, York: Joseph Rowntree Foundation.

2000a, "Ethnic Employment Penalties in Britain," *Journal of Ethnic and Migration Studies*, 26, 3: 389–416.

2000b, "Ethnic Minority Children and their Grandparents," unpublished paper.

2001, "Teenage Births to Ethnic Minority Women," *Population Trends 104* (Summer): 12–16.

Brown C., 1994, *Black and White Britain*, London: Heinemann.

Coleman, D. and J. Salt (eds.), 1996, *Demographic Characteristics of Ethnic Minority Populations*, London: HMSO.

Daniel, W., 1968, *Racial Discrimination in England*, Harmondsworth: Penguin.

Dench, G., 1996, *The Place of Men in Changing Family Cultures*, London: Institute of Community Studies.

DSS, 2001, *Households Below Average Income: 1994/95 to 1999/00*, London: Department of Social Security.

Ermisch, J., 1997, "Pre-marital Cohabitation, Childbearing and the Creation of One Parent Families," in C. Jonung and I. Persson (eds.), *Economics of the Family*, London: Routledge, pp. 119–35.

Haskey, J., 1998, "One-parent Families and their Dependent Children in Britain," in R. Ford and J. Millar (eds.), *Private Lives and Public Responses: Lone Parenthood and Future Policy in the UK*, London: Policy Studies Institute, pp. 22–41.

Iacovou, M., 2002, "Regional Variations in the Transition to Adulthood," *Annals of the American Academy of Political and Social Science* 580: 40–69.

Kiernan, K., H. Land, and J. Lewis 1998, *Lone Motherhood in Twentieth-Century Britain: From Footnote to Front Page*, Oxford: Clarendon Press.

Land, H. 1969, *Large Families in London*, London: Bell.

Modood, T., S. Beishon, and S. Virdee, 1994, *Changing Ethnic Identities*, London: Policy Studies Institute.

Modood, T., R. Berthoud, J. Lakey, J. Nazroo, P. Smith, S. Virdee, and S. Beishon, 1997, *Ethnic Minorities in Britain: Diversity and Disadvantage*, London: Policy Studies Institute.

Patterson, O., 1998, *Rituals of Blood*, Washington, DC: Civitas/Counterpoint.

Peach, C., 1996, "Does Britain have Ghettoes?", *Transactions of the British Institute of Geographers* 21, 1: 216–35.

Rowlingson, K. and S. McKay, 1998, *The Growth of Lone Parenthood*, London: Policy Studies Institute.

Smith D., 1977, *Racial Disadvantage in Britain*, Harmondsworth: Penguin.

Smith P. and G. Prior, 1997, *The Fourth National Survey of Ethnic Minorities: Technical Report*, London: National Centre for Social Research.

Song, M. and R. Edwards, 1996, "Comment: Raising Questions about Perspectives on Black Lone Motherhood," *Journal of Social Policy* 26, 2: 233–44.

Stopes-Roe, M. and R. Cochrane, 1990, *Citizens of this Country: the Asian British*, Clevedon: Multilingual Matters.

Wilson, W., 1987, *The Truly Disadvantaged: The Inner City, The Underclass and Public Policy*, University of Chicago Press.

Part III

Formal structures

The papers in the preceding section of this volume look, in broad terms, at the role of race and ethnicity in the production of social mobility, through a focus on families and neighborhoods. The present section focuses more closely on how these forces translate into social mobility outcomes, with additional attention to the critical area of education and ancestry (which we will call "pre-market forces"), and a new emphasis on the way that race and ethnicity are woven into the labor market. The fundamental points of these papers taken as a whole are: (a) important social forces not usually considered in any detail by economists are at work in both arenas; (b) race and ethnicity channel and magnify these forces; and (c) the comparative study of the two countries places these forces in sharper relief.

From the perspective taken here, social mobility is the joint product of the human capital of individuals, combined with the social capital embedded in ethno-racially specific networks. This human and social capital is refracted through the social organization of work, within labor market and political systems that are structured in part by the social meaning of race. Only when all of these considerations are taken together can we have a truly rounded understanding of how groups are stratified and how individuals attain economic and social status.

The standard way of thinking about the influence of racial or ethnic categories in the labor market is the model originally introduced by Gary Becker. In this model, individuals have specific human capital attributes, and employers under conditions of a competitive, full-employment economy will hire on the basis of these attributes. The exception to this occurs when employers have a "taste" or "preference" for discrimination – that is, an essentially irrational aversion to members of certain groups. The existence of such discriminatory preferences, together with the assumption that labor markets are perfectly competitive allows Becker to deduce the implications of a racial discrimination for racial disparities in employment and wages.

For Becker, this preference for discrimination is likely to be under severe pressure from the force of a competitive market economy, since satisfying it will cause the employer, *ceteris paribus*, to hire individuals of a lower quality or a higher wage than they would otherwise. This will tend to raise the employers' costs and prices and as a result to lower his profit margin. Over the long term, so this standard economic argument goes, we would expect discriminatory behavior to be largely eliminated.

Becker's argument has been very fruitful and important in the history of economic research on this topic. But, it is certainly not beyond criticism. Notice, for instance, that it begs the question of from whence such race-conditioned employer preferences derive in the first place. Why these preferences? The papers in this section see discrimination not as an aberration at the edges of the market, but as something closer to a fundamental fact about how labor markets function. In Becker's model, employers have complete information as to the inherent quality of applicants and zero transaction costs in searching for them, and make decisions on the basis of their preferences, not that of their existing labor force. In the real world, employers have incomplete information, frequently substantial search costs and often have to adapt themselves to the preferences of the individuals currently working for them. Furthermore, in Becker's model discrimination occurs primarily because employers have aversions to certain groups – but in the real world (as Waldinger's paper reminds us) discriminatory behavior is due as much to employers' preference *for* certain groups as it is due to any distaste they may harbor *against* others.

If the preceding description of the real world of the labor market is realistic, how do race and ethnicity fit in? On the one hand, given that employers have imperfect information, they will often be inclined to use racial and ethnic markers as proxies for individual qualities. That is, employers will often hire from particular groups because they believe that the average quality of those groups is higher, and avoid others that they believe are generally untrustworthy. This is especially likely to be the case where there are few formal qualifications that can attest for individual characteristics (as in the low-wage labor market).

Furthermore, consider what happens when we recognize the importance of search costs for employers. Where search costs are high employers will seek methods that reduce these costs while providing them with generally reliable employees. (This is particularly the case if employee turnover rates are also high, so that employers cannot amortize search costs over a long-term employment relationship.) One way to do this is for employers to rely on "network hiring" – that is, using their existing labor pool as a source for the referral of prospective new employees. Where incumbent employees are embedded in strong ethnic or racial networks, they will tend to refer individuals from those networks while excluding outsiders. What is more, search costs aside employers may prefer an ethnically or racially homogenous workforce if they believe such homogeneity will be valued by their employees (thereby reducing the monetary wage they have to pay) or where such homogeneity reduces transaction costs on the shop floor. Over time employees will treat these arrangements as a form of "entitlement," hoarding opportunity for "their own kind" while excluding others.

Thus, the ethnic or racial "niche" in the labor market effectively shields the group from full competition while giving those individuals already placed within the niche powerful leverage over fellow group members (since the insider has an asset of value to coethnics not yet in the niche). It follows that groups with strong niches will also have profound incentives for continuing group identity on the part of individuals, since it is that identity which qualifies individuals for employment in the niche. While this process is not designed with exclusion of outsiders as its objective, it can nonetheless be a very efficient exclusionary mechanism.

Furthermore, in the standard economic model employers themselves have no strong ethnic or racial identification, and the distinction between the sources of business finance, on the one hand, and of labor on the other, is sharp. But especially with immigrant communities (as Heath and Robinson emphasize) self-employment is a very common pattern. Faced with a labor market where their qualifications (which may be difficult to evaluate as they are often obtained abroad) are undervalued, or where their grasp of the language is imperfect, or where they anticipate discrimination, immigrants will often choose to work for themselves rather than sell their labor in the market. What is more, self-employment may allow labor practices that would be difficult (or illegal) in the formal labor market. An owner of a business may employ his family with little or no compensation, and may himself work very long hours that would be prohibitively expensive if he employed others to work them. While the hourly wage from such an arrangement may be low, the total compensation from such intensity of labor – both economically and in terms of status amongst peers – may be high, and this appears to be a common pattern in self-employment, what might be called "self-exploitation."

In addition, the "ethnic entrepreneur" will tend to hire coethnics and shun those from outside his group, for a number of reasons. On the one hand, employing coethnics may give the entrepreneur additional social standing in his community – and conversely there may be strong social stigma to hiring outsiders. Second, the information that flows through ethnic networks may allow ethnic entrepreneurs greater confidence in their hires – and the extent to which the employee is embedded within that network may cause shame if his work is of low quality. Finally, especially in immigrant communities, coethnics may be willing to trade off lower wages for employment in an environment where they can speak their native language, and the shielded nature of the immigrant community may make it difficult for the immigrant employee to recognize the labor standards that prevail outside that community.

But the informal economy that characterizes the previous discussion is not the entire economy – perhaps not even the predominant part of the economy. One important fact of the modern economy, and of modern society more generally, is the increasing reliance on formal qualifications as a substitute for informal knowledge. The most important consequence of this shift is the reliance on educational qualifications as a signaling device for individual qualities. Where groups are immigrants, the first generation may in large numbers be absorbed into the informal economy whose characteristics track closely with those described above. But there are strong incentives for subsequent generations to move out of that ethnically and racially encoded economic system into the formal system driven by educational qualifications, where networks and niches are less important. Thus differences in educational attainments across ethnic and racial groups must be an important part of our analysis.

Attainment of educational qualifications may also be a reflection of the impression of discrimination. Model finds in her analysis evidence that discrimination in employment is somewhat higher in Britain, while Modood finds that higher levels of ethnic minority young people value the attainment of educational qualifications than whites. These two factors may be linked – the expectation of discrimination may lead minorities to compensate by getting higher qualifications than they would otherwise. The downside of this, as Heath suggests, may be a somewhat higher unemployment rate, as some percentage of ethnic minorities become "overqualified," or in another interpretation, increase their reserve wage.[1] This pattern was also found in the United States by Waldinger, who observed that American blacks sought relatively higher educational attainment to compensate for their exclusion from niche economies (Waldinger 1996). In any event, what is clear is that the educational attainment of ethnic minorities is partially a function of group norms and family structure, as suggested by papers in the preceding section, but may also be a reflection of rational adjustments to the structure of the labor market and patterns of perceived or real exclusion therein.

A final factor in social mobility that papers in this section address is the importance of timing. All groups do not enter the economy at the same time, and when they enter may be as important as the internal characteristics of the group or the generic structure of the economy. On the one hand, as Robinson emphasizes, where groups enter the economy is partially a function of the structure of opportunity upon their arrival. Pakistanis went into industrial occupations less because of any specific capacity or taste for such jobs, and more because the movement of whites out of the low end of industry opened up a niche for them there. Afro-Caribbeans were found in government employment in hospitals and transport because of persistent labor shortages that caused the government to actively recruit them for such jobs. Waldinger makes a similar point, observing that where groups place themselves in the labor queue is largely a function of where space is being evacuated – it is there that niches form that subsequent waves of coethnics filter into. Groups may acquire a cultural affinity for such labor after the fact, or employers may associate them as a "good fit" for such jobs, but the reasons for their placement in particular parts of the economy cannot simply be understood in terms of the group's specific cultural attributes. It is important, therefore, to distinguish where ethnic niches form because of deep cultural group characteristics, and where they form because of the accidents of timing.

It is important to recognize, however, that the flip side of opportunity is almost always exclusion. Where groups hoard opportunity and distribute it to coethnics, individuals from excluded groups are denied those opportunities. It is an interesting irony that many of these papers suggest, that a free-market economy that is supposedly driven by the rational, calculating behavior of free and equal individuals creates such powerful incentives for group attachment and identity. And there are reasons to believe that groups whose structure is not as collectively oriented and institutionalized (such as Afro-Caribbeans in Britain and African-Americans in the United States) may be relatively disadvantaged by an economy that organizes at least some parts of the labor market on ethnic and racial lines.

NOTE

1. An alternative view is that overqualification may sometimes be disadvantageous, usually when combined with stereotypes (such as, "Asians are clever but can't manage people"). But, on the whole, the overqualification of some immigrant workers is simply a fact of life for newcomers and it has helped minorities to become more competitive and thus better jump over discriminatory hurdles.

REFERENCE

Waldinger, R. 1996, *Still the Promised City: African-Americans and New Immigrants in Postindustrial New York*, Cambridge, MA: Harvard University Press.

9 Educational progress for African-Americans and Latinos in the United States from the 1950s to the 1990s: the interaction of ancestry and class

Michael Hout

Introduction

In the 1950s and 1960s the civil rights movement challenged the legal basis of American-style apartheid. Through civil disobedience, litigation, and legislation, activists and movement organizations riveted the nation's attention on the contradiction between Americans' professed belief in equal treatment and the country's history of racial exclusion. The public confrontation between these contradictions caused millions of Americans to rethink their exclusionary views (Schuman et al. 1998). The net result was that African-Americans' access to public education, voting rights, and public places increased. These changes in white people's outlooks and black people's opportunities raised the expectation in the African-American community – and in other quarters, too – that blacks and whites were on the road to equality.

In the 1990s a countermovement pushed back the resources institutions had been using to increase access for African-Americans and people from other formerly excluded racial and ethnic groups. Under the rubric of "no preferences," critics of affirmative action have used lawsuits, ballot initiatives, and other means to halt or halter the use of race as a criterion when evaluating candidates for education or employment.

Much of the action in the civil rights movement and in the 1990s backlash has been in schools and universities. Civil rights activists and their opponents focus on education because it is the gateway to opportunity. Educational opportunity has been a resource for the propertyless of all ancestries at least since the nineteenth century. Early in the industrial era Americans charged schools with the task of incorporating the excluded and bringing opportunity to the disadvantaged (e.g., Fischer et al. 1996: Chapter 6). Today, in the era of small government, education is the one institution that politicians can turn to as a venue for public action.[1] But education itself has never been free from exclusionary practices and outcomes. A review of specific practices – those promoted as opening opportunities and those suspected of resulting in exclusion – would be informative. This chapter looks instead at results. I organize the evidence of educational opportunity and use data about the experience of people who passed through American schools from the 1950s to the 1990s. In developing this results-oriented view I will take special note of the transmission of inequality across generations as it has consequences for people in different racial and ethnic categories and for people in different social classes.

Initial conditions and expectations

The scale of African-American exclusion in the first half of the twentieth century was staggering. Bowen and Bok's (1998: 1) statistical portrait of Black America in 1940 illustrates the extent of this exclusion:

In 1940 most black men and women lived out of common view in rural communities chiefly in the South. Approximately 90 percent lived in poverty (Jaynes and Williams 1989, p. 277). Their annual earnings were less than half those of whites. The education they received was markedly inferior in quality. African American children in the South went to predominantly black schools in which (on average) pupil-teacher ratios were one-quarter greater than those in white schools, school terms were 10 percent shorter, and black teachers were paid half the salary of white teachers (Card and Krueger 1992, p. 167). The median amount of education received by blacks aged 25–29 was about seven years (Jaynes and Williams 1989, p. 334). Only 12 percent of blacks age 25–29 had completed high-school; less than two percent could claim a college degree (US Department of Education 1997: 17).

Against that background any progress would be welcome. But against the aspirations that the successes of the late 1960s generated, anything short of parity by the year 2000 must be regarded as disappointing. The United States in 2000 is far short of racial and ethnic parity in education, employment, wages, health, and happiness. That is because the impressive gains of the first postwar generation have not been matched since then. For example, African-American family poverty fell from 90 percent in 1940 to 26.9 percent of families by 1974; it rose through the late 1970s and early 1980s and did not get back down below 27 percent until 1995 (US Bureau of the Census 1999). Wages and annual earnings likewise increased rapidly through the 1960s and first half of the 1970s but little since. African-American men now earn 73 percent as much as white men (compared to 43 percent in 1940). The grossest educational inequities have been eliminated but most observers concede that the resources available to inner-city schools lag seriously behind those of suburban and even some rural schools. Three-fourths of African-Americans now earn a high-school diploma but only 14 percent earn a college degree (Mare 1995).

Latinos, that is Americans who trace their origins to the countries of Latin America, were barely visible in 1940. There were fewer than 4 million persons of Hispanic origin resident in the United States at the time of the 1940 Census. By 1996 that number was approaching 40 million – a tenfold increase in less than two generations. American-born Latinos today are achieving about the same amount of education as African-Americans. Immigrants from Latin America typically have much less schooling. Barely one-third of the Latino immigrants who were 25–29 years old in 1990 had a high-school diploma; 6 percent had a college degree (Mare 1995).

While contemporary inequalities may pale in comparison with the gross disparities of fifty years ago, most of the progress occurred in the first half of the postwar era. The United States has made little progress in closing the gap between blacks and whites through the stagflation of the late 1970s, the restructuring of the 1980s, and the expansion of the early 1990s (Danziger and Gottschalk 1996). There are some indications that the prosperity in the second half of the 1990s began to spread beyond the top 20 percent of the income distribution. Poverty once again began moving downward, median earnings rose for African-Americans and Latinos, and the gap between whites' wages and those of others narrowed slightly (US Bureau of the Census 1999).

"Hurry up and wait" is a good shorthand for postwar trends in racial disparity. After the revolutionary progress of the 1960s, the waiting has now held up a whole generation. The college-graduating classes of 2000 were born in 1977 and 1978. Their lives began just when the pace of racial progress ground to a halt. The few who made it all the way through to a bachelor's degree deserve their diplomas. America can feel good that so many have succeeded; education is more just now than it was in 1950. But a bachelor's degree is still twice as likely for whites as for African-Americans and Latinos. Out there somewhere in American society are unseen and untold young people who would have joined the graduation procession had progress not stopped the year they were born. The nation was once on a course that would equalize educational opportunity. The evidence in this chapter shows how falling racial and class exclusion increased educational opportunity in the 1960s and 1970s and how stalled racial progress, coupled with resurgent class exclusion, reversed the trends in the 1980s and 1990s.

Educational mobility

The problem of mobility looms large in the public consciousness. Impatient in many things, Americans seem to be paradoxically content with an economy that makes progress a generation at a time. They subscribe to the idea that each generation does at least a little better than the preceding one did. The focus on mobility masks the reality of unequal opportunity because those who start off with the biggest advantages can be downwardly mobile and still attain far more education, income, or wealth than an upwardly mobile person who started out poor. For that reason, sociologists began over thirty years ago to analyze how educational and occupational destinations depend on family origins and to treat mobility as an epiphenomenon (Duncan 1966, 1979).

The link from educational origins to educational destinations is important because a strong link perpetuates the legacy of past discrimination. The stronger the connection between parents' educations and their children's opportunities, the longer the exclusionary practices of the past live on, even if they have been discontinued. So the focus of this research is the interaction of ancestry and class – less because mobility is intrinsically interesting than because of what it can tell us about the long-term consequences of past exclusion and the class character of contemporary inequality.

Data and measurement

Large data files with long histories and detailed information on family origins are rare. Large government data bases, such as the Current Population Survey, reach back to the 1960s and beyond but lack data on social origins. Cohort studies typically include good data on social origins but lack the time span we need to understand long-term change in the life chances of African-Americans and Latinos. The General Social Survey (GSS) is an annual cross-section of the English-speaking adult population of the United States that has been conducted almost every year since 1972. It includes good measures of social origins and provides a longer historical perspective than we can get from cohort studies.

The GSS uses probability sampling methods to select nationally representative households.[2] The interview is carried out face to face with a randomly selected adult in a sample household. The GSS has maintained a 77 percent response rate since it implemented full-probability sampling (see Davis, Smith, and Marsden 1998, or consult the GSS Data and Information Retrieval System at http://www.icpsr.umich.edu/gss99).

Educational categories. The GSS obtains information on the highest grade in school that the respondent completed and the respondent's highest educational credential. From that information, I constructed four categories: did not graduate from high-school, graduated from high-school and stopped, entered a post-secondary program but did not earn a four-year degree, and earned a bachelors or advanced degree. Detailed analyses show that the use of more educational details complicates the analysis without revealing any regularities not evident in the results reported herein.

Family origin. In the study of educational inequality and mobility, the education of the respondent's mother and father are paramount among the many facets of family origin (e.g., Fischer et al. 1996: Chapter 4). This conforms to a regularity that has emerged from the sociological literature: like goes with like in intergenerational studies. That is, the dimension of social origins most important for an outcome of interest is the place of the subject's parents in the distribution of that variable; parents' income matters most for their offspring's economic outcomes (wages, poverty, etc.), their marital status matters for their offspring's marital histories, and their educations matter most for the offspring's educational opportunities.

To classify parents' educations I constructed seven categories:

1) elementary education (less than 9 years of schooling completed),
2) incomplete secondary education (from 9 to 12 years of schooling completed but no high-school diploma),
3) complete secondary education (from 9 to 12 years of schooling completed and a high-school diploma),
4) some college (a high-school diploma and 13 or more years of schooling completed, but no degrees earned),
5) a two-year degree (13 or more years of schooling completed and a diploma or certificate from a two-year college),
6) bachelor's degree (13 or more years of schooling completed and a degree from a four-year college or university),
7) a graduate degree (16 or more years of schooling completed and an advanced degree from a university).

I experimented with alternative ways of scoring the categories and settled on a simple scheme that uses the category numbers as scores.

Many respondents do not know or cannot remember their parents' educations. Some people simply do not remember (or never knew) their parents' educations; this problem increases sharply with age for respondents who were over fifty-five years old at the time of the interview. These cases are deleted from the analysis. For other people the problem is family breakup. One of their parents did not live with them while they were growing up, and they do not know about the absent parent's education. An absent parent can be a serious handicap for a child's social and cognitive development. Censoring the data by leaving out the cases for which a parent's education is unknown because the parent was absent from the household has the potential to bias the other results.[3] For descriptive purposes I report "father absent from family" and "mother absent from family" as separate categories. For regressions, I scored the missing parent's education as "high-school graduate" and also included a dummy variable equal to 1 if the father was absent and zero otherwise and an analogous variable for whether the mother was absent.[4]

The income of the family of origin and the occupational status of the main earner's occupation are also important aspects of social origins. Including them with parental education yields a more complete picture of educational stratification (e.g., Hauser and Featherman 1976). Measuring income accurately is very difficult in a retrospective survey. The GSS measure is a simple question about income in comparison to other families: "Thinking about the time when you were 16 years old, compared with other American families in general then, would you say your family income was far below average, below average, average, above average, or far above average?" Almost 10 percent of the people who are interviewed say at first that they cannot answer that question, but when asked to provide their "best guess," nearly all provide some indication of their family's standard of living. Half of the GSS respondents (52 percent to be precise) say that their family's income was "average." One-fourth (24 percent) say "below average," 14 percent say "above average," 8 percent say "far below average," and only 2 percent say "far above average." The crudeness of this measure means that using it in statistical procedures like the model I use herein will underestimate the true effect of family income on educational attainment. But including a crude estimate seems preferable to ignoring class differences that are independent of parents' education. Moreover, because the measure is equally crude for all cohorts, we can probably get a fair assessment of change in its effect; that is, even if the effect is underestimated for each cohort, the difference between the coefficient for one cohort and the next approximates to what we would obtain if we had access to a more accurate measure. The GSS discontinued this measure after the 1994 survey, so using it eliminates the two most recent surveys from the analysis. This is a serious exclusion so I present descriptive statistics for all available cases – including the 1996 and 1998 interviews that have no income data. Furthermore, I have appended regression results that leave income out of the equation. This nearly doubles the sample size for the last cohort. Since the potential rise in the importance of income for educational opportunities is a major concern, I highlight the results that include the crude income measure.

The GSS data on occupation presents two difficulties. First the rules NORC used to code job descriptions were changed in 1988 to bring the GSS into line with changes that the Census Bureau had made. The change is well-documented and the GSS data file provides three years of double coding with which to integrate the two coding schemes. But this cannot overcome the fundamental incompatibility of the schemes. A good approximation of the Erikson-Goldthorpe class model (Erikson and Goldthorpe 1992) is possible from each scheme, and I have implemented it here (details available on request). The Erikson-Goldthorpe scheme, as modified, results in the following categories: Professionals (upper), Professionals (lower), Managers (upper and lower combined), Routine white-collar employees, Proprietors, Farmers, Skilled blue-collar workers, Semi- and Unskilled blue-collar workers. Various kinds of service employees are coded as managers, routine white-collar employees, and unskilled blue-collar workers according to rules specified by Erikson and Goldthorpe.

The second problem with the GSS occupation data is that mother's occupations were not ascertained prior to 1994. Thus for the minority of households that had a female principal earner, occupation is missing. Father's occupation must serve as the measure of occupational origins even for families that had no male present. As one might expect, that measure is missing for many of the affected cases – about 12 percent of the total cases. Missing father's occupation overlaps so much with missing father's education, however, that only one "absent father" code is needed to correct the regression estimates for the missing data on this variable.[5]

The GSS also asks about the composition of the family of origin around the time when the respondent was sixteen years old. I make use of two aspects of family structure: whether the father and mother were living with the respondent then and the number of his or her siblings.[6] Information on whether the respondent was living in the United States or abroad at age sixteen, and, for US residents, in which region of the country they lived give a broad indication of educational and occupational opportunity. In particular, schools in the South are usually ranked lower than those in the rest of the country. The multivariate analysis will contrast persons who were living in the South with the rest of the United States. As this is a study of educational stratification in the United States, I decided it was best to exclude the cases that were resident in foreign countries at age 16 years (but not foreign-born respondents who were living in the United States at that age). The GSS also asks a random two-thirds of its respondents whether they were born in the United States. Preliminary analyses failed to find a significant effect of foreign birth. I do not present those null results because too many cases have to be deleted to accommodate using the foreign-born variable.

Sample restrictions. The GSS samples households. Persons in group quarters – most notably college dormitories and old-age homes – are excluded. Therefore, the GSS underestimates the educational attainment of the youngest cohorts in any given survey. To guard against this bias, I have excluded respondents who were less than thirty years old at the time of interview. Even though their individual reports were undoubtedly as accurate as those of any other GSS respondents, collectively they misrepresent their cohort because significant members of the cohort were outside the sampling frame. At the other end of the life cycle, less-educated persons die younger than college graduates. Therefore, the GSS respondents over seventy years old are more educated than their cohort was before it was eroded by significant mortality. To guard against this bias, I also exclude all persons over sixty-nine years of age. The interview is done in English, so persons who do not speak English well enough to be interviewed are excluded.[7]

Multivariate results are obtained using maximum likelihood methods. The statistical model is an ordered logit model corrected for features of the GSS sampling design. The model is discussed and justified in the appendix. A table of descriptive statistics for all variables is appended (Table 9.A1) as are the multivariate results that do not use the income measure (Table 9.A2).

Trends in educational attainment

Educational progress can be gauged by monitoring rates of high-school graduation, college enrollment, and college graduation. Comparing cohorts born 1955–68 with those born earlier in the century gives us an indication of which ancestry groups – African-American, Latino, or others – are making the most educational progress. Table 9.1 shows the trends. After discussing them, I will turn to multivariate results that show how much of the trend is due to racial dynamics per se and how much should be attributed to the interaction between ancestry and class.

High-school graduation rates almost doubled for African-Americans across the three cohorts. Less than half of the African-Americans born prior to 1940 graduated from high-school; 87 percent of those born between 1955 and 1968 earned a high-school diploma. Much of the change actually took place earlier as the 1940–54 cohort registered a 78 percent rate. Latinos made similar progress from 35 percent of those born

Table 9.1 *Successful educational transitions by ancestry and birth cohort: persons 30–69 years old, United States, 1974–1998*

	Birth cohort		
Educational transition/Ancestry	Before 1940 (%)	1940–54 (%)	1955–68 (%)
Graduate from high school			
African-American	45	78	87
Latino	35	71	82
Other	72	90	93
Total	68	88	92
Enter post-secondary			
African-American	21	42	54
Latino	11	39	50
Other	34	56	60
Total	32	54	59
Graduate from college			
African-American	7	14	14
Latino	3	16	18
Other	17	29	31
Total	16	27	28
Number of cases	8,980	7,685	3,332

Source: General Social Survey, 1974–1998.

prior to 1940 to 71 percent of those born between 1940 and 1954 and 82 percent of those born between 1955 and 1968. The other ancestry groups (mostly from European origin) started out close to the graduation rates of African-Americans and Latinos of the middle cohort – at 72 percent – and moved on up to 90 and ultimately 93 percent. Even though all groups moved upward, the gap between the groups that made up the majority, on the one hand, and African-Americans and Latinos on the other, narrowed. The initial deficit in high-school graduations was 27 percentage points for African-Americans and 37 percentage points for Latinos; for people born between 1955 and 1968, African-Americans and Latinos are still behind but the gaps have closed to 6 and 11 percentage points respectively.[8]

About half of the oldest high-school graduates of each ancestry group went on to some kind of post-secondary institution (i.e., among cohorts born before 1940). Because of the huge gaps in high-school graduation

Table 9.2 *Maximum likelihood estimates of the parameters of the ordered logit model by cohort: persons 30–69 years old, United States, 1974–1998*

	Cohort		
Independent variable	Before 1940	1940–54	1955–68
Ancestry			
African American	−.398	.201	.308
Latino	−1.017	.038	.081
Other	a	a	a
Woman	−.261	−.295	.036
Father's education	.128	.233	.250
Mother's education	.259	.330	.359
Father absent	−.027	−.291	.319
Mother absent	−.727	−.967	−.760
Main earner's occupation			
Professional, upper	1.289	.612	.832
Professional, lower	1.069	.630	.635
Manager	.996	.535	.760
Routine white-collar	.797	.524	.951
Proprietor	.986	.739	.776
Farmer	.031	.105	.978
Skilled blue-collar	.331	.133	.512
Less-skilled blue-collar	a	a	a
Family income	.202	.036	.201
Number of siblings	−.142	−.142	−.072
Region at age 16			
South Atlantic	−.409	−.383	−.480
East South Central	−.497	−.391	−.711
West South Central	−.198	−.372	−.113
Other	a	a	a
Cohort	.033	.023	−.030
Cut points			
0/1	.635	−.184	−1.824
1/2	2.581	2.056	.488
2/3	3.724	3.456	2.077
Number of cases	8,210	6,072	1,525

Note: Coefficients in **bold** type are significant at the .05 level (two-tailed).
a-Category deleted from the regression as an identifying restriction.

rates, though, some post-secondary education was achieved by 21 percent of African-Americans, 11 percent of Latinos, and 34 percent of others. As high-school graduation rates rose, even the 50 percent continuation rate would have increased post-secondary enrollment rates. But continuation rates actually rose among all groups, accelerating the rise in educational attainment. The acceleration was not as rapid for African-Americans and Latinos as for the others, so the middle cohort shows post-secondary enrollment rates of 42 percent, 39 percent, and 56 percent for African-Americans, Latinos, and others, respectively. Subsequent developments in higher education, especially the expansion of community colleges in big states, pushed post-secondary enrollments upward again and closed the gaps among ancestry groups. In the last cohort, two-thirds of young people in each group continued to some form of post-secondary education. Compounded with record-high high-school graduation rates, these continuation rates resulted in 54 percent of African-Americans, 50 percent of Latinos, and 60 percent of others going on to post-secondary education.

Only one-third of African-Americans who started post-secondary education prior to 1958 earned a four-year degree; amounting to 7 percent of their cohort. A similarly low fraction of Latinos who continued beyond high-school earned four-year degrees, netting just 3 percent of the first cohort. Post-secondary enrollees from other ancestry groups had a graduation rate of 49 percent, adding up to 17 percent of the first cohort. The relative graduation rates did not change significantly from the first to the second cohort; among African-Americans with some post-secondary education one-third earned degrees, among Latinos 40 percent earned degrees, and among others half earned degrees. Compounded by rising proportions enrolling, the overall effect was that, in the 1940–54 cohort, 15 percent of minority ancestry groups and 29 percent of the other ancestries earned college degrees. Graduation rates dropped by 7 percentage points for African-Americans and 5 percentage points for Latinos born into the 1955–68 cohort. Some minority students may have abandoned four-year programs without graduating, but some of the change came from the dramatic rise of minority enrollments in two-year schools. Successfully completing a two-year degree can lead to higher attainment, but it usually does not – especially among African-Americans (Brint and Karabel 1989). The 50 percent graduation rate among others persisted, resulting in a significantly bigger gap in the attainment of college degrees in the 1955–68 cohort than in the preceding ones.

The question for this research is whether parity is a realistic expectation when comparing groups that are not equal at the starting line. African-American and Latino parents have significantly less education than their counterparts from other ancestry groups. Is it reasonable to expect the gap to disappear in one generation? Should we not expect some residual difference in gross comparisons of the sort reported in Table 9.1? It is more reasonable to expect negligible differences in outcomes for people from similar class backgrounds but different ancestry groups. That implies a focus on educational origins and destinations – the topic of the next section.

Patterns of educational mobility

All but one of the major findings in this paper are visible in simple charts showing the fraction of a cohort that crosses the major thresholds in the educational process conditioned by mother's or father's educational attainment and ancestry (Figures 9.1 and 9.2). Each panel of each figure represents a different combination of educational threshold and cohort. The percentage of persons from the cohort in question that achieves success in crossing a stated educational threshold is arrayed by either mother's (Figure 9.1) or father's (Figure 9.2) education, with a separate mark for each ancestry category. African-Americans are represented by filled circles, Latinos by "X"s, and the comparison "other" group – mostly whites – are shown by open circles. The charts also show lines that aid in interpretation by smoothing over the sampling error in the raw data.[9]

Comparing the left, middle, and right panels of the top row of Figure 9.1, we see progress in the achievement of secondary education for each ancestry group, especially for those whose mothers had less than secondary education. In the oldest cohort over 95 percent of "others" whose mothers had high-school diplomas achieved their own too. Among African-Americans and Latinos, high-school graduation was significantly less likely at each level of mother's education; if she was missing or had never completed any secondary education, the respondent's chances of graduating from high school were barely one in four. Among whites and others whose mother had little education, graduation from high school was relatively rare – barely half made it. In the cohort born between 1940 and 1954 (the beginning of the baby boom), the minimum graduation rates among African-Americans and Latinos were 50 percent for the now much less common category of unschooled parents; among whites and others the minimum graduation rate was 75 percent. For the middle-education groups, ancestry differences diminished. The youngest cohort closely resembles its predecessor. Black–white disparity disappeared altogether. Latino–white disparity was restricted to the offspring of the least-educated parents. Thus in high-school graduation, the residual differences among ancestry groups are almost completely attributable to differences among the groups in their educational origins.

Changes in the probability of entering college are much smaller in part because the initial differences among ancestries were smaller. In the oldest cohort, African-American and Latino college enrollment rates lagged

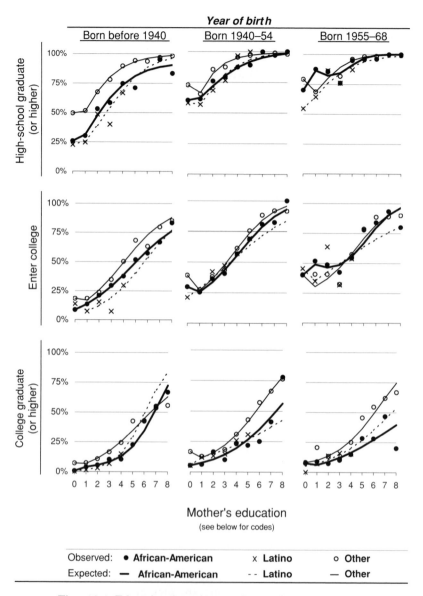

Figure 9.1 Educational attainment by mother's education, ancestry, and birth cohort: persons 30–69 years old, United States

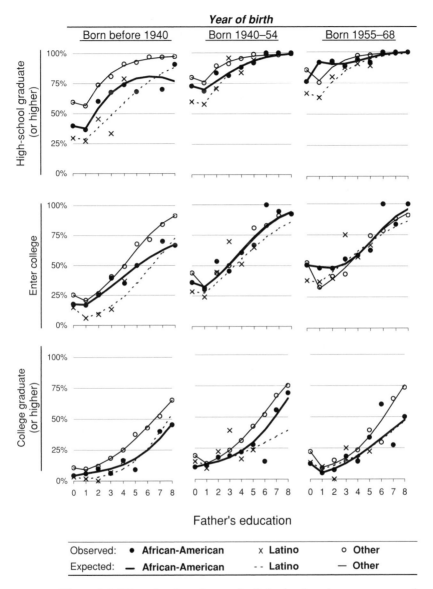

Figure 9.2 Educational attainment by father's education, ancestry, and birth cohort: persons 30–69 years old, United States

behind whites and others by between 12 and 21 percentage points for each level of parental education. For cohorts born since 1940, ancestry is barely a factor once parental education has been taken into account. The large disparities in college enrollment noted in Table 9.1 appear to stem from the legacies of past discrimination. The evidence here implies that youths seeking to enroll in college in the 1980s and early 1990s faced class barriers consistent with their parents' educational achievements but had small additional burdens related directly to ancestry. They do not appear to have any particular advantages that might indicate the intervention of "preferences" in advancing people of color. The class gaps faced by all ancestry groups were formidable. Half of the youths whose parents had not completed high school entered some form of post-secondary education; that is half of the African-Americans, half of the Latinos, and half of the others (up from 25 percent a generation earlier). Between 85 and 90 percent of those young people whose parents had graduated from college or gone on to graduate or professional school enrolled in post-secondary education. Thus the educational class gap in college enrollment was between 35 and 40 percentage points. Disparities within classes that can be tied to racial and ethnic ancestry are barely perceptible.

The last row shows that whites are still at an advantage when it comes to turning post-secondary enrollment into a college degree. African-Americans' and Latinos' rates of college graduation – which were 7 to 10 percentage points behind whites' in the oldest cohort – are 8 to 24 percentage points behind those of whites and others with equal amounts of parental education. No group shows a statistically significant change in college-graduation rates between the middle cohort and the youngest cohort. The youngest cohort is better-educated, but the reason is primarily the greater education of their parents. For people with the same parental education and ancestry, there is no net increase in college graduation from the middle to the last cohort.

These figures also reveal the strong intergenerational component to education. Both parents' educations exert a strong effect on the respondent's own educational attainment. The lines, circles, and Xs in each panel slope sharply upward to the right, indicating a strong association from one generation to the next. The curvature induced by the floor of zero percent and the ceiling of 100 percent are well-modeled by the logistic transformation that I used to smooth over sampling error. The effect of parents' educations on college graduation is significantly weaker for African-Americans and Latinos than for others. Interactions between educational origins and ancestry are nil for the other two outcomes.

Multivariate results

Differences in the educational origins of African-Americans, Latinos, and others explains nearly all of the difference we see in recent high-school graduation rates and all of the difference we see in recent post-secondary enrollment. But ancestry persists as a significant feature of the attainment of college degrees, at least as far as the kinds of analyses presented thus far can tell. To be certain that I have correctly accounted for educational differences and to account more fully for social origins, I turn now to a multivariate analysis of each educational transition. The model enters father's and mother's education simultaneously, adds family income, father's occupation, and family size as additional elements of family origins, and takes account of gender differences (significant only in the first two cohorts) and regional differences – which are very important throughout. Statistical modeling also allows for a more fine-grained approach to cohort comparisons. To expose interactions between cohort and other important variables, I obtain separate estimates of the model's parameters for each cohort. To allow for fine-grained cohort effects within each broad cohort, I add a linear cohort trend term to the model.

The multivariate results confirm conclusions about the way parental education and ancestry affect educational success already drawn after considering the evidence in Figures 9.1 and 9.2. The other variables in the multivariate model have net effects worth noting. The most important results concern parental income. Even though the measure is subjective and fraught with error, its effects are significant in the cohorts prior to the 1940s and since 1955 but not in between. The significant income effects in the first and third cohorts have nearly identical values (.201 and .202). This on-off-on pattern in the effect of family income on educational attainment coincides with important changes in the funding of higher education at four-year colleges and universities. More aid is now provided in the form of loans and less in outright grants that need not be repaid; meanwhile the tuition and living expenses associated with attending college are racing far ahead of the inflation rate for most goods (Lucas 1996; Kane 2000).

Class differences associated with the occupation of the family's main earner diminish significantly across cohorts. Still significant at the end of the series, occupation, nonetheless, has a weaker effect in the 1955–68 cohort than it had in previous cohorts.

Regional differences, sibling effects, and mother's absence work as expected. Father's absence is a weak predictor of educational success. This does not mean that an absent father is not a significant disadvantage. The comparison group for "father absent" is high-school graduates with unskilled jobs. Having an absent father is the equivalent to having one with the lowest prestige job. Cohort effects persist within the broader cohorts up until 1955.

The experience of more recent cohorts

The foregoing analysis breaks off with the cohort born in 1968. That is a group of people who were just finishing advanced schooling in 1998. Since key transitions – from incomplete secondary education to high-school graduation and from high-school graduation to post-secondary enrollment – take place about a decade earlier, it is possible to sneak preview the 1969–76 cohorts, at least for these first two transitions. This portion of the analysis gives us some purchase on the experience of cohorts who left high school in the early 1990s (with or without a diploma).

Table 9.3 compares the 1955–68 cohort with the 1969–76 cohort, limiting the comparison to those who were 23–29 years old when they were

Table 9.3 *Successful educational transitions by ancestry and birth cohort: persons 23–29 years old, United States, 1977–1998*

	Birth cohort	
Educational transition/Ancestry	1955–68 (%)	1969–76 (%)
Graduate from high-school		
African American	86	82
Latino	74	83
Other	90	94
Total	89	91
Enter post-secondary		
African American	46	44
Latino	36	60
Other	54	67
Total	52	63
Graduate from college		
African American	10	12
Latino	8	15
Other	25	28
Total	22	25
Number of cases	2,766	772

Source: General Social Survey, 1974–98.

interviewed. The high-school graduation data show glaring differences by ancestry group. African-Americans lost ground; high-school graduation fell from 86 percent to 82 percent. Latinos, on the other hand, improved dramatically from 74 percent to 83 percent.[10] Others show a modest increase from 90 to 94 percent.

Post-secondary enrollments also fell slightly for African-Americans from the 1955–68 to the 1969–78 cohort. This is not an artifact of these data nor a statistical fluctuation. Hauser (1995) has focused on this problem. His detailed analyses make clear that family resources and family structure cannot explain the deterioration of African-American enrollments. The changes took place before the all-out attack on affirmative action in college admissions. Hauser considers and rejects the conjecture that the military provided an attractive alternative for African-Americans (especially males).

Latinos, in sharp contrast, show significant improvement. Some of the improvement is attributable to the decline in high-school dropout already noted. With more Latinos graduating and a constant 50 percent enrollment rate among graduates, a significant increase in the percent enrolling in post-secondary education is to be expected, but the 60 percent entering post-secondary education exceeds expectation because it represents a 63 percent conditional enrollment rate. In plain English, the data indicate that Latino high-school graduates are increasingly likely to go on to post-secondary education. The rates for other ancestries also indicate increasing college enrollment; post-secondary enrollments among those aged 23 to 29 is up from 54 percent to 67 percent. Thus the declines for African-Americans are in stark contrast to rising rates of post-secondary attendance for Latinos and others.

The college-graduation data are incomplete and will ultimately register increases for all groups as people in their late twenties complete their degrees. The initial reconnaissance shows a slight increase for African-Americans (not statistically significant), a doubling for Latinos, and a three-point increase for others (significant at the .06 level). The college graduation rates for the 1955–68 cohort assessed once respondents were past 30 years of age were higher than registered here for those aged 22 to 29, so the rates for the 1969–76 cohort will probably rise for all three ancestry groups. But unless African-Americans catch up suddenly through a spate of late-twenties graduations, they will lag behind not only whites but also Latinos. The more than two-to-one advantage of the mostly white "other" group will probably still hold in the 1969–76 cohort.

The multivariate results show that about half of the gap between African-Americans and others is class-based, i.e., it follows from the disadvantaged socioeconomic origins that I have interpreted as the legacy of past discrimination. But the other half is independent of the measured effects of class; the academic prospects of African-Americans fall behind those of others who have similar backgrounds. Whether that residual difference reflects differences in background not captured by the variables in the GSS (e.g., school quality differences discussed by Card and Krueger 1992 and Fischer et al. 1996) or ongoing discrimination against African-Americans cannot be resolved with the data in hand. What seems clear in Figures 9.1 and 9.2 above and in a corresponding chart that could be made for the 1969–76 cohort is that the black–white college-graduation gap is greatest for those young people whose parents have some college education. Disadvantaged African-Americans do as poorly as disadvantaged youths from other groups. The African-American deficit in college graduation appears among African-Americans who have some of the advantages that previous generations had been denied.

Conclusion

Class processes – reflected in differential educational opportunity for persons whose parents had little education or money or both – have impeded progress in erasing educational differences among racial ancestry groups in the United States. For people whose parents had similar amounts of education and money, African-Americans or Latinos bear less in the way of a direct burden than they did twenty-five or fifty years ago. But because a person's educational opportunities depend on how much education his or her parents had and African-Americans and Latinos have parents who did bear the full racial burden, large gaps persist today. Thus the class dynamics of educational stratification pass on to the present generation the discrimination and exclusion of previous generations.

The United States made significant progress in erasing class differences in educational opportunity for cohorts born between 1900 and 1950. Since then progress has slowed to a halt. Money mattered more for the educational success of recent cohorts than it did for the cohorts born between 1940 and 1954. Whether this is tied to rising tuition and falling financial aid (Karen 1991, Lucas 1996, Kane 2000) is hard to say with these data, but these two contributors to the family's cost of a young person's college education are certainly the leading suspects. The effect of mother's and father's educations and father's occupation decreased steadily for all racio-ethnic groups through the 1968 cohort. Subsequent cohorts are divided by the same parental-education effects as the 1950 cohort experienced. Family finances were playing a smaller and smaller role in educational opportunity until recently. The cohorts born since 1960 are divided by a sharp resurgence of economic inequality.

Nations can encourage educational opportunity in two ways: they can make educational institutions less selective or they can change the selection criteria in ways that make class less relevant (Hout and Dohan 1996). The easiest way (but not necessarily the least expensive way) to make education less selective is to expand educational facilities. Since advantaged classes are typically utilizing the available facilities in great numbers already, expansion usually benefits the previously disadvantaged (Raftery and Hout 1993). The other approach is to go directly at the mechanisms of exclusion. Public and private institutions can make sure that lack of money and parental education do not impede a young person's educational progress by keeping costs low and considering "hardship" in evaluating applicants. Some have even proposed this kind of class-based affirmative action as a way around the University of California's current problems with its regents and voters. Some have argued in favor of class-based affirmative action, but Kane's (1999) results clearly show that class-based affirmative action will not effectively substitute for race-based affirmative action because most young people who would qualify are neither African-American nor Latino. The results presented here suggest that the converse may also be true. Racial equity will remain out of reach as long as class barriers remain as high as they have been recently in the United States. The interaction of class and race has put another generation of African-Americans at risk. Progress by Latinos is more encouraging. They remain behind whites, but they are gaining faster than African-Americans are.

Appendix: The ordered logit model

The ordered logit model begins with the idea that the continuous variable of interest, in this case "educational attainment" (Y), is unobserved but that we have observations on a categorical indicator of Y, in this case categories formed from information on years of schooling and educational credentials (Z). Z is formed by cutting Y at $K-1$ points, call these cutpoints κ_k for $k = 1, \ldots, K-1$. For completeness, define $\kappa_0 = -\infty$ and $\kappa_K = \infty$. It is not necessary to assume that the κ_k are evenly spaced, only that they are ordered, i.e., $\kappa_1 < \kappa_2, < \ldots < \kappa_{K-1}$ (and by definition $\kappa_0 < \kappa_1$ and $\kappa_{K-1} < \kappa_K$). Now suppose that Y is linearly related to some exogenous variables, call them X_p for $p = 1, 2, \ldots, P$, and an error term, call it u, that is uncorrelated with the X_p:

$$Y = \Sigma_p \beta_p X_p + u. \qquad [1]$$

Table 9.A1 *Descriptive statistics for the total population and for ancestry groups: persons 30–69 years old, 1974–1998*

Variable	Total %	Cohort		
		Before 1940 %	1940–54 %	1955–68 %
Dependent variable				
Dropout of high school	23	33	13	9
Graduate from high school	36	36	36	32
Enter college	21	16	26	30
Graduate from college	21	15	26	29
Independent variables				
African-American	10	10	10	12
Latino	3	2	4	4
Woman	55	56	55	56
Father's education[a]	2.74	2.14	2.76	3.32
Mother's education[a]	3.15	2.13	2.76	3.21
Family income at age 16[b]	2.76	2.67	2.83	2.94
Father absent	16	34	24	13
Mother absent	5	11	6	4
Siblings	3.93	4.29	3.60	3.59
Main earner's occupation				
Professional, upper	5	3	6	9
Professional, lower	2	1	3	4
Manager	7	5	9	12
Routine white-collar	4	4	5	3
Proprietor	7	7	8	8
Farmer	15	21	9	5
Skilled blue-collar	23	22	24	26
Unskilled blue-collar	25	25	26	20
No earner or missing	12	12	12	13
Region at age 16				
South Atlantic	16	17	15	15
East South Central	8	9	8	7
West South Central	9	9	9	8
Elsewhere in the USA	67	65	67	71
Number of cases	15,807	8,210	6,072	1,525

[a] Father's and mother's educations are measured on identical seven-point scales. See text for details.
[b] Parental income is coded 1 "far below average," 2 "below average," 3 "about average," 4 "above average," and 5 "far above average."

Table 9.A2 *Maximum likelihood estimates of the parameters of an alternative specification of the ordered logit model by cohort: persons 30–69 years old, United States, 1974–1998*

	Cohort		
Independent variable	Before 1940	1940–54	1955–68
Ancestry			
African American	−.432	.143	.221
Latino	−1.099	−.056	.053
Other	a	a	a
Woman	−.259	−.222	.102
Father's education	.121	.221	.297
Mother's education	.271	.335	.336
Father absent	−.036	−.228	.079
Mother absent	−.739	−.760	−.738
Main earner's occupation			
Professional, upper	1.370	.750	.755
Professional, lower	1.216	.721	.357
Manager	1.072	.651	.642
Routine white collar	.882	.581	.607
Proprietor	1.108	.812	.767
Farmer	.037	.171	.544
Skilled blue-collar	.371	.227	.277
Less-skilled blue-collar	a	a	a
Family income	.000	.000	.000
Number of siblings	−.139	−.127	−.076
Region at age 16			
South Atlantic	−.412	−.377	−.255
East South Central	−.551	−.387	−.497
West South Central	−.183	−.353	−.114
Other	a	a	a
Cohort	.036	.020	−.024
Cut points			
0/1	.190	−.376	−2.116
1/2	2.121	1.839	.228
2/3	3.265	3.244	1.838
Number of cases	8,980	7,685	3,332

Note: Coefficients in **bold** type are significant at the .05 level (two-tailed).
a-Identifying restriction.

Note that since Y is latent and scale-free, there is no loss of generality in leaving out the intercept, i.e., letting $Y = 0$ when $X_1 = X_2 = \ldots . =X_P = 0$.

The ordered logit model specifies the relationship between the latent continuous variable Y and the observed categorical outcomes Z in terms of the parameters that determine Y and the cut-points. In particular, it specifies a log-linear relationship between the odds on being in a category above k to being in category k or below and the Xs (with the cutting point κ_k as the intercept (as long as the errors conform to the logistic distribution and have a mean of zero, they cancel out):

$$\ln\left(\frac{\text{Prob}(Z > k)}{\text{Prob}(Z \le k)}\right) = \Sigma_p \beta_p X_p - \kappa_k. \quad [2]$$

Equation [2] can be solved for the probability of observing a case in category k as a (nonlinear) function of the X values and the parameters (the βs and the κs):

$$\text{Prob}(Z = k) = \text{Prob}(\kappa_{k-1} < Y \le \kappa_k)$$
$$= [1 + \exp(-\kappa_k + \Sigma_p \beta_p X_p)]^{-1} - [1 + \exp(-\kappa_{k-1} + \Sigma_p \beta_p X_p)]^{-1}. \quad [3]$$

Note that although there are $K - 1$ logistic regressions of the form given in equation [2], there is only one vector of regression coefficients, i.e., the logistic regressions differ only in their intercepts, which are -1 times the cut-point values. To get a sense of whether that constraint is reasonable, a researcher can run the $K - 1$ logistic regressions and compare the β values for successive regressions (Long 1997: 141–2). If the estimates of any of the β parameters vary substantially from regression to regression, then a less parsimonious model, e.g., multinomial logistic regression, might be more appropriate. Long (1997: 142–5) presents formal tests that can be employed.

NOTES

This research was supported by a grant from the Andrew W. Mellon Foundation and the Committee on Research at the University of California, Berkeley. I presented a version of this paper at the meeting of the International Sociological Association's Research Committee on Stratification, Madison, WI, August 13, 1999. I would like to acknowledge the useful comments that I received from participants at the UK/US conference in Bath and from Claude S. Fischer, Charles Halaby, John A. Logan, Samuel R. Lucas, and Adrian E. Raftery on previous drafts of this paper. Phillip Fucella and Erendira Rueda provided research assistance for which I am also grateful. The author bears sole responsibility for the errors that remain and for the views expressed in this paper.

1. Of course, some politicians and voters question the quality of public education and seek to foster competition through vouchers and other means.
2. The first three surveys used modified probability sampling that had a quota element at the block level. The 1975 and 1976 surveys blended the modified and full probability methods. Since 1977 all cases have been drawn using full probability methods.

3. As we shall see, having a missing parent significantly lowers educational attainment, all else being equal.

4. The choice of how to score the missing parent's education is arbitrary; it merely establishes the baseline against which the coefficients for the "father absent" and "mother absent" variables are normed. The substantive meaning of the results would not change if I made another category the baseline (as long as I keep the baseline clearly in mind when interpreting the coefficients).

5. Using the same dummy variable for "father absent" data on education and occupation means that the reference for that coefficient is the father who has both a high-school diploma and an unskilled job.

6. A few respondents report very large numbers of brothers and sisters; the maximum is 63. Tom Smith of the GSS has verified these reports. Most people count step- and half-siblings, only some of whom were co-resident with the respondent while he or she was growing up. These extreme cases have some leverage over the statistical results, so I recoded them all to a value of 20.

7. In the 1980s an average of 2.5 percent of total contacts were excluded for language problems. In the 1990s that average increased to about 2.9 percent of total contacts.

8. Recall that this analysis excludes immigrants who came to the United States after they turned sixteen years old. Including immigrants who obtained most of their schooling abroad dramatically lowers the high-school graduation rate observed for Latinos in the last cohort from 82 to 75 percentage points. A study of human capital in the labor force would want to take this latter figure into account, but this study of educational stratification draws a more accurate picture of American schooling by excluding those who got most or all of their schooling elsewhere.

9. The "smoothed" lines show the probabilities fitted using binary logistic regression. The dependent variable in the regression is the log-odds of a successful transition; the independent variables are the education of the parent in question, parent's education squared, and a dummy variable for having a missing parent. I calculated the regressions for each combination of ancestry, cohort, and educational transition (27 regressions in all).

10. Note that the data for the 1955–68 cohort after 30 years of age show a 75 percent high-school graduation rate for them. Either 9 percent completed high school between age 22 and age 30 or a significant fraction of Latino college students under 30 are not in households (therefore out of the sample frame).

REFERENCES

Bowen, W. G. and D. Bok, 1998, *The Shape of the River: Long-Term Consequences of Considering Race in College and University Admissions*, Princeton University Press.

Brint, S. and J. Karabel, 1989, *The Diverted Dream: Community Colleges and the Promise of Educational Opportunity*, New York: Oxford University Press.

Card, D. and A. Krueger, 1992, "School Quality and the Relative Earnings of Blacks and Whites," *Quarterly Journal of Economics* 107: 151–200.

Danziger, S. and P. Gottschalk, 1996, *America Unequal*, Cambridge, MA: Harvard University Press.

Davis, J. A., T. W. Smith, and P. V. Marsden, 1998, *The General Social Survey Cumulative Codebook, 1972–1998*, Storrs, CT: Roper Center.

Duncan, O. D., 1966, "Methodological Issues in the Analysis of Social Mobility," in N. J. Smelser and S. M. Lipset (eds.), *Social Structure and Mobility in Economic Development*, Chicago: Aldine, pp. 51–97.

 1969, "Inheritance of Poverty or Inheritance of Race?" in D. P. Moynihan (ed.), *On Understanding Poverty*, New York: Basic Books, pp. 85–100.

 1979, "How Destination Depends on Origin in Social Mobility," *American Journal of Sociology* 84: 793–804.

Erikson, R. and J. H. Goldthorpe, 1992, *The Constant Flux: Class Mobility in Industrial Societies*, Oxford: Clarendon Press.

Fischer, C. S., M. Hout, M. S. Jankowski, S. R. Lucas, A. Swidler, and K. Voss, 1996, *Inequality by Design: Cracking the Bell Curve Myth*, Princeton University Press.

Hauser, R. M., 1995, "Trends in College Entry among Whites, Blacks, and Hispanics," in C. T. Clotfelter and M. Rothschild (eds.), *Studies in the Supply and Demand for Higher Education*, Chicago: University of Chicago Press, pp. 61–120.

Hauser, R. M. and D. L. Featherman, 1976, "Equality of Schooling: Trends and Prospects," *Sociology of Education* 49: 99–120.

Hout, M. and D. P. Dohan, 1996, "Two Paths to Educational Opportunity: Class and Educational Selection in Sweden and the United States," in R. Erikson and J. O. Jonsson (eds.), *Can Education Be Equalized?*, Boulder, CO: Westview Press, pp. 207–32.

Jaynes, G. D. and R. Williams, 1989, *A Common Destiny: Blacks and American Society*, Washington, DC: National Academy Press.

Kane, T. J., 1999, "Racial and Ethnic Preferences in College Admissions," in C. Jencks and M. Phillips (eds.), *The Black-White Test Score Gap*, Washington, DC: Brookings Institution, pp. 431–56.

 2000, *The Price of Admission*, New York: Brookings Institution.

Karen, D., 1991, "The Politics of Race, Class, and Gender: Access to Higher Education in the United States, 1960–1986," *American Journal of Education* 99: 208–37.

Long, J. S., 1997, *Regression Models for Categorical and Limited Dependent Variables*, Thousand Oaks, CA: Sage Publications.

Lucas, S. R., 1996, "Selective Attrition in a Newly Hostile Regime: The Case of 1980 Sophomores," *Social Forces* 75: 999–1019.

Mare, R. D., 1995, "Changes in Educational Attainment and School Enrollment," in R. Farley (ed.), *State of the Union*, New York: Russell Sage Foundation, pp. 155–213.

Raftery, A. E. and M. Hout, 1993, "Maximally Maintained Inequality: Expansion, Reform, and Opportunity in Irish Education, 1921–1975," *Sociology of Education* 66: 41–62.

Schuman, H., C. Steeh, L. Bobo, and M. Krysan, 1998, *Racial Attitudes in America: Trends and Interpretations*, Cambridge, MA: Harvard University Press.

US Bureau of the Census, 1999, "The Changing Shape of the Nation's Income Distribution, 1947–1998," Current Population Reports: 60–204.

US Department of Education, 1997, *Digest of Educational Statistics*.

10   The educational attainments of ethnic minorities in Britain

Tariq Modood

By European standards Britain has good data-sources for identifying the current educational profile of the key ethnic minorities, and for tracking them over time. Data-sources include the census, though it was only in 1991 that an explicit ethnic group question was included; the PEP-PSI (Policy Studies Institute) surveys; the Labour Force Surveys (LFS); local education authority data; the Youth Cohort Survey; and national data on university entrants collected by the Universities Central Admissions Survey (UCAS) and the Higher Education Funding Councils. There is also an ethnographic literature about schools and young people, and a related theoretical and policy literature. In general, however, the data are nothing like as extensive or as detailed as those available in the USA.

The statistical data tend to show that scholastic achievement does vary by ethnicity but that at least on some measures racial disadvantage is declining and the circumstances of the minority groups are diverging. Some groups are poorly placed in educational and occupational hierarchies, others have overtaken the white population in the acquisition of qualifications and, consquently, in entry to some prestigious professions, though perhaps all minorities are underrepresented as managers in large establishments.

A developing pattern

The importance of educational attainments lies not just in their importance in accessing the better jobs and achieving social mobility. It is also significant because the attainments of (most) ethnic minority groups have proven to be quite remarkable, bearing in mind that one of the main stimuli to research on the educational attainments of nonwhite ethnic minority groups was the concern in the 1970s that children from these groups were "underachieving" in schools.

The circumstances of the minorities have changed considerably in this period. The PSI survey of the mid-1970s found that Caribbean and Pakistani men were less qualified than their white peers, while Indians

and African-Asians were best qualified. There was, however, a considerable polarization among the South Asians. In each ethnic group they were
disproportionately highly qualified as well as disproportionately having
persons without any qualifications. Moreover, South Asian women, especially the Pakistanis, were much less qualified than the men. West Indian
women, however, were as well qualified as West Indian men (Smith 1977:
58–60).

A decade later it was found that this pattern held for those over 44 years
old, but, among those aged 25–44 years, whites were better qualified than
the ethnic minority people. On the other hand, among the 16–24 age
group, South Asian men had higher qualifications than whites (Brown
1984: 145–7). In the period between the two surveys, considerable anxiety about the "underachievement" of pupils of West Indian origin in
British schools had surfaced, leading to a Committee of Inquiry led initially by Anthony Rampton and later by Lord Swann. Research carried
out on its behalf found that, while South Asians were achieving similar academic examination results to their white peers, West Indians were
performing less well (Swann 1985). This finding was repeated in other
major studies in that decade (e.g., Smith and Tomlinson 1989, Drew,
Gray, and Sime 1992; for a detailed review, see Gillborn and Gipps
1996).

Most of the earlier research failed to distinguish between different
South Asian groups. An analysis of the Labour Force Survey of the late
1980s which was able to go beyond the "Asian" category found that,
while African-Asians and Indians had higher average qualifications than
whites, the position of Pakistanis and Bangladeshis was much worse, in
fact was the worst of all ethnic groups. For example, while African-Asian
and Indian men were half as likely again as whites to have a degree,
more than half of the Pakistanis and Bangladeshis had no qualification (Jones 1993: Table 3.4). About the same time, higher educational
institutions started recording the ethnic origins of applicants and those
who were offered places. These data showed that all minority groups
except the Bangladeshis were very well represented in the polytechnics
(as they were then called), but only the Chinese and Indian/African-
Asians were so represented in the universities (Modood 1993). Analysis of
applicants in 1992 confirmed this pattern, while revealing that Pakistani
and Caribbean applicants, but not those from other ethnic minority groups, were less likely than equally qualified white candidates to
have gained admission to the "old" universities (Modood and Shiner
1994).

The 1991 Census too is a source of relevant information, though only
about qualifications higher than A levels[1]. On the basis of a 10 percent

Table 10.1 *Qualifications of 17–64 age group by ethnicity,
2001 census*

Ethnic group	Without GCSE or equivalent (%)	Degree level (%)
British	36.64	18.17
Irish	44.26	25.09
White-other	25.10	42.61
White and Black Caribbean	30.20	14.64
White and Black African	44.26	25.09
White and Asian	21.16	29.84
Mixed other	21.16	32.39
Indian	30.62	30.69
Pakistani	45.03	18.32
Bangladeshi	50.97	13.55
Asian-other	23.28	32.89
Black Caribbean	34.26	19.69
Black African	19.03	38.78
Black-other	25.35	21.11
Chinese	29.61	37.25

Source: ONS

sample of the population, it found that more than a quarter of adult Black Africans and Chinese were qualified beyond A levels, which was double that of Whites. Indians and African-Asians were also relatively more qualified than Whites, but the other minority groups were less so; though Pakistani and Bangladeshi men were more likely than Caribbean men to have degrees. Caribbean women were, however, much better qualified than all women except the Black African and the Chinese at the level between A levels and degrees (OPCS 1993, Table 17).

The latest data we have from the 2001 Census confirms previous patterns. The Black Africans, Chinese, and Indians are much more likely to have a degree than the White British, as are White-Other and Asian-Other and all the Mixed categories except White and Black Caribbean, who together with the Bangladeshis are the only two groups less likely to have degrees than the White British (see Table 10.1). The Pakistanis are about as likely as Whites to have degrees and Black Caribbeans are slightly more likely. The polarities too are apparent, with the Irish (included as a separate census category for the first time), the Pakistanis, and White and Black African Mixed all having a combination of having more of their group with no GCSEs[2] and with more degrees than the White British.

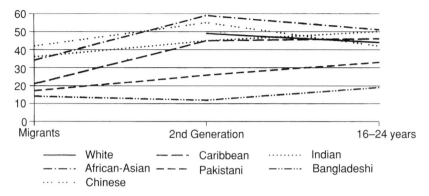

Figure 10.1 Percent within groups with A level or higher qualifications by generation

From diverse beginnings

The pattern, then, is not temporary and is very well established. Broadly speaking, the minorities can be divided into two: the Caribbeans, Pakistanis, and Bangladeshis have lower average qualification levels than whites; while the Indians, African-Asians, Chinese, and Africans are more likely than whites to have a higher qualification. I would like to explore aspects of this pattern further by using the Fourth National Survey of Ethnic Minorities.[3] It does not include Africans but does include the other six of the main nonwhite minority groups.

Among the critical factors in explaining the qualification levels of these groups today is the qualification profile at the time of migration. This can be seen in Figures 10.1 and 10.2. Figure 10.1 shows the proportion among the minority groups without qualifications divided into three "generations"[4] and also shows the qualification levels of whites for the most recent two generations. Beginning with the migrant generation, we see that from the start the six minority groups covered by the Fourth Survey fall into two groupings. The Caribbeans, Pakistanis, and the Bangladeshis had high proportions without GCSE or equivalent qualifications, between 60 and 75 percent. On the other hand, only about 45–50 percent of Indian, African-Asians, and Chinese migrants were without this level of qualifications. All six groups, however, have made educational progress across the generations, though among Bangladeshis it is only among the young that the proportion without qualifications has declined. It was the Caribbeans (taking men and women together) that initially made the most progress. This meant that the second-generation Caribbeans were no longer in the same band as Pakistanis

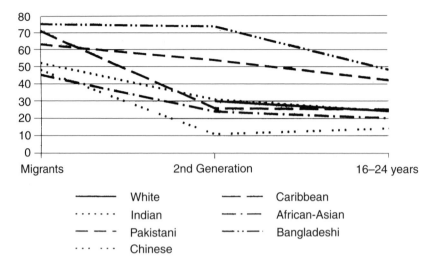

Figure 10.2 Percent within groups with no GCSE or equivalent qualification by generation

and Bangladeshis but had caught up with the other minorities and, in fact, their white peers. As native English speakers whose qualifications were from British examination boards, they were the migrant group that one would expect to make most initial progress, though note that we are not discussing the acquisition of a high-level qualification but the possession of any qualification at all. Moreover, the progress has been made much more by Caribbean women than men. That Caribbean women were more likely than other women to have a qualification certainly contributed to the good overall average achieved by the second-generation Caribbeans. By the time of today's twenty-year-olds, the gender gap has widened to the point that while exactly the same proportion of whites and Caribbeans have no qualifications (a quarter), with white women a little more likely than men not to, among Caribbeans nearly a third of men have no qualification compared to a sixth of the women.

It is, however, the Pakistanis and the Bangladeshis who have made the least progress in reducing the proportion within the group with no qualifications. While among all other groups about a fifth to a quarter had no GCSEs, the proportions among these two groups was about double this. What Figure 10.1 shows, then, is, in terms of having no qualifications, some of the ethnic minority groups were similarly or better placed than their white peers, and some much worse; and that this is not something that has just been achieved recently but has been true for some time and partly reflects migrants' starting points. The groups who are worse placed than whites are the Bangladeshis and the Pakistanis, and also Caribbean males.

Figure 10.1, however, is only part of the story. What is perhaps more important to look at is not those who have a qualification but those who have higher qualifications. Figure 10.2 presents the original profile and generational progress in relation to those who have an A level or higher qualification. Once again three migrant groups stand out as well qualified, namely, the Chinese, African-Asians, and Indians. And three groups were much less well qualified, the Bangladeshis especially, but also the Pakistanis and the Caribbeans. Again, all groups except the Bangladeshis made progress in the second generation, though the progress of the Pakistanis was quite minor. Once again the Caribbeans made the most dramatic progress though the African-Asians were the best qualified at this level, considerably ahead of whites. What Figure 10.2 does not show is that while all other groups, even the Bangladeshis, were well represented at degree level, very few Caribbeans with higher-level qualifications had degrees (just 2 percent of the migrants and 7 percent of the second generation). Many of their higher qualifications were vocational qualifications like HNCs or in nursing. In contrast, nearly 10 percent of Pakistani and Bangladeshi migrants and a quarter of Indian, African-Asian, and Chinese migrants had degrees. This meant that some groups like the Pakistanis and Bangladeshis were very internally polarized, with disproportionate numbers of highly qualified and unqualified. But it meant that all these groups had significant proportions of university-educated persons. It is therefore not surprising, as we shall see below, that these groups have gone on to be well represented in higher education in their second and third generations. That they have not all made equal progress in this regard can partly be correlated to the extent that they had British or overseas qualifications. Thus the relatively limited progress of second-generation Indians may be a reflection of the fact that the migrants disproportionately had Indian degrees, compared to the Chinese and African-Asians, whose qualifications in the main were from British examination boards and institutions.

Two other important factors need to be noted. Firstly, gender differences: male migrants were better qualified than women, especially amongst the Bangladeshis, Indians, and Pakistanis. In all groups men were much more likely to have degrees; Caribbean women, however, were and remain much more likely than the men to have higher qualifications. Secondly, a further factor accounting for the divergent profiles is that in the pursuit of qualifications some groups are more vocationally than academically qualified, and so the qualified among them are less likely to have degrees. This is particularly the case with the Caribbeans and whites, who are much more likely to have a higher vocational qualification than the South Asian groups, who have a stronger academic orientation.

Schools and young people

In most ethnic minority groups, then, the second and third generations have made significant progress, as have their white peers. Amongst the 16–24 age group, far fewer are without a qualification than the older generations. The position of Indians, African-Asians, Chinese, and Africans is comparable with that of whites, except at degree level where the position of these minorities is distinctly better. Ethnic minority women have made particular progress. By 1995, girls were more likely than boys to achieve five higher grade GCSEs in each of the principal minority groups (Gillborn and Mirza 2000: 24). Pakistanis and Bangladeshis, however, continue to have the largest proportions without qualifications and the positions of young Caribbean men is not better than that of their elders.

Data from local education authorities suggest that at the beginning of schooling, and at the time of the first national tests at age seven, the difference between Caribbeans and whites are relatively slight, and sometimes in the favor of the Caribbeans. It is the South Asian children, often coming from homes in which English, if spoken at home, is a second or third language, that begin their school careers with low averages. But while in secondary school the Asians slowly catch up, and in the case of some groups, overtake the whites, the Caribbeans' average steadily drops behind that of the national average (Richardson and Wood 1999, Berthoud et al. 2000: 10, Gillborn and Mirza 2000 and Owen et al. 2000).

Explanations of these differences have tended to focus on Caribbean males, who experience very high rates of disciplinary action and exclusion from school (Gillborn and Gipps 1996: 50–3). There is general agreement that they have the most confrontational relations with teachers and are the group that teachers report feeling most threatened and frightened by. One type of explanation emphasizes teacher racism (Connolly 1998, Gillborn 1998). This can be based upon the perceptions of teachers, acquired and fostered through a staff-room culture and through disciplinary problems with previous pupils, that lead to low expectations about the behavior and work of Caribbean boys, and can lead teachers to interpret certain behavior more negatively than the same behavior exhibited by white or Asian males and perhaps lead to pre-emptive disciplining (Gillborn 1990 and 1998). There can also be forms of indirect discrimination at play, whereby procedures and organizational arrangements that may have nothing to do with "race" and ethnicity directly, may nevertheless have disproportionately negative impacts on Caribbean boys. Setting is one example, for it is an arrangement which may result in Caribbean boys being disproportionately placed in lower sets and thereby less likely to be prepared for certain exams (Gillborn and Youdell 2000). (Of course, it is quite possible for an arrangement that negatively impacts upon one minority group to have positive impacts upon another.)

An alternative type of explanation in relation to Caribbean boys emphasizes that the high levels of confrontation and disciplining are at least partly due to what the boys bring into school with them (Sewell 1997, Mac an Ghaill 1988). It is argued that they draw on a youth/street culture and specifically "on a Black collectivist anti-school ideology, on a pro-consumerism and phallocentrism" (Sewell 1997: 108). This culture gives black boys strength to resist racism but it undervalues academic achievement. Indeed, academic aspirations are disparaged as a form of "acting white" and the living out of this black masculinity inevitably leads to failing to meet the norms of school behavior. "In this way, a vicious cycle can develop in which what is perceived as a lack of respect from teachers is met by an aggressive response from pupils who in turn are punished for the behavior" (Pilkington 1999: 415). Aspects of this view are gathering support amongst the black community, with the development of a "gangsta" culture and the absence of good male role models at home, as well as in schools, being mentioned as causes of concern (Abbot 2002, Clunis 2002, Phillips 2002), but these controversial matters continue to be a matter of contention (Jasper and Sewell 2003).

Both explanations may be true, but the former raises an unnoticed paradox: if racism leads to victims being "turned off" school and dropping out, why do Asians have such high staying-on rates and make academic progress? While recognizing that there are significant differences between the racism experienced by Caribbeans and Asians, as captured in the plural idea of *racisms* (CMEB 2000: Chapter 5), ethnographic research suggests, in ways consistent with surveys, that Asians experience more frequent and more violent racial harassment from other pupils than the Caribbeans (Gillborn 1998, Virdee, Modood, and Newburn 2000). As far as I know no one has tried to research why this high level of peer racism and bullying does not stop Asians from persisting with high levels of motivation and performance.

Suffice to say that, as far as I know, no convincing explanations exist to account fully for the above differentials. My two suggestions here are firstly, that the research and policy focus for the last three decades has been on why Caribbean males do not make progress in British schools and not on why some Asian groups do make progress; some focus on the latter must surely help us to understand better some of the processes

Table 10.2 *Proportion of qualified 16 to 24 year-olds in full-time education*

	White	Caribbean	Indian African-Asian	Pakistani/ Bangladeshi	All ethnic minorities
			cell percentages		
Has O level or higher and is in full-time education:					
Men	21	34	63	71	58
Women	28	40	47	48	46
Weighted count					
Men	163	105	166	105	413
Women	145	137	187	101	471
Unweighted count					
Men	116	48	110	119	293
Women	119	73	124	119	334

Source: PSI Fourth Survey of Ethnic Minorities (Modood et al. 1997: 76).

in relation to ethnicity, racism, schooling, and attainments. Secondly, it seems to me that what happens in schools is probably only a small part of the story. I return to this issue later when I offer some speculation about causal processes.

What cannot be denied is that ethnic minorities in general manifest a strong drive for qualifications, and once they begin to acquire qualifications, they seek more. For example, when we look at those with a GCSE or higher qualification who were continuing in (or had returned to) full-time education we see a degree of minority commitment quite different from that of whites (Table 10.2). While amongst qualified whites aged 16 to 24, about a quarter were likely to be in full-time education (slightly more for women, slightly less for men), nearly half of the ethnic minority women and well over half of the men were. The commitment to education is manifest in groups that were not particularly well qualified at the time of migration: qualified Caribbeans of both sexes in this cohort were considerably more likely to be in full-time education than their white peers, and the qualified Pakistanis/Bangladeshis had the highest participation rate in the Fourth Survey for each sex.[5]

Some of the high level of minority participation in post-compulsory full-time education is likely to be a reflection of the fact that ethnic minorities used to take longer to achieve their qualifications, but this has declined. Moreover, whites, especially white men, are more likely to be in work, and to be pursuing their further education and training while in work or in training that is linked to work (Drew, Gray, and Sime 1992, Drew 1995, Hagell and Shaw 1996). Furthermore, the presence of high rates of youth unemployment, especially amongst those without qualifications, and the knowledge that ethnic minorities suffer much higher rates of unemployment, may all be thought to add to the explanation of why the ethnic minorities have high staying-on rates. The evidence is, however, that the ethnic minority youngsters who do, or who are allowed to stay on, do so for positive reasons. A study of sixteen-year-olds in six inner-city areas also found that minority ethnic individuals were more likely to stay on than whites; of those that stayed on, half wanted to go to university eventually, while less than a fifth gave as one of their reasons for staying on that it was better than being unemployed (Hagell and Shaw 1996: 88). Further analysis of that survey shows that Asians were no more likely than whites, and Caribbeans little more likely to say that they stayed on in education because it was better than being unemployed. On the other hand, ethnic minorities were much more likely than whites to say that they wanted to improve their educational qualifications or go to university. The knowledge that qualifications are necessary for getting a (desirable) job may well motivate ethnic minorities more than whites, but it seems to do so positively rather than negatively (see also Basit 1997 and Wrench and Qureshi 1996). There may, however, be features about schools that ethnic minorities wish to avoid, for they disproportionately transfer from school to Further Education Colleges to study subjects and for exams that are available at school. Moreover, some minority groups, especially the Caribbeans, drop out of school at the age of sixteen and pick up their studies at Further Education at a later date (Owen et al. 2000).

Higher education

Thus far we have seen higher participation rates in post-16 education amongst the ethnic minorities. It will come as no surprise to learn then that, contrary to the claims of most commentators at the time, when admissions to higher education began to be monitored in 1990, it did not reveal an under-representation of ethnic minorities (Modood 1993). Moreover, all minority groups, with the possible exception of the Caribbeans, have increased their share of admissions since then. Ethnic minorities as a whole are about 50 percent more successful in achieving university entry than white applicants, but not evenly so. The proportion of Africans, Chinese, Asian-Others, and Indians in the 18–24 age group who enter university is more than twice that of whites, and no minority group is under-represented as such, as can be seen in Table 10.3 below. Some gender differences persist, however, as Caribbean men and Bangladeshi women are under-represented, but in the latter case there is a trend toward equal/over representation. Otherwise, it is only the whites

Table 10.3 *Domiciled first-year full-time and part-time students,*
1997–1998

	% in higher education	% 18–24s in higher education	% of 18–24s in Great Britain	18–24s Gender balance in higher education (m – f)
Whites	84.9	85.2	92.0	48*–52*
Indians	4.1	4.7	2.0	51–49
Pakistanis	2.5	2.7	1.8	56–44
Bangladeshis	0.7	O.7	0.7	58–42*
Chinese	0.9	1.0	0.4	50–50
Asian-other	1.2	1.2	0.4	52–48
Africans	2.1	1.4	0.6	48–52
Caribbeans	1.3	1.0	0.9	40*–60
Black-other	0.6	0.5	0.7	38*–62

* denotes underrepresentation
Source: Higher Education Statistics Agency, 1991 Census, and LFS, 1999–2000

that are underrepresented in both genders. So, the minority groups, with
the exception of Caribbean men, are on different points of an escalator,
all moving upwards relative to whites and in fact some groups exceeded
the government's target of 50 percent participation by age thirty some
years ago (Connor et al. 2004, 43, 150).

While some minorities are very well represented in competitive subjects, they are, except the Chinese, still generally more likely to be in
the less prestigious, less well-resourced post-1992 universities (which till
1992 were called "Polytechnics"). This is especially true of Caribbeans
(Modood and Acland 1998), who are also more likely to be mature students (Owen et al. 2000, Pathak 2000) (more than half of Caribbean
women students are over twenty-five years old), and part-time students
(Owen et al. 2000) – all factors which have implications for career
prospects. A-level scores, subject preferences, preference for local institutions, and type of school or college attended are all factors that explain the
concentration of ethnic minority groups, except the Chinese, in the new
universities. Nevertheless, a recent analysis shows that even accounting
for these factors, there is a clear institutional effect (Shiner and Modood
2002). The analysis shows that lower A-level predictions by schools on
UCAS forms do not seem to be a factor. In fact, schools make more generous predictions for ethnic minority candidates, with the most optimistic
forecasts made about Black African and Caribbean students, contrary to
what one might expect on the basis of the teacher racism we considered
earlier (Shiner and Modood 2002: 217). Table 10.4 presents the results
of a multivariate analysis which shows that comparing similarly qualified

Table 10.4 *Probability of eliciting an initial offer by ethnicity (estimated on the basis of an average application, results of multivariate analysis)*

	[Type of institution applied to]	
	Old	New
White	0.75	0.73
Black Caribbean	0.65**	0.75
Black African	0.57**	0.76
Indian	0.58**	0.85**
Pakistani	0.57**	0.77
Bangladeshi	0.57**	0.82**
Chinese	0.68#	0.83**

** p = <0.01 ns = not significant (p = > 0.01)
For each type of institution, significance tests compare the probability of success for each minority group with that of whites.
p = 0.018
Source: Shiner and Modood 2002.

candidates and controlling for factors such as public schools, gender and so on, new (post-1992) universities respond more positively than old universities to nonwhite applicants and, within this sector, Chinese, Bangladeshi, and Indian candidates appear to be favored over whites. White candidates have a 73 percent chance of eliciting an offer from a new university, which is lower than that of their ethnic minority peers. When applying to old universities, however, there is strong evidence that minority candidates face an ethnic penalty. Institutions within this sector are most likely to select white and, to a lesser extent, Chinese candidates from among a group of similarly qualified applicants. Given the much larger proportion of applications from ethnic minority groups, although ethnic minority applicants may be admitted to old universities in reasonable numbers, they generally have to perform better than do their white peers in order to secure a place. Given that few university places involve interviews and that different A-level scores are required for different courses, this is not a kind of discrimination that will be perceivable by the victims, so it is perhaps not altogether surprising that a recent survey of ethnic minority students who successfully got into a university found few reports of discrimination in the selection process (Connor et al. 2004: 56). As the type of institution from which you graduate can make a big difference to your career prospects, this bias can have serious, long-term implications for ethnic stratification (Shiner and Modood 2002). It ought to be borne in mind, however, that some ethnic minority groups have a disproportionately large number of people aged 18 to 24 in higher education, and therefore are digging deeper into the natural talent available in that age group. Hence, it is not in itself surprising that a larger proportion of their applicants enter institutions that require lower A-level entry scores. For, if we were to compare like with like, the peers of some who enter these universities are whites who are absent from higher education. This does not, however, negate the generalization that ethnic minorities have to do better than whites to get into older universities, who, therefore, are complicit in an institutional discrimination which is hindering and slowing down the dismantling of an ethnic stratification.

Some speculation about causes   Other than the factors mentioned above, social class is probably the most powerful one in explaining the educational outcomes discussed here. But its effect is heavily qualified. It is, for example, clearly qualified by gender norms and expectations in different communities, as we see in the contrasting effects amongst the Bangladeshis and the Caribbeans. Though of course we must not assume that cultural identities governing gender or other kinds of norms are static. There is both quantitative and qualitative data indicating that cultures which till recently might have been portrayed as opposed to the education of and employment of women seem to be producing growing cohorts of highly motivated young women (Ahmad, Modood, and Lissenburgh 2003). Other than through a distinctive gender effect, Caribbean ethnicity, however, has a lesser effect than the others on class and sometimes diminishes the class-based likelihood of success (Penn and Scattergood 1992, Taylor 1992, Gillborn and Gipps 1996). The class position of Pakistanis and Bangladeshis is made worse by the fact that on the whole they have larger households and that married women are unlikely to be in paid employment outside the home, resulting in fewer earners and more dependents in a household. South Asians and the Chinese, however, seem to do better than one might reasonably expect, given their parental class. This can be seen from Table 10.5, which shows university entrants of 1998 by ethnicity, gender, and parental social class. It shows an absence of gender difference but, unsurprisingly, that class is a major factor: in nearly every group, the offspring from non-manual parents exceed, sometimes by a large margin, those from manual parents. This is particularly the case amongst whites but is also of considerable magnitude amongst Africans and Caribbeans. But it has much less significance for Indians and Chinese, groups in which entrants are almost equally likely to come from non-manual as from other backgrounds, including unemployment. And the conventional class analysis does not

Table 10.5 *UCAS 1998 entrants by ethnicity, gender, and parental social class*

	Whites		Chinese		Indians		Pakistanis		Bangladeshis		Afro-Caribbeans*		Black Africans	
	M	F	M	F	M	F	M	F	M	F	M	F	M	F
Non-manual	67.1	67.4	52.5	52.7	48.5	48.4	36.5	36.1	36.3	35.8	52.1	56.4	51.5	54.8
Manual	25.2	24.6	33.7	33.7	39.5	39.7	39.7	38.2	39.2	38.9	26.9	24.4	20.5	19.3
Unknown**	7.7	8.0	13.8	13.6	12.1	12.0	23.8	25.8	24.5	25.3	21.0	19.2	28.1	25.9

* Includes "Black Caribbean" and "Black-other."
** The vast majority of parents whose Social Class UCCA classifies as unknown appear to have been unemployed.
Source: Ballard 1999.

hold at all for Pakistanis and Bangladeshis, amongst whom households headed by a manual or unemployed worker supply nearly two-thirds of the entrants.

To some extent, it can be countered, this was because the South Asian and Chinese entrants' parental social class and educational capital was better than that suggested by their parents' occupations, for their occupational levels were depressed by migration effects and discrimination in the labor market. Owing to this racial discrimination migrants often suffered a downward social mobility on entry into Britain (Modood et al. 1997: 141–2). The only jobs open to them were often below their qualification levels and below the social class level they enjoyed before migration. This meant that not only did many value education more than their white workmates but saw it as part of the process of reversing the initial downward mobility, especially in the lives of their children. If we recall the qualification levels of the migrants as presented in Figures 10.1 and 10.2, this argument that some migrants' occupational class in Britain is not reflective of their true class and hence of their attitudes to education seems to have some plausibility. It is particularly plausible in the case of the African-Asians and perhaps also the Indians, but less so with other groups. In any case, class analysis by itself, even after taking initial downward mobility into account, is incomplete without acknowledging the economic motivation of migrants, the desire to better themselves and especially the prospects for their children. The belief in the value of education in achieving upward mobility and respectability is related to this, as is the strong academic orientation of groups such as the South Asians and the Chinese. The same factors are likely to be operative in the case of Africans, who emerged in the 1991 and 2001 censuses as the group with the highest proportion of persons with higher qualifications (Owen, Mortimore, and Phoenix 1997; Frean 2003).

It is here worth noting the general sociological claim that there is such a thing as an "Asian trajectory" or an "Asian future," which includes social mobility by education, self-employment, and progression into the professions (Cross 1994). The implication is that it is wrong to divide South Asian groups into the "successful" and the "disadvantaged," for this situation may arise only because the latter are likely to have less longevity of residence in Britain (measuring families and communities, not just individuals) or to have suffered temporary setbacks (perhaps due to economic restructuring). Today's successful Asians (like the Indians) are yesterday's disadvantaged Asians; today's disadvantaged Asians are tomorrow's successes. This view probably over-homogenizes South Asians, ignoring the differential educational and employment backgrounds at the time of migration of different South Asian groups, differential degrees of segregation, and factors peculiar to Muslims (Modood et al. 1997: 146–8). Nevertheless, there may still be something in it and it does have the merit of consistency with some perceivable trends. It is, for example, supported by the fact, visible in Table 10.5, that South Asian university entrants are less likely than other groups to come from non-manual backgrounds. More particularly, when we compare the three disadvantaged groups – the Pakistanis and the Bangladeshis and the Caribbeans – members of the last of those groups are much more likely to come from non-manual backgrounds than the other two groups, even though they have a similar manual/non-manual profile in the workforce, at least as regards male workers (see Tables 4.10 and 4.13 in Modood et al. 1997: 100 and 104). This does lend some weight to the idea that there is an ambition to be university-educated amongst South Asians, which is not constrained by class, but on the contrary is seen as integral to social mobility ambitions.

I imagine that ethnic minority parents, especially the South Asians and Chinese, are probably less knowledgeable of the school system and participate less in school activities than their white peers. I also doubt that they spend more time on helping with or discussing schoolwork with their children at home, the content of which will be less familiar to them than to white parents. Yet what they do is to foster high expectations (even to the point of pressuring the children), give encouragement, maintain discipline (e.g., ensure that homework is done), send children to and help with supplementary classes, and so on. In short, what they give is not a transfer of knowledge and skills but a sense that education is important, that teachers should be obeyed, and academic success takes priority over other pursuits, especially recreational youth culture.

I would emphasize here that it's not just the parents that are critical but the wider family and ethnic community too. For family aspirations need to be reinforced. Min Zhou's work in New York's Chinatown, using the concept of ethnicity as social capital, shows how the orientation is reinforced by the whole community in all kinds of ways (Zhou 1997 and this volume). One of these is the protection of the children and youth from certain kinds of influences – including street and youth cultures. In contrast, Elijah Anderson's work brings out the difficulties that African-Americans have in avoiding these anti-scholastic influences (Anderson 1994, see also Ferguson, this volume). So, even where parents from different groups may have the same aspirations for their children, they may, quite independently of class, have access to quite different forms of social capital to materialize their aspirations (Modood, 2004).

Of course material resources are important, too. While they relate closely to the class configuration of an ethnic group, it is quite likely that the extent of savings and spending priorities is shaped not just by the availability of resources but by cultural preferences. These preferences are likely to have a class character but they will also have a significant ethnic dimension. For example, I guess that ethnic minority parents spend a larger proportion of their disposable income on education than white parents. There is no systematic evidence for testing this hypothesis but I would offer the following in its support. The 1998 data on university entrants showed that Indians were slightly more likely than whites to have come from independent schools and the Chinese were twice as likely to do so (Ballard 1999, see also Berthoud et al. 2000: 82). Bearing in mind that these minority groups still have slightly more children per family than whites (Modood et al. 1997: 40–1) and a much higher proportion of young people applying to universities than whites, it means, I estimate, that on a per capita basis, Indians are 2.5 times more likely than whites to be in fee-paying schools and the Chinese five times more so.[6] That's a lot of personal financial investment in educational success, despite the fact that the minority groups still have lower spending power per capita than whites, after one adjusts for pensioner households (Modood et al. 1997). Pakistanis and Bangladeshis do not have the same kind of representation in fee-paying schools but exactly the same argument about ethnic preferences can be made in their case too, when one bears in mind that despite four out of five Pakistani and Bangladeshi households being in poverty (Modood et al. 1997) these groups produce a larger proportion of university entrants than the white population.

The continuing presence of racial discrimination has also meant that nonwhite persons have been particularly dependent on qualifications for jobs and economic progression, especially as they lacked the social networks, such as those associated with elite universities or certain working-class occupations, to help them get on. Hence, each of the kinds of factors that I have been referring to, those that are "internal" to the group and those that are "external" have worked together, interacting with and reinforcing each other, to make qualifications and higher education of more value and urgency to ethnic minority than white people.[7]

Persisting/growing polarities

The research frameworks favored by researchers in the 1980s assumed that the African-Caribbean experience would be paradigmatic for children of color ("black" people). It is, however, more accurately seen as one strand in a multifaceted story (Richardson and Wood 1999). It is clear, nevertheless, that significant polarities exist among the ethnic minority groups and within specific minority groups. No convincing explanation exists that accounts for both pairs of polar ends. Typically, most researchers focus on one end of one of the polarities and try to explain that, sometimes proceeding as if their chosen end was the whole story. The most polarized groups happen to be the ones that were particularly in the news in 2001 (the year of the riots and the start of the "war against terrorism"),[8] namely the Pakistanis and Bangladeshis. While they continue to be much more likely than all other groups to leave school with no qualifications, before one makes generalizations about the group, it is best to remember that in 40 percent of LEAs that monitor by ethnic origin, Pakistanis are more likely than whites to attain five A*–C GCSEs (Gillborn and Mirza 2000), and that on a *per capita* basis there are more Pakistanis than whites at university. Caribbean men, too, are a continuing cause of concern, and if they are less polarized than other groups, it is because they are largely absent at the top end of the pole. Any social inclusion policy needs to target "the truly disadvantaged" but it would be no less a mistake to assume that, in relation to educational attainments, any minority group is homogeneous, than to assume that an explanation of the educational profile of one minority group explains them all.[9]

NOTES

This is an expanded and updated version of my chapter from D. Mason (ed.), 2003, *Explaining Ethnic Differences*, Bristol: Policy Press.
1. Public examinations typically sat at the end of year 13 and on the results of which university entry is determined.
2. GCSEs are public examinations typically sat at the end of compulsory education (year 11, age 16).
3. The Fourth Survey, conducted in 1994, covered many topics, including employment, earnings and income, families, housing, health, racial harassment, culture, and identity. The survey was based on interviews, of about an hour in length, conducted by ethnically matched interviewers, and offered in five South Asian languages and Chinese as well as English. Over five thousand persons were interviewed from the following six groups: Caribbeans, Indians, African Asians (people of South Asian descent whose families had spent a generation or more in East Africa), Pakistanis, Bangladeshis, and Chinese. Additionally, nearly three thousand white people were interviewed, in order to compare the circumstances of the minorities with that of the ethnic majority. Unfortunately, for reasons of costs and logistics, Africans were not included in the survey. Further details on all aspects of the survey are available in Modood et al. 1997.
4. The "generations" are: (1) the migrants, those who came to Britain over the age of 16; (2) the second generation, those who came to Britain under the age of 16 and so had some schooling in Britain, or were born in Britain, and were between 25 and 44 years old at the time of the survey; (3) the new generation, those who were between 16 and 24 years old, most of whom were born in

Britain and had most if not all of their education in Britain. Strictly speaking, these are not generations as there could be an age overlap between (1) and (2), and the years are not evenly spread across the three categories.

5. Other data suggest that Africans have the highest participation rate of all groups (Berthoud et al. 2000: 9).

6. Thus it needs to be borne in mind that the widening access policies in some prestigious universities that aim to reduce the proportion of entrants from fee-paying schools, if successful, should lower the proportion of Chinese and Indians admitted to those universities, while increasing that of other minority groups. Interestingly, taking the HE sector as a whole, it has been found that after controlling for A-level scores and a number of other factors, attending an independent school slightly reduced a candidate's chance of admission (Shiner and Modood 2002: 229, note 8).

7. Whether this investment in education has paid dividends in terms of jobs and incomes is a complex question but it seems not to have done so for at least the Africans (Berthoud 1999 and 2000).

8. These events precipitated a moral panic about "faith schools" without anyone offering any evidence that anyone in Britain involved in the riots or any Islamist organizations had been to a "faith school."

9. More detailed support for the arguments in this chapter can be found in Modood et al. 1997: Chapter 3, and in Modood 1998.

REFERENCES

Ahmad, F., T. Modood, and S. Lissenburgh, 2003, *South Asian Women and Employment in Britain: The Interaction of Gender and Ethnicity*, London: Policy Studies Institute.

Abbot, D., 2002, "Teachers Are Failing Black Boys," *The Observer* (January 6) (observer.guardian.co.uk)

Anderson, E., 1994, "The Code of the Streets," *The Atlantic Monthly* (May), 273: 80–94.

Ballard, R., 1999, "Socio-Economic and Educational Achievements of Ethnic Minorities," unpublished paper submitted to the Commission on the Future of Multi-Ethnic Britain. London: The Runnymede Trust.

Basit, T. N., 1997, *Eastern Values; Western Milieu: Identities and Aspirations of Adolescent British Muslim Girls*, Brookfield: Ashgate.

Berthoud, R., 1999, *Young Caribbean Men and the Labour Market: A Comparison with Other Groups*, York: Joseph Rowntree Foundation.

2000, "Ethnic Employment Penalties in Britain," *Journal of Ethnic and Migration Studies* 26: 389–416.

Berthoud, R., M. Taylor, and J. Burton (with contributions by T. Modood, N. Buck, and A. Booth), 2000, *Comparing the Transition from School to Work among Young People from Different Ethnic Groups*, A Feasibility Study for the Department of Education and Employment, Institute for Social and Economic Research, University of Essex.

Brown, C., 1984, *Black and White Britain. The Third PSI Survey*, London: Policy Studies Institute.

Clunis, A., 2002, "Stop Our Failing Children," *Voice Newspaper* (March 25): 20–1.

Connolly, P., 1998, *Racism, Gender Identities and Young Children*, London: Routledge.

Connor, H., C. Tyers, T. Modood, and J. Hillage, 2004, *Minority Ethnic Students in Higher Education: Interim Report*, Research Report 552, London: Department of Education and Skills.

Commission on Multi-Ethnic Britain (CMEB), 2000, *The Future of Multi-Ethnic Britain*, London: Profile Books.

Cross, M., 1994, *Ethnic Pluralism and Racial Inequality*, University of Utrecht.

Drew, D., 1995, *"Race", Education and Work: The Statistics of Inequality*, Brookfield: Avebury.

Drew, D., J. Gray, and N. Sime, 1992, *Against the Odds: The Education and Labour Market Experiences of Black Young People*, England and Wales Youth Cohort Study, Report R & D No. 68, Sheffield University, Employment Department.

Frean, A., 2003, "Black Africans in Britain Lead Way in Education," *The Times*, May 8, London (http://www.timesonline.co.uk).

Gillborn, D., 1990, *"Race", Ethnicity and Education*, London: Unwin Hyman.
  1998, "Race and Ethnicity in Compulsory Schooling," in Modood and Acland (eds.), pp. 11–23.

Gillborn, D. and C. Gipps, 1996, *Recent Research on the Achievements of Ethnic Minority Pupils*, London: Office for Standards in Education.

Gillborn, D. and H. Mirza, 2000, *Educational Inequality: Mapping Race, Class and Gender, A Synthesis of Research Evidence*, London: Office for Standards in Education.

Gillborn, D. and D. Youdell, 2000, *Rationing Education: Policy, Practice, Reform and Equity*, Philadelphia: Open University Press.

Hagell, A. and C. Shaw, 1996, *Opportunity and Disadvantage at Age 16*, London: Policy Studies Institute.

Jasper, L. and T. Sewell, 2003, "Look beyond the Street," *The Guardian* (July 19).

Jones, T., 1993, *Britain's Ethnic Minorities*, London: Policy Studies Institute.

MacGhaill, M., 1988, *Young, Gifted and Black: Student–Teacher Relations in the Schooling of Black Youth*, Philadelphia: Open University Press.

Modood, T., 1993, "The Number of Ethnic Minority Students in British Higher Education," *Oxford Review of Education* 19: 167–82.
  1998, "Ethnic Minorities and the Drive for Qualifications," in Modood and Acland (eds.), pp. 24–38.
  2004, "Capitals, Ethnic Identity and Educational Qualifications," *Cultural Trends* 13(2): 87–105.

Modood, T. and T. Acland (eds.), 1998, *Race and Higher Education*, London: Policy Studies Institute.

Modood, T., R. Berthoud, J. Lokey, J. Nazroo, P. Smith, S. Virdee, and S. Beishon, 1997, *Ethnic Minorities in Britain: Diversity and Disadvantage*, London: Policy Studies Institute.

Modood. T. and M. Shiner, 1994, *Ethnic Minorities and Higher Education: Why Are There Differential Rates of Entry?* London: Policy Studies Institute.

Office of the Population and Census Surveys (OPCS), 1993, *1991 Census: Ethnic Group and Country of Birth (Great Britain)*, London: HMSO.

Owen, C., P. Mortimore, and A. Phoenix, 1997, "Higher Educational Qualifications," in V. Karn (ed.), *Ethnicity in the 1991 Census*, Vol. IV: *Employment, Education and Housing Among Ethnic Minorities in Britain*, London: OPCS.

Owen, D., A. Green, J. Pitcher, and M. Maguire, 2000, *Minority Ethnic Participation and Achievements in Education, Training and the Labour Market*, London: Department for Education and Employment.

Pathak, S. 2000, *Race Research for the Future: Ethnicity in Education, Training and the Labour Market*, Research Topic Paper, London: Department of Education and Employment.

Penn R. and Scattergood, 1992, "Ethnicity and Career Aspirations in Contemporary Britain," *New Community* 189: 5–98.

Phillips, T., 2002, "The Time Has Come for Zero-Tolerance," *Mail on Sunday* (February 3): 26.

Pilkington, A., 1999, "Racism in Schools and Ethnic Differentials in Educational Achievement: A Brief Comment on a Recent Debate," *British Journal of Sociology of Education* 20: 411–17.

Richardson, R. and A. Wood, 1999, *Inclusive Schools, Inclusive Society: Race and Identity on the Agenda*, Staffordshire: Trentham Books.

Sewell, T., 1997, *Black Masculinities and Schooling, Stoke on Trent*, Staffordshire: Trentham Books.

Shiner, M. and T. Modood, 2002, "Help or Hindrance? Higher Education and the route to Ethnic Equality," *British Journal of Sociology of Education* 23: 209–30.

Smith, D. J., 1977, *Racial Disadvantage in Britain*, London: Penguin.

Smith, D. J. and S. Tomlinson, 1989, *The School Effect: A Study of Multi-racial Comprehensives*, London: Policy Studies Institute.

Swann, M., 1985, *Education for all*, CMND 9453, London: HMSO.

Taylor, P., 1992, *Ethnic Group Data for University Entry*, Project Report for CVCP working Group on Ethnic Data, University of Warwick.

Virdee, S, T. Modood, and T. Newburn, 2000, "Understanding Racial Harassment in School," A Project Report to the ESRC.

Wrench, J. and T. Qureshi, 1996, *Higher Horizons: A Qualitative Study of Young Men of Bangladeshi Origin*, Research Study 30, London: Department for Education and Employment.

Zhou, M., 1997, "Social Capital in Chinatown: the Role of Community-Based Organizations and Families in the Adaptation of the Younger Generation," in L. Weis and M. S. Seller (eds.), *Beyond Black and White: New Voices, New Faces in the United States Schools*, Albany, NY: State University of New York Press, pp. 181–206.

11   Why America's black–white school achievement gap persists

Ronald F. Ferguson

Beginning when Europeans first shipped Africans across the Atlantic Ocean to be slaves in America, blacks and whites have worked together building a nation. However, only in the past several decades has the possibility been seriously considered that blacks should be equal-status partners in this nation-building endeavor. Even after the abolition of slavery in 1863, white supremacists conspired for generations to discourage and obstruct black strivings for respect and social mobility. In the view of white supremacists, blacks were an inferior breed, preordained to serve white society as menial, uneducated, subsistence workers. The Jim Crow system of racial separatism and its ideology of white supremacy dominated the American South and influenced the North as well, beyond the middle of the twentieth century. Its influence still survives. In virtually every domain of social, political, and economic life, the nation today is living with the consequences of white supremacy.

This chapter considers why well over a century past emancipation and fifty years after the Supreme Court of the United States outlawed forced racial segregation in schools, there continues to be test-score disparity between school-aged African-American and European-American children. The topic is important for two reasons. One is that test-score disparities among children turn into other forms of disparity among adults. For example, studies in the 1980s and 1990s found that test-score disparities predicted at least half of the hourly earnings gap between black and white young adult workers (e.g., Johnson and Neal 1998). As Christopher Jencks and Meredith Phillips have written, "If racial equality is America's goal, reducing the black–white test-score gap would probably do more to promote this goal than any other strategy that commands broad political support" (Jencks and Phillips, 1998: 3).

A second major reason that the topic is important concerns the future of the US economy. The US labor force is changing. The size of the prime-aged workforce – adult workers who are aged 25–55 – grew by 54 percent during the last two decades of the twentieth century.[1] In sharp contrast, it will grow hardly at all during the first two decades of the twenty-first century. However, its racial and ethnic composition will be shifting: by the year 2020 the number of prime-aged non-Hispanic whites in the labor force will decline by 10 percent. Eventually, whites will be a minority in both the population and the workforce. No single racial or ethnic group will be a majority. Consequently, leaders in the USA are beginning to understand that the future of the economy will depend in large measure on the skills of its nonwhite citizens. Indeed, it seems clear that whether the USA continues to thrive or begins to decline in the twenty-first century will depend upon whether it can educate children of all racial and ethnic backgrounds to participate effectively at all levels of both the economy and the democracy. Achievement test scores measure the degree to which people have acquired various skills and bits of knowledge that can help this ideal to unfold.

The good news is that scores have risen for black youth over the past thirty years and black–white gaps have narrowed. Anyone who asserted in 1970 that racial gaps in achievement could not be substantially reduced has been proven wrong by the progress that occurred between 1970 and 1990. Nationally, standardized test scores in reading and math rose faster for blacks than for whites on the National Assessment of Educational Progress (NAEP) Trend Assessment, which measures achievement trends for the nation's 9-, 13-, and 17-year-olds. The same pattern of progress holds for the Scholastic Achievement Test (SAT), the nation's most widely used college entrance exam. There is also evidence of narrowing earlier in the century. Hauser and Huang (1996) find that the black–white vocabulary gap for adults narrowed by half from 1909 to 1969.

The bad news is that black–white gaps are slightly larger now than at the end of the 1980s, and the average reading and math scores of black 17-year-olds on the 1999 NAEP Trend Assessment equal those of white 13-year-olds. The challenge is to find ways of reestablishing the positive trends that narrowed the black–white gap among birth-cohorts born in the late 1960s and early 1970s, who were 17 years old during the 1980s. Toward that end, this chapter assesses a number of popular explanations for continuing achievement disparity, including problems with preschool parenting practices, class size, instructional quality, grouping and tracking, teacher expectations, and youth culture. I emphasize that there remain large racial gaps in preschool preparation, deficiencies in schools that black children attend, distractions in youth culture that interfere with school achievement, and too many routine practices in homes, schools, and communities that help to sustain achievement disparities.

Gaps exist by kindergarten

The US Department of Education's Early Childhood Longitudinal Study (ECLS-K) for the kindergarten class of 1998–9 has assembled data from a nationally representative sample of 20,000 children (and their parents and teachers) who entered kindergarten in the fall of 1998. In addition to numerous family background variables, the data include measures of cognitive skills and knowledge. The ECLS shows that by the time children are five years old, there is a gap in school-related skills and knowledge between African-American and European-American children, even when their mothers have equal years of schooling.[2]

Using data from the ECLS, Table 11.1 shows that black children arrive at kindergarten less well-prepared than same-gender whites in reading, math, general knowledge (about social studies and science), and familiarity with conventions of print.[3] Each number in the table represents the black–white gap in average scores for a particular subject, measured in standard deviation units, among children whose mothers have similar years of schooling. The gaps are similar for girls and boys but differ across topics. Gaps are highly statistically significant and moderately large for math, knowledge of print conventions, and general knowledge of science and social studies. Gaps for reading are smaller, but statistically significant at conventional levels (i.e., 0.05 or better), except among girls whose mothers have sixteen or more years of schooling.

Measured family background and home environment effects

The best available analysis of achievement gaps for young children at school entry is by Meredith Phillips et al. (1998).[4] Phillips and her colleagues use data from the Children of the National Longitudinal Survey of Youth (CNLSY), which covers the children of participants in the National Longitudinal Survey of Youth (NLSY). The NLSY is a nationally representative longitudinal survey that tracks people who were ages fourteen to twenty-two in 1979. The study by Phillips et al. focuses on 1,626 African-American and European-American five- and six-year-olds born between 1980 and 1987 who took the Peabody Picture Vocabulary Test-Revised (PPVT-R).

Phillips and her colleagues begin their analysis using a traditional list of family income, wealth and education variables. They find that parents' income, years of schooling, and other employment-related variables explain no more than a third of the black–white gap in PPVT-R scores. In addition, they find that household wealth is not a significant predictor.

Using only this basic list of family background measures, Phillips et al. seem to confirm the finding by Richard Hernstein and Charles Murray (1994), in the Bell Curve, that socioeconomic status explains about a third of the black–white test-score gap. Hernstein and Murray attribute a large share of the rest to genetic endowments.

However, when Phillips et al. use a longer, more detailed list of indicators, they are able to explain much more – up to two-thirds – of the PPVT-R gap. The additional indicators measure grandparents' educational attainment, mother's household size as a teen, mother's high-school quality, mother's perceived self-efficacy, mother's test score, the child's birth weight (as a proxy for prenatal environment), the child's household size, and mother's parenting practices.

According to Phillips et al., "Blacks are much more disadvantaged than whites when ranked on this set of measures than when ranked on the measures of socioeconomic status considered by Hernstein and Murray." Phillips et al. estimate that racial inequalities on these supplementary measures alone predict more than half of the test-score gap between black and white five- and six-year-olds. They speculate that a more complete and well-measured set of background measures might explain the entire test-score gap. Phillips et al. cannot rule out that some of the estimated background effects may actually be capturing genetic effects. However, scientists have not established that there are any genetic differences among racial and ethnic groups (Nisbett 1998) and there are many ways that what appear to be genetic effects – including IQ differences – can be environmental (Dickens and Flynn 2001).

Family resources and parent–child activities

Environmental differences that affect school readiness for kindergarteners can take many forms. These include differences in how much time families spend with children; differences in day care and preschool experiences; differences in home-learning resources such as toys, computers, and books, and differences in routines such as reading or watching television together or going to the library.

Accordingly, the ECLS-K survey for parents asks how often families do particular activities with their kindergarten children. The data reveal differences in home-learning activities between children whose mothers have different amounts of schooling and also differences between blacks and whites within each mother's schooling category.

Tables 11.2 and 11.3 show disparities in family routines and resources that help to explain the skill disparities in Table 11.1. Panel A of Table 11.2 shows at each level of mother's education, that roughly 10 percent

Table 11.1 *Black–white skill and knowledge gaps measured in the first semester of kindergarten, by gender and mother's years of schooling, fall semester 1998 (in standard deviation units)*

Mother's years of schooling	Reading readiness skills		Math readiness skills		Knowledge of print conventions		General knowledge**	
	Boys	*Girls*	*Boys*	*Girls*	*Boys*	*Girls*	*Boys*	*Girls*
12 years or fewer	−0.25	−0.32	−0.46	−0.40	−0.46	−0.53	−0.81	−0.85
13 to 15 years	−0.14	−0.25	−0.48	−0.43	−0.39	−0.42	−0.77	−0.80
16 or more years	−0.21	−0.16*	−0.70	−0.52	−0.43	−0.41	−0.91	−0.90

* indicates *not* significant at the 0.05 or better level in a simple difference of means test.
** This rating of "general knowledge" of science and social studies comprises responses to questions that the teacher answers about the child's knowledge.
Source: Author's calculations using ECLS-K public use files.

more white than black families report that they read to their children daily. Among families where mothers have twelve or fewer years of schooling, 40 percent of blacks read to their children no more than once or twice per week, while for whites the number is half as large, at 20 percent. Panel B of Table 11.2 shows that white parents are more likely than black parents to discuss nature and science with their children. For each level of mother's education, blacks are almost twice as likely as whites to report that they *never* discuss nature or science with their kindergarten children. Panels C and D of Table 11.2 report things that blacks do more than whites. Specifically, blacks sing, play games, and solve puzzles with their children more than whites do. (Playing games is not distinguished from solving puzzles in the way that the question is asked.)

Table 11.3 shows the number of children's books, records, tapes, and CDs in the home, as reported by the parent. I report both the median and the mean for each racial group and mother's education level. The differences are surprisingly large: the average white child in each mother's education category has twice as many books as the average black child, and more records, tapes, and CDs as well.[5]

To summarize, Tables 11.2 and 11.3 indicate in each mother's education category that African-Americans play and sing with their children more than whites do. However, whites buy more books, records, tapes, and CDs and engage more with their children in reading and academic enrichment activities, such as talking about nature. Simple correlations (not shown) between the variables from Table 11.1 and the home activity and resource variables in Tables 11.2 and 11.3 show a clear pattern.

Table 11.2 *Selected family and child learning practices, by mother's years of schooling, fall 1998 (row percentages)*

Mother's years of schooling	Never	Once or twice a week	Three to six times a week	Daily	Total row percent	Sample size
African-American		Panel A: Family members read books to the child				
12 years or fewer	2.0	38.0	29.1	30.9	100	1313
13 to 15 years	0.6	25.5	36.6	37.4	100	828
16 or more years	1.2	14.2	37.3	47.3	100	260
European-American						
12 years or fewer	1.0	19.4	38.1	41.6	100	3118
13 to 15 years	0.3	11.5	41.4	46.8	100	3074
16 or more years	0.1	5.7	34.1	60.1	100	2815
African-American		Panel B: Adults discuss nature or do science projects with the child				
12 years or fewer	37.0	40.1	13.1	9.8	100	1311
13 to 15 years	24.8	47.6	17.8	9.9	100	828
16 or more years	16.5	53.9	20.0	9.6	100	260
European-American						
12 years or fewer	22.2	48.4	20.2	9.2	100	3116
13 to 15 years	14.6	51.2	23.7	10.6	100	3071
16 or more years	8.5	49.5	31.0	11.0	100	2814
African-American		Panel C: Family members sing songs with the child				
12 years or fewer	5.5	21.5	19.2	53.9	100	1313
13 to 15 years	3.1	18.0	24.4	54.5	100	829
16 or more years	2.3	18.9	24.6	54.2	100	260
European American						
12 years or fewer	5.5	25.3	25.8	43.4	100	3118
13 to 15 years	3.6	21.9	30.7	43.8	100	3075
16 or more years	2.6	21.5	33.3	42.7	100	2815
African-American		Panel D: Family members play games or do puzzles with the child				
12 years or fewer	6.5	36.3	27.0	30.2	100	1313
13 to 15 years	3.9	33.3	36.3	26.5	100	829
16 or more years	4.6	29.3	38.5	27.7	100	260
European American						
12 years or fewer	3.6	36.7	39.8	20.2	100	3118
13 to 15 years	2.4	34.2	44.0	19.4	100	3076
16 or more years	1.7	30.4	48.6	19.3	100	2815

Source: Author's tabulations using ECLS-K Base Year Public Use File.

Table 11.3 *Numbers of children's books (panel A) and records, audio tapes, or CDs (panel B) (standard deviation and sample size in parenthesis)*

Mother's years of schooling	African-Americans		European-Americans	
	Median	Mean	Median	Mean
	Panel A: "About how many children's books does your child have in your home now, including library books?"			
12 years or fewer	20	30 (33, 1304)	50	76 (55, 3099)
13 to 15 years	30	46 (40, 826)	100	97 (59, 3042)
16 or more years	50	65 (51, 258)	100	114 (59, 2777)
	Panel B: "About how many children's records, audio tapes, or CD's do you have at home, including any from the library?"			
12 years or fewer	4	8 (13, 1306)	10	15 (18, 3114)
13 to 15 years	8	13 (16, 827)	12	18 (18, 3072)
16 or more years	10	16 (16, 260)	20	22 (19, 2814)

Source: Author's tabulations using ECLS-K Base Year Public Use File.

Specifically, even within each racial group, having more books and recordings in the home and reading to children are much more strongly correlated with kindergarten skills and knowledge, than are playing games with children and singing.

Why are there differences in parenting?

The differences tabulated in Tables 11.1, 11.2, and 11.3 are not simply racial; they also vary with mother's education. For example, within each racial group, the numbers of books and recordings in the home and the percentage of families who read daily to their children and talk with them about nature is higher for children where mothers have more years of schooling. Accordingly, one interpretation of the data might be that differences are mainly socioeconomic and that blacks, for historical reasons, are simply a generation or two behind whites (with similar years of schooling) in adopting "middle-class" parenting practices.

However, there could also be stable racial differences. Namely, it may be that blacks have values, norms, and worldviews that are likely to remain somewhat different from those of whites (note I said different from, not inferior to) even after several generations of middle-class life. Most parenting practices are learned informally from parents, friends, extended family, and informal associates. Others are learned from less socially proximate sources, such as books and television, but still get adapted and blended with more customary practices that may differ between groups.

These are cultural issues. Socioeconomic status is important, but so also are race and ethnicity. While people may debate the particulars, it is undeniable that cultivated ways of being (i.e., cultures) among African-Americans and European-Americans differ from one another, on average, for historical reasons. We should not be surprised to find differences in how whites and blacks have coped and adapted over time to their positions in the nation's hierarchy of power and privilege. These differences reflect not only psychological self-defense mechanisms, but also social interaction patterns and disparities in access to opportunity. Such patterns help determine not only the economic wherewithal of families to provide for their children, but also the child-rearing methods that families grow accustomed to using and the ways that they understand and interact with mainstream institutions such as schools. There is no question that black parents love their children. However, as a black parent myself, I acknowledge that there may be changes in what we do with our preschool children that would put them on a more equal footing with whites on the first day of kindergarten.

The story here is not that all white children are better prepared than all black children. Nonetheless, most school officials and teachers are quite familiar with the patterns discussed above in which the average black child begins kindergarten with fewer academic skills than the average white classmate. Then, over the next twelve years, the gap can narrow, stay constant, or widen (in standard deviation units), depending in large measure upon the effectiveness of schools.

Schools and the black–white gap

For most of the nation's history, there was no pretense among public policymakers that black (or other children of color) should have the same access to high-quality schools as whites. Indeed, racial disparity was taken for granted and legally sanctioned. However, over the past half-century, public discourse and the goals that leaders articulate have shifted dramatically. Laws no longer explicitly protect racial preferences and financial resources for schooling are more equally allocated. For example, by 1990, the percentage of black students in a school's student body was no longer a predictor of pupil-to-teacher ratios, as it had been until that time.

Still, inequities remain. Quality teaching is the most important service that schools are supposed to provide. I argue below that the main disadvantage that blacks continue to suffer compared to whites is in the quality of the instruction that they receive, even when they attend the same schools. There are reasons to believe that poor teaching, due in part to low expectations regarding what black children have the potential to achieve, is the primary remaining form of educational disadvantage that blacks suffer more than whites. Centuries of socialization to believe that blacks are naturally less able than whites has surely dampened the enthusiasm with which schools, teachers, parents, and society at large search for better ways of cultivating black children's latent potential.

School resources, desegregation and integration

From the abolition of slavery through the first half of the twentieth century, the vast majority of African-Americans lived in the South. Affirmed by the 1896 US Supreme Court decision in the case of *Plessy v. Ferguson*, the South kept virtually all public and private facilities, including schools, racially segregated.[6] Officials devoted far more resources to the education of whites than blacks. For example, in 1915, there were three students in black classrooms for every two in white classrooms. The length of the school year for blacks was only two-thirds that for whites.[7] In addition, black teachers earned less than half of what white teachers earned. Gunnar Myrdal quotes the following from a Southern commission report on teacher salaries. "An additional argument in favor of the salary differential [between black and white teachers] is the general tradition of the South that negroes and whites are not to be paid equivalent salaries for equivalent work . . . the custom is one . . . that the practical school administration must not ignore" (Myrdal 1944: 215).[8]

The Supreme Court's decision in *Plessy v. Ferguson* protected the South's way of life until 1954, when another Supreme Court rejected the idea that separate could be equal in the landmark case of *Brown v. Board of Education*. The latter Court interpreted the 14th Amendment to the US Constitution to mean that black children could not legally be restricted from attending school with whites. Later, the Civil Rights Act of 1964 set in motion a series of events that forced widespread desegregation of schools across the South, after the original Supreme Court decision of 1954 (and the implementation order in 1955) had been successfully resisted in most Southern communities. Consequently, schools in the South became the most desegregated in the nation by the early 1970s.

Desegregation has been more difficult to achieve in the North. Compared with the South, blacks and whites live more often in different legal jurisdictions and frequently there are too few whites in mostly black school districts to achieve any meaningful degree of integration. Beginning with a Detroit Michigan case in the mid-1970s, federal courts have been unwilling to issue desegregation orders that require transporting children across district boundaries. Inside districts, courts have ordered school bussing to achieve racial balance in a few Northern cities, such as Cleveland, Ohio, and Boston, Massachusetts, but bussing has ended as court orders have expired. Desegregation in the North occurs mostly as a consequence of residential mobility, when black families move to suburban communities where whites predominate.

Evidence regarding how much either forced or unforced integration has raised achievement among black children or helped to narrow the black–white achievement gap is mixed. One likely reason is that most studies are methodologically flawed. The best studies (e.g., Ludwig, Ladd, and Duncan, forthcoming) do not find effects that are particularly large. Based on a more extensive review in Ferguson with Mehta (2002), Mehta and I conclude that racial and socioeconomic mixing in schools often seems to improve outcomes – particularly non-test-score outcomes (e.g., college-going rates) – for nonwhite students who might otherwise attend low-income segregated schools. I also agree with Harvard Professor Gary Orfield, who often says that trying to raise achievement in highly segregated, high-poverty schools that are isolated from the mainstream society is a gargantuan task and that more integration by race, ethnicity, and socioeconomic status seems warranted. However, studies that estimate the achievement effects of such mixing generally suffer from methodological problems that limit their usefulness for drawing firm, confident conclusions.

From desegregation to school finance

School desegregation cases in the North have become, in effect, finance equalization cases, because, as indicated above, the courts have refused to impose desegregation remedies that cross district boundaries. They impose financial remedies instead, involving state-aid formulas to supplement education expenditures in poorer districts where blacks and other racial minorities are more heavily represented. These school desegregation (turned financial equalization) cases typically make their appeals by alleging violations of the equal protection clause of the US Constitution. However, this is not the only strategy plaintiffs have used. Another is to appeal to state instead of federal courts, by alleging violation of equity or adequacy provisions in state constitutions. These cases (when successful) have not completely equalized spending among districts, but expenditures have risen as a consequence of these cases in a number of states (Evans, Murray, and Schwab 1997 and 1999).

Despite the large number of school finance cases that plaintiffs have launched, there is no consensus among researchers who study school finance about whether increased spending helps to raise achievement.

Different researchers reach different conclusions regarding whether schools use resources effectively. The vast majority of researchers agree that to improve instruction, in particular, is an important goal. However, studies have not clearly established that districts are routinely willing and able to do so. There are other disagreements as well. Some of the most important from a financial point of view concern class size, which I discuss next, before returning to issues of instructional quality below.

Class size

Based on the Tennessee STAR Class-Size Experiment and the quasi-experimental SAGE class size study underway in Wisconsin, there is rather broad agreement that small class sizes raise standardized achievement test scores in kindergarten and first grade, especially for black children.[9] Both the Tennessee and the Wisconsin studies follow children from kindergarten through third grade. The Tennessee study randomly assigned teachers and students to different class sizes. The Wisconsin study did not use random assignment but, instead, used carefully selected comparison classrooms. In both studies, achievement scores were higher in smaller than in larger (more typical) classes by the end of the first grade. After first grade, the test score difference between large and small classes remains but does not grow (measured in standard deviation units). Because neither study moves students from small- into regular-sized classes after the first or second grade, it is impossible to know whether remaining in small classes through second and third grades confers any additional advantage. Currently, there is no consensus among researchers concerning whether class size matters other than for black children in kindergarten and first grades. We simply have not conducted the types of studies that would give us definitive answers.

Alan Krueger and Diane Whitmore (2001) report, based on their analysis of data from the Tennessee STAR Class-Size Experiment, that the benefits of smaller classes in first grade are larger for all children (not only black children) in schools where more black children attend. As a possible explanation, economist Edward Lazear (1999) has shown theoretically that the achievement gains from reducing class size should be larger in classrooms where the probability that any randomly selected student will be disruptive is higher. Disruption can take many forms, ranging from misbehaving to requesting individualized attention for a learning task. Data from a number of sources, including the ECLS-K, show that teachers regard the behavior of black children, and especially black boys, as a bit more disruptive than the behavior of white children. The reasons are not well understood. Racial biases are high on the list of possibilities that researchers consider (see below). In any case, combined with Lazear's theoretical argument, teacher reports of greater disruption point to a possible explanation for the racial differential in class-size effects that both the Tennessee and Wisconsin studies find empirically.

Actual pupil-to-teacher ratios in American schools decreased for much of the twentieth century (Boozer, Krueger, and Wolkon 1992). They decreased more rapidly in predominantly black schools than in places where more whites attended (Krueger and Whitmore 2001). Consequently, by roughly 1990, national data show no clear relationship between the pupil-to-teacher ratio and the percentage of black children in a school or even to the percentage (of all students) eligible for federal school-lunch subsidies (Ferguson 1998b: Table 9–11).

However, this racial and socioeconomic parity in average class sizes has no implications for whether class size reductions might be important (or not) for some students, in some schools, at some times. It is possible that reductions in class size at some grade levels, even past the early elementary years, might help black students or socioeconomically disadvantaged students more than whites or the non-disadvantaged. For more carefully calibrated class-size policies, we need more experimental and quasi-experimental studies of class-size effects.

Teacher (and teaching) quality

Linda Darling-Hammond and Lisa Hudson (1989) distinguish teacher quality from teaching quality. Teacher quality pertains to distinct characteristics of teachers that are believed to predict teaching quality. Teaching quality is effectiveness at helping students to learn. There are reasons to believe that black students on average are disadvantaged, compared to whites, with regard to both teacher and teaching quality.

The single strongest measure of teacher quality in the education literature seems to be teachers' own test scores. Robert Greenwald, Larry Hedges, and Richard Laine (1996) pool findings from all published studies that fit their quality-control criteria for inclusion.[10] Ten of the studies include measures of teacher test scores among the predictors of student achievement. Among 24 independent coefficients measuring the relationship of teachers' scores to their students' standardized achievement scores, 21 are positive and only 3 are negative. Among the 21 positive coefficients, 12 are statistically significant at the .05 level. In their statistical metaanalysis, the authors address whether this pattern of coefficients across all of the studies might result purely by chance if there is no relationship in general between students' and teachers' scores. Their answer is unambiguously, "No."

However, a methodological problem with these studies is the possibility of reverse causation. Namely, if good students attract good teachers, then it may be misleading to interpret the positive relationship between teachers' and students' scores as an indication that higher-scoring teachers produce higher-scoring students. Random assignment experiments that might answer the question definitively have not been conducted. However, in my own work, where I have used statistical specifications likely to minimize the role of reverse causation, the positive relationship of teachers' to students' scores remains.[11] Further, in predicting why some school districts have higher average student test scores than others, I find that teachers' average scores are roughly as important as parents' education (Ferguson 1991 and 2000; Ferguson and Ladd 1996).

In each dataset of which I am aware in which students' races and teachers' own test scores are available, the teachers in predominantly black schools and districts have lower average scores than the teachers in predominantly white schools and districts.[12] This is not simply because black teachers may have lower scores on average than white teachers. Instead, it is sometimes because teachers of every race and ethnicity in predominantly black schools and districts have lower average scores than similar teachers in predominantly white districts. For example, the state of Texas tested all of its teachers in 1986. Using the data from that test, I find that the teachers' average scores in districts where black students are more than 50 percent of the student population are a full standard deviation lower than in districts where blacks represent under 10 percent of the student body.

Similarly, Stephen Raudenbush (2000) has shown disparities using data from the Trial State Assessment (TSA) in Mathematics of the National Assessment of Educational Progress. His data cover roughly 100,000 eighth-graders attending 3,537 schools in forty-one states. Generally, he finds that students whose parents have more education are more likely to have math teachers who report they majored in mathematics and emphasize math reasoning. However, these relationships of teacher training and practices to parents' education are weaker for blacks, Hispanics, and Native Americans than for Whites and Asians. Specifically, among students whose parents have less than twelve years of schooling, Raudenbush finds that math teachers are similar. However, whites and Asians whose parents are college graduates have the "best" math teachers. For example, among students whose parents are college graduates, 62 percent of those who teach Asians and 51 percent of those who teach whites report an emphasis on reasoning in math instruction. The same is true for only about 40 percent of those who teach blacks, Hispanics, or Native Americans (Raudenbush 2000: 31).

To summarize, compared to schools and classrooms where whites pre-dominate, those attended mostly by black students are prone to have access to less skilled teachers. Lower skill is indicated by lower certification test scores, fewer college majors in the subjects taught, and weaker intellectual emphases (e.g., math reasoning). In my view, these and other disparities in teacher (and teaching) quality are the most important black–white differences that remain in access to educational opportunity.

Grouping and tracking

When black students attend the same elementary schools as whites, especially in well-to-do communities, blacks are more likely than whites to be in the lowest-level groups for reading and math instruction.[13] Similarly, blacks in racially integrated middle schools and high schools are less likely than whites to be in higher-level courses (e.g., honors and advanced placement courses).

Ability grouping in elementary schools and academic tracking in middle and high schools are suspected by many to be reasons that black children in racially integrated schools remain academically behind their white peers (e.g., see Braddock and Slavin 1993, Oakes, 1995). They provide means by which students attending the same schools may have different instructional experiences. Ability grouping refers to elementary-school practices that separate children for instruction either within or between classrooms, based on teachers' judgments. After elementary school, de facto ability grouping occurs often in the context of what historically has been called tracking and what more recently has been called "leveling" because "tracking" has acquired a pejorative connotation associated with more rigid structures of the past (Loveless 1998). Courses at higher levels cover more advanced material and may require more work.[14]

Debates about the impacts of ability grouping and tracking on black–white achievement disparities confuse at least three questions. The first is whether groups at all levels receive the same quality of instruction and, if not, what the implications are for whether the grouping should continue. The most common conclusion is that children in lower-ability groups (and tracks) receive a lower quality of instruction than those in higher-ability groups (and tracks), and therefore that grouping and tracking hurt students at the lower levels (Metz 1978, Schwartz 1981, Finley 1984, Oakes 1985, Gamoran and Berends 1987).

However, the authors who conclude that ability grouping hurts students in lower-level groups or tracks and that it should therefore be abandoned, assume that the same students would receive better instruction in more heterogeneous groups or classrooms. This may, or may not, be correct. There is ample evidence that even in heterogeneous, mixed ability classrooms, low-achieving students often receive what seems like inferior treatment. Thomas Good (1987) reviewed a large number of studies in which researchers had conducted classroom observations. Citing multiple studies for each item, he identified the following ways that teachers were found to treat "highs" and "lows" differently when they were in the same classroom. They did so by waiting less time for "lows" to answer; giving low achievers answers or calling on someone else rather than trying to improve their responses (by giving clues or repeating or rephrasing questions); rewarding inappropriate behavior or incorrect answers by low achievers; criticizing low achievers more often for failure; praising low achievers less often than highs for success; failing to give feedback to the public responses of low achievers; paying less attention to low achievers or interacting with them less frequently; calling on low achievers less often to respond to questions; seating low achievers farther away from the teacher; demanding less from low achievers (e.g., teaching them less, accepting low quality or even incorrect answers, providing unsolicited help); interacting with low achievers more privately than publicly, and monitoring and structuring their activities more closely; grading tests or assignments in a different manner, in which the high achievers but not the low achievers are given the benefit of the doubt in borderline cases; having less friendly interaction with low achievers, including less smiling and fewer other nonverbal indicators of support; providing briefer and less informative feedback to the questions of low achievers; providing less eye contact and other nonverbal communication of attention and responsiveness; evidencing less use of effective but time-consuming instructional methods with low achievers when time is limited; evidencing less acceptance and use of low achievers' ideas.

I believe that researchers are correct when they conclude that instruction for lower-level tracks is routinely inferior to what higher-level tracks receive at middle-school and high-school levels. An analogous statement may apply for ability groups at the elementary school level. However, it does not follow directly that moving students into heterogeneously grouped arrangements will typically improve learning outcomes. As Good's list reminds us, even in heterogeneously grouped schools and classrooms, minority students in integrated schools may receive inferior instruction if they are overrepresented among low achievers or among students from whom not much is expected (see below).

A second question to consider is whether ability grouping matters if the curriculum and the quality of instruction are similar across different grouping arrangements. The best studies to address this question are experimental and quasi-experimental studies in which students are randomly assigned (or carefully matched) to be grouped by ability, or not. Kulik (1992) presents findings from a metaanalysis of many such studies. The studies find overwhelmingly that ability grouping makes no difference to learning if there is no tailoring of curriculum or instruction to fit the proficiency of the group. In other words, if what is taught is the same, classmates' proficiencies seem not to matter.[15] Kulik's review also indicates that when students are placed in relatively homogeneous ability groups, and instruction and curriculum are tailored to the group, then *students at all levels can benefit at least modestly from ability-grouped instruction.* Moreover, self-esteem of low achievers is raised.[16] Again, Kulik's review is for random assignment and quasi-experimental studies, where teacher quality is likely to be roughly equal across the various ability-grouped levels.

A final issue with regard to grouping and tracking concerns whether students of color, and black students in particular, are especially likely to be misplaced – i.e., to be placed in lower-level groups or sections than their skills warrant. If teachers or guidance counselors use race, gender, or socioeconomic status as indicators of current or potential proficiency, there may be race, gender, or socioeconomic biases in placements. However, the studies that I have found that seek to measure this bias, controlling for measures of proficiency, such as past grades and test scores, tend to find it neither at the elementary level[17] nor at the middle- or high-school level.[18] Using the nationally representative data set *High School and Beyond*, Lee and Bryk (1988) find no residual racial difference in course taking during the early 1980s after accounting for academic background and prior test scores. Similarly, Loveless (1998) uses the *National Education Longitudinal Study* (NELS) that began with eighth graders in 1988 and followed them for several years afterward. He reports: "Once test scores are taken into account, a student's race has no bearing on track assignment."

The bottom line is that when grouping and tracking are hurting children – perhaps contributing to the achievement gap – it is usually because lower-level groups and tracks are not receiving high-quality instruction. In addition, it is sometimes because children get trapped in tracks where the curriculum is bad and from which they cannot move up to do more advanced coursework. The focus among agents for positive change should be on finding the best ways within any particular school context of tailoring instruction to produce the best outcomes for the students being served. Loveless (1998) is correct when he advises that this should be done in the context of individual schools, with consideration for their own specific capacities and student needs.

Are teachers' expectations and behaviors biased against black students?

Bias, by definition, is deviation from a benchmark that represents *no* bias. Elsewhere (Ferguson 1998a) I have reviewed the teacher expectations literature in some detail as it relates to the black–white achievement gap. Three implicit definitions of bias are common in this literature and failure to distinguish among them is the source of much confusion. It is useful, as well, to distinguish a teacher's expectations from the way that he or she treats students. A teacher can be biased with regard to expectations, but not with regard to how he or she treats students, or vice versa.

First, consider the benchmark that I call *unconditional neutrality*. To be unconditionally neutral with regard to their *expectations* for black and white students, teachers must expect the same of students, irrespective of which group they belong to; to be unconditionally neutral with regard to *treatment* is to treat members of both groups equally.[19]

Using the *unconditional-neutrality* benchmark, experimental researchers seek to learn whether teachers expect less of black students and treat them less supportively than they treat whites. Usually, the researcher conducting the study arranges for each teacher in the experiment to do one of several things: to coach or test a student who is behind a screen and cannot be seen; to grade an assignment written by a student who cannot be seen; or simply to express an expectation. In some fashion, the teacher is made aware of the student's race, but attending to race is not part of the assignment.

In fact, the unseen "student" in the experiment is actually a confederate who is collaborating with the researcher. Responses from the confederate to the teachers in the experiment are carefully randomized, so that the only systematic differences among the phantom students is what the teachers believe about their racial identities.

Similar to the non-experimental literature, the experimental research on teachers' expectations and behaviors typically finds that teachers are not unconditionally neutral. They expect black students to do less well on average than white students. In addition, teachers in experiments tend to react more supportively to whites, by giving more unscripted encouragement and feedback.

It is difficult to know what to conclude from the experimental studies, because they are artificial one-time encounters in which the teacher and student do not actually see one another. There is no building of relationships. All teachers have to go on is their pre-existing stereotypes. In most cases, these stereotypes are based on the actual experience that black children, on average, do not perform as well as whites. Indeed, in many cases, the experimental studies are looking for answers that conflict with teachers' past experiences. Instead of being unconditionally neutral, teachers' expectations in these experiments are probably biased in the direction of experience.

Indeed, another type of study calls into question whether the experimental studies that use unconditional neutrality as their benchmark are useful. This second type of study uses data from real classrooms and takes care to control for students' past academic performances. The benchmark for judging the absence of bias is *neutrality conditioned on past performance*. In other words, to be unbiased, teachers should have similar expectations of students who have similar academic histories. The general finding in such studies is that teachers do indeed have similar expectations of black and white students who have similar past grades and test scores. They are neutral, *conditioned on past performance*.

The third benchmark to consider is neutrality *conditioned on potential*. By "potential," I mean what the student is potentially capable of achieving. No student has demonstrated all of his or her potential. Much remains latent. The problem is that teachers might base judgments about a student's potential too much on what they have actually seen the student achieve.

Glenn Loury (this volume) gives examples of how socially sub-optimal routines can persist over time because individuals believe they are doing the best they can, given what others seem willing and able to do in response. Teachers who learn to expect the black–white gap in skill and knowledge that they routinely observe may believe that there is little that they can do to help close it. Particularly when experience with student performance seems to confirm the beliefs that inform and justify particular instructional routines, teachers are likely to continue those routines on the assumption that the beliefs on which they are based are correct. To have their beliefs shaken, sometimes requires "seeing-is-believing" experiences in which teachers observe others who are clearly more effective. However, for most teachers, such experiences are quite rare.

The typical black student has lower grades and test scores than the typical white classmate. If we assume that black and white students are born with equal potential, then it seems likely that teachers probably underestimate black students' potential by a greater margin than for white students. Stated in terms of bias, teachers' instructional practices are probably biased insofar as they set less ambitious goals for black than for white students, based on expectations about potential that rely too much on observations of past performance.

Since latent potential is not measurable while still latent, it is impossible to prove or disprove my speculation here that teachers are biased in this third way. However, if I am correct, then black student performance is depressed in part by the failure of teachers (and students and parents) to set sufficiently ambitious goals for their achievement. When people fail to search for what they do not expect to find, they miss what they *would* find *if they searched*. The Reverend Dr. Robert Schuller captures the essence of the issue with the following saying: "Any fool can count the seeds in an apple, but only God can count the apples in a seed." Points on a test are like seeds in an apple. Anyone can count them, then assign a grade. However, apples in a seed are latent, unharvested potential. The number of apples that a seed will produce depends upon the skill and care with which that seed is cultivated.

Cultivating latent potential

While far from the norm, there are many examples around the USA in which African-American students have performed to very high levels due to effective "cultivation." For example, the Mount Royal Elementary-Middle School in Baltimore, Maryland, is 99 percent African-American and nearly 80 percent low income. Nonetheless, this school has achieved the highest passing rate in the whole state of Maryland on the state's fifth-grade math test (Haycock, Jerald, and Huang 2001). Another twenty-one schools that are highly effective with low-income black children are described in a small book by Samuel Casey Carter, entitled *No Excuses* (2000). Carter found them in a number of different cities and towns. Schools qualified to be in the book if at least three-quarters of their students were from low-income households and if building-wide median test scores were above the 65th percentile on nationally normed academic achievement tests. School performances ranged from this lower cutoff, upward. Eleven had average scores at the 80th percentile or above. These and other examples are proof of the proposition that African-American children, including those from low-income, disadvantaged backgrounds, can excel academically if their potential is effectively cultivated.

Past trends and future possibilities

In the late 1960s, the US Congress mandated that there should be a way of tracking the academic progress of the nation's children. The answer for making comparisons over time was the National Assessment

Table 11.4 *National Assessment of Educational Progress Trend-assessment reading and math scores for blacks and whites, 1971–1999*

	Black			White			BW Gap		
Age:	17	13	9	17	13	9	17	13	9
Year tested:				*NAEP reading scores*					
1971	239	222	170	291	261	214	52	39	44
1975	241	226	181	293	262	217	52	36	36
1980	243	233	189	293	264	221	50	31	32
1984	264	236	186	295	263	218	31	27	32
1988	274	243	189	295	261	218	21	18	29
1990	267	241	182	297	262	217	30	21	35
1992	261	238	185	297	266	218	36	28	33
1994	266	234	185	296	265	218	30	31	33
1996	266	234	191	295	266	220	29	32	29
1999	264	238	186	295	267	221	31	29	35
				NAEP math scores					
1973	270	228	190	310	274	225	40	46	35
1978	268	230	192	306	272	224	38	42	32
1982	272	240	195	304	274	224	32	34	29
1986	279	249	202	308	274	227	29	25	25
1990	289	249	208	309	276	235	20	27	27
1992	286	250	208	312	279	235	26	29	27
1994	286	252	212	312	281	237	26	29	25
1996	286	252	212	313	281	237	27	29	25
1999	283	251	211	315	283	239	32	32	28

Source: National Center for Education Statistics, National Assessment of Educational Progress (NAEP), 1999 Long-Term Trend Assessment.

of Educational Progress (NAEP) Trend Assessment. Beginning in the early 1970s, essentially identical tests have been administered roughly every four years through 1990, every two years from 1990 through 1996 and, after a three-year interval, in 1999. The tests are administered to nationally representative samples of youngsters aged 9, 13, and 17.

Columns one to six of Table 11.4 show the average NAEP trend scores by age and race for each year that the NAEP trend assessment has been administered. The top half of the table shows reading scores and the bottom half math scores. Columns seven through nine show the black–white gap in scores for each year, age group, and subject. To put these differences in perspective, be aware that the standard deviation of scores in any given year for a particular age group is roughly 30 points for math and 40 points for reading.

Note that the gap in scores for both reading and math is substantially smaller in 1999 than in the early 1970s. Indeed, in the early 1970s, black children's scores at age 17 were lower than white children's scores at age 13. Then there was progress. Average scores among black 17-year-olds rose more than among white 13- and 17-year-olds, catching and passing white 13-year-olds and narrowing the gap with white 17-year-olds. However, after 1988 for reading and 1990 for math, scores for black 17-year-olds declined a bit, while scores for white 13-year-olds rose; those for white 17-year-olds were mostly static. Hence, the black–white gap for 17-year-olds widened. Black 17-year-olds ended the twentieth century at parity with white 13-year-olds.

While the description above is the typical way that NAEP trend scores get summarized, it is more illuminating to compare birth-year cohorts. The Educational Testing Service (ETS) when administering the NAEP does not sample exactly the same children three times – at ages 9, 13, and 17. However, it *does* draw a nationally representative sample at each round of testing. Consequently, with a four-year testing interval, the children tested when they are 9 years old are from the same birth-year cohort as those tested four years later at age 13 and four years after that, at age 17. Statisticians use special techniques to adjust for the difficulty of questions and this enables them to express all NAEP trend scores along a single scale from zero to five hundred points. The interval properties of the resulting scale permit scores for 9-, 13- and 17-year-olds to be compared.

Figure 11.1 (for reading) and Figure 11.2 (for math) are bar diagrams in which each bar represents a birth cohort for either blacks or whites.[20] Each bar has three sections. The height of the bottom segment represents the average score within the racial group for the cohort at age 9. To this, the middle segment adds the gain in average score from ages 9 to 13. Similarly, the top segment adds to the bottom two sections the gain from ages 13 to 17, so that the height at the top is the average score for the cohort at age 17. The bar diagrams highlight the idea that the trend over time for 17-year-olds equals the trend for 9-year-olds plus the gains from ages 9 to 13 and 13 to 17. The scores for 9-year-olds represent gains from birth to age 9, so that the entire height of each bar can be regarded as a measure of gain – i.e., learning – from birth to age 17.

Why such volatility for black teens

A curious feature of the pattern in Figure 11.1 is that test-score gains for blacks fluctuate more over time than they do for whites. In each segment of the bar – i.e., 9-year-olds' score, the 9–13 gain or the 13–17 gain – the

Bottom = scores at age 9; Middle = gain from ages 9–13; Top = gains from ages 13–17.

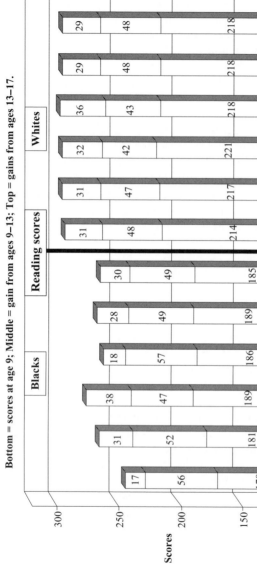

Figure 11.1 NAEP Reading scores for 9-year olds plus gains from ages 9–13 and ages 13–17, for blacks and whites, by birth-year cohorts

Source: Compiled by author, using data from the National Center for Education Statistics, *National Trend Assessment of Educational Progress (NAEP)*, 1999 Long-Term Trend Assessment.

Bottom = scores at age 9; Middle = gain from ages 9–13; Top = gains from ages 13–17.

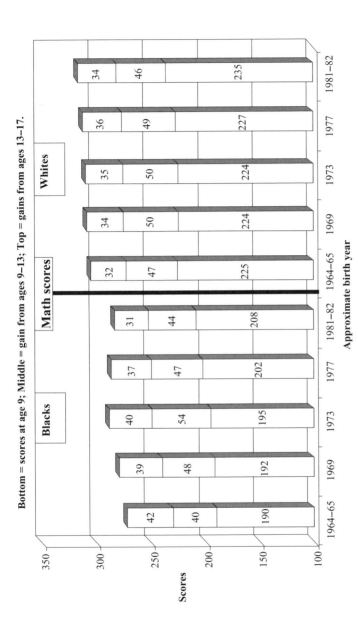

Figure 11.2 NAEP Math scores for 9-year olds plus gains from ages 9–13 and ages 13–17, for blacks and whites, by birth-year cohorts

Source: Compiled by author, using data from the National Center for Education Statistics, *National Trend Assessment of Educational Progress (NAEP)*, 1999 Long-Term Trend Assessment.

difference between the birth-year cohort with the highest gain and the cohort with the smallest gain is larger for blacks than for whites.

The most striking difference is between the cohort of blacks that was born in 1971 and turned 17 years old in 1988, and the cohort that was born in 1975 and turned 17 in 1992. At age 13, the younger of these two cohorts had higher reading scores than any black cohort before or after it. This is mostly because it had a large gain from ages 9 to 13. However, during the ages of 13 to 17, this same cohort gained less than half of what the previous cohort achieved. The only other cohorts with such meager gains as teens were those that were teenagers in the 1970s. The cohort that turned 17 in 1975 is not shown on Figure 11.1, because we do not have its score as 9-year-olds. But it too had a very small gain (19 points) from ages 13 to 17.

Evidence is growing that the reason the 1975 birth cohort gained so little as teenagers is that there may have been a shift in black youth culture at the end of the 1980s. There are a number of signs that something out of the ordinary was happening: the drop in NAEP reading scores for 17-year-olds occurred in every region of the nation.[21] At the same time, the percentage of 17-year-old NAEP test-takers reporting daily or almost daily reading for pleasure dropped from 35.3 percent in 1988, to 14.7 percent in 1992. Figure 11.3 illustrates the correspondence in time of the movement in reading scores among 17-year-olds in all four major census regions (the top four lines) and the movement in leisure reading (the bottom line). Not shown, is that the same up-and-down pattern of test-score gains between 1984 and 1992 for black 13- to 17-year-olds shows up for all levels of parent education and in all three types of communities that NAEP officials distinguish. There are no such unusual fluctuations for whites.

Additional support for the idea that black youth culture changed is the finding that class attendance patterns changed (also in a manner different from that for whites). Researchers at the University of Michigan conduct a large nationally representative survey of high-school seniors annually in order to gather data on drug use. Its name is "Monitoring the Future," and the yearly data go back to 1976. It is a totally independent data source from the NAEP. Nonetheless, it too shows a change for blacks at the end of the 1980s in all four major census regions. Specifically, as shown in Figure 11.4, class attendance dropped *in all four regions* during the four-year period from 1988 to 1992, when reading-score gains and leisure reading were falling as well.

The reasons for this apparent shift among black youth are not clear. No similar pattern appears for whites. To the contrary, white youth made

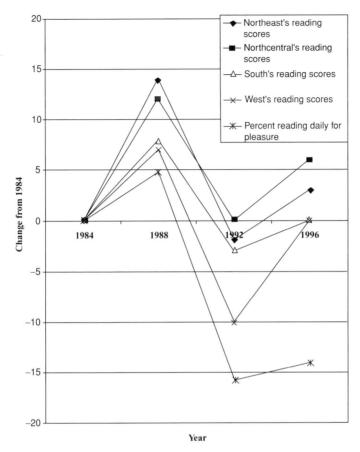

Figure 11.3 Changes from 1984 in black 17-year-olds' mean NAEP reading scores, by region, and in the national percent who read daily or almost daily for pleasure
Source: Graphed by author, using unpublished National Assessment of Educational Progress (NAEP) data, obtained from the Education Testing Service.

their largest reading gain from ages 13 to 17 during the same four-year period from 1988 to 1992 when blacks gained little.

The only phenomenon I have identified that coincides in time with the drop-off in reading gains, leisure reading, and class attendance for black teenagers, is the commercial take-off of rap music.[22] Rap music and hip-hop culture had been evolving since the 1970s (e.g., see George 1998).

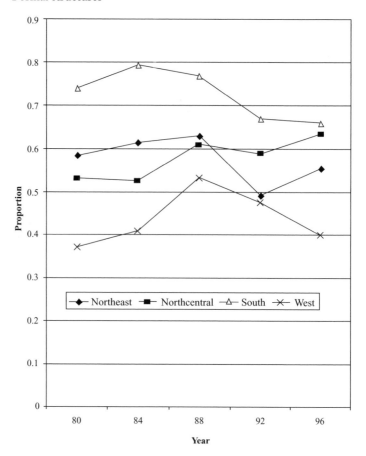

Figure 11.4 Proportions of African-American 12th-graders who report that they never cut class, by major US census region
Source: Compiled by author, using data from University of Michigan Survey, *Monitoring the Future.*

However, it was not until 1988 that it gained a strong national foothold commercially. According to *Billboard Magazine*, hip-hop artists had one gold record in 1985, none in 1986, two in 1987 and 17 in 1988. After 1988, the number rose rapidly – 1988 was the year when youth across the nation began buying this popular new music.

Presumably, if the hip-hop hypothesis is correct (and I hasten to caution that it may not be), time spent listening to and talking about the music diverted time from leisure reading and associated activities.[23] Why rap's take-off should not have had the same effect on leisure reading, class attendance, and reading scores among whites is uncertain. Perhaps this new music was not as important to them; perhaps it was entertainment for whites, but "identity" for young blacks because it was so assertively distinct from white culture. Even by the year 2000, it seems that rap has not penetrated the white youth market to the degree that it has the black youth market. In a survey of more than 30,000 students in fifteen suburban school districts from across the nation during the Fall of 2000, 87 percent of black sixth- to twelfth-graders identified rap or hip-hop among the forms of music that they listen to, while only 54 percent of white students did.[24]

After 1992, reading gains for black 13- to 17-year-olds roughly equaled those for whites in the same age range, with a 28-point gain for the 1979 birth cohort and a 30-point gain for the 1982–3 birth cohort. However, gains never returned to the 38-point jump achieved by the cohort that turned 17 in 1988, when blacks' reading scores peaked.

Closing the gap

The black–white gap in NAEP trend scores by 1999 was 31 points in reading and 32 points in math. Hence, closing the gap by age 17, if white scores remained constant, would require black scores at age 17 to be higher by approximately 30 points. If blacks were to gain an additional 10 points in each age-segment of the bar diagrams in Figures 11.1 and 11.2 – i.e., between birth and age 9, between 9 and 13, and between 13 and 17 – then the gap in NAEP trends scores would be essentially closed.

Consider the following hypothesis. Summing the highest reading score blacks achieved at age 9 (189 points), together with the largest gains they attained from ages 9 to 13 (57 points) and 13 to 17 (38 points), totals to a score of 284. Compared to the analogous hypothetical maximum score of 305 for whites, this leaves a gap of only 21 points, which is one-third smaller than the actual gap as of 1999. Further, compared to whites' actual score of 295 in 1999, a black score of 284 would leave a gap of only 11 points, which would be two-thirds smaller than the gap actually is. Performing the same exercise for math produces a maximum hypothetical black score of 302, which is only 13 points behind what whites actually scored that year and 19 points behind whites' hypothetical maximum.

Again, this is a totally hypothetical exercise and probably misleading if it makes closing the gap look easy. However, it does highlight the possibility that accumulated maximal gains across the years from birth to age 17 could substantially narrow and perhaps even close the black–white test-score gap.

Conclusion

Black–white achievement gaps persist because US history gave whites a head start while blacks were enslaved and suppressed and because current routines in homes, schools, communities, and society at large are not configured to accelerate the disappearance of historic disparities. Even so, the situation is not static and hopeless. A great deal of progress has occurred since 1863 when President Abraham Lincoln signed the Emancipation Proclamation, and even since 1964 when President Lyndon Baines Johnson launched the War on Poverty and signed the landmark Civil Rights Bill. More advancement will come as struggles to overcome opposition and to change routines continue and as it becomes increasingly clear that educating all children well is in the long-term national interest, and feasible.

While acknowledging that there are deeper root causes, this chapter has described ways that parents, teachers and youth culture seem to contribute to the persistence of the black–white achievement gap. The evidence reviewed indicates that if parents become more active as teachers of preschool children, if teachers become less accepting of poor performance and more aggressive in seeking ways to unlock potential, and if youth do their schoolwork and also engage in high-yield leisure activities, such as reading for fun, then achievement is likely to rise. More and better research is needed to increase the certainty with which such proposals can be asserted and refined.

Finally, while the focus of the chapter is on blacks and whites, the prescriptive implications are critically important for *all* children. *All* children deserve the opportunity to reach their full potential and to make whatever their distinct contributions might be to the well-being of the society. A burden on leaders is to mobilize sufficient resources for this work, including attracting more talent to the teaching profession, so that progress will not be perceived as a zero sum game, in which helping some groups to excel requires denying opportunities to others.

NOTES

1. The numbers in this paragraph are from Ellwood 2001.
2. Of course, equal years of schooling is not the same as equal quality of schooling. There is no measure in this data of parents' own test scores or the quality of the schools that the parents attended.
3. "Familiarity with conventions of print" counts the number of correct answers on the following three tasks, administered while the child is looking at an illustrated story: 1. indicating that reading goes from left to right; 2. going to the beginning of the next line after a line ends; 3. finding the end of the story.

4. Another important paper on this topic (Fryer and Levitt 1994) has appeared since the present chapter was prepared for publication. It strengthens the case even further that parenting is important in affecting achievement disparities.

5. Parents were also asked whether the child watched *Sesame Street* (the preschool educational television program) at least once a week for a period of three months or more. Eighty-one percent of blacks but only 53 percent of whites answered yes. Our very preliminary analysis found very few differences in kindergarten readiness associated with whether children do or do not watch *Sesame Street*. However, rather than conclude too quickly that *Sesame Street* has no effect, future work should investigate the degree to which children not watching *Sesame Street* are typically engaged in other, alternative educationally productive activities. It seems quite possible that if children stop watching *Sesame Street* and instead do things with no educational content, they could miss out on valuable learning.

6. The *Plessy v. Ferguson* case concerned a dispute about railway accommodations, but its reach was much further.

7. These facts about schools in 1915 are from sources cited in Card and Krueger 1992.

8. Racial differences in what society pays to educate children have declined steadily since early in the twentieth century. Differences are much smaller today than they were in 1900. However, some still exist. An analysis by the Education Trust for 1997 established that nationally, school funding per pupil in the quarter of districts with the highest nonwhite enrollments was between 80 and 85 percent of per-pupil funding in the quarter of districts with the lowest nonwhite enrollments (Haycock, Jerald, and Huang 2001: 20).

9. Both studies include blacks and whites but few Latinos, Asians, or American Indians.

10. They reviewed what are called education production function studies. The standards for a study to be included in their review were (1) the study was in a scholarly publication (e.g., a refereed journal or a book); (2) the data were from schools in the USA; (3) the outcome measure was some form of academic achievement; (4) the level of aggregation was at the level of the school district or a smaller unit; (5) the model controlled for socioeconomic characteristics or for prior performance levels; and (6) each equation was stochastically independent of others, such that only one of several equations from a study that used the same students but different outcome measures (e.g., math scores in one equation but reading scores in another) was kept for the Greenwald, Hedges, and Laine (1996) analysis.

11. See Ferguson 1998b, Table 9.10, column 7, and Figure 9.2.

12. See Coleman et al. 1966 using data from a national sample; Ferguson and Ladd 1996 using data for Alabama; Ferguson 2000 using data for Texas; and unpublished analyses by Hampton Lankford of the State University of New York at Albany, using data for school districts in the state of New York.

13. This discussion of grouping and tracking is an abbreviated version of discussions in Ferguson 1998b and Ferguson with Mehta 2002.

14. Currently, the standard arrangement is that no student is officially forbidden from entering a course at any level. Nonetheless, race, gender, and socioeconomic imbalances frequently develop. Explanations include differences

in proficiency, in the advice received from parents, counselors and teachers, and students' own preferences to be with their friends. For example, we often hear anecdotal reports about minority youth who forgo advanced courses because they would be one of only a few black or Latino students in the classroom (Fordham 1996, Ferguson 2001a).

15. See Tables 9.4 and 9.5 of Ferguson 1998b for tabulations of effect-size estimates from Kulik's study.

16. The self-esteem effect is presumably because compared to more heterogeneous classrooms, interpersonal comparisons at the classroom level are, on average, more favorable.

17. See: Pallas et al. 1994, Sorensen and Hallinan 1984, Dreeben and Gamoran 1986, Haller 1985.

18. See: Garet and Delaney 1988, Gamoran and Mare 1989, Argys, Rees and Brewer 1996.

19. Thomas Good's list of differences in the ways that teachers in real classrooms treat "highs" and "lows" (see above) indicates that teachers frequently are not unconditionally neutral in either their expectations or their treatment of individuals. To the extent that black students are overrepresented among low achievers, they are likely to be overrepresented among students receiving the types of low-achiever treatment that Good describes.

20. Birth cohorts born in 1969, 1973, and 1977 were each tested at all three ages (i.e., 9, 13, and 17) for math. Those born in 1971, 1975, and 1979 were tested at all three ages for reading. For other cohorts, there were times when one test was given one year too late or too early. In these cases, we took the test from the "late" or "early" year as a proxy. These are the cases on Figures 11.1 and 11.2 where the birth year is expressed as a blend of two years, as in "1962–3."

21. Even the SAT college entrance exam shows a leveling off for blacks at the end of the 1980s after rapidly rising scores for black students during the 1980s.

22. I explore this hypothesis in more detail in Ferguson 2001b.

23. I find no clear change in time on homework or on time watching television during this time period.

24. The same was true of 63 percent of Latinos and 52 percent of Asians.

REFERENCES

Argys, L. M., D. I. Rees, and D. Brewer, 1996, "Detracking America's Schools: Equity at Zero Cost?" Working Paper Series #9501, Center for Research on Economic and Social Policy, University of Colorado Denver.

Boozer, M. A., A. Krueger, and S. Wolkon, 1992, "Race and School Quality Since Brown v. Board of Education," *Brookings Papers on Economic Activity, Microeconomics*.

Braddock, J. and R. E. Slavin, 1993, "Why Ability Grouping Must End: Achieving Excellence and Equity in American Education," *Journal of Intergroup Relations* 20, 2: 51–64.

Card, D. and A. B. Krueger, 1992, "School Quality and Black–White Relative Earnings: A Direct Assessment," *Quarterly Journal of Economics* 107: 151–200.

Carter, S. C., 2000, *No Excuses: Lessons from 21 High-Performing, High-Poverty Schools*, Washington, DC: Heritage Foundation. (Downloadable from http://www.noexcuses.org)

Coleman, J., E. Campbell, C. Hobson, J. McPartland, A. Mood, F. Weinfield, and R. York, 1966, *Equality of Educational Opportunity*, Washington, DC: Government Printing Office.

Darling-Hammond, L. and L. Hudson, 1989, "Teachers and Teaching," in R. J. Shavelson, L. M. McDonnell, and J. Oakes (eds.), *Indicators for Monitoring Mathematics and Science Education*, Santa Monica, CA: Rand Corporation.

Dickens, W. T. and J. R. Flynn, 2001, "Heritability Estimates Versus Large Environmental Effects: The IQ Paradox Resolved," *Psychological Review* 108, 2: 346–69.

Dreeben, R. and A. Gamoran, 1986, "Race, Instructions, and Learning," *American Sociological Review* 51: 660–9.

Ellwood, D. T., 2001, "The Sputtering Labor Force of the 21st Century: Can Social Policy Help?" Harvard University, John F. Kennedy School of Government. Working Paper No. 01–022.

Evans, W. N., S. Murray, and R. Schwab, 1997, "Schoolhouses, Courthouses, and Statehouses after Serrano," *Journal of Policy Analysis and Management* 16, 1: 10–31.

1999, "The Impact of Court-Mandated School Finance Reform," in H. F. Ladd, R. Chalk, and J. S. Hanson (eds.), *Equity and Adequacy in Educational Finance: Issues and Perspectives*, Washington, DC: National Academy Press, pp. 72–98.

Ferguson, R. F., 1991, "Paying for Public Education: New Evidence on How and Why Money Matters," *Harvard Journal on Legislation* 28: 465–98.

1998a, "Teachers' Perceptions and Expectations and the Black–White Test Score Gap?" in C. Jencks and M. Phillips (eds.), *The Black-White Test Score Gap*, Washington, DC: Brookings Institution Press, pp. 273–317.

1998b, "Can Schools Narrow the Black-White Test Score Gap?" In C. Jencks and M. Phillips (eds.), *The Black–White Test Score Gap*, Washington, DC: Brookings Institution Press.

"Certification Test Scores, Teacher Quality and Student Achievement," in D. W. Grissmer and J. M. Ross (eds.), *Analytic Issues in the Assessment of Student Achievement*. Washington, DC: National Center for Education Statistics, pp. 133–56.

2001a, "A Diagnostic Analysis of Black–White GPA Disparities in Shaker Heights, Ohio," in D. Ravitch (ed.), *Brookings Papers on Education Policy, 2001*, Washington, DC: Brookings Institution Press, pp. 347–96.

2001b, "Test-Score Trends Along Racial Lines 1971 to 1996: Popular Culture and Community Academic Standards," in N. Smelser, W. J. Wilson, and F. Mitchell (eds.), *America Becoming: Racial Trends and Their Consequences*, Washington, DC: National Academy Press, pp. 348–90.

Ferguson, R. F. and H. F. Ladd, 1996, "How and Why Money Matters: An Analysis of Alabama Schools," in H. F. Ladd (ed.), *Holding Schools Accountable: Performance Based Reform in Education*, Washington, DC: Brookings Institution Press, pp. 265–98.

Ferguson, R. F. and J. Mehta, 2002, "Why Racial Integration and Other Policies Since Brown v. Board of Education Have Only Partially Succeeded at Narrowing the Achievement Gap," in T. Ready, C. Edley, and C. Snow (eds.), *Achieving High Standards for All*, Washington, DC: National Academy Press, pp. 183–217.

Finley, M. K., 1984, "Teachers and Tracking in a Comprehensive High School," *Sociology of Education* 57: 233–43.

Fryer, R. Jr., and S. Levitt, 2004, "Understanding the Black–White Test Score Gap in the First Two Years of School," *Review of Economics and Statistics* 84, 2 (May): 447–64.

Fordham, S., 1996, *Blacked Out: Dilemmas of Race, Success and Identity at Capital High*, University of Chicago Press.

Gamoran, A. and M. Berends, 1987, "The Effects of Stratification in Secondary Schools: Synthesis of Survey and Ethnographic Research," *Review of Educational Research* 57, 4 (Winter): 415–35.

Gamoran, A. and M. Berends, 1987, "The Effects of Stratification in Secondary Schools: Synthesis of Survey and Ethnographic Research," *Review of Educational Research* 57, 4: 415–35.

Gamoran, A. and R. G. Mare, 1989, "Secondary School Tracking and Educational Inequality: Compensation, Reinforcement, or Neutrality?" *American Journal of Sociology* 94: 1146–83.

Garet, M. S. and B. Delaney, 1988, "Students, Courses and Stratification," *Sociology of Education* 61: 61–77.

George, N., 1998, *Hip Hop America*, New York: Viking Press.

Good, T. L., 1987, "Two Decades of Research on Teacher Expectations: Findings and Future Directions," *Journal of Teacher Education* 38, 4: 32–47.

Greenwald, R., L. V. Hedges, and R. D. Laine, 1996, "The Effect of School Resources on Student Achievement," *Review of Educational Research* 66: 361–96.

Haller, E. J., 1985, "Pupil Race and Elementary School Ability Grouping: Are Teachers Biased Against Black Children?" *American Educational Research Journal* 22, 4: 465–83.

Haycock, K., C. Jerald, and S. Huang, 2001, "Closing the Gap: Done in a Decade," *Thinking K-16: A Publication of the Education Trust* 5, 2: 1–21.

Hernstein, R. J. and C. Murray, 1994, *The Bell Curve: Intelligence and Class Structure in American Life*, New York: Free Press.

Hauser, R. M. and M. Huang, 1996, "Trends in Black–White Test Score Differentials," University of Wisconsin, Madison, Institute for Research on Poverty, Discussion Paper 1110–96.

Johnson, W. R. and D. Neal, 1998, "Basic Skills and the Black–White Earnings Gap," in C. Jencks and M. Phillips (eds.), *The Black–White Test Score Gap*, Washington, DC: Brookings Institution Press, pp. 480–97.

Krueger, A. B., 2000, "Understanding the Magnitude and Effect of Class Size on Student Achievement," *Economic Policy Institute*, Working Paper No. 121.

Krueger, A. B. and D. Whitmore, 2001, "Would Smaller Classes Help Close the Black–White Achievement Gap?" Paper presented at the Brookings Institution Conference, "Closing the Gap: Promising Approaches to Reducing the Achievement Gap" (January).

Kulik, J. A., 1992, "An Analysis of the Research on Ability Grouping: Historical and Contemporary Perspectives," A publication of the National Center on the Gifted and Talented, the University of Connecticut.

Lazear, E. P., 1999, "Education Production," Working Paper No. 7349. Cambridge, MA: National Bureau of Economic Research.

Lee, V. E. and A. S. Bryk, 1988, "Curriculum Tracking as Mediating the Social Distribution of High School Achievement," *Sociology of Education* 61: 78–94.

Loveless, T., 1998, "The Tracking and Ability Grouping Debate," *Fordham Report* 2 (http://www.edexcellence.net/library/track.html).

Ludwig, J., H. F. Ladd, and G. J. Duncan, 2001, "The Effects of Urban Poverty on Educational Outcomes: Evidence from a Randomized Experiment," *Brookings-Wharton Papers on Urban Affairs.*

Metz, M. H., 1978, *Classrooms and Corridors: The Crisis of Authority in Desegregated Secondary Schools*, Berkeley, CA: University of California Press.

Myrdal, G., 1944, *An American Dilemma: The Negro Problem and Modern Democracy*, New York: Harper.

Nisbett, R. E., 1998, "Race, Genetics and IQ," in C. Jencks and M. Phillips (eds.), *The Black–White Test Score Gap*, Washington, DC: Brookings Institution Press, pp. 86–102.

Oakes, J., 1985, *Keeping Track: How Schools Structure Inequality*, New Haven, CT: Yale University Press.

Pallas, A. M., D. R. Entwisle, K. L. Alexander, and M. F. Stluka, 1994, "Ability-Group Effects: Instructional, Social, or Institutional?" *Sociology of Education* 67: 27–46.

Phillips, M., J. Brooks-Gunn, G. J. Duncan, P. Klebanor, and J. Crane, 1998, "Family Background, Parenting Practices, and the Black–White Test Score Gap," in C. Jencks and M. Phillips (eds.), *The Black–White Test Score Gap.* Washington, DC: Brookings Institution Press, pp. 103–45.

Phillips, M., 2000, "Understanding Ethnic Differences in Ethnic Achievement: Empirical Lessons from National Data," in D. W. Grissmer and J. M. Ross (eds.), *Analytic Issues in the Assessment of Student Achievement*, Washington, DC: National Center for Education Statistics, pp. 103–32.

Raudenbush, S. W., 2000, "Synthesizing Results from the NAEP Trial State Assessment," in D. W. Grissmer and J. M. Ross (eds.), *Analytic Issues in the Assessment of Student Achievement*, Washington, DC: National Center for Education Statistics, pp. 3–42.

Ryan, J. E., 1999, "Schools, Race and Money," *Yale Law Journal* 109: 249–316.

Schwartz, F., 1981, "Supporting or Subverting Learning: Peer Group Patterns in Four Tracked Schools," *Anthropology and Education Quarterly,* 12: 99–121.

Sorensen, A. B. and M. Hallinan, 1984, "Effects of Race on Assignment to Ability Groups," in P. L. Peterson, L. C. Wilkinson, and M. Hallinan (eds.), *The Social Context of Instruction*, New York: Academic Press, pp. 85–103.

12 Networks and niches: the continuing significance of ethnic connections

Roger Waldinger

At the top of the immigration research agenda stands the question of how the newcomers change after they have arrived. The conventional wisdom, both academic and popular, says that immigrants *should* change by entering the American mainstream. The concept of assimilation stands as a shorthand for this point of view.

In its canonical form, the theory of assimilation began with the assumption that immigrants would arrive as "ethnics," an identity reinforced by their tendency to recreate their own social worlds. Cultural change would come first, as Americanization made the second generation quite different from their forebears in tastes, everyday habits, and preferences. But Americanization could proceed even as the ethnic social structure of interpersonal relations largely stood still: as long as immigrants and their descendants remained embedded in ethnic neighborhoods, networks, and niches, integration into the fabric of American society would have to wait. Once ethnic boundaries were crossed, however, increasing exposure probabilities to outsiders would inevitably pull ethnic communities apart: with the move from ethnic ghetto to suburb, interethnic friendships, networks, and eventually marriages would all follow in due course. Thus, the advent of structural assimilation, to borrow the influential term coined by Milton Gordon, signaled entry into the "mainstream," and the beginning of the end for any distinctiveness associated with the immigrant generation (Gordon 1964).

All this is now entirely familiar to the students of American ethnicity. But perhaps too much so, since the canonical view had little, if anything to say, about the driving force behind changing contact probabilities – namely, movement out of the socioeconomic cellar. All that one can do is to infer the likeliest answer: that economic progress took the form of dispersion from the occupational or industrial clusters that immigrants initially established. After all, from the assimilationist standpoint, concentration is a source of disadvantage, to be explained by lack of skills and education. With acculturation and growing levels of schooling and American experience, immigrants and their children would naturally move upward by filtering outward from the ethnic niche.

Today's scholars, however, tend not to agree. The emphasis, instead, is on the connections that bind the newcomers together and the resources generated by the contacts that crisscross the immigrant communities. These ties constitute a source of "social capital," providing social structures that facilitate action, in this case the search for jobs and the acquisition of skills and other resources needed to move up the economic ladder. Networks tying veterans to newcomers allow for rapid transmission of information about openings in workplaces or opportunities for new business start-ups. Networks also provide better information within workplaces, reducing the risks associated with initial hiring, and similarly connecting coethnic entrepreneurs, who take membership in the community as an index of trust (Bailey and Waldinger 1991). Once in place, the networks are self-reproducing, since each incumbent recruits friends or relatives from his or her own group, and entrepreneurs gravitate to the cluster of business opportunities that their associates in the community have already identified. Relationships among coethnics are likely to be many-sided, rather than specialized, leading community effects to go beyond their informational value, and engendering both codes of conduct, and the mechanisms for sanctioning those who violate norms (Portes and Sensenbrenner 1993). In other words, concentration is the way to go, with the search for advancement taking a *collective*, not an individual form, as network-dense communities provide the informational base and support mechanisms for a pattern of parallel movement up the economic ladder.[1]

So goes the now conventional wisdom among many of today's immigration specialists. These views are most likely to resonate with sociologists and anthropologists, but they are hardly confined to these particular disciplinary tribes alone. The economist Glenn Loury was one of the first to invoke "social capital" as a factor facilitating movement up from the bottom, arguing most recently that "each individual is socially situated, and one's location within the network of social affiliations substantially affects one's access to various resources" (Loury 1998). George Borjas, certainly a card-carrying, neoclassical economist, has essentially endorsed the same point of view, showing that access to resources shared by the group as a whole can redound to the individual's benefit (Borjas 1994). And similar perspectives can be found among political scientists and other authorities of the same type.

Of course, not everyone has signed on to the program. There remain numerous defenders of the old-time religion, who continue to argue that dispersion remains the best, and more importantly, the most common way by which immigrants and their descendants move up the economic ladder (Alba and Nee 1997). And even the exponents of the new point of view are divided on almost as many points as they agree. There is uncertainty as to how best to characterize the clusters that immigrants have established – are they ethnic economies, ethnic enclaves, ethnic niches, or perhaps even some other neologism that better captures the phenomenon? Just what name to use matters, because each concept denotes a somewhat different phenomenon, each varying in nature and extent. Whether one opts for the most restricted or most expansive appellation, questions of how to explain the emergence and persistence of ethnic niches remain in play. So too is the future of the phenomenon: is this simply a matter of cultural lag, found only among the most disadvantaged of workers and in the most traditional of work settings? Or do the circumstances that foster the consolidation of ethnic networks reappear among more skilled workers engaged in complex tasks and in up-to-date organizational settings? And is the ethnic niche simply a property of immigrants or rather a recurrent form of social organization, in which case the concentrations established by other, earlier-established groups of outsiders shape the options open to today's newcomers? These are the questions to which this paper is addressed.

Ethnic enclaves, economies, or niches: the play of debate

That immigrants tend to gravitate toward a narrow set of economic activities and then stay there is neither new nor news. The historical literature on American immigration is replete with observations on the predilections of immigrants for trades and occupations of various kinds. Scholars studying chain migration naturally noticed that newcomers moving from the same hometown not only became neighbors in the new world but often worked alongside one another. As is the case today, clustering was always more pronounced among some groups than among others. Jewish immigrants from Poland were a particularly noticed and noticeable example, establishing not only *landsmannschaften* – hometown associations – but also a *landsmannschaft economy*, a striking concept coined by Moses Rischin, but one that somehow never got much intellectual circulation (Rischin 1962).

So immigration scholars were always sensitive to the specializations with which the newcomers so frequently began. But ideological and academic preoccupation with assimilation led attention to wander elsewhere: the social science analysis of immigrant adaptation developed analytic tools and concepts to study such phenomena as intermarriage or residential change, but not the ethnic structuring of the occupational order. For the most part, the state of thinking was pretty much captured by Stanley Lieberson, in his influential 1980 book *A Piece of the Pie*, who used the term "special niches" to note that "most racial and ethnic groups tend to develop concentrations in certain jobs," reflecting cultural characteristics, special skills, or opportunities available at the time of arrival, but pretty much left the matter there (Lieberson 1980).

The ethnic enclave

What led social scientists to think differently was renewed interest in, and appreciation of, that much maligned social category, the *petite bourgeoisie*. Small business had always been an immigrant and ethnic specialty, but too insignificant to get more than the passing academic nod, until Ivan Light wrote his seminal *Ethnic Enterprise in America*. Light's central point, that ethnic solidarity propelled business growth among Japanese, Chinese, and West Indian immigrants, can now be seen as a formulation of embeddedness *avant la lettre*; but widely as the book was read, its historical focus blunted its broader impact on the ways in which social scientists thought about immigrant progress (Light 1972).

Instead, the catalytic intellectual development resulted from the publication of Franklin Wilson and Alejandro Portes' article on the Cuban "Immigrant Enclave" in Miami, almost twenty-five years ago (Wilson and Portes 1980). Reporting on the initial wave of a longitudinal survey of newly arrived Cuban refugees and their labor market experiences in Miami from 1973 to 1976, Wilson and Portes (1980) found that a sizable proportion of the newcomers went to work for coethnics. They also discovered that those who worked for immigrant bosses were doing better than refugees employed in white-owned, secondary-sector firms – which in turn prompted a piece of scholarly revisionism that became known as the "ethnic enclave hypothesis." What earlier observers had seen as a sweatshop, Wilson and Portes recast as an apprenticeship: low wages for a couple of terms of labor in the ethnic economy – dubbed the "enclave" – in return for which one learns the tools of the trade in order to set up on one's own and thus move ahead.

The scholarly news about Miami's Cuban ethnic economy and its impact provoked immense interest, for reasons having to do with policy and theory. After all, the central question in immigration research concerns the prospects for immigrants and their children. The research on the Cubans suggested that at least some would move ahead successfully; and more startlingly, they would do so on their own, turning disadvantage to good account. But if Cubans, and possibly other, entrepreneurially active groups, could use business as a stepping stone, how was one to account for this state of affairs? An earlier wave of research had shown that other visibly identifiable minorities were trapped in the "secondary labor market," unable to move into the "primary labor market," where employment was more stable, job arrangements allowed for upward mobility, and workers were rewarded for investments in skill and training (Gordon 1972, Piore 1979). Indeed, Portes' own research showed that this same pattern persisted among recent Mexican immigrants (Portes and Bach 1985). The puzzle was all the more compelling because the industries that comprised the Cuban ethnic economy also made up the "secondary sector." The same structural factors that impeded skill acquisition, attachment (to a particular firm, industry, or labor market), and upward mobility in the secondary sector also characterized the ethnic enclave. Yet, workers in the enclave appeared to enjoy some of the advantages associated with the primary sector.

As to be expected with any attention-grabbing piece, the ethnic enclave hypothesis quickly led to an ethnic enclave debate. It soon became apparent that the phenomenon to which Portes drew attention was not so easily identified in the other capitals of immigrant America. In the unusual immigrant metropolis of Miami – where the largest group of newcomers were also middle-class refugees – Cubans appeared to provide ample employment to others of their own kind. Though by definition, employment of coethnics served as a distinguishing feature of the enclave, scholars eventually noted that this characteristic was relatively uncommon: immigrant entrepreneurship could be found aplenty; instances where immigrant owners *and* workers were overrepresented in the very same activity was a good deal more rare (Logan, Alba, and McNulty 1994).

The concept of the ethnic *enclave* also proved limiting. *Enclave* denotes segregation within a particular territorial configuration. And Portes' original elaboration made the enclave into a case of a still more special kind, depicting the enclave as not only geographically distinct, but as a self-supporting economy generating a variety of inputs and outputs itself. The notion of self-sufficiency was a non-starter from the very beginning: if the largest cities are far from self-supporting, how could small ethnic enclaves do any better? Moreover, our knowledge of immigrant economies shows that they are not spread throughout the economy, but rather highly specialized in a few industries or business lines where ethnic firms can enjoy competitive advantages. Likewise, the emphasis on spatial concentration proved a red herring: though many immigrant neighborhoods serve as the fount of business activity, immigrant entrepreneurs spring up throughout the urban landscape – whether there are lots of coethnic customers to be found or not. Clearly, space may be a variable affecting immigrant entrepreneurial outcomes, but there seems little reason to treat it as a defining characteristic.[2]

But the greatest problems had to do with the central finding itself: that immigrant workers laboring for a coethnic boss did better than those employed in *comparable jobs*, but engaged by an Anglo employer. The immediate issue was how to explain this apparent anomaly; the initial literature didn't help matters by offering a number of different accounts. Ethnic solidarity was one of the possibilities invoked: "Immigrant entrepreneurs," wrote Portes and Bach in *Latin Journey*, "rely upon the economic potential of ethnic solidarity." They continue:

[E]thnicity modifies the character of the class relationship – capital and labor – within the enclave. Ethnic ties suffuse an otherwise "bare" relationship with a sense of collective purpose in contrast to the outside. But the utilization of ethnic solidarity in lieu of enforced discipline in the workplace also entails reciprocal obligations. If employers can profit from the willing self-exploitation of fellow immigrants, they are also obliged to reserve for them those supervisory positions that open in their firms, to train them in trade skills, and to support their eventual move into self-employment. It is the fact that enclave firms are compelled to rely on ethnic solidarity and that the latter "cuts both ways," which creates opportunities for mobility unavailable in the outside. (Portes and Bach 1985: 345)

This story was plausible, but *Latin Journey* didn't adequately tie down the case. In the end, one is forced to conclude that Portes and Bach *assumed* solidarity, a presupposition which they never had any necessity to entertain. A more parsimonious view would simply have suggested that the development of ethnic networks would generate the infrastructure and resources for ethnic small businesses *before* a sense of group awareness or solidarity need develops. In the end, Portes himself moved on to a view of this sort, arguing that "bounded solidarity" and "enforceable trust" – *emergent* community characteristics related to the development of ethnic networks – provided the necessary ingredients for both mobilizing resources and limiting obligations, thereby making exchanges within the ethnic enclave reciprocal, and *not* exploitative.[3]

Conceptual niceties aside, the nub of the problem involved replication. Victor Nee and Jimy Sanders fired the opening salvo: looking at the Chinese in San Francisco and the Cubans in south Florida, they found that self-employment was good for the immigrant bosses, but much less satisfactory for the immigrants most likely to work in their shops (Sanders and Nee 1987). Min Zhou and John Logan then added nuance, showing that male Chinese immigrants in New York did indeed benefit from working in industries of Chinese concentration, but that their female counterparts had no such luck (Zhou and Logan 1989, Zhou 1992).

Greta Gilbertson, who examined the experience of Colombians and Dominicans in New York, came up with results that essentially supported Nee and Sanders' critique (Gilbertson and Gurak 1993 and Gilbertson 1995). Portes, needless to say, fired back, but with conclusions a good deal more modest than those that he had originally advanced – namely, that workers in the enclave *do no worse* than those at work elsewhere.[4] Debate on the matter continues, but in the meantime the theoretical action has moved elsewhere.[5]

The ethnic niche

As we have noted above, the particular economic configuration identified as an "enclave" is a relatively rare element in the immigrant employment scene. Miami may have an enclave, as conventionally defined, of sizable dimensions; so too, do the Chinatowns of San Francisco and New York, but one then quickly begins to run out of cases. Moreover, some of the immigrant groups with the highest self-employment levels seem to be particularly unlikely to exhibit the pattern associated with Miami's Cubans. The Koreans, for example, are renowned for their entrepreneurial success, with self-employment rates well above the levels attained by the Cubans. But Korean owners largely make do with a non-Korean workforce, in part, because small business ownership has simply swept up so many Korean immigrants that there are too few coethnics for Korean bosses to hire.[6] And the Korean story is hardly unique, as Ivan Light and his collaborators have shown in their work on the Iranians in Los Angeles. Admittedly, this group is not typical, as they are refugees with the good fortune of arriving with ample capital and entrepreneurial experience to boot (Der-Martirosian 1996, Light and Karageorgis 1994). But even so the example is entirely relevant: Iranians have scored tremendous business success and doing so without a coethnic labor force. Similar stories can be told for Israelis, Arabs, Russians, Greeks, Indians, and a variety of other immigrants who have made their mark in small business.[7] In effect, the old middleman minority pattern, exemplified in earlier immigration history by American Jews, remains alive, well, and a good deal more common than the ethnic enclave of immigrant bosses and their coethnic workers.

Moreover, the underlying sociological processes — involving the mobilization of information, capital, and support through ethnic social networks – characterize both the middleman minority phenomenon and the ethnic enclave as well. While there may well be differences between immigrant-owned firms that recruit outsiders and those that rely on insiders, these seem to be differences of degree, not kind, with plenty of within-group variation along the coethnic employment axis, as well as movement over time. Just as one would consider immigrant businesses that sell to a coethnic clientele and those that sell on the general market as variants of a common type, so too does it seem appropriate to think of the ethnic enclave and the middleman minority situation exemplified by Koreans or Iranians as special cases of the "ethnic economy" writ large – as convincingly argued by Ivan Light (Light and Karageorgis 1994).

Self-employment is a particularly prominent, and these days, much discussed, instance of immigrant economic specialization; but it is hardly the major feature. As an *ethnic* phenomenon, employment concentration shows up elsewhere – most notably, in the well-known propensity to find jobs in the public sector, a tradition pioneered by the Irish, and taken up by others, most notably African-Americans. As we have shown elsewhere, the public-sector story has some distinctive elements, but the crucial ingredients involved in the establishment of an employment concentration seem much the same, whether the locus is private or government sector, or for that matter, wage and salary work as contrasted to entrepreneurship (Waldinger 1996: Chapter 7).

Most importantly, immigrants tend to cluster in activities where others of their own kind have already gotten established. Initial placements, just as in Lieberson (1980), may be affected by any range of factors – prior experience, cultural preferences, or historical accident. But once the initial settlers have established a beachhead, subsequent arrivals tend to follow behind, preferring an environment in which at least some faces are familiar and finding that personal contacts prove the most efficient way of finding a job. More importantly, the predilections of immigrants match the preference of employers, who try to reproduce the characteristics of the workers whom they already have. Managers appreciate network recruitment for its ability to attract applicants quickly and at little cost; they value it even more for its efficiency. Hiring through connections upgrades the quality of information, reducing the risks entailed in acquiring new personnel; since sponsors usually have a stake in their job, they can also be relied on to keep their referrals in line. The process works a little differently in business, where early success sends later arrivals an implicit signal about the types of companies to start, and the business lines to seek out or avoid. An expanding business sector then provides both a mechanism for the effective transmission of skill and a catalyst for the entrepreneurial drive: the opportunity to acquire managerial skills through a stint of employment in immigrant firms both compensates for low pay and motivates workers to learn a variety of jobs.[8] Thus, the repeated action of immigrant social networks yields the ethnic niche: a set of economic activities in which immigrants are heavily concentrated.

Networks and social closure

A network-based account, such as the one offered above, suffers from a built-in contradiction: it does a nice job of explaining why tomorrow's workforce looks a good deal like today's; it doesn't tell us how today's labor force configuration came to be.[9] The relationship between today and tomorrow is not difficult to understand: the established immigrant workers learn about job openings before anyone else; once in the know, they run to tell their friends and relatives. They also reassure the boss that their referrals are just the right candidates to fill the vacancies, a pledge that sounds all the more meaningful when the boss thinks that birds of a feather flock together, and likes the birds he currently has.

But today is *not* like yesterday: at some point, today's immigrant veterans were outsiders, knocking on doors, with few if any contacts inside. How did the tables turn? To some extent, we have already provided the answer. On the one hand, conditions at the very bottom of the labor market are such that workers engage in extensive churning; in other words, a high turnover rate produces constant vacancies. On the other hand, we can expect that immigrants will be more apt to apply for entry-level jobs than anyone else, precisely for the reasons mentioned above: the conditions and stigma associated with the economy's "bad jobs" motivates natives to seek other options whenever possible. So even if once excluded, immigrants can rapidly build up concentrations in these jobs. In the process, the number of immigrants with the ability to help a friend or family member get a job and keep it quickly increases. Given bosses' usual preference for recruiting from inside, the immigrant presence automatically grows.

This type of explanation tells us why there are lots of immigrant sweepers and kitchen helpers, but if those were the only possibilities, opportunities would be very limited and low-skill migration streams would be a good deal smaller than they are today. Network theory, however, contends that migration quickly becomes a self-feeding process and that once the first crop of migrants takes hold, the networks will normally continue to grow.[10] For that to happen, some immigrant job-holders must come to possess more than the inside dope about the next dishwasher or janitor to be hired; they need to be in the position to grant access to better and more varied positions to their needy friends and kin. In other words, they have to either rise to positions of authority, or else somehow compel the authorities to comply with their wishes. But how do stigmatized outsiders manage to gain such leverage?

The answer to that question lies in the power that social networks acquire when they are imported into the workplace. In general, workers will use their networks to find jobs, and employers will use workers' networks to hire workers because networks give both sides the *information* they need. Workers learn about job openings and job characteristics through the networks, while employers learn about worker availability and worker characteristics. Networks can also improve the employment relationship by serving as the conduit for a set of understandings shared by both workers and managers. Thus, a quid pro quo develops. Social control within the workers' network keeps their recalcitrant comrades in line. In return, the employer gives special consideration to the friends and relatives of incumbent workers.[11]

Over time, however, the balance of power in the relationship between workers and employer may shift. As network penetration of the workplace solidifies, the ties linking veteran workers with their associates looking for work can serve goals not in line with those of the employer. Employers turn to immigrant networks to fill specific hiring needs, but as long as newcomers keep flowing into the network, it will eventually reach up and attempt to bite into management's normally sacrosanct authority. To begin with, incumbents are naturally positioned to exercise influence over the hiring process. If one group enjoys privileged access to information about job vacancies, outsiders automatically find themselves at a disadvantage. Secondly, the connections that bring ethnic communities into the workplace also become the means for excluding workers who aren't members of the same ethnic club. If work is a fundamentally social activity, and if the necessary skills are learned through interaction with others on the job, a worker must earn the acceptance and cooperation of the numerically dominant group – otherwise one can't learn the needed skills or function on the job. In other words, once a group has constructed a stronghold, it is likely to both put forward its own candidates and block the integration of others hired over its opposition. Thus, the ties that bind the workforce comprise a resource that group members can use to maintain and expand their share of employment in a firm, even against management's wishes.

Of course, the reader should realize that the properties described above aren't unique to *immigrant* networks alone. The Old-Boy network of private boarding schools and country clubs need take lessons from no one when it comes to using connections to exclude. Craft unions in the construction trades know how to use informal ties among their (skilled) workers to play the same game, stomping on the employer's ability to run the firm as he (usually it is a he) would like. African-Americans have also successfully implanted networks in particular sectors of the economy, especially government, and these have expanded in much the same way described above, as we shall now see.

African-Americans and the public sector

Government employment offers the one bright light in the generally dim black jobs scene: the public sector now looms as the largest, highest-quality employer of African-Americans. In 1990, one out of every four employed blacks held a government job; close to half of the country's African-American civil servants worked on municipal payrolls.[12] Blacks hold a much higher share of upper-level jobs in the public than in the private sector; discrimination exerts a less powerful influence on public-sector employees than on their private-sector counterparts; and the public sector seems to do better as a ladder of mobility into the middle class for blacks than for whites (Fainstein and Fainstein 1994).

Government may now be a prime concentration of black employment; that wasn't always the case. As I explained in Waldinger (1996), a book about African-Americans and immigrants in New York, African-American convergence on the public sector involved a protracted process, in which African-Americans simultaneously replaced Euro-American workers in the least desirable public functions, while contending with Euro-American workers and their organizations over access to the more desirable jobs. Blacks entered municipal service at the bottom during the first half of the twentieth century; there, they found a structure – bequeathed to them by interethnic conflicts among Irish, Italians, and Jews – that made it hard to get ahead. In the 1960s and the 1970s, the search for mobility led to open and intense conflict with these Euro-American, ethnic workers, who had earlier colonized the civil service. While these first confrontations were partly successful at best, due to changes in the power and social structure of Euro-America, incumbent groups yielded a new ethnic division of labor in the 1980s. Blacks replaced Euro-American ethnics who moved up the labor queue and fell out of the city's labor supply, a process facilitated by political changes that opened up civil service structures. By 1990, African-Americans had emerged as the successors to the Irish, while other outsider groups, most notably Hispanics, enjoyed much scantier access to the public's jobs (Waldinger 1996: Chapters 4 and 7).

While Waldinger (1996) tells the story of an important case, one might still ask whether the New York experience is unique, or reappears in other contexts as well. As Lim (2001) shows in a study of America's five key immigrant urban regions – New York, Los Angeles, Chicago, Miami, and San Francisco – government is the key African-American concentration in each place. More importantly, trends over the 1970 to 1990 period demonstrate growing isomorphism, both in the degree of public-sector concentration and in the specific public functions in which

African-Americans concentrated. In 1970, African-American niches often varied from region to region, with concentrations reflecting the particular types of opportunities available in each place – for example, blast furnaces in Chicago, or apparel in Los Angeles. By 1990, six public sector industries – welfare services, mass transit, the postal service, other health service, hospitals, and federal public administration – had become black niches in all five regions, a trait characteristic of local public administration in all regions but San Francisco. Furthermore, such industries as domestic services, hotels, or laundries, that had historically absorbed high levels of black employment in almost all five places, shifted from over- to underrepresentation during the 1970–90 period. Most striking was the thinning out in the number of black niches, as the remaining concentrations, which still absorbed a large proportion of total black employment, were now clustered in a very small number of industries. Examining the ten largest African-American niches in each region, Lim found that these fifty cases actually involved only eighteen separate industries.

As Lim argued, the isomorphic nature of the African-American niches in all five regions underscores the ethnic nature of the black employment pattern: clustering in the public sector represents one of the distinguishing traits of this group. The isomorphic nature of the niches further suggests that the underlying force producing concentration was likely to have been endogenous. Though the five regions encompass America's leading immigrant places, they do vary greatly in the relative size and composition of their immigrant populations. And yet, the types of concentrations toward which blacks have gravitated differ little from place to place: roughly the same set of clusters show up in Miami – where immigrants comprise 41 percent of the workforce – as in Chicago – where the foreign-born workforce is just over 15 percent. Much the same can be said for the specializations from which African-Americans exited: for example, why should laundries have disappeared as an African-American concentration in all five regions, were there not some other set of factors – independent of immigration – that should have weakened African-Americans' attachment to this industry?

The pattern unlocked by Lim may help explain why so many researchers have concluded that immigration has had only a modest, if any, negative impact on the employment chances of blacks. In converging on government, African-Americans also moved into a niche whose properties impeded immigrant penetration. In general, government work requires modest levels of skills and schooling, producing a formidable barrier to the entry of immigrants without a high-school education – roughly one quarter of the US total. Getting a government job usually requires formal application and passage of an examination, requirements which further hinder the route to newcomers who, if literate, may be leery of government and unfamiliar with established procedures. And the powerful civil service unions, themselves highly responsive to the interests of their African-American members, when not headed up by African-American leaders, consistently act in ways that keep job requirements high – and therefore in reach of people just like the existing union members.

That African-Americans found employment gains in the public sector also highlights the positive factors associated with immigration. The decades following 1970 were years when America's leading immigrant places were losing their hold on their native-born population. Were it not for immigration, their populations would have almost certainly shrunk, which in turn would have made for a greatly reduced demand for public services and public funds allocated for such services. To the extent that immigrants swelled the demand for public employment, even as the employment structure of the public sector remained unusually closed to foreign-born workers, the inflow of immigration may have generated distinctive benefits for native-born African-Americans, whose dependency on public-sector jobs has grown over the years.

On the other hand, the same traits that impede immigrant entry into the public sector also tends to exclude African-American workers with limited schooling from those industries of greatest African-American densities. For instance, skill or credential requirements in the public sector make it difficult, if not impossible, for the least skilled of African-American workers to exploit the ethnic networks implanted in government employment. At the same time, these least-skilled workers must find employment in a market increasingly saturated with immigrants, where the likelihood of working as a member of a small, quantitative minority – and therefore, easily harassed and vulnerable – grows steadily. Moreover, the circumstances under which African-Americans moved into the public sector no longer hold. For much of the time in question, government was a growth sector, which made it easier for federal, state, and local governments to incorporate African-American workers without totally alienating the established white rank and file. Now, however, government is clearly a declining enterprise.

What is more, immigrants – or if not immigrants, then their descendants – increasingly want greater access to those public-sector jobs that remain. In this light, it is important to note that the same processes that opened up public jobs for African-Americans in the late twentieth century are likely to work in the opposite direction in years to come. The visibility of public-sector employment made it a particularly convenient target for the application of affirmative action. Transparency made it difficult for government officials to defend functions that did a poor job of recruiting African-Americans and likewise made it easier for advocacy groups to focus their efforts on those departments that were lagging in the effort. That same characteristic, however, now highlights the degree of African-American overrepresentation in a situation where their population shares are at best stagnant, if not declining, and where the new immigrant populations have generally yet to attain parity. What is more, the changing demographic situation is also steadily undermining black political influence in the leading immigrant cities, a process bound to accelerate as rates of immigrant naturalization and voting grow.

Networks and niches in a high-tech economy

The sociological literature prepares us to expect that niches are the refuge for immigrants lacking in skill, education, or language ability; others, more equipped to enter the mainstream of the US labor market, should disperse out of the ethnic concentration in short order. The matter is of no small moment, since contemporary immigration to the United States is characterized by socioeconomic diversity: unlike the past, when the newcomers were concentrated at the bottom of the socioeconomic ladder, today's arrivals span the entire occupational spectrum, with a sizable portion moving into the middle or above.

But the extraordinarily high concentration of immigrant engineers at the very heart of America's high-tech economy – Silicon Valley – suggests that ethnic clustering is not simply a vestigial phenomenon, but rather a distinctive aspect of the immigrant phenomenon, wherever it may appear.[13] In the conventional ethnic concentrations, lovingly studied by the literature, low standards of compensation, whether measured in relative or absolute terms, make the native-born labor force chronically unstable. Native workers seize the chance for better opportunities further up the ladder whenever economic expansion makes mobility possible. Moreover, the repeated association between low-quality jobs and the stigmatized outsider groups who fill them has the lasting effect of reducing the *social* desirability of these positions, well below the level one would expect based on monetary rewards and conditions of work alone. Once natives flee and immigrants step in, the process is difficult to reverse.

In high technology, however, the long-term instability in the demand for high-skilled labor created the conditions whereby immigrant networks could take root and get implanted. The production of scientific and engineering workers is a protracted process, especially at the high end, where it takes four years of college and at least two years of graduate studies to obtain the necessary skills. But for the past thirty years, the demand for highly trained scientific and engineering personnel has gone through many gyrations. Consequently, the market for high-technology labor has been characterized by a cobweb cycle, in which new workers have been successively over- and then underproduced, a pattern with particularly pronounced effects on the highest-skilled workers, for whom the monetary and opportunity costs of skill-acquisition are particularly great.

Under these circumstances, the growth of the high-technology sector has repeatedly swollen the demand for professional and technical labor in a way that prompted sourcing from abroad. India, Taiwan, Korea, and other newly industrialized countries built up their own capacity to produce scientific labor, with all the proficiencies required to meet industry's needs in the United States. Moreover, the US system of postgraduate training offered a convenient point of entry: while the cobweb cycle has persistently discouraged the bachelor's graduates of American institutions from pursuing additional formal training, it has also left the graduate schools of engineering with underutilized capacity, for which the turn to a heavily foreign-born and-trained student body has been a source of relief. In this respect, foreign students have a very different cost/benefit calculus than their US-trained counterparts, for whom the diminishing relative returns associated with each year of postgraduate study are the most relevant considerations. For foreign students, however, entry into a US graduate engineering program greatly increases the probability of subsequent entry into the US labor market. And permanent migration to the United States remains attractive, since notwithstanding rapid economic growth in the Asia-Pacific region, the United States still offers far superior employment and career opportunities, not to speak of the social amenities associated with an American lifestyle.

And thus, in an ironic reversal of the expected pattern, the pattern of immigrant concentration is most marked at the highest end of the high-tech labor market. As of the late 1990s, engineers and systems analysts had a slight tendency toward immigrant concentration, as the foreign-born index of representation in these occupations stood at 1.09. But the degree of concentration varied with sector and skill. Within high technology, the index of immigrant representation stood at 1.3. And within the high-tech sector, immigrants were still more overrepresented among those best-educated workers with a Master's degree or more: within the high-tech sector overall, these best-educated foreign-born workers had a representation rate of 1.9, topped at 2.6 by the best-educated immigrants among the ranks of engineers and systems analysts working in high tech.[14]

So succession processes operate at the high – and not just at the low – end of the labor market. While the factors that facilitate immigrants' entry into high tech take a somewhat different form from those at work in less-skilled sectors, the role of networks is much the same. The costs of recruitment are high, which is why high-tech firms mobilize the contacts of the existing workforce whenever possible. Once firms learn to recognize the skills that foreign-born professionals possess, and also negotiate any of the obstacles that might impede access (such as the elaborate system of visas for "temporary" professional workers), they then return to the source. Experienced workers are preferred to those without the immediately relevant skills, a category that includes new graduates, since the costs of training are high, the organizational resources are lean, and the proficiencies general. Globalization essentially diffuses the same skills worldwide, which means that a technical proficiency learned in a foreign context can easily be put to use in an American setting; that foreign professionals may have previously worked in a transnational American corporation makes their expertise all the more transferable. Moreover, foreign graduate students in US universities develop a high level of groupness: living in an alien context, experiencing high levels of ethnic density, living and studying under conditions of frequent interaction, they build up the networks that facilitate parallel action during and after graduate school. Finally, the distinctive regional clusters associated with high technology lend a highly localized form to ethnic ties and, thus, facilitate the mobilization of ethnic resources. And so it should be no surprise that Silicon Valley, with its high levels of immigrant density, has spawned an elaborate infrastructure of organizations run by and oriented toward immigrant, high-technology entrepreneurs.

Conclusion

In a sense, this paper tells the oldest of stories, confirming that today's immigrants are following the timeworn paths of immigrants' past: linked by connections to established residents, and moving with the help and guidance provided by veterans, newcomers gravitate to the jobs where their compatriots have gotten started. Because migration is driven by networks, it also involves a process of social reproduction, in which the current crop of workers begets a new bunch that looks very much like themselves.

But there is also something new under the sun: the ethnic niches of the turn of the twenty-first century are not quite the same as the ethnic niches of yore. Yes, they are to be found at the bottom rungs of the occupational ladder, where workers with no other resource but social support necessarily rely for help from others of their own kind. But the distinctively new breed of immigrants – the newcomers who arrive with high levels of education – turn out to be no less likely to converge on niches than their less-skilled counterparts.

Of course, the pattern of ethnic niching is not an immigrant phenomenon alone. In older urban, immigrant regions, like New York or Chicago, earlier immigration histories set in motion a process of ethnic succession, which shaped both the timing and the sectoral destination of the pattern by which immigrants have moved into economic concentrations. Since groups concentrate in niches in response to disadvantage, it is no surprise that ethnic niching distinguishes African-Americans as well. To some extent, the contemporary African-American concentration in government reduces the potential for competition with immigrants; it would also seem to establish the preconditions for conflict in the relatively near future.

At once pervasive and persistent, the ethnic niche shows that ethnicity is not simply an imported cultural characteristic, but rather a principle of social organization, deeply shaping the role that immigrants play in America's dynamic economies at the turn of the twenty-first century America. The product of the largely unconscious actions of employers and workers, natives and immigrants, insiders and outsiders among the US-born, the niche also activates a set of boundary creating and maintaining mechanisms, providing groups with the motivation and the opportunity for excluding all those who aren't members of the same ethnic club.

NOTES

1. For a fuller elaboration of this argument, see Waldinger 1996.
2. For further elaboration along these lines, see Waldinger 1993. For a further discussion of the impact of spatial factors on ethnic economies, see Waldinger, McEvoy, and Aldrich 1990, Kaplan 1998. Of course, the paragraph above constructs the problem in relatively narrow terms, implying that the issue at hand involves the relationship between the spatial configurations of ethnic entrepreneurs and a set of economic outcomes (such as wages or business foundings), and nothing else. But, as Portes and Rumbaut argued in *Immigrant America*, to considerable success, the ethnic enclave, as *form of immigrant community*, can affect the process of immigrant incorporation in any number of ways. That effect is largely due to the enclave's status as an encompassing entity, cross-cut by a web of complex relations among coethnics of various sorts, where the density and multiplexity of ties produces considerable social control. The question is how those social control effects vary according to the spatial configuration of a community: are they dependent on recurrent face-to-face contacts, or do they persist under conditions of greater decentralization? To my (very possibly imperfect) knowledge, this question has not been systematically addressed.

3. Portes and Sensenbrenner 1993; for a fuller elaboration of these concepts see Portes and Zhou 1992 and Portes and Stepick 1993.

4. Portes and Jensen. For a more detailed review of the controversy, readers might want to consult Waldinger 1993. But I should note that many of the criticisms lodged at the enclave hypothesis strike me as mainly suited for scoring points, as opposed to illuminating our understanding of the question at hand. In particular, the conclusions arrived at by Sanders and Nee (1987) were clearly related to their own change in the terms of comparison, never clearly signaled to the reader. Whereas Portes and Bach (1985) mainly emphasized the advantages of the ethnic economy relative to the secondary sector, Sanders and Nee made the open economy (consisting of secondary *and* primary firms) the point of reference. This framing of the question seems to verge on straw-manning: to make the case for the ethnic economy one only need compare mobility opportunities in a Chinese restaurant to McDonald's – not to General Motors'. And it is precisely the fact that, in contrast to days of old, immigrants are unlikely to find employment among the dwindling General Motors-type employers, that makes the enclave an alternative worth taking seriously.

   As suggested in an earlier footnote, my summary of the debate may be framing the debate in excessively narrow terms. To some extent, the discussion may simply have taken a different turn, no longer concerned with the narrow economic effects of the enclave, but rather with its broader, and possibly longer-term social consequences. If it is the case that participation in an ethnic enclave exposes members to broader social resources not available to those group members with lower levels of community attachment, then the economic consequences of employment in an enclave firm – whether positive, negative, or simply benign, as compared to the generally unattractive alternatives – may be of lesser significance. For an argument along these lines, see Zhou and Bankston 1997. In my view, again possibly mistaken, the case is not settled.

5. It is also the case that the hypothesis has been loosened over time. At root, the original formulation simply specified a particular interaction between two variables – employment in primary, secondary, or ethnic sectors, on the one hand, and education on the other – contending that the return to education was greater in the ethnic enclave than in the secondary sector. The more recent renderings involve considerable broadening, as in Portes 1997, where he argues that "The real questions, from the standpoint of (the ethnic enclave) theory, are the viability of these firms, their capacity to spawn new enterprises, and the extent to which workers can become entrepreneurs themselves." This formulation seems to allow for the possibility that returns to education or experience among *workers* employed in enclave firms might be no different from those among workers in secondary firms. The impact of employment in an ethnic enclave would be observable only *after* that employment had ceased, enclave workers varying from the secondary sector counterparts in the greater probability that self-employment would succeed a stint of wage and salary work.

6. On the Koreans, Kim (1981) adds depth, brings the story up to date, and highlights the growing dependence of Korean entrepreneurs on non-Korean labor.

7. See, e.g., Gold and Phillips 1996.
8. Waldinger 1996: Chapters 1, 9, and *passim*; see also Waldinger 1994.
9. This section draws on my book, Waldinger and Litcher 2003. There, the argument is developed at much greater length, backed up with supporting material, based on extensive interviews with employers in Los Angeles.
10. As argued by Massey, Alarcon, and Durand 1987.
11. On the role of networks in matching workers with jobs, Granovetter 1995 is a basic source. See also Granovetter and Tilly 1988, Stevens 1978, Grieco 1987, and Powell and Smith-Doerr 1994.
12. Calculated from 1990 Census of Population, Table 47.
13. This section draws on my unpublished report on immigrants in the science and technology complex in California, prepared for the Alfred P. Sloan Foundation, 2000.
14. Representation rates calculated from a merged sample of the 1994–8 Current Population Survey; data for employed persons, 25–64 years old only. In this sample, 12.4 percent of all workers were foreign-born.

REFERENCES

Alba, R. and V. Nee, 1997, "Rethinking Assimilation Theory for a New Era of Immigration," *International Migration Review* 21: 826–74.

Bailey, T. and R. Waldinger, 1991, "Primary, Secondary and Enclave Labor Markets: A Training Systems Approach," *American Sociological Review* 56: 432–45.

Borjas, G., 1994, "Long-run Convergence of Ethnic Skill Differentials: The Children and Grandchildren of the Great Migration," *Industrial and Labor Relations Review* 47: 553–73.

Census of Population 1990, U.S. Summary Volume, United States Bureau of the Census: Washington, DC.

Current Population Survey 1994–1998, United States Bureau of the Census: Washington, DC.

Der Martirosian, C., 1996, "Economic Embeddedness and Social Capital of Immigrants: Iranians in Los Angeles," PhD dissertation, University of California Los Angeles.

Fainstein N. and S. Fainstein, 1994, "Urban Regimes and Black Citizens: The Economic and Social Impacts of Black Political Incorporation in US Cities," *International Journal of Urban and Regional Research* 20, 1: 22–37.

Gilbertson G., 1995, "Women's Labor and Enclave Employment: The Case of Dominican and Colombian Women in New York City," *International Migration Review* 29: 657–70.

Gilbertson, G. and D. Gurak, 1993, "Broadening the Ethnic Enclave Debate," *Sociological Forum* 8: 3.

Gold, S. and B. Phillips, 1996, "Israelis in the United States," *American Jewish Yearbook 1996*: 51–101.

Gordon, D., 1972, *Theories of Poverty and Unemployment: Orthodox, Radical, and Dual Labor Market Perspectives*, Lexington, MA: Heath.

Gordon M., 1964, *Assimilation in American Life*, New York: Oxford University Press.

Granovetter, M., 1995, *Getting a Job*, University of Chicago Press.

Granovetter M. and C. Tilly, 1988, "Inequality and Labor Processes," in N. Smelser (ed.), *Handbook of Sociology*, Newbury Park, CA: Sage, pp. 175–231.

Grieco, M., 1987, *Keeping it in the Family: Social Networks and Employment Chance*, London and New York: Tavistock.

Kaplan, D., 1998, "The Spatial Structure of Urban Ethnic Economies," *Urban Geography* 19: 489–501.

Kim I., 1981, *The New Urban Immigrants*, Princeton University Press.

Lieberson, S., 1980, *A Piece of the Pie*, Berkeley, CA: University of California Press.

Light, I., 1972, *Ethnic Enterprise in America*, Berkeley, CA: University of California Press.

Light, I. and S. Karageorgis, 1994, "The Ethnic Economy," in N. Smelser and R. Swedberg (eds.), *The Handbook of Economic Sociology*, Princeton University Press and New York: Russell Sage Foundation, pp. 647–71.

Light, I., G. Sabagh, M. Bozorgmehr, and C. Der-Martirosian, 1994, "Beyond the Ethnic Enclave Economy," *Social Problems* 41: 65–80.

Lim, N., 2001, "On the Back of Blacks? Immigrants and the Fortunes of African Americans," in R. Waldinger (ed.), *Strangers at the Gates: New Immigrants in Urban America*, Berkeley, CA: University of California Press, pp. 186–227.

Logan, J. R., R. Alba, and T. L. McNulty, 1994, "Ethnic Economies in Metropolitan Regions: Miami and Beyond," *Social Forces* 72: 691–724.

Loury, G. C., 1998, "Discrimination in the Post-Civil Rights Era: Beyond Market Interactions," *Journal of Economic Perspectives* 12: 117–26.

Massey, D., R. Alarcon, and Jorge Durand, 1987, *Return to Aztlan*, Berkeley, CA: University of California Press.

Min, P. G., 1996, *Caught in the Middle: Korean Communities in New York and Los Angeles*, Berkeley, CA: University of California Press.

Piore M., 1979, *Birds of Passage*, Cambridge University Press.

Portes, A., 1997, "Immigration Theory for a New Century: Some Problems and Opportunities," *International Migration Review 1997* 31: 799–825.

Portes, A. and R. Bach, 1985, *Latin Journey*, Berkeley, CA: University of California Press.

Portes A. and J. Sensenbrenner, 1993, "Embeddedness and Immigration: Notes on the Social Determination of Economic Action," *American Journal of Sociology* 98: 1320–50.

Portes A. and A. Stepick, 1993, *City on the Edge*, Berkeley, CA: University of California Press.

Portes, A. and M. Zhou, 1992, "Gaining the Upper Hand: Old and New Perspectives in the Study of Ethnic Minorities," *Ethnic and Racial Studies* 15: 491–522.

Powell, W. and L. Smith-Doerr, 1994, "Networks and Economic Life," in N. Smelser and R. Swedberg (eds.), *The Handbook of Economic Sociology*, Princeton University Press and New York: Russell Sage Foundation, pp. 368–402.

Rischin, M., 1962, *The Promised City*, Cambridge, MA: Harvard University Press.

Sanders J. and V. Nee, 1987, "Limits of Ethnic Solidarity in the Enclave Economy," *American Sociological Review* 52: 745–67.

Stevens, D., 1978, "A Reexamination of What is Known About Jobseeking Behavior in the United States," in *Labor Market Intermediaries, National Commission for Manpower Policy, Report no. 22*, pp. 55–104.

Waldinger, R., 1993, "The Ethnic Enclave Debate Revisited," *International Journal of Urban and Regional Research* 17, 3: 428–36.

1994, "The Making of an Immigrant Niche," *International Migration Review* 28: 3–30.

1996, *Still the Promised City? African-Americans and New Immigrants in Post-Industrial New York*, Cambridge, MA: Harvard University Press.

Waldinger, R. and M. Lichter, 2003, *How the Other Half Looks: Immigration and the Social Organization of Labour*, Berkeley, CA: University of California Press.

Waldinger, R., D. McEvoy, and H. Aldrich, 1990, "Spatial Dimensions of Opportunity Structures," in R. Waldinger, H. Aldrich, R. Ward, and associates (eds.), *Ethnic Entrepreneurs: Minority Business in Industrial Societies*, Newbury Park, CA: Sage, pp. 106–30.

Wilson, K. and A. Portes, 1980, "Immigrant Enclaves: An Analysis of the Labor Market Experiences of Cubans in Miami," *American Journal of Sociology* 88: 295–319.

Zhou, M., 1992, *Chinatown: The Socioeconomic Potential of an Immigrant Enclave*, Philadelphia: Temple University Press.

Zhou, M. and C. Bankston, 1997, *Growing Up American*, New York: Russell Sage.

Zhou, M. and J. Logan, 1989, "Returns on Human Capital in Ethnic Enclaves: New York City's Chinatown," *American Sociological Review* 54: 809–20.

13 Nonwhite origins, Anglo destinations: immigrants in the USA and Britain

Suzanne Model

Until very late in the twentieth century, the USA was the setting for most statistical studies of ethnic inequality; Canada ranked second, Australia a distant third. This situation reflected the high proportions of immigrants in these countries and the large amount of information that researchers could obtain about the foreign born. After World War II, however, the numbers immigrating to Europe began to grow. Today, annual immigration to Europe is twice as high as annual immigration to the "New World" (Widgren 1994). As a result, Europe's immigrants have attracted increasing amounts of research attention. Indeed, several European nations now field surveys explicitly designed to illuminate the experiences of their ethnic minorities.

Studies of Britain's ethnic minorities stand at the forefront of this new scholarship. The first survey specifically devoted to this population was launched in 1966; more exhaustive studies followed in 1974, 1982, and 1994. To be sure, in the early years, the data collected in these surveys were available only to a small group of scholars. But today researchers can obtain the responses to the 1994 National Survey of Ethnic Minorities on CD-ROM from the Data Archive at Essex University. Of course, already in the late 1980s, the British Labour Force Survey was available on computer tape; by 1993 the UK Census was accessible on the University of Manchester's mainframe. And each year new sources of information on Britain's immigrants and minorities become available.

Several scholars have taken advantage of these sources to examine the position of ethnic groups in the British labor market (Cheng and Heath 1993, Fieldhouse 1996, Heath, Roberts, and McMahon 1997, Heath and McMahon this volume, Holdsworth and Dale 1997, Leslie 1998). A related development has been the emergence of cross-national comparisons of the economic attainment of ethnic minorities. Since many of the immigrant groups settling in Britain have settled in other countries as well, scholars have begun to compare the economic well-being of ethnic minorities across receiving countries. In the main, they find that America's ethnic minorities are more advantaged than their British counterparts. One of the earliest of these studies compared Chinese immigrants in the USA and the UK (Cheng 1994). Another contrasted Black Caribbeans in four countries (Model, Fisher, and Silberman 1999). Others have expanded the number of immigrant groups but limited the destination to London and New York (Model and Ladipo 1996, Model 1997).

Building on this strategy, the present chapter uses three data sets, two from the UK and one from the USA, to explore the economic well-being of six ethnic minorities: Black Caribbeans, Indians, Pakistanis, Bangladeshis, Chinese, and Black Africans. Although these "New Commonwealth" immigrants comprise only a fraction of the American immigrant stream, they are the largest foreign-born groups in England, the region to which the present study is limited. The data contain enough members of the first two groups to support analysis of both a foreign- and a native-born sample; the other groups appear only as immigrants. Both men and women are included, except for Bangladeshis, for whom the sample is large enough to sustain only the study of men.

The first step in the research strategy is to measure the difference between each ethnic minority's economic well-being and the economic well-being of its native white counterpart. The gap between each ethnic minority and native whites in the UK is then compared to the gap between the same ethnic minority and whites in the USA. Finally, the same set of comparisons are undertaken after multivariate statistical techniques have controlled for individual differences in human capital, family characteristics, and region. As a result of this strategy, the remaining variations in the cross-national gap between ethnic minorities and whites should not be due to these three sets of factors. Rather, other theoretically based explanations must be considered, a task begun in the next section and completed in the last.

The chapter is organized in the following way. First, a discussion of the theoretical alternatives is offered. Then, the data and research methods are described. The next section presents the results of the gross and net cross-national comparisons of economic well-being. Both comparisons uncover several cross-national differences, most of which favor the USA. The goal of the paper's conclusion is to ascertain which one of the theoretical possibilities posited at the outset best explains these empirical results.

Theoretical expectations

The expectation that America offers New Commonwealth immigrants stronger economic outcomes than Britain is based on two alternatives: one is that white US employers discriminate less, in general, than their

British counterparts; the second is that white US employers discriminate less *against New Commonwealth immigrants* than their British counterparts. Several considerations motivate each possibility.

Historical differences between the two nations offer a foundation for the first hypothesis. As Hickman emphasizes in this volume, Britain has a hereditary aristocracy at home and a colonial legacy abroad. In addition, it has been a population-exporter far longer than a population-importer. In contrast, the USA has been a nation of immigrants for most of its history. Moreover, American ideology holds that social class origins are less important than talent and ambition. Some experts say that, relative to Britain, economic opportunity in America is "exceptional" (Lipset 1991). Rex and Tomlinson (1979: 6) summarize these national differences by observing that in the USA "capitalist enterprises, free of most of the aristocratic restraints to be found in European contexts, drew upon a seemingly endless supply of immigrant labor, so that, instead of an ethnically homogeneous society being divided into classes by the bargaining of the labor market, one had a society of gradually assimilating immigrants." In other words, compared to Britain, class mattered little in America, and, over time, ethnic divisions would not matter either.

Whether or not ethnic divisions matter, one reason that American employers may be less likely to react to ethnic differences than their British counterparts is that the US legal system condemns discrimination more effectively than the British (Lieberman, this volume). A UK law prohibiting job discrimination dates only from 1976, some twelve years after the US Civil Rights Act. The British law has been criticized for its small number of convictions and modest compensation to victims (Brown and Gay 1994: 326). A review of the efficacy of the British law in 1992 indicated that "its most significant weakness remains its failure to impose sanctions which are strong enough to force major employers and service providers to review their practices in order to secure compliance in the short term" (MacEwen 1995). In the USA, on the other hand, the percentage of successful complaints and the size of awards are impressive.

In addition, no parallel to affirmative action, a policy which encourages employers to recruit, hire, and promote minorities, has emerged in the British Isles, although some observers report that local authorities have felt compelled to hire ethnic minorities, especially for "race relations" and related work (Small 1994). To be sure, affirmative action may have little direct impact on New Commonwealth minorities. Most analysts find that it has primarily benefited African-Americans (Rose 1994, Smith and Welch 1994). However, even with this limitation, the very existence of the program is evidence of the US government's commitment to ethnic equality. In short, American anti-discrimination policies are stricter, more comprehensive, and better publicized than British anti-discrimination policies.

Yet another reason why British employers may be more willing to act on their prejudices is that the cost of hiring and firing is higher there than in the USA. For example, UK law requires that employers compensate employees declared redundant after two or more years of continuous service (Buxton 1995). As Esping-Andersen (1999) has observed, such labor market "rigidities" heighten the "insider–outsider" cleavage, by which he means the cleavage between workers deemed desirable and undesirable. In some nations, women or youth constitute the less desirable group, but ethnic minorities are also prime candidates. Of course, the absence of a meaningful anti-discrimination law may well reinforce British employers' willingness to act on these prejudices. To sum up, the arguments above are compatible with the expectation that US employers discriminate less against ethnic minorities *in general* than British employers do.

An entirely different logic underlies the second possibility, which is that some (rather than all) ethnic minorities will do better in the USA than the UK. This hypothesis rests on the assumption that discrimination is selective, not monolithic. More specifically, if US employers view some groups as less desirable than New Commonwealth immigrants, then New Commonwealth immigrants will do better in the USA. The relevant insights come from queuing theory, a perspective that conceptualizes workers as filling an imaginary line, or queue, with members of the most favorably ranked group at the beginning and members of the least favorably ranked group at the end. When ethnic minorities are involved, their position in the eyes of employers determines their position in the queue (Hodge 1973, Thurow 1975, Lieberson 1980).

In a single labor market, queuing is simply a way of describing the amount of discrimination or favoritism specific groups experience. In two or more markets or one market at two or more points in time, however, the relevance of the theory becomes obvious. One key variable is the number of competing groups. Suppose that one of two labor markets contains three contending groups: whites, browns, and blacks, ranked in that order. Assume the other market contains only two groups: whites and browns. In this situation, browns will do better in the first than the second market because the presence of blacks benefits browns. A second key variable is the size of the competing groups. Browns will secure additional benefits as the size of the favored white group shrinks and/or the size of the black group grows. Thus, in their study of whites, Mexicans, and blacks in the southwestern US, Frisbie and Neidert (1977) found that the greater the percentage of blacks in a labor market and the smaller the percentage of whites, the higher the occupational status of Mexicans.

These considerations suggest the relevance of demographic composition for any US–UK comparison. According to the most recent census, about 27 percent of the US labor force consists of immigrants and/or ethnic minorities, compared to 10 percent of the English labor force. Assuming that most employers in both countries prefer native-born whites to immigrants or minorities, these demographic disparities imply that those New Commonwealth minorities ranking near the top of the queue in the USA will fare better than their compatriots in England. Furthermore, the fact that the USA contains two large, low-ranking groups not present in Britain enhances the chances that New Commonwealth minorities rank near the top of the US labor queue. More specifically, 9.4 percent of its labor force is African-American and 8.1 percent is Hispanic. If African-Americans, Hispanics, or both hold a lower position in the American "hierarchy of discrimination" than do some New Commonwealth immigrants, then those immigrants, *ceteris paribus*, are likely to be more successful in the USA than in England (Arnold 1984).

Although information about the relative position of New Commonwealth immigrants in the eyes of American employers is meager, the results of the 1989 General Social Survey provide some clues. Respondents were asked to rank groups in terms of their "social standing," which ranged from 9 (high) to 1 (low). Not surprisingly, native whites scored highest (7.03). Other relevant rankings include Chinese (4.76), Asian Indians (4.29), Negroes (4.17), African Blacks (3.58), Arabs (3.57), Black Caribbean (3.56), Mexicans (3.52), Puerto Ricans (3.32), and Iranians (2.99) (Smith 1991). If these rankings are accurate, then, with the possible exception of Pakistanis and Bangladeshis, most New Commonwealth immigrants will do better in the USA than the UK because they rank higher than African Americans, Hispanics, or both. The relative ranking of Muslim groups is hard to gauge, since no questions about Pakistanis or Bangladeshis were included. The survey shows only that one Muslim group (Arabs) ranks above Hispanics and another (Iranians) ranks below. Moreover, the NORC findings should not be taken too literally. The results of a 1997 survey of employers in four cities – Los Angeles, New York, Atlanta, and Philadelphia – indicated that employers who distinguished among backgrounds usually ranked Asians above whites, placed Latinos in the middle and viewed blacks least favorably (Lim 1999). If these rankings are accurate, then the relative rankings of Black Caribbeans and Black Africans are also hard to gauge since the Four City Survey did not explore whether or not American employers distinguish among these black immigrant groups and African-Americans.

Even if these rankings are relatively accurate, a caveat must be appended to all the explanations offered so far because they assume that discrimination is the basic mechanism responsible for a US advantage. The difficulty is that, in order for discrimination to matter, members of a minority must depend on members of the dominant group for job opportunities. Furthermore, when such dependency obtains, the superordinate group must be free to act upon its preferences. There are at least three situations in which ethnic minorities may enjoy immunity from discrimination: they may be self-employed, they may work for coethnics, and they may receive preferential treatment on political grounds. With respect to working for oneself or under the auspices of coethnics, an adaptation often called "ethnic economy employment," scholars find that at least part of the motive for this adaptation is the desire to circumvent discrimination by dominant group employers (Robinson, this volume). Furthermore, research suggests that at least some ethnic economy jobs offer better rewards than jobs in the mainstream economy. At minimum, ethnic economy jobs are assumed to reduce a group's vulnerability to unemployment (Light et al. 1994, Phizacklea and Ram 1996, Waldinger 1996).

Because all three datasets identify the self-employed, the multivariate analysis of occupational prestige and of earnings can control for this form of participation in the ethnic economy. But the multivariate analysis of unemployment cannot control for self-employment because analyses of unemployment do not include job characteristics. In addition, the immunity from discrimination that accrues to ethnic economy employees remains uncontrolled throughout the study because the data do not contain sufficient information about the ethnicity of employers. Britain's National Study of Ethnic Minorities offers some insight on the extent of this immunity because half its respondents were asked the racial/ethnic origin of their "immediate boss." Unfortunately, their replies were coded rather broadly: White, Black, Chinese, Asian, or Other. Still, limiting the calculations to groups of 100 or more within race/ethnic/nativity/gender categories, the proportion reporting that their immediate boss was Asian – an admittedly crude measure of ethnic economy employment – was 9.7 percent for Indian immigrant men, 11.3 percent for Indian immigrant women, 11.4 percent for Pakistani immigrant men, and 31.9 percent for Bangladeshi immigrant men. These numbers suggest that, in the British side of the analysis, the results most contaminated by the inability to identify ethnic economy employees are the Bangladeshi. But the Chinese figures are also in doubt because, according to several sources, a large proportion of Chinese immigrants in Britain are ethnic economy employees (Cheng 1994, Model 1997, 2000).

Unfortunately, analogous figures have never been collected for a representative sample of ethnic minorities in the USA. Research on ethnic economy employees in America relies primarily on qualitative studies or on attributions based on the industry in which employees work. Of the groups included in the American side of this study, research indicates that the Chinese have the most extensive ethnic economy but this form of employment may also absorb a meaningful proportion of South Asians (Zhou 1992).

In the USA, in addition to ethnic economy employment, affirmative action grants immunity from discrimination to some groups. As mentioned above, scholars doubt that New Commonwealth immigrants reap much advantage from this policy. Yet, according to queuing theory, their well-being will depend upon the position of African-Americans and Hispanics in the US labor queue. Of major interest is whether white employers rank New Commonwealth minorities above or below African-Americans and Hispanics. To test this possibility properly requires controlling for the favoritism that affirmative action might impart to these groups. A frequent strategy for accomplishing this goal is to add controls for public sector employment, a step defended on the ground that many of the benefits of affirmative action apply disproportionately to public sector employment (Zipp 1994, Waldinger 1996, Durr and Logan 1997). This strategy is therefore adopted below.

To summarize the arguments offered in this section, there are four reasons for expecting that immigrants in Britain suffer more discrimination than their US counterparts. These include a culture less tolerant of diversity, a legal system with weaker anti-discrimination laws, an economy that offers greater worker protections, and a labor force comprised of fewer nonwhites. Any one or more of these reasons might hold, but they can apply only to those minorities who are dependent on the actions of discriminatory employers. Immune to discrimination are the self-employed, their coethnic employees and the beneficiaries of affirmative action policy. The analysis below makes every effort to control for these immunities but only partially succeeds in doing so.

Additional confounding factors

In addition to the problems already mentioned above, any claim that cross-national differences in the quality or quantity of discrimination explain cross-national differences in ethnic minority attainment rests on the unstated and potentially problematic assumption that there are no meaningful differences between immigrants from a specific country who choose to settle in America and their compatriots who choose to settle in Britain. Unfortunately, there are at least three reasons to question this assumption. Emigrants from the same sending country may vary on culture, on social class background, and on the selectivity of migration.

In this chapter, the term "culture" refers to the attitudes, values, and behaviors that all individuals of a given heritage share, regardless of their socioeconomic status (Light 1984). Scholars who favor cultural explanations emphasize that migrating groups differ in their attitudes toward school, work, marriage, indeed toward relocation itself (Sowell 1994). Such pre-migration attitudes may translate into post-migration differences in job preferences and productivity. Some of these attitudes, family size for instance, have measurable behavioral consequences and, therefore, a multivariate analysis can control for them. Others do not easily lend themselves to such treatment. In this study, however, the problems associated with controlling for culture are largely, though not entirely, overcome. This follows because the research strategy compares persons in different host countries from the *same* sending nation, that is persons whose cultural heritage, at least at the outset, is the same. Whether the cultural effect on economic performance is positive, negative, or neutral, it should be similar – at least in the short run.

In the long run, the malleability of culture could create a problem for this interpretation, however. Emigrants may depart with similar values but those values may change. For instance, American sociologists have noticed that some Black Caribbean immigrants respond to racism by identifying with African-Americans in general and with lower-class ghetto values in particular (Waters 1996). British anthropologists have noted that some British-born Bangladeshis respond to "Paki-bashing" by identifying with Muslims in general and with fundamentalist values in particular (Gardner and Shukur 1994). These are not resurrected old values but responses to the way natives treat newcomers. And, since natives in different receiving countries (for instance in the USA and the UK) may treat newcomers from identical sending countries (for instance, from the Caribbean or Bangladesh) in different ways, the values of culturally similar immigrants do not necessarily remain the same wherever they settle.

Social class background is the second factor that might vary systematically across immigrant streams who leave the same sending country for different destinations. Among the causes of such variation are the number of years the migration to the destination has persisted, the cost of relocation, and the motives for moving. Whatever the cause, unless controlled, differences in class origins may contribute to cross-national intra-ethnic differences in economic attainment (Heath and McMahon, this volume, Nee and Sanders forthcoming). To some degree, this danger is mitigated by the fact that educational credentials are highly correlated with social class background. The data at hand do contain indicators of such credentials; hence, the multivariate analysis can control for education, the strongest mechanism through which parents transmit their class background to children. Still, educational credentials are but one of the many avenues through which family background is reproduced. Other advantages – for instance, resourceful social contacts, good health, a perception of efficacy – also accrue disproportionately to the better off. These considerations mean that differences in the social class composition of migrant streams will translate into differences in the socioeconomic attainment of migrant workers. For instance, if Indian immigrants to the USA emanate from higher class origins than Indian immigrants to the UK, then controlling for educational credentials cannot fully eradicate the advantages of the former over the latter.

A third factor that could generate cross-national differences in economic well-being is the selectivity of migration. "Selectivity" refers to characteristics that distinguish movers from stayers. Some writers use the term to describe easily measurable characteristics, occupation, for instance. Thus, Foner (1979) argues that Black Caribbeans settling in the USA are more skilled, on average, than those who settled in the UK. Such a situation would certainly advantage the former relative to the latter. However, occupational selectivity poses few problems for most multivariate analyses because datasets usually contain this variable; hence it can be controlled. Other writers use the term "selectivity" to describe traits that rarely appear in standard datasets, ambition or diligence, for instance. George Borjas (1994) maintains that persons who move from nations with high income inequality, such as Third World countries, to nations with low income inequality, such as First World countries, are negatively selected. By this he means that they are less ambitious and diligent than the persons they leave behind. Other scholars place more emphasis on the motives for migration, arguing that economically motivated movers are positively selected, while politically motivated movers are not. Yet another hypothesis is that the greater the obstacles for relocation, the more positively selected the migrant (Lee 1966).

These formulations provide a theoretical basis for expecting differences in the selectivity of immigrants who relocate from identical sending nations to different receiving countries. For instance, Borjas (1993) expected that countries with demanding admissions criteria would attract more positively selected immigrants than countries with modest admissions criteria. But his research did not support this prediction. Similarly, Model's (1997) effort to measure the selectivity of nonwhite immigrants to London and New York likewise found no such effects. Thus, the analysis below proceeds under the assumption that differences in the selectivity of migrants from the same sending area to the USA and UK are small. Yet, the absence of definitive evidence means that this interpretation cannot be wholly ruled out.

To sum up, the motivating hypothesis of the present study is that New Commonwealth immigrants will do better economically in America than in Britain. Two sorts of explanations have been proposed: a weaker propensity to discriminate against immigrants in the USA and the upgrading associated with the presence of America's "indigenous minorities." If some version of the first alternative is accurate, all groups should fare better in the USA; if the second is accurate, all groups save those more stigmatized than African-Americans and Hispanics will fare better in the USA. Yet, there is a third scenario. The complexities of culture, social class, and selectivity may intervene in ways that affect each immigrant group uniquely. In this case, rather than foster generalization, the results can best be interpreted as a series of case studies.

Data and methods

The data come from the 1991 UK Sample of Anonymised Records (SARs), 1 and 2 percent samples combined, the Fourth National Survey of Ethnic Minorities (NSEM), and the 1990 US Public-Use Microdata Sample (PUMs), 5 and 1 percent samples combined. Since the number of nonwhites residing outside England is small, the SARs data were limited to England. The NSEM study, which includes Wales, was undertaken by the Policy Studies Institute in 1994. It represents a valuable addition because of the many variables it contains. Compared to the SARs, it incorporates more questions about education, a question about government employment, a question on earnings, and so on. On the other hand, like most surveys, it has a smaller case base and lower response rate than a census (Simpson 1996, Smith and Prior 1996). The smaller case base of the NSEM also means that fewer ethnic minority groups were available for study in the NSEM than in the SARs. The reason for this is that, in order to maximize reliability, the analyses in this chapter are limited to ethnic/nativity/gender groups containing at least 100 cases. Thus, only the SARs analysis extends to immigrants from China and Africa. Conversely, the number of native-born whites in the PUMs and the SARs is so large that, in order to keep the analysis within a manageable size, these groups were sampled. All analyses are limited to prime age individuals; i.e. those between 25 and 64.

With respect to the included variables, group membership was the only outcome which involved considerable recoding. This step was necessary because the three datasets do not define ethnicity in a comparable fashion. The main difficulty arose in the SARs, where some individuals are described as "Black Other" or "Asian Other." In the case of immigrants, this problem was handled by classifying "Black Others" born in Africa as "Black Africans;" "Asian Others" born in Pakistan as Pakistanis, and so on. However, native-born individuals could not be assigned an ethnic group and were, therefore, relegated to a residual "Other" category. Cases in the NSEM also underwent minor recoding. For instance, Indians born neither in Britain nor the subcontinent were recoded "Other," as were Black Caribbeans born neither in the West Indies nor the British Isles. Finally, in the USA, group membership was assigned on the basis of replies to the nativity, Hispanicity, and race questions, with the exception that the ancestry question was also utilized in the case of native-born Black Caribbeans.[1]

Three dependent variables were selected for analysis: unemployment, occupational prestige, and logged weekly earnings. As mentioned above, for each dependent variable, the first step of the analysis is a comparison of means. Do members of a particular group fare better in one country or the other? The second step is to ask the same question, controlling for as many individual and structural factors as possible. This is done by multivariate regression – probit in the case of unemployment, which is dichotomous; ordinary least squares in the case of occupational prestige and earnings, which are continuous.[2] The resulting group membership coefficients convey the size of the gap between native whites and members of an ethnic minority in each country. Still, cross-national comparison of these coefficients must be done cautiously because statistical analyses are subject to sampling error. Therefore, the last step is to test each US–UK difference in order to identify whether or not the difference between them stands up to conventional statistical tests of reliability.

For each dependent variable, a theoretical rationale motivated the choice of independent variables. For instance, in the case of unemployment, the model included human capital (age, age squared, and, when the data allowed: years since migration, years since migration squared, and English ability), marital status, and the regional unemployment rate. For women, number of children ever born was included as a rough control for years out of the labor force. Models of occupational prestige contained the same indicators of human capital and family responsibilities, but regional dummies substituted for unemployment rates. The occupational prestige regressions also included dummy variables for two job characteristics: self-employment and, when the data allowed, public sector employment. As suggested above, the motive for including these variables was to introduce at least partial controls for "queue jumping." Finally, models of earnings mimicked those for occupational prestige, with the exception of the inclusion of occupational prestige as a predictor.

As might be expected, there were difficulties in creating cross-nationally comparable codes for some of these variables. For instance, educational qualifications differ between the two countries, the 2 percent SARs offers a two- (rather than a three-) digit occupational code, the NSEM does not report the number of weeks worked per year, and so on. Although every effort was made to create meaningful values, no cross-national comparison is without comparability problems. Another source of cross-national variation is the proportion of the population "missing" on each of the dependent variables, which is not the same in the two countries. Consider, for instance, unemployment. This measure is traditionally limited to labor force participants. According to their respective censuses, about 89 percent of white men born in the USA and UK participated in the labor force, but among black African immigrant men the figure was 71 percent in the SARs and 88 percent in the PUMs. A discrepancy this large is unusual, but attention to cross-national variation in the proportion of missing cases on unemployment, occupation, and earnings (not shown) reveals a marked tendency for British ethnic minorities to register higher proportions missing than their American counterparts. The list of potential reasons for this pattern include the higher unemployment rate in the UK, that country's more generous transfer payments, the stronger enforcement of civil rights violations in the USA, and so on. Whatever the reasons, economists believe that individuals who do not report labor market outcomes are disproportionately less qualified and less assiduous. If this is so, then the ethnic minorities appearing in the British side of a US–UK comparison will constitute a more elite sample (economists say a "more positively selected sample") than their counterparts in America. This disparity, in turn, might lead to an overestimate of the attainment of ethnic minorities in the UK relative to the USA.

Economists have developed a number of techniques to correct for sample selection bias, as this problem is known; two of them are implemented in the present analysis. Both involve developing an equation to distinguish the missing from the non-missing cases and using the results of that prediction to calculate a "selection bias term." This term, when included in the final analysis, controls for the omitted observations. In the case of the dichotomous dependent variable, unemployment, this procedure involves estimating labor force participation, using those results to calculate a variable known as the inverse Mills ratio, and adding that variable to the unemployment equation (Maddala 1983). In the case of the continuous dependent variables, occupational prestige and earnings, Heckman (1976) has developed an analogous procedure that can be accomplished in a single step. All the results reported below incorporate corrections of this kind.

Results

For each gender/ethnicity/nativity category, Table 13.1 presents descriptive statistics on the three dependent variables and their most important determinants. Because there are two British datasets, the table contains two British entries for each category. Calculations based on the NSEM appear first, followed by calculations based on the SARs. Four variables are only available in the NSEM: percentage who have no secondary diploma, years since migration, English skills, and weekly earnings. Note too that the NSEM statistics are weighted, though the figure in the "number of cases" column is unweighted. Weighting is needed because all individuals were not equally likely to be selected to participate in the NSEM and, of those selected, some could not be found or refused to participate (Smith and Prior 1996).[3]

Before moving to concrete comparisons, it is useful to point out that there are some differences between the NSEM results and the SARs results. In particular, compared to SARs respondents, a higher proportion of NSEM respondents report a university degree and a higher proportion of NSEM respondents describe themselves as unemployed. The most plausible interpretation for these disparities is that well-educated people and unemployed people are especially likely to respond to surveys. The first generalization reflects the greater sympathy and understanding for "science" that accompanies a good education; the second reflects the greater accessibility of the unemployed. Also interesting is that these discrepancies are smaller for native whites than for ethnic minorities. Indeed, in the case of native-born white men, *fewer* NSEM than SARs respondents report a university degree (12.0 percent vs. 13.2 percent). Conversely, according to the SARs 7.98 percent of foreign-born Indian women have a university degree, compared to 26.9 percent of NSEM respondents. Because census enumerations generally provide more reliable figures than surveys, this chapter treats disparities of this kind by giving priority to the SARs figures.

To begin with unemployment, British rates are invariably higher than American, especially among ethnic minorities. In absolute terms, the largest cross-national gap obtains for Bangladeshi men, whose rate is 37.4 percent in Britain but 9.38 percent in the USA. Yet, in both countries, among males, Bangladeshi immigrants have the highest rate in the table, followed by Pakistanis. Among women, a shortage of cases motivated omitting Bangladeshis. Perhaps this is why Pakistanis have the highest unemployment rate among females in both nations (29.4 percent in the UK, 12.2 percent in the USA). Another observation is that in the UK the gap in unemployment vulnerability between native whites and minorities

Table 13.1 Means or percentages on major variables: men and women 25–64 in the labor force

	Age	% Univ. degree[3]	% No diploma[4]	Post-migration years	English[5]	% Unempl.	Occupat. prestige	Earnings per week	No. of cases[6]
MEN									
Eng FB Bl C[1]	48.7	6.58	56.9	30.8	1.12	31.9	36.2	278.55	304
Eng FB Bl C[2]	47.5	2.70				9.83	36.5		2184
US FB Bl C	39.8	17.3	29.0	14.4	0.08	8.56	39.7	430.28	8159
Eng NB Bl C[1]	30.7	8.47	10.2	na	1.04	22.2	38.4	314.90	236
Eng NB Bl C[2]	30.0	5.49				25.9	39.2		1074
US NB Bl C	39.8	25.6	14.0	na	0.05	7.82	41.6	492.75	1023
Eng FB Ind[1]	42.4	30.8	31.5	23.1	1.64	17.0	41.2	289.87	454
Eng FB Ind[2]	42.0	16.0				12.9	42.5		3117
US FB Ind	39.5	68.9	8.51	11.3	0.87	3.63	52.0	685.91	12139
Eng NB Ind[2]	30.4	19.0		na		15.8	45.0		385
US NB Ind	36.1	63.6	6.15	na	0.45	3.93	48.8	544.00	265
Eng FB Pak[1]	40.0	12.7	45.5	22.6	2.00	37.3	36.8	234.44	387
Eng FB Pak[2]	39.8	9.47				30.0	37.9		1832
US FB Pak	37.3	58.9	9.39	9.72	0.98	4.79	47.3	557.93	1334
Eng FB Bang[1]	41.1	9.73	69.2	20.6	2.10	51.1	33.0	200.83	185
Eng FB Bang[2]	42.0	9.47				37.4	36.1		644
US FB Bang	36.5	44.5	8.51	9.38	1.39	9.33	40.7	448.97	224
Eng FB Ch[2]	39.6	23.8				9.62	42.8		852
US FB Ch	40.2	48.4	21.9	12.8	1.51	0.04	46.4	509.95	18363
Eng FB Bl Af[2]	38.9	25.3				27.6	43.4		894
US FB Bl Af	35.5	56.9	7.28	9.70	0.80	5.64	44.1	413.52	3645
Eng NB Wh[1]	39.1	12.0	23.8	na	na	11.4	42.5	350.72	1047
Eng NB Wh[2]	41.7	13.2				9.05	43.1		2184
US NB Wh	40.5	29.9	12.4		0.03	3.27	44.3	554.29	2786

WOMEN

Eng FB Bl C[1]	44.2	4.02	29.8	28.0	1.02	8.31	38.6	236.74	373
Eng FB Bl C[2]	44.7	3.14				8.90	39.8		2134
US FB Bl C	39.8	16.3	23.2	14.1	0.06	5.76	43.7	355.98	9462
Eng NB Bl C[1]	29.9	6.64	9.96	na	1.01	27.0	39.8	233.21	241
Eng NB Bl C[2]	30.3	6.35				13.7	41.8		1024
US NB Bl C	40.2	27.4	10.7	na	0.06	5.45	47.5	384.02	1155
Eng FB Ind[1]	39.3	26.9	37.1	20.0	1.91	10.9	38.8	211.33	294
Eng FB Ind[2]	39.4	7.98				12.5	38.2		2056
US FB Ind	38.1	55.3	13.0	11.1	0.94	6.94	47.4	419.12	6859
Eng NB Ind[2]	30.9	14.7				12.0	41.7		292
US NB Ind	35.1	57.8	5.13	na	0.37	4.61	52.0		170
Eng FB Pak[2]	37.5	9.60				29.4	40.7		354
US FB Pak	38.1	51.4	11.5	10.2	1.10	12.2	46.6	349.09	367
Eng FB Ch[2]	38.5	14.2				5.59	42.2		697
US FB Ch	39.5	40.0	25.9	12.5	1.55	4.99	43.2	345.50	15364
Eng FB Bl Af[2]	36.7	11.3				21.2	39.9		750
US FB Bl Af	34.1	38.0	8.34	9.32	0.82	9.04	43.1	333.65	1651
Eng NB Wh[1]	40.4	11.4	22.5	na	na	5.21	41.2	199.64	921
Eng NB Wh[2]	41.1	8.24				4.75	41.0		4102
US NB Wh	40.4	24.9	9.90	na	0.03	4.28	45.0	310.15	2302

[1] Cases come from the NSEM.

[2] Cases come from the SARs.

[3] For England, university degree means "first degree" or equivalent. For the USA, it means at least a bachelor's degree.

[4] For England, no secondary diploma means no qualification or credential whatever; for the USA, it means no high school diploma.

[5] The NSEM does not score native-born English whites on language skills. For analytic purposes, they were assigned a value of "1."

[6] The N of cases in the SARs and PUMs is unweighted; the N of cases in the NSEM is weighted. For all groups, the N of cases is a maximum; on some variables the available case base is lower than the figure reported here.

Bang = Bangladeshi; Bl Af = Black African; Bl C = Black Caribbean; Ch = Chinese; Eng = English; FB = Foreign-born; Ind = Indian; NB = Native-born; Pak = Pakistani; US = United States; Wh = White.

is far greater than in the USA. To illustrate, UK Bangladeshi males are over four times (4.13) more likely to be jobless than UK native whites, whereas US Bangladeshi males are under three times (2.85) more likely than their US counterparts.

Attention to the cross-national gaps in occupational prestige yields a less pernicious conclusion. Among men, the occupations of US native whites are 1 to 2 points more prestigious than those of UK native whites, but – more to the point theoretically – in both countries, some ethnic minorities do at least as well as their native white counterparts. In both countries, Indian, Chinese, and African males fall in this category, and, in the USA, Pakistani men also outrank native whites (47.3 vs. 44.3). Among women, the occupations of US native whites are 4 points more prestigious than those of UK native whites, but ethnic minority outcomes are again occasionally superior to those of their native white counterparts. In Britain, occupational superiority holds for Caribbeans and Indians, provided they are native born, and for Chinese and Pakistani immigrant women. In the USA, the women with higher occupational prestige than native whites are native-born Black Caribbeans and both generations of Indians and Pakistani immigrants.

For men, the earnings results resemble unemployment more than occupation: the USA has an absolute and a relative advantage. The weekly earnings of native white British men were 63.3 percent of those of their American counterparts. Within Britain, the ethnic minority with earnings closest to native white male earnings was native-born Black Caribbeans at 89.8 percent; the lowest earners were Bangladeshi males at 57.3 percent. In the USA, on the other hand, foreign-born Indians earned 23.7 percent *more* than native white men. Next in line were foreign-born Pakistani males, who earned about the same as their native white counterparts. In the USA, Black Africans are the lowest-earning male group in the table; they earned 74.6 percent as much as native white males. For women, the cross-national pay differential is roughly the same (64.4 percent) as for men. But here the parallel ends, for, in both countries, ethnic minority women consistently outearn their native white sisters. In Britain, foreign-born Black Caribbean women are at the top, with 18.6 percent higher earnings than native whites; in the USA, foreign-born Indian women hold this position, with 35.1 percent higher earnings than native whites. Additional comparisons indicate that the frequency and magnitude of the minority advantage is larger in the USA than in Britain.

To sum up, relative to their native white compatriots, British minorities are much more likely to be jobless than American minorities. With respect to occupational prestige, the cross-national difference is less pronounced, with some minorities ranking above whites in both countries. Finally, the earnings effects vary by gender. In Britain, minority males consistently earn less than whites but in America a few outearn whites. Among females, minorities consistently earn more than whites in both countries, but the surfeit is more pronounced in America.

In addition to these outcome variables, Table 13.1 presents group differences on variables that theorists generally associate with economic attainment. Space limitations mean that only a few of these patterns be presented here. The most noteworthy pattern is that Britain's immigrants are older and have lived abroad longer than their American counterparts. Partly as a by-product of the age difference, immigrants to the USA have more schooling than their British counterparts but immigrants to the USA usually have more education than white Americans as well. To be sure, Britain contains some immigrant groups with higher educational credentials than native whites, for instance Black Africans. Both nations also have a few groups who are well represented in the high and low end of the educational spectrum, for example, Indian immigrants in England and Chinese immigrants in the USA. Finally, on the four-point English ability scale, US immigrants have slightly better skills. However, the NSEM relies on interviewers' judgments while the US Census relies on the opinion of whoever completes the questionnaire. Thus, the finding that, in both nations, Bangladeshis and Pakistanis have the most language problems is doubtless correct, but to conclude that the problem is more serious in Britain than America, as Table 13.1 suggests, would be unwise.

The next three tables present the multivariate results. Within genders, the first two columns in each table come from identical models estimated separately on the NSEM and on the PUMs; the second two columns come from identical models estimated separately on the SARs and on the PUMs. Within identical models, statistical tests determined if each ethnic minority coefficient in the UK sample was significantly different from its US counterpart.[4] Whenever such a test confirmed a difference, the cell containing the more advantaged national context was shaded. In all, 51 such tests were undertaken; 22 yielded a significant result; 20 of these favored the USA, 2 favored the UK. Interestingly, about a third of the cross-national comparisons that could be estimated using both the NSEM–PUMs and the SARs–PUMs attained statistical significance only in the SARs analysis. Because the NSEM allows the investigator to control for more variables, this discovery implies that some of the disparities between the USA and the UK in the SARs analyses stem from cross-national differences in the attributes of the immigrants themselves. At the same time, the lower response rate of the survey and the

Table 13.2 Unemployment by race/ethnicity/gender and nation

	MEN				WOMEN			
	UK NSEM	US PUMS1	UK SARS	US PUMS2	UK NSEM	US PUMS1	UK SARS	US PUMS 2
FB Bl C	0.6233**	0.4227***	0.2932***	0.3779***	0.4246	0.3280***	0.2751***	0.2446***
	(0.2113)	(0.0572)	(0.0410)	(0.0503)	(0.3284)	(0.0573)	(0.0559)	(0.0536)
NB Bl C	0.5320***	0.2902***	0.3873***	0.2642***	0.7986***	0.1557*	0.2932***	0.1898*
	(0.1502)	(0.0761)	(0.0516)	(0.0757)	(0.1849)	(0.0777)	(0.0657)	(0.0773)
FB Ind	0.1881	0.1421*	0.2792***	0.1781**	0.3816	0.2033*	0.5157***	0.1958***
	(0.2036)	(0.0577)	(0.0386)	(0.0515)	(0.3248)	(0.0610)	(0.0510)	(0.0534)
NB Ind			0.3451***	0.1461			0.4830***	0.1245
			(0.0838)	(0.1470)			(0.1028)	(0.1635)
FB Pak	0.6181**	0.2119**	0.8494***	0.2694***			0.7264***	0.1938
	(0.2069)	(0.0795)	(0.0404)	(0.0748)			(0.1035)	(0.1070)
FB Bang	0.8003***	0.3595**	0.9091***	0.4409**				
	(0.2108)	(0.1354)	(0.0573)	(0.1323)				
FB Ch			0.0971	0.0836			0.1462	0.0188
			(0.0711)	(0.0494)			(0.0999)	(0.0500)
FB Bl Af			0.6723***	0.3169***			0.7286***	0.3832***
			(0.0551)	(0.0577)			(0.0671)	(0.0644)
African-Americans		0.3698***		0.3618***		0.3154***		0.3323***
		(0.0587)		(0.0586)		(0.0603)		(0.0604)
FB Hispanics		0.1073		0.2572***		0.2914***		0.3489***
		(0.0768)		(0.0680)		(0.0818)		(0.0718)
NB Hispanics		0.3025***		0.3473***		-0.0192		0.0415
		(0.0727)		(0.0730)		(0.0854)		(0.0852)
Pseudo R^2	0.1905	0.0612	0.0952	0.0626	0.2344	0.0520	0.0809	0.0397
No. of cases	2,160	62,342	22,786	62,342	1,444	49,792	15,762	49,792

*p < .05; **p < .01, ***p < .001.

Bang = Bangladeshi; Bl Af = Black African; Bl C = Black Caribbean; Ch = Chinese; FB = Foreign-born; Ind = Indian; NB = Native-born; Pak = Pakistani overrepresentation of the jobless and the more schooled within its ranks mean that differences between the NSEM and the SARs should be interpreted with caution.

The findings for unemployment appear in Table 13.2. A positive number means that the ethnic minority faces more unemployment than similarly qualified native whites; one or more asterisks convey the extent to which such a result might be due to chance. The entries in the table are all positive, but a few fail to attain statistical significance. For example, in Britain, Chinese immigrant men and women are not significantly more likely to be unemployed than their native white counterparts. In explaining this result, it is tempting to credit the group's ethnic economy since ethnic economies are widely assumed to reduce unemployment. Furthermore, as already explained, the models estimated here cannot control for self-employment; therefore, the coefficients in Table 13.2 underestimate rather than overestimate the unemployment vulnerability of entrepreneurial groups. Yet, unemployment among Bangladeshi males, another entrepreneurial group, is the highest in the table (0.8003*** in the NSEM and 0.9091*** in the SARs). Why might one ethnic economy more successfully reduce unemployment than another? One possibility is that the Chinese ethnic economy is larger. Support for this hypothesis comes from the SARs, which report that 35.3 percent of Chinese men are self-employed, compared to 22.3 percent of Bangladeshi. Another possibility is that those Chinese and Bangladeshis who seek jobs in the mainstream economy receive very different responses from British employers. Yet a third is that the Chinese ethnic economy is a "preferred route" to success, while the Bangladeshi is a mechanism to avoid "blocked mobility" (Robinson, this volume). One or both of these explanations may be correct.

The relative position of the remaining British groups are that Indians and Black Caribbeans rank in the middle of the hierarchy, Pakistanis near the bottom. Among the surprises is that being born in Britain does not grant Black Caribbeans or Indians greater immunity from unemployment than their foreign-born compatriots (tests not shown). Another intriguing result is that, among women, Black Caribbeans are far less vulnerable to unemployment than Indians, a pattern that does not arise in the men's results.

In terms of rankings, some British findings are replicated in the American case. For instance, Chinese men and women are not significantly more likely to be jobless than similarly qualified native whites, and Bangladeshis record the highest unemployment of any group (0.3595*** in PUMs1 and 0.4409*** in PUMs2). Yet, the Bangladeshi coefficients in the USA are far smaller than in Britain. Perhaps the American advantage is due to Bangladeshi Americans having a larger ethnic economy than Bangladeshi Britons. A cross-national comparison of Bangladeshi self-employment rates challenges this interpretation. According to the SARs, 22.3 percent of Bangladeshis are self-employed, whereas the PUMs figure is 8.9 percent. Thus, Bangladeshis in America are probably more dependent on the goodwill of native white employers than Bangladeshis in Britain are.

Further attention to the American results indicates that, controlling for nativity, Indians usually rank ahead of Black Caribbeans. But only about half of these comparisons attain statistical significance (tests not shown). Interestingly, Pakistani-born men have significantly lower unemployment rates than Caribbean-born men, a result that contradicts the hypothesis that Muslim groups invariably rank near the bottom. Of course, Bangladeshis do fare poorly on this indicator, but several other groups are equally vulnerable: Black Caribbean immigrants, Black African immigrants, African-Americans, and native born Hispanics. This final comparison illuminates an important trend: the American coefficients cluster around a maximum of about 0.4; the British coefficients continue to climb to about 0.9. Thus, the two countries differ slightly in the way they rank specific groups and differ strongly in the magnitude of the shortfall they impose on those groups.

Moving to the cross-national comparison and focusing first on males, observe that in the SARs Black Caribbean immigrants in Britain are *less* vulnerable to unemployment (0.2932***) than their US counterparts (0.3779***). This finding, however, does not replicate in the NSEM. On the other hand, three groups of immigrant males do better in the USA: Pakistanis, Bangladeshis, and Black Africans. Among women, significant US–UK differences occur among native-born Black Caribbean women (in the NSEMs only), among foreign-born Indians (in the SARs only), and among foreign-born Pakistanis.

To test whether or not the American advantage can be attributed to cross-national differences in ethnic composition requires scrutinizing the African-American and Hispanic coefficients. The former are about the same size as the coefficients for all US groups except Indians and Chinese, whose vulnerability is significantly lower. As for the Hispanic coefficients, they vary in size by gender and nativity. These results are more compatible with the hypothesis that American employers generally discriminate less than their British counterparts than with the hypothesis that America contains some groups whose low status "upgrades" New Commonwealth minorities relative to their British counterparts. Put simply, ethnic minorities in both countries exhibit a hierarchy of disadvantage, but the hierarchy in the USA is shorter.

However, it is too early to conclude that the queuing hypothesis has failed. The findings for occupational prestige and earnings have yet to be examined. The results of the former analysis appear in Table 13.3. Note that both negative and positive coefficients appear; i.e., minorities may have lower or higher occupational prestige than their native white counterparts. Looking first, again, at Britain's Bangladeshis and Chinese, the former are relatively advantaged in the NSEM and relatively disadvantaged in the SARs. The Chinese appear only in the SARs, where both men and women attain low occupational prestige. The discovery that Bangladeshis suffer a weaker penalty in the NSEM implies that some of their occupational shortfall is due to the failure of the SARs to incorporate variables that reflect their handicaps, such as years since migration and English skills. If so, the large occupational deficits incurred by Chinese men (-4.5795^{***}) and Chinese women (-4.4137^{***}) in the SARs might also decline if controls for recency to the British Isles and for language skills were available.

These groups aside, Britain's "hierarchy of occupational disadvantage" offers some surprises. In the NSEM, Black Caribbean men suffer a much larger penalty (-8.2635^{***}) than in the SARs (-3.3873). It is tempting also to attribute this discrepancy to differences in the variables that the two models include, but the small difference between the NSEM (0.9808) and SARs (-1.0895^{**}) coefficients for foreign-born Black Caribbean women undermines this interpretation. Another noteworthy SARs result is that Africa-born black men (2.8999^{***}) fall roughly in the middle of the queue but Africa-born women stand near the bottom (-4.4741^{***}). The frequent difference in the size of the penalty that men and women of the same background incur is a trend theorists have yet to account for.

The relative position of groups in the USA is sometimes in line with the rankings in the NORC. Controlling for nativity, the Indian deficit is small or nonexistent, placing this group ahead of Black Caribbeans, who in turn have higher occupational status than African-Americans. Contradicting the NORC rankings, Black Africans have about the same occupational prestige as African-Americans; indeed, in most models they suffer the greatest occupational shortfall of any New Commonwealth minority. Equally unexpected is that Pakistanis of both genders perform relatively well, a challenge to the hypothesis that Muslims encounter exceptional discrimination. Conversely, Bangladeshis do not do well, at least the men do not. This difference in the occupational attainment of two ethnically and religiously similar groups is surprising; it is unlikely that employers in either country perceive a great difference between people born in Pakistan and people born in Bangladesh.

Table 13.3 Occupational prestige by race/ethnicity/gender and nation

	MEN				WOMEN			
	UK NSEM	US PUMS1	UK SARS	US PUMS2	UK NSEM	US PUMS1	UK SARS	US PUMS2
FB Bl C	-8.2635***	-2.4449***	-3.3873***	-1.3048***	-0.9808	-1.2548***	-1.0895**	0.0105
	(2.2141)	(0.3045)	(0.3175)	(0.2733)	(2.7339)	(0.2867)	(0.3203)	(0.2631)
NB Bl C	-2.6700	-1.7591***	-0.5517	-1.4083**	-0.1684	0.5995	0.2137	0.0283
	(1.6151)	(0.4281)	(0.4443)	(0.4357)	(1.6062)	(0.3867)	(0.4347)	(0.3977)
FB Ind	-4.9413**	1.2015***	-1.0459***	0.2466	-1.6964	-0.2584	-2.3582***	-1.0689***
	(1.8996)	(0.2957)	(0.2716)	(0.2626)	(2.7609)	(0.3136)	(0.3515)	(0.2741)
NB Ind			1.4105*	-0.1461			-1.2954	1.7311*
			(0.6403)	(0.7766)			(0.6944)	(0.8194)
FB Pak	-4.4092*	-0.4849	-3.6018***	-1.8318***			-1.2684	-0.5662
	(2.0763)	(0.4253)	(0.3637)	(0.4081)			(0.9275)	(0.6262)
FB Bang	-1.5172	-3.4431***	-4.2763***	-5.5500***				
	(2.4302)	(0.8371)	(0.5785)	(0.8446)				
FB Ch			-4.5795***	-1.1143***			-4.4137***	-2.4204***
			(0.4692)	(0.2548)			(0.5674)	(0.2513)
FB Bl Af			-2.8999***	-4.2464***			-4.4741***	-3.7096***
			(0.4966)	(0.3094)			(0.5320)	(0.3550)
African-Americans		-3.4905***		-3.8033***		-2.2020***		-2.6120***
		(0.3309)		(0.3366)		(0.3164)		(0.3265)
FB Hispanics		-2.5394***		-5.7219***		-1.8614***		-4.3148***
		(0.4278)		(0.3890)		(0.4525)		(0.4160)
NB Hispanics		-0.9578*		-2.3915***		0.5853		-1.1720**
		(0.4322)		(0.4404)		(0.4274)		(0.4386)
No. of cases	1,290	66,447	18,565	66,447	926	57,172	13,765	57,172

* p < .05; ** p < .01; *** p < .001

Bang = Bangladeshi; Bl Af = Black African; Bl C = Black Caribbean; Ch = Chinese; FB = Foreign-born; Ind = Indian; NB = Native-born; Pak = Pakistani.

In the cross-national comparison, among men, immigrants from the Caribbean, India, Pakistan, and China do significantly better in the USA. The Chinese result probably has little to do with differences in the position of the Chinese in the eyes of white employers. As for the other groups, queuing theory predicts the Caribbean and Indian advantage, but not the Pakistani. Also unexpected is that Black African immigrant men incur a smaller prestige deficit in England than in America. However, examining the African-American and Hispanic coefficients illuminates the two anomalies. One or both of these groups incur greater deficits than Indians, Pakistanis, and Black Caribbeans. And, as already pointed out, Black Africans and African-Americans experience statistically identical penalties. These results fit a slightly different "hierarchy of discrimination" than the NORC survey predicts. Pakistanis and Black Caribbeans rank above African-Americans, but Bangladeshis do not. As mentioned above, it is unlikely that Americans perceive large differences between Pakistanis and Bangladeshis.

Another challenge to the queuing model arises in the case of native-born Indian men and native-born Black Caribbeans of both sexes. These groups do not experience an occupational advantage in the USA, even though they have significantly higher occupational prestige than African-Americans in both the PUMs1 and the PUMs2 analyses. In other words, these groups do not fulfill the expectations of queuing theorists. To be sure, some of the women's results are consistent with a queuing model: immigrants from the Caribbean and India do better in the USA, as do native-born Indians. Also consonant with queuing is the finding of no significant difference in occupational prestige for Pakistani women in the two countries. However, this result was supposed to obtain because Pakistanis would rank below African-Americans. Attention to the African-American coefficients shows black women suffer the larger, rather than the smaller, penalty. In sum, the idea that the presence of African-Americans and Hispanics enhances the economic position of New Commonwealth minorities in the USA occasionally fits the occupational results, but the fit is not consistent.

The final economic outcome available for study is logged weekly earnings. These results appear in Table 13.4. Note that because data on the British side appear only in the NSEM, the number of minorities large enough to justify inclusion is small. All coefficients are negative and only one group, Black Caribbean men in Britain, has a deficit that fails to attain significance. Additional tests (not shown) indicate that, controlling for gender, there are no significant differences among the NSEM coefficients. In other words, statistics do not confirm an "ethnic hierarchy" among the groups included on the British side of the analysis.

Table 13.4 *Logged weekly earnings by race/ethnicity/gender and nation*

	MEN		WOMEN	
	UK NSEM	US PUMS1	UK NSEM	US PUMS1
FB Bl C	−0.2009	−0.4083***	−0.4485**	−0.0818***
	(0.1378)	(0.0170)	(0.1448)	(0.0174)
FB Ind	−0.4516**	−0.2888***	−0.3309*	−0.1059***
	(0.1333)	(0.0166)	(0.1587)	(0.0186)
FB Pak	−0.3316*	−0.3315***		
	(0.1455)	(0.0237)		
African-		−0.1655***		0.0414*
Americans		(0.0188)		(0.0192)
FB Hispanics		−0.3041***		−0.1684***
		(0.0243)		(0.0275)
NB Hispanics		−0.0738**		0.0448
		(0.0243)		(0.0262)
No. of cases	947	62,283	758	50,614

*p < .05; ** p < .01; *** p < .001
Bl C = Black Caribbean; FB = Foreign-born; Ind = Indian; NB = Native-born; Pak = Pakistani.

In the USA, on the other hand, there is one significant contrast: Black Caribbean males earn significantly less than men from India and Pakistan.

Turning to the cross-national comparison reveals one significant finding: Black Caribbean women in the USA have a smaller earnings deficit than their UK counterparts. Further analysis shows that the earnings of Black Caribbean women are less than those of African-American women but more than those of Hispanic immigrant women. Thus, the latter's poor showing may upgrade Black Caribbeans. Additional support for this interpretation comes from the finding that the earnings of India-born women are not significantly greater than the earnings of either African-American or Hispanic women; thus these indigenous minorities cannot upgrade Indian women. This may be why the US–UK difference is not significant for India born women. The same logic obtains among men. None of the American male coefficients is significantly higher than the coefficients of African-American or Hispanic men. Under these circumstances, upgrading cannot occur.

To sum up the empirical findings, over a third of the cross-national comparisons give ethnic minorities in America a statistically significant advantage over their British counterparts. Of the remaining comparisons, the majority also favor the USA, though not significantly so. A

US advantage arises with equal frequency in the unemployment analysis and the occupational prestige analysis, but relatively less so when earnings are considered. The results of the unemployment and occupational analysis are consistent with the interpretation that American employers are generally more willing to hire ethnic minorities than their British counterparts. To be sure, on occupational prestige and earnings, some of America's New Commonwealth minorities appear to profit from the presence of African-Americans and/or Hispanics. Yet, this phenomenon is not pervasive enough to label it a "pattern." Thus, the most parsimonious interpretation of the multivariate results is that American employers discriminate less often or less severely than their British counterparts. At the same time, the fact that some entrepreneurial groups also do better in the USA implies that more than employer sentiments are at work. The next and final section of this paper attempts to synthesize these disparate trends.

Discussion

At the outset, three explanations were offered in support of the prediction that minorities *in general* would do better in America. American employers might be more open-minded than British, American employers might be more intimidated by civil rights law, and/or American employers may be less vulnerable to "labor rigidities." Mathematically, the same result is consonant with both the first and the second of these alternatives, a fact that makes adjudication between them difficult. The result fitting this description is that culturally similar ethnic minorities fare better on all three job outcomes in America than in Britain. As for the "labor rigidities" hypothesis, this mechanism is more likely to motivate employers to be reluctant to hire minorities than to be reluctant to grant them parity on occupation and earnings. That is to say, the pattern most consistent with the "labor rigidities" hypothesis is that minorities in Britain face greater unemployment than minorities in the USA, but little difference in occupational prestige or earnings.

Clearly, since minorities in Britain register some shortfalls on all three outcomes, the results are not compatible with the last explanation. The question then becomes whether the observed differences are best accounted for by crediting American employers with greater tolerance for diversity or crediting American political institutions for developing stronger equal opportunity measures. In fact, research by Dobbin and his colleagues (1993) suggests that these two phenomena may be causally intertwined. They find that the legal initiatives of the 1960s promoted new norms of fairness, norms that became so well institutionalized that they remain in place even though enforcement of equal opportunity law has been in decline since the mid-1980s. In short, American employers may be more tolerant than British, but US law has helped bring this tolerance about.

Thus, "legally enhanced tolerance" is the interpretation most consonant with the statistical results. Nevertheless, there are enough limitations in the analysis that no interpretation should be accepted uncritically. Recall that several variables relevant to the task of explaining intergroup differences are not available to the present undertaking. These include the ability to distinguish ethnic economy employees from dominant economy employees, information about individuals' social class background, and insight into the many factors that motivate individuals to migrate. In addition, several of the variables that are available, education for example, are only approximate indicators of training and skill. Yet another problem is that censuses and surveys "miss" large numbers of people, especially the poor, those with no fixed address, and those with legal problems. When immigrants are involved, those without proper documents are also disproportionately undercounted.

The consequences of these data problems are multiple. For example, the multivariate analysis overestimates the amount of discrimination suffered by an ethnic minority with "low social origins" (Bangladeshis for example) because it does not control for social class background. Similarly, the analysis underestimates the amount of discrimination suffered by the foreign born in the USA because the least qualified, most oppressed immigrants are less well represented in the American than in the British data. Another problem is that the analysis cannot quantify the discrimination suffered by members of a heavily entrepreneurial group.

The Chinese well illustrate this last scenario. According to the analysis, Chinese immigrants are no more likely to be unemployed than native whites. Nor is there a cross-national difference in this respect. Given that Chinese stereotypes are quite favorable on both sides of the Atlantic, these results mesh with the interpretation that whites are quite willing to hire them. Yet, researchers believe that many Chinese immigrant employees work for other Chinese (Zhou 1992, Cheng 1994). Thus, their low unemployment probably is related not only to the jobs available to them in their own ethnic economy but also to their standing among employers in the dominant economy. Recall too that on occupational prestige, the Chinese fare quite poorly, especially in Britain. Is it plausible to attribute the occupational advantage of American Chinese over British to a stronger propensity for British employers to discriminate? This seems an inappropriate interpretation.

What are the alternatives? One possibility emerges from a recent study that compared the occupational status of US and UK Chinese disaggregated by birthplace (Model 2000). Like the present effort, it detected an American advantage, but only for those Chinese born in Hong Kong. Chinese immigrants born in other parts of Asia fared equally well in the USA and the UK. The birthplace distinction is relevant to US–UK differences because 48 percent of Britain's Chinese immigrants were born in Hong Kong compared to only 13 percent of foreign-born American Chinese. Since these ex-colonials fare less well in Britain than Chinese born elsewhere, in a US–UK comparison that ignores birthplace, the British Chinese emerge as less advantaged than the American. To be sure, this insight raises new questions. In particular, why the Hong Kong deficit in England and not America? Its most likely source is the liberal immigration policies that Britain adopted toward Hong Kong (Jowett et al. 1995). Such policies probably translate into a less positively selected Hong Kong population in Britain than in the USA, because, in the USA, Hong Kong residents enjoy no advantage in admission relative to Mainland Chinese, Taiwanese, and so on.

The value of this exercise is to demonstrate that statistical results often lend themselves to a variety of interpretations. Since the economic attainment of minorities is a multi-causal phenomenon, this should not be a surprise. Nevertheless, the extent of the US advantage is too great to attribute entirely to culture, class, and selectivity – all traits that immigrants bring with them. Such an attribution might be appropriate if the US advantage emerged for only a few groups, if it applied to only a few outcomes, if it developed in only a few datasets, or if it surfaced only in entrepreneurial minorities. But every group in the study registered a US advantage at least once; every outcome in the study exhibited a US advantage at least once, several datasets were brought to the undertaking, and the majority of members of all the included groups work for native whites. This suggests that there is a fundamental difference in the context of reception; it suggests that, alternative scenarios aside, white employers in America treat ethnic minorities a little better than white employers in Britain do.

NOTES

1. For more details on how ethnic groups were coded, see Model 1997.
2. Several models were estimated for each dependent variable. First, men's and women's experiences were modeled separately. In addition, because the study of unemployment and occupational prestige involved two British datasets (the NSEM and the SARs), two subsets of the PUMs data had to be created, one for use in the NSEM comparisons, another for use with the SARs. This step

could be omitted in the case of earnings, however, because only the NSEM contain an earnings variable.

3. Although weighting is appropriate when calculating descriptive statistics, it is inappropriate when calculating regression coefficients (Winship and Radbill 1994).

4. In the case of unemployment, Allison's (1999) method for comparing probit coefficients across models was utilized. Complete results of the multivariate analyses and of tests for coefficient differences are available from the author.

REFERENCES

Allison, P. D., 1999, "Comparing Logit and Probit Coefficients Across Groups," *Sociological Methods and Research* 28: 186–208.

Arnold, F. W., 1984, "West Indians and London's Hierarchy of Discrimination," *Ethnic Groups* 6: 47–64.

Borjas, G. J., 1993, "Immigration Policy, National Origin and Immigrant Skills: A Comparison of Canada and the United States," in D. Card and R. Freeman (eds.), *Small Differences that Matter: Labor Markets and Income Maintenance in Canada and the United States*, University of Chicago Press, pp. 21–44.

  1994, "The Economics of Immigration," *Journal of Economic Literature* 32: 1667–717.

Brown, C. and P. Gay, 1994, "Racial Discrimination 17 Years After the Act," in P. Burstein (ed.), *Equal Employment Opportunity: Labor Market Discrimination and Public Policy*, New York: Aldine de Gruyter, pp. 315–28.

Buxton, L. (ed.), 1995, *Employment Law in Europe*, 2nd edn., Aldershot: Coopers and Lybrand.

Cheng, Y., 1994, *Education and Class: Chinese in Britain and the US*, Avebury: Aldershot.

Cheng, Y. and A. Heath, 1993, "Ethnic Origins and Class Destinations," *Oxford Review of Education* 19, 2: 151–65.

Dobbin, Frank, J. Sutton, J. Mayer, and W. R. Scott, 1993, "Equal Opportunity Law and the Construction of Internal Labor Markets," *American Journal of Sociology* 99: 396–427.

Durr, M. and J. R. Logan, 1997, "Racial Submarkets in Government Employment: African American Managers in New York State," *Sociological Forum* 12: 353–70.

Esping-Andersen, G., 1999, *Social Foundations of Postindustrial Economies*, Oxford University Press.

Fieldhouse, E. A., 1996, "Putting Unemployment in Its Place: Using the Sample of Anonymised Records to Explore the Risk of Unemployment in Great Britain in 1991," *Regional Studies* 30: 119–33.

Foner, N., 1979, "West Indians in New York City and London: A Comparative Perspective," *International Migration Review* 13: 284–97.

Frisbie, W. P. and L. Neidert, 1977, "Inequality and the Relative Size of Minority Populations," *American Journal of Sociology* 82: 1007–30.

Gardner, K. and A. Shukur, 1994, "I'm Bengali, I'm Asian, and I'm Living Here," in R. Ballard (ed.), *Desh Pardesh: The South Asian Presence in Britain*, London: Hurst, pp. 142–64.

Heath, A., J. Roberts, and D. McMahon, 1997, "Education and Occupational Attainment: The Impact of Ethnic Origins," in Valerie Karn (ed.), *Ethnicity in the 1991 Census*, vol IV: *Employment, Education and Housing Among the Ethnic Minority Populations of Britain*, London: HMSO, pp. 91–113.

Heckman, J., 1976, "The Common Structure of Statistical Models of Truncation, Sample Selection and Limited Dependent Variables and a Simple Estimator for Such Models," *Annals of Economic and Social Measurement* 5: 475–92.

Hodge, R. W., 1973, "Toward a Theory of Racial Differences in Employment," *Social Forces* 52: 16–31.

Holdsworth, C. and A. Dale, 1997, "Ethnic Differences in Women's Employment," *Work, Employment and Society* 11: 435–57.

Jowett, A. J., A. M. Findlay, F. L. N. Li, and R. Skeldon, 1995, "The British Who Are Not British and the Immigration Policies That Are Not: The Case of Hong Kong," *Applied Geography* 15: 245–65.

Lee, Everett S., 1966, "A Theory of Migration," *Demography* 3: 47–57.

Leslie, D. (ed.), 1998, *An Investigation of Racial Disadvantage*, Manchester University Press.

Lieberson, S., 1980, *A Piece of the Pie*, Berkeley: University of California.

Light, I., 1984, "Immigrant and Ethnic Enterprise in North America," *Ethnic and Racial Studies* 7: 195–216.

Light, I., G. Sabagh, M. Bozorgmehr, and C. Der-Martirosian, 1994, "Beyond the Ethnic Enclave Economy," *Social Problems* 41: 65–80.

Lim, N., 1999, "Employers' Ratings of Work Related Qualities of Racial and Ethnic Groups," unpublished manuscript, University of California at Los Angeles.

Lipset, S. M., 1991, "American Exceptionalism Reaffirmed," in B. E. Shafer (ed.), *Is America Different?*, Oxford: Clarendon Press, pp. 1–45.

MacEwen, M., 1995, *Tackling Racism in Europe: An Examination of Anti-Discrimination Law in Practice*, Oxford: Berg.

Maddala, G. S., 1983, *Limited Dependent and Qualitative Variables in Econometrics*, Cambridge University Press.

Model, S., 1997, "An Occupational Tale of Two Cities: Minorities in London and New York," *Demography* 34: 539–50.

2000, "A Cross-National Look at Chinese Immigrant Occupations," in A. Dale, E. Fieldhouse, and C. Holdsworth (eds.), *Analyzing Census Microdata*, London: Edwin Arnold, pp. 195–200.

Model, S., G. Fisher, and R. Silberman, 1999, "Black Caribbeans in Comparative Perspective," *Journal of Ethnic and Migration Studies* 25: 187–212.

Model, S. and D. Ladipo, 1996, "Context and Opportunity: Minorities in London and New York," *Social Forces* 75: 485–510.

Nee, V. and J. Sanders, Forthcoming, "Understanding the Diversity of Immigrant Incorporation," *Ethnic and Racial Studies*.

Phizacklea, A. and M. Ram, 1996, "Being Your Own Boss: Ethnic Minority Entrepreneurs in Comparative Perspective," *Work, Employment and Society* 10: 319–39.

Rex, J. and S. Tomlinson, 1979, *Colonial Immigrants to a British City*, London: Routledge and Kegan Paul.

Rose, D. L., 1994, "Twenty-Five Years Later: Where Do We Stand on Equal Employment Opportunity Law Enforcement?" in P. Burstein (ed.), *Equal Employment Opportunity*, New York: Aldine de Gruyter, pp. 39–57.

Simpson, S., 1996, "Non-Response to the 1991 Census: The Effects On Ethnic Group Enumeration," in D. Coleman and J. Salt (eds.), *Demographic Characteristics of Minority Populations*, Vol. I, London: HMSO, pp. 63–80.

Small, S., 1994, *Racialised Barriers*, London: Routledge.

Smith, J. P. and F. R. Welch, 1994, "Black Economic Progress After Myrdal," in P. Burstein (ed.), *Equal Employment Opportunity*, New York: Aldine de Gruyter, pp. 155–82.

Smith, P. and G. Prior, 1996, *The Fourth National Survey of Ethnic Minorities*, London: Social and Community Planning Research.

Smith, T. W., 1991, *What Do Americans Think About Jews?* New York: American Jewish Committee.

Sowell, T., 1994, *Race and Culture: A World View*, New York: Basic Books.

Thurow, L. C., 1975, *Generating Inequality*, New York: Basic Books.

Waldinger, R., 1996, *Still the Promised City?* Cambridge, MA: Harvard University Press.

Waters, M. C., 1996, "Ethnic and Racial Identities of Second-Generation Black Immigrants in New York City," in A. Portes (ed.), *The New Second Generation*, New York: Russell Sage Foundation, pp. 171–96.

Widgren, J., 1994, *A Comparative Analysis of Entry and Asylum Policies in Selected Western Countries*, Vienna: ICMPD.

Winship, C. and L. Radbill, 1994, "Sampling Weights and Regression Analysis," *Sociological Methods and Research* 23: 230–57.

Zhou, Min, 1992, *Chinatown*, Philadelphia: Temple University Press.

Zipp, John F., 1994, "Government Employment and Black–White Earnings Inequality, 1980–1990," *Social Problems* 41: 363–82.

14   Social mobility of ethnic minorities

Anthony F. Heath and Dorren McMahon

Introduction

There has been remarkably little research on the social mobility of ethnic minorities in Britain. This contrasts with the huge amount of research on intergenerational social mobility among the native population of Britain (and of other Western societies), focusing in particular on the extent of social reproduction – that is, on the extent to which sons (and more rarely daughters) are able to secure similar positions in the class structure to those held by their fathers. The nature of these intergenerational processes of social mobility and stability are now reasonably well understood. Some of the major findings are that there has been substantial intergenerational continuity, particularly among the petty bourgeoisie and the more privileged groups in the salariat; but that at the same time there have been substantial opportunities for upward mobility from the working class as a result of increasing "room at the top" (see, for example, Goldthorpe 1987, Heath and Payne 2000).

In an early study, based on data from 1972, Heath and Ridge (1983) looked at the social mobility of the first generation of ethnic minority men who had migrated to Britain in the 1950s and 1960s. They suggested that migration broke the close link that usually obtains between father's and son's class position, and they found that nonwhite migrants and white migrants from the Republic of Ireland were less likely to have been intergenerationally stable, and were more likely to have been downwardly mobile, than the British-born white men. This accords with much of the other literature at this time which emphasized the disadvantages experienced by migrants in Britain (Daniel 1968, Castles and Kosack 1973).

Possible explanations for the downward mobility experienced by the migrants clearly include racial discrimination. However, as Heath and Ridge pointed out, the similarity between the experiences of the Irish and of the nonwhite migrants suggests that other mechanisms might have been at work too. A second factor might have been the lack of

British qualifications held by the migrants: it would not be surprising if British employers did not evaluate foreign qualifications as favorably as the native ones with which they were familiar. Moreover, lack of fluency in the English language might have held back some migrants, particularly those from the Indian subcontinent. Migrants might also have lacked the social contacts and connections that have been shown to be important in securing well-paid jobs. While ethnic minorities might well have strong ties with coethnics, these might be more useful within the ethnic enclave economy than within the labor market dominated by white British employers.

Lack of British qualifications, lack of fluency in the English language, and lack of British social connections would have been particularly disadvantageous for the first generation. If these explanations are correct, then the picture may now look rather different among the second generation who have been born and brought up in this country, have acquired British qualifications and fluency in English, and have had an opportunity to develop British social networks.

Iganski and Payne (1996) have indeed found evidence of considerable improvement over time in the economic position of ethnic minorities. They found that, by 1991, members of ethnic minorities had substantially closed the gap on the British-born white population. They termed this "collective social mobility." Using Labour Force Survey (LFS) data Iganski and Payne argue that

the data go a long way towards exploding the conventional myth that ethnic minorities are increasingly concentrated in two main socio-economic groups: low-skilled manual work and small-scale business activities . . . Rather than concentration, the picture is one of dispersal. While the minority ethnic groups do not have identical occupational distributions to those of the white group, they are now much closer than twenty-five years ago. (1996: 129)

Iganski and Payne do not, however, have data on the class origins of the ethnic minority members (since their main data source, the LFS, does not ascertain father's class); as they themselves emphasize theirs is not an analysis of intergenerational mobility in the conventional sense used in social mobility research. Nevertheless their results are important and suggest that the pessimistic view of early researchers on the social mobility of ethnic minorities may now need revising.

Our aims in this paper are first, to look at the intergenerational mobility, using the term in the classic sense, of ethnic minorities in Britain and in particular to see if the second generation have experienced higher rates of upwards mobility than the first. A second aim is to establish whether social class origins operate in the same way among ethnic minorities as in the white British population. Are ethnic minorities internally stratified by social class in the same way that the white British population is? Or does ethnicity override class, leading members of an ethnic minority to experience rather similar occupational fortunes irrespective of their class origins? One possibility is that class origins will have a rather smaller impact on the class destinations of the ethnic minorities than they do with the white population. This might be the case if ethnicity "trumps" class and if ethnic minorities were unable to achieve the same kind of social reproduction that is found among the British white population.

Data and measures

To explore these questions we draw on the General Household Survey (GHS), focusing on men and women aged twenty and over at the time of the survey. The GHS is a large-scale representative survey of British households conducted by the Office for National Statistics. It has the crucial advantage over the other major sources used by researchers such as the Labour Force Surveys and the Fourth National Survey of Ethnic Minorities (NSEM) that data on father's class were collected in the GHS.

In order to obtain sufficient numbers of ethnic minority members we use all the GHSs for the years 1985–92. Before 1985 the data on father's class were not obtained in a form that enables us to construct the social class distinctions that we need. After 1992 the GHS stopped collecting data on father's class altogether. We have therefore pooled the 1985–92 data and this yields a sample of the main ethnic minorities that is sufficient for some limited analysis. The numbers of second-generation ethnic minorities in the pooled dataset are unfortunately rather small, and our conclusions will therefore be rather tentative. Moreover, because of the very small numbers involved, we have to omit any discussion of the second-generation Pakistanis. However, this is the best that can be done with existing British data.

Ethnicity

The categorization used in the GHS distinguished White, Indian, Pakistani, West Indian/Guyanan, Bangladeshi, African, Arab, and Chinese with a residual category for mixed and other ethnicities. The Bangladeshi, African, Arab, and Chinese categories are excluded from the present study because their sample sizes were too small for useful analysis. The category mixed/other is also too heterogeneous for useful analysis. However, we have added an additional ethnic category, namely the Irish, whom we have been able to identify from data on country of birth (and parents' country of birth). The Irish represent the largest white ethnic minority in Britain and provide a valuable point of comparison with the other main ethnic minorities.

Social class

The GHS obtained data on the socioeconomic group (SEG) of the respondent and his/her father according to the standard official scheme. We have grouped SEGs to form the following classes:

1. Higher salariat (managers and administrators in large enterprises together with members of "old" professions such as doctors and lawyers) – SEGs 1.2, 3, 4.
2. Lower salariat (managers and administrators in small enterprises together with members of "new" professions such as teachers and nurses) – SEGs 2.2, 5.1.
3. Routine non-manual (clerical workers and their supervisors) – SEGs 5.2 and 6.
4. Petty bourgeoisie (employers and own account workers) – SEGs 1.1, 2.1, 12.
5. Farmers and farm managers – SEGs 13, 14.
6. Skilled manual (and their supervisors) – SEGs 8, 9.
7. Less-skilled (semi- and unskilled manual workers and service workers) – SEGs 7, 10, 11.
8. Farm workers – SEG 15.

This is a slightly adapted version of Goldthorpe's class schema which distinguishes classes according to their terms and conditions of employment (Goldthorpe 1987). It should be noted that this is only a partially ordered schema. For example, routine non-manual workers, skilled manual workers, farmers and the petty bourgeoisie have rather different conditions of employment, but it is not sensible to place them into a simple hierarchy. For example, the income and net rewards of skilled manual workers may be higher on average than those of routine non-manual workers, but their promotion chances and working conditions might be worse.

Generation

The first generation are defined as people who were born in countries other than the UK (Northern Ireland of course being included in the UK) other than those who migrated to the UK before age five. The second generation is defined as containing people who were born in the UK, together with people who came to Britain before age five, and who thus will have received all their education in Britain.

Birth cohort

In our analysis we distinguish two birth cohorts, the first containing respondents born in the years 1940 to 1959 and the second containing those born in the years 1960 to 1979. We restrict ourselves to these two birth cohorts since there were too few members of ethnic minorities born in earlier years in the relevant GHSs to permit useful analysis.

As noted above, we also distinguish two generations, the first generation who were born overseas and migrated to Britain in adulthood (or after starting their education) and the second generation who were brought up and received all their education in Britain. Because of the timing of the main periods of migration to Britain, most of the members of the earlier birth cohort were also first-generation, while almost all the second generation belong to the second birth cohort.

It is difficult therefore (especially given our rather small sample sizes) to differentiate generation from birth cohort. What we do instead is to make a virtue of necessity and combine the two criteria. Thus we focus on first-generation members born in the years 1940 to 1959 and on second-generation members born in the years 1960 to 1979. Broadly speaking the second-generation/birth cohort will be the children of the first-generation/birth cohort (although there will be the usual caveats, some members of the first generation not having children, and so on). Our strategy is to compare each of these two generations with British-born whites in the corresponding birth cohort. In this way we can investigate whether the second generation have obtained parity of experience with their white peers.

Class origins

We begin by describing the class origins of our two generations of respondents. Table 14.1a shows the class origins of the first generation, that is of ethnic minority members born overseas in the years 1940–59. Their class origins will therefore refer to the kinds of circumstances in which they were brought up in their countries of origin. We compare their class origins with those of whites born in Britain during the same period of 1940–59. There is inevitably a great deal of uncertainty as to whether we are comparing like with like when we compare class origins in Britain with those in the Caribbean or the Indian subcontinent. The problems are particularly large in the case of farming origins. In Britain, farms are relatively large and farmers are relatively affluent. In the subcontinent, many people who describe themselves (or in this case their fathers) as farmers will have plots of land of only a few acres and will

Table 14.1a *Class origins by ethnic group: British-born whites and first-generation ethnic minorities (men and women)*

	Respondents born 1940–59 (column percentages)				
	British-born white	Irish	Black Caribbean	Indian	Pakistani
Higher salariat	6	4	5	7	6
Lower salariat	16	7	4	12	8
Routine non-manual	5	4	5	8	3
Petty bourgeoisie	10	11	17	33	18
Farmers	3	23	13	12	23
Skilled manual	40	22	32	14	14
Less-skilled manual	19	23	20	12	25
Farm workers	2	6	5	2	5
N	46760	564	313	789	267

essentially be subsistence farmers. Irish farming probably comes somewhere in between. However, the relative position of farmers within the Indian class structure is probably not all that different from its relative position in Britain, despite the huge absolute differences in the circumstances of the two sets of farmers. Thus in India farmers with their own land, even if it is only a few acres, will still live in somewhat more privileged circumstances than landless agricultural laborers or semi- and unskilled workers engaged in manual work.

As might be expected, the class origins of the first-generation ethnic minorities are somewhat different from those of the British-born whites. Fewer of them came from managerial or skilled manual backgrounds, and more of them came from farming or (in the case of Indians and Pakistanis) from entrepreneurial origins. Perhaps the most striking difference occurs with farming origins. Only 5 percent of the British-born whites in this older birth cohort came from farming origins, compared with 29 percent of the Irish and 28 percent of the Pakistanis. Many of the migrants, therefore, will have been newcomers not just to Britain but also to an urban industrial environment.

Whereas in the case of the first generation the reported class backgrounds referred to positions in the countries of origin, in the case of the second generation it is likely that they refer to positions in Britain and that they largely reflect the experiences of the first generation in the British labor market. At any rate, in the second generation the excess of farming origins has completely disappeared and we see a pattern of class origins that is quite familiar from studies of British society.

Table 14.1b *Class origins by ethnic group: British-born whites and second generation ethnic minorities (men and women)*

	Respondents born 1960–79 (column percentages)			
	British-born white	Irish	Black Caribbean	Indian
Higher salariat	9	5	4	3
Lower salariat	18	9	5	5
Routine non-manual	4	3	2	8
Petty bourgeoisie	15	16	15	24
Farmers	2	1	0	1
Skilled manual	35	37	43	34
Less-skilled manual	15	30	32	26
Farm workers	1	0	0	0
N	21783	329	249	134

Note: figures for Pakistani women are not shown as the numbers are too small.

However, all three ethnic minorities on whom we have adequate data show larger proportions coming from working-class origins (defined as skilled manual together with the less-skilled category) than is the case for the British-born whites of the same birth cohort. In particular, we see in Table 14.1b that 75 percent of second-generation Black Caribbeans had working-class origins compared with 50 percent of the British-born whites. Irish and Indians in the second generation also showed higher proportions with working-class origins, with figures of 67 percent and 60 percent respectively.

Social mobility of men

We now turn to the question of mobility opportunities. We begin by describing the class positions achieved in Britain by the first- and second-generation members of ethnic minorities, and we then go on to consider whether this has represented upward intergenerational mobility. We focus on men in this section and then turn to women in the next section.

Among the first generation, we can see from Table 14.2a that the ethnic minorities had generally somewhat less advantaged class positions than the British-born whites. Thus there were fewer ethnic minority men in the higher salariat – the Indians being closest to the white British figures and the Pakistanis furthest away. Similarly, larger proportions, especially of Pakistanis, were in less-skilled work. This is the familiar picture of ethnic minority disadvantage, relative to British-born whites, that was demonstrated by the earlier researchers in this area.

Table 14.2a *Current class by ethnic group: British-born whites and first-generation ethnic minorities (men)*

	Respondents born 1940–59 (column percentages)				
	British-born white	Irish	Black Caribbean	Indian	Pakistani
Higher salariat	21	14	10	18	8
Lower salariat	17	16	14	12	10
Routine non-manual	5	3	3	5	7
Petty bourgeoisie	14	22	14	24	22
Farmers	1	0	0	0	0
Skilled manual	27	26	42	22	22
Less-skilled manual	13	19	18	19	31
Farm workers	1	0	0	0	0
N	23816	268	146	427	153

Table 14.2b *Intergenerational class mobility: British-born whites and first-generation ethnic minorities (men)*

	Respondents born 1940–59				
	British-born white	Irish	Black Caribbean	Indian	Pakistani
Stable	30	25	28	24	18
Upward	41	44	39	34	36
Downward	17	14	16	23	24
Sideways	12	17	17	19	21

In Table 14.2b we show some summary indices of absolute mobility rates. We distinguish between those who were stable, upwardly mobile, downwardly mobile, and who had experienced what we term sideways mobility. We have to include a category for sideways mobility since, as described above, the class schema that we are using is only partially hierarchical. In particular the junior non-manual, petty bourgeois, farming, and skilled manual classes are all at broadly similar levels. They are clearly inferior to posts in the salariat and are superior to unskilled manual work or agricultural labor but are not clearly "higher" or "lower" than each other. We therefore define movements between these four classes as sideways ones. We also define movements between unskilled manual and agricultural labor as sideways movements. We therefore restrict the term upward mobility to refer to movement from classes 7 or 8 to any of the higher classes, movement from classes 3, 4, 5, or 6 to classes 1 or 2, and movement from class 2 up to class 1. Downward mobility is the converse of this, while stability covers those respondents who were in the same class as their father. Consider first the British-born white pattern for the 1940–59 birth cohort. This shows net upward mobility in this birth cohort, 41 percent being in a higher social class than their father but only 17 percent being in a lower social class. This surplus of upwards over downwards mobility reflects the occupational changes that had been taking place in Britain in the postwar period with increasing "room at the top" (Heath 1981, Goldthorpe 1987).

All four ethnic minorities also experienced substantial net upward mobility too even in this first generation. The upward mobility was greatest among the Irish, where it slightly exceeded British-born white levels, and among the Black Caribbeans. In contrast, the Indians and Pakistanis experienced rather higher levels of downward mobility, and they showed a much smaller net surplus of upward over downward movement than did the British or Irish whites.

In addition, all four ethnic minorities showed lower rates of stability than did the British-born whites. This is largely explained by their higher rates of sideways movement. This is not at all surprising given that many came from farming origins but had moved to some kind of manual work in Britain. As we noted earlier, Britain and the various countries of origin have very different occupational structures and so this shift from farming origins to manual destinations among the first generation is precisely what we would expect.

Earlier research, particularly in the early years of migration to Britain, suggested that many of the migrants had suffered downward mobility on arrival in Britain (Daniel 1968). This may have been true at the beginning of their occupational careers in Britain but it is likely that, by the time of our surveys in the late 1980s and early 1990s, many of the migrants had managed to recapture some of the ground they had lost as they acquired more know-how about how to find jobs in Britain. (For evidence of the upward intragenerational mobility of these first-generation migrants see Robinson 1990, Fielding 1995). At any rate, the rather pessimistic accounts of the mobility experiences of the first generation would seem to be rather wide of the mark by the late 1980s and 1990s when our surveys were conducted.

In Tables 14.3a and 3b we turn to the second generation. We have to omit the Pakistanis from this analysis as the numbers in our sample are too small. We must also remember that at the time of our surveys, that is in the years 1985–92, the second generation will have been much younger than the first generation were at this time. We are therefore looking at

Table 14.3a *Current class by ethnic group: British-born whites and second-generation ethnic minorities (men)*

| | Respondents born 1960–79 (column percentages) | | | |
	British-born white	Irish	Black Caribbean	Indian
Higher salariat	12	13	6	18
Lower salariat	14	16	8	23
Routine non-manual	11	11	16	23
Petty bourgeoisie	10	11	5	11
Farmers	1	0	0	0
Skilled manual	30	28	33	14
Less-skilled manual	21	22	32	11
Farm workers	2	0	0	0
N	11193	177	125	63

Table 14.3b *Intergenerational class mobility: British-born whites and second-generation ethnic minorities (men)*

| | Respondents born 1960–79 (column percentages) | | | |
	British-born white	Irish	Black Caribbean	Indian
Stable	31	31	37	23
Upward	25	40	25	55
Downward	31	15	21	9
Sideways	14	14	17	14

them at an earlier stage of their careers and so we do not see the net upward mobility that we saw in the first generation. This applies to the British-born whites just as much as it does to the ethnic minorities. What we see instead is higher proportions of sons than of fathers in routine non-manual work, which tends to be the kind of job that people take up on entering the labor market. Over the next twenty years or so we can expect to see substantial net upward mobility for all groups alike as they move up the occupational ladder.

In Table 14.3b we then give the summary indices of absolute social mobility for the second generation, and as before we compare them with the experiences of the British-born whites of the same birth cohort. The main story from Table 14.3b is that the second-generation ethnic minorities are more likely to have experienced upward mobility than the British-born whites of the same birth cohort. For example, whereas 25 percent of British-born whites in this younger birth cohort were upwardly mobile and 31 percent were downwardly mobile, a net deficit of six percentage points, all three ethnic minorities showed net surpluses of upward mobility. However, this rather optimistic picture for ethnic minorities may simply reflect their lower starting points. As we saw in Table 14.1b, the second-generation ethnic minorities in Britain were more likely to have working-class (or farming) origins than were the British whites. This means that there was more room for them to move up the class structure. The fact that the ethnic minorities seem to have experienced greater upward mobility than the British whites does not therefore necessarily imply that they no longer suffer disadvantages in the British labor market. We need to take account of the different starting points of the different ethnic groups in order to compare their success or otherwise in the labor market.

We can explore this with multivariate models. To simplify the analysis we focus on access to the salariat and therefore use logistic regression. We begin by fitting a series of models. In model A social class origins constitutes the explanatory variable. In model B we add ethnicity and in model C we add the interaction between ethnicity and class origins. The interaction enables us to check whether class origins operate in the same way among the ethnic minorities as they do among the British whites. That is, model C enables us to test whether the associations between class origins and class destinations are the same for the ethnic minorities as they are for the British-born whites. In order to carry out a parsimonious analysis we treat class as a continuous rather than as a categorical variable in the interaction terms. By assuming that class is continuous we do lose some information and make some simplifying assumptions. However, the sample sizes are insufficient for a more complex analysis. Since, as noted above, the class schema that we are using is only partially hierarchical, we group classes 3, 4, 5, 6 at the same level, and similarly group classes 7 and 8 together. Table 14.4a shows the fit of this sequence of models. The first column shows the model fits for the first generation and the second column for the second generation. We find that, in both generations, model B gives a significant improvement in fit over model A. This means that, even after controlling for class origins, there are significant differences between ethnic groups in their chances of reaching the salariat.

However, we then find that in neither generation does model C offer a significant improvement in fit over model B. In the case of the first generation, the change in fit is only 3.2 for the loss of 4 degrees of freedom ($p > 0.10$) and in the case of the second generation the change in fit is 4.1 for the loss of 3 degrees of freedom ($p > 0.10$). This indicates

Table 14.4a *Fit (chi square) of models of access to the salariat: British-born white and first- and second-generation ethnic minority men*

	Respondents born	
	1940–59	1960–69
Model A class origins	2465.7 (7 df)	897.0 (7 df)
Model B class origins, ethnicity	2500.9 (11 df)	923.5 (10 df)
Model C class origins, ethnicity, class origins*ethnicity	2504.1 (15 df)	927.6 (13 df)
N	23,699	10,937

Note: degrees of freedom (df) are given in brackets.

that class origins have the same strength of association with access to the salariat among the ethnic minorities as they do among the British-born whites. This is not perhaps altogether surprising among the second generation, but it is an important result for the first generation. It shows that ethnicity does not "trump" class background: the same kind and extent of social reproduction exists among the ethnic minorities, and among those who migrated to Britain from overseas, as among the British whites.

In Table 14.4b we then show the parameter estimates of model B (the best-fitting model). In the case of ethnicity we take British-born whites as the reference category, and in the case of social class origins we take less-skilled manual work as the reference category. The parameter estimates for ethnicity thus tell us whether the different ethnic minorities have the same, better or worse chances of gaining access to the salariat as white British from the same class origins. Significant negative parameter estimates indicate that the ethnic minorities do less well than do white British men from the same class origin. The first column in Table 14.4b shows the parameter estimates for the first generation. It shows, as expected, that class origins have a powerful effect on class destinations. It also shows that in general the first-generation ethnic minorities had significantly poorer chances of reaching the salariat than did white British men from the same birth cohort and similar class origins (insofar as class origins can be compared across countries). All three visible ethnic minorities have large and statistically significant negative parameter estimates, but the Irish show no ethnic disadvantage once one has controlled for class origins. In other words white Irish seemed to be competing on equal terms with white British men of the same age and same class origins.

Table 14.4b *Parameter estimates of logistic regression model of access to the salariat: British-born white and first- and second-generation ethnic minority men*

	Respondents born	
	1940–59	1960–69
Constant	−1.15 (.04)	−1.84 (.07)
Ethnic group		
British-born white	0	0
Irish	0.00 (.15)	0.49 (.19)
Black Caribbean	−0.44 (.21)	−0.50 (.27)
Indian	−0.39 (.11)	1.05 (.25)
Pakistani	−0.95 (.24)	na
Father's class		
Upper salariat	2.10 (.07)	1.74 (.09)
Lower salariat	1.66 (.05)	1.64 (.08)
Routine white-collar	1.06 (.07)	0.94 (.13)
Petty bourgeoisie	0.70 (.06)	0.50 (.09)
Farmers	0.55 (.10)	0.34 (.20)
Skilled manual	0.32 (.04)	0.32 (.08)
Less-skilled manual	0	0
Farm workers	−0.53 (.12)	−0.60 (.35)
N	23,699	10,937

Note: Standard errors are given in brackets.

So although the first generation seemed to have experienced almost as much or more upward mobility as the British whites, the implication is that (with the exception of the Irish) they did not achieve as much upward mobility as would have been expected given their low starting points.

In the second generation the results look rather different from those for the first generation. We find that the ethnic parameter estimates for the second generation are positive for both the Irish and for the Indians. That is, both these groups have superior chances of gaining access to the salariat to those of white British men from similar class origins. In the case of these two groups, then, their higher rates of upward mobility are to be explained not only by their lower starting points but also by their greater competitive success in the labor market. However, the Black Caribbean men show no real change in the second generation from that in the first generation. To be sure, the Caribbean parameter estimate is not significantly different

Table 14.5a *Current class by ethnic group: British-born whites and first-generation ethnic minorities (women)*

| | Respondents born 1940–59 (column percentage) | | | | |
	British-born white	Irish	Black Caribbean	Indian	Pakistani
Higher salariat	5	6	2	4	0
Lower salariat	24	27	41	15	29
Routine non-manual	31	28	18	24	23
Petty bourgeoisie	6	5	3	12	14
Farmers	1	0	0	0	0
Skilled manual	5	5	4	6	2
Less-skilled manual	28	35	33	39	33
Farm workers	1	0	0	1	0
N	24583	330	210	332	52

from zero. However, its magnitude is effectively the same as that for the first generation, and one could not reject the hypothesis that the ethnic disadvantages experienced by Black Caribbeans in competing with whites from the same class origins have remained constant over time.

Women's social mobility

As with men we begin by reviewing the current class positions of our female respondents at the times of the surveys (that is, from 1985 to 1992). However, in the case of women it is important to remember that there are important variations in the proportions of women from the different ethnic groups who are economically active (see Holdsworth and Dale 1997). Black Caribbean women, for example, have slightly higher rates of economic activity than do British-born white women, Indians have slightly lower rates, and Pakistani women have very much lower rates of economic activity. Among those who are economically active, there are substantial differences in rates of full-time and part-time working (Holdsworth and Dale 1997). In general, ethnic minority women are more likely to work full-time than are British white women.

In Table 14.5a we show the current (at the time of the surveys) class positions of the 1940–59 birth cohort of women. The first, and well-known point, is that the class distribution of women is very different from that of men, with relatively few women in the higher salariat, in the petty bourgeoisie, or in skilled manual work. Instead, women are concentrated in the lower salariat (for example as teachers and nurses), in routine

Table 14.5b *Intergenerational class mobility: British-born whites and first-generation ethnic minorities (women)*

	Respondents born 1940–59 (column percentages)				
	British-born white	Irish	Black Caribbean	Indian	Pakistani
Stable	19	16	16	18	17
Upward	30	39	46	20	23
Downward	31	28	24	44	38
Sideways	20	17	14	19	23

white-collar work (for example as secretaries and receptionists), and in less-skilled work. This is clearly shown for the British-born white women, and the picture is more or less repeated for all four ethnic minorities as well.

As with first-generation men, first-generation women from all four ethnic minorities had somewhat larger proportions in less-skilled work than was the case for the white British. However, it is not a simple picture of ethnic minority disadvantage. In particular the Black Caribbean women had a much higher proportion in the lower salariat than did the white British. This almost certainly reflects the fact that many women were recruited from the Caribbean to work as nurses in the NHS.

We should also note that, in complete contrast to the first-generation men, first-generation Indian women were one of the least successful groups, with the highest proportion in manual work (45 percent) and the lowest percentage in non-manual work (39 percent). This could perhaps be a consequence of lack of English fluency among the first-generation Indian women. Lack of fluency might well preclude them from obtaining non-manual work and constrain them to enter (if they decided to be economically active) into less-skilled work. In Table 14.5b we show the summary indices of the first-generation women's absolute mobility rates. As before we distinguish between those who were stable, upwardly mobile, downwardly mobile, and those who had experienced what we term sideways mobility. Consider first the British-born white pattern for the 1940–59 birth cohort. Whereas the men in this cohort showed substantial net upward mobility, among white women there is a rough balance between upward and downward mobility, with 30 percent being in a higher class than their father and 31 percent in a lower class. These are much higher figures for downward mobility than we saw for men, and correspondingly we find generally much lower figures for intergenerational

Table 14.6a *Current class by ethnic group: British-born whites and second-generation ethnic minorities (women)*

	Respondents born 1960–79 (column percentage)			
	British-born white	Irish	Black Caribbean	Indian
Higher salariat	6	7	1	5
Lower salariat	22	19	26	18
Routine non-manual	37	44	47	48
Petty bourgeoisie	3	1	2	3
Farmers	0	0	0	0
Skilled manual	5	6	3	0
Less-skilled manual	26	24	22	27
Farm workers	1	0	0	0
N	11193	177	125	63

stability for women than for men. These patterns are exactly what one would expect given the distribution of women's current class positions.

In contrast, the Irish and Black Caribbean women in this cohort showed a substantial surplus of upward over downward mobility, whereas the Indian and Pakistani women showed a substantial surplus in the opposite direction, with larger numbers going down than up. Again, this is the pattern we would have expected from our inspection of the current occupational profiles. Turning next to the second generation, we see a convergence between the occupational profiles of the ethnic minorities and those of the British-born whites. The proportions in less-skilled manual work are quite similar, as are those in the salariat. On the one hand, the Black Caribbean women have lost their distinctively high proportion in the salariat; on the other hand, the Indian women have lost their distinctively high proportion in the less-skilled work.

Since the ethnic minorities tended to have less advantaged class origins than the British-born whites, the implication of this convergence in class destinations is that the minorities will have experienced more upward mobility than the British whites. This is indeed what we find in Table 14.6b; with all three ethnic minorities showing net surpluses of upward over downward mobility, in contrast with the British white surplus of downward mobility.

As before, we need to check whether this is simply a reflection of the ethnic minorities' lower starting points, and whether there are any persistent ethnic disadvantages in the second generation. We proceed as with men to fit a series of nested models. The results are broadly similar to

Table 14.6b *Intergenerational class mobility: British-born whites and second-generation ethnic minorities (women)*

| | Respondents born 1960–79 | | | |
	British-born white	Irish	Black Caribbean	Indian
Stable	18	14	8	16
Upward	26	38	42	30
Downward	35	25	19	24
Sideways	22	23	31	30

Table 14.7a *Fit of models of access to the salariat: British-born white and first- and second-generation ethnic minority women*

| | Respondents born | |
	1940–59	1960–69
Model A class origins	1446.8 (7 df)	567.6 (7 df)
Model B class origins, ethnicity	1503.8 (11 df)	569.5 (10 df)
Model C class origins, ethnicity, class origins*ethnicity	1506.1 (15 df)	574.1 (13 df)
N	24,111	11,558

Note: degrees of freedom (df) are given in brackets.

those for men: class origins are powerfully associated with access to the salariat (model A); ethnicity has a significant association with access to the salariat even after controlling for origins (model B), but the interaction between origins and ethnicity fails to yield a significant improvement in fit. However, unlike the case for men, this story applies only to the first generation. Among second-generation women we find that ethnicity itself does not have a significant association with access to the salariat once one has controlled for class origins. In Table 14.7b we then show the parameter estimates for model B. In the case of the first generation we see that class origins have the large effects that we found for men (although interestingly they are not quite as strong as the male effects). Turning to the ethnic parameter estimates, however, we find that, unlike men, both Irish women and Black Caribbean have significant positive estimates while only the Indian and Pakistani women have negative estimates.

In the second generation we then see the ethnic convergence that we had observed in the class distributions. None of the three parameter

Table 14.7b *Logit model of access to the salariat:*
British-born white and first- and second-generation
ethnic minority women

	Respondents born	
	1940–9	1960–79
Constant	−1.48 (.04)	−1.63 (.06)
Ethnic group		
British-born white	0	0
Irish	0.28 (.13)	0.09 (.18)
Black Caribbean	0.70 (.16)	0.26 (.21)
Indian	−0.75 (.15)	−0.11 (.31)
Pakistani	−0.45 (.34)	na
Father's class		
Upper salariat	1.78 (.07)	1.49 (.09)
Lower salariat	1.32 (.05)	1.28 (.08)
Routine white-collar	0.95 (.07)	0.72 (.12)
Petty bourgeoisie	0.77 (.06)	0.58 (.08)
Farmers	0.57 (.09)	1.08 (.16)
Skilled manual	0.30 (.05)	0.32 (.07)
Less-skilled manual	0	0
Farm workers	−0.10 (.12)	0.24 (.23)
N	24111	11558

Note: Standard errors are given in brackets.

estimates is significantly different from zero, indicating that the three second-generation minorities are competing on more or less equal terms with white British women from the same class backgrounds.

Conclusions

The four ethnic minorities on whom we have concentrated in this chapter – Irish, Black Caribbean, Indian, and Pakistani – have come from relatively disadvantaged class origins compared with British-born whites of the same age. This held true both in the first and in the second generations, although for rather different reasons. In the first generation, the ethnic minorities had higher proportions coming from farming or self-employed backgrounds, reflecting the occupational structures of their countries of origin. In the second generation, there was some convergence with British patterns, but the ethnic minorities were somewhat more likely to have had working-class origins than were British-born whites, perhaps reflecting the disadvantages that their parents (the first generation) had experienced in the British labor market.

Among the men we found that, in the first generation, all four ethnic minorities experienced substantial net upward mobility and not the downward mobility that had been found by earlier commentators. In this respect it was a more optimistic picture than that given by earlier researchers. However, multivariate analysis showed that, in the first generation, all three visible minorities experienced substantial disadvantages in the labor market compared with British-born whites from similar class origins (remembering that comparisons of class origins across countries must necessarily be rather rough). Only the Irish migrants appeared to compete on equal terms with white British from similar class origins.

In the second generation the picture was rather different. All three ethnic minorities for whom we have adequate data tended to have higher rates of upward mobility than the British-born whites. Irish, Black Caribbean, and Indian men all showed bigger surpluses of upward over downward mobility than did the white British men, and multivariate analysis showed that Irish and Indian men were more successful in gaining access to the salariat than were white British men from the same class origins, while Black Caribbean men were less successful.

In both generations, however, we found that class origins operated in much the same ways among ethnic minorities as they did among British-born whites. There was no sign from these data that migration disrupted processes of intergenerational social reproduction. Another way of looking at this is to say that ethnic minorities are internally stratified by social class in much the same way that British society is, and that ethnic minority sons from salaried backgrounds have much the same competitive advantages over their working-class coethnics as white British sons from salaried backgrounds have over the white British working class.

The patterns among women had some similarities with the male patterns, but there were also important differences, especially in the first generation. In the first generation, Black Caribbean women exhibited higher proportions in the salariat and higher rates of upward mobility than white British women: contrastingly, Indian and Pakistani women showed much higher rates of downward mobility than did white British women. However in the second generation, the ethnic groups had converged somewhat. As with the men, the Irish, Black, and Indian women all showed larger net surpluses of upward over downward mobility than did the white British, but the multivariate analysis showed that this could largely be explained by their lower starting points. Compared with white women from similar class backgrounds, ethnic minority women had more or less similar chances of gaining access to the salariat.

The only other recent study of intergenerational class mobility among ethnic minorities in Britain reaches broadly similar conclusions (Platt 2003). Our results are also broadly in line with other recent research on access to the salariat and on ethnic wage differences. Using the sample of anonymised records from the Census, and the Labour Force Surveys, other research has shown that ethnic disadvantages in the first generation have been reduced in the second generation (Model 1999, Heath, McMahon, and Roberts 2000, Leslie, Drinkwater, and O'Leary 1998). While this represents a rather optimistic picture of ethnic minority achievements in the British labor market, our research in this paper only applies to those in work. Other research (Berthoud 2000, Heath, McMahon, and Roberts 2000, Leslie, Drinkwater, and O'Leary 1998) has shown that, even among the second generation, there are still substantial disadvantages suffered by ethnic minority men in finding work. Black, Indian, and Pakistani men have much higher unemployment rates than British-born whites with similar education and experience. As Model (1999) argues "Native birth brings occupational improvement but does little to mitigate unemployment."

There are a number of possible explanations for this intergenerational progress. Perhaps the most plausible explanation is that the second generation have acquired British qualifications and fluency in the English language (Modood et al. 1997) and that this has given them much greater chances of access to the salariat. This could also explain why Black Caribbean men have made less progress than the Indian men: Black Caribbeans were not handicapped in the first generation by lack of fluency in English and so the second generation had nothing to gain in this respect.

However, there are still a number of puzzles that remain to be explained. In particular, why do Black Caribbean men, but not Caribbean women, remain less successful than the white British from similar class backgrounds? And why do Indian men, but not Indian women, tend to be more successful than their white peers? Simple answers in terms of discrimination or of cultural background would not seem adequate to explain the gender differences within ethnic minorities.

REFERENCES

Berthoud, R., 2000, "Ethnic Employment Penalties in Britain," *Journal of Ethnic and Migration Studies* 26: 389–416.

Castles, S. and G. Kosack, 1973, *Immigrant Workers and Class Structures in Western Europe*. Oxford: Oxford University Press.

Daniel, W. W., 1968, *Racial Discrimination in England*, London: Penguin.

Fielding, A. J., 1995, "Migration and Social Change: A Longitudinal Study of the Social Mobility of Immigrants in England and Wales," *European Journal of Population* 11: 107–21.

Goldthorpe, J. H., 1987, *Social Mobility and Class Structure in Modern Britain*, 2nd edn. Oxford: Clarendon Press.

Heath, A. F., 1981, *Social Mobility*, Glasgow: Fontana.

Heath, A. F. and C. Payne, 2000, "Social Mobility," in A. H. Halsey with J. Webb (eds.), *Twentieth-Century British Social Trends*, Basingstoke: Macmillan, pp. 254–78.

Heath, A., D. McMahon, and J. Roberts, 2000, "Ethnic Differences in the Labour Market: A Comparison of the SARs and LFS," *Journal of the Royal Statistical Society* 163: 341–61.

Heath, A. F. and J. M. Ridge, 1983, "Social mobility of ethnic minorities," *Journal of Biosocial Science*, supplement no. 8: 169–84.

Holdsworth, C. and A. Dale, 1997, "Ethnic Differences in Women's Employment," *Work, Employment and Society* 11: 435–57.

Iganski, P. and G. Payne, 1996, "Declining Racial Disadvantage in the British Labour Market," *Ethnic and Racial Studies* 19: 113–34.

Leslie, D., S. Drinkwater, and N. O'Leary, 1998, "Unemployment and Earnings among Britain's Ethnic Minorities: Some Signs for Optimism," *Journal of Ethnic and Migration Studies* 24: 489–506.

Model, Suzanne, 1999, "Ethnic Inequality in England: An Analysis Based on the 1991 Census," *Ethnic and Racial Studies* 22: 966–90.

Modood, T., R. Berthoud, J. Lakey, J. Nazroo, P. Smith, S. Virdee, and S. Beishon, 1997, *Ethnic Minorities in Britain: Diversity and Disadvantage*, London: Policy Studies Institute.

Platt, Lucinda, 2003, "The Intergenerational Social Mobility of Minority Ethnic Groups," ISER Working Papers, 2003–24.

Robinson, Vaughan, 1990, "Roots to Mobility: The Social Mobility of Britain's Black Population, 1971–1987," *Ethnic and Recial Studies* 13: 274–86.

15 Ethnic minorities, employment, self-employment, and social mobility in postwar Britain

Vaughan Robinson and Rina Valeny

1   Introduction

This chapter discusses the economic experience and social mobility of *postwar* black and Asian migrants to the UK, and their British-born descendants. While attempts will be made to generalize about this, three points need to be made explicit at the outset: these relate to historical setting, scale, and geography. Firstly, although the migrations under consideration are relatively recent, they need to be set within their historical contexts, for only by fully appreciating the historical precursors and settings can we understand the motivations and trajectories of these migrants, the mechanisms that brought them to these shores, and the responses to their arrival here. Secondly, although aggregate statistical data will be used to generalize about patterns of minority mobility, it is vital to remember that the migrations and migrants under discussion are far from homogeneous. The Caribbean migrations and migrants differ markedly from those from the Indian subcontinent, and neither is internally uniform. The South Asian population in the UK is made up of myriad different national, regional, religious, and linguistic groups, each with its own reasons for being in Britain, its own identity, and its own potentialities (Robinson 1984, 1986) and there are also internal differences within the West Indian population (Peach 1984). Our account will therefore generalize at one level but will also attempt to demonstrate the significance of these distinctive identities for social mobility trajectories. Thirdly, while we will generalize about social mobility in the UK, we also need to acknowledge the significance of place, noting that opportunity structures even within countries as small as the UK differ greatly between proximal locales, with their different industrial pasts, their different contemporary relations to the national economy, and their unique local political cultures. Where possible we will therefore seek to root our generalizations within specific localities.

414

2   Historical context

The postwar migrations from the Caribbean and the Indian subcontinent were neither unprecedented in British migration history nor were they the first association that these societies had with Britain.

Contrary to its proclaimed self-identity as an independent island "race," the British population has been forged from successive pulses of immigration from the time of the Roman invasions to the mass migrations of the nineteenth century from both Ireland and the Pale of Settlement in east Europe. And whilst these migrations contributed greatly to the constitution and reconstitution of "British identity," they also offered many individual immigrants the opportunity of social mobility. Whilst the experience of the Irish is discussed elsewhere in this volume, a vignette of another migrant group, the Italians, is instructive. Around 250,000 Italians migrated to the UK between 1861 and 1991, with early migrants walking from the valleys of northern Italy to seek work in London, and later migrants moving from the rural south of Italy to a more diversified set of regional destinations within the UK. Whilst the very early migrants were marble workers, statue makers, and musicians, later "mass" migrants soon identified and moved into another distinctive occupational niche, that of catering. Within this, they did not compete directly with local labor but, instead, provided a unique community service, a pattern that will be shown to have been repeated many times since for other ethnic groups. Colpi (1991) describes how by the mid-1920s nearly every Italian family in Wales or Scotland owned at least one business selling either ice cream, confectionery, or fish and chips. Most families, and their businesses, became welcome and accepted parts of local life. In the newly industrializing South Wales valleys, for example, Italians opened small corner cafés selling coffee, cigarettes, hot meals, confectionery, and ice cream to miners and their families. The cafes were valued as meeting places, places to exchange gossip and suppliers of cheap hot food, and they had a family atmosphere free from any association with alcohol. Moreover, the mechanisms used by Italians to enter self-employment were remarkably similar to those deployed by other ethnic groups in the UK, both before and since. Business owners preferred to recruit from within their own ethnic group and therefore sponsored and funded the immigration of workers who were known to them in their homeland. These workers repaid the cost of migration by indenturing themselves to their new employer for a fixed period, during which time they worked long hours for low pay. During this period, however, they also acquired business knowledge and skills which would later allow them to establish their own enterprises in a locality that did not compete with their former employer. The process of sponsored chain migration was thus mutually beneficial and self-reproducing. Thus, there were established prewar precedents of migrants arriving in the UK, gaining social mobility through occupational specialization and self-employment, and hiring fellow ethnics through chain migration.

However, another feature of British society that pre-dated the mass labor migrations of the 1950s and 1960s was xenophobia. Holmes (1991) addresses the question whether British society has only recently become intolerant or whether this is a long-standing characteristic of British public attitudes. His historical review juxtaposes the oft-expressed view that Britain has always been a haven of tolerance with the reality experienced by successive pulses of immigrants. He describes how both visible minorities such as the Chinese and the Jews, and other migrants such as Eastern Europeans and the Irish were all initially regarded with suspicion as cheap labor, and how debates about their immigration were vitriolic and overtly xenophobic.

Contemporary evidence confirms this conclusion. Although research has demonstrated some decline in expressed racism and some subtle shifts in how it is manifested (see Robinson 1987) there is no doubt that immigrants still face negative attitudes and unequal treatment. A recent EU survey (Eurobarometer 1997) found the following of British respondents:

- 30 percent agreed with the statement that non-European immigrants "are so different, they can never be fully accepted members of our country's society"
- 66 percent agreed with the statement "our country has reached its limits; if there were to be more people belonging to these minority groups we would have problems"
- 44 percent thought there were too many people from minority groups in Britain
- 32 percent described themselves as either "very racist" or "quite racist."
- And 37 percent thought the UK would be better off without immigrants from outside the European Union

Black and Asian migrants therefore constituted only the most recent pulse of immigration to the UK and entered a country that had a long history of hostility towards most, if not all, new arrivals. In addition, the postwar labor migrants from the Indian subcontinent and the West Indies did not forge a completely new link between the sending and receiving societies. Britain had already had a long colonial relationship with these societies, and this had both forged attitudes and expectations in all parties and established migration networks which formed the basis for later mass migration. Rex and Moore (1967) describe how substantial negative preconceptions about immigrants from these regions already existed in metropolitan British society before their arrival here en masse in the 1950s and 1960s, and how they were rooted in unequal colonial power relations. Western (1992) reports how expectations had also developed in the West Indies about what life in Britain would be like and what reception might await potential migrants. Comments from his respondents capture these expectations:

> *"I was surprised when I got here to find that my education was better than some of the English people I worked with! I had thought all English people must be wonderfully educated. When I was a child you'd pick anything up, a knife, a bowl: 'Made in England' it'd say, nine times out of ten . . . I thought, this must be a great place, this England. Must be a big powerful, country full of well-educated people."*
>
> *"We were brought up so English. When we got here, I was amazed in the cinema at the end of the film, we were the only ones who stood still for the playing of 'God Save the Queen.'"*
>
> "I remember, one of my mates came rushing into my room soon after we got here and said 'Maycock, there's a white man outside sweeping the streets.'"
>
> *"I'd never met poor English people; they were so ignorant."*
>
> *"I always had this desire to go to England, 'the omnipotent Mother Country.' The land of my great heroes like Sir Walter Raleigh, Lord Nelson, Robin Hood, Sherlock Holmes, Charles Dickens, Shakespeare. England to me was the land of wit, intelligence and the sophistication of Noel Coward. Little did I know that fact and fiction were two different ball games."*

Colonial contacts with the UK had also ensured that migrants from the Caribbean and from the Indian subcontinent had already come to the UK in small but significant numbers prior to the beginning of mass migration. Fryer (1984) and Visram (1986) chronicle the arrival of black and Indian migrants from the seventeenth century onwards.

Critically, these "pioneers" also established migration networks which later facilitated and supported chain migration of people from the same family, village, island or regional-linguistic group. As was shown earlier, with Italian migration, chain migration has been a recurrent feature of labor migration to the UK in the twentieth century, and one which has profoundly affected settlement and employment patterns (see, for example, Byron's [1994] study of the development of the Nevisian community in Leicester).

3   Mass migration to the UK from the Indian subcontinent and the Caribbean

The key to understanding mass labor migration to the UK in the immediate postwar period are selective labor shortages, brought about by postwar reconstruction and economic growth. In the immediate aftermath of World War II, Britain was a spent force. Heavily burdened with debt, ravaged by wartime destruction, living off the Victorians' investment in infrastructure, and fading in political and military significance on the world stage, Britain had much to do before it could return to some semblance of normality and attempt again to become competitive. Central to this task of reconstruction was the need for labor. Initially Britain turned to Ireland for workers, but this source proved inadequate, so the government had to look further afield, notably toward the displaced persons of continental Europe and the exile communities that had sought temporary sanctuary in the UK during the war. In total, some 100,000 Irish workers entered Britain between 1946 and 1951, and the number had swelled further to 352,000 by 1959 (Walvin 1984). An additional 100,000 European Volunteer Workers had been recruited by the mid-1950s, and some 284,000 Poles were given settlement rights in the UK after the war, although many chose not to stay.

Still, the scale of reconstruction and restructuring was such that economic growth continued to be stifled in the mid-1950s by persistent shortages of labor. These shortages tended to take two particular forms.

Firstly, local shortages were created because of rapid economic growth in certain local labor markets and the consequent increase in the number of jobs on offer (Peach 1968). This growth had two effects. New, expanding industries simply could not find enough local labor to meet their needs and therefore had to attract immigrants from elsewhere in the country and from overseas. The car industry in Essex, the West Midlands, and Oxford is the best example of this trend and helps account for ethnic settlement in these localities. Alternatively, new growth industries might have been able to fill their attractive vacancies without recourse to immigration, but only by denuding the local labor market with the result that other employers offering less attractive opportunities were then unable to fill *their* vacancies. These stagnant industries then had to recruit from new sources of labor, including the immigrant workforce. Foundry work in the West Midlands provides an example of this tendency. Because the work was physically very demanding and in many cases dangerous, former employees were lost to more attractive work in light engineering. They were replaced by ethnic workers, keen in the initial stages to maximize their income regardless of work conditions. Low-grade employment in hospitals, on the railways, and on the buses were other examples.

The second form of local labor shortages arose from economic transformation (Fevre 1984). Fevre argues that immigrant labor was needed not only to fuel the expansion of growth industries but also to ease the transformation of other industries, fighting for their survival against international competition. Fevre suggests that, again, there were two variants of this scenario. Some industries responded to competition by increasing their productivity through capital investment. In these cases, the need to ensure a return on this investment meant that jobs were degraded, either through deskilling of the work required or through an increase in expected workload. In the woollen mills of Yorkshire, for example, loom operatives were expected to oversee three new machines rather than one old machine. Under these circumstances many white workers left the industry in search of less demanding employment, thereby creating local sectoral labor shortages. In the second variant, struggling companies were unable to drive up productivity by investing in new machinery but sought to achieve the same objective through reducing labor costs. They could do this because they knew that black and Asian workers had little choice, because of racial discrimination, but to accept lower hourly rates than their white counterparts or shift work. Fevre argued that these two variants accounted for the concentration of Asian workers, in particular, within the cotton textile industry of Lancashire and the woollen textile industry of Yorkshire.

In both scenarios, then, there was thus a process of ethnic succession at work of the type described by Waldinger elsewhere in this volume. Newly arrived groups either took up opportunities abandoned by other workers or created new opportunities. They did not drive out indigenous workers by aggressively undercutting their wage rates. Nor did they challenge the might of organized labor where jobs were protected and where unions resisted the introduction of imported labor (e.g. the coal mining industry).

Unable to fill vacancies from traditional sources, employers and government turned to the Commonwealth. London Transport, the British Hotels and Restaurants Association, and the National Health Service (NHS) all established recruiting missions in the Caribbean directly to attract labor (see Brooks's 1975 account of how this system operated in Barbados). Some Caribbean governments like Barbados even provided interest-free loans to cover the cost of passage to the UK. From the arrival of the liner *Empire Windrush* in 1948, migration from the West Indies soon gathered pace. The natural peak of postwar West Indian migration came in 1955 to 1957 when net immigration was 23,000–30,000 per annum, up from only 1,000 in 1951, but the rush to enter Britain before the introduction of immigration control in 1962 led to a sharp rise in immigration to 50,000 in 1960 and 66,000 in 1961. Reflecting the matriarchal society that had arisen in the Caribbean as a result of slavery, this migration was in broad gender-balance, with female migrants even outnumbering males in several years in the late 1950s.

Mass migration from the Indian subcontinent to the UK was also a response to the needs of the British economy. But, South Asian migration was later to develop than West Indian migration and was more voluntaristic, with far less direct or officially organized recruitment. The migration had also only really begun to get underway as immigration controls were introduced. Prior to the "Beat the Ban rush," Indian net immigration had not exceeded 6,600 in any one year and net immigration from Pakistan had been no more than 5,200. Again, however, fear of missing out on the opportunity of immigration produced a sharp rise in migration to the UK with 49,000 people migrating from India and Pakistan in 1961 and 47,000 in 1962. This migration was initially highly imbalanced in gender terms with the vast majority of migrants being young males, traveling without dependants, who in turn would join them later in the 1960s.

4   Opportunity structure at arrival, and early occupational specialization

Blacks and Asians therefore initially filled very particular niches in the labor market and often became critical elements to the survival or success of those industries. The process of direct recruitment led to both economic specialization and geographical concentration (see Peach's chapter on this point) but, because different ethnic groups arrived at different times, the specialization and concentration of the first to arrive (the West Indians) was not replicated for later groups. Put simply, in the period between the arrival of West Indians in the 1950s and Bangladeshis in the 1970s the national and local opportunity structure had been transformed.

While the earliest direct recruits from the West Indies went straight into employment in the hotels, hospitals, and transport undertakings of London that had sponsored their migration, later independent migrants had to search out their own opportunities in the lacunae that existed at the time of their arrival. For these independent arrivals, the prewar ports of entry were very important since they could provide a stock of cheap accommodation and access to information and support networks that made the search for work and accommodation less difficult. As a result, early cores such as Brixton became central to West Indian settlement and numbers there grew from a handful in 1948 to 5,000 in 1955 (Patterson 1963). More broadly, though, the pattern of West Indian settlement was formed by the availability of employment at the time: in the foundries and engineering shops of the West Midlands, in the car plants of

London, Oxford, Coventry, and Birmingham, in the paper industry of High Wycombe, and the brickyards of Bedfordshire.

The beginning of the Indian pulse of immigration lagged only slightly behind the West Indian pulse, so that the earliest Indians to arrive were able to take advantage of some of the same employment niches in the same parts of the country. They worked in the London hospitals, in the car and engineering industries, on the buses and trains, and at the London airports. In contrast, the subsequent vintages of Indian migration and more particularly the later Pakistani pulse had to find alternative occupational or spatial opportunities, often located in the more distant regions of the country. Municipal public transport undertakings in northern cities such as Manchester, Preston, and Blackburn were enthusiastic employers of Asian workers, as was British Rail. Northern engineering and metal companies in cities such as Sheffield also took on Asian labor. However, perhaps the most significant difference to earlier waves was the growth of opportunities within the textile and woollen industries of Lancashire and Yorkshire, and the clothing and footwear industries of the East Midlands. In both regions Asian migrants were quick to occupy the vacant niche created by the withdrawal of white male labor and by the legal restrictions imposed on the employment of white female labor, and in many cases they made particular textile mills effectively their own. Social and kin networks continued to be vital in the acquisition of information about cheap housing and new vacancies, and ethnic work gangs with unofficial middlemen were equally important in ensuring that fellow Pakistanis and Indians were recruited when work did become available (Brooks and Singh 1979). Again, this combination of economic and temporal factors had a spatial outcome, with major nuclei of Pakistani and Indian populations developing in northern towns and cities such as Leeds, Bradford, Huddersfield, Manchester, Blackburn, Preston, Oldham, Bolton, Leicester, Nottingham, and Dundee. These cities had highly distinctive employment structures which later laid open Asian workers to the effects of globalization and deindustrialization.

Table 15.1 provides a summary of the outcome of the trends outlined above. It demonstrates how, by the early 1980s, Caribbean and Asian labor had very distinctively skewed distributions across the industrial sectors, with concentrations in the car industry (West Indians, Indians, and Pakistanis), in the textile industry (Pakistanis and Indians), and in Transport and Communications (West Indians and Indians), and a general underrepresentation in public and commercial services.

Table 15.2 provides gendered information on the job level of ethnic minority workers within these industries in 1971. It demonstrates several things. Firstly, how, at this time, Indian men and women had a

Table 15.1 *Industrial concentration of ethnic minority workers, 1982 (%)*

	White	Indian	Pakistani	Black Caribbean
Mining chemicals and metals	9	7	8	4
Engineering and metalwork	15	14	13	9
Vehicles and shipbuilding	5	13	10	12
Textiles, clothing, and footwear	2	8	20	3
Other manufacturing	10	13	19	14
Total manufacturing	41	55	70	42
Construction	8	3	2	7
Transport and communications	10	16	9	24
Distribution	8	4	3	6
Other services	23	16	13	14
Total services	49	39	27	51
Public admin and defense	7	2	0	3

Source: Brown (1984).

Table 15.2 *Social class profile of the white and ethnic minority populations, 1971, females and males (%)*

	White		Indian		Pakistani		Black Caribbean	
	M	F	M	F	M	F	M	F
Professional	5	1	10	4	3	7	1	0
Employer/manager	13	5	6	3	4	3	2	0
Junior white-collar	18	50	15	43	5	45	8	40
Total white-collar	36	56	31	50	12	55	11	40
Skilled manual	40	8	32	9	25	12	45	9
Semiskilled	16	27	24	34	38	29	27	43
Unskilled	8	8	13	6	25	3	17	8
Total manual	64	43	69	49	88	44	89	60

Source: 1971 data from 1971 census, Robinson (1990).

polarized distribution with overrepresentation in the professions and in semi- and unskilled manual work. Secondly, how Pakistani men were very compressed into low-grade manual work but Pakistani women had a social class distribution not dissimilar to that of their white peers. Thirdly, how Black Caribbean men were even more underrepresented in white-collar work than Pakistani men. Lastly, how Black Caribbean women were heavily concentrated in the two categories of junior white collar work and semiskilled manual work.

Finally, Table 15.3 provides summary data on the employment status, activity rates, and highest qualifications of the three ethnic groups

Table 15.3 *Summary data on employment status, white and ethnic minority populations, 1971, females and males (%)*

	White		Indian		Pakistani		Black Caribbean	
	M	F	M	F	M	F	M	F
Economic activity rate#	85.8	49.6	88.5	50.3	89.9	43.4	93.5	66.7
Self-employed*	12	na	8	7	7	12	6	1
No qualifications*			44	65	67	82	65	67
Degree or beyond*	10	na	7	2	2	1	1	<1

Source: *Smith (1974).
Greater London only, 1966 source Rose (1969).

under consideration. It illustrates how, because of the nature of the migration, ethnic minorities were more likely than whites to be employees, how the youthful nature of this labor migration produced high economic activity rates (except for Muslim women), and how the migrations were constituted largely, but not exclusively, of less well educated primary migrants.

5   Changing patterns of opportunity

Whilst the scale, timing, and nature of immigration from the Caribbean and the Indian subcontinent was fuelled by the needs of the British economy of the day, by the time those migrations were complete and early single target migrants and their families had become permanent settlers, the economic landscape and context had changed radically.

The past thirty years has seen a remarkable transformation of the space-economy of the UK, and this has been characterized by eight key trends.

We have seen an end to full employment and therefore the need to recruit large quantities of labor from overseas. Whereas unemployment never exceeded 3 percent during the long postwar boom in the UK, a combination of the oil shock of 1974, the declining international competitiveness of British industry, and the impact of the New International Division of Labor have raised unemployment from 5 percent in 1979 to 8.3 percent by 1996 (Evans 1996). As unemployment levels have risen in general, ethnic unemployment rates have risen much quicker, with ethnic unemployment often being three times higher than white unemployment during recessions.

As the UK became a post-industrial economy there have been sectoral shifts in the type of employment available. The number of jobs in manufacturing fell by 44 percent between 1971 and 1984, with 3.6 million jobs being lost overall (cf. the 2.7 million jobs created in the service sector over the same period). Moreover, the decline of manufacturing continued throughout the late 1980s and into the 1990s, with 2.2 million jobs being lost between 1977 and 1991 (Rice 1994). The loss of these jobs impacted heavily upon ethnic minority workers who were overrepresented in low-grade manufacturing and service work.

The contraction of manufacturing was uneven, with certain industries being particularly hard hit. The textile industry saw employment fall from over 2 million in 1945 to 517,000 by 1986, and engineering lost over a million jobs between 1975 and 1986. These were the very industrial sectors that had attracted ethnic workers in the 1960s.

Even some *service* sectors began to shed labor in order to remain competitive. Bus companies, for example, did away with conductors and railways did away with stokers and porters. As a result, the number of jobs in the Transport and Communication sector fell by 200,000 between 1971 and 1986. Again, this sector had actively recruited West Indian and Asian labor only twenty years previously.

The expansion and contraction of different parts of the economy has impacted unevenly on the national space-economy. Between 1979 and 1986 there were massive reductions in the number of jobs in some regions (the North West down by 16 percent, Yorkshire by 12 percent, and the West Midlands by 10 percent), whilst in others the number of jobs remained roughly the same or even increased a little (East Anglia +9 percent, South East –2 percent, South West –2 percent). At a finer geographical scale, there were also sharp discrepancies in the fortunes of individual places and types of places. Major conurbations and their inner cores haemorrhaged jobs (London lost half its manufacturing jobs between the 1960s and the 1980s, and Manchester lost 67,000 manufacturing jobs between 1971 and 1976), while small and medium towns in semirural environments gained both employment and population through counterurbanization.

Britain has experienced a "technologisation" (Green and Owen 1985) of its manufacturing labor force, with reduced demand for unskilled blue- and white-collar workers and greater demand for "information" workers. For example, between 1971 and 1981, there was a net gain of 85,000 intermediate and senior white-collar jobs within manufacturing.

More broadly there has also been a casualization and feminization of the labor force in the UK. Female employment in the service sector rose by 30 percent between 1971 and 1984, and two-thirds of this was in part-time work (*Social Trends* 1987). Of the 2.6 million increase in the number of employees in the service sector between 1977 and 1991, 1.9 million were women and half were part-time employees (Rice 1994).

And finally, the temporal coincidence of privatization, outsourcing, unemployment, greater availability of start-up capital, and the new "enterprise culture" of the Thatcher years produced a remarkable growth in self-employment. Daly (1991) noted how the 1980s saw a 57 percent increase in the number of self-employed people in the UK, with 80 percent of these people working full-time. This expansion was in marked contrast to the 1970s and was also unusual within Europe, where in some countries the number of self-employed fell.

In short, the economic conditions that had led to the positive recruitment of Asian and West Indian labor into particular sectors of the UK economy, particular industries, and particular local labor markets had evaporated less than twenty-five years later. Many of the jobs they had initially done had been replaced by technology, many of the industries whose existence they had helped prolong had succumbed to global competition, and many of the local economies they had lived within had been devastated by recession and restructuring. A labor force that had been shaped specifically to complete particular tasks was in effect redundant in the towns and cities within which it lived.

6　The position of ethnic minorities in the changing labor market

Past colonial relations and obligations ensured that West Indian and South Asian migrants had the right to settle in the UK, to acquire citizenship there, and to participate in electoral politics. They could not, therefore, be treated as a disposable reserve army of labor. Rather, like the remainder of the British population, they (and their British-born descendants) have had to adjust to changing national and local economic circumstances and chart their own responses to these.

In the first subsection we will consider whether ethnic minorities have engaged in internal migration within Britain either to escape the effects of recession and restructuring or to take advantage of new economic opportunities. In the second subsection we will then quantify what ethnic occupational mobility has occurred as a combined result of restructuring, recession, and the response of individuals to these forces. We will do this in two ways. Firstly, by using cross-sectional quantitative data and secondly by using individual longitudinal quantitative data. In the third subsection we will then focus on the particular issue of ethnic self-employment as a route to social mobility. And in a final major section we will then take the case study of one ethnic group in Britain (the Ugandan Asians) and use ethnographic data to understand their social mobility trajectory and how they mobilize resources associated with a variety of identities in order to achieve this trajectory.

6.1   *Geographical mobility*

Relatively little work has been undertaken in the UK on the internal migration patterns of ethnic minority groups (Robinson 1992a) or the contribution of this to any changes in geographical distributions. Census data have been used to demonstrate that there was little change in the geographical distribution of the key ethnic minority populations over the decade 1981–91 and that "the spatial distribution of all the groups is still heavily dependent upon the geography of opportunity which existed when their migration to Britain was at its peak . . . Once these patterns were established, chain migration, fertility, the attractions of ethnic clustering, tenure profiles and racial exclusionism have generally succeeded in perpetuating them" (Robinson 1993: 54).

Other work has charted the scale and pattern of inter-regional migration within the UK in the decade 1971–81 (Robinson 1992b). This demonstrated that the West Indian population was relatively immobile at this scale, that Indians were as mobile as whites, and Pakistanis were approximately twice as mobile as whites. The same study also charted the geography of net internal migration. A pattern was revealed for the Indian population which was very similar to that of whites, with a powerful drift from the industrial regions of the north and West Midlands to the South East, and a parallel movement out of that region to neighboring regions. For West Indians, there was little long distance mobility, perhaps because they live in social housing which is difficult to exchange for property in other areas and because they already live in the most prosperous regions of the UK. In contrast, although Pakistanis were very mobile they seemed to benefit little from it, with the lowest social classes being the most mobile (a pattern the reverse of that found in the white population). This spatial mobility was interpreted as flight from the effects of recession rather than strategic geographic mobility to acquire upward social mobility.

More recently, Champion (1996) has used the Special Migration Statistics dataset from the 1991 Census to investigate internal migration trends in the subsequent decade (1981–91). His key findings were similar in some respects to those for the previous decade. Notably, he found Indians and Black Caribbeans to be less mobile than whites within and between regions (even when standardized for age), but he also discovered that Pakistanis, too, had become less mobile than whites during this decade. All the black and South Asian groups moved over shorter distances than whites, with 55 percent of all ethnic minority moves being over distances of less than 5 kilometres. And net migration was achieving increases in ethnic concentration rather than net redistribution.

Table 15.4 *Social class profile of the white and ethnic minority populations, 1991, females and males (%)*

	White		Indian		Pakistani		Black Caribbean	
	M	F	M	F	M	F	M	F
Professional	7	2	11	4	6	3	2	1
Employer/manager	28	26	27	21	20	22	14	30
Junior white-collar	11	39	14	35	14	34	12	34
Total white-collar	46	67	52	60	40	59	28	65
Skilled manual	32	8	24	6	30	6	39	7
Semiskilled	16	18	18	29	24	32	24	19
Unskilled	6	8	4	4	6	3	9	8
Total manual	54	34	46	39	60	41	72	34

Source: 1991 data from 1991 census, Peach (1996).

To conclude, work on the internal migration of ethnic minorities has demonstrated that they have not adopted a strategy of responding to changes in the national or local space-economy by moving in large numbers to more favored areas. Rather, the attractions of ethnic clusters have encouraged them to pursue alternative responses to restructuring and recession in situ.

6.2   Aggregate patterns of social mobility

Table 15.4 provides data on the gendered social class profile of the three key ethnic minority groups in 1991. Table 15.5 tabulates the cross-sectional change in each social class between 1971 and 1991 in percentage points. It therefore reflects the combined impact of changes in the labor market and how the groups had responded to these.

In the two decades between the censuses the social class profile of white males and females changed considerably. For both sexes, there had been a significant reduction in manual work and junior white-collar work, and a commensurate growth in Social Class II (Employers and Managers). Indian women mirrored the white pattern, and Indian men also followed the same pattern, but in a more exaggerated form. Pakistani men reduced their overrepresentation in less-skilled manual work but achieved this by expanding their presence in skilled manual work and junior white-collar work, as well as in Social Class II. Black Caribbean men also increased their presence in the lower white-collar categories but to a lesser extent than white men did and through a sharp reduction in unskilled manual work. Black Caribbean women withdrew from manual

Table 15.5 *Change in social class profile of the white and ethnic minority populations, 1971–1991, females and males (percentage points)*

	White		Indian		Pakistani		Black Caribbean	
	M	F	M	F	M	F	M	F
Professional	+2	+1	+1	0	+3	−4	+1	+1
Employer/manager	+15	+21	+21	+18	+16	+19	+12	+30
Junior white-collar	−7	−11	−1	−8	+9	−11	+4	−6
Total white-collar	+10	+11	+21	+10	+28	+4	+17	+25
Skilled manual	−8	0	−8	−3	+5	−6	−6	−2
Semiskilled	0	−9	−6	−5	−14	+3	−3	−24
Unskilled	−2	0	−9	−2	−19	0	−8	0
Total manual	−10	−9	−23	−10	−28	−3	−17	−26

NB: note all columns will add up due to rounding of individual and aggregate numbers. For the same reason, gains and losses will not necessarily cancel each other out.

Table 15.6 *Indices of Dissimilarity between social class profiles of different ethnic groups, 1971 and 1991*

	Male		Female	
	1971	1991	1971	1991
White–Indian	18	10	11	14
White–Pakistani	39	11	12	15
White–Black Caribbean	25	16	19	6

NB: Index of Dissimilarity ranges from 0 (total similarity) to 100 (total dissimilarity).

work to an even greater extent than their white counterparts and instead entered Social Class II in large numbers, to the point where they are now over-represented in that category.

Table 15.6 summarizes the changes in a different way. Indices of Dissimilarity have been calculated between the social class profile of whites and each of the ethnic minorities for 1971 and for 1991. The table shows that this twenty-year period witnessed a general convergence of the class profiles of white men and ethnic minority men, leaving Black Caribbean men with the most different profile, skewed as it is towards manual work. Also worthy of note is the way that the social class profile of Pakistani men, which had been by far the most distinctively different in 1971, was no longer so in 1991. The picture for women is a little more complex. There has been marked convergence in the social class profiles of white women and Black Caribbean women to the point where they are now very similar. In stark contrast, the profiles of Indian and Pakistani women are becoming more different from those of white women and are also becoming more internally polarized with overrepresentation in the professional category and in semiskilled manual work.

An alternative mode of measuring social mobility is to use data from the Office of National Statistics' Longitudinal Study (LS). This allows us to chart the social mobility of individuals over each of the inter-censal decades. Although the LS has its weaknesses,[1] its data are innovative in the British context and also very valuable. Previous work on ethnic social mobility that has used these data include Robinson's (1990) analysis of ethnic social mobility in the period 1971–81, his narrower study of the social integration of East African Asian refugees in the UK (Robinson 1994), and his study of the social mobility of Indians between 1981 and 1991 (Robinson 1996).

Tables 15.7, 15.8, and 15.9 take these analyses further by considering the individual social mobility of Indian, Pakistani, and Black Caribbean men and women during the decade 1981 to 1991. Some generalizations can be derived from these tables, which relate to all the ethnic minority groups under consideration. Firstly, more people have experienced upward social mobility during the decade than downward mobility, although the ratio between the two varies across the groups, with the most favorable ratio being for Indian men and women, followed by Pakistani men, Pakistani women, Black Caribbean men and Black Caribbean women. Secondly, the most likely scenario during this decade for most members of ethnic minorities was that they would remain within the same social class, although again the probability of this varied, with Pakistanis recording the lowest probabilities of stability (0.43M, 0.44F), Indians intermediate probabilities (0.52M, 0.54F), and Black Caribbeans the highest (0.54M, 0.60F). Thirdly, those most likely to retain their social class position were Employers and Managers or Professionals (except in the case of Black Caribbean men where it was Employers and Managers and Skilled manual workers). The likelihood of falling out of employment by the end of the decade varied a good deal, from 4 percent of Black Caribbean women, through 7 percent of Indians and 12 percent of Black Caribbean men, to 16 percent and 18 percent respectively of Pakistani males and females.

Turning next to each of the groups in turn. Indians in Social Classes I and II have a strong propensity to remain there, with most of the outflows or inflows being to the other white-collar classes. The exception to this generalization is the significant movement from unemployment in 1981 to becoming an employer or manager in 1991. Between one in six

Table 15.7 *Social mobility, 1981–1991, Indians: outflow (Row),*
England and Wales

				1991				
	I	II	IIIN	IIIM	IV	V	Unemp	Total
Males								
I	91	14	6	2	2	0	10	125
II	9	175	20	13	11	4	8	240
IIIN	7	48	88	8	9	3	12	175
IIIM	8	55	13	244	59	20	46	445
IV	0	46	19	76	213	19	34	407
V	0	12	1	37	28	31	13	122
Unemp	5	39	12	50	39	10	63	218
Females								
I	29	1	3	0	0	0	0	33
II	2	71	11	3	6	0	6	99
IIIN	0	39	80	3	7	1	12	142
IIIM	1	7	5	30	30	2	11	86
IV	1	26	10	32	178	14	22	283
V	0	2	1	3	13	14	3	36
Unemp	0	16	13	12	34	5	19	99

NB: These tables use the Registrar General's Social Class categories where:
I = Professional
II = Employer or Manager
IIIN = Junior white-collar
IIIM = Skilled manual work
IV = Semiskilled manual work
V = Unskilled manual work
Unemp=Unemployed
Source: The data in Tables 15.7–15.9 are from the Office For National Statistics'
Longitudinal Study and are Crown Copyright. We are grateful for permission to
reproduce them, and to the staff of the LS Unit at City University London for
their help in extracting them.

(women) and one in five (men) unemployed Indians made this transition.
This trend was also noted in the previous decade (Robinson 1990) and
reflects the continued move into self-employment. The other trend that is
noteworthy is the churning between the manual classes although upward
mobility here exceeds downward mobility. The low economic activity rate
of Pakistani women prevents any further analysis of their data, because
the resulting sample is too small, but Pakistani males are seen to be the
least socially static of any of the groups considered here. There is considerable upward movement between the manual classes as well as out of
the labor force into unemployment. There is also a high dropout rate for

Table 15.8 *Social mobility, 1981–1991, Pakistanis: outflow (Row), England and Wales*

	1991							
	I	II	IIIN	IIIM	IV	V	Unemp	Total
Males								
I	17	9	1	2	0	0	3	32
II	2	57	6	5	4	0	18	92
IIIN	2	19	19	3	2	3	12	60
IIIM	2	29	12	129	22	10	49	253
IV	1	16	14	51	106	14	55	257
V	0	1	0	23	14	10	15	63
Unemp	1	23	11	47	24	7	61	174

Note: See Table 15.7 for Social Class Categories.

Table 15.9 *Social mobility 1981–1991, Black Caribbeans: outflow (Row), England and Wales*

	1991							
	I	II	IIIN	IIIM	IV	V	Unemp	Total
Males								
I	5	1	1	2	0	0	1	10
II	1	26	1	2	5	0	6	41
IIIN	3	15	31	9	4	2	9	53
IIIM	5	21	6	214	49	16	44	355
IV	0	7	6	45	105	11	28	202
V	0	1	2	14	14	20	13	64
Unemp	0	10	2	40	15	10	59	136
Females								
I	2	0	0	0	0	0	0	2
II	0	191	5	2	14	1	6	219
IIIN	0	33	104	4	10	2	8	161
IIIM	0	10	4	27	21	2	4	68
IV	1	8	10	16	102	49	13	199
V	0	2	1	1	6	25	2	37
Unemp	0	14	32	5	13	9	18	91

Note: See Table 15.7 for Social Class Categories.

professional workers, especially into Social Class II, which also receives considerable inflows from junior white-collar work. Again we can surmise that this reflects the growing importance of self-employment. Black Caribbean women record the highest white-collar retention rates of any of the five subgroups and also relatively high probabilities of movement into white-collar work from unemployment or skilled manual work, and from junior white-collar work into management. Within the blue-collar sector there has been considerable downward mobility from skilled to semiskilled and from semiskilled to unskilled work, producing a more polarized social class profile. For Black Caribbean men, the likelihood of upward and downward mobility is roughly the same, unlike other groups where the former exceeds the latter. Most mobility is clustered along the diagonal, representing movement up or down one social class, for example from social class IIIN into II, from skilled to semiskilled manual work or from semiskilled into unskilled manual work.

6.3   Social mobility and self-employment

In two cases above, we have commented on the growth of self-employment within certain ethnic minority populations. Table 15.3 demonstrated that in 1971 self-employment was unusual among ethnic minority workers and far less common in these populations than in the white population. However, as was noted in Section 5, the 1980s saw a remarkable increase in self-employment within the British population as a whole, with the percentage of all men who were self-employed rising from 9.1 percent in 1971, through 9.7 percent in 1981 to 14.1 percent by 1990 (*Social Trends* 1991). Nowhere was this trend more evident than within sectors of the ethnic minority population. By 1991 Indian and Pakistani men were respectively 38 percent and 18 percent more likely to be self-employed than white men, with 18.3 percent and 21.4 percent working for themselves, although Black Caribbean men were still under-represented in this category. Two possible explanations for this have been presented.

One school of thought develops an argument first seen in relation to ethnic residential segregation (Aldrich et al. 1981, Aldrich, Jones, and McEvoy 1984, Jones, McEvoy, and Barett 1994). They argue that the scale and depth of racism and racial exclusionism in the UK is such that ethnic minorities have few opportunities to exercise choice in relation to life strategies but, instead, can only occupy those vacant niches thought by whites to be undesirable. Asians therefore enter self-employment in order to avoid discrimination and racism in the labor market which would otherwise consign them to poorly paid, unfulfilling, and unattractive jobs with few prospects. Once in self-employment they have to use all their resources (including the exploitation of family labor and informal sources of capital and credit) simply to survive, and despite working more hours per week than their white counterparts earn less. Whether particular ethnic groups will enter into self-employment depends more upon external and local circumstances than upon any cultural preferences or prior experience. In localities where old manufacturing and service jobs are not being replaced by new jobs, racism will prevent ethnic minorities competing with whites for mainstream jobs. They can respond to the loss of their traditional jobs in three main ways. They can either leave the area (and therefore leave behind the support systems of ethnic clusters), remain in the locality but become unemployed, or engage in self-employment within the ethnic community. In contrast, in localities where new jobs are still being created and there are still localized labor shortages, ethnic workers can still find work and do not therefore need to establish their own businesses. Thus West Indians in London did not seek self-employment as a response to restructuring, but Asians in the industrial regions of the north did.

The evidence which Jones and McEvoy presented to support their claim that self-employment was a last resort was derived from two empirical studies completed in 1978 and 1990. They found that Asian businessmen were much better qualified than their white counterparts, were not particularly successful, and employed few people other than themselves. Their businesses catered largely for an ethnic clientele in what was rapidly becoming a saturated market and a quarter of interviewees claimed they had entered self-employment to avoid unemployment, underemployment, blocked mobility, and lack of job satisfaction.

The alternative school of thought does not deny the strength and pervasiveness of racism and exclusionism but argues that individuals will respond to this in different ways. Some ethnic groups or individuals will respond by entering self-employment, while others will adopt alternative strategies such as emphasizing the importance of education or targeting alternative employment opportunities where they have a competitive advantage. Thus, what becomes critical for this group of scholars is embedding the decision to enter self-employment within a cultural context which helps explain why certain groups value self-employment more than others and why some groups can more easily enter self-employment than others. Srinivasan (1995), for example, found that Asian businessmen in Oxford valued self-employment for culturally specific reasons. They valued their independence, the enhanced status that owning their own business gave them within their own community, and the way in which self-employment allowed them to spend more time with their families. Srinivasan (1995: 84, 86) concluded "there is little evidence of these South Asian shopkeepers and restaurant owners being pushed into self-employment. Entry into small business appears to be a deliberate strategy adopted to raise both economic and social standing . . . [and] . . . achieve ethnically oriented status aspirations." Werbner (1990) has shown how certain groups possess "cultural resources" which make it easier for them to enter self-employment. These resources include the cultural heritage of each ethnic group, the nature of their migration, and the multiplex social networks created by chain migration (Waldinger, Aldrich, and Ward 1990), which are based on trust, interdependence, and reciprocity. These networks supply privileged market information, finance, credit, and markets. Metcalf, Modood, and Virdee (1996) have shown how cultural resources are unevenly distributed among Indian, Pakistani, and African-Asian entrepreneurs in the UK. They found that the three groups have contrasting prior experience of self-employment, exhibit contrasting attitudes towards risk, use different routes into self-employment, and have derived different benefits from their chosen strategy.

Ethnic self-employment has therefore become a significant contemporary phenomenon in the UK. Jones (1993) has demonstrated the impact of ethnic self-employment upon particular economic sectors. Whilst self-employed Black Caribbeans were likely to be in the construction industry (34 percent) or "other services" (23 percent), fully 56 percent of all ethnic minority self-employed were in the one industrial "division" that covered distribution, hotels, catering, and repairs. This division was especially important for the Chinese, Indians, and Pakistanis, since it accounted for 86 percent, 62 percent and 53 percent respectively of all workers from these groups who were self-employed. Within that industrial division there was further specialization. Indians and Pakistanis were very likely to be working in retail distribution (52 percent and 46 percent respectively), whilst three quarters of Chinese were found in the hotel and catering trade. Finally, the Transport Division accounted for 10 percent of all Pakistani self-employed people, reflecting their employment as mini-cab drivers.

The impact of Asian self-employment has been marked in particular local economies. Werbner, for example, has described how Pakistani self-employment has revitalized the local economy of inner Manchester, and how the regeneration of that economy has had beneficial spillover effects for labor markets fifty–sixty miles away. Werbner (1994) described how in its heyday the central city of Manchester could boast 1,000 warehouses, and a further 99 spinning, dyeing, or printing works. However, the textile industry was decimated by cheaper imported cloth from the late 1950s onwards, with employment in this industrial sector in the city falling by 90 percent by 1981. The specialist manufacture of rainwear and cloth-caps had all but gone, as had the Jewish wholesalers who had bought the produce of local Jewish manufacturers. The collapse of the textile industry and the decentralization of other employers also undermined the dense network of small local firms. However, Werbner describes how the entry of Pakistanis into the textile trade in the 1980s "renewed an industrial past" by turning round a failing and declining sector. She records how from 1981 onwards, when there was but one major Punjabi wholesaler, retailer, and importer in the area, the sector became rejuvenated. There are now three major Asian wholesalers each with a turnover of more than £10 million, a further ten smaller wholesalers with turnovers of £3–5 million each, and there are also innumerable smaller "cash and carries" supplying a regional market. Moreover, these wholesalers sell the products created by hundreds of Asian-owned clothing manufacturers throughout the region, which in turn subcontract to thousands of smaller Asian businesses throughout the North West of England. Werbner estimates that there are now over five hundred significant Asian-owned businesses in the garment trade in central Manchester, alone. In this case, then, ethnic self-employment has created a parallel local economy owned and financed by Pakistanis, employing Pakistanis, and linked with other parts of the Pakistani diaspora both within the UK and internationally. Its only point of contact with the broader economy is when finished goods pass outside to be sold to white customers. Nor is Manchester unique. A study for Leicester City Council (CAG 1994) describes a very similar picture in that city, with 1,446 Asian-owned businesses employing between 10,000 and 20,000 workers.

While there is thus a good deal of evidence to demonstrate that Asian self-employment is having a marked effect on particular local economies, there is less agreement about why Asians have entered self-employment, the extent to which that decision is facilitated by cultural resources unique to groups, and the long-term future for ethnic self-employment. The next section takes the case study of one ethnic group in the UK and considers these questions, using data derived from original field research.[2]

7 Peopling social mobility studies: the case study of Ugandan Asians

It has been noted above that the study of ethnic social mobility in the UK has increasingly begun to see mobility as the joint product of racial exclusionism and the way in which different ethnic groups mobilize particular resources to achieve desired outcomes. For example, the strategy of entering self-employment should not be seen as a simple response to the stimulus of blocked social mobility in the mainstream labor market. Rather, it is one of a number of possible strategies that could have been deployed, and may have been selected because of prior entrepreneurial experience, access to ethnic networks that offer competitive advantage, and cultural values which are consonant with the requirements of that economic niche (e.g. a willingness to work long hours, take risks, and invest for the future). Moreover, by adopting this particular strategy, an individual may derive benefits that are valued more highly in his or her own culture than they are in the wider society. Central to all of this is seeing decision making, such as entering self-employment, not as a mechanistic response to external stimuli isolated from other aspects of an individual's life, but embedded within that individual's biography, including what might be termed its "taken-for-granted" elements. Such a biographical approach contextualizes decision making in an individual's past direct and indirect experience, the value-system that was inculcated by family socialization, the cultural norms that were formally and informally taught within his or her community, and the potentialities which that individual acquired through his or her unique life course. In short, it gets "back to the forgotten man of the social sciences, to the actor in the social world whose doing and feeling lies at the bottom of the whole system" (Ley 1977). This perspective on social mobility is an important one since it ensures that minority mobility strategies and outcomes are seen for what they are, rather than measured against some externally imposed ideal derived from a different value-system or culture.

In order to demonstrate the power of a biographical approach to mobility studies we have chosen to present a case study of the social mobility of Ugandan Asians in the UK. This minority arrived in the UK in 1972, having been expelled from their middleman trading role (Ghai 1965) in the former British colony by newly independent African governments. They were acute refugees who were allowed to take only £50 in cash with them when they left Uganda (Marett 1989, Twaddle 1975), and they were subject to geographical dispersal on arrival in the UK (Robinson 1999).

The subsequent social mobility history of the group is an impressive one that merits analysis on two levels. On the first level, statistical analysis of longitudinal data on Ugandan Asian social mobility in the UK demonstrates that after the initial loss of status on arrival in the UK (Kuepper, Lackey and Swinerton 1975), Ugandan Asians had gained considerable upward social mobility as a group from 1981 to 1991, to the point where their social class profile was superior to that of whites and earlier Indian labor migrants (Valeny 1998). Thus whilst the British media had made the

Ugandan Asians into a classic "rags to riches" story (Bose 1982, Bernoth 1994, Day 1995, Lashmar and Harris 1997), there was some substance to the claims that the Ugandan Asians had achieved exceptional social mobility. However, the focus of our field research was on another level. We sought to discover how Ugandan Asians had deployed their unique cultural resources to respond to the macro-economic and geographical situation they found themselves in after migrating to the UK. Faced with a temporally and geographically specific opportunity structures, individuals adopted different mobility strategies. These strategies were socially constructed rather than given, and they were rooted in each individual's "taken-for-granted" biography. More particularly we found that Ugandan Asians deployed different combinations of resources to achieve their desired social mobility, and that these resources were associated with six different identities. We define resources here, not simply as material assets, but also as ideologies, expectations, networks, values and human capital resources acquired from different past experiences. Some of these resources were deployed consciously while others imperceptibly suffused action.

We see these six identities (and their associated bundles of resources) as being critical to what Ugandan Asians have achieved in the UK and how they have achieved it. Each will therefore be described in turn and we will allow the voices of our respondents to demonstrate their significance and how the associated resources were mobilized to achieve, or shape, desired social mobility outcomes that responded to local economic circumstances. However, before we do this, we want to stress that we do not see these identities either as mutually exclusive or primordial in nature. Rather, we employ Cohen's (1994) idea of fuzzy frontiers of identity in which the different facets of people's identity continually merge and morph, and in which these different facets will be given varying prominence at different points in time, in different places, and for different purposes.

The first identity we recognized as being important was the set of values imbued in people by virtue of their socialization in Gujurati culture. Having researched the Gujurati community in London, the anthropologist Tambs-Lyche (1980) argued that Gujuratis have a "merchant ideology." Its key features are: a predilection for establishing businesses; the prestige attached to business ownership or business acumen; the respect accorded those in, or associated with, business; the importance attached to "making money" and having money; and a willingness to make sacrifices to achieve this. Tambs-Lyche even describes how when two or more Gujuratis get together – even if they are strangers – within ten minutes they compare their investments and their rates of return. One analyst of

Gujurati culture has even gone so far as to write that "the early Asian settlers were imbued with quasi-Protestant ethics: they were remarkable for their strong commercial sense, capacity to work long hours, low propensity to consume, and passion for the accumulation of wealth" (Ghai 1965; 103).

There are several ways in which this merchant ideology shaped social mobility trajectories after arrival in the UK. First, through the tendency to move into self-employment rather than becoming an employee, second, by means of attitudes toward economic risk, and, third, through access to Gujurati business networks for advice, information, and financing. These tendencies are illustrated in the following quotations taken from our interviews:

> "Gujuratis are brought up in such a way that even when a child is at school, he will start thinking of using his brains on how to make money."
> "The majority had business in the blood. It wasn't something they learned, it's within the family."
> "If I work hard for somebody else then I get limited amount, but if I have my own business, I work hard to get more money for myself and my family."

The second identity that we thought was important was being Indian. Intrinsic to this is having been socialized in a society which is highly status-conscious, and in which the izzet (or social worth) of the extended family is both very fragile and continually being reviewed by peers in light of changes in behavior or material wealth (see Robinson 1986 and Jeffery 1976). The need to protect and enhance family izzet manifests itself in behaviors and strategies orientated toward achievement and acceptance of the decision making of the head of household. As Helweg and Helweg (1990: 159) wrote about Indians in the USA, "failure is not an option for most Indians . . . the izzet of family and kin group is on his shoulders and therefore he cannot return to India a failure." Again this set of cultural values produces a set of goal-directed behaviors and also offers access to ethnic-specific resources, as is demonstrated by the quotations below:

> "I didn't want to be on state benefits . . . I wanted to start my way, with respect."
> "When we came here, everybody wanted to find a job . . . it's degrading to accept money from the social security if you're not working, so everybody said that we will fight and think positive and take whatever jobs are available in the factories, cleaning . . . people were willing to work, that's why they're so successful here . . ."
> "It was in my mind from the beginning. I had to do something for my children and my wife, because they can't work for somebody else. I don't like to send them to work in the factory. I said no, I got to open a business, a catering business, then they can help me."
> "My father was and still is a proud man . . . He went [to a factory] for the first day and he was so angry because he was being bossed around and made to work as a laborer,

he didn't go the second day. I think that really broke his heart. He couldn't do this kind
of work, he couldn't go back to the factory so somehow he had to start again, somehow
he must be in business."

The third identity is that of being "Twice Migrants." This term was
first coined by Parminder Bhachu (1985) to describe those Sikhs who
had voluntarily migrated to East Africa and then migrated again in the
1960s to the UK. Bhachu argued that the experience of the first migration
allowed the Sikhs to learn lessons which they were then able to apply to
their second migration, and that these lessons facilitated more rapid and
successful adaptation. Although Bhachu does not argue the point, intrinsic to her notion is the strengthened belief in self-efficacy that arises from
past performance accomplishments. Again this identity and its associated
behaviors were borne out by our respondents:

"I'm not saying it was easy. We had no money; it was hard for me. But being in
Uganda, starting with nothing and working hard and making a good business, somehow
it gave me confidence to get on and start again in this country. OK, I didn't know much
about doing business here, but I knew that somehow I could do it again."

The fourth identity is that of having lived and worked in Uganda. The
Asian community acquired two human capital resources through their
experience of living in Uganda; education and experience in a capitalist
labor market. The Asians began to build schools in Uganda as early as the
1920s (Rattansi and Abdulla 1965), but by the 1950s they had already
recognized the importance of acquiring further and higher education
qualifications to allow entry into white-collar employment. Furthermore,
these qualifications would be acquired through the medium of English-
language teaching and would therefore be portable to other parts of the
English-speaking world.

"My father was very adamant that he wanted us all to study and go for further
education, because it would mean better jobs for us."
"In Uganda we encouraged our children to study. Our children are our hope."

The second dimension to the Ugandan experience was participation
in a free market economy. Asians were so successful in Uganda that by
the 1950s they provided most of what one commentator described as
"middle-level manpower" in Uganda, and also a proportion of higher-
level manpower, too. They formed a classic middleman minority, and
by 1959 (Ramchandani 1976) 51 percent of all Ugandan Asians were
engaged in commerce and in the immediate postwar period the group
controlled 90 percent of all Uganda's trade. This history of employment
in commerce, industry, and the professions again provided the Ugandan
Asians who came to the UK with a set of competencies, qualifications,

and experiences upon which they could draw, and which helped form the social strategies they adopted. In addition, as traders and manufacturers they were already tied into a global financial system in which they could later participate from another country. And they were part of an ethnic diaspora within which information, credit, and goods could be exchanged on the basis of trust:

"In Uganda, for example, I used to employ 85 people there and I used to own a Merc. But I never used to drive, my driver used to drive me around. When we came to Britain the life was gone, you haven't got a car, you're catching the bus and things like that. But then one has to decide. You can't think about the past and so, many chose to start and build up business again because it's what they're used to doing. It's what makes money."

"Every Ugandan Asian, they want their own business, no matter how small it is. It gives them satisfaction to be self-employed."

"I come from a business background. Being in business is what I was brought up to do and enjoy, its part of my culture . . . Having my own business was my dream and the expulsion wasn't going to change that."

The fifth identity which our interviews lead us to believe has shaped the social mobility trajectories of Ugandan Asians in the UK is the experience of having become refugees The behavioral and attitudinal consequences of the refugee experience are little understood and have yet to be thoroughly researched, although there is a sizable literature on the negative aspects of the experience on mental health. Kotkin (1993), however, argues that the refugees who fled from China to the USA immediately after the last war had a "refugee mentality." One of his respondents described it as follows:

"The way I was brought up I feel that there is opportunity in hard times, that if we can be tougher and more durable we will come out ahead. This is how you look at life if you are uprooted. There are no failures in life, just setbacks." (Kotkin 1993; 185)

These same attitudes were espoused by some of our respondents. They claimed that having the fruits of their labors taken suddenly from them made them more determined to rebuild their lives, and more prepared to take risks to achieve this. In addition, some of our respondents felt that the experience of being uprooted at the whim of another encouraged them to rebuild their lives in such a way that they had maximum control over their own destiny: self-employment was felt to offer this. Some of our respondents even made a deliberate decision upon arrival in the UK to abandon their life's occupation to enter self-employment.

"Mentally I became a different person. I knew that my circumstances could change at any time. When the expulsion happened we lost everything, our home, our possessions, even our status. This experience of loss and change made me more ambitious and more determined to take risks. Once I came to England I was prepared to do anything to get things back to normal."

Others, however, were affected in a different way by the refugee experience. Some of our respondents reacted by reevaluating their priorities. Family unity and security became paramount, and these individuals planned their occupational careers accordingly. Some former entrepreneurs sought the security of being a 9–5 employee.

The sixth identity that we feel has shaped the mobility strategies of Ugandan Asians is that of being nonwhite in a society which has preformed negative attitudes towards people "of color," derived from the unequal power relations of colonialism. Our respondents were clearly aware of racial exclusionism and the limits which this might place on their ability to act, but our feeling was that they had responded to this positively and creatively either by redoubling their efforts or by emphasizing strategies based on competitive advantage.

"You don't just have to be equal to everybody, you know in terms of getting a job, but you have to be one better than the indigenous population and have more qualifications, you know like a Masters . . . because an employer's discrimination can hold you back . . . the only way to break prejudice is . . . to work twice as hard and have as many qualifications as possible."

"Our parents taught us that race matters, and it does, and to make it you have to work hard. (My son) . . . knows that if he wants the good things in life . . ., then he has to be prepared to work and be better than the rest."

"There's no point telling them that your colour doesn't matter, it damn well does. I keep telling them that what really matters . . . is that you're able to cope with that and fight it as well, fight it in a positive, not a negative, destructive way. If it means more qualifications, if it means working harder at school, then it's not bad."

"In British companies Indians can only reach a certain level and that's it . . . Maybe in the future I'll consider going it alone . . . Like my father said, at least with your own establishment you can make a real impact, as people will recognise your capabilities and your successes."

Our field research therefore led us to believe that the best way of understanding how our Ugandan Asian interviewees had responded to the particular local opportunity structure on offer to them in the UK in the 1970s, 1980s and 1990s was to understand the way in which strategies and trajectories grew out of the taken-for-granted world associated with the various identities of our respondents, and how each of these identities had associated with it a bundle of expectations, competencies, and resources which could be deployed when needed to guide and enable action. Only by contextualizing the actions of our respondents could we make sense of what was occurring and why it was occurring.

What we have not been able to do is demonstrate in this chapter how different economic, local, and historical contexts can lead the same ethnic group to respond with different strategies which rely upon different cultural resources. In the case of Ugandan Indians in Britain, they responded to racism and the restructuring of the British labor market in industrial regions by entering self-employment. To achieve this they deployed a particular subset of cultural resources (a willingness to work hard and to take risks, entrepreneurial flair, and the use of social networks to acquire capital and market information). In other circumstances, which offered other opportunities, a different strategy might well have been adopted which required a different assemblage of cultural resources. Indeed, our own research with Ugandan Asians and that of Metcalf, Modood, and Virdee (1996) suggest that the second generation of Asians in the UK have established themselves on a different trajectory; one that takes advantage of the new opportunities offered by Britain's post-industrial economy and eschews self-employment for education, the professions, and life in more affluent parts of the UK. There is already evidence that such a strategy is bearing fruit, with research showing that Asian students are attaining the same, or better, qualifications as their white peers, and that "by age 18 Asians are the most highly qualified of all groups (including whites)" (Gillborn and Gipps 1996: 5). However, understanding why any ethnic group responds to one set of macro-economic and local circumstances in one way and another set in another way requires extensive comparative biographical research across generations, countries, and localities. Whilst a start has been made on such a project (see, for example, Clarke, Peach, and Vertovec's 1990 study of Indians overseas) and much of the new work in the field of diaspora studies is starting to address this issue, it will be many years before we have definitive answers about why groups respond to circumstances in the way they do.

8   Conclusion

In this chapter we have worked at two levels. On one level we have taken what appears a relatively simple story, that of ethnic social mobility in contemporary Britain, and argued that it is far from simple. We have argued that whilst it is relatively easy to describe patterns and trends of social mobility, it is much more difficult to explain them and understand the meaning of them for those involved. Whilst social mobility can be seen as simple "event" (movement from one occupation to another), it is actually a process which begins at birth and which is at all times culturally, socially, economically, and historically embedded. Moreover, social mobility often involves people making choices, deploying strategies and enabling mechanisms which are "taken-for-granted" and embedded in that individual's biography rather than consciously invoked or purpose-designed. We therefore argue that any analysis of the mechanisms and significance of social mobility needs to be informed by biographical methods and knowledge of the taken-for-granted.

On another level we have taken the case study of the minority ethnic population of the UK and tried to put into practice what we have argued. We suggest that it is difficult to understand social mobility trends within this population without a clear knowledge of the context of their migration. We argued that the history of migration from the colonies to the UK was a vital facet of this, since it created attitudinal sets in both the migrants and the receiving society which were likely to allot the former particular societal and economic roles. Another vital facet was the opportunity structure that was available to them during the early years of their settlement in the UK. More particularly, we have described how the labor market changed radically under the pressure of globalization and recession shortly after their arrival in the UK and how this subsequently denied them the opportunities which were the *raison d'être* of their migration. Moreover these macroeconomic forces did not impact upon different localities within the UK in a consistent way, with some localities gaining from globalization and others losing heavily. We then went on to describe how one response to endemic racism and local restructuring was entry to self-employment, and how this strategy was adopted by many first-generation Asians in declining industrial cities such as Manchester and Leicester. Finally, we used a more focused case study of the Ugandan Asians in the UK to demonstrate how and why the particular strategy of self-employment was enthusiastically adopted by that group at that time, and how in order to achieve this objective they deployed a sub set of cultural resources, some of which were "taken for granted," rather than explicit. In short, we have tried to demonstrate that the "event" of social mobility can be fully understood only when it is simultaneously imbedded in its economic, geographical, and biographical context.

NOTES

1. It is important to state two caveats about the LS data. Firstly, although the LS is a large sample survey, numbers in individuals cells of cross-tabulations can be quite small by the time data have been disaggregated by ethnicity and social class. Secondly, the name Longitudinal Study is a misnomer since we are not able to track individuals continuously over the decade, simply to link their census records from April 1981 with those from April 1991, thereby knowing what occupations they held at the start and the end of the decade. We therefore know nothing of the churning which might, or might not, have taken place in the intervening period.

2. Involving interviews with fifty-seven Ugandan Asian men and women, who were all Gujarati Hindus, and lived in two different localities known to have

different opportunity structures (NW London and Leicester). Valeny (who is herself a Hindu of Indian descent) undertook the in-depth interviews, each of which lasted between 90–120 minutes, in a conversational style that allowed respondents to determine the subject matter. Interviews were recorded and later transcribed.

REFERENCES

Aldrich, H., J. Cater, T. Jones, and D. McEvoy, 1981, "Business Development and Self-segregation: Asian Enterprise in Three British Cities," in C. Peach, V. Robinson, and S. Smith (eds.), *Ethnic Segregation in Cities*, London: Croom Helm, pp. 170–93.

Aldrich, H., T. Jones, and D. McEvoy, 1984, "Ethnic Advantage and Minority Business Development," in R. Ward and R. Jenkins (eds.), *Ethnic Communities in Business: Strategies for Economic Survival*, Cambridge University Press, pp. 189–210.

Bernoth, A., 1994, "Penniless Refugees Who Moved Up to Join the Millionaires' Club," *Sunday Times* (May 8): 7.

Bhachu P., 1985, *Twice Migrants: East African Sikh Settlers in Britain*, London: Tavistock.

Bose, M., 1982, "The Ugandan Asian Success Magic," *New Society* 61: 456–8.

Brooks, D., 1975, *Race and Labor in London Transport*, London: Oxford University Press.

Brooks, D. and K. Singh, 1979, "Pivots and Presents: Asian Brokers in British Foundries," in S. Wallman (ed.), *Ethnicity at Work*, London: Macmillan, pp. 93–115.

Brown, C., 1984, *Black and White Britain: The Third PSI Study*, London: Policy Studies Institute.

Byron, M., 1994, *Post-war Caribbean Migration to Britain: The Unfinished Cycle*, Aldershot: Avebury.

CAG Consultants, 1994, *Leicester Asian Business Survey*, London: CAG.

Champion, A., 1996, "Internal Migration and Ethnicity in Britain," in P. Ratcliffe (ed.), *Ethnicity in the 1991 Census, Vol III Social Geography and Ethnicity in Britain: Geographical Spread, Spatial Concentration and Internal Migration*, London: HMSO, pp. 135–75.

Clarke, C., C. Peach, and S. Vertovec, 1990, *South Asians Overseas*, Cambridge University Press.

Colpi, T., 1991, *The Italian Factor: The Italian Community in Great Britain*, Edinburgh: Mainstream Publishing.

Cohen, R., 1994, *Frontiers of Identity: The British and the Rest*, London: Longman.

Daly, M., 1991, "The 1980s: A Decade of Growth in Enterprise," *Employment Gazette*, 99: 109–35.

Day, T., 1995, "Out of Africa and into Money," *Financial Mail on Sunday*, (January 8): 8–11.

Evans, P., 1996, "Unemployment in Britain," *Economic Review*, 14: 20–3.

Eurobarometer, 1997, *Racism and Xenophobia in Europe*, Brussels: European Commission.

Fevre, R., 1984, *Cheap Labor and Racial Discrimination*, Aldershot: Gower.

Ghai, D. P., 1965, *Portrait of a Minority: Asians in East Africa*, London: Oxford University Press.

Gillborn, D. and C. Gipps, 1996, *Recent Research on the Achievements of Ethnic Minority Pupils*, London: Office for Standards in Education.

Green, A. and D. Owen, 1985, "The changing spatial distribution of socio-economic groups employed in manufacturing in Great Britain 1971–81," *Geoforum* 16: 387–402.

Fryer, P., 1984, *Staying Power: The History of Black People in Britain*, London: Pluto Press.

Helweg, A. and U. Helweg, 1990, *An Immigrant Success Story: East Indians in America*, Philadelphia: University of Pennsylvania Press.

Holmes, C., 1991, *A Tolerant Country? Immigrants, Refugees and Minorities*, London: Faber and Faber.

Jeffery, P., 1976, *Migrants and Refugees: Muslim and Christian Pakistani families in Bristol*, Cambridge University Press.

Jones, T., 1993, *Britain's Ethnic Minorities*, London: Policy Studies Institute.

Jones, T., D. McEvoy, and G. Barett, 1994, "Labor intensive practices in the ethnic minority firm," in J. Atkinson and D. Story (eds.), *Employment, the Small Firm and the Labor Market*, London: Routledge, pp. 172–205.

Kotkin, J., 1993, *Tribes: How Race, Religion and Identity Determine Success in the New Global Economy*, New York: Random House.

Kuepper, W., G. Lackey, and E. Swinerton, 1975, *Ugandan Asians in Great Britain*, London: Croom Helm.

Lashmar, P. and A. Harris, 1997, "Who Wants to Be a Millionaire?" *Independent, Magazine Supplement* (March 1): 12–20.

Ley, D., 1977, "Social Geography and the Taken-For-Granted World," *Transactions of the Institute of British Geographers* 2: 468–512.

Marett, V., 1989, *Immigrants Settling in the City*, Leicester University Press.

Metcalf, H., T. Modood, and S. Virdee, 1996, *Asian Self-Employment: The Interaction of Culture and Economics in England*, London: Policy Studies Institute.

Patterson, S., 1963, *Dark Strangers: A Study of West Indians in London*, London: Tavistock.

Peach, C., 1968, *West Indian Migration to Britain: A Social Geography*, London: Oxford University Press.

1984, "The Force of West Indian Island Identity in Britain," in D. Ley and C. Peach (eds.), *Geography and Ethnic Pluralism*, London: Allen and Unwin, pp. 214–30.

1996, "Introduction," in C. Peach (ed.), *Ethnicity in the 1991 Census*, Vol. II: *The Ethnic Minority Populations of Great Britain*, London: HMSO, pp. 1–25.

Ramchandani, R., 1976, *Ugandan Asians: The End of Enterprise*, Bombay: United Asia.

Rattansi, P. and M. Abdulla, 1965, "An educational survey," in D. Ghai (ed.), *Portrait of a Minority: Asians in East Africa*, London: Oxford University Press, pp. 128–51.

Rex, J. and R. Moore, 1967, *Race, Community and Conflict*, London: Oxford University Press.

Rice, P., 1994, "The Changing Labor Force in Great Britain," *Economic Review* 12, 1: 22–5.

Robinson, V., 1984, "Asians in Britain: A Study in Encapsulation and Marginality," in C. Clarke and C. Peach (eds.), *Geography and Ethnic Pluralism*, London: Allen and Unwin, pp. 231–58.

1986, *Transients, Settlers and Refugees: Asians in Britain*, Oxford: Clarendon Press.

1987, "Regional Variations in Attitudes Towards Race," in P. Jackson (ed.), *Race and Racism*, London: Allen and Unwin.

1990, "Roots to Mobility: The Social Mobility of Britain's Black Population, 1971–87," *Ethnic and Racial Studies* 13: 274–86.

1992a, "Not a Lot of People Know That: Research into the Internal Migration of Britain's Ethnic Population," in A. Champion and A. Fielding (eds.), *Migration Processes and Patterns: Research Progress and Prospects*, London: Belhaven, pp. 188–201.

1992b, "Move on Up: The Mobility of Britain's Afro-Caribbean and Asian populations," in J. Stillwell, P. Rees, and P. Boden (eds.), *Migration Processes and Patterns*, Vol. II, London: Belhaven, pp. 221–92.

1993, "The Enduring Geography of Ethnic Settlement: First Results from the 1991 Census," *Town and Country Planning* 62: 53–6.

1994, "Marching into the Middle Classes? The Long-term Resettlement of East African Asians in the UK," *Journal of Refugee Studies* 6: 230–47.

1996, "Indians: Onward and Upward," in C. Peach (ed.), *Ethnicity in the 1991 Census*, Vol. II: *The Ethnic Minority Populations of Great Britain*, London: HMSO, pp. 95–121.

1999, "The Development of Policies for the Resettlement of Quota Refugees in the UK, 1945–91," in V. Robinson (ed.), *Migration and Public Policy*, New York: Edward Elgar, pp. 536–54.

Rose, E., 1969, *Colour and Citizenship*, London: Oxford University Press.

Social Trends, 1987, London: CSO.

Social Trends, 1991, London: CSO.

Smith, D., 1974, *Racial Disadvantage in Britain*, Harmondsworth: Penguin.

Srinivasan, S., 1995, *The South Asian Petty Bourgeoisie in Britain*, Aldershot: Avebury.

Tambs-Lyche, H., 1980, *The London Patidars*, London: Routledge Kegan Paul.

Twaddle, M., 1975, *Expulsion of a Minority: Essays on Ugandan Asians*, London: Athlone Press.

Valeny, R., 1998, "From Pariahs to Paragons? The Social Mobility of Ugandan Asian Refugees in Britain," PhD thesis, Department of Geography, University of Wales, Swansea.

Visram, R., 1986, *Ayahs, Lascars and Princes: Indians in Britain 1700–1947*, London: Pluto Press.

Waldinger, R., H. Aldrich, and R. Ward, 1990, *Ethnic Entrepreneurs*, New York: Sage.

Walvin, J., 1984, *Passage to Britain*, Harmondsworth: Pelican.

Werbner, P., 1990, *The Migration Process: Capital, Gifts and Offerings among British Pakistanis*, Oxford: Berg.

1994, "Renewing an Industrial Past: British Pakistani Entrepreneurship in Manchester," in J. M. Brown, and R. Foot (eds.), *Migration: The Asian Experience*, Basingstoke: St. Martin's Press, pp. 104–30.

Western, J., 1992, *A Passage to England: Barbadian Londoners Speak of Home*, London: UCL Press.

Part IV

Political institutions and processes

Politics synthetic essay

Previous chapters of this volume have explored the role of social and economic networks, labor market structure, entrepreneurship, and segregation as influences on the social mobility of ethnic and racial minorities. This final section of the book adds a factor typically lacking from studies of social mobility, the influence of political institutions and mobilization. Because of this traditional absence, we begin by explaining how and why political factors might be expected to be relevant to our inquiry. We then set the stage for the chapters that follow by examining the important structural, historical, and institutional differences between the two cases, while also laying out the basic contours of public policy in the two countries. We conclude by briefly relating the specific arguments of the papers to the approach of the book as a whole.

Why politics?

On one level, the answer to "why examine politics" is obvious. In the two countries under study, around a third of national resources flow directly through the government,[1] and a substantial percentage of what is left is influenced by patterns of regulation. State institutions determine patterns of policing and the extent of incarceration. They operate redistributive benefit systems, administer public housing, enforce anti-discrimination laws, and run extensive systems for public health. They operate schools and social services, encourage (or discourage) economic growth, regulate labor markets, and direct the shape and character of urban development. They shape patterns of migration, influencing both the number, character, and timing of immigration. All of these functions influence, directly or indirectly, the opportunity structure of ethnic and racial minorities. The findings of previous chapters are effected, in ways small and large, measurable and immeasurable, by the contours of public policy.

Political institutions are shaped by, and in turn shape, the character of ethnic minorities. They create incentives to organize in particular ways, to create coalitions of certain kinds, and to mobilize for particular ends. Over long periods of time, those institutions are also influenced by the presence of ethnic minorities, whether the goal is to control and subordinate them or to assist and support them (or, in many cases, both). In many cases political institutions help determine group identity, breaking down pre-existing bonds and reconstructing new ones. It is this dialectic – of groups being structured by, and reconstructing, the state – that is the subject of this section.

Politics and public policy are neither wholly determined by, nor wholly autonomous from, the processes described in previous chapters. For example, labor markets and informal systems of social control help determine the propensity of group members to engage in crime. But political institutions can: cooperate with social groups to help facilitate social control; partially substitute for weak group controls with formal social controls; distribute resources that make neighborhoods more or less dangerous; provide resources and shape the social and economic environment in ways that make crime more or less desirable; and influence the larger moral character of society in ways that influence the informal binding power of the law. Group characteristics are translated into social outcomes through a process that is influenced all along the way by the direct and indirect influence of political institutions.

In addition, politics interacts with the forces described in other chapters to produce patterns of social outcomes. For example, a number of the chapters discuss how groups form "niches" in the economy that protect them from competition, channel information to coethnics and away from outsiders, facilitate capital accumulation and investment in coethnic businesses, train coethnics (and also, intentionally or unintentionally, deny that training to outsiders), and, as a consequence of these processes, tend to reinforce group attachment (since identity is the mechanism that provides access to the niche). But the fact that "niching" provides opportunity for insiders necessarily entails that it has disadvantage for outsiders. These processes require that borders be enforced, or at least that they not be challenged by legal or other political means. Deborah Malamud, for example, has argued that these niche economies are, by a relatively straightforward interpretation of the civil rights laws, illegal (Malamud 2001). But the fact that ethnic entrepreneurs can take advantage of the political power of small business in American politics, combined with the fact that such enterprise is celebrated as "self-help," has effectively kept the American government from challenging such practices. A similar story could also be told about the way that the political power of unions, combined with the organization and perceived political influence of white ethnic groups such as Irish and Italians, effectively limited the ability of the American government to mount a serious challenge to discrimination in construction and other trades in the 1970s (Waldinger 1996). Political power protects niches, and it can also be used to challenge them. In that sense, the economic strategies of ethnic minorities are not just "socially constructed," but also politically constructed, locked in or made vulnerable by political power and institutions.

If the foregoing argument is persuasive, we would expect differences in the institutional, political cultural, and policy regimes of the two countries to be important factors in the social mobility of ethnic and racial minorities. Critically, that analysis suggests that it is not just those parts of the political environment that are explicitly ethno-racial in character that are relevant for our inquiry. A genuinely political analysis examines a combination of three things. First, the way that race or ethnicity are explicitly encoded in politics and public policy: for example, the representation of ethno-racial minorities in legislatures, their turn-out in elections, the way that political parties appeal or fail to appeal to ethno-racial minorities directly, and discrimination (either positive or negative) in public policy. Second, an examination of the impact of institutions and practices that are not explicitly encoded with race, but that may have important unequal effects on different groups. Here we examine the effects of a broad or narrow welfare state, separation of powers, centralization of government, the structure of political parties, etc. The effects of these institutional arrangements on racial and ethnic stratification may be intended effects of institutions (for example, the way that seniority rules in the House and the filibuster in the Senate gave white American Southerners disproportionate power to protect segregation) or through effects that are largely unintended, as when institutions evolve prior to minorities entering the polity. Authors in this section make a point of looking at both these intended and these unintended effects of institutions.

Next, we must examine how ethno-racial minorities organize for political action themselves: how they conceive of their group boundaries, where in the polity they seek political influence, in what way they imagine their collective interests, and the strategies they seek in pursuing those interests. This requires a focus on the reciprocal influence of existing political institutions on minority mobilization and the effects ethnic and racial groups have on those institutions themselves. Analyses that point the causal arrow in only one direction run the risk of being either too voluntaristic or excessively deterministic.

Finally, we need to recognize that groups enter the polity at different points in a nation's institutional development and interpretation of racial and ethnic categories, and within a system in which some groups have already staked out power and position. For example, Peter Skerry argues that, before the 1960s, immigrants were processed through a predominantly local system of political parties, and their ability to protect their interests depended critically upon the degree to which their co-ethnics were mobilized. Post-1964 immigrants, on the other hand, have been incorporated through a political system primarily designed to protect black Americans, and which reflected their peculiar status in American life. This system, based on a weakening of parties, the centrality of courts and national bureaucracy, and an emphasis on ideas and claims of right, shapes not just how newly incorporating groups pursue their collective interests, but also structures how they conceive of their interests and how the larger society views them and their rightful claims. In essence, Skerry argues that, coming after blacks, subsequent immigrants have been simultaneously "racialized" (that is, treated as "like blacks" in critical ways) and "demobilized" by a system that emphasizes justice rather than power.

In Britain, on the other hand, this process of racialization has been significantly weaker, as Tariq Modood points out. While there have been periods of interest among certain activists in the concept of "political blackness," this homogenization of Britain's ethnic groups into a racial whole has uniformly broken down. Part of the background to the story Modood tells is that there was no policy regime in Britain that gave groups an incentive to analogize themselves to another group with extraordinary claims on the polity (as in the US case), because no such group existed. To the degree that there was any such effect, it was through analogization to African-*Americans*, who, to some degree, influenced the political styles of British Caribbeans and subsequently, if somewhat marginally, British Asians. But this effect, in comparison to the United States, has been primarily internal – relating to how groups conceive of themselves and organize – but much weaker externally, in terms of how they are treated by law and public policy. Groups in Britain have been, at least in comparative terms, relatively free to organize on the basis of identities relevant to their own perceived history and the variety of conditions they faced in British society. While this may have limited the ability of Britain's ethnic groups to mobilize on a collective basis, it has also permitted policymakers to take their real diversity seriously.

The papers

Each of the papers in this section take on some of the questions discussed above. Peter Skerry's contribution examines the way that the civil rights movement has transformed the political organization of ethnic minorities in America, helping to destroy one form of organization, typified by the political machine, and helping to usher in a new form of politics, centered around interest groups, courts, and bureaucracies. Skerry argues that, as a result of this shift, immigrants face a political environment dramatically different from that faced by their predecessors, one that encourages "racialization" and problematic relationships between group representatives and those they claim to represent. Critically, he also claims that this new form of representation tends to be demobilizing, putting a premium on resources most immigrants lack, while devaluing those they possess.

Of special importance for this volume, he concludes that how groups and the larger society determine what social mobility is and "how much is enough" are politically constructed, and the political construction of access and openness that the new regime has produced is problematic for immigrants themselves, and for society as a whole.

Tariq Modood's chapter looks at the changing face of political mobilization of ethnic minorities in Britain, paying special attention to the ideas underlying shifts in the political stance of those groups. He finds that early waves of political mobilization were powerfully influenced by the American civil rights and South African anti-apartheid movement, and thus tended to view color as the central form of social exclusion and discrimination as its most important manifestation. During this period Afro-Caribbeans were clearly at the forefront of political activity, and with this dominance came a concept of "political blackness" that tended to obscure the differences between groups. Over time, however, this homogenization of identity has broken down, in large part as a result of the increasing political awareness and activity of Britain's Asian, and particularly Muslim, population. These groups have shifted political discourse away from an exclusive attention to discrimination (and with it an emphasis on assimilation) to the question of "recognition," of accepting groups on their own terms. Interestingly, this new wave of organization places somewhat less attention on economic matters, and more on religious and cultural questions. In essence, these new waves of mobilization have questioned the definition of social mobility not just of previous waves of political organization, but of British society as a whole.

Robert Lieberman's chapter is one of two directly comparative pieces in this section, looking at the way that political institutions in the two countries have influenced patterns of anti-discrimination policy. Lieberman emphasizes that, to echo a theme of this essay, timing matters. For Lieberman, race and state in the USA have "coevolved": the nation's institutions have been marked deeply by the way those institutions were used to subordinate, and later advance, black Americans. In Britain, on the other hand, Commonwealth immigrants faced a regime that was, in its essential features, already deeply rooted before their arrival. These differences don't always have the most obvious consequences. On the one hand, efforts for minority rights in the USA have required deep institutional transformation, a requirement not faced by their British counterparts. On the other hand, many of the institutional features of American federalism that existed in part to subordinate blacks (in particular political decentralization) have provided openings for effective political organization and mobilization largely absent for British minority groups.

The final chapter in this section, by Teles, Mickey, and Ahmed, takes a broad-brush look at patterns of public policy in the two countries, and their influence on the social mobility of ethnic minorities. In particular, the authors challenge the emphasis on income as a measure of social mobility, an emphasis that is still dominant in much of the literature on the subject. They argue that social mobility is in fact a very rich phenomenon, that certain aspects of the phenomenon are not well captured by income, and that at least some measures operate independent of income. In particular, they examine housing, income support, crime and health, and come up with at least a few surprising findings. In particular, they argue that many of the most important differences between groups are explained not by policies specifically targeted at, for or against particular groups, but by the way that generic policies often have differential impacts. As one example, America's use of prison as a response to drug crime has led to a black incarceration rate much higher than that of British Afro-Caribbeans, even though both groups appear to have similar offending patterns. On the other hand, Britain's increasing crime rates over the last twenty years have impacted ethnic minorities with special severity. For the most part, these are examples of how general policies have ethnically and racially differential effects. The authors suggest that policymakers looking for leverage over group inequality should look to these mechanisms, rather than policies that specifically pick out groups for differential treatment, in order to get leverage over persisting group differences.

NOTE

1. As of the year 2000, the United States' total tax revenue as a percentage of GDP was 29.6 percent, while in the United Kingdom the same figure was 37.4 percent. (http://www.oecdwash.org/DATA/STATS/taxrevenue.pdf).

REFERENCES

Malamud, Deborahi, 2001, "Affirmative Action and Ethnic Niches: A Legal Afterword," in John Skrentny (ed.), *Color Lines*, University of Chicago Press, pp. 313–45.

Waldinger, R., 1996, *Still the Promised City?* Cambridge, MA: Harvard University Press.

16   Ethnicity and political mobilization in Britain

Tariq Modood

In this chapter "ethnic minority" means people of non-European descent (nonwhites) who, or whose families, migrated to Britain, mainly in the period from the 1950s to the 1980s. Foremost amongst these are people from the former British Empire/Commonwealth in the Caribbean, Africa, South Asia, and Hong Kong, the large majority of whom entered Britain as British citizens, and their offspring. As most of the latter, even by the end of the 1990s, were young adults or children, the story of political mobilization to date is mainly about the Commonwealth-born, though of course increasingly the "second generation" are remaking this politics.

If we think of political mobilization as something like this: interaction and participation in the political system to register protest, win or support allies, defeat opponents, influence political processes, initiate, modify, or prevent policies, win public resources, or seek to achieve some other political goal, including the basic goals of gaining legitimacy for one's presence in the country and for one's existence as a collective presence of a certain sort. Then, the politics I am interested in is not simply focused on governments and political parties but is an arena in which rights and membership, cultural obligations and sense of belonging are articulated, debated, and contested, as well as enacted in laws and policies. And I am particularly interested in the public discursive dimension of mobilization. The question I want to address in this chapter is what have been the character and processes of ethnic minority political mobilization in Britain? Once we have some view on this, we can discuss the effects on the broader questions of social mobility.

My suggestion is that there seem to have been five aspects or ideological orientations to ethnic minority political mobilization in Britain. The five aspects follow a rough chronological order, at least in terms of their *emergence*, but do not necessarily supercede each other. On the contrary, they coexist as different tendencies at any one time in debate with and perhaps in open or implicit contestation with each other, informing the perspective of rival organizations or of rival groupings within the same organization, or confusedly mixed up with each other. Individuals or groups may seek to combine the different orientations. However, there is a rough chronology in the series at least in terms of emergence and, therefore, in the expansion of the types of mobilization, but also, I think, in terms of relative ascendency. It is possible that since this book project was started, a new Islamist discourse has emerged, but I don't really think so. I think the current Muslim discourses pre-date September 11 and its aftermath and so are part of what I identify in Section 4 below, but it is possible that I may be proved wrong in hindsight. For the time being I identify the ideological bases of minority mobilization as:

1. Racial equality and anti-discrimination
2. Political blackness: unity of "the Other"
3. Political blackness: racial identity
4. Ethnic and religious identities
5. Parts of Britishness

I shall now say something about each of them.

1   Racial equality and anti-discrimination

The postwar "New Commonwealth" immigration was led by West Indians, some of whom or their relatives had voluntarily fought for Britain during World War II, who hoped to "better themselves" while responding to invitations to assist in the economic reconstruction of the "Mother Country." They were soon joined by large numbers of Indian and Pakistani young men, who too had a British Imperial connection, though a much less developed sense of British identity; instead, their identities revolved around tightly organized lines of kinship, custom, religion, language, post-imperial nationhood, and so on – all of which gave them a clear and confident sense of not being British even while having admiration of the former ruling power (this sentiment being at least as common as any residual anti-colonialism).

By the end of the 1950s it was clear that racism against "colored immigrants" was widespread, capable of erupting into violence and that a popular pressure for stemming this immigration was building up. The Conservative government hurriedly brought in measures to limit immigration in 1961, which were opposed by the Labour Party at the time and in the general election of 1964, when racism was exploited by some Conservatives in some constituencies, but which were extended by the new Labour government.

The Labour governments of 1964–70 were also responsive to the pro-Commonwealth, Christian, liberal, and socialist anti-racism and introduced legislation against overt racial discrimination in employment and housing. They also set up national agencies and local government funding to support and coordinate the work of voluntary organizations concerned with the welfare of immigrants and community relations. Most of these organizations were set up and led by native whites but attracted, and therefore brought into political structures, some immigrant activists. The core belief of this internationalist anti-racism was that race as a biological concept had been scientifically destroyed. There were no races, for human beings were all the same under differently colored skins, and citizenship and all that was of value in human life was color-blind; people should be judged and respected as individuals, not as members of fictitious races. Many anti-racists of this time were inspired by and saw themselves in a common movement with Rev. Martin Luther King, Jr., anti-apartheid in South Africa, and anti-imperialism in the developing world; they saw themselves as standing for what was best in the British political tradition and the ideals of the Commonwealth. "Racial equality," then, meant that a person should not be excluded from any of the benefits of British citizenship and participation in British economic and social life that their talents and education allowed, just because they weren't white.

The Campaign Against Racial Discrimination (CARD) was the leading example of a national political organization, which united British white liberals and socialists and Commonwealth immigrant activists, committed to this form of anti-racism and which supplied public-funded community relations agencies with some of their leaders and personnel in the mid- to late 1960s. This prominent organization was short-lived for it fell apart when some of its minority activists came to develop a new anti-racist political orientation and CARD was unable to reconcile the two orientations, especially as the new orientation made the relationship with the government circles and the liberal left – which made CARD influential – untenable (Hiro 1991).

2   The unity of the "Other"

As racial equality consciousness developed in the 1960s, similar struggles in the USA and Southern Africa were influential in developing thinking in Britain. These two political movements, for civil rights and against state apartheid, were the most prominent and widely reported in the world, were conducted not just in the English language but also in a political discourse that made sense to British people (the anti-racism more than the objects of the critique). Moreover, they were in countries that were recognized as part of Britain's moral and political imperial legacy (and governmental responsibility in the case of Rhodesia) or in a political society seen as an outgrowth of the British. What is germane to my story is that in each of these cases the struggle was cast, both in its home territory and in the eyes of the world, as a struggle between white tyranny and black suffering; and had virtually nothing to do with issues of immigration. Racial equality discourse might have been aspiring towards color-blindness, but as these political contestations went on the racial black–white dualism became central to the anti-racist discourse and the ways in which the oppressed mobilized against their oppression.

Hence in the USA the idea of historically excluded individuals claiming the citizenship that was theirs by right of US nationality was joined by the idea of a black collective agency. In particular, for some young Northern urban black political leaders (Carmichael and Hamilton 1968, Cleaver, 1968) the identity of being black implied the urgent need to unite as a distinct political force and not simply in a color-blind way with white liberals; to unite not so much as a pressure group to achieve limited political goals but to become a political community (in the way that nationalists conceive of a nation as a political community, or socialists use to conceive of a self-conscious class as a political community).

The emergence of this politics created various fissures and new dynamics in the USA and so, similarly, in Britain, as these ideas filtered through to here, sometimes carried in person by their leading exponents (e.g., Malcolm X visited Britain shortly before his assassination). Some West Indian, Asian, and African intellectuals and activists began in the late 1960s/early 1970s to describe themselves as "black" (Banton 1987) and to theorize racialized populations, white people's "Other," in Britain and across the globe, past and present, as a singular collectivity standing in a particular relationship to other collectivities such as "capital" and "labor." The message was that nonwhites suffered a distinct form or forms of exploitation and oppression not recognized within socialist or liberal critiques of British society or international capitalism and so needed to define themselves theoretically and politically in contrast to other collectivities, not just as new members of pre-existing British groups and institutions (Sivanandan 1982). Above all, they needed to lead, not be led by whites, in developing an anti-racist agenda. The injection of this new black-power radicalism into the embryonic British community relations organizations, even when espoused by a small number of ethnic minority intellectuals and activists, created internal black–white, liberal–radical, class–race conflictual debates that led in some cases to the collapse of these organizations (CARD), in other cases to a "black" takeover and exit of white liberals (Institute of Race Relations) (Shukra 1998).

So, while new vigorous, exciting debates about "race" and its relation to socialism (Robinson 1983), about the necessity of developing a Third Worldist perspective, and, on a less utopian level, about developing race-based community responses to, say, police harassment, or educational underachievement (Coard 1971), or the racism in trades unions abounded, existing alliances, especially cross-racial alliances in liberal and socialist fora, were put under strain.

The biggest influence of this new anti-racism, as perhaps in the USA, was to give new currency, assertiveness, and dignity to the label "black," that is, to the creation of a positive black identity. While this has proved to be a major development in British race relations and in shaping ethnic minority political mobilization, it was not without its own internal difficulties.

3   Racial identity

"Black" could be taken as a political racial identity in two different senses: a race in the sense that a population has been conceived as a race by white people, which may have nothing more in common than how white people treat them; or, a race in the sense of a similar physical appearance ("black"), a similar territorial origin, a common history, and so on, in short, not just as a subordinated population but as a people. In the USA and in Southern Africa, where Coloreds, Indians, etc. found themselves sidelined as groups, it made sense for the racially subordinated to conceive of themselves as a people, and to seek to unite themselves, more precisely, to create themselves as a people, under the singular term "black." The development of this racial identity in the USA became much more than just a political construct but a racial–ethnic–cultural pride movement. It was a movement by and for people of African roots and origins in the enslavement of African peoples in the "New World," as symbolized in the slogan "black is beautiful." The celebration of the positive elements of the black diasporic African heritage of struggle, and of the achievements of the contemporary bearers of that heritage, became integral to the meaning of "black" as it was picked up across the world, including the UK (Gilroy 1993).

But this created a serious incoherence in the meaning of "black" as a positive political identity (Modood 1994). On the one hand, it was a non-ethnic term referring to a movement of resistance to racial subordination, and therefore, in aspiration, fully including Asians. On the other hand, it referred to a black diasporic African ethnicity and therefore by definition excluded Asians even though they were the numerical majority of nonwhites in Britain. That for many years this contradiction was not noticed or not thought problematic by advocates of political blackness – which included the majority of Asians involved in anti-racism as a political movement for most of the 1970s and 1980s – reflects I believe at least two things about this period.

Firstly, the Afro-Caribbean lead in forming minority discourses, activism and in challenging anti-racism, and in generally defining the "black" presence in popular perception and policy debates meant that it did not seem to matter that "black and Asian" could be shortened to "black." Of course, there were issues specifically about Asians, say, the funding of special English teaching or arranged marriages, and the term "Asian" gave one a handle on that: but on all matters which could be said to affect Asians *and* Afro-Caribbeans, the perception was that these were "black" issues. That in everyone's mind "black" meant first and foremost Afro-Caribbeans was not thought to be an obstacle to getting a purchase on those issues. If one solved the problem as it affected Caribbeans, then one had solved most of the problem. Secondly, most Asians were too disconnected from these public discourses or insofar as they were aware of them, these public identities did not add or detract from their ethnic and religious identities; unlike the celebrators of black pride, they had not reached a point that they needed an affirmation of their minority identity: they had not yet much entered "the politics of recognition" (Taylor 1994) but were relatively secure or encapsulated in their communal identities.

If you will accept a crude distinction between an "inside left" (the left inside the Labour Party) and an "outside left" (the left beyond the Labour Party), it would be fair to say that the idea of political blackness, whatever its specific origins, was very much developed by the "outside left" in the 1970s, but came to be part of the vocabulary and politics of the "inside left" in the 1980s, especially in London, in Black Sections, and in metropolitan local authorities, a combination perhaps best exemplified in Ken Livingstone's GLC (Shukra 1998). In terms of an ethnic minority movement in mainstream politics, therefore, political blackness has indeed been one of the most influential. Not only has it provided one of, if not the key post-immigration minority political identity and discursive formations but it has also been influential in organizational terms. In one version or another, and usually not very precisely defined, political blackness mobilized and defined anti-racism in professional racial equality work, local government, trade unions, and many public sector professions, especially those connected with social work. As a minority discourse it was politically hegemonic for much of the 1980s. It capitalized on and was part of the race equality initiatives developed in the wake of the Liverpool and Brixton riots in 1981, which enabled a tranche of activists to enter professional equality work. Perhaps its most emblematic organizational manifestation was the campaign to set up an autonomous

Black Sections organization in the Labour Party, which was widely covered in the media.

The campaign was not popular with the Labour leadership, and though some kind of compromise was achieved in the mid-1990s (regarded as a sellout by some of the original cohort), its most notable success was in getting about five or six safe Labour constituencies to adopt one of its leading lights as a parliamentary candidate in about 1986–7. This led to a historic breakthrough with two Afro-Caribbeans, one Anglo-Ghanaian and an Asian elected to Parliament in 1987 – as the first post-imperial nonwhites to sit in the House of Commons. While all four had been vociferous activists of Black Sections prior to election, as a group in Parliament, despite the efforts of Bernie Grant, MP to do so, they failed to establish a black caucus on the US Congressional model; indeed, they did not cohere much as a group. Paul Boateng, MP, emphasized that he was an MP who just happened to be black; Bernie Grant came increasingly to devote himself to African and African diaspora issues, such as reparations; Keith Vaz, MP, has cultivated Asian businessman and cultural groups, especially the prosperous Gujaratis (who are mainly Hindus; Vaz is a Catholic); and Diane Abbot, MP, has become a leading figure on the uninfluential Left, getting elected on to the National Executive Council (NEC) of the Labour Party but refusing to move rightward with the party. Despite their not becoming in any sense a distinctive political force, their election represented the single biggest breakthrough in ethnic minority political representation. Taking the number of ethnic minority MPs from nought to four in one election was not just a "first" but the size of the increase has not been repeated, and despite three subsequent general elections the number of ethnic minority MPs today is 13 (out of 651). The 1987 election marked the peak of political blackness.

Given that political blackness originated with the "outside left" it is, therefore, perhaps not surprising that criticism of this professional, municipal, and parliamentary political blackness should first appear among the "outside left" (Sivanandan 1985, Gilroy 1987 and 1992). To be sure it was not a criticism of political blackness per se, and nor was the criticism all of a piece. It was a criticism of what was taken to be a spoilt form of political blackness. Spoilt because it was, variously, a politics of careerists jumping onto a bandwagon, overly bureaucratized and professionalized (Dhondy 1987), with little appreciation of the historical and global liberation struggles, out of touch with the communities it claimed to represent, and collaborating with state structures it ought to be opposing, while at the same time steeped in dangerous appeals to culture and ethnicity (Sivanandan 1985, Gilroy 1987 and 1992).

While these radical critiques come from influential sources, they were not primarily responsible for the demise of political blackness as a hegemonic presence. The fundamental problem for political blackness came from the internal ambivalence I mentioned earlier, namely whether blackness as a political identity was sufficiently distinct from, and could mobilize without, blackness as an ethnic pride movement. This black identity movement, in a growing climate of opinion favorable to identity politics of various kinds, was successful in shifting the terms of the debate from color-blind individualistic assimilation to questions about how white British society had to change to accommodate new groups. But its success in imposing or making a singular identity upon or out of (unlike black America or South Africa) a diverse ethnic minority population was temporary (probably at no time did a majority of Asians think of themselves as part of a positive black identity [Modood et al. 1997: 294–7]). What it did was pave the way to a plural ethnic assertiveness, as Asian groups borrowed the logic of ethnic pride and tried to catch up with the success of a newly legitimized black public identity.

4   Ethnic and religious identities

Not only have British ethnic minorities not united under a single identity capable of mobilizing them all but the number of identities which generate intensity of commitment and community mobilization grows all the time. It is not just "black" and "Asian," the latter, while generally accepted by South Asians as a public identity, is quite thin and does not have the capacity to mobilize that "Pakistani," "Bangladeshi," and "Indian" do, or better still, "Sikh," "Muslim," "Hindu." One proud, much proclaimed identity often gives way to another within a few years. Many passionate Pakistanis of ten years ago today are dedicated Kashmiris (Ellis and Khan 1998).

Of course much of this is to do with context and in particular what one feels one needs to react against. Pakistanis were "black" when it meant a job in a racial equality bureaucracy, "Asian" when a community centre was in the offing, "Muslim" when the Prophet was being ridiculed, "Kashmiris" when a nationalist movement back home had taken off and blood was being spilt. These identities are pragmatic moves; they also define the field in which moves are made. And yet for me all this leaves unanswered the question: why is it ethnic (i.e., regional and national origins) and religious identities that have come to be politically prominent amongst South Asians in Britain instead of other group identities, most notably, a color-based identity?

Certainly part of the answer lies in describing what the relevant, including the "back home" conflicts and controversies, have been – if the conflict has been the right to wear a turban at school, or to resist the Indian state oppression in the Punjab, no wonder that a Sikh Khalistani identity dominates a decade, as it did for British Sikhs in the 1980s but certainly doesn't today (Goulbourne 1991). But this just pushes the question one step further back: why do *these* controversies become the controversies (in a particular time and place)?

At a time when social theory and research is dominated by constructivism and anti-essentialism of various sorts it is with some trepidation that I raise the question about whether, among alternative identities, certain ethnicities or collectivities may be more "real" than others, have a greater durability or ability to resurface – in short whether they may not have some characteristics that cannot be accounted for by radical constructivism.

When I try to explain to myself why, say, Pakistanis mobilize around "Muslim" with a conviction, intensity, and solidarity that they do not around "black," I use the distinction between a group's mode of oppression and mode of being. So that even if it were the case that white British society saw and treated Muslims as a "colored Other," it doesn't follow that Muslims accept that description of themselves. Excluded groups seek respect for themselves as they are or aspire to be, not simply a solidarity on the basis of a recognition of themselves as victims; they resist being defined by their mode of oppression and seek space and dignity for their mode of being (Modood 1992: 55). Their pride and sense of worth requires a reference to something that comes from them, both in terms of legacy and agency, and not just in terms of something that is imposed on them. All the identities that are being discussed in this chapter are in some sense reactive and are shaped by a situation that the minorities do not control (though I am impressed by the degree to which the minorities are active in these identity formations). I am not contrasting situationally or politically constructed identities with something primordial. My point is that a minority will respond to some forms of exclusion or inferiorization and not to others. The ones it will respond to are those which relate in some way to its own sense of being. Again, this sense of being is not atemporal and can change, but it does mean that neither the oppressor nor the oppressed are totally free to set the terms of a reactive identity – the oppression must "speak" to the oppressed, it must reach a sense of self, that is, if not in some sense authentic, at least "internalized."

So, part of the answer as to which identity will emerge as important to a group at a particular time lies in the nature of the minority group in question. That the Caribbeans have mobilized around a color identity and the South Asians around religious and related identities is not chance, nor just a "construction" but based on something deeper about these groups. That many Muslims in their anger against Salman Rushdie's *The Satanic Verses* found a depth of indignation, a "voice" of their own, in a way that it had not been found by most in relation to events and in mobilization in the previous decades cannot be explained just in terms of issues to do with political leaderships, rivalries, tactics, etc. Certainly, some individuals and organizations exploited the situation but they could not have done so if there was not a "situation" to exploit (Modood 1990 and 1992).

In one important way, however, the context has changed over the last couple of decades and this has influenced which minority identities have emerged, and the ways in which they have developed. Minority ethnicity, albeit white ethnicity, has traditionally been regarded in Britain as acceptable if it was confined to the privacy of family and community and did not make any political demands. Earlier groups of migrants and refugees, such as the Irish or the Jews in the nineteenth and the first half of the twentieth century, found that peace and prosperity came easier the less public one made one's minority practices or identity. Perhaps for non-European origin groups, whose physical appearance gave them a visibility that made them permanently vulnerable to racial discrimination, the model of a privatized group identity was never viable. Yet, additionally, one has to acknowledge the existence of a climate of opinion quite different from that experienced by the earlier Irish or Jewish incomers.

In the last couple of decades the bases of identity-formation have undergone important changes and there has come to be a minority assertiveness. Identity has moved from that which might be unconscious and taken for granted because implicit in distinctive cultural practices to conscious and public projections of identity and the explicit creation and assertion of politicized ethnicities. This is part of a wider sociopolitical climate which is not confined to race and culture or nonwhite minorities. Feminism, gay pride, Quebecois nationalism, and the revival of Scottishness are some prominent examples of these new identity movements which have come to be an important feature in many countries in which class-politics has declined. Identities in this political climate are not implicit and private but are shaped through intellectual, cultural, and political debates and become a feature of public discourse and policies, especially at the level of local government (Young 1990, Taylor 1994, Kymlicka 1995). The identities formed in such processes are fluid and susceptible to change with the political climate, but to think of them as weak is to overlook the pride with which they may be asserted, the intensity with which they may be debated, and their capacity to generate community activism and political campaigns.

One should also recognize the transnational influences, made possible by the cheap transport and electronic communication that exist nowadays. The Khalistani movement in Punjab in the 1980s was facilitated by the diasporic support it received, especially in the UK and North America, which amongst other things enabled news that the Indian state was trying to suppress to get out around the world almost instantaneously. Transnationalism can be an important feature of the identity too. Just as this was true of pan-Africanism or pan-Blackness in the earlier part of this story, it is true today with some British Muslims, especially the younger and better educated. The concept of *ummah*, the global community of Muslims, has been politically embraced and reinterpreted as global victims and the oppression in Palestine, Bosnia, Chechnyia, Afghanistan, Iraq, etc. has been used as an occasion to heighten a Muslim political identity, which is sometimes explicitly hostile to national identities and ethnic affiliations. Just as advocates of political blackness seek to unite all nonwhites despite more specific ethnic identities, so similarly, some Muslims are intolerant of ethnic minority identities. They argue that a toleration of ethnic diversity is a policy of "divide and rule" against Muslims, for it blinds Muslims to their real numbers and power by placing them in small ethnic groups, usually in competition with each other for limited resources (Muslim Parliament 1992) (in this and other respects the logic and rhetoric of political Islam can be similar to political blackness, Modood 1993 and 2002).

In this way the presence of organized minority religious communities is not simply diversifying religion in Britain but giving it a new policy importance. This has of course become particularly obvious after September 11 but was apparent much earlier (Modood 2002). Statham analyzed political claims-making in relation to "race relations" and multiculturalism as reported in the *Guardian* newspaper over a random six-week period. He found that nearly half of all claims were made by organizations with "Muslim" or "Islamic" in their title, thus showing that some groups have achieved a high level of autonomous organization on the basis of identities that at that time contradict the British state's categorization of them (Statham 1999). It would be no exaggeration to say that many multiculturalists are dismayed by the emergence of Muslim consciousness. They took it for granted that multiculturalism would be respectful of secularism: while in general they believe that to require minority identities to confine themselves to the private sphere is oppressive they believe religious identities to be an exception. They never intended the recognition of difference to be extended to Muslims; for them, Muslim identity

is a bastard child of British multiculturalism. Religious identity developments, then, challenge normative definitions of what should be public
and private in a way that, while deepening multiculturalism, has thrown
multicultural advocacy into disarray (Modood 2002 and 2005).

While Muslims have become the most visible and politicized minority
group, and this in due course turns out to have been indicative of a new
phase in minority stigmatization and mobilization, it should not obscure
another current development, which I identify as the fifth ideological
orientation.

5   Parts of Britishness

Stuart Hall, amongst others, has argued that from the mid- to late 1980s
"a significant shift has been going on (and is still going on) in black
cultural politics" (Hall 1992: 252). Not only does this entail a recognition of a diversity of minority identities, "a plural blackness," but also
an understanding that ethnic identities are not "pure" or static. Rather,
they change in new circumstances or by sharing social space with other
heritages and influences. Moreover, this also challenges existing conceptions of Britishness (Gilroy 1987). For, if ethnic minority identities are
not simply products of cultures of extra-British origin but owe something
to the stream of British life, then they too contribute to that stream, and so
their existence belies the dichotomy of "essentially black" and "essentially
British." What is particularly interesting about these and other ethnic
identity developments is that increasingly "ethnicity" or "blackness" is
less experienced as an oppositional identity than as a way of being British
(though as I have already indicated, the current position of Muslim identity, subject as it is to various global crises, is something of an exception
at the moment). Moreover, this is happening at a time when some in
the wider British public, including the Labour government which came
into power in 1997, is emphasizing the plural and dynamic character of
British society, and there is talk of "rebranding Britain" (Leonard 1997).
Of course, the whole issue of British identity is now a topic of national
debate, in the wake of the rise of Scottishness and the new devolved constitutional arrangements. But it is worth noting that amongst those who
first raised the issue of British identity and the need to remake it were
minority intellectuals like Stuart Hall, Bhikhu Parekh, and Paul Gilroy,
and racial egalitarians have put the need to rethink a new inclusive Britishness as critical to the prospects for racial equality (CMEB 2000).

The Fourth National Survey of Ethnic Minorities offers for the first
time some large dataset evidence that ethnicity is coming to mean new
things (Modood et al. 1997). Distinctive cultural practices to do with

religion, language, marriage, and so on still command considerable allegiance, but there is a visible decline in participation in distinctive cultural practices across the generations. This was particularly evident amongst younger South Asians who, compared to their elders, are less likely to speak to family members in a South Asian language, regularly attend a place of worship, or have an arranged marriage.

Yet this did not mean that they ceased to identify with their ethnic or racial or religious group. In this respect the Fourth Survey makes clear what has been implicit in recent "identity politics" (Hall 1992). Ethnic identification is no longer necessarily connected to personal participation in distinctive cultural practices, such as those of language, religion, or dress. Some people expressed an ethnic identification even though they did not participate in distinctive cultural practices. Hence it is fair to say a new conception of ethnic identity has emerged.

Traditionally, ethnic identity has been implicit in distinctive *cultural practices*, this still exists and is the basis of a strong expression of group membership. Additionally, however, an *associational* identity can be seen which takes the form of pride in one's origins, identification with certain group labels, and sometimes a political assertiveness.

This trend toward cultural hybridity and social mixing across racial and ethnic lines is led by and is most pronounced amongst Caribbeans (Peach, this volume). Its extent is quite remarkable as is the fact that it is not experienced as a denial or betrayal of blackness. Indeed, since about the mid-1990s leading black analysts have spoken of the vibrant strength of a black British cultural identity in the mid-1990s. Darcus Howe has spoken of black people having "a social ease and confidence now that we have not had before" (Younge 1995); Henry Louis Gates, Jr. believes that "a culture that is distinctively black and British can be said to be in full flower" (Gates 1997: 196), and Stuart Hall has argued not only that "black British culture could be described as confident beyond measure in its own identity"(Hall 1998: 39) but also that young black people have made themselves "*the* defining force in street-oriented British youth culture" (Hall 1998: 40).

It is indeed extraordinary that a group which comprises less than 2 percent of the population has, both in terms of quantity and quality, established itself as a leading-edge presence in urban youth culture in the face of racism, social deprivation, and relative exclusion from positions of power and wealth. From being pariahs many black people have become objects of desire, with many young whites envying and imitating their "style" (Hall in Gates 1997: 196). Moreover, this black British cultural success, like some other aspects of Caribbean settlement in Britain, has been highly inclusive. For while born of an assertiveness and a search for dignity, and while sometimes oppositional, it has also been a movement of integration, of wanting to be included into the British mainstream, of sharing and mutual respect (Phillips and Phillips 1998, and Part 4 of the BBC television series, *Windrush*, to which this book is an accompaniment). It has, inevitably, been largely a black–white relationship but some young Asians and others have been drawn into it too. One must note, if only in passing, that just as earlier black political formations in Britain were facilitated by the global visibility of the struggles of American blacks, so this hybridic cultural formation too rides on the global power of American black images and personnel to define international youth culture. This element of American global cultural power has implications for "British" and for that matter, "European" identities.

These, however, are not the only forms of minority hybridities visible today. Hanif Kureshi, in his novel *The Black Album* (Kureshi 1995), portrays London Asian youth being pulled by "sex, drugs and rock 'n' roll," on the one hand, and by communal religious solidarity on the other hand. Salman Rushdie, another leading celebrator of Asian hybridity, also is inclined to see such incompatible attractions in terms of hybridity and purity. But Asian youth, even Muslim youth, sometimes explicitly emphasize their Britishness, sometimes at the expense of their parents' ethnicities. They may say: my parents are Pakistanis, but I am Muslim and British (at least till the Pakistani cricket team arrives). Other Asians don't want to highlight religion but also talk in terms of (without using the phrase) hyphenated identity (a concept very familiar to Americans but it has crept into British ethnic minority identities with relatively little explicit reference to the USA). While the idea of a hybridic culture is more likely to be found amongst younger Asians, hyphenated identity certainly is not. Many new pressure groups, even those with relatively conservative cultural agendas, have "British" in their title.

One of the most significant anti-racist political mobilizations in recent years has been the campaign in the late 1990s to have the police find and prosecute the murderers of the black teenager, Stephen Lawrence. While not (yet) achieving its goal, the campaign achieved a national media prominence and a virtually unprecedented sense of shame amongst what is termed "middle England," and led to significant legislation and institutional reform. Though perhaps not so supportive amongst the white working classes, the campaign created a multiracial movement that evokes memories of liberal protests of the 1960s and the Anti-Nazi League in the 1970s and other anti-racist demonstrations at which white faces were in a majority. It sharply contrasts with an earlier campaign, the demand to find and bring to justice arsonists of a fire leading to the death of thirteen black teenagers, and injuries to another thirty in 1981 in Deptford,

South London. When a campaign march brought central London to a standstill, there was hardly a white face among the marchers (Phillips and Phillips 1998). The contrast shows how much has changed in twenty years. It also suggests that some of the liberal ideas of cross-racial solidarity of the Martin Luther King era are still alive. This history, then, has both cyclical and linear features. The British identity espoused by the 1948 Windrush hopefuls may be irrecoverable, but it may be that a new British identity is evolving which makes more sense to them than some of the politics in the period between then and now.

Conclusion

Ethnic minority political mobilization in Britain began with a set of factors that enabled it to reach a degree of ideological assertiveness, prominence, and civic impact to a scale and in a limited period of time that seems without parallel in Western Europe:

- the British imperial connection, felt by many migrants and politically acknowledged by at least some white British
- the British identity and sense of having a right to be in Britain
- automatic British citizenship and franchise from day of arrival (later qualified)
- large-scale anti-racist struggles elsewhere in the English-speaking world, especially in the USA, in which notions of "migrants and hosts" were absent, and which were borrowed from or emulated creating a confidence and assertiveness which amongst migrants-as-guests would be regarded as intolerable by "hosts."

Hence, there is real sense that these groups were not just economic immigrants but former colonials moving to the metropolis; partly through institutional fact, such as the free entry and automatic British citizenship on the day of arrival, and partly through their subsequent politics (their "attitude"), it is fair to say that what we are talking about is something in between a "country-to-country" movement and a movement from an outlying province of an empire to its ruling capital. Neither is a satisfactory description of the phenomenon. The fact that it was not pure immigration but entry into a country upon which one had a moral or political claim stands out when one compares it to migration to Western Europe or North American countries in the same period (descriptions of the mighty USA as an "invisible empire" notwithstanding).

In most/each of the respects mentioned above, the West Indians, who thought of themselves as culturally and politically British in the way that New Zealanders arriving in England in the 1950s would have done, took the lead in forging a minority political discourse and assertiveness that

South Asians gradually assimilated into, adapted for their own use, or used as a point of departure to develop a less racial dualist and more ethnic pluralist orientation. Once this minority assertiveness is part of a political culture and regarded as legitimate, perhaps even necessary to demonstrate a certain group dignity, then it can take forms which owe nothing to the original source. They can take, for example, the form of the Muslim campaign against *The Satanic Verses*, which to many observers initially bore no relation to anti-racism but has increasingly come to be seen in that light.

British "ethnic relations," then, have been characterized by a high level of political mobilization but have been constituted by different ideas and ideologies, including those which contradict official policy frameworks and are motivated by a resentment of "misrecognition" and the search for "recognition." The political opportunities structure has been initially and strongly shaped by postcolonial and American conceptions, producing a "race relations framework" embodied in official discourse, laws, and policies. It has been a framework, however, which has encouraged and been responsive to ethnic minority challenges. Thus the framework has been and continues to be modified over time and is at least partly shaped by ethnic minority political mobilization, and includes efforts to redefine race, ethnicity, racism, discrimination and, ultimately, British citizenship.

While then, one could argue that the social mobility of immigrants and ethnic minorities has been made possible by the fact that they have come to establish a certain political legitimacy for their presence in Britain and for racial equality and multiculturalism; or more precisely, that both the social and the political integration has been made possible by the post-colonial character of the migrants and the fact that they had British citizenship status from date of arrival, there is, however, no clear correlation between the two kinds of integrations. The Caribbeans have been very active in political terms, especially in political-discursive and political-cultural terms, and while this has undoubtedly led to their carving out a place for themselves in British society, it is not an enviable one in socioeconomic terms except in relation to sport, entertainment, and the related media. The other active group, the Pakistanis, continue to be one of the most materially marginal groups in the country. Indeed, minorities such as the Hindus and the Chinese, who have established and are consolidating a middle-class profile, have given little time and energy to politics; indeed, they are politically invisible. It seems to be the characteristic of British ethnic minority politics that it is the politics of the excluded and disadvantaged rather than of ethnic minorities per se. The continuing rise of Muslim assertiveness and militancy, though largely affected by global crises and increasingly by Islamist discourses, also largely fits this pattern but may yet intimate a new ideological orientation, additional to the ones discussed in this chapter (cf. Modood 2003 with Werbner 2004).

REFERENCES

Banton, M., 1987, "The Battle of the Name," *New Community* 14: 170–5.
Carmichael, S. and C. V. Hamilton, 1968, *Black Power: The Politics of Liberation in America*, Harmondsworth: Penguin.
Cleaver, E., 1968, *Soul on Ice*, New York: McGraw Hill.
Coard, C., 1971, *How The West Indian Child is Made Educationally Subnormal in the British School System*, London: New Beacon Books.
Commission on Multi-Ethnic Britain (CMEB), 2000, *The Future of Multi-Ethnic Britain*, London: Profile Books.
Dhondy, F., 1987, "Speaking in Whose Name?" *New Statesman* (April 24).
Donald, J and A. Rattansi (eds.), 1992, *"Race," Culture and Difference*, London: Sage.
Ellis, P. and Z. Khan, 1998, "Diasporic Mobilisation and the Kashmir Issue in British Politics," *Journal of Ethnic and Migration Studies*.
Gates J. H. L., 1997, "Black London," *New Yorker* (April 28–May 5).
Gilroy, P., 1987, *There Ain't No Black in the Union Jack*, London: Routledge.
  1992, "The End of Anti-Racism," in Donald and Rattansi (eds.), pp. 49–61.
  1993, *The Black Atlantic*, London: Verso.
Goulbourne, H., 1991, *Ethnicity and Nationalism in Post-imperial Britain*, Cambridge University Press.
Hall, S., 1992, "New Ethnicities," in Donald and Rattansi (eds.), pp. 252–9.
  1998, "Aspiration and Attitude . . . Reflections on Black Britain in the Nineties," *New Formations*, Frontlines/Backyards Special Issue, 33.
Hiro, D., 1991, *Black British, White British*, London: Grafton Books.
Kureshi, H., 1995, *The Black Album*, London: Faber.
Kymlicka, W., 1995, *Multicultural Citizenship: A Liberal Theory of Minority Rights*, Oxford University Press.
Leonard, M., 1997, *Britain TM: Renewing Our Identity*, London: Demos.
Modood, T., 1990, "British Asian Muslims and the Rushdie Affair," *Political Quarterly* 61: 143–60; reproduced in Donald and Rattansi (eds.), pp. 260–77.
  1992, *Not Easy Being British: Colour, Culture and Citizenship*, London and Stoke-on-Trent: Runnymede Trust and Trentham Books.
  1993, "Muslim Views on Religious Identity and Racial Equality," *New Community* 19, 3: 513–19.
  1994, "Political Blackness and British Asians," *Sociology* 28, 4: 859–76.
  2002, "Muslims and the Politics of Multiculturalism in Britain," in E. Hershberg and K. Moore (eds.), *Critical Views of September 11: Analyses from Around the World*, New York: New Press, pp. 193–208.
  2003, "Muslims and the Politics of Difference," in S. Spencer (ed.), *The Politics of Migration*, Oxford, The Political Quarterly/Blackwell, pp. 100–15.

2005, *Multicultural Politics: Racism, Ethnicity and Muslims in Britain*, Minnesota: Minnesota University Press and Edinburgh: Edinburgh University Press.

Modood, T., R. Berthoud, J. Lakey, J. Nazroo, P. Smith, S. Virdee, and S. Beishon, 1997, *Britain's Ethnic Minorities: Diversity and Disadvantage*, London: Policy Studies Institute.

Muslim Parliament of Great Britain, 1992, *Race Relations and Muslims in Great Britain: A Discussion Paper*, London: The Muslim Parliament.

Phillips, M. and T. Phillips, 1998, *Windrush: The Irresistible Rise of Multicultural Britain*, London: HarperCollins.

Robinson, C., 1983, *Black Marxism*, London: Zed Press.

Shukra, K., 1998, *The Changing Pattern of Black Politics in Britain*, London: Pluto Press.

Sivanandan, A., 1982, *A Different Hunger: Writings on Black Resistance*, London: Pluto Press.

1985, "RAT and the Degradation of the Black Struggle," *Race and Class* 26, 4.

Statham, P., 1999, "Political Mobilisation by Minorities in Britain: A Negative Feedback of 'Race Relation'?" *Journal of Ethnic and Migration Studies* 25: 597–626.

Taylor, C., 1994, "Multiculturalism and 'The Politics of Recognition'," in A. Gutmann (ed.), Princeton University Press, pp. 25–73.

Werbner, P., 2004, "The Predicament of Diaspora and Millenial Islam: Reflections on September 11, 2001," *Ethnicities* 4 (4): 451–76.

Young I. M., 1990, *Justice and the Politics of Difference*, Princeton University Press.

Younge, G., 1995, "Black in Britain: Where Are We Now?" *Guardian* (March 20).

Peter Skerry

In comparing the influence of different political institutions on minority mobility, the conventional approach is to look at social and economic outcomes. This essay will go further and scrutinize the *standards* by which such outcomes are evaluated. What levels, rates, and disparities of mobility are acceptable, or not, to minority groups and other political actors? The standards used to answer these questions are typically treated as exogenous to the political institutions being studied.[1] These standards are the product of many societal forces, to be sure. But they are fundamentally shaped by politics. Indeed, as conceptions of distributive justice, such standards are themselves political outcomes and are arguably more important than social and economic outcomes.

In the US context, such discussions inevitably address the impact of political machines[2] on the mobility of ethnic and racial groups. Machines are usually compared with trade unions, social democratic or labor parties, and Progressive reforms. Here, too, this essay will go further and compare machines with the post-civil-rights regime that has effectively replaced them. I call this regime "post-civil-rights" because it grew out of the civil rights movement of the 1960s and, like all successful movements, has become institutionalized. My intention is to show the advantages and disadvantages of each, for minorities as well as for the larger society. Again, the focus here will be on how each regime has shaped *expectations* of minority mobility. This is key, because while the shortcomings of political machines are well known, the insights they provide about today's regime have been largely ignored.

Disadvantages of political machines

In the public mind, "political machine" connotes corruption. Yet when academic observers criticize machines, they tend to downplay this aspect, agreeing with James C. Scott that corruption is endemic to politics: "Just as social banditry and piracy must be viewed as integral parts of many agrarian and maritime economies, so, for example, must vote-buying and 'rake-offs' be seen as an integral part of United States urban politics at the turn of the century" (Scott 1972: viii). For Scott and others, a more serious problem than corruption was the machines' role in reconciling immigrant workers to an unjust capitalist society: "The effect of machine rule under universal suffrage is to submerge growing collective policy demands with immediate payoffs, thereby retarding the development of class-based political interests among the lower strata" (ibid.: 151).

But Scott is not concerned that machines channeled class- or occupation-based demands into ethnic group-based claims. He suggests a more insidious outcome: "Although pork-barrel legislation provided inducements for ethnic groups and neighborhoods collectively, the machine did most of its favors for individuals and families" (ibid.: 108). Likewise, William Grimshaw writes that the Chicago machine redefined "public services" such as "patching potholes, collecting garbage, trimming trees, and the like" as "private 'favors' dispensed on a quid pro quo basis" (Grimshaw 1992: 54). Machine politics catered to constituent needs less through the passage of legislation, which would have required public rationales for broad categories of beneficiaries, than through enforcement, which allowed individual benefits to be quietly targeted and tailored (Scott 1972: 23–7). Public declarations about issues and principles ill suited the needs and often the talents of machine politicians. Hence the fabled inarticulateness of Mayor Richard J. Daley.[3]

The realist critique of machines focuses right here on their limited political vision. As Daniel P. Moynihan once quipped, "The Irish didn't know what to do with power once they got it" (Glazer and Moynihan 1970: 229). Machine politicians conceived of politics as the pursuit of power, pure and simple. They were not attuned to the articulation of broad public goals. No wonder they were overwhelmed by the national trauma of the Depression and the sacrifices demanded by World War II. It was not simply the New Deal's greater fiscal resources that hastened their end. It was also the political and intellectual resources that Roosevelt amassed in Washington in order to inspire a nation on the verge of demoralization and defeat.

After the war, those same intellectual resources engaged an increasingly affluent, educated, and issue-oriented citizenry in the pursuit of the Cold War. This further marginalized machine politicians who, like their aging constituents, had long been preoccupied with pressing material needs and therefore unaccustomed to looking very far ahead (Scott 1972: 117–18). Edward Banfield and James Q. Wilson have noted that the machines were about conflict management, not leadership (Banfield and Wilson 1966: 18–19). As they conclude, "The machines failed because bosses lacked statesmanship" (ibid.: 125).

Advantages of political machines

The virtues of political machines are also widely acknowledged. Scott highlights their ability to keep the peace: "The social setting of the machine is ordinarily one where ties to the community as a whole are weak and where the potential for violence is great. The capacity of the machine to organize and provide material inducements (often corruptly) operates as a means of solving, for the time being at least, conflicts of interest that might otherwise generate violence" (1972: 145). And while Ira Katznelson criticizes machines for discriminating against blacks and blunting working-class challenges to capitalism, he similarly acknowledges that "the machine form of political organization maintained social order in a setting where the potential for threats to the social order was high" (1981: 114).

Further, Katznelson expresses begrudging respect for the way machines "provided an organized, coherent access link to government and acted as the key distributor of political rewards" (1976a: 224). The machines' affective ties to their adherents made them better at "controlling *both* the input and output sides of politics" than the service bureaucracies that succeeded them, Katznelson argues. Having only impersonal ties to their clients, such bureaucracies cannot shape demands at the pre-political level. So they resort either to rigid enforcement of rules, which of course alienates clients, or to their relaxation, which is intended to co-opt them.[4]

Quite unlike "urban villages," the communities in which machines operated were typically disorganized and violence prone. To some extent this reflects the transience and travail of migration and assimilation. But it also reflects the fact that immigrants were – and are – "transitional" populations that have shaken off the deference patterns of traditional societies without yet acquiring the perspectives of modern society. As Scott explains:

> For portions of the modern sector where broader class loyalties and civic sentiments have begun to take root, or for the traditional sector where deference and symbolic goals are common, machine blandishments are likely to fall on barren soil. Machines therefore can manage conflict best among "transitional" populations and may be unable to alleviate strife – or may actually exacerbate it – in other social contexts. (Scott 1972: 147)

This accounts for the instability of machines. Indeed, as immigrants and their children assimilated to more modern styles of politics, the machines were left behind.

Of course, the machines themselves contributed to this process. As Scott observes, "The machine simply destroyed its own social base"

(1972: 152). It accomplished this by serving, in Morris Janowitz's term, as a "bridging institution" between immigrant neighborhoods (the private realm of family, neighbors, and friends) and the wider society (the public realm of politics) (Janowitz 1983: 19). Or as Theodore Lowi puts it, the machine combined "rational goals and fraternal loyalty."[5]

Thus did machines provide a critical nexus between the formal institutions of the state and the informal, even chaotic world of immigrants. They did so by being rooted in the face-to-face, primary group networks that still enable even the most unsophisticated individuals to travel great distances and find work in unfamiliar, even hostile settings (Massey et al. 1987: 170–1, Piore 1979: 17). For peasants unschooled in democracy, the precinct captain gave politics a concrete presence. And because immigrants – then as now – seek chiefly economic goals, the material inducements of the machines drew them into politics by connecting it directly with their families' well-being. The lesson was reciprocity: political support in exchange for economic benefits. To be sure, the machines also taught the less than ennobling lesson that votes could be sold to the highest bidder. But arguably this was a necessary first step. Unlike the Progressives, who demanded disinterested civic involvement from politically inexperienced European peasants, the machine politicians met newcomers halfway.[6]

Machines did not leave immigrant networks unaltered, however. In Steven Erie's phrase, machines were "engines of political modernization" (Erie 1988: 231). They took primary group ties and reoriented them toward rational, instrumental, political-organizational goals. Tracing the "communitarian basis" of the New York machine, Katznelson notes that "the centralized machine's political clubs organized this social impulse [of friends and neighbors] and made it the cornerstone of an electoral politics through patronage and services."[7] A measure of the social alchemy wrought by the machines was their ability, when strong, to get members of one immigrant ethnic group to vote for candidates from another. Hence one connotation of "machine" (Banfield and Wilson 1966: 115, 159).

That a trade-off is involved is captured by Samuel Huntington in his treatise on political development:

If the society is modern and complex, with a large number of social forces, individuals from any one of the social forces may have to make extensive changes in their behavior, values, and attitudes in the process of acquiring power through the political institutions of society. They may well have to unlearn much which they have learned from family, ethnic group, and social class, and adapt to an entirely new code of behavior.[8]

It is precisely such "unlearning" that was fostered by political machines. As a nation the United States may have been "born modern," but ironically, it has grown by absorbing large numbers of pre-modern peoples. The machines helped to perform this function, and they did so at a time when few other institutions did. The high-minded civic consciousness urged by Progressives did not have much to offer struggling newcomers. But neither did trade unions, which were not only weak but also less welcoming of immigrants than were machines (Shefter 1994: 161, 164, 165).

Machines and African-Americans

How many of these benefits extended to African-Americans? The short answer is – not many. Still, African-Americans fared better under machine rule than is often acknowledged.

Of particular help here are comparative studies, such as Katznelson's work on racial politics in the United States and the United Kingdom. In both liberal democracies, he argues, political elites created "buffering institutions" that "link potentially partisan black and Third World migrants to the polity *indirectly* through institutions over which the elites could exercise significant control – institutions which precluded direct group inclusion in the relevant competitive establishments" (Katznelson 1976b: 119, 175–88, 193).

Katznelson's specific evidence offers additional insights. He demonstrates that from 1900 to 1930 blacks fared better under Chicago's machine than they did with New York City's. During that era, black Chicagoans were registered to vote in higher proportions than whites. And they held municipal jobs commensurate with their proportion of the city's population. Katznelson emphasizes that most of those jobs were menial, but the significance of this is unclear, since his study does not control for group educational differences (Katznelson 1976b: 99–100).

Katznelson notes that by 1930 black New Yorkers had secured only about 20 percent of the top patronage positions that they deserved, based on their proportion of the population. Here again, he does not control for educational differences. Nor does he say anything about black voter turnout in New York – obviously a critical consideration for machine politicians parceling out patronage slots. Nonetheless, he reports that black New Yorkers did not fare much worse than Italian New Yorkers, "who in this period fared least well among the European ethnics." Based on their proportion of the population, Italians held only 27 percent of the expected top patronage jobs (Katznelson 1976b: 117).

By the 1960s, blacks in Chicago were benefiting less from machine rule. Faced with new and fundamentally challenging demands from the civil

rights movement, the Daley organization shifted its attention to white ethnics (Grimshaw 1992: 115–40). In New York, by contrast, the demise of
the machine improved political opportunities for blacks, albeit marginally
(Katznelson 1976b: 118). But by the 1970s and 80s the remnants of
machine politics in New York were doing even less for blacks, as the
whites in charge (with substantially fewer resources and patronage prerogatives) proved indifferent to black and minority inclusion.[9]

Another illuminating comparison is in Amy Bridges's study of urban
reform in the Southwest. Here, again, the evidence indicates that
machines were not as hard on blacks and other minorities as typically
assumed. While acknowledging the critique mounted by Katznelson and
others, Bridges argues that machine cities compare favorably with reform
cities:

> From the perspective of the big cities of the Southwest, machine politics does not
> look nearly so antiparticipatory . . . machine politics must be judged a veritable
> school of politics for working-class and minority voters, compared to big-city
> reform. (Bridges, 1997: 216)

As for turnout, Bridges reports that it remained greater in "machine-
descendant cities" than in "big reform cities," and concludes:

> This is hardly accidental. Party workers and leaders continued to have incentives
> to get out the vote, be present in neighborhoods, contact voters, and be responsive
> to voters' contacts. The result was, comparatively speaking, a highly participatory
> form of local politics. (ibid.: 217)

Bridges doesn't minimize the travail of blacks under machine rule. But
she also emphasizes: "It should surprise no one that the first African-
American Democrat, in the Senate, like the first African-American
Democrat in the House, came from Chicago" (ibid.).

Such comparisons – across decades, groups, and cities – are helpful,
because they move analysis beyond the global explanation of "racism."
Katznelson highlights the advantages to blacks of the intense party competition in Chicago in the years before World War II. Other scholars
reveal the structural constraints under which machine politicians tried
to manage conflict among ethnic and racial groups.[10] Still others show
that machines were more inclusive of blacks than, say, trade unions
(Katznelson 1976b: 97). Taken together, these findings suggest more
realistic standards by which to judge machine performance.

Of course, by any yardstick it must be said that African-Americans
consistently got less than their due. The simple truth is that machine
politics was not capable of addressing America's racial dilemmas in any
fundamental way. What machines could do was address the demands of

individual blacks. But by their very nature, such particularistic benefits could not begin to solve the problems facing African-Americans *as a group*. And to the extent that machine politicians did engage in bargaining among ethnic and racial groups, they could not alter the basic terms of trade.[11] But this of course is precisely what blacks needed, and eventually demanded. As short-term conflict managers, not statesmen and definitely not prophetic leaders, machine politicians could neither conceive nor articulate a broad new public purpose with regard to race.

Such a challenge had to come from outside – and it did, from the civil rights movement. The outcome is captured in an encounter between Mayor Daley and the young Jesse Jackson, depicted by Nicholas Lemann. Having recently moved to Chicago in the 1960s, Jackson called on Daley, who promptly offered the civil rights leader a job as a toll-taker on the Illinois Tollway.[12]

The problem was not simply that Daley misjudged the "price" demanded by an individual black constituent (this having skyrocketed).[13] The problem was that the benefits sought had shifted from individual to collective. Even more to the point, as black demands for desegregated public schools and neighborhoods mounted, the Daley machine began to deliver such collective goods – but to enraged white ethnics, not blacks (Erie 1988: 163–5). At that point the very basis of machine politics was crumbling. For as Scott observes: "Only in circumstances where ethnic groups do not feel threatened with physical or cultural extinction do ethnic cleavages promote machine politics. Where the threat is perceived as great, the result is often collective solidarity" (Scott 1972: 106, footnote 14).

A black nationalist postscript

A neglected irony of this story is how, despite such manifest shortcomings, machine politics still enjoys considerable respect among minorities. The antipathy that white liberals harbor toward the machines is certainly seldom voiced in minority communities.

This observation is based on years of interviewing black and Latino activists and leaders. But an echo of pro-machine attitudes can also be found in the Kerner Commission report, which counted among the causes of black civil disturbances in the 1960s "the demise of the historic urban political machines and the growth of the 'city manager' concept of government." Reform had produced more honest and efficient administration, the report conceded, but at the price of eliminating "an important political link between city government and low-income residents" (Kerner Commission 1968: 287).

A certain begrudging respect for machines can be discerned in the work of black nationalist scholar Harold Cruse (1987, 1967). This becomes explicit in Ture and Hamilton's 1967 manifesto, *Black Power*, in which blacks were reminded that "each new ethnic group in this society has found the route to social and political viability through the organization of its own institutions . . . Italians vote for Rubino over O'Brien; Irish for Murphy over Goldberg, etc."[14] In the mid-1970s Hamilton would favorably contrast the "patron-client" basis of machine politics with the "patron-recipient" politics of the emergent post-civil rights regime (Hamilton 1979: 211–27). Concerned about the rights-oriented litigation strategies then beginning to dominate black politics, Hamilton complained that such efforts were nurturing "plaintiffs instead of precinct captains" (Hamilton 1974: 191).

Thoughtful black nationalists distrust the tendency of liberals to evade the rigors of political competition, whether through over-reliance on the courts or through moralistic appeals to conscience (for which Cruse harshly criticized Martin Luther King, Jr. [Cruse 1987: 232, 236–7, 267]). Suspicious of American individualism, nationalists also argue that although the United States is formally a regime of individual rights, economic and political power have always been wielded by groups, especially ethnic groups. Granted, this perspective fails to appreciate the fundamentally individualistic ethos of machine politics (not to mention their ability to get Rubino to vote for Murphy!). Nevertheless, it is striking to see such regard for the machines among minority leaders and thinkers.

The post-civil-rights regime

The civil rights movement was a genuine grass-roots effort that helped to sweep away the remnants of machine politics. It also laid the foundation of a new style of politics – public interest politics – whose roots are either shallow or nonexistent. Unlike the civil rights movement, which was characterized by "thick" communal and organizational relationships, public interest politics (and the post-civil-rights regime of which it is a part) is notable for "thin" relationships. These have certain advantages. But when it comes to the empowerment of minorities, there are also undeniable disadvantages.

Theda Skocpol has suggested that the career of Marion Wright Edelman tracks this institutional transformation. Starting off in the front lines of the civil rights movement in Mississippi, Edelman was by the late 1960s a Washington lobbyist for Mississippi's Head Start program. Eventually, with the backing of major foundations, she founded the Children's Defense Fund (CDF), whose policy research and media savvy have made it one of the most prominent advocates in behalf of poor children and families (Skocpol 1999b: 488).

Many such efforts emerged after the 1960s, when it became apparent that various unorganized or hard-to-organize interests were not being heard in the usual din of pluralist politics. The prototype is Common Cause, founded by John Gardner in 1970.[15] Focused on issues like campaign finance reform, consumer protection, and the environment, such public interest organizations have reflected the "quality of life" concerns of middle- and upper-middle-class Americans. Yet as the example of CDF suggests, they have also sought to represent racial minorities. Even the venerable NAACP (National Association for the Advancement of Colored People), which began as a conventional membership-based organization, had by the 1990s made itself over in the public interest mold (Raspberry 1994: A23).

Because they represent diffuse, difficult-to-organize interests, public interest organizations tend to rely less on membership dues than on third-party funding from wealthy patrons, corporations, and especially foundations. Indeed, they make a virtue of the free-rider problem by greatly reducing the costs of membership. Some, like the Mexican American Legal Defense and Educational Fund (MALDEF), have reduced those costs to zero: they have no members at all but nevertheless advocate on behalf of all Latinos.

When public interest groups do have members, they tend to be widely dispersed, with weak ties to the organization and almost none to one another. Jeffrey Berry calls this "cheap" membership, because it typically requires no more time and energy than it takes to write an annual check (1989: 55). Robert Putnam notes that such "checkbook organizations" are low on "social connectedness," with most members "unlikely ever (knowingly) to encounter any other member" (Putnam 1995: 71). Bound together by abstract appeals and symbols rather than face-to-face interaction, these members rarely (in Albert Hirschman's terms) exercise "voice" or "loyalty." If dissatisfied, they simply "exit" (Hirschman 1970).

This affords leaders and staff of public interest organizations considerable discretion. But it also obliges them to sustain the interest of members and patrons through "outside strategies" aimed at attracting public – especially media – attention. Neil Komisar and Burton Weisbrod conclude that public interest lawyers maximize publicity, not profits. Favorable media attention stimulates funding, especially in a nonmarket environment where the effectiveness of public interest activities can be difficult to assess (1978: 80–101). Furthermore, as Jack Walker notes, public interest organizations rely on the media to communicate with members and patrons. These organizations do, of course, use newsletters and other internal media. But as Walker emphasizes, people drawn to *public* interest efforts want *public* results. He doesn't put it this way, but his analysis suggests a kind of public interest revivalism: a continual, public, and often contentious rededication to stated goals (Walker 1991: 106).

Another component of the post-civil-rights regime is a transformed Congress. Now that the old Southern-dominated committee hierarchies are gone, individual representatives have the resources and opportunities to be policy entrepreneurs. The "iron triangles" – in which power and influence were wielded out of public view by pressure groups, agency bureaucrats, and members of Congress – have been broken up and exposed to the light of day. Power now is more likely to be dispersed among formless, continually shifting "issue networks" of policy experts and public officials, whose ties to concrete interests are more attenuated than those binding lobbyists to interest groups (Heclo 1980: 87–125). Central to these developments are the media, which since the 1960s have become not only a more important source of information but also a more aggressively reformist player.

Again, the emphasis is on representing constituencies that are either hard to organize (illegal immigrants, taxpayers, airline passengers) or impossible to organize (snail darters, redwoods, the unborn). Hence the growing importance of class action lawsuits, facilitated again by third-party funding and by media-savvy entrepreneurs. Such efforts are in essence legal fictions, in which the formality of consciously experiencing and then voicing a grievance are relaxed or forgotten (Macey and Miller 1991). The result is what James Q. Wilson calls "vicarious representation" (1980: 370–2).

Underlying these changes is an intellectual revolution in the meaning and scope of rights. Whether recognized by the courts or granted as entitlements by Congress, rights have become, in Shep Melnick"s phrase, "the stock in trade of American political discourse" (1989: 188). The connection with public interest politics is clear. Those who make rights claims tend to conceive of their efforts as transcending mere self-interest and to regard opponents as churlish and mean-spirited. This fosters a politics of symbols and ideas that purports to be, and in many respects is, loosely tethered to material interests. Conventional interest politics has hardly disappeared. But at the cutting edge today, particularly with regard to social policy, is a politics of vaguely defined interests interpreted by elites whose accountability is much more to third-party funding sources than to the constituencies they seek to represent.

Accountability and reciprocity

This post-civil-rights regime is not without its virtues, chiefly the representation of previously excluded interests and groups. This new regime also makes it easier to overcome the inertia – or stability – of the Madisonian system. Swift policy change no longer requires public concern, much less outrage. Indeed, change may now be easily pursued against the grain of public opinion.[16] The Madisonian system is still there, but overlying it is a new one lacking the constraints that once stymied change. One could even say that the attenuation of the close-knit ties of the pre-civil-rights regime is a Madisonian remedy to the shortcomings of the Madisonian system.[17]

One virtue of public interest organizations specifically is their "long-term horizon" (Berry 1999b: 157). Indeed, their reliance on third-party funding insulates them from the pressing concerns of those for whom they speak, allowing a focus on longer-range goals. An example would be MALDEF's approach to immigration reform during the mid-1980s. At that time rank-and-file Mexican-Americans eagerly supported the amnesty for illegal immigrants then pending in Congress. But such legislation also called for sanctions against employers hiring illegal immigrants. MALDEF lawyers were so opposed to sanctions, which they argued would result in discrimination against all Latinos, that they successfully blocked any such legislation. In the end, MALDEF did relent and amnesty was enacted, but only because sanctions were rendered toothless. Such a strategy was possible only because MALDEF was not directly answerable to Mexican-Americans, who were so enthusiastic about amnesty that they would have tolerated sanctions (Skerry 1995).

In other words, the price of such long-term horizons can be lack of accountability. Absent any revealed preferences for public goods, representation of those preferences is inherently problematic. This is exacerbated when the organization speaks for a minority characterized by low levels of political participation. One reason why illegal immigration became such a controversial issue during the early 1990s was because MALDEF felt so little pressure to moderate its de facto open-borders stance in response to the views of ordinary Mexican-Americans, many of whom were – and are – as anxious about immigration as Americans generally. Indeed, during its protracted battle against immigration reform during the 1980s, MALDEF was perceived by allies and opponents alike as downright intransigent (Sierra 1989: 24–7).

As mentioned earlier, a guiding principle of machine politics was reciprocity (Scott 1972: 109). This changed dramatically in the 1960s, when mayors like John Lindsay realized that their constituencies included not just voters in their cities but also national elites. As Martin Shefter notes, Lindsay relied on federal grants to increase benefits to minorities and came to see that he no longer had "to induce members of the Board of Estimate and the City Council . . . to appropriate local revenues for this purpose." It also became clear that "the major benefit Lindsay received by working with black and Puerto Rican community activists was legitimation, not votes." The result was a decline in organization and participation: "Because black and Puerto Rican leaders were not rewarded in proportion to the number of followers they mobilized, they had no overriding incentive to mobilize large numbers of followers" (Shefter 1985: 94–5).

Echoing Hamilton's distinction between the "patron-client" politics of the machines and the "patron-recipient" politics of the new regime, Erie writes that "bureaucratic politics has acted as a depressant on electoral participation . . . Precinct workers are encouraged to mobilize loyal voters on election day. Human service workers, however, have little incentive to politically mobilize their clientele – as long as social programs and budgets grow" (Erie 1988: 265). So along with accountability, reciprocity has eroded.

The participation–representation trade-off

Viewed as a whole, the post-civil-rights regime presents a striking paradox. On the one hand, the workings of government are more transparent than ever. On the other, politics itself is more insular and more removed than ever from the lives of ordinary Americans. For minorities and non-minorities alike, political participation is now at historically low levels, and many Americans feel they have little control over the institutions that decide the fate of their families and communities. Hugh Heclo offers this explanation:

The reformers of the 1960s and 1970s were institution challengers, not builders. With the major exception of the civil rights movement, their work remained generally detached from the political lives and affiliations of ordinary Americans . . . Procedural rights of participation were a reality for only small circles of activists. Their efforts penetrated the arcane world of administrative law and legal maneuverings but not street-level politics. The reformers could capture media attention, but they were much less interested in the mundane work of grass-roots organizing and precinct politicking. (1989: 304)

Clearly, there is a trade-off here between participation and representation. After weighing them, Jeffrey Berry comes down squarely in favor of representation. This is noteworthy because in the past Berry has been highly critical of public interest organizations (Berry 1980: 42–7). Now, it seems, Berry is reconciled to them. "Membership in a national interest group is, in its own way, a search for community," he writes. "It is not, of course, the same kind of community that face-to-face interaction offers, but by identifying with a cause, people also identify with others who join the same group" (Berry 1999a: 369–71). As the center of political gravity has shifted to Washington, Berry now defends public interest organizations as the obvious way to address "a set of issues that could not be resolved without the involvement of Congress, the president, and the federal courts" (1999a: 369–71, 1999b: 166–7).

Yet Berry also acknowledges that this new regime is biased against certain segments of society. Noting that the power of unions has declined, he admits that public interest organizations "represent middle-class and upper-middle-class citizens" and "*empower only part of the population*" (emphasis added).[18] In fact, the problem is worse. Not only does the post-civil-rights regime favor resources lacking among the disadvantaged, such as money and media; it also devalues resources, like social capital, that they have relatively more of. Indeed, such resources are bypassed by the depersonalized, professionalized politics of campaign consultants, media buys, and computerized direct mail.[19]

Perhaps most troubling is the failure of today's regime to facilitate the political learning – or "unlearning," as Huntington describes it – that is necessary for marginal groups to attain political power. Public interest organizations are not deliberative. Whether for affluent suburbanites or impoverished minorities, they offer scant opportunities to weigh conflicting interests and perspectives. This reflects an overall trend in contemporary American politics emphasizing interest *articulation* over interest *aggregation* (Fiorina 1999: 395–427). As Michael Walzer observes more generally about "thinness" in moral argument and politics, it is "less the product of persuasion than of mutual recognition" (1994: 17).

But while the system has changed, the needs of the disadvantaged have not. Uprooted immigrants and disconnected minorities still need to learn about "loyalty" and "voice," not just "exit" (Hirschman 1970). Such lessons are not taught by public interest organizations (McFarland 1984: 96–9). Political machines were not very deliberative, to be sure. But by drawing newcomers into face-to-face interactions based on accountability and reciprocity, machines provided at least a rudimentary political education to those most in need of it. Today the need still exists, but school is no longer in session.

The new corporatism

The post-civil-rights regime has other shortcomings. Berry has observed that despite their label, "public interest" organizations represent a decidedly narrow set of interests and have actually helped to weaken the one institution that has a much stronger claim to representing broader societal interests – political parties.[20] A consequent irony, which redounds to the specific disadvantage of minorities, is that organizations like MALDEF work outside the party system and end up looking a lot like the "buffer institutions" criticized by Katznelson (1976b: 119, 175–88, 193).

Another problem with the current regime is its formalism, which relates back to the participation–representation trade-off. In our eagerness to ensure that diverse groups are represented, we Americans have grown accustomed to paying little or no attention to the substantive nature of that representation. More specifically, we seldom look at its organizational basis.

In fact, today's regime contains a strong element of corporatism. Michael Piore argues that in recent decades the United States has fashioned a "new corporatism" based on ascriptive traits such as gender, race, and ethnicity. Indeed, he writes that "blacks are the first of the new noneconomic corporate groups in American society" (Piore 1995: 25).

Like peak labor and business organizations in more traditionally corporatist regimes, the organizations that represent blacks, women, Latinos, Asians, and other such groups enjoy something like a representational monopoly – in return for which the state seeks social peace. The obvious problem, of course, is that corporatism fails to acknowledge that individuals have multiple, even competing interests. Indeed, corporatist regimes are predicated on assigning individuals interests that *by definition* do not overlap with others.

As a result, corporatist arrangements tend to be particularly thin and rigid. This certainly applies to the racial and ethnic groups targeted by American policymakers. As the demographer William Petersen notes, these are often "categories" more than "groups." The ubiquitous term "group" implies a level of self-conscious cohesion and solidarity lacking in what are often mere statistical aggregates. For Petersen, the difference between a "category" and a "group" is analogous to Marx's differentiation of a "class in itself" from a "class for itself." Moreover, Petersen distinguishes a "group" from a "community": each has an awareness of being different from other groups, but only the latter has an organizational structure (Petersen 1987: 206–8). In this typology, only some racial and ethnic categories are groups; very few are communities.

In this light, one would not prudently characterize African-Americans as a "category." But the term does seem to fit looser designations such as "Hispanic" or "Asian or Pacific Islander." When we look at the organizational life underlying these various "groups," they are revealingly "thin." Of course, as Arlene Saxonhouse reminds us, the conventional groupings of political life are inescapably arbitrary (1992). But there are degrees of fit, and in the context of American individualism and voluntarism, the racial and ethnic categories we rely on seem especially concocted and ill-fitting.

Still more troubling is the point raised by Ralf Dahrendorf:

The risk of the corporatist perversion of the democratic class struggle is that it creates rigidity in the place of movement. Corporatism enters into an easy union with bureaucracy, and both tend to rob the constitution of liberty of its essence, the ability to bring about change without revolution . . . fundamentally corporatism takes life out of the democratic process. (1988: 110–11)

One way of overcoming such rigidity is, of course, corruption. As Roger Waldinger highlights elsewhere in this volume, formal institutions typically rely on informal relationships to achieve their goals.[21] The machines illustrated this, and so do today's post-civil-rights institutions. For example, the "old girl network" of feminist activists and foundation executives has come to rely on longstanding, face-to-face relationships not unlike the "old boys network" that the women's movement once denounced (Cigler and Nownes 1995: 92).

Similarly, Bridges highlights how in reform cities the "nonpartisan slating groups" intended to replace political parties as a way of endorsing candidates functioned like parties – except that as private organizations their deliberations were shielded from public scrutiny (1997: 121). Thus do corporatist arrangements ossify over time, efforts at transparency lead to opaqueness, and thin politics become thick.

Conclusion: conflict and impatience

Finally, the thin politics of the post-civil-rights regime is highly volatile. Its capacity for change carries with it a certain faddishness, especially among elites.[22] And as a politics of symbols and ideas, it encourages conflict (albeit of a unique and curious sort) while discouraging bargaining and compromise. As one journalist has quipped, "Symbols cannot be split in two" (Schnur 1999: B9).

Critical are the new regime's structural underpinnings. As discussed earlier, public interest organizations rely heavily on the media to communicate with tenuously connected members. So it's hardly surprising that these organizations would share the media's taste for the dramatic and outrageous, using 'the-sky-is-falling' rhetoric to gain the attention of members and third-party benefactors (Easterbrook 1989: 304–5). As Walzer suggests, thin politics unites people by focusing not on common commitments but on common enemies (1994: 17–18). Donald Brand underscores the point: "It is highly likely . . . that public-interest groups will always be more combative than their interest-based counterparts because conflict generates publicity and allows public-interest groups to mobilize their constituents."[23]

This dynamic is illustrated by the contrasting styles of two organizations – MALDEF and the Alinsky-inspired Industrial Areas Foundation (IAF) – during the campaign to reform school finance in Texas during the 1980s. Ever since MALDEF's defeat in the 1973 *Rodriguez* decision, increased state aid to poorly funded local school districts had been a popular issue among Mexican-Americans (San Antonio Independent School District v. Rodriguez). Yet when the IAF got recalcitrant Texas legislators to agree to a compromise package (which was eventually enacted), MALDEF balked out of concern to avoid undermining its litigation strategy charging the legislature with racial discrimination.

The difference could not be more stark. Committed to building a network of church-based community organizations, the IAF was able to get the attention of state elected officials by busing into Austin thousands of Mexican-American (and some African-American) parents from across the state. Justifiably known for their confrontational style, the Alinsky organizers had aroused their members to action – and by the same token were reluctant to disappoint them. From their perspective, a reasonable compromise with the state legislature was clearly desirable as a way to reward members and build the organization. By contrast, MALDEF had no members to mobilize or reward – which allowed it to remain focused on the long-term litigation strategy that funders like the Ford Foundation want public interest law firms to pursue. In other words, MALDEF had every reason to prolong and nurture the conflict.

But such conflict, so characteristic of today's post-civil-rights regime, is curious. It is not the "unrealistic" conflict that Lewis Coser identified (1956: 48–55). Nor is it the irrational, "expressive" conflict that Wilson has analyzed (1995). Rather it is a highly rationalized mode of conflict, perpetuated chiefly to maintain the peculiar institutions of this regime. Such conflict is rarely resolved – in part because the issues it places on the agenda are hard to resolve, and in part because the players have few incentives to resolve them. Writes Heclo: "It appears that a great deal of postmodern policy-making is not really concerned with 'policy-making' in the sense of finding a settled course of public action that people can live with. It is aimed at crusading for a cause by confronting power with power" (1996: 34–63).

Perhaps this is why so many Americans turn away from politics as pointless bickering – not because they reject politics or conflict per se, but because they intuitively grasp that today's ritualized, self-reinforcing conflict is dysfunctional. By contrast, Machiavelli of course saw political conflict as benefiting republics by arousing citizens to heroism and love of glory (Crick 1970). In our own era, Skocpol inveighs against the "neo-Durkheimian stress on social trust as the essence of democracy" and notes that "in a very real sense, first liberal-parliamentary regimes and then democracies were a product of organized conflict and *distrust*" (Skocpol and Fiorina 1999: 14).

Similarly, Dahrendorf sees conflict as promoting social progress, but stipulates: "To be fruitful conflict has to be domesticated by institutions" (1988: 111). And this was precisely what political machines did – perhaps to a fault (Banfield and Wilson 1966: 25–7). But today we see the opposite: political institutions that fuel conflict for their own organizational ends.

Yet this organization-maintaining conflict is also curiously selective – particularly with regard to racial minorities. On the one hand, conflict between the white majority and racial minorities is presumed to exist everywhere as a deep-seated, endemic problem. On the other hand, conflict between various minority groups is presumed not to exist at all. Indeed, a basic premise of the post-civil-rights regime is that all protected minority groups share the same fundamental experience of debilitating racial discrimination, and that their basic interests are therefore congruent. As John David Skrentny characterizes this perspective, blacks, Latinos, Asians, and other protected minorities are "the same, but different" (2002). Thus, for all its fueling of conflict, the post-civil-rights regime does the opposite when it comes to relations among racial minorities.

There is a striking similarity between this presumed homogeneity of racial minority interests and the eighteenth-century republican view of "the people" as a coherent entity whose interests were opposed to those of the Crown. It was this theory, embraced by statesmen like Burke, which undergirded the notion of "virtual representation" of the colonies in Parliament (Wood 1969: 174–9). Like its eighteenth-century predecessor, today's presumption is a kind of corporatist fiction – one of those areas of political life where consensus is assumed to have supplanted conflict (Dahrendorf 1988: 111). I say "presumed" because there are, of course, many conflicts among minority groups – between blacks and Latinos during the 1992 Los Angeles riots, between Korean greengrocers and African-Americans in New York City,[24] and between MALDEF and the old-line black-oriented Leadership Conference on Civil Rights over employer sanctions.[25] Now and then one of these conflicts breaks through the surface, but because the regime has no way of acknowledging or dealing with it, it quickly sinks back out of sight.

This denial of conflict – or, for that matter, difference – among minority groups profoundly impacts the way we assess minority social mobility. This is particularly true with regard to one of the most fundamental but overlooked variables in political life: time. Bernard Crick reminds us that time is how politics is able to reconcile the inevitable tensions between ideals and realities.[26] Yet time is what our post-civil-rights regime affords us precious little of. Certainly when it comes to minority mobility, time has been foreshortened.

How are we to interpret the social and economic progress of Mexicans who recently immigrated to the United States, say within the last twenty years? By the same standard applied to African-Americans who have been here for twenty generations? Framed thus, this standard seems inappropriate. Yet it is the one we use. Relying on the policy paradigms developed in response to the black civil rights movement, we interpret statistical disparities in income, education, residential settlement, and other outcomes between Latino immigrants and their children, on the one hand, and non-Latino natives, on the other, the same way we interpret disparities between blacks and nonblacks – through the lens of racial discrimination. In essence, we have institutionalized impatience.

Now, impatience is understandable, even laudable, toward the continuing inequalities experienced by the descendants of African slaves. But when transposed to immigrants, this same impatience overlooks what a long and arduous process it is for newcomers to become full participants in American life. We forget our own history – not just that of Mexicans in the Southwest, but of European immigrants in the last century. Indeed, we seem unable to wait for today's recent arrivals to settle in and adapt to their new home before declaring them to be victims of a society intent upon excluding them.

In a political culture characterized by self-reinforcing conflict and institutionalized impatience, the crucial question is whether the progress of immigrants will be fast enough to satisfy either them or the rest of us. The answer will not come from social science, I hasten to add, but from politics. Which means that it will be critically shaped by the post-civil-rights regime, whose institutions may be less tolerant of social disadvantage than political machines but also less capable of bringing newcomers into the mainstream. But whatever they accomplish, today's political institutions will not do it individually and discretely, as the machines did, but collectively and stridently.

NOTES

1. My point here parallels Martin Shefter's critique of "the neoclassical theory of patronage." See Shefter 1994: 22–25.
2. In this essay I use the term "political machine" broadly to encompass the important distinction between a stable, citywide organization (a political machine) and a patronage-driven style of politics that does not necessarily result in such an organization (machine politics). See Wolfinger 1972: 365–98.

3. On the aversion of machine politicians to debate issues and principles, see Banfield and Wilson 1966: 116 and Scott 1972: 108.

4. Katznelson 1976a: 226. See also Katznelson 1987a: 129–30 and Erie 1988.

5. Lowi 1967: 86. James C. Scott pushes this insight further and argues that the rationalized, bureaucratic structures of modern societies depend for their day-to-day functioning on the flexibility of informal relations such as characterized machines (see Scott 1998: 352).

6. So did astute Progressives like Jane Addams. See J. B. Elshtain 2002: 77, 104, 157.

7. Katznelson 1981: 70. Here Katznelson's analysis of the machine echoes that of Polish mutual-aid societies in Thomas and Znaniecki 1958: 1590.

8. Huntington 1968: 83. On the transformative role of patronage parties, see Schmidt 1977: 326–7.

9. Katznelson 1981: 108–34; see also Jones-Correa 1998: 69–90.

10. Examples of these structural constraints can be found in Erie 1988: 163–5, Grimshaw 1992, Scott 1972: 108. Shefter 1985: 33, 34, 71.

11. On how this bargaining ethos persists today in New York City politics, to the advantage of immigrants, see Kasinitz 2000.

12. Lemann 1991: 91. My thanks to Steven Teles for bringing this episode to my attention.

13. By contrast, a few years earlier Wilson had noted that blacks in Chicago had "not priced themselves out of the market" established under machine incentives (see Wilson 1965: 54). For parallel developments in New York City, see Shefter 1985: 71. On the fundamental tension between the civil rights movement and Daley, see Grimshaw 1992: 125.

14. Ture and Hamilton 1992: 44–55. The irony here of course is that Ture and Hamilton got it wrong; at least according to my analysis here, machines did not work so exclusively on ethnic, solidaristic incentives.

15. The classic work on Common Cause is McFarland 1984. See also McFarland 1976.

16. See, for example, Schuck 1995: 47–87.

17. See McWilliams 1995.

18. Berry, 1999a: 391. Theda Skocpol argues that the new regime is "open but oligarchical": Skocpol 1999a.

19. On this point, Marshall Ganz's work is particularly instructive. Specifically, Ganz cites how the effort to mobilize California Latinos for Robert Kennedy's 1968 presidential campaign would not likely be undertaken in today's world of rationalized, consultant-dominated politics. See Ganz 1994: 100–9. On the other hand, community organizing efforts under the aegis of the Industrial Areas Foundation (IAF) *do* build on the social capital of the disadvantaged. See Skerry 1995: 144–74. See also Warren 2001.

20. See Berry 1980. It is worth noting that Berry's stance on public interest organizations became more positive over the years.

21. Waldinger in this volume; and as pointed out above, this classic sociological insight pervades Scott 1998.

22. See Wilson 1995: 249–268; also Shapiro 1995: 3–20.

23. See Brand 1989: 38, Gilmour 1995, Skerry 2000: 251.

24. For an interesting analysis of black-Korean conflicts, see Kim 2000.

25. See Kirschten 1991.
26. Crick 1982: 156. A similar point is made in Nisbet 1975: 176.

REFERENCES

Banfield, E. C. and J. Q. Wilson, 1966, *City Politics*, New York: Vintage Books.
Berry, J. M., 1980, "Public Interest Vs. Party System," *Society* 17 (May/June): 42–8.
  1989, *The Interest Group Society*, 2nd edn. Glen View, IL: Scott, Foresman/ Little, Brown.
  1999a, "The Rise of Citizen Groups," in Theda Skocpol and Morris P. Fiorina (eds.), *Civic Engagement in American Democracy*, Washington DC: Brookings Institution Press.
  1999b, *The New Liberalism: The Rising Power of Citizen Groups*, Washington DC: Brookings Institution Press.
Brand, D. R., 1989, "Reformers of the 1960s and 1970s: Modern Anti-Federalists?" in R. A. Harris and S. M. Milkis (eds.), *Remaking American Politics*, Boulder, CO: Westview Press, pp. 27–51.
Bridges, A., 1997, *Morning Glories: Municipal Reform in the Southwest*, Princeton University Press.
Cigler, A. J. and A. J. Nownes, 1995, "Public Interest Entrepreneurs and Group Patrons," in A. J. Cigler and B. A. Loomis (eds.), *Interest Group Politics*, 4th edn. Washington DC: Congressional Quarterly.
Coser, L. A., 1956, *The Functions of Social Conflict*, Glencoe, IL: Free Press.
Crick, B. (ed.), 1970, *Machiavelli: The Discourses*, New York: Penguin Books.
  1982, *In Defence of Politics*, 2nd edn. New York: Penguin Books.
Cruse, H., 1967, *The Crisis of the Negro Intellectual*, New York: William Morrow and Company.
  1987, *Plural But Equal: A Critical Study of Blacks and Minorities and America's Plural Society*, New York: William Morrow and Company.
Dahrendorf, R., 1988, *The Modern Social Conflict: An Essay on the Politics of Liberty*, New York: Weidenfeld and Nicolson.
Easterbrook, G., 1989, "Why the Sky Is Always Falling," *The New Republic*, 201, 8 (August 21): 21–4.
Elshtain, J. B., 2002, *Jane Addams and the Dream of American Democracy*, New York: Basic Books.
Erie, S. E., 1988, *Rainbow's End: Irish Americans and the Dilemmas of Urban Machine Politics 1840–1985*, Berkeley and Los Angeles: University of California Press.
Fiorina, M. P., 1999, "Extreme Voices: A Dark Side of Civic Engagement," in Skocpol and Fiorina (eds.), pp. 395–427.
Ganz, M., 1994, "Voters in the Crosshairs," *The American Prospect* 16: 100–9.
Gilmour, J. B., 1995, *Strategic Disagreement: A Stalemate in American Politics*, University of Pittsburgh Press.
Glazer, N. and D. P. Moynihan, 1970, *Beyond the Melting Pot: The Negroes, Puerto Ricans, Jews, Italians, and Irish of New York City*, 2nd edn. Cambridge: The MIT Press.

Grimshaw, W. C., 1992, *Bitter Fruit: Black Politics and the Chicago Machine 1931–1991*, University of Chicago Press.

Hamilton, C. V., 1974, "Blacks and the Crisis of Political Participation," *The Public Interest* 34: 191.

1979, "The Patron-Recipient Relationship and Minority Politics in New York City," *Political Science Quarterly* 94: 211–27.

Heclo, H., 1980, "Issue Networks and the Executive Establishment," in Anthony King (ed.), *The New American Political System*, Washington DC: American Enterprise Institute for Public Policy Research, pp. 87–124.

1989, "The Emerging Regime," in R. A. Harris and S. M. Milkis (eds.), *Remaking American Politics*, Boulder, Co: Westview Press, pp. 289–320.

1996, "The Sixties False Dawn: Awakenings, Movements and Postmodern Policy Making," *Journal of Public History* 8: 34–63.

Hirschman, A. O., 1970, *Exit, Voice, and Loyalty: Responses to Decline in Firms, Organizations, and States*, Cambridge, MA: Harvard University Press.

Huntington, S. P., 1968, *Political Order in Changing Societies*, New Haven: Yale University Press.

Janowitz, M., 1983, *The Reconstruction of Patriotism: Education for Civic Consciousness*, University of Chicago Press.

Jones-Correa, M., 1998, *Between Two Nations: The Political Predicament of Latinos in New York City*, Ithaca: Cornell University Press.

Kasinitz, P., 2000, "Beyond the Melting Pot: The Contemporary Relevance of a Classic?" *International Migration Review* 34: 248–55.

Katznelson, I., 1976a, "The Crisis of the Capitalist City: Urban Politics and Social Control," *Theoretical Perspectives on Urban Politics*, Englewood Cliffs: Prentice Hall, pp. 214–29.

1976b, *Black Men, White Cities: Race, Politics and Migration in the United States, 1900–30, and Britain, 1948–68*, Chicago and London: University of Chicago Press.

1981, *City Trenches: Urban Politics and the Patterning of Class in the United States*, Chicago and London: University of Chicago Press.

Kerner Comission, 1968, *Report of the National Advisory Commission on Civil Disorders*, New York: Bantam Books.

Kim, C. J., 2000, *Bitter Fruit: The Politics of Black-Korean Conflict in New York City*, New Haven: Yale University Press.

Kirschten, Dick, 1991, "Lobbying-Not Black-and-White," *National Journal* (March 2) 9: 496–500.

Komesar, N. K. and B. A. Weisbrod, 1978, "The Public Interest Law Firm: A Behavioral Analysis," in Burton A. Weisbrod, Joel F. Handler, and Neil K. Komesar (eds.), *Public Interest Law: An Economic and Institutional Analysis*, Berkeley, CA: University of California Press, pp. 80–101.

Lemann, N., 1991, *The Promised Land: The Great Black Migration and How It Changed America*, New York: A. A. Knopf.

Lowi, T., 1967, "Machine Politics – Old and New," *The Public Interest* 9.

Macey, J. R. and G. P. Miller, 1991, "The Plaintiffs' Attorney's Role in Class Action and Derivative Litigation: Economic Analysis and Recommendations for Reform," *University of Chicago Law Review* 58: 1–118.

Massey, D. S., Rafael Alarcon, Joreg Durand, and Humberto Gonzalez, 1987, *Return to Aztlan: The Social Process of International Migration from Western Mexico*, Berkeley, CA: University of California Press.

McFarland, A. S., 1976, *Public Interest Lobbies: Decision Making on Energy*, Washington, DC: American Enterprise Institute.

   1984, *Common Cause: Lobbying in the Public Interest*, Chatham: Chatham House.

McWilliams, W. C., 1995, "Two-Tier Politics and the Problem of Public Policy," in M. K. Landy and M. A. Levin (eds.), *The New Politics of Public Policy*, Baltimore: Johns Hopkins University Press, pp. 268–76.

Melnick, R. S., 1989, "The Courts, Congress, and Programmatic Rights," in R. Harris and S. M. Milkis (eds.), *Remaking American Politics*, Boulder, CO: Westview Press.

Nisbet, R., 1975, "Public Opinion versus Popular Opinion," *The Public Interest* 41: 166–92.

Petersen, W., 1987, "Politics and the Measurement of Ethnicity," in W. Alonso and P. Starr (eds.), *The Politics of Numbers*, New York: Russell Sage Foundation, pp. 206–8.

Piore, M. J., 1979, *Birds of Passage: Migrant Labor and Industrial Societies*, New York: Cambridge University Press.

   1995, *Beyond Individualism: How Social Demands of the New Identity Groups Challenge American Political and Economic Life*, Cambridge, MA: Harvard University Press.

Putnam, R. D., 1995, "Bowling Alone: America's Declining Social Capital," *Journal of Democracy* 6: 65–78.

Raspberry, W., 1994, "What Ails the NAACP?" *Washington Post* (November 7): A23.

San Antonio Independent School District v. Rodriguez (411 U.S. 1 1973).

Saxonhouse, A. W., 1992, *Fear of Diversity: The Birth of Political Science in Ancient Greek Thought*, University of Chicago Press.

Schmidt, S. W., 1977, "The Transformation of Clientelism in Rural Colombia," in Stephen W. Schmidt, Laura Guasti, Carl H. Laude, and James C. Scott (eds.), *Friends, Followers, and Factions*, Los Angeles: University of California Press.

Schnur, D., 1999, "Everybody's Mad at Davis on Prop. 187," *Los Angeles Times* (April 29): B9.

Schuck, P. H., 1995, "The Politics of Rapid Legal Change: Immigration Policy in the 1900s," in M. K. Landy and M. A. Levin (eds.), *The New Politics of Public Policy*, Baltimore: Johns Hopkins University Press, pp. 47–87.

Scott, J. C., 1972, *Comparative Political Corruption*, Englewood Cliffs, NJ: Prentice-Hall.

   1998, *Seeing Like a State: How Certain Schemes to Improve the Human Condition Have Failed*, New Haven: Yale University Press.

Shapiro, M., 1995, "Of Interests and Values: The New Politics and the New Political Science," in M. K. Landy and M. A. Levin (eds.), *The New Politics of Public Policy*, Baltimore: Johns Hopkins University Press, pp. 3–20.

Shefter, B. M., 1985, *Political Crisis/Fiscal Crisis: The Collapse and Revival of New York City*, New York: Basic Books.

1994, *Political Parties and the State: The American Historical Experience*, Princeton University Press.

Sierra, C. M., 1989, "Mexican Americans and Immigration Reform: Consensus and Fragmentation," Paper presented to the annual meeting of the Western Political Science Association, Salt Lake City, Utah.

Skerry, P., 1995, *Mexican Americans: The Ambivalent Minority*, Cambridge, MA: Harvard University Press.

2000, *Counting on the Census?: Race, Group Identity, and the Evasion of Politics*, Washington, DC: Brookings Institution Press.

Skocpol, T., 1999a, "Associations Without Members," *The American Prospect* 10: 66–73.

1999b, "Advocates without Members: The Recent Transformation of American Civic Life," in T. Skocpol and M. P. Fiorina (eds.), *Civic Engagement in American Democracy*, Washington DC: Brookings Institution Press, pp. 461–510.

Skocpol, T. and M. P. Fiorina (eds.), 1999, *Civic Engagement in American Democracy*, New York: Russell Sage Foundation.

Skrentny, J. D., 2002, *The Minority Rights Revolution*, Cambridge, MA: Harvard University Press.

Thomas, W. and F. Znaniecki, 1958, *The Polish Peasant in Europe and America*, New York: Dover Publishers.

Ture, K. and C. V. Hamilton, 1992, *Black Power: The Politics of Liberation*, New York: Vintage Books.

Walker, J. L., 1991, *Mobilizing Interest Groups in America: Patrons, Professions, and Social Movements*, Ann Arbor: University of Michigan Press.

Walzer, M., 1994, *Thick and Thin: Moral Argument at Home and Abroad*, University of Notre Dame Press.

Warren, M. R., 2001, *Dry Bones Rattling: Community Building to Revitalize American Democracy*, Princeton University Press.

Wilson, J. Q., 1965, *Negro Politics*, New York: Free Press.

1980, "The Politics of Regulation," in James Q. Wilson (ed.), *The Politics of Regulation*, New York: Basic Books.

1995, "New Politics, New Elites, Old Publics," in M. K. Landy and M. A. Levin (eds.), *The New Politics of Public Policy*, Baltimore: Johns Hopkins University Press, pp. 249–68.

1995, *Political Organizations*, Princeton University Press.

Wolfinger, R. E., 1972, "Why Political Machines Have Not Withered Away and Other Revisionist Thoughts," *Journal of Politics* 34: 365–98.

Wood, G. S., 1969, *The Creation of American Republic*, University of North Carolina Press.

18 Race, state, and policy: the development of employment discrimination policy in the USA and Britain

Robert C. Lieberman

Long a central feature of American politics, racial diversity increasingly emerged as a critical dividing line in British politics as well in the last half of the twentieth century. Despite its imagery of homogeneity, Britain's national identity and political development have long been infused by racial and ethnic constructs (Curtin 1964, Colley 1992, Hickman 1998). In the wake of the British Empire's dissolution, immigration from former colonies in Asia, Africa, and the Caribbean has heightened the prominence of racial diversity in Britain and spawned a familiar litany of problems: racism, discrimination, political powerlessness, and violence. In the United States, these are the common disorders of a society that has long been divided by race, in particular by the color line between African-Americans and all others (Smith 1997, Jacobson 1998, Lieberman 1998, Marx 1998). In Britain, however, postwar immigration produced new patterns of race politics that redrew the racial and ethnic lines that had come to prevail in British society (Paul 1997, Hansen 2000, Hickman, this volume).

Despite differences in the way national "color lines" are drawn, racial diversity poses similar policy problems in the two countries, encompassing particularly issues of state protection against discrimination in a variety of domains. Moreover, the United States and Britain share a common ideological and cultural approach toward defining race as a political category and framing issues of race policy. For both countries, the problem of race policy has come to be defined in race-conscious and multicultural terms: how to allow different groups to coexist and flourish, while protecting individual rights and equality of opportunity (Favell 1998, Bleich 2003). Moreover, British intellectuals and policymakers have quite explicitly seen their own evolving problems of racial conflict as similar to American ones and sought to emulate American successes and avoid American mistakes in policymaking (Rose 1969, Bleich 2003).

Despite their generally compatible approaches to race as a political category, however, the United States and Britain have adopted quite different approaches to racial policy. In particular, they have responded differently to one of the most important barriers to the social mobility of minorities and hence a serious policy challenge for any multiracial society: job discrimination. American and British employment discrimination policy differ both in the explicit policies they enacted – the kind of discrimination that is proscribed, the structure of the institutions established to fight discrimination, and the powers available to those institutions – and in the ways in which those policies have been implemented. Briefly, British law as enacted by Parliament in the Race Relations Act of 1976 takes a much broader view of discrimination and gives greater potential power to the state than American law as enacted by Congress in the Civil Rights Act of 1964. Ironically, however, American anti-discrimination practice has produced group-based, compensatory policies, enforced through a variety of public and private mechanisms. Despite apparently weaker legislation, the United States has produced a welter of policies and practices known collectively as affirmative action, while Britain, whose law explicitly authorizes "positive action," has shied away from such practices. In this essay I offer an explanation for these differences in the evolution of employment discrimination policy in the United States and Britain that focuses on political institutions and the historical evolution of race politics in the two countries. I argue that the critical factor that accounts for these divergent outcomes is the nature of political institutions in the two countries, and in particular the historical trajectories that situated racial minorities differently in two different political systems (Orloff and Skocpol 1984).

History and institutions in the development of race politics

The histories of nonwhites in the United States and Great Britain differ dramatically. The United States has a long history of slavery that predates even the formation of an autonomous American politics, with the result that American political institutions and processes have, from the beginning, been built on a foundation of racial hierarchy (Marx 1998, Lieberman 1999). In Britain, by contrast, the racialization of politics is in general a more recent phenomenon, bound up with imperial politics and postcolonial migration, particularly from the so-called New Commonwealth – although the formation of Britain's political institutions and national identity were premised on the deeply ambiguous and often racialized position of the Irish in Great Britain (Hickman 1998, this volume). These historical differences might seem to preclude a comparison between these two countries as a route toward understanding the political dynamics of race policy, since these divergent histories have produced different patterns of racial politics.

But these historical differences also present an opportunity to isolate factors that can account for national differences in race policy. One important consequence of these contrasting historical trajectories is that the relationship between minority groups and national political institutions developed along different paths in the two countries, with profoundly important consequences for the shape of race policy in the late twentieth century. Like any policy development, the formation of employment discrimination policy is a story of the formation of coalitions for particular policy choices, and particularly of the capacity of minority groups to participate in such coalitions. This approach suggests attention to such factors as group size, cohesion, and status; electoral participation; patterns of political mobilization; and strategic alliances with other groups. These factors, in turn, depend on political institutions, which allocate political power, shape the strategic context for coalition formation, and structure the translation of power resources into political deliberations and policy outcomes (Thelen and Steinmo 1992). For racial minorities, distinctive national histories of racial formation have been decisive both in defining group identities and in shaping the links between racially defined groups and national political institutions (Omi and Winant 1994, Lieberman 1995). It is precisely the divergent histories of minorities in the United States and Britain that produced different configurations of political conditions in which similar ideas about race and discrimination were translated into different policies, and it is these historically constructed political configurations that constitute the central axis of comparison (Katznelson 1997).

The distinctive position of African-Americans in the American political system resulted from the co-evolution of racial politics and American political institutions (Lieberman 1998: 230–4). American political institutions were themselves structured to accommodate slavery and contain the political conflict surrounding it. Although the Civil War emancipated the slaves and Reconstruction promised citizenship to African-Americans, the failure of Reconstruction effectively ended national protection of citizenship rights and relegated African-Americans to an evolving local structure of segregation and white supremacy in the South (where nearly all African-Americans lived until the twentieth century) (Woodward 1974, James 1988). In the twentieth century, the persistence of Jim Crow combined with the American pattern of federated non-programmatic political parties, Democratic party dominance in the South, and the decentralized, seniority-bound structure of Congress to protect the local dominance of Southern whites and prevent

African-Americans from forging political links with national forces (Key 1949, Bensel 1984, Katznelson, Geiger, and Kryder 1993, Shefter 1994). Thus the development of American public policy reflected and reproduced racial imbalances, linking white workers firmly to a protective national state while leaving African-Americans disproportionately attached to discriminatory local power structures.

At the same time, the place of African-Americans in American politics was changing dramatically. Millions of African-Americans moved north in the twentieth century (Grossman 1989, Lemann 1991). As they did so, they acquired political rights and became an important part of the Democratic Party's electoral coalition, in which they coexisted uneasily with still-powerful Southern Democrats. African-Americans also sought influence through other means, particularly the courts. Finally, the mobilization of the civil rights movement gave African-Americans an unprecedented platform for political influence in the 1950s and 1960s. Civil rights issues increasingly drove wedges both between the parties and between wings of the Democratic Party. Racial politics was an essential element in party strategies in the mid-twentieth century, and thus was a critical component of the American political order. And while the links between African-Americans and the American state were changing, they remained rooted in historical patterns of decentralization and local attachment.

In Britain, by contrast, the political construction of race began as a process of distinguishing between "white" Britons at home and colonial subjects abroad. Just as British liberal imperialism encompassed beliefs about the "white man's burden" and the "backwardness" of colonial societies, the politics of British social reform at the turn of the twentieth century revolved partly around the need to preserve an "imperial race" at home (Semmel 1960, Mehta 1999). Thus unlike the creation of the American welfare state, which perpetuated institutional decentralization, the development of the British welfare state was a relatively centralizing affair (at least as regards income-support policies) creating links between citizens and the state that did not depend on racial differentiation. Colonial subjects were connected with the British state through a national government ministry, the Colonial Office, which also claimed jurisdiction over the affairs of colonial subjects in Britain proper (Tabili 1994, Hansen 2000).

When nonwhite commonwealth citizens, made British citizens by the Nationality Act of 1948, began to migrate to Britain in large numbers after World War II, they thus entered a political universe in which questions of race had largely been erased both from official political discourse and from the institutional fabric of the state (in part due to willful obfuscation of the status of the Irish in Britain) (Hickman 1998). British race politics through the 1950s thus embodied what Ira Katznelson (1976) has called a "pre-political consensus," in which the two major parties did not differ on racial issues, not so much because they agreed on principles or policies but because there were no surface racial issues to speak of. That began to change in the 1950s and 1960s, as continuing immigration and growing racial conflict provoked a series of political and policy responses from national institutions, centering on immigration restriction and protective legislation for racial minorities (Foot 1965, Paul 1997, Hansen 2000). Although the leaders of the Conservative and Labour Parties strove to uphold this emerging political consensus, race increasingly divided the parties in the 1960s and 1970s, as nonwhite voters came to favor Labour strongly and the parties diverged in their approaches to race policy (Katznelson 1976, Crewe 1983, Messina 1989, Saggar and Heath 1999). Finally, the political mobilization of ethnic and racial minorities in Britain, while more extensive than is commonly recognized, has not produced a concerted national social movement to match the American civil rights movement of the 1960s (Modood, this volume).

One important institutional similarity between the American and British experiences is the localization of racial politics. In Britain before the 1960s, it fell to local governments to address problems of racial conflict and integration, an arrangement that was institutionalized by the community relations policies of the 1960s and 1970s (Katznelson 1976, Rex and Tomlinson 1979, Young 1990). Thus as in the United States, the chief organizational and political linkages between British minorities and the state arose at the local level, to the detriment of minorities (Katznelson 1976).

But local political attachments do not have the same meaning and impact in British politics, whose basic institutions are more centralized and less permeable to influence from local sources. As a result, despite its prominence as an issue, race did not dominate British political institutions in the 1960s and 1970s as it did in the United States. Although there are certainly parliamentary constituencies in which minorities comprise a dominant or pivotal voting bloc, there is no British analogue to the electoral college, which effectively makes some constituencies (that is, states) more important than others in the national partisan balance. The party discipline of the British parliamentary system makes intraparty splits, although they no doubt occur, less prominent as strategic openings for policymaking. Thus, despite strong Labour advantages in minority voting patterns, the Labour Party has made relatively little progress in incorporating British minorities, whether by offering policy concessions, forging links with leaders of immigrant communities, or working to mobilize minority voters. For example, it resisted for a long time calls for the formation of "black sections" within the party organization to represent and mobilize minority voters, and it has been slow to recruit minority members and elect and appoint blacks and ethnic minorities to national or local offices (Crewe 1983, Messina 1989: 160–77, Skellington 1996: 235–41, Teles 1998: 1022–3). To be sure, this pattern mirrors the limitations of the representation of African-Americans by the Democratic Party and reflects the influence of an electoral system that rewards moderation while punishing militancy (Frymer 1999). Moreover, beginning with the race-baiting Smethwick parliamentary campaign in 1964 and continuing with Enoch Powell's truculent "rivers of blood" speech in 1968 and with Margaret Thatcher's later campaigns, the Conservative Party has traded on racial and ethnic resentment to gain votes among whites. These partisan transformations clearly played a role in disrupting the uneasy policy consensus of the 1950s, but the tight structure of British parliamentary government dampened the impact of these changes on the process of coalition-building for policymaking.

Above all, the presence of racial and ethnic division in British politics has done little to reshape the pre-existing institutional patterns of British politics. While racial issues have moved on and off the British national agenda, race has not played the same role in shaping British politics as in the United States. Thus the historical sequence of race and political development in Britain left British minorities and their allies less well poised to shape the development and implementation of equal employment opportunity law when employment discrimination arrived on the agenda.

This comparative historical exploration suggests that two institutional characteristics of American and British state structure will be especially prominent in any convincing explanation of the divergence of anti-discrimination policy. The first is the extent of the consolidation or fragmentation of government authority. Here the strong party government model of Britain contrasts with the fragmented and diffuse institutional structure of American governing institutions (Steinmo 1993). This dimension encompasses factors such as the politics of coalition-formation in Congress and Parliament; the nature of the administrative state and its potential independence from political control; and the existence of independent courts and other avenues for political influence outside regular legislative policymaking channels, all of which combine to shape policymaking constraints and opportunities. The second is the role of local governments and local patterns of political organization and attachment in shaping politics and policymaking. On this dimension, the two countries are more similar, but because of differences in the underlying structure of policymaking institutions and the role of local units in national politics, similar patterns of local race politics have had different consequences for national race policy.

Political development and employment discrimination policy: a comparative approach

These developmental patterns had important consequences for race policy in the two countries, particularly for policies aimed at guaranteeing equal employment opportunity. While it is not the only element of race relations policy, employment discrimination is certainly a critically important one. The right to work is generally considered to be a central element of modern citizenship, and access to jobs remains one of the most important sources of group inequality in modern industrial economies (Marshall 1964, Shklar 1991, de Beijl and Böhning 1995, Gordon 1995). Moreover, employment discrimination has become a central policy problem in both countries in the last generation, and the role of the state in enforcing employment rights has grown more complex and controversial. The principle of employment discrimination enforcement is disarmingly simple: no one should be denied a job or a promotion or be fired simply because of his race. But this simple proposition conceals a nest of thorny legal and political questions about the state's role in defining and enforcing racial fairness in employment; establishing legal guidelines, procedures, and sanctions; and devising coercive mechanisms to ensure compliance. There is no better example of the politically explosive nature of these questions about the form and extent of state power in employment than the current controversy over affirmative action in the United States. Although the American debate is, in one sense, an argument between color-blind and race-conscious views of employment policy, it is also a conflict over the nature of state power and the structure of political institutions (Graham 1990, Edley 1996, Skrentny 1996).

Such controversy over the state's role in non-discrimination enforcement is not unique to the United States. All the member states of the European Union, among others, have anti-discrimination policies in force, and more than one hundred countries are parties to the United Nations Convention on the Elimination of All Forms of Racial Discrimination, which was adopted by the United Nations General Assembly in 1965 (United Nations 1979, Forbes and Mead 1992, Ireland 1995). Among European countries, Britain is among the most vigorous pursuers of anti-discrimination policy, and it rivals the United States in the emphasis it places on preventing and punishing employment discrimination.

During the 1960s and 1970s, both countries passed major laws aimed at (among other things) outlawing employment discrimination. These laws – the American Civil Rights Act of 1964 and the British Race Relations Act of 1976 – had much in common. Each forbade employers to refuse to hire or promote or to fire a person on racial grounds, making such discrimination a civil offense that gives rise to legal action between private parties. Each provided the national government with new and unprecedented power to enforce this prohibition against private employers. Each created a new government agency dedicated exclusively to enforcing racial equality, whether exclusively in employment (the US Equal Employment Opportunity Commission, or EEOC) or generally (the British Commission for Racial Equality, or CRE).

But these similarities mask two important differences. First, while the Civil Rights Act added a new agency, the EEOC, to a growing alphabet soup of civil rights agencies, the Race Relations Act consolidated several institutions into a single, overarching agency, the CRE. Second, American enforcement power was, at first, exclusively individual in nature; the EEOC was empowered to resolve individual claims of employment discrimination, and not to investigate or remedy collective patterns of discrimination.[1] In Britain, by contrast, the CRE had both sorts of power from the outset, and it was weighted toward collective over individual enforcement activities. Finally, and ironically, the United States built, atop its relatively weak foundation, a vigorous (if controversial) policy of affirmative action, while British enforcement remained relatively passive despite the strong language of the law.

The politics of racial conflict, of course, differs across these two countries in ways that importantly affect the comparison. The legacies of colonialism and slavery have produced different histories of racial division in the two societies, and race policy is more closely linked with immigration and naturalization policy in Britain than in the United States. Racial minorities make up a smaller percentage of the total population in Britain than in the United States – about 8 percent in Britain (excluding the Irish) compared to approximately 13 percent African-Americans and 23 percent total nonwhites in the most recent national censuses – and the minority population in Britain is more diverse and often divided than in the United States (Owen 1996, Berthoud and Beison 1997, Teles 1998; the American data are from the 2000 Census). These factors doubtless play a role in any comprehensive explanation of differences in policy. Nevertheless, they operate through the workings of political institutions and processes that structure political decision-making. Thus a comparison of the institutional settings of policy choices in these countries will provide a platform for further investigation of how such factors influence policy and politics to produce important difference in race policies.

The development of employment discrimination policy

Political differences led the United States and Britain to diverge on two institutional dimensions of anti-discrimination policy. The first is the consolidation and coordination of anti-discrimination policy: is policy streamlined and is power vested in a single agency, or is it fragmented and dispersed among several state organs? The fragmentation of policy and power might indicate coordination problems that could lead to weak enforcement, with important racial consequences. The second institutional dimension is the individual or collective nature of the enforcement power. Is the state's enforcement role to resolve individual claims of discrimination, or is it empowered to regulate employment practices more generally through collective powers of coercion?

Together, these two dimensions of anti-discrimination institutions have shaped policy implementation and the development (or non-development) of affirmative action or other practices that entail some form of race-conscious positive action. Once they were established, these anti-discrimination policy institutions interacted with the political and institutional configurations in which they were forged to produce often unintended and unexpected results. In the United States, fragmented and decentralized politics produced a fragmented and individualistic enforcement regime. The multiple veto points, the inhibition of coalition formation combined with the radically localized nature of linkages between African-Americans and the state frustrated the more comprehensive designs of civil rights advocates. Ironically, however, the localism of African-American politics and the fragmentation and multiple access points of American political institutions paved the way for political strategies that led to the construction of a powerful anti-discrimination enforcement regime. In Britain, by contrast, the centralized structure of party and parliamentary politics produced a more coordinated and collective anti-discrimination regime. But the structure of British politics – not only party and parliamentary structure but also the lack of independent courts and the relatively top-down and inflexible structure of local-national relations – lacked institutional mechanisms that could allow locally oriented immigrant political organization and attachments to "filter up" to the national level to shape the implementation of anti-discrimination policy (Ashford 1982).

The United States

The struggle for passage of the Civil Rights Act of 1964 reflected the United States' distinctive, race-laden institutional configuration. The fundamental problem facing President Lyndon Johnson was assembling a coalition that would pass a bill in both houses of Congress, over the absolute objections of most Southern Democrats and the ambivalence of many Republicans. The problem was particularly acute in the Senate, where a two-thirds vote was required to end debate and bring the bill to a vote. At the same time, African-American political pressure strengthened the political imperative for Northern Democrats to pass serious civil rights legislation.

Title VII of the resulting act outlawed racial discrimination in employment, and created the Equal Employment Opportunity Commission to enforce the new law. Civil rights advocates envisioned this new body as a full-fledged regulatory agency that would wield comprehensive authority over job discrimination, including the power to conduct investigations and impose sanctions against employers. A subcommittee of the House Judiciary Committee approved such an agency in October 1963, but it was too much for conservatives and moderates on the committee and in the Kennedy administration. The House ultimately passed a compromise version that dropped the EEOC's cease-and-desist authority and gave it instead the authority to file lawsuits against recalcitrant employers (Graham 1990: 131–4, Loevy 1990: 52–4).

The Senate filibuster that followed forced a further compromise, particularly in respect of the language in Title VII, ensuring that only intentional, individual discrimination would be a violation of the act, and not so-called "statistical discrimination" (inferred from numerical imbalances). But equally important was a compromise over the EEOC's structure and power. First, the EEOC lost the power to file lawsuits directly. Second, it had to defer to state employment discrimination agencies (Graham 1990: 145–9). These two provisions did two things. They lowered the EEOC from its status as the lead regulatory agency in the field of job discrimination, and they limited its power to mediating in individual cases.

The EEOC was further handicapped by Johnson's failure to appoint its members until nearly a year after the act's passage. Meanwhile, the coordination of anti-discrimination enforcement was a problem for the administration.[2] A series of false starts and dead ends culminated in October 1965 with the promulgation of Executive Order 11246, which abolished several existing civil rights agencies in the executive branch.[3] But rather than consolidating anti-discrimination power in the EEOC, the order transferred jurisdiction over discrimination in federal contracts to the Department of Labor, which created the Office of Federal Contract Compliance (OFCC). Thus began the most important jurisdictional battle of the EEOC's brief career.

The OFCC quickly emerged as the EEOC's chief rival in the employment discrimination enforcement game. In its early years, the commission's enforcement efforts ran up against the limits of both its statutory power and its position in a fragmented executive civil rights establishment. Unable to marshal full regulatory power, the EEOC began inching pragmatically toward enforcement based on the notion of statistical discrimination. Meanwhile the OFCC also began working toward a pragmatic strategy to police discrimination in the construction industry, and particularly in construction unions working on federally funded projects (Skrentny 1996: 111–44, Graham 1990: 282–97). This strategy, which led ultimately to the Philadelphia Plan, was unsuccessful under the Johnson administration, coming to fruition, ironically, only after Richard Nixon's election. Despite its obscure origins and relatively subordinate place in the executive hierarchy, the OFCC had what the EEOC lacked: an effective sanction against noncompliant employers (or unions), the power to withhold federal contracts (Skrentny 1996: 134, Graham 1990: 284–7).

The EEOC coveted this power along with power to issue "cease-and-desist" orders in egregious cases. Without these powers it could only mediate individual cases and act as a sideline cheerleader (and sub rosa advisor) in discrimination suits in federal courts. Both additional powers had substantial support in the administration and in Congress. In 1966 the House passed legislation granting the EEOC cease-and-desist authority but the bill died in the Senate. Two years later, an interagency task force headed by the attorney general recommended that contract compliance functions be transferred to the EEOC, but the measure languished at the end of the Johnson administration.[4]

Despite these limitations imposed by institutional fragmentation, anti-discrimination policy flourished in the United States well beyond the apparent confines of the Civil Rights Act. For one thing, affirmative action evolved, a development made possible by the confluence of institutional conditions in the late 1960s and early 1970s. These conditions included the independence of the federal courts, the continued activities of civil rights organizations in a variety of political and legal arenas, and continuing contest over the place of African-Americans in the partisan and coalitional patterns of American politics (Frymer and Skrentny 1998).

Affirmative action – a set of practices that allow (and often require) group-conscious treatment of individuals – arose out of the pragmatic alignments of politicians and bureaucrats, to make anti-discrimination policy work within the limitations of institutional weakness and fragmentation (Skrentny 1996). The highly localized political attachments of African-Americans, long a political handicap, now proved empowering. This development occurred not primarily in official Washington but in a variety of local settings, involving courts, movement activists, unions, state and local governments, and others, taking advantage of the multiple points of access available in American governing institutions. Thus the localism of race politics was able to "filter up" through this variety of political settings to shape anti-discrimination policy and practice, not least because of the "fit" between patterns of African-American politics and American political institutions.

What made the ironic development of affirmative action possible was precisely the same set of factors that conditioned the development of American anti-discrimination law in the first place – particularly the fragmentation of American political institutions and the locally inflected links between African-Americans and the American state. Hamstrung by its limited power, inundated with an overwhelming caseload, and limited by the legal requirement of proving discriminatory intent in individual cases, the EEOC turned to a variety of tactics to pursue its aims. It was able to exert influence through informal channels precisely because of the organizational slack in the federal government, because its enforcement role was so ill defined, and because it was able to find outside partners and allies. It used its limited regulatory power to prevent newspapers from publishing job advertisements that specified the race of acceptable applicants. It held a series of high-profile hearings on employment practices in New York City in 1968 that shone an embarrassing spotlight on, among other employers, the *New York Times*.[5] It participated with the NAACP and other organizations in precedent-setting lawsuits, including *Griggs* v. *Duke Power* (1971), the key case in the consolidation of affirmative action practices (Stein 1998). Finally, the EEOC has also had an indirect but profound influence on American corporate structure, inducing companies to institutionalize equal employment opportunity practices without the actual exercise of coercive authority or legal action (Dobbin et al. 1993, Dobbin and Sutton 1998). The flip side of institutional fragmentation has been a level of improvisatory suppleness that has enabled the EEOC and the rest of the American race relations establishment to overcome institutional limitations in pursuit of policy goals. These institutional opportunities, in turn, were the result not simply of the structure of American political institutions but of the way in which African-Americans had been incorporated in those institutions through the historical processes of political development.

Great Britain

Britain's approach to the problem of race relations was similar to the liberal integrationism of the Civil Rights Act. In the early 1970s the interparty consensus on race and immigration began to break down. In the first of two general elections held in 1974, neither party won a majority in the House of Commons; in the second, Labour won a three-seat majority. Some analyses suggested that nonwhite voters had provided the margin of victory (Messina 1989: 143–9). Whether or not these voters were decisive, the Labour leadership felt compelled to advocate stronger state protection for racial minorities, at least as compensation to the party's left wing for its continued acceptance of strict immigration restrictions (Bleich 2003, Hansen 2000: 225–8).

Thus when the government proposed a new Race Relations Act in 1976, it was responding not only to increasing racial tension but also to increasing partisan pressure to act on race relations, as the Johnson administration had. The political imperative was similarly to attack discrimination in employment, education, and public accommodations, and to ensure equal treatment to all regardless of race.[6] Racial division in British society would not go away, said the Home Secretary, Roy Jenkins, in introducing the bill, and the government ought to address it forthrightly.

The British government, however, faced different institutional pressures than the Johnson administration had in 1964. Most important were the different dynamics of coalition building. Under the British parliamentary system, which nearly always produces majority governments, the process of policymaking does not depend on the piecemeal assembly of legislative coalitions, nor does it allow either concerted minorities or fragments of the majority party to block government-sponsored legislation. Moreover, because of the limited incorporation of minorities into British party politics, a function partly of the localization of British race politics, the parliamentary process was more insulated than its American analogue from electoral pressure. The government had no opponents, whether within their own party or in the opposition, who could block the legislation. Rather, it could enact the government's favored policy without complicating amendments. Thus, despite similar ideological moorings, British race relations law departs substantially from its American counterpart. Nevertheless, the parliamentary debates on the Race Relations Act of 1976 reveal disagreements over issues of institutional structure and power similar to those that shaped American anti-discrimination policy debates of the 1960s.

As in the United States, arguments over the structure and power of the anti-discrimination agency were at the center of the politics of the Race Relations Act. Rather than creating a fragmented set of enforcement institutions, the act consolidated two older agencies into a new Commission for Racial Equality, which was charged with the comprehensive enforcement of anti-discrimination law in employment and other areas.

Moreover, the CRE was to have fairly extensive powers to address collective discriminatory patterns in addition to remedying individual claims of discrimination. In both respects, the British institutional pattern departed from the American model, despite the similarity of general approach.

Jenkins emphasized both aspects of the bill, arguing particularly that the greater coordination and more extensive power represented by the new commission would allow the government "not only to combat discrimination and encourage equal opportunity but also to tackle what has come to be known as racial disadvantage." The act explicitly defined discrimination to include "not only deliberate and direct discrimination but also unjustifiable indirect discrimination. A particular practice may look fair in a formal sense," Jenkins explained, "or at least neutral in its original intent, but may be discriminatory in its operation."[7] The CRE was empowered to investigate and sanction employers who engaged in such collective discriminatory practices, as well as to help individuals bring cases in the courts. Moreover, there was little problem of overlapping jurisdiction or fragmented authority concerning race relations in the British government; the CRE was given sole authority over these matters, to some extent coexisting with but largely preempting the locally oriented community relations approach.

Both aspects of the CRE – collective power and the superseding of local authority – were controversial. Although the Conservative leadership supported the act, many Conservative members of Parliament worried that the commission's powers would "be used in a bureaucratic and harrying manner," or worse. Others worried that the Home Office, which was to oversee the CRE, was notoriously disorganized and overloaded, and suggested that a more modest individual approach might get better results. Similarly, some members opposed combining the existing Community Relations Councils and the Race Relations Board into a single body, largely on the grounds that they served two different purposes (enforcement and education, respectively) that should remain separate.[8] Proponents of the newly configured CRE argued that it was precisely this consolidated, collective power that would render the CRE effective. Alexander Lyon, the Minister of State for the Home Office and the government's leading spokesman on race relations, explicitly cited the EEOC's weakness and ineffectiveness as reasons to give the CRE both broader jurisdiction and greater power.[9]

The resulting legislation was, on paper at least, a strong antidiscrimination measure, certainly among the strongest in Europe and stronger in many ways than the Civil Rights Act in terms of the power it conferred on the state to punish racial discrimination in employment (Forbes and Mead 1992, MacEwen 1994, Boothman and MacEwen

1997). In fact, unlike the Civil Rights Act, which seemed explicitly to rule out affirmative action (at least for private employers), the Race Relations Act of 1976 seemed to invite it, by defining discrimination to include indirect discrimination, endowing the CRE with strong regulatory enforcement power, and even enabling (though not requiring) limited forms of "positive action." Although the law distinguished clearly between "positive action" – action to expand minority employment opportunities – and "positive discrimination" – compensatory preferential treatment for members of minority groups, its definition of discrimination deliberately went well beyond the Civil Rights Act's explicit disavowal of indirect, statistical discrimination. But the consequences of the Race Relations Act were quite limited in comparison with the ironic development of affirmative action in the United States. Like the EEOC, the CRE lacks strong coercive sanctions with which it could compel employers to adopt affirmative hiring programs. Unlike the EEOC, however, the CRE had little access to other coercive means, such as the courts, to foster affirmative action. Although it had legal sanction to pursue and enforce certain kinds of "positive action," the CRE took little action to do so, even in some instances opposing preferential hiring actions (Teles 1998).

A number of institutional factors constrained the CRE from pursuing even the limited forms of "positive action" that fell within its statutory purview. First, disagreements within the Home Office and the Labour Party over the role of the state in acting against racial discrimination made it difficult for the CRE to act vigorously (Katznelson 1976: 181, Lyon 1976, Observer 1976, Times 1976a, 1976b, 1976c, 1976d, Freeman 1979: 58, 126). Moreover, the government's indifference, if not outright hostility, to vigorous anti-discrimination enforcement increased further when Margaret Thatcher's Conservatives swept into office in 1979 (Messina 1989, Steinmo 1993, MacEwen 1994, Boothman and MacEwen 1997). The Labour government had intended to increase the CRE's budget by nearly 25 percent in 1979, suggesting a strengthening commitment to enforcement; Thatcher's increase was less than 5 percent, and her government actually cut the CRE's budget in real terms over the next six years (Messina 1989: 134). The Thatcher government also repeatedly ignored proposals that the CRE be given expanded powers (MacEwen 1994: 363–7, Honeyford 1998: 67–72).

Perhaps most important, the British political system provided few openings for alternative routes to positive action, and the integration of British minorities into this non-receptive polity was weak. Only marginally integrated into the party system, without institutionalized recourse to other sources of power, and without the backing of a social movement on the scale of the American civil rights movement, British minorities were unable to convert the potential embodied in the Race Relations Act into actual outcomes (Modood, this volume). In particular, the British judicial system, which is not predisposed to grant claims based on constitutional rights as are courts in the United States, is a weak vehicle for advancing anti-discrimination claims. To the extent that the courts were involved in the anti-discrimination enforcement, their effect was to impose limits on the commission's powers through judicial review of its procedures rather than to provide a point of access for aggrieved individuals or groups to seek redress for harms done them (McCrudden 1983: 68–71, Lustgarten and Edwards 1992, MacEwen 1995: 194–6). The rigidity of executive control under the British parliamentary system and the rapidity of the Conservative takeover after the creation of the CRE produced unfavorable conditions for strong state action against collective patterns of discrimination or for the pursuit of "positive action." Some years later, the Home Office considered and rejected implementing a contract compliance system for public contractors, modeled on the successful American practice, leaving it instead to local government to pursue such policies at their own option (Dubourdieu 1998: 95).

Finally, and most paradoxically, the relative centralization of British anti-discrimination policy actually hindered the consolidation of the CRE's enforcement authority. The British pattern of localized race politics, which had relegated racial issues to lower levels of government without the crushing injustice of institutionalized white supremacy as in the American South, had important advantages for the pursuit of anti-discrimination enforcement and other policies for racial incorporation, offering more proximate opportunities for active coalition-building with white elites and for partnerships across party lines in support of local developmental policy that could assist natives and immigrants alike (Peterson 1981, Ball and Solomos 1990). In addition to mandating national action, the Race Relations Act required local authorities to take steps to eliminate racial discrimination, leading to a flurry of activity by local anti-racist organizations, Community Relations Councils, party organizations (especially Labour), and other groups at the local level. These efforts have resulted in gains for minorities, especially in public-sector employment and the adoption of equal opportunity policies by some local authorities, but these have not come without conflict nor have they been uniform (Ben-Tovim and Gabriel 1986, Young 1990). But such local attachments have corresponding disadvantages for minorities, especially the susceptibility to domination and exploitation by local majorities, which can be heightened by the lack of access to and leverage over national political institutions (McConnell 1966, Katznelson 1976, Lieberman 1998). In the United States, the particular configuration of historical and political circumstances in the 1960s and 1970s – including significantly the heightened level of minority political mobilization – gave African-Americans and their allies such leverage, allowing them to exploit openings in American political institutions from their highly localized positions when more centralized avenues were closed to them. In Britain, by contrast, local attachments, while often locally empowering, proved nationally disadvantageous because the structure of British politics did not provide a foothold for locally attached minorities to enter into national processes of coalition building and policymaking.

The fundamental difference between the British and American cases, then, was not the acceptance of group-based remedies for discrimination in one country and their rejection in the other, but the political and institutional avenues available for their adoption. Despite its vaunted advantages of capacity and effectiveness, the British parliamentary system actually produced weaker enforcement of fair employment laws, even with stronger "parchment" institutions. As Kent Weaver and Bert Rockman (1993) have suggested, institutional differences, while not entirely determinative of outcomes, created both opportunities and constraints for strategic action that elites in both countries exploited to pursue anti-discrimination policy. In the British case, the relative rigidity of these institutions in the context of an increasingly multiracial society meant that British minorities had few routes to power. Not only was the policy-making system less directly porous than in the United States – less open to influence through the courts, the bureaucracy, or social movement pressure – but the policymaking and coalition-building strategies of British political actors were more effectively buffered from minority pressures and interests (Katznelson 1976). Thus the historical pattern of racial and political development proved decisive in the United Kingdom as well as in the United States: pre-existing British political institutions were relatively less malleable in the face of racial division and so offered a less robust policy response. Whether they will prove more brittle in the face of current strains remains an open question.

Conclusion: history, institutions, and race politics

This comparison of the development of equal employment opportunity policy in these two countries, and particularly the juxtaposition of the historical and political contexts in which these two national policies evolved, serves to clarify the reasons for the differences in the policy trajectories of two apparently similar nations. In this regard, it points toward an explanation of policy outcomes that emphasizes how particular configurations of factors – ideas, interests, and institutions – combine to produce

policy. But by emphasizing such configurations, it also demands specification of the causal mechanisms that connect these factors, without
giving explanatory priority to one factor over another.

In the United States, the clash among the multiple ideological traditions underpinning debates about American citizenship – Gunnar
Myrdal's (1944) liberal "American creed" and its illiberal, ascriptive challengers – were clearly fundamental to midcentury debates about civil
rights in general and equal employment opportunity policy in particular
(Smith 1997). These broad cultural and ideological traditions framed the
debate, focusing attention on certain kinds of ideas about how the state
should recognize and manage racial difference and inequality in society.
But these ideas were situated in a political and historical context in which
institutions clearly defined and delimited the role of African-Americans
in the political economy, so that the interests of African-Americans and
their allies and supporters in equal employment opportunity policies were
constituted and organized in particular ways that reflected configurations of power and the political opportunities they offered to a variety
of actors. American policy was made in institutions that incorporated
African-Americans only on particular terms, the result of a long, often
antagonistic history of engagement between blacks and the American
state. The result was a relatively circumscribed law that ironically proved a
relatively strong instrument for the vigorous pursuit of affirmative action.

Britain began with a similar ideological tradition, and British policy
leaders even self-consciously modeled their ideas about race and race
policy on the American experience, although not without dissent. British
policy debates were similarly framed, but they occurred in a different
institutional context, in which interests were constituted, organized, and
represented in different ways. British minorities did not have a long history of engagement – constructive or otherwise – in British politics, and
British political institutions thus offered them little leverage to shape policy outcomes; at the same time, opposition to anti-discrimination policy was also less deeply rooted in British politics than in the United
States and a higher degree of consensus prevailed on racial issues than
in America's deeply race-laden political landscape. The result was that
Britain adopted a law that appeared to settle on an alternative paradigm
of anti-discrimination policy but that in the end provided a weak platform for the energetic pursuit of anti-discrimination efforts, particularly
through positive or affirmative action.

For both the United States and Britain this comparison offers possibilities and perils. For the United States, these are one and the same.
Race and American politics are deeply and historically interconnected,
mutually constitutive, and, for racial minorities, double-edged. Much

of American political development consists of the reproduction of race-laden structures of power and inequality, which have imposed a heavy burden on African-Americans in politics and policy. America's fragmented and decentralized political institutions have often been the agent of these inequalities, but have also provided sites of access to the political system that have supplied leverage in surprising and often inspiring ways. In Britain, by contrast, the state offers greater potential for authoritative and decisive action to mitigate racial inequality in the labor market and elsewhere, but the limited access to power that British institutions have historically afforded to minorities restricts the ameliorative potential inherent in that power. The question facing both countries is whether they can mobilize their very different sources of political strength in the service of their common ideals.

NOTES

I am grateful to the Russell Sage Foundation, the German Marshall Fund of the United States, and the Lyndon Baines Johnson Foundation for financial support and to Lisa Kahraman and John Smelcer for research assistance. For their generous advice, I thank Sheri Berman, Frank Dobbin, Dan Kryder, Michèle Lamont, Glenn Loury, Tariq Modood, Lauren Osborne, John Skrentny, Steve Teles, and the Bath and Boston conference participants.

1. In 1972, Congress granted the EEOC limited power to file lawsuits, but not cease-and-desist power (Graham 1990: 434–45).

2. Memorandum, William L. Taylor to Lee White, June 17, 1964, Office Files of Lee C. White, Box 2, Lyndon B. Johnson Library (hereafter cited as LBJL); Memorandum, Lee C. White to Johnson, 28 September 1964, LE, White House Central File (hereafter cited as WHCF), Box 167, LBJL; Graham 1990: 177–9.

3. Memorandum, Hubert H. Humphrey to Johnson, September 24, 1965, in *Civil Rights During the Johnson Administration, 1963–69: A Collection from the Holdings of the Lyndon Baines Johnson Library, Austin, Texas*, part 1, reel 11; Executive Order 11246, *Federal Register* 30 (1965): 12319; Memorandum, Nicholas deB. Katzenbach to Humphrey, November 23, 1964, *Civil Rights During Johnson*, part 1, reel 2; Johnson to Humphrey, December 2, 1964, *Civil Rights During Johnson*, part 1, reel 2; LeRoy Collins, "Analysis of Civil Rights Functions of the Federal Government and Recommendations for their Consolidation in a Single Agency," July 1965, HU 2, Confidential File, WHCF, Box 56, LBJL; Memorandum, Joe Califano to Harry McPherson, August 20, 1965, HU, WHCF, Box 3, LBJL; Memorandum, Humphrey to Johnson, September 17, 1965, *Civil Rights During Johnson*, part 1, reel 7; Graham 1990: 161–2, 180–7; Skrentny 1996: 133–4.

4. Memorandum, Steve Pollak to James Gaither, October 30, 1968, *Civil Rights During Johnson*, part 1, reel 10; Reps. William F. Ryan, Philip Burton, John Conyers Jr., Edward R. Roybal, and Charles C. Diggs to Johnson, June 20, 1968, *Civil Rights During Johnson*, part 1, reel 7; Memorandum, Lee C. White

to Johnson, October 5, 1965. *Civil Rights During Johnson*, part 1, reel 5; William L. Taylor to Lee C. White, December 8, 1965, *Civil Rights During Johnson*, part 1, reel 11; Memorandum, W. H. Rommel to Harry McPherson, April 22, 1966, *Civil Rights During Johnson*, part 1, reel 11; Memorandum, Nicholas deB. Katzenbach to Joseph Califano, December 13, 1965, LE, WHCF, Box 65, LBJL; Ramsey Clark to Humphrey, February 17, 1967, *Civil Rights During Johnson*, part 1, reel 10; Graham 1990.

5. Graham 1990; Memorandum, Luther Holcomb to Marvin Watson, December 16, 1965, HU 2–1, WHCF, Box 57, LBJL; Memorandum, Luther Holcomb to Marvin Watson, March 25, 1966, FG, WHCF, Box 380, LBJL; Memorandum, Clifford L. Alexander, Jr., to Lloyd Hackler, December 28, 1967, FG, WHCF, Box 380, LBJL; Memorandum, Clifford L. Alexander, Jr., to Henry Fowler, April 12, 1968, HU 2–1, WHCF, Box 44, LBJL.

6. *Parliamentary Debates* (Commons), 5th ser., vol. 906, cols. 1547–8.

7. *Parliamentary Debates* (Commons), 5th ser., vol. 906, cols. 1548, 1552. See also McCrudden 1983.

8. *Parliamentary Debates* (Commons), 5th ser., vol. 906, cols. 1574, 1588–9, 1591, 1607–8.

9. *Parliamentary Debates* (Commons), 5th ser., vol. 906, 1663–4.

REFERENCES

Ashford, D. E., 1982, *British Dogmatism and French Pragmatism: Central-Local Policymaking in the Welfare State*, London: George Allen and Unwin.

Ball, W. and S. John (eds.), 1990, *Race and Local Politics*, London: Macmillan.

Bensel, R. F., 1984, *Sectionalism and American Political Development: 1880–1980*, Madison: University of Wisconsin Press.

Ben-Tovim, G., J. Gabriel, I. Law, and K. Stredder, 1986, *The Local Politics of Race*, Houndmills, Basingstoke: Macmillan.

Berthoud, R. and S. Beison, 1997, "People, Families, and Households," in T. Modood et al. (eds.), *Ethnic Minorities in Britain: Diversity and Disadvantage*, London: Policy Studies Institute, pp. 18–59.

Bleich, E., 2003, *Race Politics in Britain and France: Ideas and Policymaking since the 1960s*, Cambridge: Cambridge University Press.

Boothman, C. and M. MacEwen, 1997, "The British Commission for Racial Equality as an Enforcement Agency," in Martin MacEwen (ed.), *Anti-Discrimination Law Enforcement: A Comparative Perspective*, Aldershot: Avebury, pp. 155–73.

Colley, L., 1992, *Britons: Forging the Nation, 1707–1837*, New Haven: Yale University Press.

Crewe, I., 1983, "Representation and the Ethnic Minorities in Britain," in N. Glazer and K. Young (eds.), *Ethnic Pluralism and Public Policy: Achieving Equality in the United States and Britain*, Lexington, MA: D.C. Heath, pp. 258–81.

Curtin, P. D., 1964, *The Image of Africa: British Ideas and Action, 1780–1850*, Madison: University of Wisconsin Press.

De Beijl, R. and W. R. Böhning, 1995, "Labour Market Integration of Migrants and Legislative Measures to Combat Discrimination," Geneva: International Labour Office, Employment Department.

Dobbin, F., J. R. Sutton, J. W. Meyer, and W. R. Scott, 1993, "Equal Opportunity Law and the Construction of Internal Labor Markets," *American Journal of Sociology* 99: 396–427.

Dobbin, F. and J. R. Sutton, 1998, "The Strength of a Weak State: The Rights Revolution and the Rise of Human Resources Management Divisions," *American Journal of Sociology* 104: 441–76.

Dubourdieu, E., 1998, "The Theory and Practices of 'Positive Discrimination'," in J. Edwards and J. Revauger (eds.), *Discourse on Inequality in France and Britain*, Aldershot: Ashgate.

Edley, C., Jr., 1996, *Not All Black and White: Affirmative Action and American Values*, New York: Hill and Wang.

Favell, A., 1998, *Philosophies of Integration: Immigration and the Idea of Citizenship in France and Britain*, Houndmills, Basingstoke: Macmillan.

Foot, P., 1965, *Immigration and Race in British Politics*, Harmondsworth: Penguin.

Forbes, I. and G. Mead, 1992, *Measure for Measure: A Comparative Analysis of Measures to Combat Racial Discrimination in the Member Countries of the European Community*, Southampton: Equal Opportunities Study Group, University of Southampton.

Freeman, G. P., 1979, *Immigrant Labor and Racial Conflict in Advanced Industrial Societies: The French and British Experience, 1945–1975*, Princeton University Press.

Frymer, P., 1999, *Uneasy Alliances: Race and Party Competition in America*, Princeton University Press.

Frymer, P. and J. D. Skrentny, 1998, "Coalition-Building and the Politics of Electoral Capture During the Nixon Administration: African Americans, Labor, Latinos," *Studies in American Political Development* 12: 131–61.

Gordon, I., 1995, "The Impact of Economic Change on Minorities in Western Europe," in K. McFate, R. Lawson, and W. J. Wilson (eds.), *Poverty, Inequality, and the Future of Social Policy: Western States in the New World Order*, New York: Russell Sage Foundation, pp. 521–42.

Graham, H. D., 1990, *The Civil Rights Era: Origins and Development of National Policy, 1960–1972*, New York: Oxford University Press.

Griggs v. Duke Power Company, 401 US 424 (1971).

Grossman, J. R., 1989, *Land of Hope: Chicago, Black Southerners, and the Great Migration*, University of Chicago Press.

Hansen, R., 2000, *Citizenship and Immigration in Post-war Britain: The Institutional Origins of a Multicultural Nation*, Oxford University Press.

Hickman, M. J., 1998, "Reconstructing Deconstructing 'Race': British Political Discourses About the Irish in Britain," *Ethnic and Racial Studies* 21: 288–307.

Honeyford, R., 1998, *The Commission for Racial Equality: British Bureaucracy and the Multiethnic Society*, New Brunswick, NJ: Transaction Publishers.

Ireland, P. R., 1995, "Migration, Free Movement, and Immigrant Integration in the EU: A Bifurcated Policy Response," in S. Leibfried and P. Pierson (eds.),

European Social Policy: Between Fragmentation and Integration, Washington, DC: Brookings Institution, pp. 231–66.

Jacobson, M. F., 1998, *Whiteness of a Different Color: European Immigrants and the Alchemy of Race*, Cambridge, MA: Harvard University Press.

James, D. R., 1988, "The Transformation of the Southern Racial State: Class and Race Determinants of Local-State Structures," *American Sociological Review* 53: 191–208.

Katznelson, I., 1976, *Black Men, White Cities: Race, Politics, and Migration in the United States, 1900–1930, and Britain, 1948–1968*, University of Chicago Press.

   1997, "Structure and Configuration in Comparative Politics," in M. I. Lichbach and A. S. Zuckerman (eds.), *Comparative Politics: Rationality, Culture, and Structure*, Cambridge University Press, pp. 81–112.

Katznelson, I., K. Geiger, and D. Kryder, 1993, "Limiting Liberalism: The Southern Veto in Congress, 1933–1950," *Political Science Quarterly* 108: 283–306.

Key, V. O., Jr., 1949, *Southern Politics in State and Nation*, New York: Alfred A. Knopf.

Lemann, N., 1991, *The Promised Land: The Great Black Migration and How it Changed America*, New York: Alfred A. Knopf.

Lieberman, R. C., 1995, "Social Construction," *American Political Science Review* 89: 437–41.

   1998, *Shifting the Color Line: Race and the American Welfare State*, Cambridge, MA: Harvard University Press.

   1999, "Constructing Race Policy in the United States and Great Britain: History and Politics in the Development of Employment Discrimination Policy," Working Paper No. 147. New York: Russell Sage Foundation.

Loevy, R. D., 1990, *To End All Segregation: The Politics of the Passage of the Civil Rights Act of 1964*, Lanham, MD: University Press of America.

Lustgarten, L. and J. Edwards, 1992, "Racial Inequality and the Limits of the Law," in A. Braham, A. Rattansi, and R. Skellington (eds.), *Racism and Antiracism: Inequalities, Opportunities and Policies*, London: Sage Publications, pp. 270–90.

Lyon A., 1976, "Race: Why We Must Act Now," *Sunday Times* (May 23): 16.

McConnell, G., 1966, *Private Power and American Democracy*, New York: Alfred A. Knopf.

McCrudden, C., 1983, "Anti-Discrimination Goals and the Legal Process," in N. Glazer and K. Young (eds.), *Ethnic Pluralism and Public Policy: Achieving Equality in the United States and Britain*, Lexington, MA: D.C. Heath, pp. 55–72.

MacEwen, M., 1994, "Anti-Discrimination Law in Great Britain," *New Community* 40: 353–70.

   1995, *Tackling Racism in Europe: An Examination of Anti-Discrimination Law in Practice*, Oxford: Berg.

Marshall, T. H., 1964, "Citizenship and Social Class," in *Class, Citizenship, and Social Development*, Garden City, NY: Doubleday, pp. 65–122.

Marx, A. W., 1998, *Making Race and Nation: A Comparison of the United States, South Africa, and Brazil*, Cambridge University Press.

Mehta, U. S., 1999, *Liberalism and Empire: A Study in Nineteenth-Century British Liberal Thought*, University of Chicago Press.

Messina, A. M., 1989, *Race and Party Competition in Britain*, Oxford University Press.

Myrdal, G., 1944, *An American Dilemma: The Negro Problem and Modern Democracy*, New York: Harper and Brothers.

Observer, 1976, "Alex Lyon invited sacking" (April 18): 3.

Omi, M. and H. Winant, 1994, *Racial Formation in the United States: From the 1960s to the 1990s*, New York: Routledge.

Orloff, A. S. and T. Skocpol, 1984, "Why Not Equal Protection?: Explaining the Politics of Public Social Spending in Britain, 1900–1911, and the United States, 1880s–1920s," *American Sociological Review* 49: 726–50.

Owen, D., 1996, "Size, Structure and Growth of the Ethnic Minority Populations," in David Coleman and John Salt (eds.), *Ethnicity in the 1991 Census*, Vol. I: *Demographic Characteristics of the Ethnic Minority Populations*, London: HMSO.

Paul, K., 1997, *Whitewashing Britain: Race and Citizenship in the Postwar Era*, Ithaca: Cornell University Press.

Peterson, P. E., 1981, *City Limits*, University of Chicago Press.

Rex, J. and S. Tomlinson, 1979, *Colonial Immigrants in a British City: A Class Analysis*, London: Routledge and Kegan Paul.

Rose, E. J. B., 1969, *Colour and Citizenship: A Report on British Race Relations*. London: Oxford University Press.

Saggar, S. and A. Heath, 1999, "Race: Towards a Multicultural Electorate?," in G. Evans and P. Norris (eds.), *Critical Elections: British Parties and Voters in Long-Term Perspective*, London: Sage Publications, pp. 102–23.

Semmel, B., 1960, *Imperialism and Social Reform: English Social-Imperial Thought, 1895–1914*, London: George Allen and Unwin.

Shefter, M., 1994, *Political Parties and the State: The American Historical Experience*, Princeton University Press.

Shklar, J. N., 1991, *American Citizenship: The Quest for Inclusion*, Cambridge, MA: Harvard University Press.

Skellington, R., 1996, *"Race" in Britain Today*, 2nd edn., London: Sage Publications.

Skrentny, J. D., 1996, *The Ironies of Affirmative Action: Politics, Culture, and Justice in America*, University of Chicago Press.

Smith, R. M., 1997, *Civic Ideals: Conflicting Visions of Citizenship in US History*, New Haven: Yale University Press.

Stein, J., 1998, *Running Steel, Running America: Race, Economic Policy, and the Decline of Liberalism*, Chapel Hill: University of North Carolina Press.

Steinmo, S., 1993, *Taxation and Democracy: Swedish, British, and American Approaches to Financing the Modern State*, New Haven: Yale University Press.

Tabili, L., 1994, *"We Ask for British Justice": Workers and Racial Difference in Late Imperial Britain*, Ithaca: Cornell University Press.

Teles, S. M., 1998, "Why is There No Affirmative Action in Britain?," *American Behavioral Scientist* 41: 1004–26.

Thelen, K. and S. Steinmo, 1992, "Historical Institutionalism in Comparative Politics," in K. Thelen, S. Steinmo, and F. Longstreth (eds.), *Structuring Politics: Historical Institutionalism in Comparative Analysis*, Cambridge
University Press, pp. 1–32.

Times, The, 1976a, "10 Promotions, Four Resignations in Callaghan Reshuffle"
(April 15): 1–2.

  1976b, "Mr Callaghan Accused on Racial Harmony" (April 17): 2.

  1976c, "Former Minister Tells of Clash with Civil Servants over Immigration"
(April 26): 2.

  1976d, "Callaghan Denial of Change in Race Relations Policy" (April 27): 3.

  1976e, "Mr Lyon Describes how Reform Attempts Were Frustrated" (May 10
1976): 3.

United Nations, 1979, *Committee on the Elimination of Racial Discrimination and
the Progress Made Towards the Achievement of the Objectives of the International
Convention on the Elimination of All Forms of Racial Discrimination*, New York:
United Nations.

Weaver, R. K. and B. A. Rockman, 1993, "Assessing the Effects of Institutions,"
in R. K. Weaver and B. A. Rockman (eds.), *Do Institutions Matter?: Government Capabilities in the United States and Abroad*, Washington, DC: Brookings
Institution, pp. 1–41.

Woodward, C. V., 1974, *The Strange Career of Jim Crow*, 3rd rev. edn, New York:
Oxford University Press.

Young, K., 1990, "Approaches to Policy Development in the Field of Equal
Opportunities," in B. Wendy and J. Solomos (eds.), *Race and Local Politics*,
London: Macmillan, pp. 22–42.

19 Regime effects: ethnicity, social mobility, and public policy in the USA and Britain

Steven M. Teles, Robert W. Mickey, and Fawzia S. Ahmed

1 Introduction

What accounts for the social mobility of racial and ethnic groups in liberal capitalist democracies? How do polities, consciously or not, accelerate or retard these groups' advancement? And how might these polities differentially affect the opportunities of various groups to "get ahead"? Drawing on a broader understanding of social mobility than is traditionally employed, this paper compares contemporary racial and ethnic groups in the USA and Great Britain on three crucial aspects of social mobility. In doing so, we emphasize what might be called the *regime effect*: the consequences for different ethnic groups inhabiting polities that differ in their mix of political institutions and policy instruments. After outlining below our understanding of social mobility, we proceed by tackling in turn three essential, if underappreciated, aspects of social mobility: wealth accumulation; crime; and health.

Scholars have traditionally conceived of social mobility in terms of an individual's position in the labor market, whether measured by occupational strata or income level (Blau and Duncan 1978, Duncan 1984, Erikson and Goldthorpe 1992). "Mobility" refers either to individuals over the course of their life cycle, or across generations. By generating income and by securing status benefits that accompany various employment categories, individuals are conceived of as climbing up, slipping down, or remaining on the same rung of a social ladder common to all in the polity. While the traditional focus of scholars in this field is on classes, they have also drawn on these same tools to chart the mobility of members of racial and ethnic groups.

Scholars' relentless focus on labor market position, whether viewed in terms of income level or occupation, is understandable, this position is obviously crucial for understanding how individuals interpret their place in society. Our primary argument is that this focus on labor markets is incomplete, not incorrect.[1] First, it ignores the significance of capital markets, intergenerational transfers of wealth, asset accumulation, and the returns individuals derive from those assets. After all, social mobility is a process that occurs over time, and for which the intergenerational transfer of resources (material, cultural, organizational) can be critical in affecting social mobility. The distribution of well-being in society, and especially the goods necessary for maintaining and improving social status, are as shaped by financial capital as by the human and social capital rewarded in the labor market. Second, labor markets are not the only site of distribution in capitalist democracies. Upwards of one-half of the national income produced in Western societies is redistributed through political institutions. Some of this income is allocated to goods consumed collectively, while some is redistributed across generations and income classes. At this point, it suffices to note that groups vary substantially in their ability to leverage government as a channel for group mobility.[2]

Third, and most important, not all socially relevant goods are distributed through the labor market or are even distributed through goods that have obvious financial equivalents. Safety, health, residential location, education, and other goods are essential components of most individuals' idea of living a dignified, satisfying life, but their production and distribution occur as much through political and informal social practices as through private markets. Educational attainment, for example, may be thought of as a means to achieving a higher income. However, education may be considered by group members as an end in itself, and one which is an independent indicator of social mobility. Thus, merely ascertaining income or occupational strata may omit much of importance in whether and how individuals conceive of themselves as "getting ahead." (Unfortunately, to recognize this fact is to render social mobility a much messier concept, since indicators of social mobility are simultaneously themselves social mobility "destinations.")

Social mobility, then, should be viewed much more broadly than labor market status. This is particularly true of members of minority ethnic and racial groups. While these groups may differ in myriad ways, they often share a history of subjugation, of possessing a level of citizenship that has long fallen far short of that taken for granted by members of the majority group (see Shklar 1992). For these groups, social mobility may mean securing symbolic goods dispensed not by markets, but by private and public institutions (e.g., language policy) (Horowitz 1985). Moreover, because ethnic and racial groups draw on different historical experiences and cultures, they may develop unique understandings of social mobility, of what it means to achieve individual or group progress. Some groups may possess different priorities in securing some goods (e.g., education) rather than others and attach different meanings to these goods. Thus, they may deploy different individual and collective choices and strategies in pursuing social mobility. In sum, an approach to social mobility that concentrates on the attainment of a single destination runs up against obvious difficulties, since groups are constituted in large part by their (heterogeneous) answers to the question, "mobility to/for what?"

Broadening our conceptual palette in this way also points toward the central role of the state, both as a collection of institutions through which decisions are made, and as a producer of goods. Since many of the means by which individuals in these groups seek to advance themselves are profoundly shaped by public policies, understanding the determinants of social mobility requires a much more explicitly political analysis than scholars have heretofore offered. Given these complexities, we do not attempt to chart relevant racial and ethnic groups' subjective understandings of social mobility, or to describe and analyze all relevant indicators of social mobility. Rather, we direct attention to three areas of importance for all ethnic groups in the USA and Great Britain: asset accumulation, with special focus on homeownership; crime; and healthcare access and outcomes. As we will show, each of these three interrelated areas is crucial both as an indicator, and a determinant, of social mobility. Moreover, we emphasize the interaction effect of public policies, processes, and institutions with group-level characteristics. It is often those policies that are nominally non-ethnic/racial in nature which have the most bearing on these groups' social mobility. What is more, these policies often differentially affect ethnic groups both within and across the two polities.

2   Assets and social mobility

This section consists of three parts. First, we argue that asset accumulation is central to the social mobility fates of ethnic groups. Second, we examine the role of asset accumulation in social mobility in detail, drawing on literature examining the American case, followed by a shorter examination of Britain. Finally, we examine how the design of seemingly non-asset-related policies can measurably effect asset accumulation.

Why assets matter

In liberal welfare regimes, wealth accumulation is a critical contributor to social mobility, although it may be less important for some groups than for others. Some groups may place more emphasis on the accumulation of human capital, for instance, while underinvesting in housing or other capital assets. That said, assets are connected to social mobility in two principal ways. First, assets, especially housing equity, can accelerate the pace of (upward) social mobility for future generations. Second, assets can serve as shock absorbers, interrupting what could become a downward slide in socioeconomic and status attainments. Of course, housing equity and cash gifts from family and close associates far from exhaust the possible ways in which family members, particularly parents, help their kin: in-kind assistance in the form of housing, child care, and transportation assistance are often important, as are less tangible transfers of human and cultural capital. However, the presence (or absence) of financial assets has enduring implications for the social mobility prospects of the disadvantaged. Space permits only a cursory review of three paths by which assets facilitate improvements in social status and higher economic attainments. First, levels of accumulated assets are important in determining future levels of accumulated assets, especially for one's offspring. Primarily through the intergenerational transfer of real estate and cash, households can place children on a solid footing for a lifetime of effective asset accumulation. Central here is the role of parental assistance in allowing young households to purchase more valuable real estate than would otherwise be possible, and to make a larger down-payment, and/or secure lower interest rates, both of which lower the long-term costs of homeownership. The value of such investments, of course, is more than just financial, for "residential location is a well-established indicator of people's social standing" (Logan and Alba 1993: 243).

Second, assets facilitate higher educational attainment, a chief component of social mobility. Greater educational attainment results in increased earnings, independent of family background or other variables.[3] For example, as Dalton Conley argues, the great majority of American households, white and black, cannot afford to pay for college expenses out of income. As a result, "individuals from low-income families tend to enroll in less selective colleges, net of academic ability, achievement, or educational expectations, since there is an association between selectivity and cost" (Conley 1999: 59).[4] Also, asset levels may affect high-school graduation rates by providing additional resources for tutoring, or for private schools (which experience lower dropout rates) (ibid.: 74–9). Given that the USA increasingly relies on subjective perceptions of prestige in higher educational achievement as a social sorting mechanism (Lemann 1999), financial assets emerge again as important in assisting parents in boosting their children's prospects for social mobility.

Third, assets are important in increasing the rates, and relative success, of self-employment and firm creation. Both in their inter- and intragenerational guises, assets can be critical in securing loans for start-up firms.

Even after controlling for creditworthiness and many other differences between black- and white-owned firms, black firm owners remain about twice as likely to be denied credit, and to pay higher interest rates. Given that America's minorities continue to suffer from racial discrimination in small business credit markets, intergenerational transfers may be even more critical for low-income groups (Blanchflower, Levine, and Zimmerman 1998).[5]

Who owns assets in the USA?

By the 1980s, the USA already possessed the largest wealth inequalities across households of any advanced industrial nation. In 1989, the wealthiest 1 percent of households held 48 percent of all financial assets (Oliver and Shapiro 1995: 62). With the explosion of stock prices in the 1990s, these inequalities have widened further. From 1983 to 1989, median net worth rose about 7 percent nationally, and then dropped 17 percent from 1989 to 1995. Meanwhile, *mean* net worth over the seventeen-year period rose by about 3 percent, suggesting that the "vast bulk of household wealth is concentrated in the richest families" (Wolff 1998: 131). Amidst this highly stratified distribution of wealth, African-Americans form "the sediment of the American stratificational order" (Oliver and Shapiro 1995: 5–6). African-American households during the postwar period have substantially reduced the gap between black and white incomes, but the wealth gap remains high. As of 1995, the median African-American household had only about 12 percent of the wealth of the median white household (Wolff 1998: 140).[6] Analysis of a slightly different dataset revealed that in 1988, median white households held approximately $44,000 in net worth, as compared to about $4,000 for the median black household (Oliver and Shapiro 1995).

Moreover, this median white household also retained about $7,000 in net financial assets that could be drawn upon during periods of lost or lowered income or unexpected expenses. The median African-American household, on the other hand, possessed *zero* net financial assets (Oliver and Shapiro 1995: 56 and passim). While 61 percent of African-American households held zero or negative net financial assets, only 21 percent of black households maintained sufficient financial assets to remain above the poverty threshold for three months in the event of a complete loss of income, compared to 62 percent of white households. Thirty-eight percent of whites and 17 percent of blacks, had resources on hand to remain above the poverty level for six months (Oliver and Shapiro 1995: Appendix). Asset levels maintained by America's Hispanic households are basically similar to those of African-Americans. In 1988, 54 percent of Hispanic households had zero (or negative) financial assets, while 27 percent and 23 percent of these households were able to remain above the poverty level for three and six months, respectively.

The black middle class

Over the past forty years, black middle-class Americans have substantially narrowed the racial gap in income. Even so, middle-class black households have struggled to keep pace with white middle-class households, rely heavily on two earners, and find it very difficult to accumulate wealth. In the late 1980s, white white-collar households maintained a net worth and net financial assets of $56,000 and $2,000, respectively, while black white-collar households had $8,000 in net worth and no net financial assets. More troubling, a similar gap existed among median young (aged 25–35) two-earner African-American middle-class households: while their share of white income reached 81 percent, their net worth of $4,000 was only 18 percent of similarly situated whites, and the median white household held a net financial assets advantage of $1,150 to zero (Oliver and Shapiro 1995: 97). Additionally, Oliver and Shapiro find that the net worth of black "moderate" income households is $2,000, lower than that held by *white households with incomes under the poverty level*. Black middle-income households possess a mere 3 percent of the net financial assets of their white counterparts, and only 26 percent of moderate-income whites (Oliver and Shapiro 1995: 197).

Black middle-class households are both more vulnerable to downward mobility and face additional constraints in accumulating wealth. First, they are proportionately more reliant on state employment, and they are more at risk to private sector layoffs during economic downturns. Second, to the extent that their kin are more likely to face economic hardship, these households face greater pressures to make asset transfers to others. Third, an obvious point should be kept in mind: since members of the black middle class are much more likely than white middle-class members to have working-class parents, they can expect much smaller intergenerational wealth transfers. These are often crucial in securing better, more valuable, and cheaper housing. The greater the parental assistance with a first mortgage, of course, the larger the possible down payment and the lower subsequent mortgage payments will be.

The data seem to bear out these assertions. Oliver and Shapiro show that until the late 1960s, few older African-Americans were able to save or invest much at all. In 1988, the average African-American household headed by an individual aged 65 had no financial assets to pass on (Oliver and Shapiro 1995: 7). And Wolff finds that in 1995, 24 percent of white households had received an inheritance, as compared to 11 percent of black households.

The differential in average transfer size was also large: $115,000 for whites, and $32,000 for blacks (Wolff 1998: 142). An analysis based on the National Survey of Family and Households in the late 1980s concluded that controlling for need, resources, family structure, and parent-grandparent ties, race differentials persist in intergenerational exchange. Contrary to a highly influential ethnographic portrait of African-American intergenerational assistance, blacks are consistently *less* likely than whites or Hispanics to be involved in any sort of inter-generational assistance. They are only half as likely as whites to be "high exchangers," and two-thirds as likely to receive unreciprocated support from parents.[7] Additionally, whites are four times as likely as blacks to receive parental help on making a down payment toward the purchase of a home (Charles and Hurst 2000: 18).

Racial differences in the composition of asset portfolios

As mentioned above, different assets assist households in different ways. The current boom in both mass participation in and the value of heav-ily traded stocks is likely to have enduring effects on the distribution of wealth in the USA. The most recent data suggest that 90 percent of all equity owners, individual stock owners, and stock mutual fund shareowners are white, and 5 percent are African-American. Black and Hispanic equity owners are more common (7 percent and 6 percent respectively) among Generation X (ages 19 to 35 during 1999) than among boomers (5 percent and 4 percent). This generational differ-ence is much smaller than that between boomers and the "silent genera-tion" (those aged 55–74), among whom blacks and Hispanics were only 2 percent and 1 percent of all equity owners (Investment Company Insti-tute 1999: 61, 68, and 74). However, in generating net financial assets and transferable net worth among these groups, aggregate participation levels in these markets are less important than the amounts invested. Oliver and Shapiro found that as of 1988, about 9 percent of the median white household's financial assets were held in stocks, as opposed to 1 percent of black households. Similar gaps held for the relative impor-tance of IRA/Keough accounts (Oliver and Shapiro 1995: 106). Here, the central fact of African-American household wealth accumulation, which is true for most of the black middle class, must be kept in mind: these households simply possess no net financial assets with which to invest in speculative markets.[8]

Moreover, there may be "stickiness across generations" in the portfolio choices of blacks, in which parents pass on a propensity to invest (or not) in equity markets. Historically, blacks have preferred to invest in life insurance, and have shown an aversion to (and/or have been discriminated by) formal financial institutions. The upshot has been that black participation in equity markets has been low, controlling for income. Recent analysis suggests that, controlling for a variety of factors, including income and inheritance, those blacks whose parents owned stock are more likely to do so (Chiteji and Stafford 1999: 377–80). Even indirect ownership of equities shows substantial gaps between whites and blacks: 69 percent of whites and 54 percent of nonwhites[9] report involvement in a pension. Another racial difference emerges from the data: whites are twice as likely as nonwhites (20 percent vs. 10 percent, respectively) to have pensions which combine Defined Contribution (DC) and Defined Benefit (DB) plans. These are financially more lucrative than a plan that is based on either DC or DB alone (McGarry and Davenport 1998: Appendix A, Table 1).

What explains racial and ethnic gaps in asset levels?

Economists offer many answers to this question. In the US case, one widespread argument is that African-Americans, for whatever reason, save at lower levels than whites. However, this claim has been disputed by many analysts.[10] Both Conley and Oliver and Shapiro argue instead that a household's accumulation of assets is best predicted by the level of assets held by the prior generation of kin (Conley 1999: Chapter 3, Oliver and Shapiro 1995: Chapter 6). Their quantitative analysis is subject to criticism due to possibilities of omitted variable bias. However, the broader claim – that previous generations affect the wealth of subsequent generations – seems well-established, as several analysts have demonstrated.[11]

Besides parental levels of wealth, family structure of the prior generation has important independent effects on asset holdings. Sons in families that experience disruptions are more likely to enter low-status occupations, net of other factors. Family structure also weakens intergenerational inheritance and resemblance, even after direct effects are controlled for. Thus, any accumulated advantages in terms of skills, networks, and other resources may be de-linked from the social mobility prospects of children (Biblarz and Raftery 1993: 97–109). Moreover, the breakup of a two-parent household places enormous stress on adults, particularly women and mothers, in securing sufficient income and replacing social networks. As the data presented below will indicate, substantial losses in levels of net worth and net financial assets follow the demise of two-parent households. More broadly, for a variety of reasons, single-parent households often possess *no* net worth or net financial assets, even controlling for income and other variables.

Third, asset accumulation is highly influenced by neighborhood effects. As will be discussed later in the paper, high-crime areas have direct effects on educational attainment, as well as indirect effects (mediated by, among other things, the health of children and parents). Assets allow households to purchase homes in better neighborhoods. When transferred by the state, assets may even allow the very poor currently residing in dangerous public housing areas to move to mixed housing in better neighborhoods, with positive effects on health, exposure to crime, and social networks.[12] Fourth and finally, asset accumulation is often affected by self-employment rates, since some forms of ethnic firm growth may produce wealth quickly for one's household and for others; depending upon the group's spatial location and the prior assets of group members and kin, rates of asset accumulation may vary greatly. In sum, understanding the rates of asset accumulation of ethnic minorities requires an understanding of their family backgrounds and structure, neighborhood and economic strategies, rather than simply differences in individual-level savings behavior.

Housing: the cornerstone of wealth accumulation

Homeownership was the motor that propelled the enormous expansion of the white middle class emerging from the Depression and World War II.[13] As with that generation, the social mobility prospects of African-Americans and Hispanics today are bound up with their opportunities to purchase and maintain valuable owner-occupied housing. Below, we briefly discuss the ways in which homeownership fuels asset accumulation, and how assets are needed to make homeownership likely.

In 2002, American homeownership rates reached an all-time high of 68 percent, with whites at an even higher 75 percent (Joint Center 2003: 35). Blacks, however, had a homeownership rate of 48.9 percent, while Hispanics had a rate of 47.4 percent and Asians 53.9 percent. The differences in homeownership are partially a function of income, but racial and ethnic differences in spatial positioning also constrain opportunities for asset accumulation through homeownership, due to differences in urban and suburban housing markets. While 28 percent of whites lived in central cities in 1997, almost twice as many lived in the suburbs (57 percent). For African-Americans, however, 64 percent lived in central cities, and only 31 percent lived in suburbs. Seventy-two percent of suburban residents owned their own homes, compared to only 49 percent of urban residents (Conley 1999: 38, citing Joint Center for Housing Studies' 1997 report). But some recent trends seem favorable for African-American and Hispanic would-be homeowners. From 1994 to 1998, given high rates of economic growth and all-time annual highs in housing starts, ethnic minority households contributed more than 40 percent of the blistering growth in the rate of homeownership. And as of 1999, minorities now comprise 30 percent of first-time homebuyers, compared to 19 percent in 1985 (Joint Center 2000: 4 and 2). However, central cities have lagged behind in the boom. While suburban and nonmetropolitan homeownership rates increased about 2 percent each, to 73 percent and 75 percent, respectively, the central city homeownership rate increased just a half of one percent (to 49 percent). In fact, the homeownership rate for northeastern cities suffered a net decline of almost 3 percent (Joint Center 2000: 18).

Besides aggregate rates of homeownership, two other issues are of importance here. First, which whites and blacks own housing? Drawing on 1968–94 PSID data, Conley found that among households with incomes between $25,000 and $35,000, 62 percent of white households owned homes, compared to 45 percent of black households (producing a black rate 35 percent smaller than that for whites even given some controls on income level). When similar rates are compared at income levels between $35,000 and $50,000, the racial gap shrinks: 77 percent of whites own homes, as opposed to 67 percent of blacks (Conley 1999: 109). These numbers suggest that while growing African-American incomes can eventually make up ground in homebuying, African-Americans are less likely to be able to purchase homes as early as whites; and, given the large disparities in net worth, those homes they do purchase are likely to be of lesser value. Conley notes that the median value of housing equity held by white and black homeowners was $45,000 and $31,000, respectively.

Of course, the degree to which homeownership can spur asset accumulation for ethnic and racial minorities is dependent upon their access to valuable investments in homeownership. Here, residential segregation works to restrict this access. More than one-third of America's blacks reside in sixteen metropolitan areas in hypersegregated neighborhoods (Massey and Denton 1993: 77). These neighborhoods are also marked by substantial concentrations of poverty and poor housing stock (Massey, Gross, and Shibuya 1994). Segregation effectively shrinks the housing market open to blacks. On the demand side, blacks in segregated areas are much more likely to be financially strapped, and unable to secure funds necessary for homeowning. They are probably more likely to face discrimination in securing financial assistance, and to be discouraged from applying for mortgage financing on this basis. On the supply side, predominantly black neighborhoods may be marked by a shortage of single-family detached homes. Given that a critical part of the decision to buy a home is its expected increase in value, many potential homeowners may choose not to buy within these neighborhoods, even as they are priced out of more expensive housing in other neighborhoods. Indeed, Herbert found support for this supply constraint phenomenon in his analysis of fifty US metropolitan areas, especially in the northeast, which featured the largest gap between actual and predicted rates of homeownership (Herbert 1997: 176–7, 211). Additionally, segregation may also stigmatize black-owned homes, thereby suppressing its present value and reducing its long-term appreciation. Thus, housing already owned by blacks is unlikely to increase in value at the same rate as that of whites, which makes it more difficult to "trade up" to more valuable housing.

Finally, housing costs in the form of rental payments constitute a large and often extremely burdensome expenditure for poor and very poor African-American and Hispanics, and one that adds nothing to long-term wealth accumulation. Two aspects of current trends are worrisome in this regard. First, as the 1999 Joint Center's report demonstrates, affordable unsubsidized rental units for extremely low-income households are declining, as is "the stock of subsidized housing units . . . as property owners increasingly opt out of federal subsidy programs in search of higher returns" (Joint Center 2000: 25–6). In this sense, economic good times are a mixed blessing for the African-American community. While the inflation of real estate prices associated with good times is good for most white families, who are seeing their housing investment increase in value, it is bad for African-Americans, who are disproportionately renters. This means that not only do African-Americans face higher rents, but the wall separating them from homeownership continues to get harder and harder to climb.

Housing and assets in Britain

It is much harder to assess the role of assets for the social mobility of racial and ethnic minorities in the UK than it is in the USA, due to limitations in available data.[14] Because of these limits, in this section we focus on only one aspect of wealth accumulation in this section, housing, an area for which relatively detailed analysis based on ethnicity is possible. This focus also makes more sense substantively, since in Britain, net housing equity represents well over half of total wealth, as compared to under a third in the United States (Banks, Blundell, and Smith 2000: 55).

What can we say about the trajectory of ethnic minority housing mobility over time? One measure on which solid data are available is housing tenure. Modood et al. report the proportions of each ethnic group that lived in the more valuable "detached or semi-detached" type of accommodation at two points in time, 1982 and 1994. The proportion of Indians living in this type of housing increased by a remarkable 83 percent, from 30 percent to 55 percent, and Bangladeshis and Pakistanis more than 100 percent, to 28 percent and 20 percent respectively. Caribbeans, however, increased their residency in such housing at a rate of only 32 percent (from 22 percent to 29 percent), the lowest of all ethnic groups, while the white proportions remained relatively constant (Modood et al. 1997: 219). These patterns of housing type are partially explained by presence in social housing.[15] Twenty-three percent of whites, 46 percent of Caribbeans, 35 percent of Caribbean/white mixed households, 45 percent of Bangladeshis, 24 percent of Chinese, 15 percent of Pakistanis, 13 percent of Asian/white mixed households, and 9 percent of Indians live in social housing (Modood et al. 1997: 199).

Ultimately, however, our concern is not with the type of housing that ethnic minorities occupy, but whether they own their own home and thus are able to accumulate wealth. Table 19.1[16] shows that rates of homeownership vary widely across groups, with Black Africans at the bottom (due no doubt to their very recent migration) and Indians at the top, at nearly the same level as whites. At the top of the income scale, the Indians have rates of homeownership, relative to whites, that are what one would predict from their relative earnings. In addition, as seen in Table 19.2, while there are substantial gaps between Indians and whites over age sixty, these gaps mostly disappeared for those under forty. Most strikingly, when one calculates groups' housing equity, there is even clearer evidence of progress over time: while the housing equity for Indians over sixty trails that of whites' by 24 percent, for the younger cohort mean Indian housing equity is 27 percent *more* than that of whites. The Indian housing equity advantage relative to other ethnic minority groups holds even at lower levels of income, as Table 19.3 indicates. This difference even at lower levels of income may suggest that group attachment has an independent effect on housing wealth, possibly through the mechanism of intragroup transfers (such as bequests or loans). Overall, however, the experience of Indians appears to be one of substantial wealth mobility for those groups' youngest members, an advantage that makes it reasonable to surmise that their wealth relative to whites will rise as this cohort ages.

The situation for other ethnic groups is more complicated. Perhaps the most interesting contrast in these data is between Pakistanis and

Table 19.1 *Characteristics of benefit units by ethnic group*

				Ethnic group				
Benefit unit characteristics	White N = 114,697	Black Caribbean and Black Other N = 1,393	Black African N = 576	Indian N = 1,574	Pakistani N = 851	Bangladeshi N = 277	Chinese N = 224	Other N = 1,101
Age of benefit unit head								
Mean ± s.d.	48.1 ± 19.5	40.8 ± 16.0	35.3 ± 11.9	41.1 ± 16.1	37.6 ± 15.1	39.5 ± 15.8	38.7 ± 15.6	38.2 ± 14.5
No. adults in benefit unit								
Mean ± s.d.	1.5 ± 0.5	1.3 ± 0.4	1.3 ± 0.5	1.6 ± 0.5	1.6 ± 0.5	1.7 ± 0.5	1.5 ± 0.5	1.4 ± 0.5
No. dependent children in benefit unit								
Mean ± s.d.	0.5 ± 0.9	0.7 ± 1.1	0.9 ± 1.2	0.9 ± 1.2	1.6 ± 1.8	1.9 ± 2.0	0.7 ± 1.1	0.8 ± 1.2
Total no. people in benefit unit								
Mean ± s.d.	2.0 ± 1.2	2.0 ± 1.2	2.2 ± 1.4	2.4 ± 1.5	3.1 ± 2.1	3.6 ± 2.2	2.1 ± 1.4	2.2 ± 1.4
Homeowners								
N (%)	64,271 (56.0)	480 (34.5)	87 (15.1)	852 (54.1)	400 (47.0)	77 (27.8)	106 (47.3)	414 (37.6)
Income relative to Whites at the same percentile								
Median	0%	−15%	−19%	1%	−14%	−10%	−11%	−7%
75th percentile	0%	−24%	−25%	−1%	−30%	−28%	−10%	−8%
95th percentile	0%	−23%	−21%	−1%	−33%	−40%	−7%	−4%
Housing equity relative to Whites at the same percentile								
Median	0%	NA	NA	−42%	NA	NA	NA	NA
75th percentile	0%	−68%	NA	−14%	−46%	−96%	−29%	−60%
95th percentile	0%	−38%	−68%	−19%,	−44%	−53%	−2%	−22%

Notes: NA indicates instances where the ethnic group has no housing equity at the given percentile. Data pools Family Resources Survey for years 94/5, 95/6, 96/7, and 97/8.

Table 19.2 *Housing equity relative to whites at the same percentiles by age group*

| | Age of benefit unit head | | | | | | | | | | | | | | |
| | <40 | | | | | 40-59 | | | | | ≥60 | | | | |
Ethnic group	N	P 50	P 75	P 95	Mean	N	P 50	P 75	P 95	Mean	N	P 50	P 75	P 95	Mean
Black Caribbean and Black Other	821	NA	NA	−31%	−51%	324	−95%	−34%	−35%	−45%	247	NA	−23%	−28%	−35%
Black African	409	NA	NA	−88%	−81%	131	NA	−92%	−59%	−80%	34	NA	−32%	−29%	−51%
Indian	803	NA	77%	21%	27%	523	10%	2%	−5%	2%	242	NA	−14%	−9%	−24%
Pakistani	510	NA	−31%	−19%	−26%	252	−35%	−30%	−25%	−17%	87	−64%	−38%	−45%	−44%
Bangladeshi	158	NA	NA	−21%	−43%	71	NA	−48%	−43%	−57%	48	NA	NA	−69%	−77%
Chinese	124	NA	−63%	21%	−5%	74	−25%	−11%	16%	−9%	23	NA	21%	−9%	−6%
Other	671	NA	NA	−16%	−35%	312	−64%	−16%	−23%	−30%	113	−47%	17%	8%	−3%

Notes: NA indicates instances where the ethnic group has no housing equity at the given percentile. Data pools Family Resources Survey for years 94/5, 95/6, 96/7, and 97/8.

Table 19.3 *Housing equity relative to whites at the same percentiles by income group*

| | Benefit unit income group | | | | | | | | | | | | | | | | | | | |
| Ethnic group | <£150 | | | | | £150–£224 | | | | | £225–£299 | | | | | >£300 | | | | |
	N	P 50	P 75	P 95	Mean	N	P 50	P 75	P 95	Mean	N	P 50	P 75	P 95	Mean	N	P 50	P 75	P 95	Mean
Black Caribbean and Black Other	681	NA	NA	−28%	−52%	348	NA	−86%	−23%	−54%	166	−67%	−27%	−24%	−33%	197	−52%	−41%	−49%	−51%
Black African	301	NA	NA	−71%	−83%	126	NA	NA	−79%	−92%	59	NA	NA	−49%	−79%	88	NA	−82%	−65%	−78%
Indian	652	NA	−54%	−5%	−15%	316	NA	−17%	−19%	−16%	202	40%	−5%	−14%	2%	398	−6%	−12%	−17%	−15%
Pakistani	422	NA	−55%	−33%	−37%	239	NA	−40%	−41%	−43%	99	−56%	−36%	−34%	−43%	89	−44%	−28%	−9%	3%
Bangladeshi	129	NA	NA	−52%	−66%	86	NA	−98%	−61%	−76%	38	NA	−35%	10%	−29%	24	NA	−67%	−54%	−61%
Chinese	104	NA	8%	12%	1%	40	NA	−39%	0%	−27%	26	NA	−80%	−29%	−58%	51	−42%	−13%	−2%	−24%
Other	490	NA	NA	−4%	−41%	230	NA	−47%	−13%	−34%	128	NA	−55%	−13%	−41%	248	−63%	−38%	−39%	−46%

Notes: NA indicates instances where the ethnic group has no housing equity at the given percentile. Data pools Family Resources Survey for years 94/5, 95/6, 96/7, and 97/8.

non-African blacks (which for our purposes includes both those identifying as Black Caribbean and Black Other). In terms of income, these
groups are closely matched, although Pakistanis lag behind non-African
blacks higher up in the income distribution. Insofar as housing equity is
a proxy for wealth, however, it appears that non-African blacks are more
disadvantaged than their income suggests, and Pakistanis more advantaged. Thirty-five percent of non-African black families are homeowners, compared to 47 percent of Pakistani families.[17] The non-African
black 75th percentile of housing equity is 68 percent behind the white
75th percentile, compared to 46 percent for Pakistanis. While older non-
African blacks are somewhat less disadvantaged in terms of housing
equity, the differences at younger ages are especially stark: Pakistanis
under forty trail whites by 27 percent, and non-African blacks trail by
54 percent.

Especially interesting are the differences in homeownership and housing equity between non-African blacks and Pakistanis at the lower end
of the income spectrum. Only 18 percent of non-African blacks earning less than £150 per week own their own home, as compared to
33 percent of Pakistanis, with similar figures in the £150–224 range.
These differences in homeownership disappear, however, above £300 per
week (although differences in housing equity at these higher incomes are
very substantial). In short, gaps in housing wealth between non-African
blacks and Pakistanis are starker the younger the age cohort, and the
lower the income bracket. This suggests, at first blush, that poverty is
likely to be a deeper and more debilitating condition for non-African
blacks, since they have little accumulated wealth (in the form of a home)
and little prospect for economic improvement outside the labor market.

While there is only so much that can be gleaned about social mobility
from non-panel data, the difference across age cohorts suggests generational improvement for Pakistanis, with serious generational decline for
non-African blacks. How can we explain this seemingly divergent pattern?
One explanation for the non-African black decline is that it is largely a
statistical artifact produced by the "graduating out" of black identity for
those born in Britain and especially for children of mixed marriages. This
argument has substantial weight for the Black Caribbean category, but
the most likely identity destination for those exiting this category is not
the white or "Other" group, but the "Black Other" category, which we
fold together. This would mean that to the degree that there is substantial
movement out of the Black Caribbean category over time, we are probably capturing most of it. That said, there is still some reason to believe that
at least part of the seeming disadvantage of younger non-African blacks
is a consequence of stronger black identity at lower income levels, while

studying those of Caribbean descent is inherently difficult given their high rates of interracial intimacy, as discussed in Ceri Peach's chapter in this volume.

Assuming that the deterioration in the relative wealth of non-African blacks across age cohorts is a real phenomenon, what might explain it? We suggest three hypotheses, although these are by no means exhaustive. First, data from the PSI Survey of Ethnic Minorities shows that Caribbean ownership of consumer durables, especially when one controls for family type, is substantially higher than that for Pakistanis and Bangladeshis (Modood et al. 1997: 171). This suggests that non-African blacks have a higher propensity to consume than Pakistanis, driven perhaps by their greater assimilation in British society, with its emphasis on consumption as a measure of status. Pakistanis, on the other hand, being less assimilated than non-African blacks, may be more insulated from British standards of material comfort. If true, this would translate into a higher savings rate among Pakistanis, and a lower rate for non-African blacks, which is consistent with our data.

A second interpretation of the comparative wealth accumulation of Pakistanis and non-African blacks focuses on the two groups' family structures. While single-parent families were not dominant among Caribbean immigrants a generation ago, they are increasingly the non-African black norm. While 54 percent of Black Caribbean families are headed by a lone parent, only 15 percent of Pakistani families are, as compared to 23 percent of white families (Office of National Statistics 2002: 8). Whatever its other merits or flaws, the nuclear (or extended) family takes advantage of domestic economies of scale: since Pakistanis maintain fewer separate family units for a given number of individuals, they are more able to take advantage of economies of scale to accumulate wealth. Combined with the former conjecture on propensity to consume, this would help to explain how Pakistanis seem able to squeeze more housing equity and homeownership out of less labor market income.

A third explanation looks at claims on group assets from abroad. Another determinant of differences in wealth, especially for groups of recent migration, is the degree to which they send money abroad. While it may be a source of prestige for high-senders, remitting money abroad inevitably siphons away income from wealth accumulation and intragroup, in-country redistribution. Modood et al. found that "a fifth or a sixth of Indians, African Asians and Bangladeshis," about one-third of Pakistanis and Chinese and "well over a third of Caribbeans" transferred assets to family outside the household (1997: 166). Significantly, of these groups, only the Caribbeans included a large number of respondents who reported sending funds back to home "regularly" (Modood et al. 1997:

166). While some of these funds undoubtedly go to parents and children who remain at home, it is striking that even in those households in which all adults were born in Britain, 14 percent of Caribbeans regularly send funds abroad (compared with 4 percent of the much wealthier South Asians). When at least one adult per household was born abroad, these proportions jump to 42 percent of Caribbeans and 20 percent of South Asians (Modood et al. 1997: 168). Thus, part of the explanation of lower Caribbean asset holdings may be this relatively large disbursement of funds abroad.

A final illuminating comparison is that of Bangladeshis and Pakistanis, two groups that are typically grouped together in studies of ethnic minorities. While their income profiles are not radically dissimilar, their housing profiles are. In our sample, 28 percent of Bangladeshis are homeowners, as compared to 47 percent of Pakistanis.[18] This difference is not easily accounted for by the relative age of the two groups: Bangladeshis are only slightly younger than Pakistanis (Office of National Statistics 2002: 6). However, Bangladeshis did not begin to migrate to Britain in substantial numbers until the 1980s, while a substantial cohort of Pakistanis arrived in the 1960s: this has given the Pakistanis longer to set down roots and accumulate assets. Even more suggestive are the two groups' employment experiences: Bangladeshis have lower rates of both female and male labor force participation than Pakistanis, and higher rates of unemployment (Office of National Statistics 2002: 9). At this point, the figures for housing are suggestive enough that future analysts should be aware that the two groups' somewhat similar labor market experience may be an insufficient guide in and of itself to their relative economic prospects.

Overall, our most surprising findings are the rapid progress of Indians and the relatively high rates of homeownership for Pakistanis. In the first case, what is unexpected is that, despite the fact that they have only recently caught up with whites in terms of income, younger Indians now far surpass them in housing equity. This is surprising because of the reasonable expectation that housing wealth takes multiple generations to accumulate, with each generation leveraging the previous generation's wealth. With so few generations of wealth and higher incomes to build upon, we would expect to see younger Indians still lagging whites. In addition, the Pakistani levels of homeownership are also unexpected, given their relatively low incomes, high unemployment, and relatively recent migration. Together with the other findings in this section, these findings highlight the importance of looking at both income and wealth as measures of economic well-being and social mobility, and not simply assuming that the one naturally translates into the other.

Policy design and asset accumulation

In this section, we have argued that wealth is fundamental to the social mobility prospects of racial and ethnic minorities. Asset accumulation can help individuals secure other instruments of social advancement, such as income, education, and more desirable residential location. Wealth, both through intra- and intergenerational transfers, can both limit a downward slide and spur upward mobility. While *income* inequalities have decreased steadily in both countries, *wealth* disparities proceed apace. These disparities have many sources, but critical among them is the spatial location of minorities. As Massey and Denton put it, "barriers to spatial mobility are barriers to social mobility" (1993: 14). Segregation is in itself a barrier to homeownership. As we make clear in Sections 3 and 4, numerous neighborhood effects that accompany segregation, including exposure to crime and poor health and healthcare access, feed back onto asset accumulation, and groups thereby may face even greater difficulties in creating wealth.

How might policymakers go about addressing the substantial gaps in asset accumulation across ethnic minorities, gaps that public policies helped to produce? First and foremost, it should be recognized that most public policies in both countries oriented toward savings are oriented toward the more affluent.[19] Moving resources from these sorts of distributively ineffectual and expensive policies to those aimed at those with lower incomes, such as "endowment" schemes (which provide a non-means-tested, lump-sum grant to everyone), would be likely to have a dramatic effect on ethnic minorities, despite not being targeted on them. But how existing policies are structured may also have powerful effects (albeit not as powerful as policies that represent additional redistribution) on wealth accumulation, and thus on the social mobility of racial and ethnic minorities.

The structure of in-work benefits illustrates such policies. Both the USA and Britain have increased redistribution to the working poor over the last decade, in the USA through the Earned Income Tax Credit (EITC), and in Britain through the Working Families Tax Credit (WFTC).[20] The basic structure of both programs is quite similar, but they differ substantially in their mode of delivery and generosity. Both subsidize low-wage labor by eliminating taxation for some poor persons, and by creating a "negative" tax rate for others.

The spending levels of the EITC and WFTC are far from trivial, at least in comparison to past spending in the USA and UK to support the incomes of the low paid. In the USA in 1986, an unmarried woman with children who left welfare and earned $10,000 would have ended up

Table 19.4 *Persons and children lifted out of poverty by EITC, by race, 1996*

	Number lifted out of poverty by EITC (millions)	Percentage of pre-transfer poor lifted out of poverty
All Persons	4.6	**8.0 percent**
White non-Hispanic	1.8	5.5 percent
Black non-Hispanic	1.0	8.1 percent
Hispanic	1.5	14.8 percent
Children only	2.4	**14.5 percent**
White non-Hispanic	0.9	14.8 percent
Black non-Hispanic	0.5	11.0 percent
Hispanic	0.8	18.0 percent

(*Source:* Table 4 from Porter et al. 1998)

with only an additional $1,861 (in 1998 dollars) in "disposable income," once federal taxes, child-care expenses, AFDC[21] benefits, and various tax credits were taken into account, and her children would have lacked medical coverage. By 1998, the same job would have increased her disposable income by $6,876 and her children under 15 would be covered by Medicaid (Ellwood 2000: 1069). Clearly, in the USA the tax/benefit system has dramatically increased the rewards from work, and between 1992 and 1998, employment rates of the least-skilled and lowest-wage unmarried mothers grew from 33 percent to 50 percent, a "truly unprecedented rise," according to David Ellwood (2000: 1079).[22]

As would be expected from a program primarily targeted at the poor, the EITC has disproportionately benefited blacks and Hispanics. Table 19.4 (taken from Porter et al. 1998) shows that the EITC is most powerful in reducing Hispanic poverty rates – one survey estimates that about 15 percent of poor Hispanics have been lifted above the federal poverty line, compared to 8 percent of blacks and 5.5 percent of whites. The case of EITC demonstrates how social policies, even nominally neutral ones, often have dramatically different impacts across ethnic/racial groups. Hispanics are most advantaged by EITC because, while on average very poor,[23] they are more likely than blacks to be working. To the degree that work obligations push more black women into the labor market, this relative impact may diminish over time.

The British system of in-work transfers is more generous than that of the United States, but also more limited. While the EITC goes to all households with positive annual income, the British credit applies only to those working sixteen or more hours per week (Brewer 2001: 62).[24]

On the other hand, WFTC makes up a much larger percentage of the gain in income from moving from welfare to work than EITC. While in-work benefits comprise between 39–60 percent of the gain to work for a single mother with two children in the USA, similar benefits in the UK amount to 82 percent of the gain to work (Brewer 2001: 59).[25] In sum, the EITC is less than one-quarter of most families' income, while WFTC "can represent over 40 percent of total income for low-income parents" (Brewer 2001: 67). While there are clearly differences in spending levels between the two countries, both policies have dramatically increased in-work benefit caseloads over the last twenty years, as have expenditures per claimant (Brewer 2001: 63).

To speculate how this policy shift might differentially affect members of various ethnic and racial groups, it is useful to consult these groups' average earnings. Consider the UK case, where 51 percent of Pakistani and Bangladeshi working families have weekly average earnings below £149 (as compared with 24 percent for whites) (Berthoud 1998: 15). Assuming that they place their child in formal care and worked more than thirty hours per week, a family at the top of this range would receive approximately £183 – more than doubling its income. The credit would be even larger for families with lower incomes. All ethnic minority groups have higher poverty rates than that of whites,[26] ranging from 20 percent for Caribbeans to 60 percent for Pakistanis/Bangladeshis. Of particular importance for our purposes, the Caribbean and African poverty rate for working families approximates that of whites, while Indians, Pakistanis/Bangladeshis, and Chinese all had rates of poverty substantially higher than the white rate. Thus, they are most sensitive to increases in in-work benefits.[27] In sum, while there is little indication that WFTC was designed to assist ethnic minorities, the improvements that the WFTC has made on Family Credit are likely to have a substantial redistributive impact on minorities, especially the most poverty-stricken groups.

Most of the interest in this policy shift has focused on labor force attachment, but there are good reasons to believe that the new tax/benefit regime, at least in the USA, may have even broader consequences than simple redistribution. Smeeding, Phillips, and O'Connor note that EITC has an unusual, rarely commented-upon characteristic – almost all of its recipients (95 percent) choose to take it as a lump sum at the end of the year, rather than requesting that up to 60 percent be added to their weekly or monthly checks (2000: 1189). So, for example, the unmarried woman earning $10,000 mentioned above would receive a $3,656 EITC check at the end of year (more if the Dependent Care Tax Credit, which provides a refundable tax write-off for child-care expenses, is included). This is the equivalent of more than four monthly paychecks.

Smeeding, Phillips, and O'Connor investigated how EITC recipients allocated these substantial lump sums, dividing the uses between what they called "making ends meet" (paying regular bills, purchasing clothing, household appliances, and furniture) and "social mobility" (debt-reduction, tuition and medical bills, car payments, moving expenses, home improvements, and saving). They report that almost 70 percent of those receiving the EITC planned to use it, at least in part, for some social-mobility-related purpose (2000: 1200). They conclude that "the EITC does seem to provide opportunities for investments that may not be as likely were those beneficiaries to receive a smaller but continuous transfer during the previous year" (ibid.). These findings suggest that EITC recipients were using their refund at least in part as a form of "forced saving" by denying themselves their refund until the end of the year and then using it at least in part for mobility-related purposes.[28]

However, there is one very significant difference between WFTC and EITC, stemming from the manner in which the credits are administered, which may have significant effects on social mobility. Unlike the EITC, the WFTC can only be taken in the weekly or monthly pay packet and thus is probably more likely simply to increase consumption. Policymakers presumably took this approach to increase work levels, on the belief that an immediate, rather than delayed credit, would have more powerful effects. However, even with the end-of-the-year payment, EITC seems to have increased work levels. Controlling for levels of income-supplements, the American approach may be preferable to policymakers who seek to facilitate ethnic minorities' rates of social mobility.

4   Crime, criminal justice regimes, and social mobility outcomes

In this paper, we have argued for a conception of social mobility broader than that of labor market outcomes. It is thus imperative that we come to grips with crime. First, criminal behavior and/or punishment, for its perpetrator, amounts to an important social mobility "destination." Second, the degree of personal security enjoyed by law-abiding citizens is an important *determinant* of social mobility, arguably as important as wealth, income, or education. In this section, we chart the often surprising ways, direct and indirect, in which crime, criminality, and the incarceration regimes developed and maintained by the USA and Great Britain affect the social mobility of different ethnic minorities.

Criminal behavior has widespread effects: on the criminal, and those with whom he shares strong ties; the victims, and their networks of family and others; and the character of the community in which both criminal and victim are situated. Crime's potential effects upon the criminal are obvious – the criminal gains psychic or material benefits from the commission of a crime but risks incarceration, physical harm, and estrangement from the community, while forgoing other behaviors that may have produced greater long-term benefits.

The criminal's victim loses life, limb, or treasure, and also, perhaps, a more general sense of well-being. This effect will apply to the victim as an individual, but also to the victim's circle of intimates, and to some degree to the community at large, by weakening residents' sense of security. Finally, the community may be affected by crime in a number of other ways. Communities with high crime rates may: attract less business investment; suffer due to their residents' withdrawal from civic, social, and political participation; experience a shortage of marriageable men;[29] induce the exit of frightened middle-class members and their resources, including their tax contributions; and stigmatize residents as "bad risks" among employers, creditors, and others. To the degree that ethnic minorities are spatially situated in communities with high levels of crime, we expect that, in some combination with other measures of status attainment, they will achieve lower levels of social mobility.

How, then, do crime and punishment interact with other forces under discussion in this paper? To what degree are certain ethnic minorities disproportionately victims of crime, situated in neighborhoods with greater-than-average levels of crime, or criminals themselves? And how do these outcomes vary across the two polities?

In Britain, blacks[30] make up 11 percent of the prison population, or six times their share of the general population (Smith 1997: 127). In addition, ethnic minorities who are in prison are more likely to be serving longer sentences than whites (defined as four years or more) (Home Office 2000: 41). The disproportion is especially large for certain crimes, such as drug-related offenses, for which blacks are twenty-six times more likely to be imprisoned, controlling for their share of the general population, and rape and robbery, for which they are eight times more likely than whites to be imprisoned (Smith 1997: 131). South Asians, on the other hand, are not generally marked by higher levels of incarceration, with the large exceptions of drug offenses (for which they are over four times more likely to be incarcerated than whites), and fraud (for which they are incarcerated at two and one-half times the white rate) (ibid.).

What explains the dramatically higher rates of criminalization among Afro-Caribbeans? In their landmark work, *Crime in the Making*, Robert Sampson and John Laub found that weak marital attachment and unstable labor force participation were critical factors in determining whether individuals with difficult childhood backgrounds were more likely to engage in crime (Sampson and Laub 1993: 240).[31] In other research, Sampson found that these factors applied more specifically: "rates of black violent offending, especially by juveniles, are strongly influenced by variations in family structure . . . the effects of family structure are strong and cannot be easily dismissed by reference to other structural and cultural features of urban environments" (Sampson 1987: 376–7).[32]

More Afro-Caribbeans are single than married, a pattern utterly unlike that of any other ethnic group in British society (Modood et al. 1997: 24).[33] Forty-seven percent of Caribbean families are headed by a never-married woman, as compared to 16 percent of whites and negligible percentages of other groups (Modood et al. 1997: 35). One possible mechanism by which family structure affects the propensity for criminal behavior could be that children from single-parent families are subject to less stringent supervision and control, or that they had experienced high levels of family disruption. But Sampson and Laub's work suggests a more likely cause: high rates of female-headed families mean that more adult men live alone. This means that they lack the need to give an account of themselves on a daily basis, and that their everyday socialization occurs among other unattached males. Sixty-three percent of Caribbean men between the ages of 22–35 are "unattached," as compared to 47 percent of whites, 31 percent of Indians, and 23 percent of Bangladeshis/Pakistanis (Berthoud 1999: 31).

In addition to the relatively greater isolation of Afro-Caribbean men, their position in the British labor market is especially difficult. Among non-manual workers, Afro-Caribbean men have an unemployment rate of 24 percent (versus 8 percent for whites), and among manual workers, the problem is worse (28 percent versus 17 percent) (Modood et al. 1997: 94). For young men, the rates are even higher (for managed 20–24 years the rate is 34 percent versus 14 percent of whites) (Berthoud 1999: 43). This gap narrows somewhat at higher ages, but at least with respect to crime, it is too late: serious involvement in crime occurs in great part among the young. In short, setting aside some obviously important childhood experiences, the combination of the relative absence of marital and labor force attachments among young Caribbean men becomes a dangerous concoction, leaving them without many of the social bonds that prevent criminality among other poor minority groups. At least on the matter of criminal behavior, this suggests the existence of a common path shared by many Afro-Caribbeans and American blacks, both in terms of rates of offending as well as certain causal factors. Despite their similar risk profile for engaging in criminal behavior, there is one critical factor that differentiates the two groups, sharply: the nature of their countries' criminal justice regimes. Afro-Caribbeans and American blacks are being compared here not because of phenotypic similarities, but because they are the social groups with the most disproportionate rates of criminal behavior. Along other dimensions, especially cultural integration into their home societies, the two groups share little. We take up this matter below.

As stated above, criminal victimization must be included in an analysis of social mobility. Lesser, but still substantial, disproportionate rates of victimization occur as well. Afro-Caribbeans are significantly more likely to be the victim of a physical attack than whites: 5 percent reported such an attack in the previous twelve months, versus 3 percent for whites, 2 percent for African-Asians and Indians, 4 percent for Pakistanis, 3 percent for Bangladeshis, and 1 percent for Chinese (Smith 1997: 265). They are also much more likely to be the victims of murder: between 1996/7 and 1998/9, 8 percent of all homicide victims in Britain were "black" (a disproportion of approximately 4:1), while Asians comprised 6 percent of homicide victims (a disproportion of approximately 2:1) (Home Office 2000: 17). Shooting deaths were particularly prevalent among British blacks: 37 percent of all murders for blacks, but just 5 percent for whites (ibid.: 18).

A wider range of statistics on crime and victimization of racial/ethnic minorities are available in the United States, and here blacks stand out both for their rates of victimization and for their rates of offending and incarceration. In 1997, African-Americans were more than eight times as likely to be imprisoned than whites in the USA, as compared to six times for blacks in Great Britain (relative to whites). But the relative proportions conceal the fact that blacks in Britain are disproportionately imprisoned in a system that incarcerates significantly fewer people on the whole than does the United States. For example, 3.2 percent of all black males were imprisoned in 1997, as were 1.3 percent of Hispanics, compared to less than 0.4 percent of whites. The numbers for younger offenders are especially shocking: 8.6 percent of black males between the ages of 25–29 are imprisoned, compared to 0.9 percent of whites (All figures: Bureau of Justice Statistics 1999: Table 15). By way of comparison, approximately 1.7 percent of all black males were imprisoned in Great Britain in 1998, and 0.25 percent of all "Asian" males.[34]

In exploring the consequences of criminal regimes, the issue of drugs is paramount. Blacks in both countries are disproportionately incarcerated for drug-related crimes, a pattern that does not appear to track actual drug *use* (Substance Abuse and Mental Health 1998, Office of National Statistics 1996). To judge how important these disproportionate rates are in the lives of British and American blacks – that is, to isolate one important social mobility-related outcome of the criminal justice regime – we compare the proportions of the two populations that were, at any one time, incarcerated on drug charges. In the United States, 0.36 percent of the black population is in state or local prison for drug charges, while in Britain 0.17 percent is in prison. Thus, more than twice as many blacks per capita are imprisoned in the USA; and this proportion, because it excludes federal prisoners, is probably conservative.[35] These are rough estimates, but they do give a sense of the impact of the drug enforcement regime in the two countries.

In both countries, the racial disproportion in the prison population roughly approximates patterns of actual offending. But the important fact to keep in mind here is that the American criminal justice system is *dramatically* more dependent upon incarceration than the British system, and is becoming more so, both in absolute and in relative terms.[36] The two countries differ substantially in terms of severity of sentence. The average murder sentence in the USA is 266 months, compared to 230 in Britain, the result of a dramatic increase in severity on the British side between the mid-1980s and mid-1990s (Langan and Farrington 1998: 31). But this growing similarity does not carry over to rape and robbery, for which American sentences double those of Britain (ibid.).

The two systems differ mainly in how they treat the less severe, and more common, forms of crime. In the USA, 62 percent of convicted assaulters, 60 percent of burglars, and 55 percent of motor vehicle thieves are sentenced to incarceration (as compared to 27 percent, 38 percent, and 30 percent, respectively, in Great Britain) (ibid.: 23). Sentencing differentials are even greater for these lesser crimes than for more severe ones, on average approximately three times more so in the USA than in England and Wales (ibid.: 31).[37]

Things were not always so. Twenty-five years ago, in the living memory of most Americans and Britons, the exact inverse of this pattern held true. Britain incarcerated a much larger percentage of convicted felons than did the USA, and featured a much lower rate of crime. Examining the subject, James Q. Wilson found that in 1971, "England, which had only one-sixth the number of reported robberies, actually sent more persons to prison or its equivalent than did the state of California" (Wilson 1976: 19). In 1973, there were 1,680 murders and 72,750 robberies in New York, but only 110 murders and 2,680 robberies in London (ibid.: 6).

Presumably, rates of victimization and offending for ethnic minorities tracked the overall rate twenty-five years ago, but crime data by ethnicity, to the degree they were collected at all, were held very closely by the Home Office. Since then, for all but the most violent crimes (such as rape and murder), British and American rates of crime have substantially converged. Britain now features more per capita assault, burglary, and motor vehicle theft; in the case of the last two, about *twice* as much as the USA (Langan and Farrington 1998, 4–5). Most of the patterns we have been describing, in short, are of quite recent vintage. Britain was once a much more orderly society than the USA, and also a more punitive one: the USA was once more disorderly, and less punitive. Ethnic minorities in Britain once had the advantage of living in a remarkably orderly and lawful society, albeit one with unquestionably differential rates of harassment by the police. Both these advantages and disadvantages appear to have waned significantly. Criminal justice outcomes in the USA constitute a much more pervasive influence on the life chances of criminals, and of social groups with high rates of criminality, than they do in Great Britain. What might those outcomes be? Criminal activity is more widely studied as a *consequence* than as a *cause* of socioeconomic status. Obviously the former is important – poor people steal cars more often than the rich for a reason. Of course, only a small minority of poor persons engages in criminal behavior, in part because of the mediating effects on socioeconomic status of family and neighborhood. That said, there are reasons to believe that crime has a number of important effects on social mobility, especially when understood within the larger arguments of this chapter. Below, we focus on three: labor market effects; suburbanization; and neighborhood effects.

Labor market effects

Crime and legal employment are not, as sometimes assumed, mutually exclusive. In fact, up to one-quarter of all criminals in the USA held legitimate jobs at the same time as they were committing crimes. Thus, it is impossible to cleanly divide impacts of punishment on the "law-abiding" and "criminal" population: punishing criminals will inevitably affect both their legal and illegal earnings. Richard Freeman found that "a young man incarcerated in 1979 worked about 25 percent less in the ensuing eight years than a young man who had not gone to prison" (Freeman 1995: 188).[38] Other studies come to similar conclusions. It is unclear whether this relationship is due to one's engaging in criminal behavior itself, or the punishment that may result from it; for public policy purposes, this question would be critical. If the former holds, then it is primarily *the extent of criminal behavior* that would have the largest effect on social mobility, and the extent to which policy was deterring crime would be the primary factor affecting employment. If the latter holds, then it is *the shape of the criminal justice regime* that would be crucial, and limiting the damage wrought by incarceration, as opposed to probation or other alternative means of treatment and punishment, would be essential.

Most of the evidence on this question seems to point to "punishment" rather than "criminal behavior" (ibid.: 189). This conclusion is advanced with caution, for a number of reasons. First, criminal behavior is harder to measure than punishment status, thereby raising uncertainty over the labor market outcomes of different regimes. Second, there are sound reasons to believe that engaging in crime itself affects social mobility. For example, the availability of illegal work may create incentives for moving back and forth between licit and illicit economies, thereby creating gaps in one's employment record. Third, it is quite difficult to disentangle punishment from the offending that leads to it. That said, the empirical ties between punishment and employment are more direct and speak for themselves. Substantial numbers of jobs flatly forbid those with a criminal record from employment, while many others use criminal background as an informal disqualification (at least when labor markets are sufficiently loose to allow flexibility in choosing applicants). A prison sentence usually means that an individual must cease his legal employment, possibly having to re-enter the labor market at a lower level than he exited it, and having lost whatever wages, on-the-job skills, and upward mobility he would have otherwise secured. Finally, the very process of maneuvering through court deliberations (regardless of verdict) can create stress and time away from work, thereby increasing one's risk of being fired. All of these factors suggest that we need to take seriously the incarceration levels of different groups as a causal force in affecting labor market outcomes.

Crime is also likely to affect the community in which an individual is embedded. We differentiate between two types of such effects: suburbanization and neighborhood effects.

Suburbanization

Most ethnic minority groups in both the USA and Britain are located in central cities. Therefore, the political and economic condition of central cities is of special importance to the quality of life experienced by individuals in these groups. The financial health of an urban area may determine the levels of resources allocated to schools, streets, economic development, and urban amenities. What is more, the presence of substantial numbers of middle- and upper-class individuals in an urban jurisdiction may provide the city's civic organizations with financial and other forms of support. Finally, the exodus of middle- and upper-class individuals from cities substantially suppresses the demand for urban housing, leading to declining property values.

Obviously, a large number of factors affect suburbanization: economic and cultural changes, racial animus, and public policy. In addition to these, evidence from the USA strongly suggests that crime spurs suburbanization. Cullen and Levitt find that in the USA, "each reported city crime is associated with approximately a one person decline in city residents" and that "migration decisions of high-income households are much more responsive to changes in crime rates than those of the poor" (1999: 167). Shihadeh and Ousey (1996) find that the degree of suburbanization is itself a significant predictor of black center-city crime. The two claims need not be competing: there is every reason to believe that urban crime causes suburbanization, which then reduces informal social control and concentration effects, thereby increasing crime and further increasing suburbanization.

Neighborhood effects

Crime also has consequences for the neighborhood in which it is committed. To the degree that ethnic minorities live in neighborhoods with higher rates of crime, they will face these neighborhood effects as well. Neighborhood effects are of varying sorts. The most obvious is that children raised in neighborhoods with high rates of crime may have to develop a repertoire of situational identities, some even violent, simply as a form of self-protection, identities that make involvement with the judicial system highly likely (Anderson 1999). In addition, a high rate of neighborhood crime tends to lower the bar on what is considered acceptable individual behavior: what would be punishable (privately or publicly) in a low-crime neighborhood may seem trivial in one with a high crime rate.[39] Because ethnic minorities are located in neighborhoods with higher crime rates, they may be forced to accept behavior in their neighbors that they would otherwise prefer to see sanctioned, and to find their children socialized into those same standards, unless they can generate strong group-specific countermeasures.

High-crime areas are also likely to be subject to different patterns of policing than low-crime areas, in part because of police officers' fears for their own safety. Whereas low-crime areas can adopt what James Q. Wilson (1968) called a "service strategy," high-crime areas are more likely to be subject to an "occupying army" or "respond and retreat" approach. The consequence of this is that police officers spend little of their time on order maintenance and most of it responding to discrete violations of law. This is especially likely where police use the racial make-up of a community as a cue for policing strategy, or when relations between the police and the community are frayed.[40]

So how might we judge the differences in criminal justice regimes in the USA and UK in their impact on ethnic minorities? Perhaps equivocally. On the one hand, were they operating under contemporary US laws, roughly twice as many British blacks (mainly Afro-Caribbeans) would be imprisoned, and therefore twice as many British blacks would have a prison record.[41] Conversely, were they in the British system, half of the black Americans currently in prison would probably be out in the streets and would not have a prison record.

On the other hand, rates of criminal activity in the two countries appear to be diverging quite sharply. Between 1994 and 1998, the murder rate dropped 30 percent in the United States (US Department of Justice 1999: 15). Of more importance for this study, 6,619 black persons were murdered in the USA in 1998, down from 9,694 in 1995, a 32 percent drop in four years. It would be too rash to argue that increases in incarceration in the USA have reduced rates of offending, and downright implausible to argue that increased incarceration has reduced drug trafficking – everything we know about the operation of the drug market suggests that incarceration simply moves new drug dealers into the slots opened up by those in prison (Kleiman 1997). On the other hand, there is some evidence to suggest that increased incarceration, in combination with changes in policing and the buoyant economy, have reduced rates of violent and property crime. Britain, at least in recent years, has followed an opposite path, reducing quite dramatically the days of prison risked by any given crime. Rates of almost all crimes have risen at a rapid pace over the last two decades. Since ethnic minorities are more likely to be victims of crime, and more likely to live in cities which suffer middle-class flight when crime increases, this must be considered a disturbing outcome, whatever its causes.

If there is a larger point that issues from the foregoing analysis, it is this: at least some ethnic minorities in both countries are disproportionately likely to be the victims of crime, to live in neighborhoods with high levels of crime, and to suffer from the side effects of incarceration-based responses to it. Both countries desperately need to do more to reduce crime in ways that rely as little as possible on increases in prison populations, through, especially in Britain, increases in the number of police and, probably more important, by the way they are deployed and administered. Especially in the USA, the most important such change would be the expansion of non-prison punishments that can control criminals, impose real punishment outside of prison, and reduce their likelihood of recidivism (see Kleiman and Teles 2000).

5   Health, healthcare access, and social mobility

If one were to ask most reasonably intelligent nonspecialists to identify the most important differences between American and British society, two common answers would be that Britain is a substantially more orderly society than the USA, and that Britain, unlike the USA, features a national health service that delivers care free to all citizens. While the former, as the last section makes clear, is increasingly untrue, Britain does continue to maintain a system of nationalized healthcare, while the United States has a combination of private and public insurance, accompanied by a large uninsured population. In this final section we ask how health policy contributes to the social mobility prospects of ethnic minorities. In one sense, health is an end in itself: many people would trade off large amounts of annual income for longer life expectancy, responsive healthcare, and fewer health problems. As such, the quality of health and healthcare are relevant to measures of social mobility. In another sense, health and healthcare can have important effects on other dimensions of social mobility: for instance, prolonged illness can interrupt career trajectories and drain family assets.

Unlike the last two sections, our conclusion here is much less equivocal – ethnic minorities in Britain appear to be substantially advantaged relative to their American counterparts by living in a polity in which healthcare is free at the point of use and unconnected to employment status. While larger social forces seem to generate substantial inequalities in the underlying health of different groups, America's healthcare system tends to *reinforce* those factors that exacerbate health inequalities. In Britain, the healthcare system *ameliorates* or at least does not exacerbate these forces. What problems there are with the British healthcare system are not primarily distributive, but systemic; these chiefly include long waits for procedures and backlogs with specialists caused by insufficient commitment of resources. But whereas in the United States the entire healthcare debate centers around profound distributive questions, primarily due to the division between those with and without private healthcare, in Britain there is a basic commonality of interest in healthcare reform among ethnic minorities and whites, all of whom have to deal with more or less the same system.[42] Improvements generated by the power of the (white) political majority ultimately redound to the advantage of the poor and ethnic minorities, in a way that does not happen automatically in the American system.[43]

Here, we examine the overall health of ethnic minorities in Britain and the USA, then consider access to care, and then draw some conclusions concerning the importance of regime differences in the delivery of medical care. We separate health from healthcare for an important analytical reason – to a large degree, health is a function of forces outside of the formal provision of medical services. As important as preventive medical care is, diet, exercise, access to clean air and water, and neighborhood risks are more important in determining why members of some groups are more frequently ill, on average, than others. These factors, like others discussed in this chapter, are the result of socio-economic status mediated by group-specific characteristics. Usually, poor health tracks along with other forms of privation. The primary question here is how the underlying inequalities in health across social groups are either reinforced, or ameliorated, by the structure of the healthcare system itself.[44]

The health of ethnic minorities in the USA

In the United States, both health surveys and other data make clear that black and Hispanic[45] populations suffer from substantially worse levels of overall health than whites, and for some subpopulations these differences are truly disturbing. Taking self-reported well-being first, 68 percent of whites aged 18–64 reported being in excellent or very good physical health, compared to 56 percent of blacks and 54 percent of Hispanics (Weigers and Drilea 1999). More objective measures corroborate these figures for blacks, although not uniformly for Hispanics. One objective measure of health status is the ratio of minority to white death rates. Hispanics have slightly higher death rates from ages 1–44, but lower rates than whites thereafter, while Asian/Pacific Islanders have lower rates than whites at every age level (Nickens 1995: 154). Blacks, on the other hand, have dramatically higher death rates than whites, in some cases more than twice the white rate: this does not equalize until around age 80 (ibid.).[46] The black–Hispanic difference is especially perplexing, given both groups' combination of low income and poor access to health services (as will be described below). Nickens observes that "were it not for Hispanic health data, researchers might conclude that poverty overwhelmingly drives health status" (ibid.: 150).

This black–Hispanic difference reflects, and may be driven by, the many distinct characteristics of these two groups that exist despite their common economic fortunes: Hispanics are more likely to be raised in two-parent households than blacks, and to face lower levels of segregation and discrimination. They also have lower rates of criminal offending and victimization, and have higher rates of labor force participation. The impact of this difference on health can be seen, for example, in studies that have examined the correlation of residential segregation and health. Collins and Williams found that mortality is positively correlated with residential segregation (as measured by black social isolation), net of socio-economic status (1999: 509–10). In a study of thirty-eight large metropolitan areas, Polednak found that segregation was a much better predictor of infant mortality rates than the black poverty rate (1996: 101). This mirrors the "concentration effects" that other analysts have found in such areas as crime and labor force participation.

Overall, blacks have more difficulty being born than whites and other minorities.[47] Life expectancy at birth is a full eight years lower for black men than white men, and five and one-half years for black women (Collins, Hall, and Neuhaus 1999: 25–6). Infant mortality rates are dramatically higher for blacks: 14 percent, versus 6 percent for whites. Interestingly, there is no significant difference in Hispanic infant mortality rates, and the rate for Asian-Americans, at 5 percent, is actually lower than that for whites (ibid.: 32). Much of this difference can be accounted for by the dramatically higher black rate of low-birthweight births: 13 percent for blacks, versus 6 percent for whites and Hispanics, and 7 percent for Asian-Americans (ibid.: 34).[48] Finally, blacks have a much higher risk of premature birth: 1.9 percent of all black births, versus 0.5 percent for whites and 0.7 percent for Hispanics (Centers for Disease Control and Prevention 1995: 6). Breaking down the black category, native blacks are much more likely to have infants with congenital anomalies than Haitians, West Indians, and Cape Verdeans (7 percent of all births versus 4 percent, 5.6 percent, and 2.9 percent respectively, versus 3 percent for whites). Similar results are found when examining "abnormal conditions": 18.6 percent of all births for native blacks, versus 9.9 percent for Haitians, 16 percent for West Indians, 5.6 percent for Cape Verdeans, and 10 percent for whites (Friedman et al. 1993: 259). Blacks and Hispanics, but not Asian-Americans, are substantially less likely than whites to receive first-trimester prenatal care (Collins, Hall, and Neuhaus 1999: 99). But this fact does not explain why similarly low levels of prenatal care between blacks and Hispanics do not translate into similar rates of problem pregnancies – controlling for prenatal care, rates of black fetal death remain at more than twice the Hispanic rates (Centers for Disease Control 1996: 18–19). Despite our emphasis in this section on health*care*, the persistent differences between native blacks and Hispanics reinforce the findings on adult mortality: *health* and *healthcare* do not always go together.

The health of ethnic minorities in Britain

In Britain, ethnic minorities on the whole have a higher probability of reporting fair or poor health, but important variations exist. Chinese, Indians, and African-Asians do not differ markedly from whites in self-reported health. *All* of the difference in ethnic minority health is generated by Caribbeans (whose self-reports on fair/poor health were 25 percent higher) and Pakistanis/Bangladeshis (who were 50 percent more likely to report fair/poor health) (Nazroo 1997: 229). However, when health quality is disaggregated by individual ailments, the picture becomes less clear. Only Pakistanis/Bangladeshis report higher rates of heart disease or severe chest pain than whites, and only Caribbeans report higher rates of hypertension (ibid.: 230–3). All ethnic minorities in Britain report much higher rates of non-insulin-dependent diabetes, by multiples ranging from two to seven (ibid.: 234). But all ethnic minorities also report substantially lower rates of respiratory disease (although most of this difference disappears when controlling for smoking) (ibid.: 235). Returning to a measure analyzed earlier in the US section, all ethnic minorities in Britain have substantially higher percentages of low-birthweight children (on average approximately 150 percent of the white rate), with rates varying from 8.8 percent for Bangladeshis to 12.4 percent for East Africans (compared to 6.6 percent for those whose mother was born in Great Britain) (Parsons, MacFarlane, and Golding 1993: 65). However, some measures show improvement in this general area. Prenatal mortality rates for all ethnic groups declined dramatically from the mid-1970s to the mid-1980s, both in absolute terms and relative to those whose mother was born in Britain (Kurtz 1993: 69).[49]

Nazroo has asked to what degree differences in self-reported health could be explained by socioeconomic differences between ethnic minorities and whites. Despite numerous controls (including age, gender, class, and housing tenure), Indians and African-Asians continued to track closely with those of whites. But none of these standard controls could account for the differences between whites and Caribbeans or Pakistanis/Bangladeshis. However, when he introduced a measure of "standard of living" with a richer set of socioeconomic controls, he found that "relative risks that were significantly greater for ethnic minorities compared with whites became no longer or only just significantly different once standard of living had been controlled" (Nazroo 1997: 250–1).[50] These findings seem to suggest that differences in health between ethnic minorities are due not to differences in medical care, but to underlying social deprivation.

Access to medical care in the USA

Most ethnic minorities in both the USA and Britain suffer from worse health than do whites. Given their poorer health, how does the healthcare system respond? Before answering this question, one important regime difference should be noted. There is little evidence that the NHS has developed special outreach programs for ethnic minorities or sought to adapt its programs to suit their particular needs. The health of ethnic minorities is not a high-profile subject, and there is no special data collection devoted to the health of ethnic minorities (which might keep their well-being at the forefront of policymakers' minds). On the other hand, there are excellent data in the United States, numerous studies examining the subject, and a number of targeted programs aimed at ethnic minorities. Simply as a question of visibility, ethnic minority health disparities have a much higher profile in the USA than in Britain.

Despite their almost invisible status in the health debate, ethnic minorities in Britain seem to be distinctly advantaged by the British healthcare system. Despite their high visibility in the USA, ethnic minorities are put at a distinct disadvantage by a system oriented around private insurance, with government acting primarily as a residual provider. Below, we describe and attempt to account for these differences.

At the most basic level, all ethnic minorities in Britain have health coverage: care through the NHS is a right of citizenship, paid for out of general revenue. By contrast, in the USA in 1996, 34 percent of Hispanics and 23 percent of blacks lacked any private or public health insurance, compared to 13 percent of whites (Kass, Weinick, and Monheit 1999: 6). Seventy-five percent of whites have private healthcare, compared to only 44 percent of Hispanics and 49 percent of blacks (ibid.: 6). Similarly large differences exist for young Americans (19–24): 59 percent of young Hispanic males and 61 percent of young black males lack health insurance, compared to 34 percent of white males.

Lacking medical insurance, blacks and Hispanics must fall back on a crazy-quilt of alternative sources of care. Fifty-three percent of Hispanics and 47 percent of blacks use a hospital emergency room as a source of medical care, as opposed to 30 percent of whites (Collins, Hall, and Neuhaus 1999: 89). What is more, adjusting for age and poverty status, African-American women are twice as likely to use an emergency room as their *usual* place of care (such adjustments erase most of the Hispanic–white difference, however) (Mays, Cochran, and Sullivan 2000: 107). Forty-six percent of Hispanics and 39 percent of blacks reported having no regular doctor, compared to 26 percent of whites (ibid.: 77). It is unlikely that access to care is the only medical care variable likely to affect the health of ethnic minorities. One person may take advantage of every opportunity for preventive care, demand more intensive attention while under a doctor's care, question a doctor's judgments and demand second opinions, and transfer to a different primary care physician when dissatisfied. Another individual may schedule or show up for preventive care intermittently, accept whatever care they are given, and defer to a doctor's judgment, even when it is not in their own interest.

There is evidence that ethnic minorities in the USA experience something closer to this latter pattern. Overall, whites are more satisfied with their care than African-Americans and Hispanics (72 percent, 66 percent, and 57 percent respectively). This greater level of overall white satisfaction may reflect, ironically, the fact that whites are more dissatisfied about particular experiences with the healthcare system, and do more about it, than African-Americans and Hispanics. For example, 9.4 percent of white women felt they were "treated badly or felt uncomfortable when getting healthcare in past year," compared to 5.5 percent of African-Americans and 8.3 percent of Hispanics" (ibid.: 112).[51] White women notice what they see as inadequate treatment more frequently than ethnic minorities, and they also seem to act on that perception: 45 percent report having changed doctors because they were dissatisfied, as compared to 33 percent of African-Americans and Hispanics (ibid.: 112), while 20.3 percent received a second medical opinion, compared to 13.7 percent of African-Americans and 12.6 percent of Hispanics (ibid.: 110). Finally, white women use discretionary care much more intensively than do ethnic minorities: 8.6 percent of white women saw a mental healthcare provider, compared to 4.1 percent of African-Americans and 4.6 percent of Hispanics, while 14.3 percent of whites were treated by a chiropractor, compared to 4.2 percent of African-Americans and 8.9 percent of Hispanics (ibid.: 110). These differences might be explained by whites' greater likelihood to be high-demanders where healthcare is concerned: both for reasons of knowledge and power, blacks and Hispanics may be more likely to react passively to the healthcare system, taking what care is given and accepting the judgments of healthcare professionals. As we show below, however, this matter is quite ambiguous; it is unclear whether the difference is caused by cultural predispositions, or rather by minorities' adaptation to their generally lower-status position in the healthcare system.

Studies that draw on administrative data, rather than survey-based research, suggest that blacks' impressions of lower-quality care have a basis in reality. Significantly, however, the brunt of this research suggests that these differences are driven primarily by type of insurance coverage, rather than by the race of the individual. Kahn et al. (1994) found that for hospitalized Medicare patients (all of whom, of course, have insurance coverage), blacks received care inferior to that received by whites within the same institution. However, "because patients who are black or from poor neighborhoods receive more of their care in urban teaching hospitals [where quality of care has been shown to be superior], there are no differences in overall process of care by race and poverty status" (ibid.: 1171). The black Medicare population is obviously not representative of blacks as a whole, since the healthcare fact most characteristic of blacks is their lower rate of insurance. Burstin, Lipsitz, and Brennan (1992) found that blacks were at higher risk of negligent care than whites, but that almost all of this difference was explained by type of insurance. They concluded that "lack of insurance, but not race, income, or gender, is the major individual socioeconomic risk factor for substandard care" (ibid.: 2387). Other studies reveal a similar pattern – racial and ethnic differences are largely (although not completely) driven by variations in insurance status (Andrulis 1998: 412–16).[52]

Access to medical care in Britain

Despite some complexities, the British story, at least where the most basic services are concerned, is the inverse of the US story. One is almost tempted to state that Britain has universal access to healthcare through the NHS, and the United States does not, and to leave it at that. However, as suggested earlier, *access* to healthcare and *utilization* are not identical. It is conceivable that, despite ethnic minorities' access to healthcare in Britain, they could receive substandard care in practice, due to different patterns of utilization. Fortunately, there are data on the British side which can help resolve this question. Two sets of studies, one based on the PSI's Fourth National Survey, and another based on the General Household Survey, posited basically the same question: controlling for self-reported illness, how extensively do ethnic minorities in Great Britain use the health service? This question taps the relevant issues much better than merely asking whether ethnic minorities use the health service at the same rate as whites, since, given their greater need (as analyzed earlier), we would expect greater use. The important question is, do ethnic minorities utilize the health service at the same rate as whites with the same need for service?

The answer, at least provisionally, seems to be "yes," with some important qualifications. Nazroo divided the PSI respondents into three categories: good/excellent, fair, and poor/very poor health. He found that ethnic minorities in all categories reported significantly higher rates of having visited a general practitioner in the last month, with the striking exception of the Chinese. Greater use as a function of need was especially marked for those in the worst health, where 69 percent of whites reported visiting a GP, compared to 89 percent of Pakistanis/Bangladeshis, 83 percent of Indians/African-Asians, and 81 percent of Caribbeans (Nazroo 1997: 253).[53] A pattern closer to parity emerged with inpatient stays in the past year. No significant differences emerged for those in the best health, small differences for those in fair health, and no significant differences for those in poor/very poor health (ibid.: 254).[54]

Smaje and LeGrand corroborate these findings with a highly useful measure of medical care use. They measure need as a function of the number of individuals reporting different types of illness. If the health service were perfectly neutral, all groups would receive the same value of care predicted by their self-reported need. They then apply a monetary value to GP, outpatient and inpatient procedures: the use measure for each group was the sum of the value of all the procedures that they received ("cost per person reporting illness"). Thus, they estimate a "use/need ratio" for each group. The use/need ratios for each group were: 1.01 for Africans, 1.09 for Indians, 1.16 for mixed/no race, 1.23 for Caribbeans, 1.33 for Pakistanis, and 1.57 for Bangladeshis (Smaje and LeGrand 1997: 11). Because of the nature of their sample, finer breakdowns by group for different kinds of service were difficult, but both those Indians and Pakistanis who reported illness had noticeably higher rates of GP utilization. On the other hand, among those reporting no illness, Indians, Pakistanis, Chinese, and mixed race respondents reported statistically significant lower rates of outpatient utilization, and Indians reported significantly lower rates of inpatient use (a use/need ratio of 0.74) (Smaje and LeGrand 1997: 13).[55]

It is unclear how much of a discrepancy must be explained here. On the one hand, for services outside the core of the health service, such as dentists, physiotherapists, psychotherapists, and social workers, all ethnic minority groups report lower levels of utilization (Nazroo 1997: 255). Clearly, ethnic minorities underutilize outpatient service, but do not appear to underutilize more costly inpatient services. While ethnic minorities see GPs at a higher rate than whites, this may be a function of their difficulty in being referred to specialists (ibid.: 254–6). Conversely, it may be due to poorer quality service, requiring repeated procedures. Finally, some groups may be overutilizing GPs because there are more doctors at this level who speak their native tongue, while there are fewer specialists (e.g., cardiologists) who speak, say, Sylheti or Gujerati. Clearly, there are important ethnic inequalities in service that the NHS could probably remedy.

As important as these differences may be, they should not obscure one central fact: the NHS spends £900 per year per Indian, £1,095 per Pakistani, £1,298 per Bangladeshi, £1,015 per Caribbean, and £836 per African reporting illness, compared to £825 per white Briton (Smaje and LeGrand 1997: 11). If these numbers are accurate, there is little reason to believe that ethnic minorities have been relegated to the more inexpensive end of the NHS, being given superficially equal care but actually a lower level of service. Quite the contrary – ethnic minorities in Britain appear to get more out of the universal system of healthcare than do whites.

Implications of regime differences on health outcomes

Why does the British system seem so much better at cutting across socio-economic disadvantage? One important difference between the two cases is their respective political economies. Ethnic minorities in Britain are less politically powerful than their counterparts in America, as measured either by the number of minority representatives in Congress or Parliament, or by the priority their claims have in political discourse. But in Britain, ethnic minorities operate within a universal system, as opposed to America's three-tiered system of private health insurance, public insurance (Medicare and Medicaid), and an uninsured population. Schoen et al. (2000) found that those with below average income in Britain reported, across a wide range of measures, a much greater satisfaction with their medical care than low-income individuals in the United States. Fifteen percent of low-income Britons stated that they found it "difficult to get needed medical care," as compared to 48 percent of low-income Americans (ibid.: 75). Thirty percent of those Britons reported difficulty in seeing a specialist, compared to 51 percent of Americans (ibid.: 75), and 16 percent of Britons stated that they had no regular doctor, compared to 37 percent of the Americans (ibid.: 77). Only on waiting for non-emergency surgery does America look substantially better than Britain from the perspective of low-income persons.

Ethnic minorities in Britain are advantaged by being situated in a healthcare system that is, in comparative terms, relatively good at serving the needs of poorer citizens. Efforts to improve, for example, the operation of HMOs, which is a central feature of the US healthcare debate, do not respond in any serious way to the needs of Hispanics and blacks, who are disproportionately outside of the system of private healthcare. In Britain, on the other hand, the central debate around healthcare concerns the overall level of spending in the system. Any increases in spending for the NHS, as are currently flowing into the system, will indirectly affect ethnic minorities. That is, given the political economy of the British healthcare system, it is not easy to make improvements in the overall system that do not redound to the advantage of ethnic minorities. In the USA, it is quite easy, through improving the quality of private healthcare, to deliver better healthcare to whites in a way that does not reach most ethnic minorities. What is more, efforts to improve the health of ethnic minorities, without addressing the overall structure of the healthcare system, are the equivalent of trying to swim upstream. At least in this area, universality (even without substantial ethnic outreach) appears significantly advantageous to ethnic minorities, as compared to a two-tiered system of care.

6   Conclusion

At this point in our research, it is reasonable to be modest as to the conclusions that follow from the foregoing analysis. For now, we are prepared only to point to a few directions that seem fruitful.

First, each of the subjects examined in this paper constitutes an independent variable affecting social mobility outcomes. Assets clearly impact prospects for status attainment and economic advancement in a number of ways. However, some policies may unintentionally be countering these effects. For example, the large lump-sum transfers in the USA to the working poor under the EITC (but not, interestingly, in Britain) may serve as a "shock absorber" akin to net financial assets to be used in difficult times. This is critical, for often when we think of social mobility, the importance of defending against downward mobility is overlooked.

Second, each is a significant dependent variable in that each serves as a "destination" of social mobility; often, these dependent variables are influenced causally by one another. For example, high-crime areas are inimical to asset accumulation; health suffers in high-crime areas.[56] Meanwhile, the lack of net financial assets among most, and especially poor, African-American households contributes to crime rates.[57]

Third, in each policy area, state policies and features of the polity unrelated to politicians' electoral or policy goals vis-à-vis ethnic minorities were often *more* influential on social mobility outcomes than those policies and features of the polity that were *directly* designed to influence these outcomes. That is, the generic structure of the policy regime, at least within the subjects we analyzed in this paper, seems more important than whatever ethnic targeting occurs within that larger structure. Of greater importance is the way that those generic policies interact with group-specific characteristics, and the outcome of that interaction, especially where it appears highly damaging (for example, the very high rates of incarceration for young black men). But this, as with our other conclusions, is highly preliminary.

NOTES

1. For an argument that indices of "occupational status" are undertheorized as a way to get at socioeconomic status, see Hodge 1981.
2. See, for example, Waldinger 1996, especially Chapters 6 and 7.
3. For a review of studies and strong new evidence of this link, see Ashenfelter and Rouse 2000.
4. Conley's own multivariate analysis points to parents' liquid assets, but not their net illiquid assets, or even the child's race or family structure, as statistically significant and sizable predictors of college graduation (72–3).
5. As the authors note, their findings probably underestimate the problem, given the numbers of potential entrepreneurs dissuaded from attempting to develop businesses because of their (seemingly accurate) perceptions of racial discrimination (25–8).
6. Of course, comparisons of *mean* household wealth greatly inflate this race differential.

7. Stack 1972 offers the former view. See Hogan, Eggebeen, and Clogg 1993. These findings are corroborated in Benin and Keith 1995.

8. Conley 1999: 26, using a different data set, concurs with Oliver and Shapiro that the median African-American household possesses zero financial assets. His data are from 1994.

9. Thus, these data do not allow us to draw inferences concerning Hispanic vs. African-American vs. Asian-American differences.

10. For example, see Conley 1999: 29, who reviews some findings.

11. Several of these models are reviewed in Lundberg and Starz 2000.

12. This argument is supported by the outcomes of the Moving To Opportunity program in the United States, which helped to place public housing residents in the suburbs. Katz, Kling, and Liebman 2001.

13. Those same policies, of course, also helped to fuel the out-migration of whites from central cities into highly segregated suburbs. See Sugrue 1996, Hirsch 1983, Jackson, 1985.

14. One substantial exception to the paucity of analysis in this area is found in Warren and Britton 2003. The primary problem with replicating the research done on the American side of this paper is the small number of ethnic minorities in Britain's main source of panel data, the British Household Panel Survey.

15. Social housing includes both that provided by local government ("council housing") and that provided by not-for-profit housing associations.

16. All of the tables in this section are based on the Financial Resources Survey (FRS), pooling data from the years 1994/5 through 1997/8, with the exception of income data, which is taken from the Households Below Average Income (HBAI) survey. Details on the methodology used in generating this analysis can be found at: http://people.brundeis.edu/~teles/. Housing equity data is presented relative to whites, rather than in absolute terms, both for ease of presentation and to prevent the need to adjust home values across years. In addition, the reader should take note, in particular, of the relatively low sample sizes for Bangladeshis and Chinese, and thus interpret the data on these groups with this in mind. Finally, while we report data for Black Africans, we are hesitant to interpret these figures, in part because of the very substantial heterogeneity of the group, coming as they do from such disparate backgrounds, and because the age distribution of the group is so substantially tilted toward the under-40 cohort that little of interest can be said about change in the group over time.

17. These numbers are non-tabulated.

18. While we report figures for Bangladeshis broken down by income and age, the size of the sample for Bangladeshis makes reading too much into these figures hazardous, and so in the text we rely primarily on group averages.

19. Orszag and Greenstein (2000: 8) find that only 1 percent of the present value tax expenditure benefit from pensions and IRAs goes to the bottom 20 percent of families, while 66.4 percent goes to the top 20 percent.

20. A good summary of the WFTC can be found at http://www.inlandrevenue.gov.uk/wftc/index.htm.

21. AFDC (Aid to Families with Dependent Children) was, until the 1996 Personal Responsibility and Work Opportunity Act, the program that most Americans referred to when they discussed "welfare." Post-reform, the program is now called TANF (Temporary Assistance for Needy Families).

22. Ellwood gives equal credit to changes in welfare policy and the strength of the economy as an explanation for this shift in labor force participation.

23. For example, 27.2 percent of Hispanics live in households with annual income under $25,000 (US Department of Commerce 2003).

24. Brewer's calculations of the EITC in the USA are slightly different than Ellwood's, and based on different years, so the reader should note that the studies are not exactly comparable.

25. The difference is even sharper when one examines part-time, minimum wage work, where WFTC makes up over 100 percent of the gain to work, and for some families amounts to over 200 percent of the gain.

26. Poverty here defined as 50 percent or less of average income.

27. The low rate of Caribbean working poverty might seem initially surprising, given the group's lower overall income than Indians. However, much of the lower rates of Caribbean income is explained by low rates of economic activity.

28. Romich and Weisner (2000), in an ethnographic study of EITC recipients in Wisconsin, found strong evidence for the use of lump-sum receipt of EITC as a self-control mechanism.

29. This is true especially if crime is accompanied by high levels of incarceration, as opposed to other means of punishment.

30. Crime statistics in Britain do not break down on an ethnic basis, as do those from the Modood et al. (1997) study, but on a racial basis – hence the term "black" rather than the more descriptive "African" or "Afro-Caribbean."

31. Sampson and Laub's model is developmental in nature – marital and labor force attachment are factors which determine whether individuals who had already had a history of delinquency moved on to a life of crime. Other factors determined whether individuals had a predisposition to delinquency, such as family disruption, poverty, poor education, etc.

32. In this detailed analysis of mid-century cases, Sampson also found that joblessness had an important impact on criminality, but primarily through its effects on family disruption.

33. Despite this significant variation from the pattern of all other groups, it is important to be very hesitant before attributing this pattern to inherited cultural patterns from Caribbeans' countries of origin. In 1974, the Caribbean rate of lone parenting was only 13 percent, but by 1982 it had risen. This suggests that explanations for this pattern need to begin with factors in British society, such as the economic position of Caribbean men relative to Caribbean women, and cultural changes within British society which may have disproportionately affected this group. One interpretation of those factors can be found in Dench 1996.

34. The black figure was taken by dividing the total number of black males in prison (approximately 7,388, Bureau of Justice Statistics 1999 : Table 7.1) by the total number of black males in the population, based on the British

census (approximately 445,000). The "Asian" (meaning Indian, Pakistani, or Bangladeshi) figure was derived by dividing the total number of Asian males in prison (1,878, Bureau of Justice Statistics 1999: Table 7.1) by the total number of Asian males in the population (approximately 740,000). These numbers are meant to give a rough approximation, but we do not claim for them absolute scientific precision.

35. The US numbers came from dividing the entire black population, 35 million, into the total number of blacks in prison for drugs offenses, 127,000 (Bureau of Justice Statistics 1999). The GB figures came from dividing the total number of blacks (based on the 1991 census), 890,700, by the total number of blacks in prison for drugs offenses, 1,500 (Home Office 2000: 44).

36. For the most severe crimes, rates of incarceration across the two countries are not much different: 96 percent of murderers in the USA are sentenced to some term of incarceration, compared to 94 percent in England and Wales; and in England and Wales, convicted rapists are substantially *more* likely to be sent to prison (95 percent versus 82 percent). Differentials are also relatively low for robbers, with 79 percent of convicted US robbers sentenced to incarceration, compared to 67 percent in England and Wales (a differential that did not emerge before the mid-1980s) (Langan and Farrington 1998: 23).

37. These differentials in sentencing closely track with those in actual time served (Langan and Farrington 1998: 33).

38. Asking a similar question, Grogger found that arrests had a strong impact on unemployment, explaining between a third and two-thirds of the black/white employment differential.

39. Daniel Patrick Moynihan (1996: 136–67) calls this process "defining deviancy down." Drawing on Durkheim and Kai Erikson, he argues that the recognition of deviancy is essentially zero-sum: increases in more serious crimes mean that lesser offenses must be redefined as normal. Not to do so would be to overstress the supervisory and punishment instruments of any community.

40. On the difference between "crime control" and "order maintenance" as alternative policing strategies, see Kelling and Coles 1996. For an interesting analysis of how race and policing can influence each other, and how one city seems to have pulled itself out of highly conflictual police–black community relations, see Winship 1999.

41. That is, unless they changed their rate of offending in response to higher rates of incarceration.

42. The statement that ethnic minorities and whites deal with "more or less the same system" is certainly true when compared with the United States, so long as the phrase "more or less" is kept in mind. Some wealthier individuals in Great Britain have access to supplemental private insurance, which allows them to avoid lengthy waits for procedures and to have access to more comfortable hospital rooms.

43. An excellent analysis of the political consequences of universal programs on disadvantaged populations can be found in Skocpol 1995.

44. Healthcare is, of course, an enormously complex area of study, accounting in and of itself for one-seventh of the American and one-fourteenth of the British economy – by necessity this section will only skim the surface, both for reasons of space and due to the preliminary nature of our research.

45. "Hispanic" is obviously not a very helpful category, conflating as it does a large number of groups with quite variant characteristics on matters of interest. We use this category in the USA, as we did "black" in Britain, because the collection of statistics left us no other choice.

46. This higher black survival rate after age eighty has been hypothesized to be driven by a form of survivor bias: blacks who make it to age eighty represent a much smaller slice of black births than is the case for whites, and one that is selected for superior underlying health (such as genetic predisposition to illness).

47. Infant mortality is a critical indicator, since there are reasons to believe that at least some of the differential in later-life outcomes for various ethnic groups may be explained by the conditions of their birth. Low-birthweight children have a significantly higher chance of having very low (<70 IQ) or subnormal intelligence (70–84 IQ), as well as a greater risk of educationally sensitive behavioral disorders, such as difficulty concentrating and hyperactivity (Hack, Klein, and Taylor 1995). This suggests that the mechanisms of intergenerational disadvantage among American blacks operate directly through biological, in addition to the usual socioeconomic, mechanisms.

48. Blacks are especially at risk of giving birth to very low (less than 1500 grams) birthweight babies: 2.7 percent of all black births, versus 0.9 percent for whites and 1 percent of Hispanics (Centers for Disease Control 1995: 6).

49. Despite this improvement, rates of prenatal mortality were still higher for most ethnic minorities, dramatically so for Pakistanis.

50. Nazroo's standard of living measure included overcrowded accommodation, lacking sole access to one or more amenity, few consumer durables, and number of cars. Pakistanis/Bangladeshis reported extremely low levels of standard of living – 50 percent were poor versus 8 percent for whites, while only 9 percent reported good, versus 43 percent of whites. Both Indians and Caribbeans reported lower levels than whites, but nowhere near the Pakistani/Bangladeshi rates (Nazroo 1997: 249).

51. All the data reported in this paragraph are adjusted for age and poverty status.

52. See also Hargreaves 2000.

53. The Chinese figures, at 45 percent, were very low, but were also based on a very small number of observations, rendering them unreliable.

54. Again, Chinese use of the health service was markedly lower than for other groups, but the same caution noted before applies here as well.

55. Nazroo 1997 also found a discrepancy between GP and other, more expensive forms of service. Peculiarly, what lower levels of use there appear to be are for those reporting that they were "not sick" while those reporting illness appear to be at parity across different types of service.

56. The physical health of children and the emotional well-being of adults are worsened in stressful and unsafe public housing, where, for example, the presence of cockroach allergens causes alarmingly high rates of asthma among children. See Katz, Kling, and Liebman 2001.
57. See Freeman 1995 for a related argument.

REFERENCES

Anderson, E., 1999, *Code of the Street*, New York: W. W. Norton.

Andrulis, D. P., 1998, "Access to Care is the Centerpiece in the Elimination of Socioeconomic Disparities in Health," *Annals of Internal Medicine*, 129: 412–16.

Ashenfelter, O. and C. Rouse, 2000, "Schooling, Intelligence, and Income in America," in K. Arrow, S. Bowles, and S. Durlauf (eds.), *Meritocracy and Economic Inequality*, Princeton University Press, pp. 89–117.

Banks, J., R. Blundell, and J. P. Smith, 2000, "Wealth Inequality in the United States and Great Britain," London: Institute for Fiscal Studies, Working Paper 00/20.

Benin, M. and V. M. Keith, 1995, "The Social Support of Employed African American and Anglo Mothers," *Journal of Family Issues* 16, 275–97.

Berthoud, R., 1998, *The Incomes of Ethnic Minorities*, Essex: Institute for Social and Economic Research.

1999, "Young Caribbean Men and the Labour Market: A Comparison with Other Groups," Joseph Rowntree Foundation Report.

Biblarz, T. J. and A. E. Raftery, 1993, "The Effects of Family Disruption on Social Mobility," *American Sociological Review* 58: 97–109.

Blanchflower, D. G., P. B. Levine, and D. J. Zimmerman, 1998, "Discrimination in the Small Business Credit Market," Working Paper 6840, NBER Working Paper Series, Cambridge: National Bureau of Economic Research (December).

Blau, P. and O. D. Duncan, 1978, *The American Occupational Structure*, New York: Free Press.

Brewer, M., 2001, "Comparing In-work Benefits and the Reward to Work for Families with Children in the US and UK," *Fiscal Studies* (March), 41–77.

Bureau of Justice Statistics, 1999, *Prisoners in 1998*, NCJ 175687 (August).

Burstin, H. R., S. R. Lipsitz, and T. A. Brennan, 1992, "Socioeconomic Status and Risk for Substandard Medical Care," *JAMA* (November 4): 2383–7.

Centers for Disease Control and Prevention, National Center for Health Statistics, 1996, "Fetal Mortality by Maternal Education and Prenatal Care, 1990," *Vital and Health Statistics* (July).

1995, "Infant Mortality by Hispanic Origin of Mother: 20 States, 1985–1987 Birth Cohorts," *Vital and Health Statistics* (October).

Charles, K. K. and E. Hurst, 2000, "Racial Differences in the Transition to Home Ownership," paper presented at the Institute on Race and Social Division, Boston, January 12.

Chiteji, N. S. and F. P. Stafford, 1999, "Portfolio Choices of Parents and Their Children as Young Adults: Asset Accumulation by Afro-American families," *AEA Papers and Proceedings* (May).

Collins, C. and D. Williams, 1999, "Segregation and Mortality: The Deadly Effects of Racism?" *Sociological Forum* 14: 495–523.

Collins, K. S., A. Hall, and C. Neuhaus, 1999, *US Minority Health: A Chartbook*, New York: Commonwealth Fund.

Conley, D., 1999, *Being Black, Living in the Red: Race, Wealth, and Social Policy in America*, Berkeley: University of California Press.

Council of Economic Advisers, 1998, *Changing America: Indicators of Social and Economic Well Being By Race and Hispanic Origin*, Washington, DC: President's Initiative on Race.

Cullen, J. and S. Levitt, 1999, "Crime, Urban Flight, and the Consequences for Cities," *Review of Economics and Statistics*: 159–69.

Dench, G., 1996, *The Place of Men in Changing Family Structures*, London: Institute for Community Studies.

Duncan, G., 1984, *Years of Poverty, Years of Plenty*, Ann Arbor, MI: ISR.

Ellwood, D., 2000, "The Impact of the Earned Income Tax Credit and Social Policy Reforms on Work, Marriage and Living Arrangements," *National Tax Journal*, 1063–106.

Erikson, R. and J. Goldthorpe, 1992, *The Constant Flux*, Oxford: Clarendon.

Freeman, R., 1995, "The Labor Market," in J. Q. Wilson and J. Petersilia (eds.), *Crime*, San Francisco: ICS, pp. 171–91.

Friedman, D. J., B. B. Cohen, C. M. Mahan, R. I. Lederman, R. J. Vezina, V. H. Dunn, 1993, "Maternal Ethnicity and Birthweight Among Blacks," *Ethnicity and Disease*: 255–69.

Hack, M., N. K. Klein, and H. G. Taylor, 1995, "Long-term Developmental Outcomes of Low Birth Weight Infants," *The Future of Children*: 176–96.

Hargreaves, M., 2000, "Uninsurance and its Impact on Access to Health Care," in C. Hogue, M. Hargraves, and K. Collins (eds.), *Minority Health in America: Findings and Policy Implications from The Commonwealth Fund Minority Health Survey*, Baltimore: Johns Hopkins University Press, pp. 142–59.

Herbert, C. E., 1997, "Limited Choices: The Effects of Residential Segregation on Homeownership Among Blacks," PhD thesis, Harvard University.

Hirsch, A., 1983, *Making the Second Ghetto: Race and Housing in Chicago, 1940–1960*, Cambridge University Press.

Hodge, R. W., 1981, "The Measurement of Occupational Status," *Social Science Research* 10: 396–415.

Hogan, D. P., D. J. Eggebeen, and C. C. Clogg, 1993, "The Structure of Intergenerational Exchanges in American Families," *American Journal of Sociology* 98: 1428–58.

Home Office, 2000, *Statistics on Race and the Criminal Justice System*, London: HMSO.

Horowitz, D., 1985, *Ethnic Groups in Conflict*, Berkeley: University of California Press.

Investment Company Institute, 1999, *Equity Ownership in America*, Washington, DC: Investment Company Institute.

Jackson, K. T., 1985, *Crabgrass Frontier: The Suburbanization of the United States*, New York: Oxford University Press.

Joint Center for Housing Studies, 2000, *The State of the Nation's Housing: 1999*, Cambridge, MA: Joint Center for Housing Studies.

2003, *The State of the Nation's Housing: 2003*, Cambridge, MA: Joint Center for Housing Studies.

Kahn, K. L., M. L. Pearson, E. R. Harrison, K. A. Desmond, W. H. Rodgors, L. V. Rubertstein, R. H. Brook, and E. B. Celer, 1994, "Health Care for Black and Poor Hospitalized Medicare Patients," *JAMA* (April 20): 1169–74.

Kass, B. L., R. M. Weinick, and A. C. Monheit, 1999, *Racial and Ethnic Differences in Health, 1996*, Rockville, MD: Agency for Health Care Policy and Research. MEPS Chartbook No. 2. AHCPR Pub. No. 99-0001.

Katz, L. F., J. R. Kling, and J. B. Liebman, 2001, "Moving to Opportunity in Boston: Early Results of a Randomized Mobility Experiment," *Quarterly Journal of Economics* 116: 607–54.

Kelling, G. and C. Coles, 1996, *Fixing Broken Windows*, New York: Free Press.

Kleiman, M., 1997, "The Problem of Replacement and the Logic of Drug Law Enforcement," *Federation of American Scientists Drug Policy Report* (September). http://fas.org/drugs/issue3.htm#3.

Kleiman, M. and S. Teles, 2000, "Escaping the Over-incarceration Trap: A Political Strategy for Reducing America's Reliance on Prisons," *The American Prospect* (September 11): 30–4.

Kurtz, K., 1993, "Better Health for Black and Ethnic Minority Children and Young People," in A. Hopkins and V. Bahl (eds.), *Access to Health Care for People From Black and Ethnic Minorities*, London: Royal College of Physicians of London, pp. 63–87.

Langan, P. and D. Farrington, 1998, *Crime and Justice in the United States and in England and Wales*, Washington, DC: Bureau of Justice Statistics (October).

Lemann, N., 1999, *The Big Test: The Secret History of the American Meritocracy*, New York: Farrar.

Logan, J. R. and R. H. Alba, 1993, "Locational Returns to Human Capital: Minority Access to Suburban Community Resources," *Demography* 30: 243–68.

Lundberg, S. J. and R. Starz, 2000, "Inequality and Race: Models and Policy," in K. Arrow, S. Bowles, and S. Durlauf (eds.), *Meritocracy and Economic Inequality*, Princeton University Press, pp. 269–95.

Massey, D. S. and N. A. Denton, 1993, *American Apartheid: Segregation and the Making of the Underclass*, Cambridge, MA: Harvard University Press.

Massey, D. S., A. B. Gross, and K. Shibuya, 1994, "Migration, Segregation, and the Geographic Concentration of Poverty," *American Sociological Review* 59: 425–45.

Mays, V., S. Cochran, and J. G. Sullivan, 2000, "Health Care for African-American and Hispanic Women," in C. Hogue, M. Hargraves, and K. Collins (eds.), *Minority Health in America: Findings and Policy Implications from The Commonwealth Fund Minority Health Survey*, Baltimore: Johns Hopkins University Press, pp. 97–123.

McGarry, K. and A. Davenport, 1998, "Pensions and the Distribution of Wealth," in D. Wise (ed.), *Frontiers in the Economics of Aging*, University of Chicago Press, 463–85.

Modood, T., R. Berthoud, J. Lakey, J. Nazroo, P. Smith, S. Virdee, and S. Beishon, 1997, *Ethnic Minorities in Britain: Diversity and Disadvantage*, London: Policy Studies Institute.

Moynihan, D. P., 1996, *Miles To Go*, Cambridge, MA: Harvard University Press.

Nazroo, J. Y., 1997, "Health and Health Services," in Modood et al. (eds.), *Ethnic Minorities in Britain: Diversity and Disadvantage*, London: Policy Studies Institute, pp. 224–58.

Nickens, H., 1995, "The Role of Race/Ethnicity and Social Class in Minority Health Status," *Health Services Research* (April): 151–62.

Office of National Statistics, 1996, "Dataset ST29A5 – People Taking Any Drug in the Last Year, By Ethnic Group and Age: 1994–1996," London: Office of National Statistics.

2002, *Social Focus in Brief: Ethnicity 2002*, London: Office of National Statistics.

Oliver, M. L. and T. M. Shapiro, 1995, *Black Wealth/White Wealth: A New Perspective on Racial Inequality*, New York: Routledge.

Orszag, P. and R. Greenstein, 2000, "Toward Progressive Pensions: A Summary of the US Pension System and Proposals for Reform" (Prepared for the conference on "Inclusion and Asset Building: Research and Policy Symposium"), Washington University, St. Louis. http://www. sbgo.com/Papers/csdconf.pdf.

Parsons, L., A. MacFarlane, and J. Golding, 1993, "Pregnancy, Birth and Maternity Care," in W. I. U. Ahmad (ed.), *"Race" and Health in Contemporary Britain*, Buckingham: Open University Press, pp. 51–75.

Peach, C., 1998, "South Asians and Caribbean Ethnic Minority Housing Choice in Britain," *Urban Studies* 35: 1657–80.

Polednak, A., 1996, "Segregation, Discrimination and Mortality in US Blacks," *Ethnicity and Disease* (Winter/Spring): 99–108.

Porter, K. Katunju 1998, *Strengths of the Safety Net: How the EITC, Social Security and Other Government Programs Affect Poverty*, Washington, DC: Center for Budget and Poverty Priorities.

Romich, J. and T. Weisner, 2000, "How Families View and Use the EITC: Advance Payment Versus Lump Sum Delivery," *National Tax Journal*: 1245–66.

Sampson, R., 1987, "Urban Black Violence: The Effect of Male Joblessness and Family Disruption," *American Journal of Sociology*: 348–82.

Sampson, R. and J. Laub, 1993, *Crime in the Making*, Cambridge, MA: Harvard University Press.

Schoen, C., K. Davis, C. DesRoches, K. Donelan, R. Blendon, and E. Strumpf, 2000, "Health Insurance Markets and Income Inequality: Findings from an International Health Policy Survey," *Health Policy* 51: 67–85.

Shihadeh, E. and G. Ousey, 1996, "Metropolitan Expansion and Black Social Dislocation: The Link Between Suburbanization and Center-city Crime," *Social Forces*: 322–41.

Shklar, J., 1992, *American Citizenship*, Cambridge, MA: Harvard University Press.

Skocpol, T., 1995, "Targeting Within Universalism: Politically Viable Policies to Combat Poverty in the United States," in T. Skocpol (ed.), *Social Policy in the United States: Future Possibilities in Historical Perspective*, Princeton University Press, pp. 250–74.

Smaje, C. and J. LeGrand, 1997, "Ethnicity, Equity and the Use of Health Services in the British National Health Service," LSE Health Discussion Paper No. 5 (February).

Smeeding, Timothy, Katherin Ross Phillips, and Michael O'Connor, 2000, "The EITC: Expectation, Knowledge, Use and Economic and Social Mobility," *National Tax Journal* (December) 1187–210.

Smith, D., 1997, "Ethnic Origins, Crime and Criminal Justice in England and Wales," in M. Tonry (ed.), *Ethnicity, Crime and Immigration: Comparative and Cross-National Perspectives*, University of Chicago Press, pp. 101–82.

Sugrue, T., 1996, *Origins of the Urban Crisis: Race and Inequality in Postwar Detroit*, Princeton University Press.

Stack, C. B., 1972, *All Our Kin: Strategies for Survival in the Black Community*, New York: Basic Books.

Substance Abuse and Mental Health Services Administration, 1998, *National Household Survey on Drug Abuse Population Estimates 1998*, Home Office, British Crime Survey. Dataset ST29A5. Available at: http://www.samhsa.gov/OAS/NHSDA/Pe1998/Pop98web3-2-02.htm#P678_2154.

US Department of Commerce, 2003, *Statistical Abstract of the United States*, Washington, DC: GPO. Table 652: http://www.census.gov/prod/2003pubs/02statab/income.pdf.

US Department of Justice, 1999, *Crime in the United States: Uniform Crime Reports*, Washington, DC: FBI.

Waldinger, R., 1996, *Still The Promised City?* Cambridge, MA: Harvard University Press.

Warren, T and N. J. Britton, 2003, "Ethnic Diversity in Economic Wellbeing: The Combined Significance of Income, Wealth and Asset Levels," *Journal of Ethnic and Migration Studies* 29 (January): 103–19.

Weigers, M. E. and S. K. Drilea, 1999, *Health Status and Limitations: A Comparison of Hispanics, Blacks and Whites, 1996*, Rockville, MD: Agency for Health Care Policy and Research. MEPS Research Findings No. 10. AHCPR Pub. No. 00-0001.

Wilson, J. Q. 1968, *Varieties of Police Behavior*, Cambridge, MA: Harvard University Press.

1976, "Crime and Punishment in England," *The Public Interest* (Spring): 3–14.

Winship, C., 1999, "Boston Cops and Black Churches," *The Public Interest* (Summer): 52–68.

Wolff, E. N., 1998, "Recent Trends in the Size Distribution of Household Wealth," *Journal of Economic Perspectives* 12: 131–50.

Part V

Normative analysis

20 Race, inequality, and justice in the USA: some social-philosophic reflections

Glenn C. Loury

1 Introduction

The concerns of this essay are normative and conceptual. Seven generations after the end of slavery, and a half-century past the dawn of the civil rights movement, social life in the United States is still characterized by a significant degree of racial stratification and inequality. Numerous indices of well-being – wages, unemployment rates, income and wealth levels, ability test scores, incarceration and criminal victimization rates, health and mortality statistics – all reveal substantial disparity among different racial groups. Indeed, over the past quarter-century the black–white gap along some of these dimensions has remained unchanged, or even widened. Although there has been noteworthy progress in reversing historical patterns of racial subordination, there is today no scientific basis upon which to rest the prediction that a rough parity of socio-economic status between blacks and whites in the USA will obtain in the foreseeable future.[1]

"So what?" one might reasonably ask. As long as the individual members of a disadvantaged racial minority group are not being discriminated against, why should citizens in the United States, or in any liberal democracy for that matter, care about racial inequality per se? This is an important question for anyone reflecting on matters of social justice in a pluralistic society. It is especially crucial for adherents of political liberalism, who hold that a properly structured analysis of the justness of social arrangements should derive from a consideration of the welfare of individuals, and not from the economic or social position of population subgroups.

I believe this position – that only individuals and never groups can be the subjects of a discourse on social justice – to be mistaken. As such, I undertake here to criticize the manner in which liberal political theory deals with the ethical problems raised by the pronounced and durable social-economic disadvantage of African-Americans. My topic, then, is "racial justice." Now, it would be nice, were this possible, to avoid a philosopher's quibble over this use of words but, alas, I expect not to get off so easily. Taking "racial" as modifier of "justice" inevitably raises hackles, because doing so hints that the well-being of *groups* of persons – groups defined in terms of something called "race" – can have moral significance. Liberals (rightly) worry that the freedom, dignity, integrity, autonomy, and/or rights of persons may be trod underfoot in a mad rush to obtain justice for fictitious "races."[2] Just beneath the surface of what is ostensibly progressive rhetoric about "racial justice" liberals detect the distinct odor of an unjustifiable essentialism – a retrograde belief in racial essences. While acknowledging that "racial justice" talk courts these dangers, I nevertheless hold that such talk is necessary for an intellectually rigorous and historically relevant social criticism in the USA. Moreover, I think it possible to conceive of social justice in regard to matters of race in such a way that these pitfalls are avoided.

To fix ideas, consider the formidable intellectual edifice that is modern social choice theory. This literature at the junction of economics and philosophy pursues the formal, logical derivation of implications for public decision making that issue from various postulates chosen to capture our ethical intuitions about social justice.[3] A near universally imposed constraint on collective decision making in this literature is the so-called *Anonymity Axiom*. This postulate denies the ethical legitimacy of distinguishing for purposes of social choice between two states of affairs, A and B, that differ only in the identities of the people located in various positions of the social order. Thus, imagine that states of affairs A and B entail the same number of persons living in poverty, suffering from inadequate health care, held in prison, and the like, but that a different group of people suffer these conditions in state A than in state B. The Anonymity Axiom then requires that a just public decision-making process be indifferent between these two states. It follows as an immediate corollary of this requirement that the diminution of racial inequality for its own sake would not be a legitimate social goal.

I argue here against this implication of the Anonymity Axiom (and, perforce, against the axiom itself.) For, despite its apparent reasonableness, this position of race-neutrality in the realm of social justice is profoundly counterintuitive in the USA, denying as it does the appropriateness of what has been a preoccupation for progressive social critics, scholars, and activists over the past two generations. More generally, I call into question the adequacy of political liberalism as a normative theory, in view of the historical facts of racial subordination, and the continuing reality of racial inequality. There seem to be questions of social justice arising under these conditions, in societies such as the United States that are sharply stratified along racial lines, to which liberalism gives no good answers.

2   What's wrong with liberalism?

The argument to be advanced here relies on the vast body of empirical work in the social sciences that has been devoted to establishing the
central place of race in the *relational structures* that mediate social life in
the USA. These are matters having to do with patterns of family formation, with the shaping of personal identities, with adolescent peer interactions, residential segregation, and job referral networks. My position is
that the normative issues of concern require for their proper exploration
that attention be paid to patterns of interaction among persons within
and across those social boundaries that have come through history to be
organized around the category of race.[4]

This argument is also constrained by a baseline presumption that I have
elsewhere called *anti-essentialism* (Loury 2002). Explaining protracted
and durable racial inequality becomes relatively easy if one admits the
possibility of inherent racial differences in human attributes that significantly influence the ability of individuals to act effectively (intelligence,
for example). I reject this possibility *a priori*. Although adopted as a postulate, I believe this stance is empirically plausible. The evidence that
inherent racial differences can account for the observed socioeconomic
disparity between blacks and whites in the USA does not persuade me.
But I think it necessary to stipulate the anti-essentialist position *a priori* for
two reasons: one cannot prove empirically that innate racial differences do
not exist. One can only show this view to be more or less plausible, and
not everyone will be persuaded. More importantly, in a "raced" polity
committed to democratic values, public discourses imputing inherent
incapacity to some "raced" group of citizens are fundamentally inconsistent with espoused democratic ideals. Policy argument in such a political
setting, I hold, must as a matter of civic duty proceed under the maintained hypothesis of anti-essentialism.

This anti-essentialist position amounts to the assertion that, like the
social convention of "race" itself, the social fact of widespread, durable,
large-scale disparity in the status of different racial groups within the
same society is also a constructed, not a natural, outcome. It follows,
then, that a successful and consistent theory will need to account for the
relatively disadvantaged position of African-Americans by reference to
processes that systematically block the realization of the human potential
of the members of this racial group. One can account for racial inequality
without reference to essential racial difference in only two ways: one can
show that the rewards accruing to members of the disadvantaged group,
given their productivity, are lower than the rewards garnered by others; or,
one can show that, through processes unrelated to their innate capacities,
members of the disadvantaged racial group lack opportunity to realize

their productive potential. (These means of argument can, of course, be used in combination; it need not be either one or the other.)

In the first mode of argument, one shows that, systematically, productivity is rewarded differently for members of distinct racial groups. Call this the *reward bias* argument. In the second mode, one shows that, systematically, opportunity to acquire productivity is unequally available to the members of distinct racial groups. Call this the *development bias* argument. There is a significant distinction to be drawn between these two modes of argument, one that is critical for the enterprise being undertaken here.

Another name for the reward bias argument is *discrimination*. I am not high on this concept, and would like to see it demoted, removed from its current prominent place in the conceptual discourse on racial inequality in American life. Instead, I argue that the concept of *racial stigma* should have a more prominent place in this discourse. While I cannot here develop a theory of racial stigma, it is desirable to give some general sense of the intellectual work I hope the concept can do, and the place it occupies within my larger theoretical enterprise. The basic point is that racial discrimination, as an analytical category, deals mainly with the reward bias problem, and cannot effectively reach the problem of development bias. And yet, it is development bias, not reward bias, that explains more fully the extent and durability of current racial inequality.

Racial stigma, on the other hand, takes us some way toward understanding the persistence in US society of development bias affecting African-Americans. Confronted with the experience of racially disparate achievement, racially disproportionate transgression of legal strictures and racially unequal development of productive potential, observers need to give an account. They need to tell themselves a story. They must, in effect, answer the question: where do the problems lie – with US or with THEM? Their willingness to examine taken-for-granted assumptions about the extent to which their nation's civic arrangements correspond to its professed ideals will depend upon the answers they give to this question. Indeed, their very processes of social cognition, of discernment, their awareness of anomaly, their capacity for empathy, their stirrings of conscience are all conditioned by beliefs in this regard. Faced with manifestations of extreme marginality and dysfunction among some of the racially marked, will the citizenry indignantly cry out, "What manner of people are THEY, who languish in that way?" Or, will they be moved, perhaps after overcoming an instinctual revulsion, to ask themselves reflectively (and reflexively!), "What manner of people are WE who accept such degradation in our midst?"

I hold the latter response ("What manner of people are WE . . .") to be less likely, the greater credit is given to the essentialist view (that the "races" really differ in some deep ways that can account for durable and pronounced racial inequality). And, I understand a "raced" population subgroup to be *stigmatized* in the perception of an external observer when this latter response comes less easily to that observer's mind. "Racial stigma," then, is (tacitly) presuming an essentialist cause for racial inequality, thereby ascribing a "virtual social identity" to (some) blacks that implies they are, in some inherent sense, "damaged goods," "not like the rest of us," "people for whom negative social outcomes are not particularly anomalous or surprising."

I believe that the phenomenon of racial stigma poses intractable problems for liberal individualism. For there is a sphere of intimate social intercourse, governed to some degree by "raced" perceptions in individuals' minds, that, out of respect for liberty and the dignity of human beings, should not become the object of political or bureaucratic manipulation. Yet, I hold that such race-preferential associative behavior helps perpetuate a regime of development bias against blacks, largely because of a protracted, ignoble history during which reward bias against blacks was the norm. Thinking in terms of racial stigma, I believe, provides insight into race-constrained social interactions and into race-impacted processes of social cognition, helping us to see the forces at work in a "raced" society like the USA that create causal feedback loops perpetuating racial inequality, and that impede their identification. Moreover, as expanded upon below, this way of looking at things has an important implication for political philosophy. In particular, it leads me to reject color-blindness (or the related notions of race-neutrality, or racial impartiality) as *the* moral standard in regard to issues of social justice and racial inequality in the USA.

Indeed, I argue that color-blindness – a quintessential icon of liberal neutrality – is a superficial moral standard, one that reveals how starkly undersocialized is the entire intellectual project within which it is embedded. It will be important now to stress that I do not think of this weakness as irremediable. The root of my argument is not to announce a bedrock philosophical inadequacy; it is to decry a sociological naïveté. I do not attack liberalism in a wholesale manner. But I long to see liberalism enriched by taking seriously the relational structures that mediate the contacts between the autonomous, dignity-bearing subjects of liberal political theory. I want the socially situated context of these subjects to be integrated into the philosophical project itself. Thus, I do not defend simpleminded racial utilitarianism – the idea that we aggregate the incomes or utilities of people defined by superficial racial characteristics, and use this sum as an indicator of the goodness of society. But I insist that reflection about the rights of individuals and the vitality of the institutions that influence individual interactions, should take seriously the "raced" historical and social structures within which those individuals function.

So, my core objection to liberalism has to do with this sociological naïveté and the limited place for historical developments to enter when liberal political theory is brought to bear on the problem of race. Sure, the so-called "underclass" in the ghettos of America is behaving badly, in self-destructive and threatening ways. But those patterns of behavior, embodied in those individuals, reflect structures of human development mediated by social relations that are biased against those persons because of a history of racial deprivation and oppression. The result then is to produce, in our time, wide disparities in some indicia of behavior across racial groups. What does the abstract individualism of liberal theory suggest that we do now? Throw up our hands? There are no questions of justice raised? Scratch our heads? We don't quite know what to do. Too bad. We lament, but . . . There is, I believe, a gaping hole in liberalism as a normative framework if no better answer is to be had.

My fundamental point is that the selves that are the enshrined subjects of liberal theory are not given *a priori*. Rather, they are products of social relations, and of economic and political institutions. They are creatures, to some not inconsiderable degree, of the very system of laws, social intercourse, and economic relations that normative political theory is supposed to assess. Neither their ideas about the good life, nor (crucial for my purposes here) their self-understandings as "raced" subjects, come into being outside of the flow of history and the web of culture.[5] The diminished selves, the self-doubting, alienated, nihilistic selves – these are social products, and I want to attend to this fact within the project of political theory. This leads to a rejection of color-blindness as a normative standard because I cannot abide the imposition of abstract strictures of neutrality upon a game in which, systematically, non-neutral practices have left so many "raced" and stigmatized outsiders with so few good cards to play. My core concern is about racial stigma and development bias. Succinctly stated, my argument with liberalism is that it fails to comprehend the following. *Stigma-influenced dynamics in the spheres of social interaction and self-image production lead to "objective" racial inequality which is de-coupled from the discriminatory acts of individuals, carries over across generations, shapes political and social-cognitive sensibilities in the citizenry, makes racial disparity appear "natural" and non-dissonant, stymies reform, and locks-in inequality.*

3   Beyond discrimination

Most discussion of the topic of race and social justice in the United States, whether in the social sciences or in social philosophy, has been centered on the concept of *discrimination*. It was animus against racial discrimination that prompted those monumental achievements – the Supreme Court's 1954 *Brown* decision and the Civil Rights Act of 1964 – that ultimately established equality of citizenship for the descendants of slaves as a matter of law in the USA. The legal apparatus erected on this foundation endeavors to enforce equality of treatment of individuals in public and quasi-public spaces – the public schools, the labor market, the voting booth. Although this is a classic way of stating the problem of group-based social injustice, I nevertheless suggest that a focus on the discriminatory treatment of individuals is now misplaced, because it obscures the most crucial normative questions raised by the fact of large racial disparities in life chances.

To see this more clearly, consider an elemental distinction between two kinds of behavior – *discrimination in contract* and *discrimination in contact*. The phrase "discrimination in contract" is meant to invoke the unequal treatment of otherwise like persons based on race in the execution of formal transactions – the buying and selling of goods and services, for instance, or the interactions with organized bureaucracies, public and private. By contrast, "discrimination in contact" refers to the unequal treatment of persons on the basis of race in the associations and relationships that are formed among individuals in social life, including the choice of social intimates, neighbors, friends, heroes, and villains. It involves discrimination in the informal, private spheres of life. An important difference is to be noted between these types of discrimination. Discrimination in *contract* occurs in settings over which a liberal state could, if it were to choose to do so, exercise review and restraint in pursuit of social justice (subject, of course, to the limitations of information and authority that inhibit any regulatory enterprise.) Thus, the US courts no longer enforce racially restrictive covenants in real estate deeds, or allow employers to advertise that "no blacks need apply," etc. Such discrimination is legally proscribed, and this proscription is regarded not only as consistent with, but as necessary for, the realization of liberal ideals.

However, in any liberal political order some forms of discrimination in *contact* must remain a prerogative for autonomous individuals. Preserving the freedom of persons to practice this discrimination is essential to the maintenance of liberty. This is so for two reasons. The social exchanges from which such discrimination arises are so profoundly intimate and cut so closely to the core of our being that all but the most modest interventions in this sphere would have to be avoided if liberty and autonomy are to have any real meaning. More fundamentally, while the ethical case against racial discrimination in formal (e.g., market) transactions is relatively easy to make, it is far less obvious that there is anything wrong in principle with forming or avoiding close association with another person based, in part, on racial identity.[6]

So we have on the one hand a formal sector of *contract*. We have on the other hand, what I am referring to as the informal sector of *contact*. When discrimination in contract takes place, the tendency is to say that individuals are being treated unfairly, not given their due. But when discrimination in contact occurs, it is more likely to be seen as a necessary if not always desirable consequence of our commitment to liberal principles. Given that individuals socialized in the USA understand themselves partly in racial terms, and that they must in any liberal political order be endowed with autonomy regarding their choices of association, it is inevitable that the selective patterns of social intercourse that are the stuff of discrimination in *contact* will arise.

And yet, *mechanisms of status transmission and social mobility depend critically upon the nature of social interactions in both spheres – that is, on the patterns of contact as well as on the rules of contract.* The provision of resources fundamental to the development of human beings is mediated both by formal and informal, by contractual and non-contractual, social relations. I have in mind here the roles played in the shaping of persons by the family, the social network, and (using the word advisedly) the "community." I am thinking about infant and early childhood development, and about the influences of the adolescent peer group. I mean to provoke some reflection on how people come to hold the ideas they, in fact, do hold concerning who they are (their identities), which other persons are essentially like them (their social identifications), and what goals in life are worth striving toward (their ideals). The fundamental empirical claim, taken here to have important philosophic implications, is this: In US society, where of historical necessity patterns of social intercourse are structured by perceptions of race, it is inevitable that developmental processes operating at the individual level will also be conditioned by race. From this I hold it to follow that, in a racially divided society like the USA, fighting discrimination in the sphere of *contract* while leaving it untouched in the sphere of *contact* will generally be insufficient to produce a baseline circumstance of equality of opportunity for all individuals. And yet, a commitment to political liberalism would seem to require precisely this – hence the dilemma.[7]

There are, however, influential traditions of social inquiry in which this basic point seems to have been insufficiently appreciated. For instance, the scholarly literature on racial inequality in economics focuses almost entirely on the differential treatment of individuals, based on race, in formal market transactions (jobs, housing, credit, etc.). Little attention is paid to underlying social processes that lead to racial differences in the acquisition by individuals of productive skills. The primary normative claim in this approach is that such discrimination (in *contract*) is morally offensive, a legitimate object of regulatory intervention, and a significant contributor to the scourge of race and sex inequality in society. These claims are true. But implicit here also is the notion that, to the extent that racial inequality is due to supply-side differences – in the skills presented to employers by black and white employees, for example – the same moral issues are not raised, nor is comparable warrant given for intervention. This notion I hold to be both wrong and dangerous.

In the USA, while it is clear that some discrimination in contract against blacks still exists, it is also clear that such discrimination can no longer be taken as the major explanation of racial inequality. Indeed, it is entirely possible that ending discrimination in markets will not lead, even in the very long run, to a solution for the problem of racial economic inequality. The substantial gap in skills between blacks and whites is a key factor in accounting for racial inequality in the labor market. Yet, this skills gap is itself the result of processes of social exclusion that deserve to be singled out for explicit study and, where possible, for policy remedy. This skills gap is in part a reflection of social and historical factors – geographic segregation, deleterious norms and peer influences, and poor educational quality – all of which have racial dimensions.[8] In this view, inequality between blacks and whites in the USA is a phenomenon that cannot be understood, or remedied, with a focus on market discrimination alone.

There is a long history of justified concern that approaching the problem of racial inequality with less of a focus on employer discrimination and more on skills differences could foster dangerous stereotypes and undermine arguments for policies to narrow the racial wage gap. In the decade after the enactment of US anti-discrimination laws, researchers who began to find evidence of a decline in labor market discrimination were sometimes criticized for giving aid and comfort to political conservatives.[9] This reaction, however, accepts the implicit normative assumption that racial inequality based on skill disparities is not as important a moral problem and does not warrant as vigorous a corrective intervention as does inequality based on *discrimination in contract* (in the labor market, say). But that assumption is much less compelling when one recognizes that persistent racial skill disparities are in part the result of *discrimination in contact*.

4   Social capital and social opportunity

The conventional economist's approach to social analysis begins with an atomized agent, acting more or less independently, and seeking to make the best of opportunities at hand. This way of thinking has been very fruitful for economics, but it cannot adequately capture the ways that racial inequality persists over time. In actuality, individuals are embedded in complex networks of affiliations: they are members of nuclear and extended families; they belong to religious and linguistic groupings; they have ethnic and racial identities; they are attached to particular localities. Each individual is *socially situated*, and one's location within the network of social affiliations substantially affects one's access to various resources.

Opportunity travels along the synapses of these social networks. Thus, a newborn is severely handicapped if its parents are relatively uninterested in (or incapable of) fostering the youngster's intellectual development in the first years of life. A talented adolescent whose social peer group disdains the activities that must be undertaken for that talent to flourish is at risk of not achieving his or her full potential. An unemployed person without friends or relatives already at work in a certain industry may never hear about the job opportunities available there. An individual's inherited social situation plays a major role in determining his or her ultimate economic success.

In earlier work, I introduced the term "social capital" to suggest a modification of human·capital theory designed to provide a richer context within which to analyze group inequality.[10] This idea builds upon the observation that family and community backgrounds play an important role, alongside factors like individual ability and human capital investments, in determining individual achievement. Some important part of racial inequality, in this view, is seen to arise from the way that geographic and social segregation along racial lines makes an individual's opportunities to acquire skills depend on present and past skill attainments by others in the same social group.[11]

In cities across the country, and in rural areas of the Old South, the situation of the so-called black underclass and, increasingly, of the black lower-working classes, is bad and getting worse. This is certainly a race-related problem. The plight of the black poor is not rightly seen as another (albeit severe) instance of economic inequality, American-style. But conventional market discrimination is only one small part of it. These black ghetto dwellers are a people apart, susceptible to stereotyping, ridiculed for their cultural styles, isolated socially, experiencing an internalized sense of helplessness and despair, with limited access to communal networks of mutual assistance.[12] Their purported criminality, sexual profligacy, and intellectual inadequacy are the frequent objects of public derision. They suffer a stigmatized, pariah status (Goffman 1963). It should not require enormous powers of perception to see how this degradation relates to the history of black–white race relations in the USA.

Here is where the implicit normative model that accompanies the emphasis on discrimination in contract is most seriously flawed. And, here is where the challenge to political liberalism is also the greatest. Given social segregation along race lines, the effects of past discrimination can persist over time by adversely affecting the skills and social contacts acquired by the victims of discrimination, to be sure, but also by those closely connected to them – their children, for instance. Moreover, discrimination in one market can leave its victim less well prepared to compete in another market. The cumulative impact of an act of discrimination – within a single lifetime, over generations within a family, or between various venues of social interaction – should be no less problematic, as an ethical matter, than was the original offense. But these effects will be far more difficult to counter because such historical causal processes are near impossible to quantify. One can rarely say with any confidence what portion of an observed racial disparity is due to the indirect effects of past *discrimination in contract*, as mediated and reinforced by contemporary *discrimination in contact*. Moreover, the most effective means of disrupting these causal chains usually run afoul of the cherished liberal ideal of individual autonomy.

Thus, we have now in the USA a curious and troubling situation. The civil rights struggle, which succeeded brilliantly in winning for blacks the right to be free of discrimination, failed for the most part to secure a national commitment toward eradicating the effects of such discrimination as had already occurred. When those effects manifest themselves in patterns of behavior among poor blacks which lead to seemingly self-imposed limits on their acquisition of skills, the tendency of many who think only in terms of market discrimination is to argue that society is not at fault. This is the grain of truth in the insistence of some conservative observers that, while overt racism was implicated in the past, it is behavioral differences that lie at the root of racial inequality in the USA today.[13] But the deeper truth is that, for many generations now, the communal experience of the descendants of the African slaves has been shaped by political, social, and economic institutions that, by any measure, must be seen as racially oppressive. When we look at the so-called "underclass culture" in US cities today we are seeing a product of that oppressive history.[14] In the face of the despair, violence, and self-destructive behavior of these people, it seems to me to be both morally obtuse and scientifically naïve to argue, as some conservatives now do, that "if those people would just get their acts together then we would not have such a horrific problem." Yet for closely related reasons, I also hold it to be a mistake to argue, as some liberals do, that the primary cause of continuing racial inequality is ongoing market discrimination.

This analysis would seem to have an important ethical implication: because the creation of a skilled work force is a social process, the meritocratic ideal should take into account that no one travels the road to economic and social success alone. The facts that generations overlap, that much of social life lies outside the reach of public regulation, and that prevailing social affiliations influence the development of the intellectual and personal skills of the young imply that present patterns of inequality – among individuals and between groups – must embody, to some degree, social and economic disparities that have existed in the past. *To the extent that past disparities are illegitimate, the propriety of the contemporary order is called into question.*

5   Historical causation and social justice

One aspect of this perspective should be commented upon. History has been invoked here as a factor conditioning the ethical assessment of contemporary social arrangements. And yet, the explicit channels of historical influence, on which social scientific work can shed some light, must of necessity remain opaque, and vaguely specified. What might be called an "epistemological fog" obscures the causal dynamics at work across the generations and limits our ability to know in detail how past events have shaped current arrangements. Thus, it may be reasonable to assert in a general way that past racial discrimination in contract, together with present discrimination in contact, disadvantages blacks by impeding their acquisition of skills. But it is nearly impossible to say with any quantitative precision just *how much* of current racial inequality is due to this source of disadvantage.[15]

Now one could take the view, as some conservatives have done, that this knowledge limitation should short-circuit claims for racial egalitarianism that rely upon the past unjust treatment of some racial group.[16] While acknowledging the plausibility of this view, I nevertheless reject it. Rather, I hold that a compensatory model, familiar from tort and liability law, is the wrong way to think about this question. My position, contrary to what I believe are simplistic applications of liberal neutrality that issue in mandates of color-blindness, is that past racial injustice is relevant in establishing a general presumption against indifference to present racial inequality (thereby militating against the implications of the Anonymity

Axiom mentioned earlier). But the degree to which social policy should be oriented toward reducing present racial inequality and the weight to be placed on this objective in the social decision calculus is not here conceived in terms of "correcting" or "balancing" for historical violation. Thus I argue that, even though quantitative attribution of causal weight to distant historical events is not possible, one can still support qualitative claims.[17]

This distinction between quantitative and qualitative historically based claims is important, I think, because it casts doubt on the adequacy of purely procedural theories of justice when analyzing matters of race. Color-blindness as understood by critics of affirmative action is one such theory. In general, procedural theories of social justice turn on the answers to two kinds of questions: What are people entitled to? And, what actions affecting the distribution of claims are legitimate? Then, any state of affairs that respects individuals' entitlements and comes about from procedurally legitimate actions is held to be just. Notice, however, that procedural theories are essentially incomplete because they cannot cope with the consequences of their own violations.

Suppose we are given a set of rules about how people are to treat one another. Suppose further that people happen not always to follow these rules. As just noted, history can be messy stuff. Teasing out causal implications across the centuries of historic procedural violations is impossibly difficult. So, if procedurally just requirements are not adhered to at some point – people entitled to the fruits of their labor are not rewarded accordingly, say – then, at some later point, perhaps a century on, there will be consequences rife in the interstices of society. But, as argued above, it will be impossible in principle to identify and to quantify these effects. What then would a procedural account have to say about this? Simple notions about providing compensation for identifiable historic wrongs may work when individual interactions are being considered, but they cannot possibly work for broad social violations – chattel slavery, for instance. A procedural theory leaves us with no account of justice under such circumstances. This is a fundamental incompleteness in the theory, one that is especially pertinent to a consideration of racial justice in the USA.[18]

To pursue this point somewhat more formally, let us call a system of rules about social justice *procedural* if it satisfies the following: (1) A list of rules or procedures is specified about how people are supposed to deal with one another. And (2) a state of affairs is held to be just if it evolves from a just original state, where every step in the evolution is brought about by the freely chosen actions of mutually consenting agents, all of which are consistent with the rules specified in (1). Furthermore, call such a system *closed to moral deviation* if it meets the following test. Whenever some state of affairs is brought about through actions by some agents that breach the rules specified in (1), it is in principle possible to "recover" from the effects of this breach through a series of counteractions that are themselves consistent with the rules set out in (1).

In other words, a *procedural* account of social justice is *closed to moral deviation* if one can correct the consequences of rule violation through actions that are themselves consistent with the rules. In the absence of this "closure" property, a procedural theory would need to be supplemented by some non-procedural account of how to manage the states of affairs arrived at in the aftermath of the commission of procedurally unjust acts. Elsewhere I have demonstrated (in the context of a theoretical example) that notwithstanding the effective prohibition of discrimination in contract, historically engendered economic differences between racial groups can persist indefinitely when discrimination in contact continues to be practiced (see Loury 1977 and 1995). That is, non-discrimination, once having been established in the sphere of contract but not in the sphere of contact, can admit of an indefinite perpetuation of the racial inequality originally engendered by historic contractual discrimination. Stated in terms of the language just introduced, my demonstration implies that the color-blindness derived from the Anonymity Axiom – treat all subjects interchangeably and take note of no person's racial identity in the execution of social choice – when viewed as a procedural account of racial justice, is not closed to moral deviation. This, then, is the basis of my larger argument that, as a matter of social ethics, policies should be undertaken to mitigate the economic marginality of members of historically oppressed racial groups. This is not a reparations argument. *When the developmental prospects of an individual depend on the circumstances of those with whom he is socially affiliated, even a minimal commitment to equality of opportunity for individuals requires such policies.*

6   The affirmative action controversy and the poverty of proceduralism

The current dispute about affirmative action throws some light on the arguments being advanced here. My general view is that the affirmative action debate receives too much attention in US policy discourses about racial inequality, obscuring as much as it clarifies. However, by exploring some aspects of this hotly contested public question, I hope to illustrate more incisively the conceptual distinctions that drive my larger argument.[19]

Consider, then, the issue of achieving (or not) racial integration at selective colleges and universities in the USA. In a recently published study, two former Ivy League university presidents assert a prerogative on behalf of administrators in the great American educational philanthropies: that these decision-makers be granted sufficient autonomy in their affairs to pursue a vitally important educational objective – more racial diversity in their student bodies.[20] William Bowen and Derek Bok present data to suggest that, through the prudent use of racial identity in the admissions process, this objective is being achieved at a tolerable cost. The evidence offered in support of these claims persuades me, though, of course, reasonable people can disagree. Yet, even if the evidence were more equivocal, the authors' articulate defense of their goal – to integrate elite higher education by race – would remain enormously controversial, and it is useful to ask why. I see two reasons for the intensity of this controversy. First, the goals and purposes openly espoused by a nation's leading colleges are public purposes. (And, given their considerable influence on national life and culture, this is no less true of the private institutions. What a Harvard or a Princeton seeks to achieve is, in some measure, what America strives after.) Public purposes are worth arguing about, and these arguments necessarily entail disputed moral judgments.

Second, the venue of this dispute – elite higher education – heightens its intensity. Education is a special, deeply political, and almost sacred, civic activity. It is not a merely technical enterprise – providing facts to the untutored. Inescapably, it is a moral and aesthetic enterprise – expressing to impressionable minds a set of convictions about how most nobly to live in the world. Moreover, this is a venue where access to influence and power is rationed. As a result, the selection of young people to enter prestigious educational institutions amounts to a visible, high-stakes exercise in civic pedagogy. These "selection rituals" are political acts with moral overtones. Their perceived legitimacy is crucial in a stratified society where one's place in the status hierarchy can turn on access to elite institutions. (Imagine, for example, what it would mean for civic life in the USA if, due to the expense, only wealthy families could send their children to the most prestigious institutions.)

Two normative concerns appear to be elemental in this controversy:
(1) To establish non-discrimination, or race-blindness, as a procedural ideal. People should be treated without regard to their racial identity. Race is a morally irrelevant trait. [Race-blindness]
(2) To pursue racial equality, or racial justice, as a substantive public good. Given a history marred by racial injustice, we should try to reduce group inequalities in wealth and power. [Race-egalitarianism]

Both of these concerns bear on the issue of race and social ethics, but in different ways. The first looks to how people are treated in discrete encounters, affirming as a value that such treatment should not be conditioned on race. The second normative concern looks to broad patterns of social disparity between racial groups, advancing as an ethical ideal that such differences should be reduced. The first concern deals with the rights of individuals; it is process-oriented, and a-historical. The second concern is motivated by the status of groups; it is focused on outcomes, and rooted in history.

Among the most important conclusions emerging from *The Shape of the River* is that, though not mutually inconsistent, these two ideals are in tension with one another: pursuit of racial equality can be powerfully abetted by violating race-blindness. This is because, given the differences in test score distributions among blacks and whites, achieving racial integration at highly selective colleges requires the admission probability conditional on test scores to be higher for black than for white applicants. As a matter of simple logic, a college with limited places to fill can achieve more racial diversity only if some black applicants are admitted who would otherwise have been rejected, while some nonblack applicants are rejected who would otherwise have been admitted. Selective institutions will naturally try to reject the least qualified of the otherwise admissible nonblack applicants, while admitting the most qualified of those black applicants who would otherwise have been rejected. Yet, in doing so, the college necessarily uses a racially preferential admissions policy. Thus, with resources limited, and with a college committed to remaining highly selective, the two normative concerns come clearly into conflict with one another. A choice between them must be made.

Now, the relevant point for the purposes of this essay turns on the conceptual distinction between procedural and egalitarian moral interests. To develop this point, I suggest a terminological convention: Let us adopt the term "race-blind" to identify the practice of not using race when carrying out a policy. And, let us employ a different term – "race-indifferent" – to identify the practice of not thinking about race when determining the goals and objectives on behalf of which some policy is adopted. If a selection rule for college admissions can be applied without knowing the racial identity of applicants, call that rule "race-blind." On the other hand, if a selection rule is chosen with no concern as to how it might impact the various racial groups, then call the choice of that rule "race-indifferent." I can now restate my claim: the key moral question in matters of race is about indifference, not blindness. (This is not to deny, of course, that "blindness questions" can sometimes matter a great deal.)

The power of this distinction between race-indifference and race-blindness becomes clear when one considers that both ameliorating the social disadvantage of blacks, or exacerbating this disadvantage, can alike be achieved with race-blind policies. Yet, whereas a race-blind policy explicitly intended to harm blacks could never be morally acceptable, such policies adopted for the purpose of reducing racial inequality are commonplace, and uncontroversial. Put differently, given the facts of US history, departures from race-indifference are, and should be, evaluated asymmetrically: those that harm blacks are universally suspect, whereas non-indifferent undertakings that assist blacks are widely recognized as necessary to achieve just social policy.

For example, when a court ruling forbade the practice of affirmative action in college admissions in Texas, the legislature responded by guaranteeing a place at any public university to the top ten percent of every high school class in the state. This so-called "ten percent rule" mainly benefits students with low test scores and good grades at less competitive high schools – disproportionately blacks and Hispanics – and certainly this was the intent. That is, this rule, while being race-blind, is most decidedly is not race-indifferent. Thus, we have a situation in Texas where the explicit use of race in a college admissions formula is forbidden, while the intentional use of a proxy for race publicly adopted so as to reach a similar result is allowed. Can there be any doubt, had a different color-blind proxy been adopted in order to exclude black and Hispanic students from public institutions in Texas, that this would be morally unacceptable?

This example illustrates why the key moral issues having to do with race are most often about indifference, and not blindness. The moral intuition being drawn on in the example derives from the fact that in the USA most citizens see reversing the effects of our history of immoral race relations as a good, while seeing the perpetuation of those effects as an evil. The choice of instruments used to achieve these ends is often of less moment than the choice among the ends themselves. Indeed, this is the case in other policy arenas as well: the primary normative concern is not discrimination as such, but rather it involves deciding how much account to take of racially disparate consequences when choosing among what may be alternative, non-discriminatory policies. Thus worthy racial goals can be pursued by race-blind means. Moreover, race-indifferent public purposes are sometimes most effectively pursued by non-race-blind (shall we say, "race-sighted"?) means.

Consider, to further illustrate, a state's governor who seeks to appoint judges to the courts. He might reason as follows:

I need to have a diverse group of appointees both for my own political protection and in the long-term interest of preserving the legitimacy of the administration of the justice in this jurisdiction. If I appoint all white men, even when they appear to be the best qualified, I may do damage not only to my reputation, but also to the institution of the court itself. This is because I may create a situation where some people doubt that the institution fairly represents them. I have a responsibility as governor to ensure this does not happen.

Maintaining the legitimacy of the institution of the court is not a racial goal; it is something that everybody has a stake in. And yet in order to do it, the governor might have to take racial identity into account to see whether his or her list of possible appointees contains a sufficient number of racial minority group members.

On the other hand, consider a federal anti-drug policy concentrating on arresting street-level traffickers and putting them away for a long time. This is a race-blind policy – formulated to pursue nonracial public ends, but having pronounced racially unequal results. Such policies have led to the incarceration of young people of color in vastly disproportionate numbers – young people, it might be argued, who to some degree are engaged in the illicit traffic precisely because they are at the margin of society and their alternative opportunities are scant.[21] As a result of this and similar policies, out of the 2 million people under lock and key on any given day in the USA, some 1.2 million are blacks, though blacks are only about one-eighth of the national population. A concern solely for the race-blindness of policy instruments – are the police and courts applying the laws without racial discrimination? – would fail to raise the larger question: Is this not a public policy that should be examined because of the cost it is imposing on a particular community?

Of course, the example of USA anti-drug policy is controversial, but at a minimum reasonable people must accept the central logical claim here: that this race-blind policy instrument raises a question of social justice, the answer to which turns in part on the policy's racially dispro-portionate effects.[22] And, it is *this* distinction – between "blindness" and "indifference" – that I seek to emphasize, because one can slide quickly from a forceful critique of race-sighted policy instruments (arguing that they should be *race-blind*) into a denial of the legitimacy of any discussion of public issues that is formulated in racial terms (arguing that such discussions should be *race-indifferent*).

The relevance of the affirmative action controversy to my larger argument about liberalism can now be seen more clearly. I have just asserted a priority of moral concerns – racial justice before race-blindness. The broad acceptance of this moral ordering in US society would have powerful consequences. When exclusive colleges and universities use racial preferences to ration access to their ranks, they tacitly and publicly confirm this ordering in a salient and powerful way. This confirmation is the key civic lesson projected into American national life by these disputed policies. At bottom, what the racial preference argument, in college admissions and elsewhere, is really about is this struggle for priority among competing public ideals. This is a struggle of crucial importance to the overall discourse on race and social justice in the USA.

The priority of concerns asserted here has far-reaching consequences. It implies, for example, that an end to formal discrimination against blacks in this post-civil rights era should in no way foreclose a vigorous public discussion about racial justice. More subtly, elevating racial equality above race-blindness as a normative concern inclines us to think critically, and with greater nuance, about the value of race-blindness. It reminds us that the demand for race-blindness – our moral queasiness about using race in public decisions – arises for historically specific reasons – slavery and enforced racial segregation over several centuries. These reasons involved the caste-like subordination of blacks – a phenomenon whose effects still linger, and that was not symmetrical as between the races. As such, to take account of race while trying to mitigate the effects of this subordination, though perhaps ill advised or unworkable in specific cases, cannot plausibly be seen as the moral equivalent of the discrimination that produced the subjugation of blacks in the first place. To do so would be to mire oneself in a-historical, procedural formalism.

Yet, this is precisely what some critics of affirmative action have done, putting forward as their fundamental moral principle the procedural requirement that admissions policies be color-blind. "America, A Race-Free Zone," screams the headline from a recent article by Ward Connerly, leader of the successful 1996 ballot campaign against affirmative action in California, and now at the helm of a national organization working to promote similar initiatives in other jurisdictions. Mr. Connerly wants to rid the nation of what he calls "those disgusting little boxes" – the ones applicants check to indicate their racial identities. He and his associates see the affirmative action dispute as an argument between people like themselves, who seek simply to eliminate discrimination, and people like the authors of *The Shape of the River*, who want permission to discriminate if doing so helps the right groups.[23]

This way of casting the question is very misleading. *It obscures from view the most vital matter at stake in the contemporary affirmative action debate – whether public purposes formulated explicitly in racial terms are morally legitimate, or even morally required.* Anti-preference advocates suggest not, arguing from the premise that an individual's race has no moral relevance, to the conclusion that it is either wrong or unnecessary to formulate public purposes in racial terms. But this argument is a *non sequitur*. Moral irrelevance does not imply instrumental irrelevance. Nor does the conviction that knowing an individual's race adds nothing to an assessment of personal worth require the conclusion that patterns of unequal racial representation in important public venues are irrelevant for accessing the moral health of our society.

The failure to make these distinctions is dangerous, for it leads inexorably to doubts about the validity of discussing social justice issues in the United States at all in racial terms. Or, more precisely, it reduces such a discussion to the narrow ground of assessing whether or not certain policies are race-blind. Whatever the anti-preference crusaders may intend, and however desirable in the abstract may be their color-blind ideal, their campaign is having the effect of devaluing our collective and still unfinished efforts to achieve greater equality between the races. Americans are now engaged in deciding whether the pursuit of racial equality will continue in the century ahead to be a legitimate and vitally important purpose in our public life. Increasingly, doubts are being expressed about this. *Fervency for color-blindness has left some observers simply blind to a basic fact of American public life: we have pressing moral dilemmas in our society that can be fully grasped only when viewed against the backdrop of our unlovely racial history.*

Consider the stubborn social reality of race-consciousness in US society. A standard concern about racial preferences is that they promote an unhealthy fixation on racial identity among students. By classifying by race, it is said, we are further distanced from the goal of achieving a color-blind society. Many proponents of race-blindness as the primary moral ideal come close to equating the use of racial information in administrative practices with the continued awareness of racial identity in the broad society. Yet, consciousness of race in the society at large is a matter of subjective states of mind, involving how people understand themselves, and how they perceive others. It concerns the extent to which race is taken into account in the intimate, social lives of citizens. The implicit assumption of race-blind advocates is that, if we would just stop putting people into these boxes, they would oblige us by not thinking of themselves in these terms. But, this assumption is patently false.[24] Anti-preference advocates like to declare that we cannot get beyond race while taking race into account – as if someone has proven a theorem to this effect. But, no such demonstration is possible.

The basic point needing emphasis here is this: The use of race-based instruments is typically the result, rather than the cause, of the wider awareness of racial identity in society. To forgo cognizance of the importance of race, out of fear that others will be encouraged to think in racial terms, is a bit like closing the barn door after the horses have gone. One cannot grasp the workings of the social order in which we are embedded in the USA without making use of racial categories, because these socially constructed categories are etched in the consciousness of the individuals with whom we must reckon. Because they use race to articulate their self-understandings, we must be mindful of race as we conduct our public affairs. This is a cognitive, not a normative point. One can hold that race is irrelevant to an individual's moral worth, that individuals and not groups are the bearers of rights, and nevertheless affirm that, to deal effectively with these autonomous individuals, account must be taken of the categories of thought in which they understand themselves.

Indeed, one easily produces compelling examples where the failure to take race into account serves to exacerbate racial awareness. Consider the extent to which our public institutions are regarded as legitimate by all the people. When a public executive (like the hypothetical governor considered above) recognizes the link between the perceived legitimacy of institutions and their degree of racial representation, and acts on that recognition, he or she has acted so as to *inhibit*, not to *heighten*, the salience of race in public life. When the leaders of elite educational philanthropies worry about bringing a larger number of black youngsters into their ranks, so as to increase the numbers of their graduates from these communities, they have acted in a similar fashion. To acknowledge that institutional legitimacy can turn on matters of racial representation is to recognize a basic historical fact about the American national community, not to make a moral error. The US Army has long understood this.[25] It is absurd to hold that this situation derives from the existence of selection rules – in colleges and universities, in the military, or anywhere else – that take account of race.

So much may seem too obvious to warrant stating but, sadly, it is not. In the 5th US Circuit Court of Appeal's *Hopwood* opinion, Judge Smith questions the diversity rationale for using racial preferences in higher education admissions. He argues that, because a college or university exists to promote the exchange of ideas, defining diversity in racial terms entails a pernicious belief that blacks think one way, whites another. But this argument is fallacious for reasons just stated. Suppose one begins with the contrary premise, that there is no "black" or "white" way of thinking. Suppose further that conveying this view to one's students is a high pedagogic goal. The students being keenly aware of their respective racial identities, some racial diversity may be required to achieve the pedagogic goal. Teaching that "not all blacks think alike" will be much easier when there are enough blacks around to show their diversity of thought. That is, *conveying effectively the ultimate moral irrelevance of race in our society may require functional attention by administrative personnel to the racial composition of the learning environment. Whether, and to what extent, this may be so is a prudential, not a principled, question. It cannot be resolved a priori.*

7   Concluding observations

There is, however, an objection to be raised to the position being developed here that I wish to consider. At the consequentialist level, a critic may concede that some departures from color-blindness are needed, though they should be "narrowly tailored" to meet only the most "compelling interest" as the language of recent Supreme Court rulings on affirmative action would have it. But at the most profound moral level, doesn't someone who abhors the consequences of racial stigma have to affirm a kind of moral blindness to the race of agents? I think this is in fact the case, and am not the least bit reluctant to say so, but I continue to urge clarity on this point. Let us distinguish between three distinct domains of concern about race-based behavior in a racially divided society. One is the *domain of policy implementation.* Here we are admitting students to college, hiring firefighters, distributing public benefits, and the like. A second is the *domain of evaluation of the consequences of public action.* Here we are deciding whether to build a prison or a school and if a school, then at what level of elite pedagogy to focus it. We are framing a war on drugs and deciding whether to focus attention on the buying or selling side of the transaction, we are determining whether it is necessary to induce a recession in order to prevent a bout of inflation, and so on. Finally, there is the *domain of the construction of national community* – the development of our sense of nationhood, through civic pedagogic enterprises of all sorts – the building of monuments, proffering of public ritual, and, of course, the making of public policy which, inescapably has an expressive as well as more directly instrumental dimension. (Capital punishment either does or does not deter murder. It most definitely, however, is the state-sanctioned taking of human life which, for good or for ill, contributes to civic pedagogy in the sense in which I intend that term here. So, too, does the racial imbalance imbedded in the practice of capital punishment.)

Now, eschewing the use of race in the domain of implementation is what most critics of affirmative action mean by race-blindness. No more of those "disgusting little boxes," as Ward Connerly, leader of the national political campaign to end affirmative action, has put it. I wish here to stress that, given US history, fewer people are prepared to import their love of the race-blind principle into the domain of evaluation of public actions. That is, while they may object to race-based selection rules, they do not object to the pursuit of explicitly race-egalitarian outcomes through public policies taking no notice of race at the point of implementation. That is, using my linguistic convention introduced above, though they may embrace race-*blindness* they reject race-*indifference*. Thus, there is much (I think plausible) disquiet at the thought of constructing race-based electorates for the purpose of giving blacks greater political voice, but hardly any opposition to moving from at-large to non-racially drawn single-member voting districts when the intent is to produce a similar outcome. And, as mentioned, policies like the ten-percent plan in Texas, implemented through race-blind decision rules but adopted with the intent of benefiting blacks and Hispanics, are not controversial – either politically or constitutionally – among most affirmative action opponents.

Now consider the domain of the construction of civic community. What would race-blindness mean here? Roughly what I have in mind is what the sociologist Orlando Patterson has called the *principle of infrangibility* (i.e., the absence of boundary) – saying that we are One Nation, Indivisible, and taking that idea seriously enough to try to act (whether in a race-blind or a race-sighted fashion) so as to bring that circumstance about. Those people, languishing at the margins, even if they are strange and threatening, are going to be seen as being, in the way that most fundamentally counts for our politics and civic life, essentially like *us*. We're going to move prudently and constitutionally, but determinedly and expeditiously, so as to tear down, or certainly build no higher, the boundaries of race that rend the body politic.

There should be no race-mediated civic boundary, and where a boundary exists, it becomes our work to rub it out. That is a kind of race-blindness, too. Thus, when elite college presidents say, in effect, "while administering multibillion dollar philanthropies that enjoy (for the public good) the protection of tax exemption, we endeavor, among other things, to construct an elite leadership cadre of African-Americans at the end of the twentieth and at the beginning of the twenty-first century," they say a very modest thing. In the elite schools studied by Bowen and Bok (1998), the average admissions rate for whites is about 25 percent. Getting rid of all the affirmative action is calculated to raise that rate to about 27 percent. So, for every seventy-five whites rejected under the regime of race-preferential admissions currently being practiced, seventy-three would still be rejected after the eradication of affirmative action. Why, then, all the energy, why all the angst, why all the hand wringing, why all the clamor, why all the concern that America is being run aground, that our standards are being trashed, that the barbarians are at the gates. Why? When in fact, as the data in that book show, the boundary of racial hierarchy is being erased just a little bit by the trickling through of a few students who, at the margin, because of the colleges' practice of affirmative action are being inducted into the leadership cadres of the US. I hold that there is nothing in political liberalism, rightly understood, that should lead us to reject that practice. There is nothing wrong with a liberal, concerned about social justice, undertaking to fight racial stigma. There is nothing wrong with constructing a racially integrated elite in America. There is nothing wrong with fretting over 1.2 million African-American young bodies under the physical control of the state. Indeed, I am led to wonder how any thoughtful person aware of the history and the contemporary structure of USA society could conclude otherwise.

NOTES

1. See, for example, United States, Office of the President 1998: Chapter 4, Farley 1996: Chapter 6, Loury 2000, and 2002: Appendix for documentation of these claims.
2. There has been much discussion among social philosophers writing in the liberal tradition about the ontological status of "race" – are there any things in the world that may be taken as corresponding to the word "race," etc. (See, for example, Appiah 1992: Chapter 2). Some writers have even taken to putting that word in quotation marks, by way of emphasizing its problematic scientific and philosophical status. Their claim is that no objective criteria are available – biological, cultural, or genealogical – through use of which the set of human beings can be consistently partitioned into a relatively small number of mutually exclusive, collectively exhaustive subsets that may be taken as "races." Belief in the existence of races, on this view, is rather like belief in the existence of witches – mischievous superstition, nothing more.

   I do not dispute the core claim here, but neither do I find this exercise in linguistic philosophy to be of much interest. Rather, as any good social scientist would be, I am impressed by the fact that so many behaviors have come to be organized around the "race" category, despite its evident lack of an objective basis in human biology. This is what needs to be explained. Objective rules of racial taxonomy are not required to study, as I do here, the subjective use of racial classifications. It is sufficient that influential observers (policemen, employers, bankers, and passersby on the street) have classificatory schemes, and act on those schemes. They need not make the schemes explicit. Their classificatory methods may well be mutually inconsistent. They are unlikely to be able to give cogent reasons for adopting these methods; but then, they are also unlikely to be asked to do so. Still, if a person is aware that others in society are classifying him or her by reference to certain markers, and if this classification, in turn, constitutes the basis of differential actions affecting his or her welfare, then such markers will become important to this person. He or she will attend to them, become conscious (and self-conscious) in regard to them. He or she will, at some level, understand and identify himself or herself as "raced." This, I assert, will be a rational cognitive stance on this person's part, not a belief in magic of some kind, and definitely not a moral error. Thus, following Cornell and Hartmann (1998) I define "race" as:

a human group defined by itself or others as distinct by virtue of perceived common physical characteristics that are held to be inherent. A race is a group of human beings socially defined on the basis of physical characteristics. Determining which characteristics constitute the race – the selection of markers and therefore the construction of the racial category itself – is a choice human beings make. Neither markers nor categories are predetermined by any biological factors. These processes of selection and construction are seldom the work of a moment. Racial categories are historical products and are often contested. (p. 24)

3. Further elaboration can be found in Arrow 1963 and Sen 1970.
4. I am much encouraged in this way of thinking by Charles Tilly's recent contribution to social theory (1998) and, in particular, by his emphasis on *categorical inequality*:

Durable inequality among categories arises because people who control access to value-producing resources solve pressing organizational problems by means of categorical distinctions. Inadvertently or otherwise, those people set up systems of social closure, exclusion, and control. Multiple parties – not all of them powerful, some of them even victims of exploitation – then acquire stakes in those solutions . . . Through all of these variations, we discover and rediscover paired, recognized, organized, unequal categories such as black/white, male/female, married/unmarried, and citizen/noncitizen. (pp. 7–8)

One may regard the present essay as an initial exploration of some of the philosophical implications of this social theoretic point of view.
5. My critique of liberalism is thus similar in spirit to the communitarian arguments found in the work of Michael Sandel (1982) and Charles Taylor (1992), among others.
6. Recall, in this context, that even the Civil Rights Act of 1964, which undertook to regulate discriminatory behavior only in the formal, contractual sector of US society, was (and still is, see Epstein 1992) opposed by libertarian conservatives worried about the threat to personal liberty posed by laws of this kind.
7. My argument here is influenced by the work of James Fishkin (1983). Fishkin defines a "tri-lemma" for liberalism, insofar as it is committed at one and the same time to the ideals of equality of opportunity, reward according to merit, and autonomy of the family. He observes that autonomous but differentially endowed families will pass along developmental advantages to their children who, because rewards are distributed in reference to merit alone, will have superior life chances, unearned by them, thus defeating the goal of achieving equal opportunity. A difficult choice, he concludes, must be made among these ideals.
8. I cannot here undertake to review the voluminous literature that supports this claim. Loury (1998a) cites some of this literature. It should be noted that some recent work in economics, both empirical (Cutler and Glaeser 1997) and theoretical (Akerlof 1997) moves in the direction I urge here.
9. A classic example is the reception by some on the political left of William Julius Wilson's book, *The Declining Significance of Race* (1978).

10. See Loury 1977, 1981, 1987, and 1995.
11. There is fairly strong support for this view of the lagging economic position of blacks in the literature. Akerlof (1997) provides a theoretical argument, supported by a wealth of evidence from social anthropology, for the notion that concerns for status and conformity are primary determinants of individuals' educational attainment, childbearing, and law-breaking behavior. Anderson (1990, 1999) provides ethnographic accounts of life in inner-city Philadelphia, where peer influences significantly inhibit skill acquisition by adolescents in poor neighborhoods. Waldinger (1996), in a study of immigrant labor in New York City, concludes that poor blacks suffer less from the racism of employers than from the fact that they do not have access to the ethnic networks through which workers are recruited for jobs in construction and service industries. Glaeser and Cutler (1997), comparing US cities with varying degrees of racial population concentration, find blacks to be significantly disadvantaged by residential segregation; they estimate that a 13 percent reduction in segregation would eliminate about one-third of the black–white gap in schooling, employment, earnings, and unwed pregnancy rates. Mills and Lubuele (1997) argue that a central problem for students of urban poverty is to explain why "low income black residents actually or potentially eligible for jobs that have moved to suburbs (have) not followed such jobs to the suburbs."
12. See Wilson 1996 for an extended discussion.
13. See Thernstrom and Thernstrom 1997 for an example of this conservative view, and Loury 1997 for a vigorous critique of it.
14. This point about the long historical shadow of racial categorization is powerfully developed in Thomas Sugrue's Bancroft Prize-winning study of race and inequality in postwar Detroit (1996).
15. Consider the recent argument of Orlando Patterson (1998) on behalf of the proposition that the high rates of paternal abandonment of children among contemporary Afro-Americans is due to the devastating consequences for gender relations among blacks of American slavery, and of the racist system of Jim Crow segregation that followed. In my view, Patterson's argument is persuasive. But, even so, he can provide no answer to this crucial counterfactual query: What would family patterns look like among today's blacks in the absence of these historical depredations? This question is important because, without some sense of the *extent* of damage caused by past violation, it is difficult to gauge the appropriate scope of remedy.
16. Thomas Sowell is perhaps the leading exponent of this view. A representative work is Sowell 1983.
17. A sharp contrast can be drawn between two different ways of dealing with the problem of a morally problematic racial history. One seeks "reparations," conceiving the problem in compensatory terms. The other conceives the problem, let us say, in interpretative terms – seeking public recognition of the severity, and (crucially) contemporary relevance, of what transpired. In this latter view, the goal is to establish a common baseline of historical memory – a common narrative, if you like – through which the past injury and its ongoing significance can enter into current policy discourse. (A crude analogy might

be drawn here, suggested by the debate over the Truth and Reconciliation Commission in post-apartheid South Africa: the compensatory approach is rather like putting as many past offenders as possible on trial, punishing them for their wrong doing and getting justice for survivors of the victims. The interpretative approach is a bit like waiving the pursuit of individual criminal liability in the interest of bringing to public light the true nature of what took place under apartheid.) What seems conceptually important, though, is to clarify that, while some reckoning with the racist history of the USA remains to be done, this reckoning may, for political as well as epistemological reasons, be inappropriately specified when cast in terms of "reparations." What is required, instead, is a commitment on the part of the public, the political elite, the opinion-shaping media, etc., to take responsibility for such situations as the contemporary plight of the urban black poor, and to understand them in a general way as a consequence of an ethically indefensible past. Such a commitment would, on this view, be open-ended and not contingent on demonstrating any specific lines of causality.

18. Nozick (1974) provides a prototype of the procedural approach, in the sense being criticized here. I hasten to note that Nozick is himself aware of these difficulties and proposes various amendments to his procedural theory in an effort to deal with them.

19. The argument of this section draws on the previously published essay, Loury 1998b.

20. Bowen and Bok 1998.

21. See Tonry 1995 for an extended critique of US drug policy along precisely these grounds, and for compelling evidence in support of the claim that US drug policy has led to young blacks being imprisoned disproportionately.

22. Obviously, there are also benefits to blacks from anti-drug law enforcement. This illustration is by no means intended to suggest that those benefits are slight. Taking them into account, and calculating the net impact of the policy on blacks as a group, would be entirely consistent with the spirit of the argument here.

23. Connerly's recently published memoir, *Creating Equal* (2000), provides an extended exposition of his views.

24. Thernstrom and Thernstrom (1997) argue explicitly in just this way.

25. See Moskos and Butler 1996 for documentation of this rationale for racial affirmative action in the US Army personnel policies.

REFERENCES

Akerlof, G., 1997, "Social Distance and Social Decisions," *Econometrica* (September), 65: 1005–28.

Anderson, E., 1990, *Streetwise: Race, Class, and Change in an Urban Community*, University of Chicago Press.

1999, *Code of the Streets*, New York: Norton.

Appiah, K. A., 1992, *In My Father's House: Africa in the Philosophy of Culture*, Oxford University Press.

Arrow, K. J., 1963, *Social Choice and Individual Values*, New Haven: Yale University Press.

Bowen, W. G. and D. Bok, 1998, *The Shape of the River: Long-Term Consequences of Considering Race in College and University Admissions*, Princeton University Press.

Connerly, W., 2000, *Creating Equal: My Fight Against Race Preferences*, San Francisco: Encounter Books.

Cornell, S. and D. Hartmann, 1998, *Ethnicity and Race: Making Identities in a Changing World*, Thousand Oaks, CA: Pine Forge Press.

Cutler, D. and E. Glaeser, 1997, "Are Ghettos Good or Bad?" *Quarterly Journal of Economics*: 827–72.

Epstein, R., 1992, *Forbidden Grounds: The Case Against Employment Discrimination Laws*, Cambridge, MA: Harvard University Press.

Farley, R., 1996, *The New American Reality: Who We Are, How We Got Here, Where We Are Going*, New York: Russell Sage Foundation.

Fishkin, J. S., 1983, *Justice, Equal Opportunity, and the Family*, New Haven: Yale University Press.

Goffman, E., 1963, *Stigma: Notes on the Management of Spoiled Identity*, New York: Simon and Schuster.

Loury, G. C., 1977, "A Dynamic Theory of Racial Income Differences," in P. A. Wallace and A. Lamond (eds.), *Women, Minorities and Employment Discrimination*, Lexington, MA: Lexington Books, pp. 153–810.

1981, "Intergenerational Transfers and the Distribution of Earnings," *Econometrica* 49: 843–67.

1987, "Why Should We Care about Group Inequality?" *Social Philosophy and Policy* 5: 249–71.

1995, *One by One from the Inside Out: Essays and Reviews on Race and Responsibility in America*, New York: Free Press.

1997, "The Conservative Line on Race," *The Atlantic Monthly* (November): 1144–54.

1998a, "Discrimination in the Post-Civil Rights Era: Beyond Market Interactions," *Journal of Economic Perspectives*, 12: 117–26.

1998b, "Foreword," paperback edition of W. G. Bowen and D. Bok, *The Shape of the River*, Princeton University Press, pp. xxi–xxx.

2000, "Twenty-Five Years of Black America: Two Steps Forward and One Step Back?" *Journal of Sociology and Social Welfare*, 27: 19–52.

2002, *The Anatomy of Racial Inequality*, Cambridge, MA: Harvard University Press.

Mills, E. S. and L. S. Lubuele, 1997, "Inner Cities," *Journal of Economic Literature* 35: 727–56.

Moskos, C. C. and J. S. Butler, 1996, *All That We Can Be: Black Leadership and Racial Integration the Army Way*, New York: Basic Books.

Nozick, R., 1974, *Anarchy, State and Utopia*, New York: Basic Books.

Patterson, O., 1998, *Rituals of Blood: Consequences of Slavery in Two American Centuries*, Washington, DC: Civitas.

Sandel, M., 1982, *Liberalism and the Limits of Justice*, Cambridge University Press.

Sen, A., 1970, *Collective Choice and Social Welfare*, San Francisco: Holden-Day.

Sowell, T., 1983, *The Economics and Politics of Race: An International Perspective*, New York: William Morrow.

Sugrue, T. J., 1996, *The Origins of the Urban Crisis: Race and Inequality in Postwar Detroit*, Princeton University Press.

Taylor, C., 1992, *Multiculturalism and the Politics of Recognition*, Princeton University Press.

Thernstrom, S. and A. Thernstrom, 1997, *America in Black and White: One Nation, Indivisible*, New York: Simon and Schuster.

Tilly, C., 1998, *Durable Inequality*, Berkeley: University of California Press.

Tonry, M., 1995, *Malign Neglect: Race, Crime, and Punishment in America*, New York: Oxford University Press.

United States, Office of the President 1998, *Economic Report of the President*, Washington DC: US Government Printing Office (February).

Waldinger, R., 1996, *Still the Promised City: African-Americans and New Immigrants in Postindustrial New York*, Cambridge, MA: Harvard University Press.

Wilson, W. J., 1978, *The Declining Significance of Race: Blacks and Changing American Institutions*, University of Chicago Press.

1996, *When Work Disappears: The World of the New Urban Poor*, New York: Alfred A. Knopf.

21   Achieving racial equality

Bhikhu Parekh

In this paper I do three things. I begin with a general discussion of the nature and basis of equality and show why human beings should be treated equally. Although racial equality shares much in common with other forms of equality, it is distinct in its nature and logic. I analyze its specificity and end by suggesting how best it might be achieved.

Why equality?

Equality is an extremely elusive concept. In mathematics, its original home, it generally means identity or substitutability. To say that "two plus two equal four" is to say that "four" is the same as and can always be substituted for "two plus two," and vice versa. It cannot have the same meaning in relation to human beings who are unique and by definition nonsubstitutable and different. Basically equality in a human context implies a status or a standing. To maintain that human beings are (or should be) equal is to say that they enjoy the same moral status, that none of them is inherently superior or inferior, and that none should be treated differently from another unless they are different in relevant respects.

Human beings do not have a status in the same way that they have eyes and ears. It is something that we ascribe to or rather confer on them. Empirically human beings are similar or different, not equal or unequal. The fact that they have common basic needs and are in that respect similar does not by itself tell us if and why their needs should be equally met or why they have equal claims to the satisfaction of their needs, for one might argue that some human beings are inherently superior and have a stronger claim to the satisfaction of their needs. In order to defend equality, we need to show why we think we should confer the same moral status on all human beings. This is a matter of judgment and should be based on good reasons. In other words equality is a moral principle or practice, a way of treating human beings, which we think we have good reasons to adopt. These reasons have to do with how we understand human beings, define their humanity, what we value in them, and so on, and call for a wider philosophical theory.

Bentham thought that such a theory was neither necessary nor possible, and that the question of equality should be best discussed in scientific terms.[1] Rather than ask whether human beings are "really" equal or should be treated equally, we should ask why inequalities are undesirable and how they should be reduced. Invoking the concept of diminishing marginal utility, he argued that an additional sum of one hundred pounds gave far more pleasure to a person earning fifty pounds a month than one earning ten times as much. The principle of maximizing general happiness therefore entailed giving them to the former, and a broad policy of economic redistribution or minimization of economic inequality. Bentham justified political and social equality or rather equalization on similar grounds and made out a strong case for the welfare state.

Although Bentham's approach has its merits and has rightly encouraged ways of measuring and calculating the consequences of inequality, it suffers from fatal weaknesses. As he himself realized, the general happiness in a racist society is maximized by lynching or distributing blacks as slaves. He rightly condemned this but could not give good reasons for it. He had similar difficulty justifying his belief in the abolition of slavery. He also assumed that in any utilitarian calculation, every human being was to count as one and none as more than one, but gave no good utilitarian reasons for his view. The greatest happiness principle does not allow us to prefer the pleasure of human beings over that of the animals when the quantities of the pleasure involved are equal, and yet Bentham rightly insisted that human happiness was to be preferred.

In recent years some writers have proposed yet another way of defending equality.[2] In their view it is self-evident that those who are equal in relevant respects should be treated equally, that unequals should be treated unequally, that no distinctions should be made between individuals unless there are relevant differences between them, and that when pared to its barest essentials, there is nothing more to the principle of equality than the principle of impartiality or moral consistency. If the right to vote requires certain capacities, then all those possessing them should all enjoy that right. If two or more persons have equal qualifications for a job, they should all be considered for it, and those lacking these are clearly not entitled to equal treatment. At a more general level, since all human beings have common basic needs such as food, clothing, and shelter, they all have a right to their satisfaction. In short, these writers argue that equality is about how to treat two or more individuals in a given context, and that the nature of the treatment depends on whether they are equal in the relevant respect.

Although this way of dealing with equality has something to be said for it, it is seriously flawed. It is not enough to say that equals should be treated equally, for we need to decide *who* should be included among equals. Human beings need food, and so do the animals, but we rightly do not treat them both equally. We do not concentrate on needs per se but privilege human beings, and must show why. Furthermore, the rule that equals should be treated equally does not tell us anything about the nature and content of the treatment. When confronted with equal needs and capacities, we could either satisfy or starve, and develop or stifle, them equally. Since the principle of impartiality does not by itself tell us which response is justified, we need to go beyond it and introduce some notion of human worth and well-being. We cannot discuss "equality of what" without discussing "equality for what." Again, the principle of impartiality or equal treatment of equals does not explain why we think it right to give additional help to those severely disadvantaged by decades of neglect or oppression, or to assign equal worth to the mentally handicapped. For these and other reasons we cannot defend equality without understanding a wider philosophical inquiry and showing why we should adopt the moral practice of assigning equal status or worth to all human beings.

Human beings are endowed with several distinct capacities which mark them out from the rest of the natural world. These include the capacity to think, reflect, reason, use language, imagine things unseen, form visions of the good life, enter into moral relations with one another, fall in love, dream dreams, and so on. Although these capacities are interrelated, they are different in their nature, origins and modes of operation, and cannot all be reduced to any one of them. The capacity for rationality, often taken to be the most basic of all, does not by itself explain why humans are able to construct myths, fall in love, compose music, or dream dreams of a better life.

Thanks to these capacities, human beings are able to build a rich inner life of their own as well as a world of interpersonal relationships, and experience emotions such as love, joy, grief, sadness, pride, shame, fear, loyalty, and deep personal attachments, which give richness and depth to their lives and make the latter uniquely human. They are also able to exercise self-determination, carve out spaces of freedom, understand, control, and humanize their natural environment, rise above the automatic and inexorable processes of nature, create a public world of aesthetic, literary, scientific, moral, religious and other great achievements, give meaning to their lives, and introduce a wholly novel form of existence. Their humanity is not limited to and exhaustively defined by their rationality or morality as the dominant rationalist or moralist account of human beings maintains. They are certainly rational and moral beings, but they are also artistic, sensual, sexual, vulnerable and needy beings, and the interplay of all these constitutes and defines their humanity. The fact that they can experience moments of great joy as well as sadness, die for a cause as well as kill for it, is as much a part of their humanity as the fact that they can reason, imagine and create great and beautiful works of art and literature.

As beings capable of creating meaning and values and leading lives based on these, human beings deserve to be valued themselves, are worthy of respect, or have intrinsic worth. Worth is not a natural fact like eyes and ears but something we ascribe to or confer upon human beings. It is a moral judgment and, like all judgments, is based on and can be defended by reasons and arguments. Human beings have worth because they are capable of doing worthy things, and their worth is intrinsic because it is based on capacities and achievements that are not contingent but constitutive of their humanity. Since they have worth by virtue of being human or membership of the human species, it is their species or collective entitlement. It is, of course, possible that human capacities and achievements are all trivial in the eyes of God, and that the high value we place on them reveals our species-bias. However, that does not diminish their value in our eyes, for we have no other standards to judge them by than those derived from as detached and objective a perspective as we can bring to bear on the subject. We cannot leap out of ourselves and judge ourselves and the world from nowhere. Even if we believed in God and looked at ourselves from His point of view, we would have to rely on our own judgment as to who to accept as God, and how to define Him and interpret His intentions. Since we value human beings because of their capacities and the kind of life they are capable of leading, we reduce our species-bias by conferring value on apes and other higher forms of animal species who too display some of these capacities.

It is true that some human beings have more intelligence or reason than others, but that does not make them morally superior or more worthy. They might be less caring and compassionate, or possess less practical or intuitive intelligence, common sense or artistic ability, or be less able to relate to and love others. Since these and other capacities are both valuable and incommensurable, human beings cannot be graded or declared inherently superior or inferior. It is true that some categories of humans such as mad or mentally handicapped persons lack some of the distinctively human capacities and might appear to have less or no worth. However, they are rarely devoid of these capacities altogether, and are mad and handicapped in a way that only humans can be. Besides, they are also the sons, daughters, brothers, and friends of normal human beings, to

whom they are deeply bonded and in whose worth they therefore participate. Conferring dignity and worth on such persons also tests, affirms,
and intensifies our general commitment to human worth for, if we are
able to value them, we are even more likely to value our more fortunate
fellow-humans. Furthermore, madness and mental handicap are not easy
to define. Once we start denying worth to such persons, we open the way
to denying it to other classes of human beings as well. Since this is a dangerous road and can be and has been grossly misused, it is better to avoid
it altogether. For these and other reasons, it is both right and prudent to
insist not only on the intrinsic but also on the equal worth of all human
beings.

We can also give other reasons why human beings should be assigned
equal worth or value. They share common needs, as compelling in the
case of one human being as another. They share common vulnerabilities
such as mortality, susceptibility to fear, pain, and frustration, and sadness
at the loss of their loved ones, and these are as much a part of one person's
life as of any other. They can all without an exception flourish only under
certain common conditions and wither away in their absence. Although
these and other commonalities do not by themselves entail equality, they
imply that human beings should be treated alike in respect to them unless
there are compelling reasons to the contrary, and thus create a strong
presumption in favor of equality. Furthermore, treating human beings
equally enables them to realize their potential and help create a rich and
vibrant communal life from which all benefit. And it also increases their
self-worth and respect for others, and conduces to a relaxed and humane
society.

As Aristotle, Machiavelli, Rousseau, and others have shown in their
own different ways, equality is also indispensable for the creation of
a genuine community, especially a democratic one. It fosters common
interests, shared life experiences, common conditions of social existence,
social transparency, ease of mutual understanding, empathy and communication, and so on, all of which are necessary to create and sustain a
common collective life and to deliberate about its affairs in a consensual
and disinterested manner. In a grossly unequal society, different groups
lead lives that share little in common. The rich and the privileged live
within their gated communities, send their children to separate schools,
go to private hospitals, provide for their own security, enjoy their own
separate parks and sport clubs, and have their own separate channels to
those in power. The police harassment, traffic jam, crowded trains and
buses, ill-equipped hospitals, substandard schools, noisy streets, pollu-
tion, and a sense of powerlessness that are the daily lot of most of their
fellow-citizens have little relevance for them. The two groups naturally

make very different assumptions about the world and each other, share few common experiences, hardships, interests, and intuitions, and lead parallel lives. No cohesive, democratic, and deliberative political community can be built on such a basis.

We can give these and other reasons why human beings should be assigned equal worth, and show why those holding the opposite view are wrong. Since humans have equal worth, they should enjoy equal access to those conditions and capacities without which they cannot lead a worthy, worthwhile or the good life. The conditions include such things as the satisfaction of their basic needs, good health, physical security, control over their environment, social and political stability, access to the cultural resources of their society, education, and basic civil liberties. The capacities that human beings need include such things as independent and critical thought, ability to organize and plan their lives, self-discipline, a sense of responsibility for their actions, ability to form stable relationships, and self-respect and self-worth without which they lack the will to aim high and take advantage of the opportunities available to them.

Although human beings should enjoy equal access to the conditions of the good life, they vary greatly in their talents, drive, resourcefulness, capacity for hard work, ambition, background, luck, and so on. As a result some individuals wield greater political power than others, earn higher income and accumulate greater wealth, get into prestigious universities and obtain better degrees, acquire greater moral authority, and enjoy a higher social standing and recognition. Some of these inequalities are justified on grounds of justice. We rightly think that those who work harder or acquire superior talents and skills deserve better than those who do not. Some inequalities are justified on consequentialist grounds. Higher rewards are necessary to spur individuals to greater efforts, to foster rare talents, or to attract individuals to socially valuable activities that for some reason they tend to avoid. For obvious reasons, there is much to be said for the market economy and consumer choices, and these too lead to inequalities of various kinds. Although we might feel deeply troubled by the ridiculously vast sums of money earned by managers of industries, film stars, comedians, sportsmen and media pandits, we might decide to live with such inequalities out of respect for the choices of our fellow-citizens, as unfortunate products of the free market which we have good reasons to allow, or because eliminating them requires extensive government intervention which we have reasons to fear. Some inequalities, again, are a product of pure luck. And although we might be unhappy about them, we might decide to tolerate them because they are not unfairly secured, or because the role of luck in human life cannot be eliminated. John Rawls' view that inequalities are justified only when they work to the benefit of the worst off is too simplistic to accommodate these and other grounds on which they can be justified.

As long as human beings remain what they are, namely, unequally endowed beings who are competitive and possess limited degrees of public spirit, altruism, and love of their fellow humans, inequalities would continue to remain an inescapable part of human life. There are, however, limits to the range and depth of inequalities that a society committed to the equality of human worth can tolerate. The inequalities should not threaten the basic equality of access to the conditions of the good life, or give some so much political and economic power that others are virtually at their mercy and lack a sense of self-respect and self-worth. Different kinds of inequalities should not be so interlocked that those enjoying one kind of power, say, the economic also wield political, social, cultural, and other kinds of power, for they then create a tightly knit elite exercising such a stranglehold over society that the rest feel excluded and powerless to change the prevailing social structure. The inequalities should not be self-perpetuating either, as others then have no hope of breaking through their barriers and feel demoralized. Nor should inequalities be so widespread and deep that they lead to parallel lives and undermine the spirit of common citizenship. Since these kinds of inequalities spring up in all societies, the state committed to the principle of equal human worth must find ways of preventing, regulating, and countering them.

What is racial equality?

Having discussed equality in general, we shall now turn to racial equality, which is one of its several forms. The term racial equality is ambiguous both because the term race itself is problematic and because it is not always clear what equality means and implies when extended to racial groups.[3]

The term race is commonly used in two senses. In its first and older sense, which dominated eighteenth- and nineteenth-century thought on the subject and is not entirely absent today, it refers to the division of humankind into static and quasi-natural groups on the basis of their phenotypical features. Races are supposed to be homogeneous, separate, unchanging, and easily distinguishable by their shared physical features.[4] In its second sense, the term refers to ethno-cultural groups, that is, those based on a combination of shared physical and cultural characteristics, a common history, real or imaginary homelands, a shared sense of collective identity, and their own and others' perception of them as distinct groups.

The first sense of the term is deeply problematic. Unlike animals, human beings do not fit into a neat pattern and cannot be exhaustively defined and classified on the basis of shared physical features alone. And thanks to migrations, intermarriages, and close interactions between the races, there are no pure races, there being as much physical variety within as between them. Physical features, further, tell us nothing about the individuals involved and have no descriptive, explanatory, or normative significance. In its second sense the term "race" has some usefulness. Although ethno-cultural groups too are rarely homogeneous and static and share much in common, they are broadly united and distinguishable in terms of a shared culture, history, common name and origins, a sense of collective identity, and so on. Although they are best called ethnic or ethno-cultural groups, I shall, in deference to common usage, use the term race to refer to them.

When the term "race" is used in this sense, racial equality can mean one of two things. First, it can mean equality of the races, that is, that all races should be treated equally in the same way that all human beings should be treated equally. This is an incoherent notion. Since races are not self-conscious collective agents and bearers of collective interests, they cannot make collective claims on each other. And since they do not exist independently of their members, the idea of treating them equally makes no sense except as a way of referring to equality of their members. Secondly, racial equality can mean that individuals should be treated equally irrespective of their races. This is a coherent view, and that is how I earlier argued for equality. When so understood, racial equality can be interpreted in one of two ways, and much of the current controversy surrounding it centers on this ambiguity. It can mean either that all racial differences are irrelevant and should be abstracted away in our treatment of individuals, or that these differences are sometimes relevant and should be taken into account in determining the content of equal treatment. For the former, racial equality is difference-blind; for the latter, it is alert to racial differences.

Of these two interpretations of racial equality, the former is incoherent and unjust. Human beings are both human and cultural beings, belonging both to a common species and to particular historical ethno-cultural communities. Although they have common capacities and needs, these are culturally articulated and shaped, and they also have other culturally specific needs and capacities. To ignore both these is to overlook what makes them distinctive and to treat them as other than who and what they are. Furthermore, when we ignore or abstract away their cultural identity, we run the risk of unconsciously generalizing our own cultural assumptions. Culture inescapably mediates our understanding, interpretation, and evaluation of human behavior. In the absence of an explicit recognition of others' cultural differences, we are constantly tempted to understand and judge them in terms of the categories of our own culture, and thus to assimilate them to our ways of thought. While appearing to treat them equally, we end up treating them unequally. Equality requires us both to ignore irrelevant differences and to take full account of the legitimate and relevant ones. The differences do not affect the equality of their claims and our duty to treat them equally, but they do affect the content of their claims and our view of what their equal treatment consists in.

In the light of our discussion, racial equality requires that, irrespective of their racial origins, all human beings should be treated equally, should enjoy equal access to the conditions and the capacities required to lead the good life, and that when relevant their legitimate ethno-cultural differences should be taken into account in our treatment of them. Racial inequality exists when a racial group is treated unequally because of its race. Its members might be subjected to systematic discrimination in employment, education, criminal justice system, political representation, and other areas of life. Or they might suffer from severe material disadvantages caused by present or past acts of ill-treatment, and enjoy unequal access to the basic conditions of the good life. Or they might be stigmatized, subjected to demeaning stereotypes, treated as an inferior species, and socially avoided.

Racial inequality covers a wide spectrum. Some racial groups might suffer from all these inequalities whereas others might be subjected to only some of them, and the inequalities in each case might vary in their depth and severity. The African-Americans and the Hispanics in the United States, the Pakistanis, the Bangladeshis and the Afro-Caribbeans in Britain, the Turks in Germany, the Maghrebians and Africans in France, and the Roma in almost all European countries suffer from acute forms of major inequalities. The Indians in Britain are subjected to systematic discrimination but have successfully mobilized their resources and energies and do not suffer from significant racial disadvantages or grossly demeaning stereotypes and low self-respect. Although the Jews in the West do not suffer from racial disadvantage and low self-respect, they are subjected to relatively minor forms of discrimination and demeaning stereotypes.

Although racial inequality is causally tied up with the economic, political, cultural, and other forms of inequality, it differs from them in significant respects and has its own distinct logic. First, since individuals are subjected to discrimination and treated as inferior because of their membership of a particular racial group, racial inequality has a collective dimension. None of them can fight against his race-derived disadvantages without also fighting against those of the others of his race. Their struggle therefore is inescapably collective in nature and calls for at least some degree of group solidarity.[5]

Second, although tackling racial inequality involves attacking economic and political inequalities, that is never enough. The low self-respect, poor ambition, weak motivation, poor self-esteem, and the accumulated psychological and moral legacy of decades of oppression or neglect also need to be addressed, both because they are damaging in themselves and because they adversely affect economic performance and quality of citizenship. Those with poor self-esteem or used to lowly positions in society often rule out certain careers as "not for people like them" or do not know how to take advantage of the opportunities offered to them, or lack supportive networks, or easily reconcile themselves to their failures. The struggle for racial equality requires us to raise the collective status and build up the self-esteem of disadvantaged races, and thus calls for profound changes in the cultures of both the marginalized and dominant groups.

Third, although, as we shall see later, the state can do much to tackle racial discrimination and disadvantage, it has its obvious limits. It can do little to bring about the cultural changes referred to earlier. Furthermore, discrimination and demeaning treatment often occur in interpersonal relations that are not amenable to the law. The media might resort to racially offensive jokes and stereotypes, shop assistants might be rude and sullen, store detectives might shadow members of particular racial groups, neighbors might refuse to extend cooperation or show basic decency, fellow passengers might make snide remarks, and employers and school authorities might refuse to accommodate legitimate differences or discriminate in subtle ways. Although individually trivial, these and other acts can cumulatively drive a racial group to despair and result in dissipation of its energies in self-defeating acts of impotent rage or withdrawal into the communal ghettos. Tackling casual and informal but deeply debilitating expressions of racist sentiments, and creating a climate of mutual respect and goodwill, eludes the law and requires the cooperation of schools, churches, creative writers, the media, and institutions with the power to change attitudes.

Fourth, as we saw, racial equality is tied up with respect for cultural identity. Different racial groups often subscribe to and live by different systems of meaning, values, and visions of the good life. Subject to certain basic moral principles, these need to be respected and accommodated. Racial equality involves respecting cultural differences, resisting the understandable impulse to mold others in the image of the dominant culture, and providing opportunities for different forms of life to flourish. In one way or another, racial equality requires a multicultural society with all its challenges and tensions. So long as a society insists on cultural homogeneity as the basis of its survival and unity, and extends equality only to those willing to assimilate into the dominant culture, it cannot ensure racial equality.

Racial equality then raises questions some of which are different from those raised by other forms of equality. Since much of the traditional and even the contemporary discussion of equality is preoccupied with the latter, especially economic equality, it either ignores and misinterprets these questions or gives them inadequate answers. Equality is generally assumed to be concerned with material resources, and that excludes the issues of self-respect, self-worth, social esteem, and motivation that are central to racial equality. Equality is often defined and discussed in terms of redistribution, but self-respect, etc. are not a matter of redistribution, and although redistribution of material resources is vital, it is not enough to tackle racial inequality. Equality is expected to be achieved by means of state action which, although crucial, plays a somewhat limited role in tackling the informal racism and deep-seated prejudices that lie at the basis of racial inequality. Equality is largely discussed in individualist terms whereas racial equality has an inescapable collective dimension and raises complex and neglected issues of cultural and collective rights. Relations between races and the ways in which each race perceives itself and others are historically and socially structured. They cannot therefore be understood let alone changed when approached in ahistorical and individualist terms.

Achieving racial equality

In the light of our discussion, achieving racial equality requires a comprehensive and well-coordinated four-pronged strategy, involving the removal of racial discrimination, countering racial disadvantage, challenging racist ideologies, and building up the self-esteem and self-confidence of marginalized racial groups. Since no society so far has been so successful as to be a model for the rest, the strategy is largely a matter of trial and error based, no doubt, on practices that have been successful in other societies.

So far as removing racial discrimination is concerned, the law has a vital role to play. We need laws to ban and define it in reasonably precise and narrow terms, a publicly funded and powerful agency to assist individual complainants and conduct investigations into organizations suspected of practicing discrimination, and a system of justice that does not demand impossible standards of proof. Rather than require complainants to prove discrimination, which they cannot easily do for obvious reasons, we should reverse the burden of proof, asking them to produce satisfactory prima facie evidence and requiring the defendant to disprove the charge of discrimination, as the recent European Union Directive suggests. Discrimination constantly takes new forms and occurs in unfamiliar and elusive ways. It might not be directly based on race but on other apparently neutral criteria, which intentionally or unintentionally have a disproportiate impact on a particular racial group. Our legal categories and tools need to be constantly updated to keep pace with this.

Anti-discrimination legislation, however, has its limits.[6] It only helps particular individuals, puts them to considerable inconvenience, and they might sometimes not even know that they have been discriminated against. It is also adversarial, time-consuming, makes the defendant unduly defensive, hardens attitudes, makes the working environment tense and hostile, presumes fault on the part of the organization involved, and damages its reputation even if it is later found innocent. For these and other reasons it is better to place on organizations of certain size, including government departments and other public authorities, a positive duty to promote equal opportunity for marginalized and underrepresented racial groups. They can be required to draw up employment equity plans, monitor the recruitment and promotion of their workforce, set up realistic, flexible, and long-term recruitment targets on the basis of the expected outcome if the organizations concerned and the wider society had been fair and open, to devise a program of action to remove such obstacles as stand in the way of meeting these targets, and to undertake periodic ethnic audits.

The point of all this is twofold: to get organizations to take a regular and careful look at their policies and practices lest these should unwittingly work to the disadvantage of certain racial groups, and to make them transparent and publicly accountable. Ideally they should be persuaded to undertake such practices for reasons of justice, commercial self-interest, advantages of a diversified workforce, popular goodwill, and so on, and the law should remain a final recourse to be activated only in cases of resistance or refusal. It is also important that ethnic audits should not become bureaucratic and excessively costly. One way of ensuring this is to make them as informal as possible, tailoring them to the nature of the organization, and devolving the responsibility for assessing them to the employees, consumers, and interest groups who are directly affected by and fully familiar with the running of the organization concerned.

As for reducing racial disadvantage, it requires a comprehensive program of action at both educational and economic levels.[7] Marginalized groups are often caught up in a vicious cycle. They live in poor areas with substandard schools, high rates of unemployment, high incidence of crime and violence, and so on, all of which act as disincentives to industrial investment, produce a poorly qualified workforce, throw up irresponsible local leadership, and breed a culture of despair, dependency, and powerlessness. Imaginative policies are needed to break this cycle. These can include such things as coordinated programs of urban regeneration, allocation of greater public resources to needy areas, twinning schools, paying higher salaries to attract better teachers, and partnerships between government agencies, community organizations, voluntary sector, religious bodies, and enlightened businesses. Some of these policies have been tried out in recent years in the USA, Europe, and elsewhere, and much can be learned from a critical assessment of them.

The policies for tackling racial disadvantage can take several forms. They could be directed at the disadvantaged groups in general without an explicit racial angle. When some racial groups are disproportionately disadvantaged, they benefit more from such policies than do others. Although the policies are intended to be race-neutral, they are not so in their outcome. Indeed, if the outcome is known to the policymakers, the policies, although race-neutral in intention, are not race-blind. Sometimes this is not enough, and public policies might need to be specifically directed at certain racial groups. This is the case when public resources are limited, or when the groups in question are the most severely disadvantaged, or when we want to draw attention to their plight and send out appropriate messages to them and to others, or when we intend to give them a sense of ownership of the program and build up their communal institutions and self-confidence. It is sometimes argued that taking an explicit account of race and devising race-specific policies perpetuates racial consciousness and stands in the way of creating a non-racial society. This argument is flawed. Since race is an independent source of discrimination and disadvantage, the latter cannot be tackled without taking full account of it. Furthermore, when racial consciousness is a fact of life in the society at large, ignoring it is hardly the way to eliminate it. It is only by explicitly challenging its legitimizing ideology and removing its disadvantages that we can hope to enable its victims to compete as equals, and create over time a society so well-integrated as to take no notice of racial differences.

Sometimes we might need to go further and practice what is called affirmative action or positive discrimination, consisting in giving preference to certain groups in the allocation of public resources, employment, and university admissions. Affirmative action can be defended on several grounds.[8] It is demanded by the principle of equality because deeply disadvantaged groups cannot be expected to compete as equals without the additional help needed to remove the damage done by the past. It is in the interest of society as a whole because it releases talent, widens the pool of available skills, and reduces the inescapable collective cost of coping with the harm the long-oppressed groups do to themselves and to others. It also fosters social cohesion by integrating them into the mainstream society and reassuring them that the rest of the society cares enough for them to want to make such sacrifices as are needed to remove their disadvantages.

Affirmative action is not without its critics. Some argue that it does injustice to those of greater merit who are passed over in jobs and university admissions. The argument is suspect, for it all depends on how we define merit. If the criteria of university admission include, as they should, not only the examination results but also the potential ability, the hurdles overcome, providing incentives to these who have never been to university, and the diversity of background, then no injustice is done to those who only excel in the examination results.[9] And if some injustice is done to some individuals in some cases, it is justified on the grounds of, and more than compensated by the gains in terms of equality, collective interest, social cohesion, role models for the disadvantaged groups, and so on.

Affirmative action is also criticized on the ground that it privileges some racial groups. As we saw, it is really an equalizing measure intended to remove historically inherited disadvantages and to enable their victims to compete as equals. Affirmative action is also said to demean its beneficiaries who are widely seen as recipients of charity. This is to misunderstand its rationale, for it is designed to rectify past injustices and remove present disadvantages, and is a matter of justice and not charity. It is, of course, possible that the program of affirmative action might foster a culture of dependency, discourage effort, serve as electoral bribes, or become excuses for not tackling the deeper roots of economic and other inequalities. These and other criticisms pertain to the way the program is designed and implemented and do not affect the validity of the principle of affirmative action.[10]

I argued earlier that achieving racial equality involves countering racist ideologies and building up the self-esteem and self-confidence of marginalized groups. As the economic and social conditions of the latter improve, their collective self-esteem tends to rise and the appeal of the racist ideology in the wider society begins to decline. Their political visibility and empowerment, brought about by their democratic mobilization, struggles, and imaginative appointments to high places, also has a similar effect. Although racism has economic and political roots, it also has its own independent history and dynamics and needs to be tackled in its own terms. A systematic critique of the dominant culture, exposing its crude and subtle racist assumptions and categories and their pervasive presence in literature, the arts, the social sciences, and popular forms of thought, is vitally necessary. A similar critique of the culture of marginalized groups is also needed, including the ways in which they sometimes glorify their sense of victimhood, seek solace in self-pity, and expect others to solve their problems for them. Anti-racist and multicultural education also plays an important role, the former countering prejudices and stereotypes and the latter fostering a positive respect and creative engagement with other cultures. The political and economic struggles and the cultural critiques address related but different aspects of the problem, one being primarily concerned with the structure of power, the other with its legitimizing ideology; and need to be conducted together.

Racial inequality scars all contemporary societies, and eliminating it is one of the great moral and political challenges of our age. It degrades and deeply damages human beings, wastes talent, undermines common life, distorts democratic processes, and creates pockets of festering discontent and violence. Although I have proposed some ways of dealing with it, they are general, tentative, and need to be backed up by well-considered policies. A great deal of serious research is needed in the area if we are to develop an effective strategy capable of shaking its deepest roots.

NOTES

1. For a further discussion and references to Bentham's works, see Parekh 1970.
2. This view is common in the writings of analytical philosophers. For good examples, see Benn and Peters 1959 and Peters 1966: Chapter 4. Although his overall position is more complex, Amartya Sen (1992: Chapter 1) seems to show sympathy for this view. In his view "equality of what" rather than "why equality" is the central question facing the theorist of equality, and once it is answered, equality is largely a matter of impartial treatment.
3. Much of the discussion of inequality homogenizes its different kinds, and fails to appreciate the differences in their justification.
4. For a useful discussion, see Cornell and Hartmann 1998. The authors define race as "a human group defined by itself or others as distinct by virtue of perceived common physical characteristics that are held to be inherent": 24.
5. See Loury 1987.
6. For a valuable discussion, see Hepple, Coussey, and Choudhury 2000.
7. For a good analysis of racial disadvantage, see Modood et al. 1997.
8. I have discussed this more fully in Parekh 1992.
9. Such "value-added admission policies" are becoming fairly common in British universities and are used by some Oxford and Cambridge colleges to increase their student intake from poor schools and families.
10. See Loury 1997, and the articles by Gwnneth Pitt, Werner Menski, Vera Sacks, and Josephine Shaw in Hepple and Szyszczak 1992.

REFERENCES

Benn, S. I. and R. S. Peters, 1959, *Social Principles and the Democratic State,* London: Allen and Unwin.

Cornell, S. and D. Hartmann, 1998, *Ethnicity and Race: Making Identities in a Changing World,* California: Fine Forge Press.

Hepple, B., M. Coussey, and T. Choudhury, 2000, *Equality: A New Framework,* Oxford: Hart Publishing.

Hepple, B. and E. M. Szyszczak, 1992, *Discrimination. The Limits of Law,* London: Mansell.

Loury, G., 1987, "Why Should We Care About Group Inequality?" *Social Philosophy and Policy* 5, 1 (Autumn): 249–71.

1997, "How to Mend Affirmative Action," *The Public Interest,* 127 (Spring): 33–43.

Modood, T., R. Berthoud, J. Lokey, J. Nazroo, P. Smith, S. Virdee, and S. Beishon, 1997, *Ethnic Minorities in Britain: Diversity and Disadvantage,* London: Policy Studies Institute.

Parekh, B., 1970, "Bentham's Theory of Equality," *Political Studies,* 18.

1992, "A Case for Positive Discrimination," in B. Hepple and E. M. Szyszczak (eds.), *Discrimination: The Limits of Law,* London: Mansell, pp. 261–80.

Peters, R. S., 1966, *Ethics and Education,* London: Allen and Unwin.

Sen, A., 1992, *Inequality Reexamined,* Oxford: Clarendon Press.

Author index

618

Subject index